Mysterium & Medulla Bibliorum
THE
Mystery and Marrow of the B I B L E
NAMELY:

God's Covenants

WITH MAN

In the *First Adam* before the Fall, and in the *Last Adam*, JESUS CHRIST, after the fall, From the beginning to the end of the world:

Unfolded & Illustrated

In positive *aphorisms* & their *explanations*.

WHEREIN

The general nature, several kinds, gradual discoveries, sanctions and administrations of all God's *Holy COVENANTS*, from first to last, throughout the whole *Scriptures*: together with their peculiar terms, occasions, author, federates, matter, end, properties, agreements, disagreements, and many other their noted excellencies are largely and familiarly expounded: the blessed person and office of *JESUS CHRIST*, the *soul of all the Covenant of Faith*, and sole *Mediator* of the *NEW COVENANT*, is described: many choice fundamental points of Christianity, are explained, sundry practical questions, or cases of conscience are resolved; various puzzling controversies about the present occasionally elucidated; and in all, the great supernatural MYSTERY of the whole Sacred BIBLE, touching God's most wise, gracious, merciful, righteous, plenary, wonderful, and eternal salvation of sinners by *JESUS CHRIST through faith*, sweetly couched and gradually revealed in his *covenant-expressions* in all ages of the church, is disclosed and unveiled.

---

by FRANCIS ROBERTS, *M. A.*

Pastor of the Church at Wrington, in the County of Somerset

Berith Press
P.O. Box 861, Kansas, OK 74347
(918) 896-2055
www.berithpress.com

God's Covenants: The Mystery & Marrow of the Bible was first published in 1657. This Berith Press reprint, in which spelling, grammar, and formatting changes have been made, is ©2023 by Berith Press. All rights reserved. Printed in the U.S.A.

ISBN 979-8-9893238-2-1

But ye are come unto Mount Sion,—and to JESUS the Mediator of the NEW COVENANT, Hebrews 12:22-24

"I will be, says God, their God, and they shall be my people. What is better than this good, what is happier than this happiness?!" Augustine, On The Spirit and Letter, Chapter 22, Tome 3

London, Printed by R.W. for George Calvert, and are to be sold at his shop at the sign of the half-moon in Paul's Church-yard. 1657.

THIS is THE COVENANT that I will make with the House of Israel after those days, saith the LORD; I will give my Laws into their mind, and write them in their hearts. And I will be to them a God; and they shall be to me a people, etc.
Hebrews 8:10-12, Jeremiah 31:33-34

Volume 1

- *Covenant Theology* (Book I)
- *The Covenant of Works and the Covenant of Faith* (Book II)
- *The Covenant of Faith under the Adamic and Noahic administrations* (Book III, chapters 1 & 2)

Editor's Note

In preparing this work, I have placed most Scripture references as footnotes rather than within the body of the text. This is because (a) this follows the pattern presented by Roberts in early publication of this work, and (b) because there are simply so many Scripture references that Roberts gives.

The numbering system may take some getting used to. Roberts makes points within points, and sub-points within these, and so on. If you do not follow his numbering system closely, it is easy to feel lost quite quickly. To remedy this issue, I have listed the points from which each further sub-point derives. The sequence of parentheses appears usually in this manner: (1) [1] {1} (i) (a) - and then back to (1).

Footnotes are generally as they appear in the original work, rather than following a standardized modern format. Missing words are mostly eliminated, although in some places I have issued an explanatory footnote.

Latin quotations have been preserved, although some translations have been provided where convenient.

I pray that this work will be a blessing to you, dear reader.

Joseph Weissman, Oklahoma, 2023

8

Contents

~~~

INTRODUCTORY MATERIAL

Preface by Todd Ruddell - page 17
A Letter from Francis Roberts - page 59

~~~

BOOK ONE - Of God's Covenants Their Names, Natures, Sorts, and Benefits, More Generally - page 81

Chapter 1: Of God's dealing with his church, in all times and ages, by way of covenant. - Page 83

Aphorism 1 - God is pleased in all times and ages, from the beginning to the end of the world, to deal with his church and people by way of covenant. - Page 86

Aphorism 2 - God in all ages pleases to deal with his church and people by way of covenant for several weighty causes and excellent ends. - Page 92

Chapter 2: Of the name, general nature, and distribution of God's Covenant. - Page 99

Aphorism 1 - The names given to God's covenant with his church in Scripture, are principally two, namely, בְּרִית *berith* in the Hebrew original of the Old Testament: and διαθήκη *diatheke*, in the Greek original of the New Testament: the true meaning and use of which two names will somewhat conduce to the understanding of God's Covenant. - page 99

Aphorism 2 - God's Covenant (in the general notion of it) is his gratuitous agreement with his people, promising them eternal happiness and all subordinate good: and requiring from them all due dependence upon God, and obedience unto him, in order to his glory. - page 105

Aphorism 3 - God's Covenant with his people is not only one, but distinct: and it is distinct in kind, degree, and circumstances. It may be thus distributed or distinguished. - page 109

BOOK TWO - Of God's Covenant more particularly - page 113

Chapter 1: Of God's Covenant of Works, with the first Adam, and his natural seed before the fall. - page 115

Aphorism 1 - God was pleased to enter into covenant with the first Adam, before his fall. - page 115

Aphorism 2 - God's entering into covenant with Adam before his fall, was an act of divine grace and favor, not of debt. - page 121

Aphorism 3 - God entering into covenant with the first Adam before his fall did, in and with him, enter into the same covenant with all his posterity. - page 123

Aphorism 4 - The Covenant which God made with the first Adam and his posterity before the fall, has upon several respects different names or denominations put upon it; but for the nature of it, it is God's gracious agreement with Adam, and with his posterity, in him, to give them eternal life and happiness, upon condition of perfect and personal obedience. - page 125

Aphorism 5 - When God entered into this Covenant of Works with the first Adam, he was completely able in his own person to keep this covenant in every point. - page 141

Aphorism 6 - This Covenant of Works, Adam utterly broke by disobedience. - page 145

Aphorism 7 - Finally, the breach of the Covenant of Works by the disobedience of the first Adam, did wonderfully make way for the establishment of the Covenant of Faith by the obedience of the second Adam. - page 182

Chapter 2: Of God's Covenant of Faith with the last Adam and his seed after the fall, more generally considered. - page 185

Aphorism 1 - The Covenant of Works being broken in the first Adam, the Lord God was pleased to reveal a Covenant of Faith in Jesus Christ the last Adam. – page 186

Aphorism 2 - The Covenant of Faith is God's gracious compact or agreement with Jesus Christ the last Adam, and in him with all his seed, after the fall; touching their recovery out of the state of sin and death, into a state of righteousness and eternal life, by Christ, that in him the Lord may be their God, and they his people: they accepting Christ and these covenanted mercies by true faith, and walking worthy of them according to the gospel. - page 197

Aphorism 2 Section 1 - The efficient cause, or author of the Covenant of Faith is God. It is God's gracious compact or agreement. - page 198

Aphorism 2 Section 2 - The parties to this Covenant of Faith are two, namely: (1) God, on the one hand. (2) Christ the last Adam, and in him all his seed, on the other hand. - page 201

Aphorism 2 Section 3: The matter of this Covenant of Faith, comes next to be considered. Which is: the recovery of Christ's seed from the state of sin and death into the state of righteousness and eternal life by Christ, that in him the Lord may be their God, and they his people; they accepting him and these covenanted mercies by true faith, and walking worthy of them according to the gospel. This is the substance and matter of this covenant, touching which

God makes agreement with Christ the last Adam, and in him with all his seed. - page 216

Aphorism 2 Section 4 - The form of this Covenant of Faith comes now in the last place briefly to be inquired into. And it is twofold, namely, 1. Inward, and more essential. 2. Outward, and more accidental. - page 246

Aphorism 2 Section 5 - Of certain corollaries, or consectaries, resulting from the nature of the Covenant of Faith, generally considered. – page 255

Aphorism 2 Section 5 Corollary 1: Hence, the Covenant of Faith is a most profound supernatural mystery. - page 255

Aphorism 2 Section 5 Corollary 2: Hence the Covenant of Faith is a wonderful compound and contrivance of mere grace. - page 260

Aphorism 2 Section 5 Corollary 3: Hence Jesus Christ is the very marrow and kernel of the Covenant of Faith. - page 265

Aphorism 2 Section 5 Corollary 4: Hence the Covenant of Faith may in a right and sound sense be acknowledged conditional. - page 270

Aphorism 2 Section 5 Corollary 5: Hence, the Covenant of Faith is a sweet paradise of believers' union to, and communion with God in Jesus Christ. - page 306

Aphorism 2 Section 5 Corollary 6: Hence, the substance and matters of this Covenant of Faith are most high and great: far surpassing the matters of all other covenants, whether of God or man. - page 308

Aphorism 2 Section 5 Corollary 7: Hence, the properties and perfections of this Covenant of Faith are various and excellent. - page 310

Aphorism 2 Section 5 Corollary 7 Property 1: The Covenant of Faith is holy. - page 310

Aphorism 2 Section 5 Corollary 7 Property 2: The Covenant of Faith is gracious. - page 313

Aphorism 2 Section 5 Corollary 7 Property 3: The Covenant of Faith is ordered in all things. - page 314

Aphorism 2 Section 5 Corollary 7 Property 4: The Covenant of Faith is sure. - page 317

Aphorism 2 Section 5 Corollary 7 Property 5: The Covenant of Faith is comfortable. - page 348

Aphorism 2 Section 5 Corollary 7 Property 6: The Covenant of Faith is everlasting. - page 367

Aphorism 2 Section 5 Corollary 8: Hence finally, the concord and discord, the agreement and difference, between the Covenant of Works, and the Covenant of Faith, is notably conspicuous from the nature of the Covenant of Faith thus unfolded in the general. - page 371

Aphorism 3 - The Covenant of Faith may be sub-distinguished, or distributed into two branches: 1. God's Covenant of Promise with one peculiar sort of people only before Christ. 2. God's Covenant of Performance, or the New Covenant, with all sorts of people, since Christ. – page 388

BOOK THREE - Of God's Covenant of Faith in Christ, in particular, namely: of the Covenants of Promise before Christ, in six remarkable expressions of it. - page 399

Chapter 1: Of the discovery and administration of the Covenants of Promise in the first period of time remarkable, namely: from Adam, till Noah. – page 401

Chapter 1 Section 1 - page 403
Chapter 1 Section 2 - page 404
Chapter 1 Section 3 - page 415

Aphorism 1 - Hence, immediately upon Adam's fall, God revealed a gracious promise touching man's recovery. - page 416

Aphorism 2 - Hence, this promise of man's recovery was revealed very imperfectly and obscurely. - page 426

Aphorism 3 - Hence, this first promise of lapsed man's recovery was revealed in Christ, the woman's seed. - page 431

Aphorism 4 - Hence, this first promise in Christ, revealed lapsed man's recovery, in the enmity threatened between the woman and the serpent, between her seed and his seed, and in the events of that enmity. - page 441

Aphorism 5 - Hence, this first promise revealed in Christ the seed of the woman, though it had not the name and complete formality of a covenant; yet had it the nature, substance and reality of a covenant, and that the Covenant of Faith. - page 479

Chapter 2: Of the discovery and administration of the Covenants of Promise, in the second period of time: from Noah until Abraham. - page 491

Aphorism 1- The Lord God, having determined to destroy the old world for its extreme wickedness, established his Covenant with righteous Noah, to save him, his family, and a seed of living creatures in the ark, from the common destruction. - page 493

Aphorism 2 - The Lord God having destroyed the wicked old world by a flood of waters, not only resolved within himself, but also covenanted with Noah, with his seed, and with the creatures, never to destroy the earth any more by a flood: annexing the rainbow for a token of the Covenant. - page 504

Aphorism 3 - These two Covenants of God, established with Noah, before and after the flood, for saving Noah and his family in the ark by water from perishing with the wicked world, and for preserving the world from future destruction by a general flood, were a renewed discovery and administration of the Covenant of Faith, touching sinners' salvation by Jesus Christ. - page 515

Preface

Covenant Theology breaks into consideration in our Confession of Faith in chapter 7, *Of God's Covenant with Man*, with a following chapter on the Mediator, Christ. Some would have it enter the discussion before then, and others after, but for the author of this preface it is, like Goldilocks' porridge, "just right." The author of the work you have before you would agree. Calling this work "The Mystery and Marrow of the Bible", he does not overcharge Covenant Theology with describing the necessary, *opera ad-intra* of the Triune God, as if covenanting were a necessary act of the Godhead, nor does he relegate it to a secondary or tertiary concept to be taken up after the bulk of necessary points of theology are well understood. As "Mystery and Marrow" Francis Roberts presents to his readers something that will help to untie certain knots of the Bible that plague the novice, and many professing Christians, with apparent contradictions and other difficulties (the *mystery*), and at the same time revealing the "fat and sweet core" of God's covenant dealing with men, through Jesus Christ (the *marrow*).

Originally a work of some seventeen hundred plus pages all bound in one volume, this is a copious and painstaking labor of tracing this marrow, this sweet thematic core that runs through the unfolding of redemptive history. I am particularly pleased to see this work republished, updated, and made accessible to the general Christian public, to pastors, seminary professors, and others, having made use of it in my own studies these last few years as I have endeavored to relate the truth of God's Covenant with man to the congregation of the Lord for their encouragement, and to their admiration of the Scriptures, and of God Himself, the Triune God, who has "been pleased to express [His voluntary condescension] by way of covenant."[1] I pray that this preface will whet the reader's appetite to begin and finish the work you have before you, for I believe it to be a necessary corrective for declensions from a

---

[1] Westminster Assembly, *The Westminster Confession of Faith*: Edinburgh Edition, (Philadelphia: William S. Young, 1851), Sect. 7.1, p45

Biblical commitment to Covenant Theology, and a setting things in good order, which will be a welcome refreshment to the Christian in every age of the Church.

Francis Roberts was born in Yorkshire, England in 1609, to parents of humble means. His father, Henry Roberts was a man of common stock, a "plebian." Not much is known about Rev. Roberts' childhood, but in 1625, at the age of sixteen, he entered Trinity College, Oxford, matriculated at the age of seventeen in November of the following year, and graduated with his Bachelor of Arts in February of 1629. In June of 1632, after further study he was awarded Master of Arts at the age of twenty-three. He studied as a curate under John Burges in Sutton Coldfield, and by 1635 was established as the resident minister at Street Martin in the Bulletin Ring, the parish church of Birmingham, where he married in 1635 and where two of his children – Mary and Elizabeth – were baptized in 1637 and 1638. While in Birmingham he founded the Birmingham Library, one of the first public libraries in England, and developed a reputation as a "famed lecturer." Roberts was appointed minister of St. Augustine's Watling Street in the City of London the same year. In 1648 Roberts was presented by his patron, Arthur Capel, first Earl of Essex, to the rectory of Wrington in Somerset, where he was to spend the remainder of his life.[2] At Somerset, he became a zealous partisan of the Somerset puritans, and was appointed in 1654 assistant to the commissioners, or triers, to eject scandalous ministers, and examine others for ordination. At the Restoration he conformed to the ceremonies and took the oaths, rejoining the Church of England. On the appointment of Lord Essex as lord-lieutenant of Ireland, Roberts was nominated (23 March 1673) his first chaplain, and was installed as Doctor of Divinity of Dublin while in that office. He died at Wrington in the end of 1675, and was buried near his wife, who preceded him to glory. Five daughters survived him. To Hannah, the fourth daughter, he bequeathed his 'virginalls with all the virginall books and lessons.'[3] Roberts possessed considerable estates in Yatton. To the church and parishioners he

---

[2] See https://prabook.com/web/francis.roberts/2440282; accessed 19 Jan. 2023
[3] A Virginal is a keyboard instrument, similar to a harpsichord.

bequeathed five folio books—his own 'Clavis Bibliorum' and 'God's Covenant'—with three volumes of Foxe's 'Book of Martyrs,' which he had some time previously 'set and chained in the church.'[4]

He was a Puritan, a Presbyterian, a member of that venerable and memorable company of the "Sundry London Ministers" from which we have the seminal work on Presbyterianism, *Jus Divinum Regiminis Ecclesiastici*, recently republished by Naphtali Press in conjunction with Reformation Heritage Books.[5] He signed petitions addressed to Parliament, to both houses, pertaining to admission to the Lord's Supper and church government. He was especially concerned with the unity and purity of the Church as it pertains to the admission of ignorant and scandalous persons to the Supper, and his pastoral care for the flock is seen in his being signatory to these documents. In a petition to the House of Lords in March 1645, he joined with six other London Ministers, assembled at Zion College with the concern recorded below:

"Nevertheless, Renowned Worthies, extreme necessity doth enforce us, with sad hearts, to present to your deep and pious Considerations the dangerous and unspeakable mischiefs, which, like a flood, break in upon us, and swell higher and higher every day; every man taking liberty to do what is right in his own eyes, because no ecclesiastical discipline or government at all is yet settled, for the guarding of the precious ordinances of Christ, especially that holy sacrament of the Lord's Supper, from profanation and contempt; whence it comes to pass, that God is much dishonoured; the tender consciences of many, both ministers and people, are offended; multitudes fall away into several and strange by-paths of separation; our parochial congregations, both in city and country, are woefully rent in pieces, through schisms and faction; the celebration of the Lord's Supper in many congregations is wholly omitted, and likely to be so in many more, unless some

---

[4] See https://en.wikisource.org/wiki/Dictionary_of_National_Biography,_1885-1900/Roberts,_Francis, accessed 7 Feb. 2023

[5] https://www.heritagebooks.org/products/jus-divinum-regiminis-ecclesiastici-the-divine-right-of-church-government-coldwell.html

sufficient remedy against the abuses of this sacred ordinance be presently applied; the pious ministers are extremely discouraged in their ministerial employments; many, that have formerly manifested good affections, being much wearied with long expectation, do daily withdraw both from the Parliament, their orthodox ministers, and from one another.

"For removal of all such evils, and the happy uniting of the well-affected both to you and one to another, may it please this Honorable House, according to your wisdoms, with the advice of the Assembly of Divines, to publish, with the Directory for Worship, some effectual course to keep back ignorant and scandalous persons from the Sacrament of the Lord's Supper."[6]

Similar petitions appeared before both the House of Lords and Commons with Rev. Roberts' signature, joining with other Puritan and Presbyterian ministers in the city of London and using that proximity to Parliament for the advancement of the Kingdom of Christ (and England!) in the reformation of the Church. Having sworn the Solemn League and Covenant, Rev. Roberts and others had covenanted for the Biblical uniformity of the religion of the realm, and so, commendably, they presented petitions, sermons, and other lawful means to the civil power of their day for the reformation of the Church, and conformity to the best reformed examples of church order on the Continent.

Joining with seventy-four other London ministers, he petitioned the House of Lords in November of 1645 for uniformity in Church government, pressing for biblical Presbyterianism. Note a portion of that petition:

"Wherefore your petitioners, in Pursuance of our Solemn Covenant, in zeal to the glory of God, the Kingdom of Jesus Christ, and to the complete establishment of purity and unity in the Church of God, for the satisfaction both of our own and our people's consciences in this weighty matter of church government, and for the general benefit, not only of the province of London,

---

[6] Journal of the House of Lords: Volume 7, 1644. Originally published by His Majesty's Stationery Office, London, 1767-1830.
See [https://www.british-history.ac.uk/lords-jrnl/vol7/pp 267-269]
<accessed 7 February 2023>

but of all the provinces in England, both for present and succeeding ages, do most humbly and earnestly beseech the Right Honourable Houses,

"That the presbyterial government, in congregational, classical, provincial, and national assemblies (agreed upon already by the Right Honourable Houses), may be speedily established, with such fullness and sufficiency of power upon all the said elderships, that they may fully, faithfully, and cheerfully, with well-satisfied consciences, submit unto, and put in execution, the said government; and that there may be, to that end, by your authority, superadded a clear explanation of things doubtful, and full supply of things defective, in the said directions and ordinance of the Right Honourable Houses, according to the schedule annexed, and herewith humbly presented to your wisdoms and piety."[7]

Other such signatory work shows Rev. Roberts to be a minister very much engaged, for the reformation of religion, with fellow ministers and statesmen of the day. Petitions appeared in the House of Commons in 1644, concerning Presbyterial Church government, and to the House of Lords in 1645 concerning the ignorant and scandalous and the Lord's Supper beside the ones quoted above.[8] The Erastian party in parliament (and in much of the episcopacy in the Church of England) desired that local representatives of Parliament would hold the key of discipline with the authority to admit and censure from the Lord's Table—which the Westminster Divines, and the Zion College Ministers most vehemently opposed. Several communications passed between Parliament and Assembly on this topic, and our Rev. Roberts joined with the orthodox party of Presbyterians, who asserted in the Confession of Faith that, "There is no other head of the church but the Lord Jesus Christ"[9] and "The Lord Jesus, as king and head of his church, hath therein appointed a

---

[7] Journal of the House of Lords: Volume 7, 1644. Originally published by His Majesty's Stationery Office, London, 1767-1830.
See:https://www.british-history.ac.uk/lords-jrnl/vol7/pp 267-269 accessed 7 February 2023
[8] See Chad Van Dixhoorn, *Minutes and Papers of the Westminster Assembly*, v. 5, Oxford University Press, 2012, 198-202
[9] Westminster Assembly, *The Westminster Confession of Faith: Edinburgh Edition*, Philadelphia: William S. Young, 1851, Sect. 25.1, p140.

government in the hand of church-officers, distinct from the civil magistrate. To these officers the keys of the kingdom of heaven are committed, by virtue whereof they have power respectively to retain and remit sins, to shut that kingdom against the impenitent, both by the word and censures; and to open it unto penitent sinners, by the ministry of the gospel, and by absolution from censures, as occasion shall require."[10]

While Roberts was never an official member of the Westminster Assembly, he joined in their labors concerning the examination of ministers, either for inception and ordination to the ministry or trial concerning maladministration of or scandal concerning ministerial duties (1644 and beyond). He also joined several others in preaching before Parliament during their regular fasts. A specimen of his preaching is preserved in his, "A Broken Spirit, God's Sacrifices."[11] This sermon is a worthy specimen of Puritan preaching, identifying particular sins, current in the days of the Assembly, and God's threatening against those sins, (opening the wound) and then pouring in the balm of Gilead, the sacrifice and righteousness of Christ, and applying to members of Parliament direction for true repentance and obedience. It was also during this time that Roberts was instrumental in keeping communication open between the Scottish Commissioners to the Westminster Assembly, and the Zion College of Ministers and other members of the London Synod through his correspondence with Robert Baillie. Several important communications are preserved in Baillie's letters and journals, speaking to the great concern these ministers had for the reformation of religion in their day and country,[12] and in the work before you Roberts will

---

[10] Ibid., Sect. 30.1-2, p154.

[11] Roberts, Francis. A Broken Spirit, God's Sacrifices. Or, The Gratefulness of a Broken Spirit unto God. Represented in a Sermon, before the Right Honourable House of Peers, in King Henry VII's Chapel in the Abbey Westminster, upon Wednesday December 9. 1646. Being a Day of Public Humiliation for Removing of the Great Judgment of Rain and Waters Then upon the Kingdom, etc. / By Fran. Roberts M. A. Minister of Christ, at Austins, London. Early English Books Online. London: Printed for George Calvert, of Austin's parish, in the Old-Change, at the sign of the Golden Fleece, 1647.

[12] See David Laing, The Letters and Journals of Robert Baillie, A. M. Edinburgh, 1841 v.2, pp. 333, 345, 358, 359

represent his Scottish fellow soldier as "my godly and learned friend," and "my worthy friend."

We alluded above to Roberts' conformity to the Church of England at the Restoration (1662). Many ministers were ejected from their posts for non-conformity, including the godly Thomas Vincent, and this act of Roberts has prejudiced the esteem that he might have otherwise enjoyed among many, given his recension of prior commitments and accepting the settlement of the monarchy. A more charitable construction is recorded in Rose's New General Biographical Dictionary, where it is said, "At the restoration, however, he conformed, tired out, as many others were, by the distractions of the contending parties, and disappointed in every hope which the encouragers of rebellion had held forth."[13] While we may not agree with his actions at this point in his public ministry, we can certainly sympathize with his desire to continue ministering to his flock, while disapproving of his compromise. He received his Doctor of Divinity with the help of his patron Lord Capel in 1672 from the University of Dublin, and passed into glory in 1675.

As a writer, Roberts reveals himself both scholarly and popular, as well as prolific. Beside the work you have before you, which is quite scholarly, he leaves for history his Clavis Bibliorum, or Key of the Bible, a work of Bible introduction and brief commentary, written primarily for the members of his Church. In the introduction to this work, Edmund Calamy, speaking of reading the Scriptures, writes,

"To read them in an orderly and methodical way; and for their better help herein, to take this ensuing treatise in their hands. It is short and pithy; it sets the whole Bible before them, in an orderly, plain and perspicuous manner, and helps them to understand every book. The author of it is a godly learned minister, well known and very well esteemed on in this famous city. The Book itself is called the Key of the Bible, because it unlocks the richest Treasury of the Holy Scriptures. Take this Key with you, whensoever you go into this

---

[13] Hugh James Rose, *New General Biographical Dictionary*, London, 1857, pp. 358-359. See also Won Take Lim, *The Covenant theology of Francis Roberts*, PhD Dissertation, Calvin Theological Seminary, 2000, pp. 31-32

Treasury. And pray unto him that hath the Key of David, that openeth and no man shutteth, and shutteth and no man openeth, that he will open this Treasury unto you."[14]

Other works of our author include his Synopsis of Theology, an outline of the main points of Scripture "for the benefit of his flock." Other pastoral works include:

• *A communicant Instructed, practical directions for the worthy receiving of the Lord's Supper*

• *The True way to the Tree of Life, or the Natural Man Directed to Christ*

• *The Chequer Work of God's Providence, towards his own people, made up of blacks and whites, of their advancements, abasements, their distresses.*

• *Believers' Evidences for Eternal Life collected out of the First Epistle of John.*

Finally in this biographical section of our preface, Roberts was also very much interested in the Psalms in Christian worship, himself translating several Psalms into English meter for singing in the congregations he served. He published his "Book of Praises" (1644) containing the translations of Psalms 90-107. In his third edition of *Clavis Bibliorum* he included a complete translation of the entire 150 Psalms, and added his own translations cited above (90-107) to this editorial augmentation. In this same work he included his *Direction for the Right Singing of the Psalms*,[15] which include:

- Have grace in the heart
- Sing with the Spirit: with the assistance, guidance, and active furtherance of the Holy Spirit of God.
- Sing with understanding.
- Sing with the heart and inward affections.

---

[14] Francis Roberts, *Clavis Bibliorum The Key of the Bible, Unlocking the Richest Treasury of the Holy Scriptures*: by Francis Roberts, Early English Books Online (London: T.R. and E.M. for George Calvert .., 1648), 7–8

[15] Francis Roberts, *Key of the Bible*, London, Peter Parker, 1675, pp. 128-131. https://archive.org/details/clavisbibliorumk00robe/page/n133/mode/2up?view=theater

- Sing with prudent accommodation.
- Sing with holy and heavenly meditation upon subject matters sung.
- Sing with impartial application of all things applicable to yourself.
- Sing psalms to the right ends for which singing of psalms was intended and ordained.

Leaving the life and works of our author, we proceed to the scope and contents of the work you have before you. As we have intimated, it is a compendious and detailed work on the covenants of the Lord as they are made historically with man. In something of a departure from conceptions of Covenant Theology contemporary to our author, he styles the two historical covenants the "Covenant of Works" and the "Covenant of Faith." The work is admirably arranged, logically sorted, and well argued. His introductory address – nearly 8,300 words — presents the scope of the work to the beloved readers, primarily Christians in England, Scotland, and Ireland, and "other annexed dominions." He justifies this work as necessary, stating that this is a, "subject so sublime, spiritual, comprehensive, transcendent, and every way excellent, in itself; so necessary, profitable, comfortable, and every way desirable, to us: that it is most worthy of all acceptation, by all that are, or desire to be, altogether CHRISTIANS. He presents his seven points of importance thusly:

"1. The author of these COVENANTS is the LORD, the most High and only wise God.

2. The original fountain and impulsives of them: the glorious riches of divine grace.

3. The confederates or federate-parties to them; God, and man either as in the first Adam before the fall, or as in the last Adam, Jesus Christ since the Fall.

4. The foundation of all the COVENANTS OF FAITH from first to last: JESUS CHRIST, God-man, our only mediator and hope, either as promised, or as performed.

5. The matters of God's covenants are: from God, all manner of blessings temporal, spiritual, and eternal, which the whole Scriptures promise: from man, all manner of duties natural in the first Adam, or supernatural in the last Adam, which the whole Scriptures require.

6. The Form of them: more inwardly, the federates' reciprocal and mutual obligation; more outwardly, the various manifestations, confirmations and administrations of God's several covenants according to the mysterious contrivances and counsels of his blessed will.

7. Finally, the intended scope or ends of them all, are: subordinately, the happiness of man in his federal enjoyment of the LORD as his Covenant God both in this and the world to come, which is absolutely the height of all possible felicity: ultimately, the glory of God in his matchless wisdom, goodness, free-grace, mercy, love, truth, faithfulness, justice, holiness, happiness, etc., all which are rendered in and through JESUS CHRIST most illustrious and glorious."

He will speak in his address of this subject as vast in extent, of great difficulty, requiring much labor, and consuming a long time in bringing it forth, requiring weekly lectures for nearly six years of labor in the Church, and that not including his work on the New Covenant in Christ, which was delayed due to illness. He writes of his labor nearly being cut short by this sickness, yet that the Lord was "ready to save" him, and so he passed on to the end of the work. The style of the author will be appreciated by many, for he often uses the pen of the rhetorician – he can be very engaging. From the introductory address, take note of a specimen from this master of seventeenth-century English:

"(1) In affliction: by withholding my disease from annoying mine animals, and from assaulting much my vitals, though it had brought my naturals almost as low as the dust. By which dispensation I comforted myself: that the LORD in sparing my animals and intellectuals intended to reserve them for some further service to himself and his Church:

(2) From affliction: by loving my soul from the pit of corruption, casting all my sins behind his back, and restoring a new life unto me that I might exalt

his glorious name in explication of his New Covenant. For which complexive mercy I desire unfeignedly to render all possible Praises to the God of my salvation."

The work before you is a Scriptural book. It is not a book on covenant theology as one might see written today, outlined as an encyclopedia article might be, beginning with a history of the topic, various other works discussing the covenants, etc., or polemics on why the author has ordered his work in this way or that, but a work unfolding Scripture, as God's covenant dealings with men are pressed out in redemptive history. It is not without reference to other theologians of the author's present day or even men of his past, but it is primarily a work bringing out the author's understanding of Scripture. It is ordered temporally, beginning with a discussion of the Covenant of Works in Paradise, and passing into a discussion of the fall of man, the proto-evangelium, and from there unfolding the Covenant of Faith as it was dispensed in the days of Noah, Abraham, Moses/Israel, David, Restoration-Israel, and finally in the New Covenant in Christ, which Roberts calls "The Glory of all God's Covenants." In his introduction, he sets forth these premises for the better understanding of this work:

"1. That a study of the covenants does not work against the Lord's own divine complacency—that is, the eternal satisfaction had among the Persons of the Trinity. God is pleased to communicate this eternal happiness to His intellectual creatures, but does not stand in need of them.

2. That God brings mankind into sweet communion with Himself by way of covenant, in all ages.

3. That God's covenant with man is of two kinds, a Covenant of works, and a Covenant of Faith, and that the latter comprises the majority of this work.

4. That the Covenant of Faith is presented in Scripture as twofold in Christ: as promised, and as performed.

5. For this premise we will hear the author in his own words, that the mystery and chief matter of all the Covenants of Faith, whether Covenants of Promise or New Covenant, though for accidents and circumstances it be very

variously represented, yet for essence and substance it is only one and the same, namely: the recovery of lapsed sinners from sin and death, to Righteousness and life by JESUS CHRIST alone through Faith. The same CHRIST, the same Faith, the same recovery of lapsed sinners by Christ through faith is Revealed in all the Covenants of Faith, but in every of them diversely.

6. The covenants progress through time in advancing and further revealing the idea of the grace of Christ for sinners, in some cases abolishing ceremonies, yet in all cases preserving the "essentials and substantials" of them.

7. The unfolding of these covenants is so capacious and comprehensive that they enclose the "grand mystery and marrow of all the Holy Scriptures."

8. That the Scripture cannot be judiciously understood apart from an understanding of God's covenants.

9. That the people of the world are miserable, or happy, as they are without or within the covenants of God.

10. His tenth and last premise is, "That, finally, the church's ministers, and members of Christ should with all possible judgment, zeal, affection and constancy, interest and exercise themselves in the Covenants of God, but especially in the Covenants of Faith whereby alone Sinners' Hope and comfort in Christ are provided for by God since the Fall, The top-excellency, perfection and glory of all which Covenants is the New COVENANT."

The work proceeds in four books. Book One speaks more generally of the covenants of God. Book Two speaks more particularly. Book Three speaks of the Covenants of Promise—those "Covenants of Faith" before the coming of Christ. This is a very lengthy section of the work. Finally we have Book Four, and the New Covenant, in Jesus Christ actually performed and exhibited. He presents his efforts by asserting his "aphorisms", and then explaining these thesis statements. This makes the work one of neat and logical structure, and more easily followed. Roberts differs from many in his own day regarding the terminology he uses, especially in his styling what Bible students regularly call the Covenant of Grace as the "Covenant of Faith." For Roberts, this is because he has identified what he calls "grace" in the Covenant of Works. Under the heading of God's covenants, beginning with the Covenant of works, he writes in Aphorism 2: "*God's entering into Covenant with Adam before his fall, was an Act of Divine Grace and favor, not of debt.*" And, while there is sound divinity in what follows this aphorism, yet we are reminded that it was a covenant of performance, or works, and that Roberts retained that designation. In other words, while recognizing God's gracious covenanting with Adam in Paradise, he affirms that it was Adam's own performance that was required to procure the reward of covenant-fidelity. His view is that God might have not covenanted with Adam at all, but simply commanded him, apart from any promissory arrangement, and then brought him to nothing as he made him from nothing.

As Roberts unfolds his aphorisms and arguments concerning this first covenant there is much to be said in favor of his construction. However, there is a caution to be observed as well. The term Covenant of Works, and Covenant of Life have been ensconced in our confessional documents with great care and reason.[16] The Apostle Paul will write to the Roman Church concerning works and grace in the eleventh chapter of that epistle. Note his words: "*Even so then at this present time also there is a remnant according to the election of grace. And if by grace, then is it no more of works: otherwise grace is no more grace. But if it be of works, then is it no more grace: otherwise work is no more work.*"[17] Roberts himself will acknowledge this difference in high-sounding terminology, saying: "If God's Covenant with the first Adam, in his integrity, was an act of divine grace, then God's Covenant with lapsed man, in Christ the second Adam, is an act of superabounding and transcendent grace." We see here that Roberts refused to confuse works and grace in practice, although not perhaps in his terminology. Many Westminster

---

[16] See WCF 7.2, 19.1; 19.6. WLC Q. 30, 97, The term "Covenant of Life" is used in WLC 20, WSC 12 due to the reward promised to Adam upon condition of personal, perfect, and perpetual obedience. We note that in none of these references in our standards do we read of God's "grace" in the Covenant of Works—only of His providence, and His condescension.

[17] *The Holy Bible: King James Version.*, electronic ed. of the 1769 edition of the 1611 Authorized Version. (Bellingham WA: Logos Research Systems, Inc., 1995), Ro 11:5–6

era theologians used this kind of language to describe the Covenant of Works, such as John Ball, who writing of the Covenant of works declared,

"The Covenant is of God, and that His free grace and love: for although in some Covenant the good covenanted be promised in justice, and given in justice for our works: yet itwas of grace that God was pleased to bind Himself to His creature, and above the desert of the creature, and though the reward be of justice, it is also of favor. For after perfect obedience performed according to the will of God, it had been no injustice in God, as He made the creature of nothing, so to have brought him to nothing: it was then of grace that he was pleased to make that promise, and of that same grace his happiness should have been continued."[18]

By way of contrast, Samuel Rutherford emphasizes God's decree, predestination, and providence in the Covenant of Works in his *Covenant of Life Opened*, not speaking particularly of grace in that covenant, but it being a temporary means to the ushering in of grace in Christ, in the Covenant of Grace. He writes,

"Therefore Adam fell from the state of Law-life both totally and finally, but not from the state of gospel election to glory. For the Lord had in the Law-dispensation a love design, to set up a theater and stage of free grace. And that the way of works should be a time-dispensation, like a summer-house to be demolished again, as if the Lord had an aim that works and nature should be a transient, but no standing court for righteousness: Hence it is now the relics of an old standing court, and the Law, is a day of assize, for condemning of malefactors, who will acknowledge no tribunal of grace, but only of works: And it is a just court to terrify robbers, to awe borderers and loose men, but to believers it is now a court for a far other end."[19]

Summarizing his handling of the Covenant of Works, Rutherford gives several reasons why there was, in it, some "out-breakings of grace" and yet immediately follows this with, "It's true, there was no gospel-grace, that is a

---

[18] John Ball, *A Treatise of the Covenant of Grace*, London, 1645, 7
[19] Samuel Rutherford, *The Covenant of Life Opened*, (Edinburgh: Andro Anderson for Robert Brown) 1655), 2–3.

fruit of Christ's merit in this Covenant."[20] Later in this section he will turn from the use of the word grace altogether and begin to speak of "undeserved goodness." Regarding the nature of the distance between the thing promised (life) and the creature-obedience offered, Rutherford writes,

"Being and dominion over the creatures is of undeserved goodness (Being, life, and self, are undeserved favors). Who looks to a borrowed body and a borrowed soul, yea and to self, and to that which is called I, as to a thing that is freely gifted? So that though thou be in a high opinion of self, self is self, and what it is, from God. And when thou rides, whence is it that I am the rider, and the wearied horse the carrier, but from God? The Covenant of Works itself, that God out of Sovereignty does not command, is undeserved condescending; that God bargains for hire, do this and live, whereas he may bide a Sovereign Lawgiver and charge and command us, is overcoming goodness. Law is honeyed with love, and hire; (it is mercy that God rewards our obedience) it is mercy that for our penny of obedience, so rich a wedge as communion with God is given."[21]

It is apparent in these comments that Rutherford is concerned to protect the uniqueness of "gospel grace" and to keep it distinct from any conception of grace that was obtained in the Adamic administration. For our part, we think this very wise, especially when many have departed from the proper conception of its uniqueness and have gone so far in their understanding as to deny the necessity of the perfect, active obedience of Christ as that *righteousness* by which a sinner stands just before God, imputed gratuitously to the sinner, being received by faith alone.[22] This error in many cases proceeds from confusing the kindness of God apparent in the Covenant of Works with the Grace of the second covenant. The perfect, personal, and perpetual obedience required in the Covenant of Works, performed by Christ the second

---

[20] Rutherford, *Covenant*, 35
[21] Rutherford, *Covenant*, 35
[22] WLC 70: Justification is an act of God's free grace unto sinners, in which he pardoneth all their sins, accepteth and accounteth their persons righteous in his sight; not for any thing wrought in them, or done by them, but only for the perfect obedience and full satisfaction of Christ, by God imputed to them, and received by faith alone.

Adam in the Covenant of Grace, (as the terms of having God as our blessedness and reward) is replaced with a partial, halting obedience expressed as "faithfulness in the Covenant," by which sinners stand righteous before God.[23] The "works" principle of the Covenant of Works is somehow subsumed and confused with the "grace" principle in the Covenant of Grace, such that apart from Christ's active obedience being imputed to the believer, sinners stand before God righteous because of their own faithfulness to the Covenant. This is a grave error, and all talk of grace in the Garden must be carefully circumscribed so as to preserve the uniqueness and necessity of Christ's active obedience imputed to the believer and reckoned to him by faith alone, that even this faith is a gift and not a work.[24] We believe a fair reading of Roberts will yield the same results as we have seen in his effusive language concerning the uniqueness of the grace of Christ in the gospel. He was careful, as we all ought to be, to follow the inspired language and ideology of the Apostle Paul in the eleventh of Romans, and let work be work, and grace be grace.

Another area of note in the work before you is the author's treatment of the Covenant that the Lord made with Noah. Our author shows that this covenant, recorded in Genesis 8 and 9, is an administration of his "Covenant of Faith," or Covenant of Grace in common parlance. His treatment appears in Book 3 "Of God's Covenants of Faith in Christ, in particular, viz. of the Covenants of promise Before Christ, in Six Remarkable Expressures Thereof." These six administrations or expressions are styled as: (1) From Adam to Noah, (2) From Noah to Abraham, (3) From Abraham to Moses, (4) From Moses to David, (5) From David to the Captive Jews in Babylon, (6) From the Captive Jews to Christ. Many students of the Scriptures have understood the covenant the Lord made with Noah not as an administration of the Covenant of Grace, but something more akin to a common grace covenant with the whole world through Noah, after the flood. Miles Van Pelt writes,

---

[23] See Guy Prentiss Waters, *The Federal Vision and Covenant Theology*, P&R Publishing, Phillipsburg, NJ, 2006, 64-65

[24] Isaiah 64:1-6; Romans 4:1-10; Ephesians 2:1-10; Philippians 3:1-11,

"The Noahic covenant recorded in Genesis 9 is a universal, unilateral, non-redemptive administration of the covenant of grace restoring and securing the principle of common grace in this world that was suspended during the judgment ordeal of the flood. This covenant of common grace ensures a period of delay from God's final, eschatological judgment until the covenant of grace should be accomplished in its various historical administrations, which include the Abrahamic, Mosaic, Davidic, and new covenants."[25]

This distinction between the Covenant of Grace and the common grace exhibited in the Noahic administration is more fully explained in a footnote in the work cited above:

"At this point it is helpful to briefly distinguish between the covenant of grace and common grace. The covenant of grace 'is a gracious bond between the offended God and the offending sinner in which God promises salvation in the way of faith in Christ and the sinner receives this salvation by believing.'[26] Bruce K. Waltke explains, 'After the fall into original sin, and the loss of Paradise, the covenant of works is no longer a possibility. In his sovereign grace, God establishes his "covenant of grace" on the basis of the benefits of Christ's active obedience and his atoning death, validated by his resurrection from the dead, his ascension into heaven, and the empowering presence of his Spirit.'[27] Common grace, on the other hand, represents a period of delay from final judgment at the consummation of history. It is 'the antithesis of the Consummation and, as such, epitomizes this world-age viewed under the aspect of a delay during which the Consummation is abeyant.'"[28]

---

[25] Miles V. Van Pelt, *"The Noahic Covenant of the Covenant of Grace,"* in *Covenant Theology: Biblical, Theological, and Historical Perspectives*, ed. Guy Prentiss Waters, J. Nicholas Reid, and John R. Muether (Wheaton, IL: Crossway, 2020), 111. For counterpoint, see Robertson, O. Palmer. *The Christ of the Covenants*. Phillipsburg, NJ: Presbyterian and Reformed Publishing Co., 1980, 124-125

[26] Geerhardus Vos, Reformed Dogmatics, vol. 2, Anthropology, trans. and ed. Richard B. Gaffin Jr. (Bellingham, WA: Lexham, 2012–2014), 92.

[27] An Old Testament Theology: An Exegetical, Canonical, and Thematic Approach, with Charles Yu (Grand Rapids, MI: Zondervan, 2007), 288

[28] Meredith G. Kline, "The Intrusion and the Decalogue," WTJ 16, no. 1 (1953): 3; Ibid, 111, fn. 1

While this is a common construction among many today, Roberts rather understands the Noahic administration as an "expressure" of the Covenant of Grace. He will write of a double covenant made with Noah, one before the flood, in which God covenanted to save him and his household, and one after the flood "superadded" to the former Covenant. In this second instance of covenanting, several things are noticed that indicate not common, but special, saving grace. The first is the occasion of it, that God "smelled the sweet savor" of Noah's sacrifice, as the outward moving cause of it, which indicates an appointment to Christ and His sacrifice, the inward "moving cause" being God's "mere grace and commiserating mercies" to Noah. Second, the parties covenanting are the appeased God on the one hand, smelling that "savor of rest" and second, Noah and his sons, and their "*seed.*"[29] Third, the matters covenanted consist on God's part that He will not again destroy all flesh. For Noah and his sons, on their part, and especially in reference to the "seed," to believe God's gracious dealing in this promise, but more, to believe in Christ the true sacrifice as the One who appeases God's wrath and restores rest to the perishing and cursed creature, preserving God's gracious design. Fourth, the token of the Covenant, the rainbow in the cloud, concerning which Roberts declares, "So then the rainbow which physically and naturally denotes rain, theologically, supernaturally and by institution signifies fair weather and security from rain and a flood." Roberts sees in the rainbow a supernaturally instituted sign—that is, while occurring naturally, the Lord claimed that sign to proclaim His covenant fidelity according to His bond never to destroy the earth by a flood. He writes, concerning its signification,

"The rainbow was no natural, but an instituted sign, and therefore it may seal the assurance of the promise, though there were no correspondence between it and the thing signified: and yet it was the fitter to be a sign of security from the future flood:

1. Because of the place, which is in the clouds of heaven, whence the rain came that drowned the world before.

---

[29] Genesis 9:9

2. Because the bow is bent upwards towards God, not towards the creature below, as when it is taken in hand to shoot at a mark; nor is there in the bow any arrow, which is said to be made ready upon the string, when hurt is intended, Psalm 11:2.

3. Because the rainbow commonly appeareth with rain, and so where men might begin to fear this judgment, there they may take comfort against it, in that it is a sign of his covenant for safety.

4. Because the rainbow appears not but when there is a clearness and a brightness in some part of the sky: but at the general flood it was all black with rain."

So, in these descriptions, Roberts sees in the Noahic Covenant an administration of the Covenant of Faith, fore-signifying Christ and His gracious work of atonement, not simply preserving the world by means of His mediation and cross-work, but by providing for the seed that should come in the preservation of the world, in seasons, in times, etc. He proves this proposition in several points which follow, remembering especially that Noah is called an heir of the righteousness which is by faith (Hebrews 11:7). He writes,

"It's styled {*the righteousness by faith*}, or *of faith*, because it is instrumentally apprehended and applied only by faith. It is opposed to the righteousness of the law, called our own righteousness, which consists in our own perfect and perpetual personal fulfilling of the law: this being not our own, but Christ's righteousness, perfectly fulfilling the law, and undergoing the curse thereof for us, accounted making his righteousness ours by faith. Of this righteousness of Christ, Noah became heir, whilst by faith he reverenced God's warning touching the flood, and prepared an ark according to God's Covenant with him, for his family's salvation. Hence therefore it is evident, that Noah, in all this federal transaction between God and him, had a special eye to Christ by faith; and that beyond the temporal salvation of his house in the ark by waters from the general deluge, he beheld and apprehended the spiritual salvation of Christ's house the Church, and peculiarly of himself from the wrath of God by Jesus Christ and his blood; otherwise how could this act of his faith have made him heir of Christ's righteousness? None can inherit Christ's righteousness, but by faith in Christ."

In addition to this, Roberts evinces with great detail that all of God's Covenants since the fall have been founded, established, and principally accomplished in Jesus Christ the Savior of sinners, that Noah was a type of Christ in his labor concerning the ark and the deluge, and that the ark itself is a type of the protection that the Church or household of Christ holds for sinners, especially for those who believe in Christ. It will be remembered that not all in Noah's extended household, subsequent to the flood, added credibility to the profession of their own personal faith. Ham, Noah's son, disrespected his father shortly after disembarking from the ark in the matter of Noah's drunkenness and shameful exposure in his tent. Instead of keeping matters private and covering the sins of his father in love,[30] Ham was forward to disrespect his father, speaking of his behavior to his two brothers, who honored their father even in his shameful actions by refusing to look upon him, and covering his nakedness.[31] Beyond this, Roberts shows how the rainbow is seen in other manifestations of God or Christ in the Scriptures, as a sign of His mercy and forgiveness,[32] and will provide several references from divines, his contemporaries, which taught that this covenant was an administration of the Covenant of Grace.[33] Roberts continues his discourse by dispelling doubts concerning his understanding of the Noahic Covenant, and in providing other material in the original printing for some forty pages of material through three of his Aphorisms identifying and reasoning from the Scriptures, theology, reason, and history why we should understand this as a

---

[30] See WLC Question 127, noting the scripture reference Genesis 9:23

[31] It is a very sad report indeed that many interpreters of the modern time imprint upon this passage the hyper-sensuality of their own age. By not seeing the heinous nature of this violation of the 5th Commandment, Ham's acting and speaking disrespectfully against this "Head of the Covenant" of his day (Noah), they miss the point of Moses' narrative. Note also that because Ham proved himself an unworthy son to his father, in disrespecting Noah and thereby the Covenant of God, his son loses the title of "Son" and instead will take the part of "servant." See Genesis 9:20-27

[32] Revelation 4:3, 10:1, to which we might add Ezekiel 1:26-28

[33] Roberts cites Pierre Rivet, David Pareus, Henry Ainsworth, and William Perkins

"covenant of faith." Nearing the close of this discourse, citing the Apostle Peter (1 Peter 3:18-20) he writes,

"That they who should be saved by this true Noah Jesus Christ in the ark of his Church, should be saved by virtue of his death and resurrection. This Peter intimates in his accommodation of the type to the antitype. While the Ark was preparing, wherein few, that is, eight souls were saved. The like figure whereunto, even baptism doth also now save us, by the resurrection of Jesus Christ, who is gone into heaven, and is on the right hand of God. When Christ purchased and wrought out our salvation, he effected it chiefly two ways:

1. By his death and humiliation. Dying for our sins, and bearing the curse of our sins in his own body on the tree,[34] for the full satisfying and pacifying of divine justice: so that now there needs no more sacrifice for sin.[35] 2. By his resurrection from the dead, and exaltation".

For our part, with respect and honor to the labors of our brethren, we are inclined to agree with Roberts that the Noahic covenant, while in some of its particulars may appear to have common grace indications, when rightly considered it will evince itself to be a species or administration of the Covenant of Faith, for the salvation of the elect, to the glory of the mediator, Jesus Christ.

Roberts' discussion of the Abrahamic Covenant is also very important, and corrective of many departures from its right understanding in the present day, and in times past. Introducing the topic, Roberts writes,

"The two former Federal Administrations, From Adam till Noah, and From Noah till Abraham, were but the daybreak, or day-dawning of the Covenant: But this, from Abraham till Moses, was as the bright sunrise of God's Covenant and promise in Christ. Let us therefore stir up our selves so much the more intentively to look into it with all diligence and delight: For the substance of it concerns us as well as Abraham, if we be the spiritual seed of Abraham."

---

[34] Romans 4:25, 1 Corinthians 155:3, 1 Peter 2:24, Galatians 3:13
[35] Ephesians 5:2, Hebrews 10:5-19

Roberts provides six separate aphorisms, spanning some 360+ folio pages, illuminating in great detail the nature, parties, matter, form, end, and inferences from this covenant. For Roberts, like many of his contemporaries, this covenant made with Abraham was for its sum and substance an expressure of the Covenant of Faith, and an advancement of God's Gospel purpose among His elect, and the Seed promised, none other than Christ Himself. Roberts will adduce several arguments in support of this idea. First, this calling of Abraham while he was yet in Ur of the Chaldees is styled the preaching of the Gospel to Abraham.[36] Second, this Covenant was confirmed of God in Christ 430 years before the law,[37] and citing Beza, "that God's Covenant graciously begun with Abram, was carried to One Christ, in whom alone that Seed of Abraham in Christ, both of Jews and Gentiles, is gathered together." Third, it is the Covenant of Faith because of the mercies and benefits promised by God in this covenant which led Abraham to faith in Christ, and because his covenanted fatherhood was not private, but public, by which he should be called the father of many nations. Further, those regardless of their earthly line, who would walk in the faith-steps of Abraham, are counted righteous through the promised seed, especially Christ, the *"eminent Seed"*[38] as was Abraham. Regarding the portion of the Covenant, the promise made concerning the land of Canaan, Roberts writes,

"The covenanted inheritance of Canaan, did lead Abraham and his posterity to Jesus Christ, and to salvation by him through faith.[39] For,

1. The Land of Canaan is styled (as has been already noted) The land of Immanuel, that is, the land of Christ the Mediator, God-man.[40]

2. Canaan, the Land of rest, was a special type of heaven, the eternal rest, as after will appear. And, as Joshua (whom the apostle calls Jesus, he being herein the type of the true Jesus Christ) brought the Israelites that believed

---

[36] Galatians 3:8 with Genesis 12:3
[37] Galatians 3:17
[38] Genesis 17:4-5; Romans 4:12, 17-18; Galatians 3:7, 16, 28-29
[39] Genesis 12:7, 13-15; 15:18-21; 17:8
[40] Isaiah 8:8

into Canaan's rest, they that believed not being unable to enter in:[41] so Jesus Christ brings the believing Israelites into heaven's rest, all unbelievers being excluded."[42]

Fourth, the conditions of the Covenant show that it was an administration of the Covenant of Faith, which were, besides others, "faith and worthy walking." Several passages of Scripture are brought to bear on this point. Fifth, the recompense also makes known that this was the Covenant of Faith, for, *"Abraham believed in the LORD, and He counted it to him for righteousness."* Sixth and finally, the confirmation, succession, and progression of these covenants God made with Abraham, all being for sum and substance the same covenant, were confirmed in Christ.

In the first of these, when Abraham was yet in Ur, we have the word of the Apostle for this, that God preached the Gospel to Abraham. In the second, when the Lord called upon Abraham to divide the animals, Roberts writes,

"That covenant which God renewed with Abraham after Melchizedeck had blessed him, was confirmed by sacrifices cut in twain, a smoking furnace, and a lamp of fire passing between those pieces.[43] These, as all corporal sacrifices appointed by God before Christ's coming, were types and figures of Christ the true sacrifice:[44] by whose death and blood the New Covenant or Testament is confirmed.[45] And the smoking furnace, and lamp of fire, passing between the parts of these divided sacrifices, seem to point out (according to the usual solemnity of covenanting)[46] the parties covenanting, namely: on the one hand, Abraham's seed, resembled by a smoking furnace, in reference to their great afflictions in Egypt before they should come to Canaan;[47] on the other hand, God in Christ, represented by a lamp of fire, who should lighten their darkness, and deliver them out of all their affliction and misery, and

---

[41] Hebrews 4:8-9; with 3:18-19; 4:6
[42] John 3:16, 18, 36. Matt. 16:16. Heb. 4: 9-11.
[43] Genesis 15:8-18
[44] Hebrews 10:1
[45] Hebrews 9:15-17, 1 Corinthians 11:25.
[46] Jeremiah 34:18
[47] Exodus 1:11, 13-14, Deuteronomy 4:20, Jeremiah 1:1, 4

bring them into Canaan. God[48] and Christ[49] in Scripture are compared to fire. This in my judgment, seems the most apposite interpretation of this vision of Abraham. And thus it notably points at Christ crucified, as the establishment of his covenant; as the redeemer and deliverer of his people."

For our part, we might also add that Roberts' second proposition in the interpretation of the Abrahamic ceremony that truly only God is seen "passing through the pieces" in the form of that smoking furnace is the better understanding. For in the Covenant of Grace, as was seen the self-maledictory bow that pointed away from mankind and toward heaven the throne of the Lord, so also here, as God comes under the bond of this Covenant, and Abraham is set aside as an observer. For in the essential work of that gracious covenant in Christ, man receives, and God gives; and the monergistic work of the Lord provides for all of the promised seed. Then, in the third of these covenant transactions of God with Abraham, we see the "covenant of circumcision" which was a seal of the righteousness of faith. Roberts writes, "and that's Christ's righteousness. And it was a type of Christ and his death, whereby our sins are destroyed, mortified and put off. *In whom also ye are circumcised with the Circumcision made without hands, in putting off the body of the sins of the flesh, by the Circumcision of Christ.*"[50]

In the second aphorism, discussing the parties of the Covenant, Roberts will distinguish three sorts of Abraham's seed: Only natural, only spiritual, both natural and spiritual. From those three we must determine which of them is the seed of promise. Marshaling several Scripture texts and with admirable logic, Roberts concludes that this seed was only one, Christ. That, although some Scriptures appear opposite in this regard, they may be "clearly reconciled, and the harmonious agreement of them evidenced, by considering how and in what sort God established his Covenant with Abraham's seed." In a remarkable use of Scripture he writes,

---

[48] Hebrews 12:29, Exodus 3:2, 20:18
[49] Daniel 10:6, Revelation 1:14
[50] Colossians 2:11

"(1) God established his Covenant with Abraham's seed as with one, and not as with many. I grant that Abraham's Covenant-seed was in itself manifold, namely: natural Jews, believing Jews, believing Gentiles, and Christ: as has been distinguished. Yet with these God established his Covenant, not in the notion of multiplicity, but in the notion of unity: not as they were many seeds; but as they were all one seed. *To Abraham and his Seed were the Promises made. He saith not, And to seeds, as of many: but as of one, and to thy Seed.*

(2) This one seed of Abraham to whom God made his Promises, and with whom he established his Covenant, was only CHRIST. *He saith not, And to Seeds, as of many; but as of one, And to thy Seed, which is Christ.*[51] Here under the word CHRIST, The Apostle comprehends all Abraham's Covenant-seed, to whom the federal Promises were made, namely: both believing Jews, believing Gentiles, and the Lord Jesus himself. All these are but one Christ, and God looked upon them all as one Christ, when he established his Covenant with them. This is a mystery which very few do aright observe. Yet it need not seem strange to us, if we intentively consider:

[1] That Christ the last Adam recollects and gathers together in one all things, as the first Adam broke, scattered and dissipated all things."

So, for Roberts, the seed of Abraham is Christ, the second Adam, and in Him with all the elect as His seed, considered together in the promise. He goes on to say that with this mystical, united body of believers in Christ, God establishes this Covenant forever, for the superabundant riches of His grace, for His own honor and glory, for the great benefit and reward He would be to His own people in Christ, and finally because of the worthiness of Christ Himself. Pursuant to this section, Roberts will give the people of God a lengthy pastoral section on self-examination, answering the question, "How may we know that we are Abraham's Spiritual seed?" He answers,

"By being Christ's. It is not enough that we are his nominally, that we are his formally, but in deed and in truth, sincerely, and altogether Christ's. We

---

[51] Galatians 3:16

must ask ourselves these questions: Have we Christ's Spirit? Are we new Creatures? Are we one with Christ? Have we crucified the flesh with its affections and lusts? Do we walk after the Spirit?

"By our walking in the steps of our father Abraham's faith: Abraham believed God, even to the point that the Lord is able to raise the dead. Abraham's faith was grounded upon God's promise. Abraham believed God's promise of Christ, the seed to come. Abraham walked by faith, not sight, and past natural impediments. Abraham doubted and staggered not at God's promises. He gave glory to God in the promises he anticipated and in which he had confidence. He was full persuaded that God would perform that which He committed to do.

"By doing the works of Abraham, which Christ discusses with the wicked Jews of His day. What were those works? His ready obedience to God's call. His submission to, and compliance with God's ordinances. His rejoicing to see Christ's day by faith. His true and brotherly love, expressed to Lot and others. His religious care and government of his family. His "eminent and admirable act of obedience to God, in sacrificing his son Isaac for a sort of burnt-offering, which was a stupendous act indeed."

It is here that we see the affection of a pastor of the flock of Christ leading and tenderly instructing the people of God in their faith and self-examination. As we said at the outset of this essay, this is a Scriptural, not a dusty theological treatise, from the heart of a pastor. Further, if the Covenant God made with Abraham is for himself only, and does not include a Seed in Christ and all His, this is all simply a nice historical example of a man who lived extraordinarily according to the light he had in his day, but would not be something to which the people of God today would aspire, or follow, seeing that they are now under a different covenant. But this is not at all the case. The student of Scripture will see that what Roberts has described above is truly the life of faith in Christ, for Abraham, and for us. The same pastoral direction, and fatherly counsel that Abraham would have given to his children, following his own example, Roberts draws from the New Testament and presses it to the people of God, who should consider themselves Abraham's seed, in Christ.

As might be expected, with the same Covenant of Faith, and in it a similar administration in Christ, Roberts will identify circumcision as the sign of that Covenant, and therefore, the Covenant sign of baptism having come in the room of circumcision, by the command of Christ in the New Testament. In several points under the title of "Covenant Inauguration" Roberts will show,

1. The New Covenant under which Abraham's Christian seed are, is for substance one and the same with this covenant under, which Abraham's Jewish seed were. Therefore as infants of his Jewish seed were circumcised: so infants of his Christian seed should be baptized.

2. The infants of Abraham's Christian Seed are in Covenant with their parents now: as well as the infants of Abraham's Jewish Seed were in Covenant with their parents then. If therefore Jewish infants were to be sacramentally initiated, because they were within Covenant, consequently Christian infants are to be sacramentally installed, because they are within covenant. And this is Peter's argument for baptizing the children of both believing Jews and Gentiles. (Acts 2:37-41)

3. This Sacramental inauguration of the infants of Abraham's seed God established and Commanded under the Old Testament, and has never forbidden it under the New Testament: therefore though the sacrament be changed, yet the sacramental inauguration and visible admission of the infants of Abraham's seed into the body of the Church, is still to be continued.

4. Citing Colossians 2:10-12, he shows that baptism has succeeded in the room of circumcision, "Here the Apostle dissuades his Colossians from the Jewish Circumcision; Partly, because they have now a better circumcision, even Christ's Circumcision made without hands, the spiritual putting off of the sins of the flesh. The type was now fulfilled and accomplished in Christ, and therefore was to vanish away."

5. The Federal Grace and Privileges of Abraham's Christian seed under the New Testament are as large and larger than those of Abraham's Jewish seed under the Old Testament: therefore if the infants of his Jewish seed were circumcised then, much more the infants of his Christian seed should be

baptized now. Nor parents, nor their infants, have lost, but gained, by becoming Christians.

6. The infants of Abraham's Christian seed now, are every way as capable of baptism as the infants of Abraham's Jewish seed then, could be capable of circumcision. Neither of them had actual faith, actual repentance, or actual understanding of Christ, covenant, sacrament, or of any divine mystery: both of them were merely passive in this administration. And as the one sort were only sensible of the sharpness of the knife; so the other sort were only sensible of the coldness of the water.

7. No objection can be made against the baptizing of the infants of Abraham's Christian seed, but the same objections will militate and may be urged as strongly every way against the circumcising of the infants of Abraham's Jewish seed.

This construction concerning the identity of the Covenant of Grace in the Abrahamic Covenant, and the sign of that covenant, circumcision, coming into the days of the New Testament and being superseded by baptism is the majority report among the Reformed.[52] This preface does not permit the space necessary to speak about several departures from this historic understanding. Suffice it to say that there are many such declensions from embracing the true nature of the Abrahamic Covenant. What they have generally in common is a separation of the complex of promises God made to the Patriarch, all which

---

[52] See Waters, Guy Prentiss, J. Nicholas Reid, and John R. Muether, eds. *Covenant Theology: Biblical, Theological, and Historical Perspectives*. Wheaton, IL: Crossway, 2020., 133-149; Smith, Morton H. *Systematic Theology, Volume One: Prolegomena, Theology, Anthropology, Christology*. Electronic ed. Escondido, CA: Ephesians Four Group, 1999, Vol. 2, 336-340, Reymond, Robert L. *A New Systematic Theology of the Christian Faith*. Nashville: T. Nelson, 1998, 503-545; Venema, Cornelis P. *Christ and Covenant Theology: Essays on Election, Republication, and the Covenants*. Phillipsburg, NJ: P&R Publishing, 2017, 256-282; Dabney, Robert L. *Systematic Theology*. Electronic ed. based on the Banner of Truth 1985 ed. Simpsonville SC: Christian Classics Foundation, 1996, 672-679; Robertson, O. Palmer. *The Christ of the Covenants*. Phillipsburg, NJ: Presbyterian and Reformed Publishing Co., 1980, 147-166, Turretin, Francis. *Institutes of Elenctic Theology*. Edited by James T. Dennison Jr. Translated by George Musgrave Giger. Vol. 1–3. Phillipsburg, NJ: P&R Publishing, 1992–1997.192-205, Samuel Rutherford, *The Covenant of Life Opened*, (Edinburgh: Andro Anderson for Robert Brown) 1655), 72-117, among many other references. Truly, these mentioned here only scratch the surface.

had a gracious contribution to the overall expression of the covenant of grace. Instead, these promises are particularized, separated one from another, in order to make, in our opinion, an unbiblical separation between the Abrahamic Covenant and the Covenant of Grace. Various kinds of separation are often set forth:

- The Covenant made with Abraham was actually two covenants, with "two distinct posterities."[53]
- There are "two circumcisions, and two posterities."[54]
- The Abrahamic covenant was not the Covenant of Grace, nor was it an administration of it, but only a way to reveal it as part of the unfolding nature of God's revelation. The Covenant of Grace waited in time until Christ came.[55]

These departures from the historic Reformed construction by many in Baptist Churches are based on dividing the Seed of Abraham. Note above, and in the reading that follows in Marrow, that Roberts understands that the seed of Abraham divided as well, but in a very different sense. The promised Seed of Abraham is Christ, including all those who have faith in Christ, like Abraham did,[56] for they too are Abraham's seed, in Christ.[57] In the sense of the promise, the promise of eternal life and the resurrection from the dead, Christ is the seed. Rather than making circumcision the sign of being Abraham's physical seed,[58] as our Baptist friends have done, or seeking to divide circumcision into "two circumcisions and two posterities",[59] Roberts sees circumcision as the sign of the Covenant of Grace that was administered

---

[53] Pascal Denault, *The Distinctiveness of Baptist covenant Theology*, Solid Ground Christian Books, Birmingham, AL 2013, 119-121

[54] Greg Nichols, *Covenant Theology, A Reformed and Baptistic Perspective on God's Covenants*, Solid Ground Christian Books, Birmingham, AL 2011, 168-172

[55] Pascal Denault, *The Distinctiveness of Baptist covenant Theology*, Solid Ground Christian Books, Birmingham, AL 2013, 70-71

[56] John 8:56

[57] Galatians 3:26-29

[58] Jeffrey D. Johnson, *The Fatal Flaw of the Theology Behind Infant Baptism*, Free Grace Press, 2010, 209-214

[59] Greg Nichols, *Covenant Theology, A Reformed and Baptistic Perspective on God's Covenants*, Solid Ground Christian Books, Birmingham, AL 2011, 172-173

in Abraham's time, as the Apostle says in Romans 4:9-13, a seal of the righteousness which is by faith, administered not only to Abraham, but to his household also: all who come under the bond of the covenant.[60]

The importance of republishing this work becomes even clearer when we come to the Mosaic Covenant. As with the covenants made with Adam, Noah, and Abraham, Roberts identifies here as well the Covenant of Grace (or in his parlance, the Covenant of Faith) manifested and advanced. Comprising chapter four of the work, spanning some 350 pages, we have yet another master-work of Bible exposition. Aphorism 1 speaks to the Law of God, as moral, ceremonial, and judicial, given for the Church under age, as well as the continuing obligation distinguished in the days after the coming of Christ. Roberts will show that there are both continuities and discontinuities, clearing several questions about the Law of God in its abiding validity. Students of Scripture will see the application of this section to the questions of theonomy, antinomianism, and what Westminster confessors call the "general equity" of the law of God, especially in the "judicials." Roberts declares that the end and scope of the moral law is love. Standing in the stream of second reformation thought, he shows that the moral law comprises all duties of religion, piety, and holiness or love to God in the first table, condemning all contrary sins, and in the second table comprising all duties of sobriety, equity, and righteousness, and condemning all opposite vices, toward our fellow men in our various places and relations. He brings together the moral law of God and the natural law written upon the heart of Adam upon his creation and being placed in paradise. Speaking of the various uses of the word "law," he writes, "Sometimes, the law of nature; consisting in certain principles of religion, righteousness, and temperance, at first con-created in man, and naturally engraven in his heart in innocency: some imperfect sparkles or relics whereof remain even in hearts of pagans, who have not God's written law."[61] Later, he will distinguish the moral law expressed in ten commandments from the law of nature written on the heart, providing some details of

---

[60] Genesis 18:18-19
[61] Romans 2:14

identification, and others of distinction. Regarding the ceremonial law he provides a good summary of reformed thought:

"(1) That the way of God's worship and service enjoined to the Jews was very chargeable, tedious and troublesome: an entangling yoke of bondage, a yoke which they were not able to bear.

(2) That their service and worship of God was more carnal and corporal, according to the dullness and incapacity of that people, the church then being under these tutors and governors, because under age;

(3) That the way of religion was then very dark under types and shadows: under all these shadows, good things to come in and by Christ, were veiled and dimly represented, which the faithful Jews did, though obscurely, apprehend, for their salvation:

(4) That God has provided better things for his church under the New Testament, wherein we are happier than the Jews."

Advancing to the judicial laws, Roberts shows great judgment speaking about them as an "appendix to [God's] moral law" in the civil regulation of equity, righteousness, and sobriety. Concerning their abiding validity, he places himself squarely in the Westminster understanding of general equity, refusing particular equity of every statute and command, but retaining proper general equity, and bringing that equity into the present day, especially regarding Christian magistrates:

"Now the LORD imposed not these judicials upon the Gentiles, but only upon the Jews during the continuance of their commonwealth. Nor are Christian commonwealths now under the New Testament formally under those laws or obliged by them, further than the moral ground and equity thereof binds analogically. God gave these judicial laws to the Jews,

1. That He might hereby let them see that Himself immediately was their King, their Judge, their Lawgiver...

2. That there might be the form of a well-ordered commonwealth in Israel; wherein vice might be suppressed, virtue encouraged...

3. That they might perceive how much God approves of government, order, public peace, honesty, righteousness, distinction of things, etc. and how much he abhors anarchy, confusion, tyranny, barbarousness, injustice, etc.

4. That they might know how great a rewarder God was of all piety and righteousness, and how severe an avenger of all sin and wickedness.

5. That in this well-constituted and well-regulated commonwealth, the Church and ordinances of God might have quiet, safe and comfortable subsistence...

6. That God might proportionably instruct all Christian magistrates under the New Testament, to govern their subjects by wise and righteous laws, made known unto the people: and not arbitrarily, by their own mere will and pleasure. The wisdom and equity of whose laws will notably appear, by comparing them in some due analogy with these of God himself, which were the most wise, full and righteous political laws that ever were contrived."

In all, this is a very profitable discussion of the law of God from a Reformed and Christian perspective and is highly recommended to the student of Christian ethics. He progresses in this discussion through the ten commandments, with a brief description of each, what obedience is, and what violations of these commands deserve, and is a proper undertaking against the antinomianism of our day. He admirably sets out the difference between legal and evangelical obedience, encouragement to obedience by promise, and shows how that evangelical obedience is not inconsistent with justification by the free grace of God. Many modern errors are anticipated by our author in this section, and rightly treated.

In Aphorism 2, Roberts sets out to show that the Law was given at Sinai as a "Covenant of Faith." Showing himself to be very well read in the divinity of his age, Roberts is aware that the Covenant at Sinai was, even in his own day, variously understood. Let us remember, as Westminster Confessors, that we have confessed that the Covenant of Sinai was an administration of the Covenant of Grace:

"This covenant was differently administered in the time of the law, and in the time of the gospel:[a] under the law it was administered by promises, prophecies, sacrifices, circumcision, the paschal lamb, and other types and ordinances delivered to the people of the Jews, all foresignifying Christ to come;^b which were, for that time, sufficient and efficacious, through the operation of the Spirit, to instruct and build up the elect in faith in the promised Messiah,^c by whom they had full remission of sins, and eternal salvation; and is called the Old Testament.^d

a. 2 Cor. 3:6–9. *b.* Heb. 8, 9, 10; Rom. 4:11; Col. 2:11–12; 1 Cor. 5:7. *c.* 1 Cor. 10:1–4; Heb. 11:13; John 8:56. *d.* Gal. 3:7–9, 14.

Under the gospel, when Christ, the substance,^a was exhibited, the ordinances in which this covenant is dispensed are the preaching of the Word, and the administration of the sacraments of Baptism and the Lord's Supper:^b which, though fewer in number, and administered with more simplicity, and less outward glory, yet, in them, it is held forth in more fullness, evidence, and spiritual efficacy,^c to all nations, both Jews and Gentiles;^d and is called the new Testament.^e There are not therefore two covenants of grace, differing in substance, but one and the same, under various dispensations.^f

a. Col. 2:17. *b.* Matt. 28:19–20; 1 Cor. 11:23–25. *c.* Heb. 12:22–27; Jer. 31:33–34. *d.* Matt. 28:19; Eph. 2:15–19. *e.* Luke 22:20. *f.* Gal. 3:14, 16; Acts 15:11; Rom. 3:21–23, 30. Ps. 32:1; Rom. 4:3, 6, 16–17, 23–24; Heb. 13:8."[62]

There are many who have turned away from these propositions in their fullness, and have, in one way or another, allowed other ideas to creep into their thinking. In the quotation below, we see that there were various ideas concerning the Sinai administration in the days of our author which persist until today:

"I find principally four several opinions touching this matter, namely:

1. The first holding, that *the Law on Mount Sinai was given as a Covenant of Works, not of Grace* (or, of Faith, as I had rather style it).

2. The second holding, that it was a *mixed covenant, partly of Works, partly of Grace.*

---

[62] Westminster Assembly. Chapter 7, "Of God's Covenant with Man" *The Westminster Confession of Faith: Edinburgh Edition.* Philadelphia: William S. Young, 1851., 7.5-7.6

3. The third holding, that *it was not purely and properly either a Covenant of Nature or of Grace, but a covenant subservient to the Covenant of Grace, and preparing thereunto.*

4. The fourth holding, *that it was a Covenant of Grace for substance, though propounded in an unusual way of terror and servile bondage, suitable to that people, time, and state of the Church under age.*

Touching these various opinions, I intend not polemically to discuss them; but rather positively, to give a brief narrative of them severally, and to annex briefly some few reasons, partly against such of them as do not satisfy; and partly for that, which is the truth. After which, I shall remove objections made to the contrary."

In this briefly stated compass, Roberts has embarked on a course of study most necessary to our day, for in it he will present the Biblical understanding of the Covenant of Sinai, that it is an administration of the Covenant of Grace, and will interact with brotherly wisdom and care against other, competing views. He will relate the Sinaiatic Covenant to former covenants of faith, show how its administration at Sinai pertains not to performance, but to salvation by the work of Christ. Suffice these few quotations as a sample of Roberts' thinking:

"The ceremonial law is presently annexed to the moral, as part of the Sinai-Covenant, to instruct them yet further in the deep mystery of this blessed prophet and mediator promised, Christ Jesus. The ark, mercy-seat, golden altar of incense, table of shew-bread, altar of burnt offering, the veil of the tabernacle, the tabernacle it self, the Priests, the sacrifices of all sorts and their bloods, the purifications, washings, etc., all being but shadows of good things to come: but the body, Christ. Whose person, office, condition, effects of his office, etc., were typified and shadowed out to the people in these things. Thus the law was contrived to be their schoolmaster to bring them to Christ, that they might be justified by faith."

In Aphorism 3, Roberts considers the federate parties of the Covenant at Sinai, God, and His Covenant Seed, the Israelites, considered His peculiar people visibly, establishing a *"dear and strong union and communion betwixt*

God and Israel, and that upon sundry and intimate relations." They are Abraham's seed in Covenant with God, they are "*the Lord's Redeemed from temporal and spiritual misery.*" They are His espoused people, spoken of as the very bride of the Lord, heirs of His promises by faith, looking forward, as a church under-age, until that time of majority in Christ. In all of these relations, had in Christ by the Israelites, Roberts concludes this section with several inferences from this covenant relation, beginning with this:

"Hence, How admirable was the loving-kindness of God to Israel, and the happiness of Israel in God, in that they were federate parties to this covenant in these sweet comfortable and excellent notions! Recollect but a little the notions and considerations wherein they became federate-parties: And consider the infinite distance and disparity between God and Israel: and then say with admiration, "Who so gracious a God as the Lord! Who so happy a people as his Israel!"

In Aphorism 4, Roberts speaks of the matter of this Sinai Covenant. In this section he shows the promises God had made to His people: to be a God to them. To raise up Christ as a mediator and savior for them; to give them the Spirit of Christ; to confer upon them in Christ blessing of a temporal, spiritual, and eternal nature.

To the Israelites was given these covenant duties: to be a people unto the Lord, his peculiar possession; to keep covenant with Him, by true faith and sincere obedience; to repent of any failings of these standards.

In great detail, over the next 100 pages, Roberts shows that this matter of covenanting was gracious, based upon faith and repentance, although it was given under a "terrible" form, even with strong legal overtones, because the Church was yet in an immature estate. Near the conclusion of this section, he writes,

"How plain is it, That this covenant at Mount Sinai was a gospel administration: because in case of Israel's failing therein it conditioned and called for their repenting! Repentance is a pure evangelical condition and duty, pressed often in the gospel-doctrine of Old and New Testament, as has been already shown: whereas the law, that is, the Covenant of Works, admits of no repentance at all, no not in the least case of failing in covenant-duties but denounces death without mercy for the smallest transgression. So then the Sinai-Covenant was a Covenant of Faith evangelical, not a Covenant of Works legal."

In Aphorism 5 we have presented to the reader the form of God's Sinai Covenant, that it spoke of God's great condescension to a people then steeped in the ways of this world, as a church under age, and in bondage in Egypt. The servile pedagogy of the Sinai Covenant was truly God's condescending mercy, along with these other mercies from the Lord:

• It had an outward glory in the gold, silver and precious stones of the tabernacle.

• It separated God in His holiness by a veil of darkness and awe-inspiring majesty.

• They heard the voice of God—the trumpet that thundered from Sinai.

• It organized the succession of an ordinary ministry to teach the Word of God and administer ordinances under the command of God.

• It was in its form made with all the people, their children, and others of the Gentiles who would covenant with God.

• It had a protective reference to their civil state, as well as ecclesiastical ordinances for their instruction and preservation as a Church.

In all of these, and many more things too numerous to be named here, Roberts shows the surpassing glory and grace of the Mosaic administration, as a "Covenant of Faith": an advancement of the Gospel in Christ. He shows that the Jews were an exceedingly intractable people, a stubborn, rebellious, and stiff-necked nation, and thus the necessary iron yoke placed upon them was not for their destruction, but for their salvation in Christ, and that the carnal Jews, who did not embrace this Covenant of the Lord, were without excuse. Finally, we will see that this covenant was a marked advance to all the covenant expressions that had come to this time, yet would be far inferior to the New Covenant in Christ.

In Aphorism 6, Roberts presents the end or scope of this Sinai covenant. Briefly here, Roberts states that it was intended to reveal Jesus Christ more fully than He had been revealed before as the promised Savior of sinners, and as the end of the law for righteousness to all those that believe. This aphorism is handled in a mere nine pages, yet some great material touched on in other sections is stated with more force. Roberts distinguishes between different ends that may exist in any undertaking, including covenant, in this way:

"Then, one and the self-same covenant may have several ends. And this without any inconvenience or absurdity: provided those ends be some of them more near and immediate, others more remote and mediate; some of them subordinate, others of them ultimate. And such are all these aforementioned ends in this covenant. Jesus Christ, the life and salvation of Israel, was the more near and immediate end of it: Israel's temporal, spiritual, and eternal happiness by Jesus Christ through faith was the more remote and subordinate end of it: The further advancement of God's glory in and by both was the principal and ultimate end of it."

He will also affirm in this section that Sinai was not a mere carnal and temporal covenant pertaining to Canaan, it was purely and only evangelical, leading to justification by faith in Christ alone. Many in our day have wrestled with these truths as Roberts has presented them, as was said above, some going even so far as saying that the Sinai Covenant was a "covenant of works."[63] Various others have come close to such an admission as well, when they have focused on the legal framework, the terrifying nature of its beginning at Sinai, with fire, smoke, the unendurable voice of words, the obvious fear that the Lord was inciting among them when He thundered the 10 Words from the top of the mount.[64] In our day this hearing the thunderings of Sinai as a covenant of works is called the doctrine of republicationism. And while this title does not represent a monolithic group of scholarly brethren, these men

---

[63] Jeffrey D. Johnson, *The Fatal Flaw of the Theology Behind Infant Baptism*, Free Grace Press, 2010, 233

[64] See T. David Gordon, *Abraham and Sinai Contrasted, in The Law is not of Faith*, Estelle, Fesko, VanDrunen eds. P&R Publishing, Phillipsburg NJ, 2009, 251

have some things in common in their understanding of Sinai. The admission of a works/merit paradigm in Sinai is allowed so that the Covenant of Works is said to be republished in some sense in the Sinai administration. For most this manifests in Israel maintaining some kind of covenant fidelity before the Lord in exchange for their tenure in the land of promise. Merideth Kline writes,

"Likewise, the Israelite people corporately could maintain their continuing tenure as the theocratic kingdom in the promised land only as they maintained the appropriate measure of national fidelity to their heavenly King. Failure to do so would result in the loss of the typological kingdom and their very identity as God's people in that corporate, typological sense. If they broke the covenant, they would suffer exile and the loss of their national, typological election. Such was, of course, the actual outcome. Israel became Lo-Ammi. The fact of this loss of the national election given to Israel in the Mosaic Covenant compels all who confess the sovereignty of God's saving grace to recognize the presence of a works principle in that covenant."[65]

Similar comments can be found in various works of our brethren.[66] This author would not count himself among the "all" who confess the sovereignty of God's saving grace who also maintain a works principle in the Sinaitic Covenant. Certainly, maintaining the sovereignty of God's grace does not require the entrance of a works principle into the Mosaic administration, any more than it requires a works principle in the promises of Ephesians 6:1-3. There the apostle enjoins obedience upon children to their own parents "in the Lord", that is, in the context of the New Covenant, and then promises long life upon their obedience, bringing the 5th Commandment into the New Testament face of a worldwide Church. Shall we say there is a works-principle at "work" here, or shall we rather say, in kindness our heavenly Father encourages obedience by holding out blessings, not meritorious rewards, for following Him? In other words, when we offer our children a prize for their

---

[65] Meredith G. Kline, *Kingdom Prologue: Genesis Foundations for a Covenantal Worldview* (Eugene, OR: Wipf & Stock Publishers, 2006), 322

[66] Multiple authors, *The Law is not of Faith*, Estelle, Fesko, VanDrunen eds. P&R Publishing, Phillipsburg NJ, 2009, 8,19,85,136,251

are we ready to disown them if they fail in that performance? Do
' their joy and felicity in being part of the family upon their
nents? Do we say that they have earned, meritoriously, the prize
:eived, or have they merely done that which is their duty—to obey
parents have desired of them? The Lord, in the Sinai
n, presented the Law to Israel in such a way that they would
hat it could not be kept. It would be a carnal and prideful
the gracious principle evident in the whole, that Roberts in his
od at identifying, to believe that the Israelites as a whole, or any
that nation, could merit tenure in the land, or any other
piritual benefit from the Lord by covenant-obedience. The
d have learned to rest upon God's mercy as they learned of their
would die in their stead, as year after year they beheld as their
ted to two goats, one slain, and one sent out to the wilderness.
nals presented to the Israelites not a covenant of works, but a
ition of the sins of the people upon a substitute to be slain in
upon a sacrifice sent away in removal of their guilt.

: makes clear that there was no law which could give life.[67] In
: interpretation of the phrase used in the Pentateuch and
ll therefore keep my statutes, and my judgments: which if a
' live in them: I am the LORD,[68] he makes plain that these
ed the impossibility of keeping the Law for meritorious
asting faith and merit in Romans 10:5, Paul categorically
orks/merit paradigm could ever obtain righteousness before
t to him that wills or runs, but it is of God who shows mercy,
usness which is obtained from God in every age is the
ich comes through the alone instrument of faith. The
d for obedience, and threatened chastisement for
simply part of God's gracious design as He deals with His

2

cus 18:5, Nehemiah 9:29; Ezekiel 20:11,13,21; Luke Romans 10:5;

weak children in every age. There are other considerations as well that sho[w] this encouragement to duty in promised rewards, and threatened chastiseme[nts] as a deterrent for disobedience was a part of God's merciful and gracio[us] covenant dealing with His people in all of redemptive history.

The first is that in the Covenant of Works, only one sin is necessary for [all] to come down—just one—and the curses of the Covenant to come upon t[he] breakers of it. But it is here that we must ask, how many times did Isr[ael] manifest their covenant infidelity? The student of Scripture will remem[ber] when the entirety of the nation committed idolatry in Exodus 32, just 40 d[ays] after the covenant ceremony of chapter 24. In testimony to their coven[ant] breaking, Moses cast the tables from his hands and broke them in the prese[nce] of the people. Deuteronomy chapter 9 gives the record of that day, and m[any] others, when the Israelites, as a nation, broke covenant with God. Did [the] curses come upon them? Were they destroyed? Not at all—rather Moses st[ood] as a mediator, a type of Christ, and interceded for them, and the Lord forg[ave] them, and took vengeance on their inventions—that is, He chastised [His] sinning people. This is a gracious act on God's part, and not a covenan[t of] works. Remember what the Lord *threatened*, and what He *actually did*. [He] threatened them with destruction, and then to make of Moses a new na[tion.] Dear reader, this is what the Covenant of Works would have demanded. [The] Lord threatened them with that destruction to show them the conseque[nces] of the Covenant of Works—that is, their own fallen estate, and the destruc[tion] deserved, but then graciously interposed a mediator, and extended mer[cy to] them, because Sinai was a Covenant of Grace after all.

The second principle is that in the Covenant of Grace the Lord [often] threatens the end of some temporal estate or other as a discourageme[nt to] disobedience, and temporal maintenance and blessing as an encourageme[nt to] obedience. This was seen above, in Ephesians 6. It also is seen in the lett[ers to] the Churches of Asia Minor in Revelation, chapters 2 and 3. This princi[ple of] blessing/promise, threatening/cursing is seen as the Lord interacts wit[h His] people, in the Covenant of Grace. The Churches of Ephesus, Sardis [and] Laodicea are threatened with an end of their estate before the Lord, s[hould] they continue in their present state of disobedience to his commands, and disloyalty to Him. They are also given promises to encourage them to repentance and new obedience. Would any declare that these three churches are subsumed under some republished covenant of works? The Lord offers blessing to his people upon their repentance and obedience as an encouragement to them. Further, he threatens His chastisement upon His people, for He loves them, *and scourgeth every son whom he receiveth*.[69] Hebrews 12 makes this clear that when the Lord shows Himself in this manner, he is dealing as a Father, under a principle of grace, and not as a Judge, under a principle of works.

The third principle used especially by Roberts in describing the Sinai Covenant is that of repentance. Dear reader, there is never, never an opportunity for repentance in a covenant of works. Once the performance principle is violated, the covenant is broken, and the curses of the covenant come in, unabated. The mere fact that the Lord accepted from the people gathered at Sinai their sin offerings, their repentance, and held out forgiveness to them, as a people and as individuals, presents one of the strongest cases that Sinai was indeed a manifestation of the Covenant of Grace.

As much as we would love to go on, it is here, dear reader, that we bring our preface to a close. Certainly, there is much more to be said, much more darkness to dispel, and more light to be let in. Our author will pass on to the Davidic Covenant, and the Covenant promises made to His people as He brought them back from captivity. And finally, He will speak of the glorious New Covenant in Christ, the surpassing glory of all of God's covenanting. Your time will not be wasted wringing every drop of sound divinity you can from this tome—there is much to be had. I hope that in these few remarks, you will have your appetite whetted to read a stalwart, a Master in Israel, as he gleaned from the Scriptures that gracious work of God in condescension, by way of Covenant, to His elect people, throughout the ages, through types, shadows, promises, prophecies, sacrifices, circumcision, the Passover, and other

---

[69] Hebrews 12:1-6

types and ordinances, prepared and pointed His people to their King, Head, Mediator, Surety, Substitute, their Savior and Lord, Jesus Christ. The work that follows is highly commended. Dear reader, *tolle lege*.

Yours in Christ Jesus,

Rev. Dr. Todd Ruddell, M.Div., Th.M., Th.D.
Pastor, Christ Covenant Reformed Presbyterian Church
Wylie, TX

The author's letter to the churches

To the churches

To the churches, ministers, and members of Jesus Christ, in England, Scotland, Ireland and others the annexed dominions, grace, mercy and peace from God our Father and the Lord Jesus Christ our mediator, and from the Holy Spirit the comforter.

Highly honored, and entirely beloved in the Lord,

The sacred covenants[70] of God with man, before,[71] and since[72] his fall, that profound *mystery* and *marrow* of the Bible, are a subject so sublime, spiritual, comprehensive, transcendent, and every way excellent, in itself; so necessary, profitable, comfortable, and every way desirable, to us: that it is most worthy of all acceptation, by all that are, or desire to be, altogether Christians,[73] for:[74] (1) The author of these covenants is the Lord, the most high and only wise God. (2) The original fountain and impulsives of them: the glorious riches of divine grace. (3) The confederates or federate-parties to them: God, and man either as in the first Adam before the fall, or as in the last Adam, Jesus Christ since the fall. (4) The foundation of all the Covenants of Faith from first to last: Jesus Christ, God-man, our only mediator and hope, either as promised, or as performed. (5) The matters of God's Covenants are: from God, all manner of blessings temporal, spiritual, and eternal, which the whole

---

[70] Luke 1:72
[71] Genesis 2:16-17
[72] Genesis 3:14-15, 6:18, etc,, 9:8-9, etc., 12:1-3, 15:18, Deuteronomy 5:2, etc., with Exodus 24:4-9, Psalm 89:3, etc., Ezekiel 37:26, etc., Hebrews 8:6-13
[73] Acts 26:28-29
[74] See all these seven particulars abundantly cleared in all God's federal expressures unfolded in the ensuing treatise.

Scriptures promise: from man, all manner of duties natural in the first Adam, or supernatural in the last Adam, which the whole Scriptures require. (6) The form of them: more inwardly, the federates reciprocal and mutual obligation, and more outwardly, the various manifestations, confirmations and administrations of God's several covenants according to the mysterious contrivances and counsels of his blessed will. (7) Finally, the intended scope or ends of them all, are: subordinately, the happiness of man in his federal enjoyment of the Lord as his covenant God both in this and the world to come, which is absolutely the height of all possible felicity: ultimately, the glory of God in his matchless wisdom, goodness, free-grace, mercy, love, truth, faithfulness, justice, holiness, happiness, etc. – all of which are rendered in and through Jesus Christ most illustrious and glorious. This transcendent and most excellent mystery, the Covenants of God, I have endeavored (according to the measure of the gift of Christ received) to explicate and illustrate in the ensuing treatise. A work (I acknowledge) of vast extent, great difficulty, much labor, and long time.

(1) *Of vast extent.* Comprising in it: all the methods of divine dispensations to the church in all ages; all the conditions of the church under those dispensations; all the greatest and precious promises, of the life that now is, and of that which is to come; all sorts of blessings promised by God to man; all sorts of duties re-promised by man to God; all the gradual discoveries of Jesus Christ, the only mediator, and savior of sinners; the whole mystery of all true religion from the beginning to the end of the world; and which as a continued thread of gold runs through the whole series of all the holy Scriptures.

(2) *Of great difficulty.* Things that are excellent are difficult. This work is difficult: partly, through the profound mysteriousness of the covenants themselves; partly, through the obscurity and seeming repugnancy of some Scriptures wherein the covenants are mentioned and revealed; partly, through the great diversity of God's covenant discoveries: partly, through the many intricate knots, doubts and perplexing controversies that all sorts of adversaries to the truth, have cast in the way. By reason of all which this precious truth

lies, like silver, very deep, and sometimes hard to come by, and must be laboriously dug out from amongst the very rocks.

(3) *Of much labor.* Being of such vast extent and great difficulty, it must needs be very laborious. God's Covenants are many, occasioning many doubts, questions, cases of conscience, etc. And the nature of some of them especially so involved in intricate difficulties and perplexities; that I confess, it has cost me no small pains and study to give myself and others satisfaction therein. It can be no easy task to take so long a journey, and of times to travel through such deep ways and unbeaten paths, yea sometimes to pass through such stony and rocky places. But because I have set my heart exceedingly to the covenants of my God, which (in my judgment) are a universal basis or foundation to all true religion and happiness, I have shunned no diligence, industry or endeavors that to me seemed requisite for the profitable unveiling of them.

(4) *Finally, this is a work of a long time.* This I have proved by much experience, far beyond my expectation. For in the treatise following is comprised the substance of all my weekly lectures for the space of almost six years complete – besides much of the New Covenant, which was never preached at all. During which time, when I had brought on the work almost to the end of God's Covenant with his captives as it were in their graves in Babylon,[75] I was for certain weeks together so captivated by a putrid fever that I was almost brought to the brink of the grave. And this was a deep aggravation of mine affliction, that now the work was likely to be left imperfect, and little or nothing spoken to the new covenant, which is the glory of all God's Covenants. But the Lord my God was ready to save me,[76] both in affliction, and from affliction.

(1) In affliction: by withholding my disease from annoying my animals and from assaulting much my vitals, though it had brought my naturals almost as low as the dust. By which dispensation I comforted myself that the Lord, in sparing my animals and intellectuals, intended to reserve them for some further service to himself and his church.

---

[75] Ezekiel 37:11-14
[76] Isaiah 38:20

(2) From affliction: by loving my soul from the pit of corruption,[77] casting all my sins behind his back, and restoring a new life unto me, so that I might exalt his glorious name in explication of his New Covenant. For which complexive mercy, I desire unfeignedly to render all possible praises to the God of my salvation.

Now therefore, having enterprized and (through the good hand of my most gracious God) at last accomplished this long, laborious, difficult and comprehensive work, I most humbly lay it at the feet of Jesus Christ my Lord and Savior, sincerely devoting and consecrating it first to his honor, next to the service, edification, and consolation of his church and all his genuine members within these islands. And the God of all grace, who has given the *manifestation of the Spirit to every man to profit withal,*[78] and who can actuate the doctrine of truth – whether preached with lively voice, or printed in a book to the saving benefit of his people's souls – so accept, bless, go forth with and prosper these poor labors of his most unworthy servant, by his Spirit's sacred influences and effectual co-operations, that thereby, some ignorant souls may be illuminated; some gainsayers to the truth and opposers of religion may be convinced; some aliens to Christ may be converted; some weak doubting and trembling Christians may be resolved, strengthened, and established; some dejected, disconsolate, afflicted, tempted or deserted saints may be refreshed and comforted, and that in some fort or other, whosoever shall read the soul-saving mysteries of God's holy covenants hereafter unfolded, may have his heart even burn within him towards God, Jesus Christ, his Covenants, and a true New Covenant state with God in Christ, that the flames of that heavenly fire within his breast may be unquenchable.

And in order to the more fruitful perusal of this treatise, and for the more speedy fixing of right notions and apprehensions in the readers' minds touching the covenants of God, I premise and earnestly recommend these few general considerations, namely:

---

[77] Isaiah 38:17
[78] 1 Corinthians 12:7, etc.

(1) *That, the Lord, the only true God, Father, Son, and Holy Ghost, though eternally and infinitely happy in himself alone, yet is pleased to communicate of his happiness to his intellectual Creatures, angels and men: but especially to men, by vouchsafing them a blessed fellowship or communion with himself, both natural, spiritual, and celestial.* In this consideration I comprise four things, namely:

[1] That the Lord, the only true God is Father, Son, and Holy Ghost.[79] A Trinity of persons, or personal subsistences in unity of essence.

[2] That the Lord God is eternally and infinitely happy in himself: for before all time and before the world or any creature was,[80] from eternity to eternity, he was God. And being eternally God, he was eternally happy in himself – the blessed and only potentate.[81] Yea being the infinite and boundless of God, he was, is, and will be infinitely happy in himself. Perfect happiness consists in enjoyment of perfect goodness, of a confluence of all goodness. Now God is all goodness; God is his own goodness. There is none good save one, that is, God,[82] namely: there is none good as God is good – essentially, independently, infinitely, immutably, eternally, etc.

And therefore God is his own happiness eternally; when nothing was, but God. The Father, Son and Holy Ghost having eternal and infinite fulness of satisfaction, complacency and acquiescence in themselves alone. And whatsoever goodness or happiness is in any creature since the creation, all that is wholly put into, and heaped upon the creature by God alone, as drops out of his ocean, as grains out of his mountain, as littles out of his all.

[3] That God notwithstanding is pleased to communicate of his own happiness to his intellectual creatures, angels and men, but especially to men. As the sun, full of light, communicates his light and glory to all the world, or as the sea, full of water, imparts his streams to all the earth. And yet the happiness of God is not at all diminished by imparting his happiness to men

---

[79] Genesis 2:4-6, etc., The Lord God, John 17:3, Matthew 28:19, 1 John 5:7
[80] Psalm 90:2
[81] 1 Timothy 6:15
[82] Matthew 19:27

and angels, as the light of the sun is not at all lessened by his diffusion and emanation of light to all the world. Nevertheless man, being brought nearest to God in the person and office of Jesus Christ,[83] has the primary impartment of the divine felicity.

[4] That God communicates his happiness to man by vouchsafing him blessed communion with himself, both natural, spiritual, and celestial. God so communicates his happiness to man, as that man must reciprocate some homage to God out of that which he has received from God. God gives of his own to man, and expects again of his own from man – and herein in the general stands that blissful and sweet communion between God and man. And this communion is threefold, namely: {1} *natural*, by creation, which was between God and Adam in paradise before the fall,[84] {2} *spiritual*, by new creation,[85] which is between God and all the elect in Jesus Christ the second Adam, since the fall, and {3} *celestial*, by glorification, which shall be between God and all the elect in Christ in the highest heavens, in the beatific vision and fruition of God in Jesus Christ face to face immediately, fully and eternally.[86]

(2) ***That the Lord God brings man into communion with himself, by that sweet familiar way of covenant, in all ages, from the foundation to the consummation of the world.*** God might have dealt with man in a more absolute lordly and majestical way, peremptorily commanding and requiring from man his duty and allegiance: but he has pleased to condescend to a more relatively familiar covenant way – and this *after the manner of man*,[87] namely, familiarly, sweetly, and condescendingly dealing with man by covenant, as one man with another. God by his covenants reveals, applies, confirms, and increases this sweet communion between himself and his people in all ages and generations of the world, from the creation to the judgment day. [1] Into

---

[83] John 1:14, 1 Timothy 3:16, Hebrews 2:16, Ephesians 1:20-22, Philippians 2:9-11
[84] Genesis 2:7 to the end
[85] 2 Corinthians 5:17, 1 John 3:2, 2 Corinthians 13:14
[86] Matthew 5:8, 1 John 3:2-3, John 17:24
[87] 1 Chronicles 17:17 with 2 Samuel 7:19

natural communion. God brought innocent man by the Covenant of Works.[88] [2] Into spiritual communion, God brings lapsed man by the Covenant of Faith,[89] gradually more and more revealed unto perfection, in all the seven periods and discoveries of it: witness Adam, Noah, Abraham, Israel, David, the captives, and Jews and Gentiles of all nations, thus brought into, and established in communion with God by his covenant. [3] Into celestial communion also they are brought by the same Covenant of Faith, assuring by many promises of a glorious life and complete happiness in heaven forevermore.[90]

(3) **That God's Covenant with man is of two kinds**, namely: [1] a Covenant of Works,[91] with man upright in the first Adam before the fall, promising the continuance of life and happiness to him upon terms of perfect and perpetual personal obedience, but threatening death and misery upon the least failing therein – which covenant being broken by Adam's disobedience in eating the forbidden fruit, was *in specie* utterly irreparable (see in this treatise, these covenants' explication).[92] [2] A Covenant of Faith,[93] with man lapsed, in Jesus Christ, the last Adam, revealing and promising lapsed sinners recovery from sin and death to righteousness and life, upon terms of unfeigned faith in Jesus Christ to that end. This distinction of God's Covenant, into a Covenant of Works and of Faith, is most proper and agreeable to Scripture. The nature whereof,[94] and of the Covenant of Faith in general, is hereafter at large unfolded.

---

[88] Genesis 2:16-17
[89] Genesis 3:14-15, 6:18, etc., 12:1-3, etc., Deuteronomy 5:2, etc., Exodus 24:4-0, Psalm 89:3, etc., Ezekiel 37:26, etc., Hebrews 8:6 to the end
[90] Hebrews 8:10, etc., Mark 16:16, John 3:16, 1 John 3:2, 1 Timothy 4:8
[91] Genesis 2:16-17, Ecclesiastes 7:29, Deuteronomy 27:26, Galatians 3:10, Romans 6:23
[92] Genesis 3 throughout. Romans 5:12, etc, 19.
[93] Dr. Andrews styles it *a Covenant of Obedience* and *a Covenant of Faith* in his *Exposition of the Moral Law*, p.72
[94] In Book 1 Chapter 2 Aphorism 3 & Book 2 Chapter 2

(4) ***That God's Covenant of Faith in Christ the last Adam*** (inchoate in the earthly, but consummate in the heavenly paradise) ***has a twofold respect to Jesus Christ***, namely: [1] as promised, and to be revealed afterward; [2] as performed, exhibited and actually revealed already, and whereupon it is sub-distinguished into, {1} the *Covenants of Promise* in Christ only promised:[95] wherein are fixed gradual discoveries of Christ and covenant mercies, still proceeding from the less to the more perfect. {2} The *Covenant of Performance*, in Christ performed and actually manifested in the flesh, namely: the New Covenant,[96] the most perfect and complete expression of all the Covenants of Faith, commencing from Christ's death, and continuing until the end of the world. The Covenants of Promise were more dark, imperfect, ineffectual and restrained to one sort of people; the New Covenant is more clear, perfect, efficacious and universally extended to all sorts and nations of people in the whole world. This distinction of the Covenant of Faith, see hereafter explicated and confirmed.[97]

(5) ***That the mystery and chief matter of all the Covenants of Faith, whether Covenants of Promise or New Covenant, though for accidents and circumstances it be very variously represented, yet for essence and substance it is only one and the same, namely: the recovery of lapsed sinners from sin and death, to righteousness and life by Jesus Christ alone through faith. The same Christ, the same faith, the same recovery of lapsed sinners by Christ through faith is revealed in all the Covenants of Faith, but in each of them distinctly.*** As:

[1] The same Christ is revealed in all the covenants since the fall. They are as many cabinets one within another: but Christ the jewel within them all. All their promises lead to him, and center in him, all their commandments refer to him, all their threats drive to him, all their ceremonies typify him, all their sacraments signify him, all their ordinances magnify him, etc. But in every of

---

[95] Ephesians 2:12
[96] Jeremiah 31:31 etc., Hebrews 8:8-13
[97] Book 2, Chapter 2, Aphorism 3

them how differently is the same Christ represented! As the seed of the woman bruising the serpent's head:[98]

In the first: as the true Noah saving an elect remnant by water by his blood, in the ark of the church.[99] In the second: as the seed of Abraham in whom all the nations of the earth should be blessed.[100] In the third: as the prophet like Moses raised up from among the people Israel, to be hearkened unto in all things, under severest penalty.[101] In the fourth: as the royal seed of David, that should sit upon his throne, ruling the house of Jacob, the church of God, forevermore.[102] In the fifth: as the true David, shepherd, prince and king of the redeemed captives forever.[103] In the sixth: and, as God manifested in the flesh, crucified, dead, buried, risen, ascended, and set down on the right hand of God,[104] for the actual accomplishment of his elect's redemption; in the seventh.

Or thus: in the three first Covenants is represented the person of Christ, God-man: his *manhood*, as the seed of the woman, the seed of Noah, the seed of Abraham; his *Godhead*, as being able to bruise the serpent's head, to save his elect remnant by water, and to bless all the nations of the earth.

In the two next covenants, his triple mediatory office is set forth: his prophecy, under the type of Moses, his priesthood under the type of Aaron, and his kingship under the type of David. In the sixth Covenant with the captives is set forth some notable efficacy of his office, in redeeming, cleansing and sanctifying his enthralled guilty and polluted people. But in the New Covenant, Christ is represented both in his person, offices and efficacy of his offices, both towards Jews and Gentiles more clearly fully and gloriously then in all the fore-going Covenants, and yet, it is Jesus Christ yesterday, and today, and forever the same.[105]

---

[98] Genesis 3:14-15
[99] Genesis 6:18, etc., 1 Peter 3:20
[100] Genesis 22:18, Acts 3:25-27, Galatians 3:13-14
[101] Deuteronomy 18:18-19; Acts 3:32, 7:37
[102] Psalm 132:11, etc., Luke 1:31-33
[103] Ezekiel 37:21 to the end
[104] 1 Timothy 3:16
[105] Hebrews 13:8

[2] The same faith is revealed in all the Covenants before Christ, as in the New Covenant after Christ. {1} The catalog of the ancient believers.[106] {2} The justification of Noah, Abraham, etc.: by faith. {3} The description of the righteousness of faith by Moses[107] and David,[108] and Habakkuk,[109] etc., are clear indications that in all time before Christ, sinners were recovered and saved by Jesus Christ through faith.[110] But before Christ, faith was revealed very darkly, obscurely and imperfectly, in comparison with the revelation of faith since Christ, which is more clear, perspicuous and complete. Hence comparatively, faith is said not to come until the New Covenant times.[111]

[3] The same recovery of lapsed sinners by Christ through faith was revealed proportionably under all former Covenants; but never so clearly, extensively and efficaciously as now under the New Covenant. Then under redemption from Egypt and reduction from Babylon. Their eternal redemption from sin and death was shadowed out; then under the sprinkling of blood, their justification, and under various washings and Levitical purifications, their sanctification, etc., was represented – but now all these spirituals in Christ are represented without veil and with open face.[112]

(6) *That consequently, whatsoever accidentals or circumstantials of foregoing Covenants of Faith from time to time were abolished upon the commencing of more perfect federal administrations, yet all the essentials and substantials of them still remain, the former being still confirmed by, yea comprized in the later, as more complete and perfect.* God proceeds in all his Covenants, from first to last, from the more imperfect to the more perfect, till at last he had brought in the most perfect New Covenant.

---

[106] Hebrews 11
[107] Deuteronomy 30:12, etc., with Romans 10:6, etc.
[108] Psalm 4:6, 7, etc.
[109] Habakkuk 2:4 with Galatians 3:11, Hebrews 10:38
[110] Hebrews 11:7, Genesis 15:6
[111] Galatians 3:22-23
[112] 2 Corinthians 3:5 to the end

As Ezekiel's wheels, were a wheel within a wheel,[113] or as the celestial orbs are supposed to be orb within orb from the lowest to the highest: so God's Covenants are, as it were, covenant within covenant, from the least to the greatest; the latter being still fuller and larger than the former. Jesus Christ was represented in the first covenant as the seed of the woman; in the second, as the true Noah; in the third, as the seed of Abraham; in the fourth, as the seed of Israel; in the fifth, as the seed of David, in the sixth, as the true David, in the seventh, which is the New Covenant, as actually God-man, Immanuel, God-with-us.

In the first covenant God promised that this seed of the woman should bruise the serpent's head;[114] in the second, that this true Noah should save an elect remnant; in the third, that this seed of Abraham should bless all nations,[115] and be a priest like Melchizedek; in the fourth, that this seed of Israel should bless and guide Israel,[116] and be their great prophet like Moses; in the fifth, that this seed of David should reign over the house of Jacob,[117] the church, forevermore; in the sixth, that this true David should redeem his captives,[118] re-unite them into one kingdom, and be their shepherd, prince and king forever; and in the seventh, that this God-man Jesus Christ actually exhibited, should bless all nations as well as the Jews, discipling them, and incorporating them into the same church body with them, writing his laws in their hearts, etc.[119]

In all these covenants before the New Covenant, there were certain accidentals and circumstantials belonging to the outward form of administration peculiar to those times and people, which were vanishing and are done away – as sacrifices, circumcision, passover, and the four extraordinary sacraments, with all the Levitical ordinances, rites, ceremonies

---

[113] Ezekiel 1:16
[114] Genesis 3:14-15
[115] Genesis 22:8, 14:18, etc.
[116] Deuteronomy 18:15-20
[117] Psalm 132:11, Luke 1:32-33
[118] Ezekiel 37:20 to the end
[119] Galatians 3:13-14, Matthew 28:18-20, Ephesians 3:6, etc., Hebrews 8:30, 11, 12

and administrations under the Old Covenant – but yet the substantials of all these covenants still remain and have their chief accomplishment in the new covenant, as the Scriptures abundantly testify of all these covenants severally.

Compare: (1) Genesis 3:14-15 with Hebrews 2:14-15, Colossians 2:14-15, Romans 16:10. (2) Genesis 6:18 and onwards with 1 Peter 3:20-21, Hebrews 11:7. (3) Genesis 22:18, 12:3 with Acts 3:25-26, Gal 3:13-14. (4) Deuteronomy 5:2 and onwards, 18:15-20 with Hebrews 8:10, Acts 2:20-22 and onwards. (5) Psalm 132:11 with Acts 2:30, Luke 1:31-33. (6) Ezekiel 36:25-26 and onwards with Jeremiah 24:5-7 with Hebrews 8:10-12.

And this will abundantly appear by comparing the matter of all these six covenants with the matter of the New Covenant hereafter explicated. Several useful consectaries hence result. As:

[1] Hence the substantial promises of mercies in all foregoing Covenants of Faith do as truly belong to us, and may be as consolatory to us, now under the New Covenant, as to any of God's people to whom they were first and immediately propounded under any former covenants.

Thus we may, from the first covenant, expect victory over the serpent, as well as Adam.[120] We may, from the second covenant, expect the world's absolute security from being universally drowned withstood forever, as also the constant course and revolution of seedtime and harvest, and cold and heat, and summer and winter, and day and night while the earth remains, as well as Noah.[121] We may, from the third covenant, assure ourselves that we (being Abraham's spiritual children by faith)[122] shall be blessed with faithful Abraham,[123] though we be Gentiles: shall have victory over our enemies, especially our spiritual enemies: shall have the true celestial Canaan for an everlasting inheritance: and shall enjoy the Lord for our Covenant-God, etc., as well as Abraham and his natural seed. The like is to be said of all the other covenants with Israel, David, and with the captives. The substantials of all

---

[120] Genesis 3:14-15
[121] Genesis 8:21-22
[122] Romans 4:12, 16-17, Galatians 3:7
[123] Genesis 12:3, 22:17-18, 17:7-8, with Galatians 3:9, 13-14; Luke 1:71, 74, Galatians 3:26-27, 29

covenants of faith being one and the same, we may apply and extract comfort from the substantial promises of them all, as well as from the New Covenant under which we live. Herein we have an admirable advantage above all the federates of former covenants; in that we have the benefit of the promises of all the Covenants of Promise, which they had; and of the New Covenant, which they had not here is much wisdom required, here is high privilege vouchsafed, for the skilful and comfortable applying and improving of God's promises in all Covenants of Faith throughout the Bible.

[2] Hence all the substantial commands – explicit or implicit – of former covenants of faith, are as obligatory and binding to us now under the New Covenant, as formerly they were to God's people under any covenant on whom they were first imposed. As former promises are still consolatory to us in regard to covenant mercies from God, so former commands explicit or implicit are obligatory to us in regard of covenant-duties to God. The analogy and proportion between these two is evident. Are not we as strongly obliged now under the New Covenant:

{1} To fight against the serpent, that in Christ we may bruise his head; as well as Adam?[124]

{2} To believe God's word and warnings, and be obedient to him in most difficult undertakings: as well as Noah?[125]

{3} To walk before God in faith and obedience, to be perfect, to initiate our infant children in the first initiating token of the present covenant of God, etc., as well as Abraham?[126]

{4} To observe all the Ten Commandments of the Moral Law; as well as the people Israel?[127]

{5} To keep God's Covenant and testimony; as well as David and his seed?[128]

---

[124] Genesis 3:14-15
[125] Genesis 6 with Hebrews 11:9
[126] Genesis 17:1-2, 9-10, etc.
[127] Deuteronomy 5, Exodus 30
[128] Psalm 132:12

{6} To remember our own evil ways and doings which were not good, and loath ourselves in our own sight for our iniquities, and for our abominations; to walk in God's statutes, etc., to be God's covenant-people, etc., as well as God's captives in Babylon?[129]

Doubtless these and like command of the substance of former Covenants, reach us, concern us, oblige us still, as well as God's people of old, for they were never abrogated, but rather most strongly reinforced and confirmed under the New Covenant.

[3] Hence we under the New Covenant have strongest consolation from such promises, and greatest obligation by such commands of all Covenants of Faith foregoing. Inasmuch as the substance of all those covenants does still remain of force and virtue; and the vigor of them is afresh revived and continued under the New Covenant. And a sevenfold cord is not easily broken.

[4] Hence this excellently directs us in the reading, applying and improving of the holy Scriptures with judgment. We wisely distinguish substantials for circumstantials, essentials from accidentals, in the promises, precepts and covenants of God – and then we shall plainly see the due portion and allotment which appertains to us.

[5] Hence the necessity and utility of the books of the Old Testament, as well as of the new, unto all New Covenant federates is evinced and described. The substantials of all promised mercies and of all commanded restipulated duties, under all former covenants still remaining of force and virtue, do both evince the necessity, and delineate the utility of the books of the Old Testament. This is the compass and polestar to sail by in this Scripture-sea: this is the golden clew and thread to be followed in this Scripture-labyrinth. What doubts, knots, difficulties, etc. will not this one thing resolve and unite about the diligent and fruitful perusal of the Scriptures!

---

[129] Ezekiel 36:31, 27, 28

(7) *That the Covenants of God in their latitude – namely: his Covenants of Works and of Faith – are so capacious and comprehensive, that they enclose and comprise within themselves the grand mystery and very marrow of all the holy Scriptures.*

This is very clear, for: [1] the whole Scriptures are a mere supernatural revelation by divine inspiration.[130] [2] The grand mystery and very marrow of the whole Scriptures, is; man's happiness in the enjoyment of God in the first Adam, before the fall, comprised in the Covenant of Works; and man's recovery from sin and death to righteousness and life, after the fall, by Jesus Christ the last Adam, through faith, comprised in the Covenant of Faith and all the gradual discoveries thereof from age to age. [3] Now these two sorts of the Covenants of God are so complex that they clearly fathom and conclude within themselves, as within their arms, this grand mystery, soul and marrow of all the Holy Bible. For,

{1} All the doctrines of Scripture come under these Covenants; they are, as so many divine truths come from them, to be referred to them as their chief heads, and are to be tried by them as their common standard or touchstone. The clearest extraction of all fundamental truths in religion is from these Covenants, and the most solid decision of all sorts of controversies and refutation of all sorts of errors is to be derived from the true state of these Covenants.[131] God's Covenants are the best umpires in all controversial divinity, and the best hammers for all errors and heresies against the truth. As might easily be demonstrated, if need were, in both cases. {2} All promises and prophecies in the whole Scripture, from the beginning of Genesis to the end of the revelation, do flow as so many streams from these fountains of God's Covenants, and meet as so many lines in these covenant-centers. The promises are but God's Covenants in their branches; the Covenants are God's promises in the root. And were I to treat of God's greatest and precious promises (as

---

[130] 2 Timothy 3:16-17
[131] This will more easily appear, by considering how many fundamentals of faith have unavoidably come to be unfolded in this *treatise* in handling the Covenants of God.

sometimes I had resolved)[132] I should count it the most clear, exact and proper way, to rank all the promises in the whole Bible under their peculiar Covenants, and federal expresures, both for the plainest explication, and for the safest and sweetest application of them to the spirits of believers. {3} Consequently, all the threats in Scripture come under God's Covenants, with the promises. Threats and promises are relatives, and arise both from the same spring-head of the Covenants, though upon different considerations. Promises chiefly are propounded upon terms of such or such covenant-performances: threatenings chiefly are denounced in case of failing in performance of such or such covenant-duties. {4} All types in Scripture come under God's Covenants, as figures or shadows of covenant-blessings, especially of Jesus Christ in his person, offices, effects of his offices, body mystical, members, etc.[133] One way or other, Christ is the substance, body, soul, and end of them all. They are all Christ veiled. {5} All histories in Scripture come under these covenants: declaring the antecedents, concomitants or consequents of these covenants; and one way or other subserving to illustrate these Covenants' manifestation, confirmation, or administration. {6} All commands in Scripture come under God's Covenants in one regard or another, but especially as impositions or explanations of the covenant-duties restipulated and required from man to God. {7} Finally, all the ordinances of God in Old or New Testament touching doctrine, worship, church-government and practice of God's people come under God's Covenants – and principally under the external forms of those covenants respectively. And therefore from all this it's very evident, how just a cause I had to entitle this treatise, *Mysterium & Medulla Bibliorum, The Mystery and Marrow of the Bible, namely, God's Covenants with man*, etc. For, God's Covenants are the peculiar display of the grand Scripture mystery, and so are the very sinew and marrow of all the blessed Bible. Oh! What a subject, what a secret, what a treasure, what a conflux of grace, wisdom, goodness, justice and mercy are the Covenants of God!

---

[132] The footnote is missing words in the text I accessed.
[133] Colossians 2:16-17, Hebrews 9:9, 10:1

(8) *That without the solid knowledge of God's Covenants, the depth of holy Scriptures, the secrets of true religion, and God's mysterious contrivances of sinners salvation can never be judiciously understood.* This evidently results from the former consideration, and needs no further illustration.

(9) *That all the people of the world, are so far miserable or happy, as they are without, or within the covenants of God.* For, the whole mystery of man's natural happiness was comprised in his being in covenant with God, according to the Covenant of Works in the first Adam; and the whole mystery of man's supernatural happiness is comprehended in man's being in covenant with God, according to the Covenant of Faith in Jesus Christ the last Adam, the Covenant of Works requiring perfect, and perpetual personal obedience, being broken by the first Adam, and by all his ordinary posterity in him, cannot afford lapsed man any happiness any more, forasmuch as lapsed man cannot any more enjoy God in that covenant.

The Covenant of Faith has provided a remedy in Jesus Christ, as the sinner's mediator and surety,[134] satisfying by his death for man's debt, and exactly fulfilling the law (the substance of the Covenant of Works) by his obedience for men's acceptance – so that whosoever shall by faith unfeigned accept this remedy provided, namely, Jesus Christ, his death and obedience, shall thereby be acquitted from sin and death, restored to righteousness and happiness in the enjoyment of God in Jesus Christ. They therefore that are effectually within this Covenant of Faith are so far truly happy, but they that are without this covenant-state are so far utterly miserable, being without Christ, without hope, and without God in the world.[135]

And therefore, having first preached in my weekly lectures upon this comfortable, comprehensive, intricate, but necessary subject of God's sacred covenants, at the importunity of many I have been induced to publish the same: [1] for the helping of poor souls out of their miserable covenantless-state

---

[134] Hebrews 8:6, 1 Timothy 2:5-6
[135] Ephesians 2:12

into a happy covenant condition with God in Jesus Christ.[136] [2] For the assisting of God's weakest doubting, yet sincere federates to discern their inward, effectual and saving interest in the covenant of God. [3] For the displaying of their matchless and transcendent felicities, who not only are savingly in covenant with God, but also have well-grounded evidence of their good covenant-state.[137] [4] For inciting: {1} both of all God's faithful ministers, (who are ministers of the New Testament)[138] to frequent preaching of God's Covenants,[139] with all prudence and diligence, {2} and of all his sincere federates, to an answerable and worthy walking with their God in Christ as his covenant-people; according to his covenant's directions, encouragements and obligations. [5] For satisfaction to my own heart and spirit about this profound, mysterious, and important subject. [6] For edification of my hearers the more abundantly by my weekly lectures upon so noble and profitable a theme. [7] For more clear illustration of those sweetest saving truths which as precious jewels are laid up for God's people in these rich cabinets of God's Covenants. And, [8] for the high advancement of the glory of the blessed God and Jesus Christ our only Lord in all.

For attainment of which high and excellent ends, I have (to my best judgment) taken the most probable and promising way in the unfolding of God's covenant-expressures in this ensuing treatise. For, [1] herein I have treated of God's Covenants, first more generally, then more especially, namely, of the Covenant of Works before the fall in the first Adam and of the Covenant of Faith after the fall in Christ the last Adam – and that in Christ, {1} as promised in all the Covenants of Promise[140] revealed in six noted periods of time especially, {2} as performed in the New Covenant.[141] This method of

---

[136] 2 Corinthians 3:3, etc
[137] Psalm 144:15
[138] 2 Corinthians 3:6
[139] Totum Del verbum à primario Subjecto appellationem suam accepit, ut Dicatur, Foedus vetus & Novum. Hinc Olevianus se appellavit, Concionatorum Foederis: quod in omnibus Conscionibus hoc Foedus Del gratuitum sibi urgendum esse videret, &c. H. Alsted. in Theolog. Catech. §. 1. c. 2. p. 26.
[140] Ephesians 2:1-2
[141] Hebrews 8:6 to the end

handling God's Covenants, being most proper and clear in itself, and most congruous to the Scriptures. Consequently the reading of this whole treatise, and not only some part, is requisite to the right notion of God's Covenants.

[2] Herein I have digested the whole doctrine of God's Covenants into: {1} certain distinct theses, positions or compendious assertions which I call *aphorisms*, comprising in brief the sum of all. {2} The *explanations* and *confirmations* of those aphorisms, as the nature of them requires. {3} Such *consectaries* or *inferences* as properly result from them. And this course I have purposely embraced. Partly, that both myself and others may have the more distinct and clear apprehension about all God's covenant-mysteries. Partly, that every thing may be the more obvious in the treatise, and the better fixed in the memory. Partly, that the whole may hereupon be more acceptable and profitable to all sorts of readers.

[3] Herein I have (so far as possible with safety to the truth) purposely waved polemical dissertations and disputes, chiefly bending myself unto *doctrinals* and *practicals*: wherein, a very considerable part of the body of divinity is unfolded, many practical questions or cases of conscience are resolved, various doubts and difficulties both about doctrine and practise are removed, and all according to the nature of particulars advantageously applied. And where I have been forced for vindication of the truth, to touch upon points controversial (disputings, wranglings, and vain janglings about religion being the epidemical and pernicious disease of these times,[142] whence very many have disputed away both truth, religion and a good conscience from themselves), I have stated the questions, confirmed the truth by arguments, and refilled the contrary objections which seemed material, I solicitously declining all logomachies, personal reflections, and other extravagances, as unavailable to truth or godliness.[143]

[4] Herein I have very frequently throughout the whole treatise insisted upon Scripture-trials, evidences and discoveries of men's covenant-condition, spiritual state, hearts, graces, dispositions, actions, etc., towards God. That

---

[142] 1 Timothy 1:5-7, 6:3-5
[143] 2 Timothy 2:16, 1 Timothy 6:3-5

hypocrites and carnal men may not think better of themselves then they have cause, and so run headlong to destruction in a golden dream; and that the true Israelites indeed, though most weak and inexperienced, may not think worse of themselves then they ought, but may be instructed how to make their calling and election sure,[144] and at last come sweetly to discover by the Spirit of God the things that are freely given them of God.[145]

And in all this great work I have most seriously and (if I know my own heart) sincerely desired the furtherance of the knowledge, faith, assurance, comfort, joy, holiness, heavenliness, and all the spirituals of such as are ordained to eternal life,[146] and especially of all my endeared relations, not only natural, but also spiritual, that ever received any converting, confirming, supporting or edifying benefit by my ministry. And I beseech the Lord of the Covenant to make these my weak and unworthy labors advantageously speak and preach to them and others, when I shall sleep in Jesus, and be silent in the grave.

The volume, I confess, has swelled too much under my hand: but I have this apology, the vast comprehensiveness, great variety, and frequent difficulties of the subject-matter; as also my earnest endeavors after practicalness and perspicuity therein to the meanest capacities, have occasioned this prolixity. And yet I hope the judicious reader, upon perusal of the whole, will acknowledge such a brief prolixity, or prolix brevity therein, that very little could have been conveniently omitted. I say therefore, (as once Augustine of his work of the City of God)[147] let such as think it too little or too much, hold me excused: but let those who think it is enough, give congratulating thanks, not to me, but to the Lord with me.

---

[144] 2 Peter 1:10
[145] 1 Corinthians 2:12
[146] Acts 13:48
[147] Videor mihi debitum ingentis hujus operis, adjuvante Domino, reddidisse. Quibus parum, vel quibus nimium est, mihi ignoscant; Quibus autem satis est, non mihi sed Domino mecum, gratias congratulantes agunt, Amen. Aug. de Civit. Dei, l. 22. c. 30. Tom. 5.

(10) *That finally, the church's ministers, and members of Christ should with all possible judgment, zeal, affection and constancy, interest and exercise themselves in the Covenants of God, but especially in the Covenants of Faith whereby alone sinners' hope and comfort in Christ are provided for by God since the fall, the top-excellency, perfection and glory of all which covenants is the New Covenant.* Therefore,

O all ye true churches of Christ, look upon the Covenants of God, as the grand mystery and very marrow of all the holy Scriptures. All the Scripture-doctrines, promises, threats, types, histories, commands and ordinances, are fully deductible from, and reducible to the Covenants of God: consequently all your information, consolation, caution, instruction, exhortation and edification depends upon God's Covenants. Mind and meditate upon them diligently. These will preserve you in the truth against error; these will direct you in purity of worship, government and all the ordinances of Christ without pollution or corruption; these will restore you unto, and preserve you in the sweet unity of the Spirit in the bond of peace, against distractions and divisions; these will engage you in the life of God,[148] and power of godliness effectually,[149] against all profaneness, formality, and hypocrisy: these will endear you unto God, Father, Son, and Holy Ghost, in all heavenly soul-ravishing communion, that spiritual paradise and heaven upon earth.[150]

O ye faithful ministers of Christ, study and preach the covenants of God with all prudence and diligence to the flocks of God whereof the Lord has made you overseers. Ye are by calling and office ministers of the New Covenant,[151] (the Lord of the covenant make us all able ministers of the New Covenant, of the Spirit and not of the letter, that the people may be through divine grace, the epistle of Christ,[152] ministered by us, written not with ink, but with the Spirit of the living God – not in tables of stone, but in the fleshy

---

[148] Ephesians 4:18
[149] 2 Timothy 3:5
[150] 1 John 1:3, 2 Corinthians 13:14
[151] 2 Corinthians 3:6
[152] 2 Corinthians 3:3-5, etc.

tables of the heart). Oh strive exceedingly to display the riches of divine grace, and the fulness of Jesus Christ, as wrapped up in the covenants, to the hearts and spirits of poor sinners; oh let all the chief tendencies of your doctrine be subservient hereunto. Hereby you shall most sweetly revive and bind up the bruised souls of broken-hearted sinners, and most happily espouse them as a chaste virgin unto Christ.

Finally, all ye members of Christ, come and see, trade and traffic daily in this spiritual mart of God's Covenants. Here are the greatest gains and richest treasures to be had in all the world. If holiness or righteousness; if conversion, confirmation, or consummation; if pardon, adoption, sanctification or communion with God; if grace or glory; if Jesus Christ, the only mediator, or the only all-sufficient God, with all the mysteries or treasures of Scripture, etc be worth the having; then come close with the sacred Covenants of God, wherein you shall abundantly find all these. This ensuing treatise is offered to you for your assistance and encouragement in this glorious employment. The Lord God and Jesus Christ the only mediator of the New covenant make it useful and effectually instrumental by his Spirit to bring aliens into covenant, and establish federates in covenant with God in Jesus Christ to all eternity. Amen.

So prays,

Your humble and faithful servant in the gospel of our Lord Jesus Christ,

Fran. Roberts

May 20th 1657

Book I

Of God's Covenants Their Names, Natures, Sorts, and Benefits, More Generally

Chapter 1

Of God's dealing with his church, in all times and ages, by way of covenant.

God, over all blessed forever,[153] is the center where all happiness meets,[154] and the fountain whence all happiness flows.[155] Man, under whose feet God has put all things here below,[156] is only so far happy as he enjoys the Lord to be his God.[157] On earth, man enjoys the Lord to be his God, either (1) more immediately, or (2) more mediately.

(1) *More immediately*, before Adam's fall, by conformity both of man's upright nature unto God,[158] through God's image in which he was created,[159] and of man's life to God's will through his personal obedience[160] – whereunto he was fully enabled.

(2) *More mediately*, after the fall, by mystical union unto the mediator Jesus Christ,[161] the *express character of the Father's person*,[162] and only way unto God.[163] Man's enjoyment of God, by natural conformity to his will before the fall, and by supernatural union to Christ since the fall, are instrumentally established and effected by God's Covenants with man: that, by his Covenant of Works,[164] this, by his Covenant of Faith.[165] So then, God's covenant is the Scripture-star that leads man unto Christ, Christ is the

---

[153] Romans 9:5, 1:25, 2 Corinthians 11:31
[154] Matthew 14:61, 1 Timothy 6:15
[155] Matthew 5:8, Acts 3:25-26 with Galatians 3:16
[156] Psalm 8:6
[157] Psalm 144:15, Ephesians 2:12
[158] Ecclesiastes 7:29
[159] Genesis 1:26-27
[160] Genesis 2:16-17
[161] 1 Timothy 1:5, 1 Corinthians 6:15, 17, Ephesians 5:30-32, John 17:21-23
[162] Hebrews 1:3
[163] John 14:6
[164] Genesis 2:10, 17
[165] Romans 3:20-29, Galatians 3:16-17, Genesis 17:7-8, Ezekiel 36:28, Hebrews 8:10

heavenly way that brings man unto God, and God is heaven itself, in whom man finds and enjoys all satisfying happiness.

In this treatise (subdivided into four distinct books), the unfolding of God's precious and mysterious covenant with man is undertaken, that Christians' happiness may be promoted by enjoying of God, that they may enjoy God by their union to Christ, that they may be united to Christ by accepting God's Covenant, and that they may be allured to accept God's Covenant by a familiar knowledge and apprehension of it.

For the more clear representation of this subject to the weakest capacity, God's Covenant shall here be laid open. Firstly, more generally in Book 1. And here shall be evidenced: (1) that God has pleased in all ages to deal with his church and people by way of covenant, (2) what God's Covenant is, for name and thing generally considered, and (3) into what kinds or sorts God's covenant is to be distributed.

Secondly, more particularly in Book 2. And here: (1) of God's Covenant of Works with the first Adam, and in him with all his natural seed, before the fall. (2) Of God's Covenant of Faith with Christ the last Adam, and in him with all his supernatural seed, after the fall. And this both in general and in particular.

In general shall be shown: (1) that the Covenant of Works being broken in the first Adam, God was pleased to reveal a Covenant of Faith in Christ the last Adam, (2) when and how soon God did first reveal this Covenant of Faith, (3) why God revealed this Covenant, (4) what this Covenant of Faith is, and (5) how this Covenant of Faith is to be distributed.

In particular shall be opened:

(1) **The Covenants of Promise,**[166] **made and confirmed in Christ only promised and to be exhibited in our flesh afterwards.** And how the Lord God did gradually disclose these covenants in Christ most obscurely at first, but afterwards still more and more clearly, until they were accomplished in Christ in the fullness of time, but most remarkably in certain periods of time, namely: [1] from Adam until Noah, [2] from Noah until Abraham, [3] from

---

[166] Ephesians 2:12

Abraham until Moses, [4] from Moses until David, [5] from David until the Babylonian captivity, and finally [6] from the Babylonian captivity until Christ – and all this in Book 3.

(2) **The New Covenant made and confirmed in Christ actually performed and exhibited in our flesh already.**[167] And how this New Covenant is substantially one and the same with the Covenants of Promise, yet accidentally far different in administration: the New Covenant. Notably surpassing all foregoing administrations, in extant spiritual privileges, efficacy, and evangelical glory – in Book 4. Now in these four distinct books all these things shall be laid down orderly in certain succinct positions or *aphorisms* (summarily comprising much in a little compass for the help of both understanding and memory) together with the explanations of them, through the direction and assistance of the covenant-making and covenant-keeping God, who has said: *The secret of the LORD is with them that fear him, and he will show them his covenant.*[168]

---

[167] Jeremiah 31:31 with Hebrews 8:8
[168] Psalm 25:12, 14

Aphorism 1

God is pleased in all times and ages, from the beginning to the end of the world, to deal with his church and people by way of covenant.

For clearing of this aphorism something is to be spoken touching:
(1) God, who thus deals.
(2) His church and people, with whom he thus deals.
(3) God's dealing thus with his church in a covenant way.

(1) *God, who deals with his church and people by way of covenant.* Touching God, thus in brief, conceive of him. The supreme Being of Beings,[169] Cause of Causes,[170] and most spiritual Spirit,[171] the one only true God,[172] Father, Son and Holy Ghost,[173] is most absolutely simple,[174] all-sufficient,[175] immutable,[176] infinite,[177] immense,[178] and eternal[179] in his life,[180] understanding,[181] truth,[182] will,[183] goodness,[184] graciousness,[185] love,[186]

---

[169] Psalm 83:18, Exodus 3:14, Revelation 1:8, Romans 11:36, Acts 17:28
[170] Romans 8:29-30, Hosea 2:21-22 with Acts 17:24-25
[171] John 4:24, 2 Corinthians 3:17, Hebrews 12:9
[172] Deuteronomy 6:4, 1 Corinthians 8:4, 6, John 17:3
[173] Matthew 28:18, 1 John 5:7, 1 Corinthians 8:6, John 1:1, Acts 5:3-4
[174] 1 John 1:5
[175] Genesis 17:1, Acts 17:25, Romans 11:35-36
[176] Malachi 3:16, James 1:17
[177] Psalm 147:5, 145:3, Job 11:7-8
[178] 1 Kings 8:27, Job 11:7-8
[179] Deuteronomy 33:17, 1 Timothy 1:17, Psalm 90:2, 102:25-27
[180] Psalm 42:2, Hebrews 10:31, John 5:26
[181] Psalm 147:, Acts 15:18, Psalm 139:1-3, etc.
[182] Deuteronomy 32:4
[183] Ephesians 1:5
[184] Exodus 33:19, 34:6, Luke 18:9
[185] Exodus 34:6, Psalm 103:8
[186] 1 John 4:16

mercy,[187] longsuffering,[188] justice,[189] holiness,[190] power,[191] dominion,[192] perfection,[193] excellency,[194] blessedness,[195] and gloriousness.[196]

(2) *Touching God's church and people, with whom God deals in a covenant-way, thus briefly apprehend.* The self-satisfying all-sufficient and all-perfect God has not only created the whole world with all things therein,[197] and more especially the intellectual creatures, angels and men, for his own self. But also in all times and ages of the world provides himself a church here on earth among the children of men. For evidencing hereof, two things especially are to be noted, namely:

[1] That God in all ages has his church (a people separated to himself peculiarly)[198] in this world, though not at all times of like equal extent. It was at first only domestic, confined within the narrow compass of particular pious families, as of Adam,[199] Seth,[200] Enoch,[201] Noah,[202] Shem,[203] Abraham, Isaac, Jacob, etc.[204] Afterwards it grew up and became national, extending itself to the families of all the twelve tribes,[205] even the whole Jewish nation, which then after the redemption out of Egypt, was fashioned and digested by God into an ecclesiastical polity called the church in the wilderness.[206] But at last, when Christ the blessed seed came, in whom *all the nations and families of the*

---

[187] Exodus 34:6-7, Psalm 103:8-9, etc.
[188] 2 Peter 3:9, Exodus 34:6, Psalm 103:8
[189] Deuteronomy 32:4, Psalm 92:15, 145:17
[190] Exodus 15:11, Psalm 22:3, Isaiah 6:3
[191] Matthew 6:13, Revelation 19:6
[192] Daniel 4, 3:22, 34, Jude 25
[193] Matthew 5:48, Job 35:7-8
[194] Amos 8:7, Exodus 15:11
[195] Mark 14:61, Romans 9:5
[196] 1 Corinthians 2:8, Exodus 15:11, Isaiah 33:21
[197] Proverbs 16:4, Romans 11:36
[198] Deuteronomy 7:6-7, 10:15, Exodus 19:5-6, Titus 2:14, 1 Peter 2:5, 1 Corinthians 1:2
[199] Genesis 2:16-17, 3:15, 4:3-5
[200] Luke 3:34 to the end, Genesis 4:26
[201] Genesis 5:22, 24
[202] Genesis 6:9, 7:1
[203] Genesis 9:27, Luke 3:36
[204] Genesis 17:7-8, Hebrews 11:8-9
[205] James 1:1, Romans 9:4, Psalm 147:19-20
[206] Acts 7:38

earth should be blessed,[207] the church began to be planted even among other nations besides that of the Jews, and so spread from nation to nation, that it became ecumenical or universal,[208] not limited any longer to that one nation of the Jews only, but diffused without restraint to the nations of the Gentiles.[209]

From Adam until Moses it was domestic, from Moses until Christ national, and from Christ until the end of the world it was ecumenical – and this triple period comprehends all times and ages. Thus the church spreads like leaven,[210] grows like a mustard seed,[211] and like the waters of the sanctuary, swells and increases from smallest beginnings to greater and greater perfection.[212]

[2] Why God in all ages thus provides himself a church amongst men. Namely: {1} from the exceeding riches of his free grace and love to mankind.[213] This the impulsive or inward moving cause why God has: (i) elected eternally in Christ a certain select number out of mankind to be his own peculiar people,[214] (ii) redeemed in fullness of time this his church and people (lapsed in Adam) by his own blood,[215] and (iii) actually applied this redemption to his people by calling them effectually out of the world unto himself in Christ.[216] Remarkably says Wisdom (the Son of God) of himself: *I was daily his delight, rejoicing always before him: rejoicing in the habitable parts of his earth, and my delights were with the sons of men.*[217] {2} That God might communicate himself and his fullness more sweetly, familiarly and completely to his church, then to all other societies and created beings in the world. For to his church and people God peculiarly unveils the mysteries of his kingdom,[218] the hidden

---

[207] Genesis 12:3, Acts 3:25, Galatians 3:8
[208] Acts 13:46-48
[209] Matthew 28:18, Ephesians 3:6
[210] Matthew 13:33
[211] Matthew 13:31-32
[212] Ezekiel 47:1-6
[213] Exodus 33:19, Ephesians 1:4-11, Titus 3:4-5
[214] Ephesians 1:4-6, Deut 7:6, 8
[215] Ephesians 1:7, Acts 20:18, 1 Peter 1:18-19
[216] Titus 3:4-6, 2 Timothy 1:9
[217] Proverbs 8:30-31
[218] Matthew 11:25-27, Ephesians 3:3-6, 1 Corinthians 2:8 to the end, Psalm 147:19

secrets of his wisdom, goodness, free grace, mercy, loving-kindness, holiness, justice, etc. He dwells and walks among them, and is a God and father unto them, they becoming sons and daughters to the Lord Almighty.[219] {3} That in and by the church the glory of all God's perfections and dispensations might be spread abroad both in heaven and earth to his everlasting praise. *In his temple everyone speaks of his glory.*[220] And, by the church, God's excellencies and the wise mysterious disposals of his grace are made known – not only unto the sons of men on earth, but also unto the principalities and powers in heavenly places.[221]

(3) *God's covenant-way of dealing with his church and people.* Finally, touching God's covenant way of dealing with his church and people: it is evident by their continued experience of his dispensations, both before, and after Adam's fall, that God pleases in all times and ages to deal with his church and people by way of covenant. For,

[1] Before the fall, God dealt with the first Adam, and in him with all his seed, then in state of innocency and integrity, by way of covenant, and that a Covenant of Works. For, besides that God had engraven in his heart the substance of the moral law – certain relics whereof remain in the hearts of pagans since the fall,[222] who have not the law written – God also gave Adam a positive law, permitting him to eat of the trees of the garden; commanding him not to eat of the tree of knowledge of good and evil; threatening him, in case he should eat, with present death; and consequently, promising him life in case of obedience. *And the LORD God commanded the man, saying, of every tree of the garden thou mayest freely eat: but of the tree of the knowledge of good and evil, thou shalt not eat of it; for in the day that thou eatest thereof thou shalt surely die.*[223] Now all this amounts to a covenant, as after shall more fully be evidenced in the particular handling of the Covenant of Works.[224]

---

[219] 2 Corinthians 6:17-18
[220] Psalm 29:9
[221] Ephesians 3:10-11
[222] Romans 2:14-15
[223] Genesis 2:16-17
[224] See Book Two, Chapter One

[2] After the fall, God deals with his church and people also by way of covenant: and that the Covenant of Faith in Jesus Christ the last Adam. This is very observable in several eminent intervals or periods of time, wherein God revealed his covenant more and more clearly by degrees, until it came to a full and complete discovery in these days of the New Testament. As God dealt by way of covenant, {1} with Adam presently after the fall, and with the fathers before the flood till the time of Noah, promising the seed of the woman, to bruise the serpent's head.[225] {2} With Noah, establishing his Covenant with him, to save him, and his family, and a seed of the creatures, in the ark, from perishing by the waters of the flood, when the whole world should be drowned.[226] Under these two dispensations of the covenant – together with the promises and other appurtenances thereof – did the fathers and church live until the days of Abraham. {3} With Abraham and his seed, covenanting and promising to be a God to them,[227] to give them the land of Canaan, and make them heirs of the world, and in his seed to make all the nations and families of the earth blessed; annexing circumcision as a confirming sign and token of the covenant. And under this and the former federal dispensations, was the church and the holy patriarchs trained up till the days of Moses. {4} With Israel, led and brought by the hand out of the land of Egypt, at Mount Sinai in the days of Moses,[228] *declaring his covenant unto them, even ten commandments written on two tables of stone, which he commanded them to perform,*[229] together with the ceremonial and judicial laws which he required them to observe. Under this and the former administrations of the covenant, the church was nurtured up, till the time of David. {5} With David and his seed God made an everlasting Covenant ordered in all things and sure,[230] promising with an oath, to establish his seed forever,[231] and build up his

---

[225] Genesis 3:15
[226] Genesis 6:18, etc., with 1 Peter 3:20-21 & Hebrews 11:7
[227] Genesis 17:1-15 with Acts 3:25-26, Galatians 3:8, Romans 4:13
[228] Jeremiah 31:32, Hebrews 8:9
[229] Deut 4:13-14, 5:2-6, with Exodus 20-32.
[230] 2 Samuel 23:5, Psalm 89, 2 Samuel 7:5-17
[231] Psalm 89:3-4, 35, 56, 37; 132:11

throne to all generations, etc., which covenant had its fullest accomplishment in Christ,[232] of the seed of David, and in his spiritual kingdom. Christ being the true David,[233] and king of his church, gathering both Jews and Gentiles into one body under his government, and subduing finally and totally all the enemies of his kingdom.[234] Under this and former dispensations of the Covenant, the church of God continued from David's days until the Babylonian captivity. {6} With the people of the Jews under the Babylonian captivity, God covenanted to return their captivity and restore them into their own land, the land of Canaan, to take away their stony heart, and to give them an heart of flesh, to cleanse them from all their filthiness and idols, etc., promising that they shall be his people, and he will be their God.[235] And under this, with the foregoing ministrations of the Covenant, the church of God was nursed up from the time of the Babylonian captivity, until the very coming of Christ in our flesh. {7} Finally, with the church and people of God under the New Testament, after Christ's incarnation, God makes a New Covenant in Christ: new not so much for substance as for circumstance and manner of administration (all the former administrations being laid aside as waxing old and wearing away), and new for continuation, in that this dispensation of the covenant should not wax old as did all the former, but should continue still fresh new and unaltered to the very end of the world.[236] And under this covenant, the promises and appendices thereof, the church of Christ is and shall be continued, built up, and perfected, from the first until the second coming of Jesus Christ.

Thus it is clear, *that in all ages and times, from the beginning to the end of the world, God pleases to deal with his church and people in a covenant-way.*

---

[232] Acts 2:30-31
[233] Ezekiel 37:21-22, 24, 26; Hosea 3:5, John 10:16, 11:51-52, Ephesians 1:10
[234] Psalm 110:1, 1 Corinthians 15:24-26
[235] Jeremiah 32:37 to the end, Ezekiel 11:16-21, 36:22 to the end of the chapter
[236] Hebrews 8:8 to the end with Jeremiah 31:35

Aphorism 2

God in all ages pleases to deal with his church and people by way of covenant for several weighty causes and excellent ends.

And these are worthy to be inquired into, and heedfully observed, by all the children of the Covenant,[237] and heirs according to the promise.[238] Now the Lord seems to deal with his church in a covenant-way.

(1) ***Of his mere grace and love to his church.*** God takes not this course by reason of any law or tie of necessity lying upon him: he is the most free unlimited agent, above all laws, and *doeth whatever he pleases both in heaven and earth*.[239] He could have dealt with man, both before and since the fall, in an absolute supreme way of Lordship, dominion and sovereignty, as a creator with his creature, as a potter with his clay, commanding what duty he pleased from him, without any covenant-obligation of himself in any respect unto man, being in no way debt-bound to the creature, but absolutely free. Nor can anything be imagined in his church or people, which could not in the least degree invite God into covenant with them, because between God and them, there are no terms of equality or proportion for a basis or remote foundation of a covenant. For:

[1] In their innocent state the distance between them is greater than between heaven and earth, then between highest angels and basest worms: even as great as between finite and infinite.[240] Now between finite and infinite there can be no proportion.

[2] In their lapsed state, sin has infinitely widened the distance, and rendered them altogether unlovely and abominable in themselves before God.[241] Yea, sin has extremely aggravated the distance, and turned it into

---

[237] Acts 3:25
[238] Galatians 3:29
[239] Psalm 135:4-6
[240] Psalm 147:5
[241] Romans 3:9-19, Titus 1:15-16

opposition and enmity between God and them.[242] So that nothing but mere grace, the mere good pleasure of his will, mere love and mercy, could possibly move or incline God to embrace them in a covenant-way. Hence God tells Israel that he set his love upon them because he loved *them*.[243] And he tells Jerusalem that *when her nativity was of the land of Canaan, her father an Amorite, her mother a Hittite, she in her birth wretched, unpitied, polluted in her blood, and cast out to the loathing of her person: even then he spread his skirt over her, covered her nakedness, sware unto her, entered into covenant with her, and she became his.*[244]

(2) ***Because the Lord would deal familiarly with his people, therefore he deals with them by way of covenant***. A covenant-way is a familiar way, as between man and man that are agreed. This David intimates in God's covenant with him, *And is this the manner of man, O LORD God?*[245] Or, as Junius renders it: "and that after the manner of men, O Lord God, that is, thou in covenanting deals familiarly with me, as man with man, as friend with friend." And, in that parallel place *and hast regarded me, according to the state of a man of high degree, O LORD God:*[246] it may be rendered: "And thou hast provided for me this excellency according to the manner of men, O Lord God." Or: "Thou hast provided for me, according to the manner of men, concerning this excellency O Lord God." That is, "Thou hast made a familiar provision for me." Now the distance is so vast between majesty and meanness, glory and baseness, God and us most despicable dust and ashes, that there cannot be a familiar reciprocal dealing between God and us but by way of covenant: wherein the most high God condescends and stoops down to us, and we base worms ascend up to God, and so meet one another friendly and familiarly.

(3) ***That God's people might more clearly and certainly know what good they may confidently expect from God, whatsoever be their present***

---

[242] Colossians 1:21, Romans 8:7, Luke 19:14, 27
[243] Deuteronomy 7:7-8
[244] Ezekiel 16:2-9
[245] 2 Samuel 7:19
[246] 1 Chronicles 17:17

condition. For all good covenanted by God, whether temporal, spiritual or eternal, is clear and sure, as God's Covenant is clear and sure. Hence David; *Although mine house be not so with God* (that is, flourishing, and without clouds) *yet he hath made with me an everlasting covenant, ordered in all things, and sure: for this is all my salvation, and all my desire, although he make it not to grow.*[247]

(4) ***That the church and people of God may be the more endeared unto God, and enlivened unto all free cheerful obedience***. God's loving kindness to us so wonderfully appears, both in his condescending to such a sweet familiar covenant-way with us, and in his storing his covenant with such rich provisions for us: that duly considered, it snatches our hearts and affections (as once David's)[248] vehemently unto him, even ravishing us with him. Besides, God's ample rewards and benefits covenanted, are as oil to the wheels of our obedience,[249] making them run smoothly in all God's paths with delight and alacrity.

(5) ***Finally, that God's Covenant with his church and people may be a distinctive and discriminating character between them and all other people in the world***. To the church pertain the covenants,[250] whilst all others are strangers to the Covenants of Promise.[251]

Corollaries resulting from the whole.

Hence, (1) ***God's condescension to his creatures is wonderful***. He stoops so low as to accept man, dust and ashes, sinful dust and ashes, in covenant with himself infinitely transcending all created beings.

(2) ***Man's ascension and advancement is admirable***. Man is brought from so low a state, and at such distance from God, to such a height of dignity

---

[247] 2 Samuel 23:5 with 7:5-17; Psalm 89
[248] 2 Samuel 7:18-20
[249] Jeremiah 31:33 with Psalm 40:8, Ezekiel 11:18-20
[250] Romans 9:4
[251] Ephesians 2:12

and nearness unto God: yea from utter enmity, to perfect amity with God, by covenant; that he may cry out, *Lord, what is man that thou art thus mindful of him, and the son of man that thou thus visitest him!*[252] Everyone in covenant with God may say with thankful David: *Who am I, O LORD God? And what is my house, that thou hast brought me hitherto?* etc.[253]

(3) ***We can never understand the mystery of God's dealing with his people, unless we know the mystery of God's Covenant***. Study therefore God's covenant diligently, be expert therein. For,

{1} This is the compendious abstract, or epitome of God's gracious dispensations to his church in all ages. Here may be seen how God dealt with his people in innocency, covenanting to give them continued life,[254] upon condition of exact personal obedience, and how he deals with his church lapsed: covenanting to restore life unto her, upon condition of faith in Christ's obedience.

And how God applies himself herein to his church's capacity: in her infancy he gives her the ABC of the covenant, teaching her to spell his grace in the promised seed of the woman,[255] and in saving a remnant in the ark by water from perishing with the world of the wicked.[256] In her youth and non-age he trains her up under a more rigid and severe discipline of Mosaical administrations, as under tutors and governors, yet in hopes of after-freedom.[257] In her full age He invests her with New Covenant liberties and enjoyments in Christ revealed, delivering her from all her former bondage.[258]

{2} This is that golden clew[259] which leads into that inmost mystery of Jesus Christ: the Son of God being the kernel and marrow of God's Covenant. For in the Covenant of Works before the fall, upon condition of perfect

---

[252] Psalm 8:4
[253] 2 Samuel 7:18
[254] Genesis 2:16-17
[255] Genesis 3:15
[256] Genesis 6:18, 1 Peter 3:20-21, 2 Peter 2:5
[257] Galatians 4:1, etc.
[258] Galatians 5:1, etc.
[259] Ball of thread or yarn

personal obedience, life is promised to be continued to Adam (think some learned men)[260] by the Son of God, in whom was life, and that life was the light of men (enlightening every man naturally, more or less) that comes into the world. And in the Covenant of Faith after the fall, Christ ast God-man, mediator between God and sinners, is the foundation of the covenant, as revealed to Adam, Noah, Abraham, Moses, David, the Jews, and to both Jews and Gentiles. At first Christ is revealed more dimly and obscurely; at last most clearly and evidently with open face and glory.

{3} Finally, this Covenant of God is the key that unlocks the whole Scriptures. Holy Scriptures do especially scope at revealing God's Covenant, in several ages, severally, God's covenant administrations like a thread of gold running through the books both of Old and New Testament. Yea God's Covenant is such a primary subject of the whole Scripture, that the whole word of God receives its denomination from God's Covenant, being styled {*the Old and New Testament*} or {*the Old and New Covenant*}. And surely no context of holy Scripture can be solidly explicated, no common place of divinity can be rightly handled, no polemical or controversial point can be dexterously decided, no case of conscience or practical question can be accurately resolved, no Christian duty can be skilfully urged or advised, without due respect and scope had to the Covenant of God. Hereupon it is reported of Olevianus that he styled himself {*concionatorem faederis*}, that is: {*a preacher of the Covenant*}.[261] And so should every faithful and skilful minister have it principally in design to be a preacher of God's Covenant, and every prudent Christian to be a hearer and practitioner of God's Covenant: God's Covenant calling for most attentive respect from them both. So that whilst we are ignorant of the mysteries of God's Covenant, we are ignorant of Scriptures, of Christ, and of all God's gracious administrations to his church.

[4] **God's Covenant is a notable character or mark of God's church and people**. For with them God deals peculiarly by way of covenant, and not with others. Therefore the way to discover whether we be members of God's

---

[260] Polanus, Partit. Theol. Book 1, p. 17
[261] H. Alsted. in Theolog. Catcechet. Sect. 1. cap. 2. p. 26. Hanov. 1622

church, and among the number of his people, is to try whether God has dealt with us by way of covenant.

Are we in covenant with God? They that are only outwardly in covenant with God, are only outwardly his people; they that are also inwardly in covenant with God, are inwardly his people also. They that were within the ark only were saved, whilst those that did cling to the outside of the ark, as well as those that came not near the ark, were drowned.[262]

---

[262] 1 Peter 2:20-21

Chapter 2

Of the name, general nature, and distribution of God's Covenant.

Aphorism 1

The names given to God's Covenant with his church in Scripture, are principally two, namely, בְּרִית berith *in the Hebrew original of the Old Testament:*[263] *and* διαθήκη diatheke, *in the Greek original of the New Testament:*[264] *the true meaning and use of which two names will somewhat conduce to the understanding of God's Covenant.*

To this end consider, (1) the notation of these two names. (2) The various acceptation of them in Scripture.

(1) **The notation of these two names, take thus briefly.**

[1] The Hebrew name בְּרִית *berith* a covenant; is by learned men derived from several roots.

{1} Some derive it from בָּרָא *bara* to create: because God's covenant hath been with his people even ever since the creation. But this seems too far-fetched as Pareus thinks.[265]

{2} Some derive it from בָּרַר *barar* to purify, make-clear, etc.,[266] because by covenants open and clear amity is confirmed, and faithfulness is clearly declared and ratified without sophistication between covenanters. And things are made plain and clear between them.

---

[263] Genesis 6:18, 9:12, 17:2, 4, 7, 9-11, 13-14, 19, 21; Deuteronomy 29:1, 2 Samuel 23:5, Jeremiah 32:40, 31:31-33
[264] Luke 1:72, Romans 9:4, Galatians 4:24, Ephesians 2:12, Hebrews 8:6, 8-10
[265] David Pareus on Genesis 6:18
[266] Mercer in Pagnin, Lexic. Ad. verb. ברך Synops, Pur. Theol. Sp.23

{3} Some derive it from ברת *berath*, which imports firmness,[267] whence בְּרוֹת *beroth*, is the name of firm and strong tree (Song of Solomon 1:17). As the ash, cypress or fig tree because covenants are firm and sure, and things are confirmed by them.

{4} Some derive it from בָּרָה *barah*, as it signifies to choose,[268] because in making covenants, there is a choice made of persons between whom, and of things or conditions about which there is covenanting. Or, from בָּרָה. *barah*, as it signifies to eat,[269] because they usually had a feast at the making of covenants.

{5} Some derive it from בָּרָא *bara*, or בָּרָה *barah*, to smite, strike, cut or divide (as both these words signify), because in making covenants commonly sacrifices were stricken and slain for confirmation and solemnity. This last is the common opinion about the original of this name, thinks that learned Rivet,[270] and doubtless to be preferred before all the former. So this word בְּרִית *berith*, covenant seems to sound as much, as כְּרִית, *kerith*, a smiting or striking, because of sacrifices slain in covenanting. Hence the word {*covenant*} is often joined with כָּרַת *karath*, which signifies the striking of a covenant. An example of this beyond all exception (says Rivet)[271] is in that sacrifice, wherein God by Moses made a covenant with all the people of Israel, and bound them to obey his law.

The description of it is Exodus 24: *For when Moses had built an altar at the bottom of Mount Sinai, and had erected twelve pillars according to the twelve tribes, he caused the young men to sacrifice burnt-offerings and peace-offerings, and he took half of the blood, and put it in basins, and half of the blood he sprinkled on the altar. And he took the book of the covenant, and read in the audience of the people: and they said, all that the LORD hath said,*

---

[267] l. Dictio vero, Berith, 1. Pactum, à firmitate nomen sortitur: und; Beroth nomen arboris firmae & fortu. Cant. 1. Oleaster. in Pentat. sup. Gen. 6. 18. Compare also Pagnin. in Lexic ad. verb ברת

[268] Buxtorf, Lex. in verb

[269] Mr. Ball in his Treatise of the Covenant, p.1

[270] Rivet, exercit. 53 in Genesis 6

[271] Rivet, in Genesis 31, Exercitation 135

will we do, and be obedient. And Moses took the blood, and sprinkled it on the people, and said, behold the blood of the covenant, which the LORD hath made with you concerning all these words. And sometimes the sacrifices slain in covenanting were cut in twain, and the parties covenanting passed between the parts for confirmation of the covenant, as Genesis 15:9-10, 17, etc., and Jeremiah 34:18-20.

And the heathen in their covenanting used sacrifices and divided them, passing between the parts, as learned men have observed, and probably in imitation of God's people. And that phrase {*a covenant of salt*},[272] denoting a perpetual covenant, is thought hence to have taken its rise, not because salt resisting putrefaction preserves things, but because salt by a perpetual law was to be used in all sacrifices, and sacrifices were still used in covenanting, as Oleaster,[273] and after him Rivet,[274] and after them both, Ball has well observed.[275]

[2] The Greek name {διαθήκη} *diatheke* – a covenant, or a testament – is the word by which, not only the Septuagint Greek translators of the Old Testament do generally, yea everywhere (except only in Deuteronomy 9:15) render the Hebrew name בְּרִית *berith*, as some learned men observe:[276] but also upon diligent search, I find that this is the only word by which the apostles and holy penmen in the New Testament render the Hebrew word *berith*.[277] And this Greek word being translated sometimes {*covenant*}, sometimes {*testament*}, is the only word that is used in the whole New Testament for covenant and testament: wheresoever either of these are mentioned, it is still *diatheke*. namely:

For {*covenant*} in Luke 1:72, Acts 3:25, 7:8, Romans 9:4, 11:27, Galatians 3:15, 17; 4:24, Ephesians 2:12, Hebrews 8:6-10; 9:1, 4; 10:16, 12:24, and 13:20. For {*testament*} in Matthew 26:28, Mark 14:24, Luke 22:20, 1

---

[272] Numbers 18:19, 2 Chronicles 13:5
[273] Oleaster in Pentateuch, ad Num. 18
[274] Rivet, in Genesis 31, Exercitation 135
[275] Mr. Ball of the Covenant, chapter 1
[276] In Synopsis Purior. Theolog. Disp. 23, Thes. 2
[277] Hebrews 8:8-10 & 10:16

Corinthians 11:25, 2 Corinthians 3:6, 14; Hebrews 7:22, 9:15-18, and Revelation 11:19. And I find it not used at all in any other places of the New Testament. So that it concerns us much to understand the meaning of this word aright.

Now {διαθήκη} *diatheke*, being derived from {διατίθεμαι}, *diatithemai*, signifying to dispose, compose, constitute, or make; generally it signifies a disposition or a disposal, but yet such a disposal wherein a promise is contained expressly or implicitly.[278] And particularly, it signifies either such a disposal as is merely federal, namely, a compact between the living: or such a disposal as is testamentary, namely, a last will or testament of one dying whereby he disposes of his goods and affairs by word or writing. This is to be noted against papists, who much mistake the genuine signification of the Greek word {*diatheke*}, restraining it only to a testamentary disposition. And in the New Testament it is used for a federal disposition,[279] as well as for a testamental,[280] as our translators have well rendered it both ways. And God's Covenant expressed by it (think some)[281] is mixed of the properties of both covenant and of testament, as the apostle shows in Hebrews 9:16-17, etc., and of both may be named *a testamental covenant* or a *covenanting testament*, whereby the disposing of God's favors and good things to us his children is declared.

(2) The various acceptation and use of these two names in Old and New Testament is also considerable for the opening of the covenant.

[1] Hebrew {בְּרִית} *berith*, is used in the New Testament for compacts or agreements, {1} Religious. {2} Civil. {3} Sinful.

{1} ***For religious compacts or agreements***, (i) of God with his church and people. (ii) Of God's people with God.

(i) *Of God with his church and people*: which is more general, with his whole church. So God's Covenant is used *properly*: (a) for God's gracious

---

[278] Synops. Purier. Theolog. Disp 23 Thes 2; Andre Rivet in Genesis 6 Exercitation 53, p.341, Lugden 1633
[279] Hebrews 8:8-10, 10:16 & 13:20
[280] Hebrews 9:15-18, Matthew 26:28
[281] Henry Ainsworth, Annotations on Genesis 6:18, Synopsis Pur. Theol. Disp. 23 Thes 3.4.

agreement with his people in Christ, for their happiness and salvation. Thus the word is used in Genesis 6:18, 17:4,11. Exodus 34:28, Jeremiah 31:31-32, and Hebrews 8:6-9. And in this sense it's used most frequently. (b) For some branch or additional only to that agreement, by a synecdoche of the part for the whole. As {covenant} for not drowning the world, Genesis 9:9-18. For continuing day and night, etc. Jeremiah 33:20, 33:25, with Genesis 8:21-22. For earthly blessings, Hosea 2:18-23. Against the particular sin of idolatry, as God's covenant with Israel in the land of Moab, Deuteronomy 29:1. *Improperly*: (a) for Christ, the mediator of the Covenant, by a metonymy. As Isaiah 42:6, 49:8. (b) For circumcision, the token and seal of the Covenant, by a metonymy of the sign for the thing signified, Genesis 17:13. *More special and peculiar*, with some particular persons, or sorts of persons only. Thus the word is used for God's covenant-agreement with: (a) priests and Levites, about their office and maintenance, Numbers 18:19, Nehemiah 13:29, Malachi 2:4-5, 8, (b) Phinehas, for an everlasting priesthood, Numbers 25:12-13, and (c) David, for a perpetual kingdom, 2 Chronicles 13:5.

(ii) *Of God's people with God, engaging themselves to duty*. And this either: (a) more solemnly in public covenants for reformation, as Joshua. 24:25, 2 Kings 11:17 and 23:3; 2 Chronicles 15:12 and 20:10, and Ezra 10:3, or (b) more secretly in private resolutions and promises touching points of sanctification, Job 31:1.

{2} *For civil compacts or agreements.* (i) Of man and woman in marriage, Malachi 2:19. Proverbs 2:17. (ii) Of particular persons, societies or states about other secular affairs, Genesis 21:27, 32. Exodus 23:32. 1 Samuel 18:3, and 20:16.

{3} *For sinful compacts or agreements.* (i) With idols: by idolatry. Metaphorically, Isaiah 57:8. (ii) With death and hell; by security. Metaphorically. Isaiah 28:15, 18.

These are the several acceptations of the Hebrew word {*berith*}, covenant in the Old Testament, and I find not any other. Now here the word is considered in the first sense, as it denotes a religious compact and agreement of God with his people, more generally, in order to their happiness and salvation.

[2] The Greek name {διαθήκη}, *diatheke*, is used also in the New Testament, {1} in a religious sense, and {2} in a civil sense.

{1} In a religious use, this name *{diatheke}* is taken more properly, and that sometimes (i) in a larger sense, for God's Covenant of Faith. As Acts 3:25, Galatians 3:17, Hebrews 8:6. etc. & 9:1, etc. (ii) In a stricter sense, for God's testament, or for God's Covenant as it is testamentary, and ratified by the death and blood of a testator. By typical blood of sacrifices: so it denotes the Old Testament. Hebrews 9:18-20. By anti-typical or true blood of Christ, the anti-type: so it denotes the New Testament in his blood, Matthew 26:28, Luke 22:20, Hebrews 9:15. More improperly and metonymically, for circumcision. By a metonymy of the sign. As Acts 7:8.

{2} In a civil use, this name {διαθήκη}, *diatheke*, in the New Testament, is applied to signify a man's will or testament whereby he disposes of his outward estate, how it shall be bestowed or employed after his decease. Galatians 3:15, Hebrews 9:16-17. Here, treating of God's covenant, we are not to consider the word *{covenant}* or *{testament}*, in a civil, but in a religious sense: and that, as it more properly signifies God's Covenant in a larger acceptation, or God's testament in a stricter acceptation.

Thus of the names given to God's Covenant in Scripture, both in respect of their grammatical notation, and of their various theological acceptations. As for the English word *{covenant}* or *{league}*,[282] and the Latin word *foedus, pactum, testamentum*,[283] I insist not upon them, because they are not in the Scripture originals. Now to the thing itself.

---

[282] *Covenant* seems to be so called from the Latin *conventio*: a convening or coming together: because in making covenants, men come together, not only into one place, but especially into one agreement, etc. *League* seems to be derived from the Latin *lego*, to send, because ambassages or messages used to be sent about making of leagues, or from *ligo*, to bind: leagues being binding to them that enter them.

[283] Auson. Popma de verb. Different. Lib 2 in verb. Fadus. Cooks Instit. Part 1, Book 3, Chapter 10, Section 58b

Aphorism 2

God's Covenant (in the general notion of it) is his gratuitous agreement with his people, promising them eternal happiness and all subordinate good: and requiring from them all due dependence upon God, and obedience unto him, in order to his glory.

This description of God's Covenant (generally considered) is of such latitude as to comprehend in it the nature of all God's covenants with his people, though most variously administered to them in their greatest varieties of conditions, both before and after the fall. This will best appear, if we view it in the particulars. In this description note: (1) the general nature of God's covenants, and (2) the special difference of them from all other covenants.

(1) **The general nature of God's Covenants with his people, it is an agreement.** All covenants, divine and human, consist in some agreement. *Can two walk together, except they be agreed?*[284] Concord is the foundation of all contracts. Now God's agreement with his people is twofold;

[1] *Implicit only*. So God's agreement with Adam was implied, partly by the inscription of his law, and covenant in his heart, which Adam was to perform.[285] Partly by threatening his disobedience with death, under which was implied a promise of life upon his obedience.[286]

[2] *Explicit*: wherein God plainly expresses his agreement with his people. This he does:

{1} Sometimes by word only,[287] as to Abraham and the fathers before Moses,[288] before any Scripture was written.

---

[284] Amos 3:3
[285] Compare Genesis 1:27 & Ecclesiastes 7:29 with Romans 2:14-15
[286] Genesis 2:17
[287] Exodus 34:28 & 24:7
[288] Genesis 6:18 & 17:7, 9

{2} Sometimes by writing also, as to Israel by Moses, and afterwards.[289] Hence such frequent mention of the tables of the covenant, and of the book of the covenant.

(2) **The special difference between God's covenants and all other covenants, is contained in the residue of the description.** Chiefly in the [1] efficient, [2] matter, [3] form, and [4] end of God's Covenant.

[1] The *efficient cause* or *author* of this Covenant is God. It is God's gracious agreement. In human covenants, where there is some proportion and equality between the parties covenanting, they jointly are con-causes, or joint authors of their covenants mutually agreed upon. But between the Most-High God and man, finite and infinite, there being no equality or proportion at all, God alone is the author of the Covenant between him and his people. And they must accept what covenant, and upon what terms, God will please to propound, or none at all. Hence the Covenants between God and his people, are seldom referred to the people as their Covenants (though in some sense they may be styled theirs, namely, as they are parties to them, and obliged to perform the conditions of them)[290] but generally they are all still in Scripture referred to God, counted his Covenants,[291] and said to be made by him with them.[292]

Thus God alone is the author of the Covenant: and his free-grace or favor, is the only inward impulsive, or moving cause why he makes a covenant with his people. It's his gratuitous agreement with them, God is a most free agent, and works all things *according to the counsel and good-pleasure of his own will*.[293] It is an act of his grace and mercy to make covenant with his people: but having made a covenant with them, it is an act of his justice, truth and faithfulness to make good and perform covenant. God freely makes himself our debtor, by covenanting; God faithfully and justly pays his debt in performing covenant with us.

---

[289] Exodus 34:28
[290] Malachi 2:10
[291] Genesis 6;18, 9:9, 17:9, Jeremiah 22:9 & 31:32,
[292] Genesis 6:28 & 17:7, Deuteronomy 5:2 & 29:1-2; 2 Samuel 23:5, Hebrews 8:7-9, etc.
[293] Ephesians 1:5, 7, 9, 11

[2] The *matter* of God's Covenant with his people is, on God's part, eternal *happiness and all subordinate good*, promised to them; on his people's part, *all due dependence upon God and obedience to him*, required of them, and restipulated by them.

{1} That eternal happiness is the subject matter in all God's Covenants after the fall, is evident by the tenor of them (as will after appear particularly) and in God's Covenant also before the fall it cannot be justly doubted. For, when death – not only corporal and spiritual, but also eternal was threatened and inflicted upon disobedience[294] – consequently not only a corporal and spiritual, but also eternal life was promised and should have been performed upon obedience. Now where eternal happiness is promised, all lesser and subordinate good must needs be included, as leading thereunto. And this is clear in all God's Covenants if exactly considered, which are bundles of promises touching the life that now is, and that which is to come.

{2} And reciprocally, God's people's due dependence upon God, and obedience unto him, is expressed or implied in all God's covenants with them. Adam must depend upon God for life, and be exactly obedient unto God, not only in keeping the law moral written in his heart, but in observing the law of trial touching the forbidden fruit.[295] Noah must depend upon God, for preservation from the flood:[296] and also be duly obedient to God in making an ark for his preservation. Abraham must depend upon God for Canaan covenanted,[297] and for the blessedness of all nations in his seed promised; and he must also duly obey God, in walking before God, in being perfect, and in circumcising all his males. And the like may be said of all God's Covenants with his people.

[3] The *form* of God's Covenant consists in God's promising to his people, and his people's restipulation to God. Promise and restipulation between federates make up the formality of federal obligation. God's promise

---

[294] Genesis 2:17 with Romans 6:23
[295] Genesis 2:17
[296] Genesis 6:14 to the end, Hebrews 11:7
[297] Genesis 17:1-2, etc.

is not always expressed, but sometimes necessarily and by consequence implied. As the promise of life is implied in the threatening of death to Adam.[298] And God's people's restipulation is sometimes only implied, as in God's Covenant with Adam after the fall, God expressly promises that *the seed of the woman shall bruise the serpent's head*,[299] and Adam implicitly restipulates by faith to accept this seed of the woman, Christ.

[4] The ***end*** of God's Covenant with his people, is his own glory. In all things God seeks his own glory, and so should we seek his glory above all. God – by his Covenant – displays his glory most gloriously. Herein shines the glory of his free grace in willing it; the glory of his wisdom in contriving it; the glory of his goodness, mercy and loving-kindness in condescending and stooping to mean man, and that so familiarly in a covenant-way; the glory of his liberty, in accepting whom, when, where, and upon what terms he pleases, into covenant with himself, and rejecting also at his pleasure; the glory of his justice and faithfulness in performing exactly all the promises and threats of his Covenant in their season; and the glory of his power in enabling his people acceptably to perform covenant with him unto the end.

---

[298] Genesis 2:17
[299] Genesis 3:15

Aphorism 3

God's Covenant with his people is not only one, but distinct: and it is distinct in kind, degree, and circumstances. It may be thus distributed or distinguished.

God's Covenant is,

(1) Of Works, in the first Adam, before the fall.[300]

(2) Of Faith, in the second Adam, after the fall.[301] This Covenant of Faith is sub-distinguished gradually and accidentally, in respect of the promise, and performance, of Christ the second Adam, into:

[1] The Covenants of Promise, under the Old Testament:[302] {1} with Adam;[303] {2} with Noah[304]; {3} with Abraham;[305] {4} with Israel at Sinai;[306] {5} with David;[307] {6} with the Jews about their return from Babylon.[308]

[2] The New Covenant, under the New Testament both with Jews and Gentiles. As in the ensuing scheme:

God's Covenant is two-fold:

(1) A Covenant of Works, in the first Adam, before the Fall.

(2) A Covenant of Faith in the second Adam, after the Fall; comprehending

[1] The Covenants of Promise, under the Old Testament: {1} with Adam;[309] {2} with Noah[310]; {3} with Abraham;[311] {4} with Israel at Sinai;[312] {5}

---

[300] Genesis 2:17
[301] Romans 3:20 to the end of the chapter
[302] Ephesians 2:12
[303] Genesis 3:15
[304] Genesis 6:17-18, etc.
[305] Genesis 15:18 & 17:1-2, etc.
[306] Exodus 24:1-0, Deuteronomy 5:2-3, 6, etc.
[307] 2 Samuel 7:5-17 & 23:5, Psalm 89
[308] Jeremiah 32:37 to the end
[309] Genesis 3:15
[310] Genesis 6:17-18, etc.
[311] Genesis 15:18 & 17:1-2, etc.
[312] Exodus 24:1-0, Deuteronomy 5:2-3, 6, etc.

with David;[313] {6} with the Jews about their return from Babylon.[314] [2] The Covenant of Performance, or the New Covenant, under the New Testament.

This distribution of God's Covenant, I like best to follow, as contriving it (without prejudice to any man's judgment) most clear, full and unexceptionable. For explaining the branches of it, consider,

(1) God's Covenant is first distributed into [1] a Covenant of Works, and [2] a Covenant of Faith. This is a division of God's Covenant, into its several species or kinds, which are directly opposite to each other. For the Covenant of Works, and the Covenant of Faith are two opposite kinds of covenants. This upon the matter seems to be the apostle's distribution; *Where is boasting then? It is excluded. By what law? Of works? Nay: but by the law of faith.*[315] Here the apostle is treating of God's free justification of us in Christ, the way to eternal happiness, which God covenants with his people: and he shows that God's justification is such, as all boasting is excluded. How? Not by the law of works, but by the law of faith. These amount to as much as the Covenant of Works, and the Covenant of Faith.

And again it is said, *the promise that he should be the heir of the world, was not to Abraham or to his seed, through the law* (i.e. the works of the law) *but through the righteousness of faith.*[316] Which intimates thus much, that God's Covenant with Abraham and his seed to make him heir of the world, was not a Covenant of Works, but of Faith. Again, this distribution arises, from the opposite stipulations required, works and faith; from the opposite foundations of the covenants, the first Adam, and the second Adam; and from the opposite states of mankind when these covenants were made, namely: before the fall, and after the fall – and therefore it seems very clear.

And inasmuch as all covenants of God with his people, may be referred to one of these two heads, namely, works in the first Adam before the fall, or faith in the second Adam since the fall, it seems very full.

---

[313] 2 Samuel 7:5-17 & 23:5, Psalm 89
[314] Jeremiah 32:37 to the end
[315] Romans 3:27
[316] Romans 4:13

Hence we may the better see what to judge of other distinctions of God's Covenant.

[1] Some distinguish God's Covenant into the Covenant of Works and the Covenant of Grace, but the members of this distinction are not opposite: for it was an act of God's grace and favor, that he would enter into a Covenant of Works with Adam, before as well as after the fall.

[2] Some, into the legal and evangelical covenant,[317] but if by {*legal covenant*} they understand the law and covenant as published on Mount Sinai, etc. (as usually men do), then that seems a great mistake: for that was a publication evangelical of the Covenant of Faith, not of Works. If by {*legal*}, they mean God's covenant with Adam before the fall, then the legal and evangelical covenant, is for substance the same with the Covenant of Works and of Faith.

[3] Some, into the covenant of nature, of grace, and subservient to the Covenant of Grace.[318] The first was made with Adam in his natural integrity; the second with Adam, Abraham; etc. after the fall, through Christ; the third with Israel at Mount Sinai which is called the Old Testament. But (though this be the distinction of a learned author, probably devised to avoid some difficulties about the Covenant of Faith, as published on Mount Sinai), yet it is not without its inconveniences. For God's Covenant with Adam in innocency was not so natural, but that it was also gratuitous and of divine favor, that God would deal so familiarly with Adam as by way of covenant, from whom as his creature he might have exacted obedience by an absolute command. And this covenant on Mount Sinai, called subservient to the Covenant of Grace, is not a distinct species or kind of covenant from the Covenant of Faith, or grace, but a distinct publication of the same covenant, the manner of administration being single, and the degree of manifestation clearer then of all before: in respect of which degree and manner, it was subservient indeed to the Covenant of Grace, namely: for clearing the foregoing publications, and for

---

[317] Mr. Edward Leigh on his Treatise of Promises, 1. 2. c.1
[318] John Cameron in Thes. de 3. Federe. Thesis 7, etc., p.544, etc. in fol. Genev. 1642

preparing to the following publications, especially to that of the New Covenant.

The Covenant of Faith: Promised & Performed

God's Covenant of Faith, in the second Adam, after the fall, is sub-distinguished into, (1) *the Covenants of Promise*, and (2) *the New Covenant*.

This distinction is grounded upon Christ the only mediator and foundation of the Covenant of Faith, and upon his different representation in this covenant. Christ is represented herein:

(1) As *promised* and to *come afterwards*, to work our redemption. And so he is set forth in the Covenants of Promise, to Adam, Noah, etc.

(2) As *performed, incarnate*, and *having suffered already*: and so he is set forth in the New Covenant or New Testament solemnly established by his death. Now the Covenants of Promise, and the New Covenant are essentially one and the same Covenant of Faith. Therefore I say that the Covenant of Faith comprehends them,b but they differ only gradually and accidentally, as after in due place will appear.

(3) In the Covenants of Promise, I find no writers observing above five eminent gradual steps or administrations; God's Covenant with Noah, being generally (but I think, causelessly) omitted by them. Therefore adding that, I produce six. And why God's Covenant with Noah is to be ranked among the eminent discoveries of the Covenant of Faith, shall be evidenced in handling of that particular.

Book II

Of God's Covenant more particularly

Chapter 1

Of God's Covenant of Works with the first Adam, and his natural seed before the fall.

Aphorism 1

God was pleased to enter into covenant with the first Adam, before his fall.

Under the term {*Adam*}, Scripture sometimes comprehends both sexes, both Adam and his wife.[319] And if any shall contend that God entered into covenant with both Adam and Eve at once as the complete root of mankind, I shall not much gainsay, and yet this will not so easily be proved – nor know I any inconvenience that would follow should it be denied: the woman coming from Adam as well as any of his posterity. Nor am I ignorant that some are of the opinion[320] that Adam received the covenant alone, and was to teach it, and did teach it to his wife – which opinion has more weight, because when God forbids the eating of the tree of knowledge under pain of death (wherein the promise of life contrariwise is implied), he speaks only in the singular number, namely: to Adam only.[321]

---

[319] See Genesis 1:26 with Genesis 5:12
[320] Augustine, On the Literal Interpretation of Genesis, 8.17.3
[321] Genesis 2:16-17

Question: But how may it be evidenced that God entered into covenant with the first Adam, even into a Covenant of Works, before the fall?

Answer: Though it be not positively and plainly said in Scripture that God gave Adam a Covenant of Works before his fall, and though the characters and footsteps of this covenant are not so expressly discovered in holy writ as with some other covenants, yet notwithstanding, upon sundry Scriptural grounds and considerations, it may be evinced sufficiently. As:

(1) *From the inscription of the Covenant of Works in Adam's heart.* Before the fall, God wrote the Covenant of Works – namely: the substance of the moral law – perfectly in Adam's heart, and in so doing, entered into covenant with him. Here are three things in this position to be cleared, namely: [1] that the moral law is the Covenant of Works, [2] that this moral law was perfectly written in Adam's heart before the fall, and [3] that God, in writing the moral law in his heart, entered into the Covenant of Works with him.

[1] That *the moral law* (abstractly and precisely in itself considered, without the additionals, namely: the preface, ceremonial law, etc. jointly promulgated with it in Horeb)[322] *is the Covenant of Works*, is manifest: {1} Because the moral law (by which is the knowledge of sin,[323] and which works wrath)[324] is styled by the apostle {*the law of works*}, and is set in opposition to the law of faith.[325] Now this law of works, and law of faith, amount in effect to as much as the Covenant of Works, and Covenant of Faith. {2} Because righteousness and life were at first by the moral law,[326] and should have been so still, had the law not become unable to give righteousness and life, in that it

---

[322] Exodus 20:2-3, etc., with 24:18 & 25:1-2, etc.
[323] Romans 3:20
[324] Romans 4:15
[325] Romans 3:27 with Galatians 3:18
[326] Galatians 3:21-22

was weak through the flesh: man through sin being unable to keep it.[327] Now the law – requiring obedience, and promising life upon that condition – must needs be a covenant, and that a Covenant of Works, works being the proper condition of it.

[2] That *this Moral Law for substance was perfectly written in Adam's heart before the fall*, is certain: {1} because man was made in God's image upright,[328] and perfect,[329] and consequently, was throughly furnished with all accomplishments of upright and perfect human nature – and particularly with the moral law, that law of nature – the substance whereof was engraven both in his mind by natural light knowing it, and in his will by natural integrity conforming unto it. {2} Because the work of the law remains imperfectly written in some dim characters in the very hearts of pagans and heathens since the fall: *they doing by nature the things contained in the law, and being a law unto themselves*, without the law of God written. Whence we may strongly conclude that much more before the fall, the moral law was perfectly written in Adam's heart, there being in him no sin to deface it in the least degree. {3} That God, in writing the moral law in Adam's heart, entered into the Covenant of Works with him, namely by real impressions upon his heart, though not by verbal expressions to the ear. For by this law written in Adam's heart, he had laid before him what obedience was required and assented to on Adam's part, and what recompense should be performed on God's part. And this was at least an implicit if not an explicit covenanting.

(2) **From God's express prescription of a positive law unto Adam in his innocent state.** God's positive law is laid down in these words, *And the Lord God commanded the man, saying, of every tree of the garden thou mayest freely eat: but of the tree of the knowledge of good and evil, thou shalt not eat of it; for in the day that thou eatest thereof thou shalt surely die.*[330]

---

[327] Romans 8:3
[328] Genesis 1:26-27
[329] Ecclesiastes 7:29
[330] Genesis 2:16-17

Here are *parties covenanting*, and agreeing upon terms, namely, God and Adam: here are also *terms agreed upon and matters covenanted reciprocally by these parties*: Adam on his part was to be obedient to God, in forbearing to eat of the tree of knowledge only; God on his part for present permits Adam to eat of all other trees of the garden; and for future (in his explicit threatening of death in case of disobedience), implicitly promises life in case of obedience herein. Now where there are parties covenanting and agreeing upon terms, and *terms mutually agreed upon by those parties* as here, there's the substance of an express covenant, though it be not formally and in express words called a covenant.

(3) ***From the intention and use of the two eminent trees***, **namely,** ***the tree of life in the midst of the garden, and the tree of knowledge of good and evil***.[331] The intended use of these two trees in paradise was sacramental. Hence they are called symbolical trees and sacramental trees. The tree of life, signifying to Adam that if he continued in his obedience and did eat of that tree, he would have life continued to him forever. God's speech, after the fall of Adam, seems to imply thus much; *and now lest he put forth his hand, and take also of the tree of life, and eat, and live forever*.[332] And some are of opinion that this tree signified Christ the Son of God,[333] *in whom was life, and that life the light of men*,[334] and that by the Son of God (but not as God-man, nor as mediator) this everlasting life was to have been confirmed, according to the sacramental signification of this tree of life. The Tree of Knowledge of Good and Evil,[335] signifying also to Adam contrariwise, that if he should become disobedient and eat of that tree, in that very day he should certainly die.[336] The former was a sacrament of life, this of death; *that* for confirmation of obedience, *this* for exploration of obedience and caution against disobedience.

---

[331] Genesis 2:9
[332] Genesis 3:22
[333] John Calvin, commentary on Genesis 2:9
[334] John 1:3-5
[335] Why so called, see hereafter in this chapter, Aphorism 4, in the [duty stipulated], Question 2, Doubt 1.
[336] Genesis 2:16-17

And learned writers both ancient and modern, count these trees symbolical, and sacramental. Augustine says, "There was a tree of life, as the rock was Christ; nor would God have man to live in paradise without mysteries of spiritual things corporally represented."[337] He had therefore in the other trees, nourishment; but in that tree, a sacrament. Bishop Hall said wittily, "Neither did these trees afford him only action for his hands, but instruction to his heart: for here he saw God's sacraments grow before him. All other trees had a natural use; these two in the midst of the garden, a spiritual. The one tree was for confirmation; the other for trial. One showed him what life he should have; the other what knowledge he should not desire to have. Alas, he that knew all other things, knew not this one thing, that he knew enough," etc.[338]

Mr. Perkins more solidly: "Now for Adam's sacraments, there were two: the Tree of Life, and the Tree of the Knowledge of Good and Evil: these did serve to exercise Adam in obedience unto God. The Tree of Life was to signify assurance of life forever, if he did keep God's commandments: the Tree of the Knowledge of Good and Evil, was a sacrament to show unto him, that if he did transgress God's commandments, he should die: and it was so called because it did signify that if he did transgress this law, he should have experience both of good and evil in himself."[339] To like effect, many other authors express themselves.[340] Now if these two trees were two sacraments, assuring of life in case of obedience and of death in case of disobedience, then hence we may collect that God not only entered into a Covenant of Works with the first Adam, but also gave him this covenant under sacramental signs and seals.

---

[337] Erat ergo & lignum viga quemadmodum petra Christus: nec sine mysteriis rerum spiritualium corporaliter praelentatis voluit hominem Deus in Paradiso vivere. Exat ei ergo in lignis caeteris Alimentum, in illo autem Sacramentum, etc. August. de Genesis ad literam l. 8. c. 4. Tom. 3. Basil. 169.

[338] Bishop Hall in his Contemplations, Book 1, *Of Paradise*, p.81

[339] Mr. William Perkins in his *Exposition of the Creed*, p.152, A. Volume 1, London 1626, and his *Order of Causes, etc.* p.17,18. *Ibid*.

[340] John Calvin. Commentary on Genesis 2:6; David. Pareus in Genesis 2:9; H. Ainsworth in his Annotations on Gen. 2. 6.—Polan. Partit. Theolog. lib. 1. p. 170. &c. Edit. 1623

(4) Finally, *from the sad event and fruit of the first Adam's fall, to all his ordinary posterity, even all mankind*: namely, guilt of sin and death. The apostle says that in one man (that is, Adam) all sinned, and that in Adam, all die. As by one man sin entered into the world, and death by sin, even so death passed upon all men (namely: by that one man), in whom all have sinned. Thus the words are best translated, as some learned men have well observed.[341] So then in one Adam's sinning, all sinned, and in one Adam's dying all died, as the apostle at large shows in Romans 5.

Question: But how did all mankind sin in Adam?

Answer: Not only by imitation of Adam as an evil example: for death seized on them that have not so sinned, not actually sinned. Nor merely by propagation, as from a corrupt root or fountain. For the apostle does not parallel Adam and Christ as two common roots only, but also as two common public or universal persons. For our immediate parents are corrupted roots, and we corrupted by them, yet their actual sins are not made ours, as Adam's is. But in Adam's first sin, we all became sinners, by imputation: Adam being an universal person, and all mankind one in him by God's Covenant of Works (as after will appear). All were that one man, as Augustine says, namely: by federal consociation.[342] God covenanted with Adam, and in him with all his posterity, and therefore Adam's breach of covenant fell not only upon him, but upon all his posterity.

---

[341] Ludovic de Dieu in Animadvers ad Romans 5:12; Mr. Anthony Burgess, Of Justification, Lecture 21, p.185

[342] Omnes ille unus homo suerunt. Augustine.

Aphorism 2

God's entering into covenant with Adam before his fall, was an act of divine grace and favor, not of debt.

For:

(1) God – the creator of Adam and of all things – has an absolute supremacy over all, and as absolute a liberty to dispose, as he will, of all. He might as creator have dealt only in a supreme way of command, requiring duty from Adam without any promise of reward: but he condescends to Adam, enters into a covenant and promise with him of his mere good pleasure, being no way necessitated or obliged thereunto. And that was mere grace.

(2) Adam though perfect and upright, and though perfectly persevering in that integrity, could merit no reward, nor any promise of reward. For when he had done all he could, he should have been an unprofitable servant, having done nothing but what was duty. And though Adam had walked in perfect obedience with God, yet might not God (without any wrong to Adam) for the manifesting of his sovereignty, power and liberty, have brought him to nothing as he made him of nothing?

Hence:

(1) Adam had great cause before his fall to serve the Lord most freely and cheerfully in all obedience. God creates him, therefore Adam owed him all. God covenants with him, therefore he owes him (if it were possible) more than all. By bonds of nature, Adam was obliged to be dutiful; by obligation of covenant-favor, to be double dutiful. For his being he owed him much; for his well-being, he owed him more.

(2) The more divine favor that shone in God's Covenant with Adam, the more heinous and inexcusable was Adam's breach of covenant with God. God's kindness heightens and aggravates Adam's unkindness. (3) If God's Covenant with the first Adam in his integrity was an act of divine grace, then God's Covenant with lapsed man in Christ the second Adam is an act of

superabounding and transcendent grace. If Adam, whilst he was without sin and able not to sin, could deserve nothing from God, then what can we deserve or challenge from God, who are nothing but lumps of sin, and can do nothing but sin?

Aphorism 3

God entering into covenant with the first Adam before his fall did, in and with him, enter into the same covenant with all his posterity.

This is evident:

(1) **By the miserable event of Adam's breach of this covenant upon all his posterity.** In Adam's sinning, all his posterity sinned, and in Adam's dying they all died. As by *one man sin entered into the world, and death by sin: and so death passed upon all men, for that all have sinned*.[343] Or as the Greek will well bear it; *in whom all have sinned*. Or (as a learned critic has well observed, whom in this particular I rather follow)[344] this verse may best be rendered thus: *as by one man sin entered into the world, and by sin, death; even so death passed upon all men, for that all have sinned*. Here's no forcing of the text, and thus the sense runs clear. But how have all men sinned, and so death passed upon them? All have not sinned *actually* as Adam sinned, for many die before they are capable of actual sinning.[345] How then? All are sinners *originally*, by reason of the corruption of nature.[346] True, yet the apostle reaches further, saying, *By the offense of one* (or, *by one offense*) *judgment came upon all men unto condemnation*.[347] Therefore by Adam's one offense, all men are condemned – and that before they actually sin, or are originally unclean. How can this be, but in reference to the Covenant wherein Adam and all his posterity were one party and God was the other?

(2) **By the analogy or proportion of God's dealing in all other covenants.** His usual course is to take in head and members, root, and branches. As, Christ the last Adam and his posterity,[348] Noah, and his

---

[343] Romans 5:12
[344] Lud. de Dieu in Animadvers. In Ep. ad Romans 5:12
[345] Romans 5:14
[346] Psalm 51:5, John 3:6
[347] Romans 5:18
[348] Genesis 3:15

family,[349] Abraham,[350] David,[351] and Israel, and their seed, and their seed's seed.[352] In like manner here, God deals with Adam and his posterity proportionably. God took them all into covenant with Adam the common head, and root of them all.

---

[349] Genesis 6:18
[350] Genesis 17:7-8
[351] 2 Samuel 7:16, Psalm 89
[352] Acts 2:39 with Isaiah 59:21

Aphorism 4

The Covenant which God made with the first Adam and his posterity before the fall, has upon several respects different names or denominations put upon it; but for the nature of it, it is God's gracious agreement with Adam, and with his posterity, in him, to give them eternal life and happiness, upon condition of perfect and personal obedience.

For opening the names and nature of this Covenant particularly, consider:

(1) **The names or denominations which learned men attribute to this covenant are several, and that upon several notions and considerations.** As,

[1] *A covenant of amity, or friendship.*[353] Because the parties to this Covenant, God and Adam with his posterity, were in perfect amity, when this Covenant was made: there was no enmity or discord at all between them. Adam (as Tertullian expresses it)[354] was innocent, a most near friend to God, and inhabitant of paradise.

[2] *A covenant of nature.*[355] Because founded upon Creation, and the integrity of man's nature; and requiring only a natural righteousness.

[3] *A covenant of life:*[356] in respect of that happy life which God implicitly promised to Adam therein. For under the threatening of death, expressed in case of disobedience, the promise of life is implied in case of obedience.

[4] *A legal covenant*, or Covenant of Works, in respect of Adam's restipulation of exact obedience required of God; legal works in all points

---

[353] Mr. John Ball, of the Covenant, chapter 2
[354] Innocens erat, & Deo de proximo amicus, & Paradisi colonus. Tertul. de Patient. lib. p. 130. 10. 1597.
[355] John Camer, de Federe, Thesis 7, 8, 9
[356] See the Westminster Shorter Catechism, advised by the Assembly of Divines

perfect being the condition of this covenant. This last denomination, unto me, seems fittest, for reasons formerly mentioned.[357]

(2) **The nature of this Covenant is in this description represented by [1] the author; [2] parties; [3] form; and [4] matter of it.**

[1] The *author of it* is God. Adam even in innocency stood not upon equal terms with God, but infinitely below him, as a creature below his creator. Therefore it concerned him not to capitulate or indent with God about the Covenant, but humbly and thankfully to accept what covenant the righteous God would impose. Now God became the author of this Covenant of Works with Adam two ways, namely: {1} by giving Adam the substance, law and rule of this Covenant, both inwardly, and outwardly. *Inwardly*, in his engraving the substance of the moral-law upon his heart – some dim characters whereof remain still even upon the hearts of pagans that have not God's written law.[358] *Outwardly*, in that express positive law about the tree of knowledge, forbidding to eat thereof under penalty of present death,[359] but implicitly promising life in case of not eating, in case of obedience: this former was the general rule for his direction in obedience – this latter was the special touchstone for exploration and detection of his obedience. {2} By annexing two tokens or sacramental signs to this Covenant, namely, the tree of life,[360] to assure Adam of the certainty of life promised, in case of perfect obedience, and the tree of knowledge, to assure him of the certainty of death, in case of disobedience. Learned men are of the opinion that these two trees were sacramental trees.[361]

[2] The *parties* to this Covenant of Works are God, and Adam together with Adam's posterity in him. God, as a creator, well-pleased with Adam, covenants with Adam as his creature, fashioned according to his own image, and perfectly upright without all spot of sin. In this notion, they were parties

---

[357] See before in Book 1, Chapter 2, Aphorism 3.
[358] Romans 2:14-15
[359] Genesis 2:16-17
[360] Genesis 2:9, 17 & 3:22
[361] Augustine, On the Literal Meaning of Genesis, Book 8, Chapter 4, Tome 3; David Pareus' commentary on Genesis 2:9

to this Covenant of Works, but in a far other notion afterwards to the Covenant of Faith.

[3] The *form* of this covenant consists in the agreement between God and Adam, namely: that Adam in his own person should yield perfect and perpetual obedience unto God, and particularly should discover his obedience in forbearing to eat of the tree of knowledge – and in so doing he should live happily, otherwise die presently.[362] This is the sum of the agreement. God propounds it, annexing two sacramental trees to confirm it, and Adam accepts it.

Now, that God should engage himself by promise and covenant to give Adam life in case of obedience, and should also annex two signs or tokens to this covenant, these were acts of mere favor and grace from God. Adam could in no respect challenge or expect the one or the other, though he had been never so obedient. Hence it may well be styled {*God's gracious agreement with Adam*}.

[4] The *matter* of this covenant was principally twofold. namely, {1} the blessing promised, and curse threatened on God's part, and {2} the duty restipulated on Adam's part.

{1} The blessing promised and curse threatened, is the matter of the covenant on God's part, for, *In the day that thou eatest thereof, thou shalt surely die.*[363] Contrariwise he implied: "Until the day that thou eatest thereof, thou shalt surely live. For clearing this, various doubts or questions hereunto appertaining, are to be resolved. As:

1. What life Adam had in his innocency?

2. What life it was which God farther promised him, upon his persisting in obedience?

3. What death it was which God threatened in case of disobedience?

---

[362] Compare and well-weigh Genesis 1:26-27 & 2:16-17, Ecclesiastes 7:29 with Galatians 3:10
[363] Genesis 2:17

4. How God's threatening of death was fulfilled, seeing Adam did not die in the self-same day; that he did eat of the tree of knowledge, but lived 930 years after?

Question 1: *What life was it which Adam enjoyed in innocency?*

Answer: It is not here the question whether Adam's life in innocency was natural, or supernatural? And I suppose it will easily be granted that, as God's law – written in Adam's heart as the rule of his life – was natural; and as God's image – wherein Adam was created, as the principle of his obedience and of his living to God – was natural; and as everything in Adam's primitive created state was natural; so his life that he lived in innocency with God and to God was natural. But the question here is: whether Adam had a mortal or immortal life in innocency? If mortal, how could it be rendered immortal? If immortal, then the promise of life seems needless.

For resolution herein, consider (as learned men well observe),[364] a thing may be said to be immortal in several ways.

(1) When it is simply, absolutely and every way incorruptible: having no possible cause of corruption, inward or outward. Thus, *God only has immortality*.[365]

(2) When it has, by reason of the perfection of its nature, no inward matter or cause of corruption, though it may be destroyed from without, as from God. Thus angels and souls of men are immortal.[366] And so Adam's soul had an immortal life in innocency; yea and every man's soul even since the fall remains still immortal in this sense.

(3) When it is in its own nature corruptible, but yet by the power or grace or justice of God, is preserved that it neither is nor can be corrupted. Thus the

---

[364] Andre Rivet on Genesis 2, Exercitations 19, 20, 21. David Pareus on Genesis 2:7
[365] 1 Timothy 6:16
[366] Matthew 10:28

spiritualized bodies of the saints in heaven; the bodies of reprobates in hell; the new heavens and new earth, etc., shall be immortal.

(4) When it has a power not to die, from some gift of the creator, or from some other supposition: yet in its own nature it is corruptible. Thus, Adam was immortal in innocency; not by an inability of dying, but by an ability of not dying. Which ability of not dying, Adam and his posterity would still have retained, according to God's Covenant and promise, if he had not fallen; and God's power, grace, and justice would have preserved him still in this immortal life, upon supposition of his perfect obedience.

Adam then before the fall had an immortal life, his soul being inwardly and in itself immortal, and his body, despite being inwardly and in itself corruptible, yet outwardly and from God rendered incorruptible. It had a remote capacity of dying, and yet an immediate ability of not dying, so that Adam in innocency had a possibility of not dying, if he sinned not. Saints in glory shall have an impossibility of both sinning and of dying. And though before the fall Adam had a mortality, or remote capacity of dying, yet since the fall both he and all his have an actual necessity of dying.

Question 2: What life it was, which God further promised Adam, upon his persisting in obedience?

Answer: (1) It seems clear that not only a temporary life only for some limited time was promised Adam, but even an eternal life without end in case of perfect obedience. Forasmuch as not only temporal, but also eternal death was threatened to Adam, and inflicted on his posterity for disobedience.[367]

(2) But whether Adam would have enjoyed this eternal life still in the earthly paradise, or would after some certain time have been translated and taken up to the heavenly paradise, that is by some disputed. Yet, [1] seeing as Scripture is silent touching any such translation, and [2] seeing as the giving of

---

[367] Compare Genesis 2:17 with Romans 5:12, 16, 18, Matthew 25:46, Romans 6:23

the heavenly paradise is the prerogative of Christ the last Adam, the heavenly Adam, as the earthly paradise came by the first and the earthly Adam, it would argue too much temerity to determine upon it. This is certain: his everlasting life would have been a most sweet and happy life with God.

Question 3: What was the death with which God threatened Adam in case of disobedience?

Answer: Whatsoever comes under the name and notion of death, was threatened to Adam, in that phrase, *thou shalt surely die*;[368] or *in dying thou shalt die* as the Hebrew phrase affords it. And the doubling of the Hebrew word seems to imply thus much, as some learned Hebrews are of opinion. Now death is the privation of life – and this, by separation of that which lives from the principle or fountain of its living. Life consists in union; death in dis-union, or separation. This, the nature of death in general. Hence particularly there is a manifold death.

(1) A death *temporal*, namely, a death for a time only.

[1] Of the soul, when by sin it is separated from God, from his image, and from the *life of God*;[369]; *Dead in trespasses and sins*;[370] *She that lives in pleasure, is dead while she liveth*;[371] *Let the dead bury their dead*.[372]

[2] Of the body, {1} when it's separated from the soul by nature's dissolution. And this, the most common acceptation of death. Thus, *Lazarus is dead*,[373] *Abraham is dead, and the prophets*.[374] {2} When it is gradually in any measure disposed or prepared for such a separation, by afflictions, pains, diseases, infirmities, etc. Hence such afflictions, etc., are called death, because

---

[368] Genesis 2:17
[369] Ephesians 4:18
[370] Ephesians 2:1, 5
[371] 1 Timothy 5:6
[372] Luke 9:60
[373] John 11:14
[374] John 8:52

they are death's harbingers and steps thereunto. As not the running out of the last sand, but also of all that went before, empties the hourglass; not the last stroke, but also the foregoing blows, fell the tree: *Take from me this death only*;[375] *There is death in the pot*;[376] *I die daily*;[377] *in deaths often.*[378]

(2) A death eternal of both body and soul, when by damnation particular or universal they shall be separated from the glorious fruition of God and his favor forevermore. This is called *the second death*,[379] *everlasting punishment*,[380] etc. These are several sorts of death mentioned in Scripture. Now all these were threatened to Adam in case of disobedience, namely:

[1] Death eternal both of body and soul. For, {1} death eternal is the most fully adequate proportional wages of sin,[381] as the apostle intimates in opposing there eternal life to death. And the due wages of sin was threatened to Adam. {2} The threatening limits not death, therefore no death can be excluded, and consequently, not eternal death either.{3} Guilt of eternal death and condemnation comes upon all Adam's posterity by his fall, as the apostle intimates;[382] and the actual execution of it shall come upon reprobates, as Christ implies. Therefore in the threatening, God intended eternal death.

[2] Temporal death of the soul in sin. For sin in its own nature alienates and separates from God and his favor, which is the spiritual death of the soul, for so long time, until the soul be reconciled to God.[383]

[3] Temporal death of the body, in separation of it from the soul, was also threatened to Adam in a special manner. For, {1} death and dying, in their most usual and proper acceptation import the dissolution of soul and body, and the most usual and proper sense of the words should here especially be taken. {2} The sentence of corporal death was denounced by God upon Adam

---

[375] Exodus 10:17
[376] 2 Kings 4:40
[377] 1 Corinthians 15:31
[378] 2 Corinthians 11:23
[379] Revelation 20:14
[380] Matthew 25:46
[381] Romans 6:23
[382] Romans 5:12, 16, 18, with Matthew 25:46
[383] Ephesians 4:17-18, Colossians 1:21, Romans 8:7

after his fall. *In the sweat of thy face shalt thou eat bread, till thou return unto the ground: for out of it wast thou taken; for dust thou art, and unto dust thou shalt return.*[384] Therefore death corporal was threatened to Adam before the fall. {3} The apostle does partly interpret this death inflicted upon all men for Adam's sin, to be the death of the body.[385] For all men do not die eternally.

[4] Finally, under the name of death, were threatened to Adam, all manner of evils and afflictions, whether in the soul, as grief, fear, horror, etc., or in the body, hunger, thirst, pains, diseases, etc. Even all inlets, preparatories, and harbingers of death. For, {1} all these are as so many gradual and partial deaths. Hence Scripture often calls them by the name of death.[386] {2} In inflicting the death threatened upon Adam and Eve, and their posterity, God lays on them these afflictions, of sorrow, sweating, toil, etc.[387] Therefore in threatening death, he intended all such afflictions. By all this, it appears it was no small matter that God threatened Adam under the name of death, in case of his disobedience.

Question 4: But how was God's threatening truly fulfilled, seeing as Adam – in the day that he did eat of the forbidden tree – did not die, but lived many hundreds of years after? (Genesis 5:5)

Answer: For clearing of this doubt,

(1) Some say that Adam, dying within a thousand years after his fall, died the same day he fell: because *with the Lord a thousand years are but as one day, and one day as a thousand years.*[388] But this is rejected as too much forced: in historical books, as this of Genesis, the word {*day*} being always taken in its proper signification. And this is a very needless shift.

---

[384] Genesis 3:19
[385] Romans 5:12, 14
[386] Exodus 10:17, 1 Corinthians 15:31, 2 Corinthians 11:23
[387] Genesis 3:16-19
[388] 2 Peter 3:8

(2) Some of the Hebrews were of the opinion that this speech of God was not peremptorily definitive and determinatory, but only minatory, like that pronounced against the Ninevites.[389] And that Adam repenting, he did not presently die, as otherwise he would have done. But Adam presently repented not till God extorted it from him, but rather did so excuse and extenuate his fault.[390] And though Adam repented, yet he died – and that immediately in some sense, as after will appear. This therefore satisfies not.

(3) Some refer this word {*in the day*} in the threatening to Adam's eating not to his dying, and take those words absolutely {*thou shalt surely die*} as if God had intimated that there was no day, no time excepted, but if they did eat any day whatsoever, they should die; but he tells them not when they shall so die. But this resolution seems too dilute, more witty then solid, and too much to force the text.

(4) Others, joining the circumstance of the day with the threatening of death, conceive that in the self-same day that Adam sinned, he did die the death, and that the threatening was presently fulfilled upon his sinning. And this, as it is the most common, so it is the best resolution. But let us see how Adam died in the same day wherein he sinned.

[1] *In his soul*, he was immediately separated from God by sin, and died spiritually.[391] Sin, in the inward nature of it, carries death in it. *Dead in trespasses and sins.*[392] Adam had no sooner sinned than he was dead in sin, being immediately deprived of the image of God, of the favor of God, and of communion with God, which was the life of his soul.

[2] *In his body* he died also in the same day wherein he sinned. But how? Not actually: for God, intending *to make of one blood, all nations of men*,[393] did respite the actual execution of bodily death on Adam until he had a considerable posterity. But in his body he died the same:

---

[389] Jonah 3:4
[390] Genesis 3:10-12
[391] Genesis 3:7-8, 10
[392] Ephesians 2:1
[393] Acts 17:26

{1} In respect of the guilt of death corporal, he – according to what he deserved – was presently condemned, and under sentence of death, though reprieved for a time. Now we count a condemned man, a dead man.

{2} In respect of the inevitable necessity of death corporal, which he contracted upon himself. He became presently mortal, though he did not presently die. He that before his fall had an ability of not dying, after his fall brought upon himself an impossibility of not dying. Hence Jerome commends Symmachus' version, who instead of {*thou shalt die*}, renders it {*thou shalt be mortal*}, as Rivet observes.[394] So then Adam in paradise before his fall had a *posse non mori*, an ability of not dying; after the fall, a *non posse non mori*, an impossibility of not dying; and in heaven he shall have, a *non posse mori*, an impossibility of dying any more.

{3} In respect of the experimental beginnings, symptoms, signs, and harbingers of death corporal. Adam presently began to feel, heat, cold, weariness, etc. – his natural heat and radical moisture began to consume one another, and so went on, until the accomplishment of death. So that as a wounded man cries out, "I am a dead man," so Adam – beginning to be wounded with afflictions – might cry out, "I am a dead man." In both his soul and body, Adam was presently liable to eternal death,[395] the proper wages of sin, and under the arrest of God's wrath and curse.

(1) Thus of the blessing promised and curse threatened – the matter of the Covenant of Works on God's part.

(2) The duty restipulated, the matter of the Covenant on Adam's part, was perfect and perpetual personal obedience. For clearing this, two questions are to be resolved.

[1] How it may appear that such obedience was required of Adam, and restipulated.

[2] What was the law rule or measure of Adam's obedience?

---

[394] Andre Rivet in Genesis 2, Exercitation 11

[395] Romans 6:23. Adam non quidem è vestigio moriebatur morte corporali; statim tamen fichat mortalis, paulatim moriebatur; & mox erat mortuus morte aeterna. D. Zach. Ursin. in Explicat. Catechet. Part 3. Question 46.

Question 1. How it may appear, that God required of Adam in this covenant such perfect and perpetual personal obedience, and that Adam restipulated such obedience?

Answer: That perfect and perpetual personal obedience was required by God and restipulated on Adam's part, is evident in several ways. As:

(1) From the manner of God's threatening. He threatens present death upon the least single act of Adam's personal disobedience: *In the day that thou eatest thereof thou shalt surely die.*[396] Consequently, God covenanted with Adam for such personal obedience as should be both perfect and constant. The least act of disobedience destroys both the perfection and constancy of obedience.

(2) From the nature of the Covenant of Works, which requires all exactness of personal obedience both for kind, degree and duration, under a curse. *Cursed is everyone that continues not in all things, which are written in the book of the law to do them.*[397] Here's obedience, personal obedience, perfect obedience, and perpetual obedience required by the legal Covenant of Works. And the law was never given as a Covenant of Works, but only to Adam in innocency.

(3) From God's process in judgment with Adam and his posterity upon one act of disobedience. He brought the threatened death upon them, as has been explained, which God would not have done, had he not covenanted with Adam, for perfect and perpetual personal obedience.

(4) From God's mysterious method in repairing the first Adam's breach of the Covenant of Works through disobedience by the last Adam's exact fulfilling and satisfying of the Covenant of Works through obedience. Now the last Adam, Jesus Christ God-man, exactly fulfilled and satisfied the Covenant of Works through obedience, both *passively* and *actively*.

---

[396] Genesis 2:17
[397] Galatians 3:10 with Deuteronomy 27:26

Passively, whilst Christ, as our surety, *humbled himself and became obedient to the death, even the death upon the cross;*[398] and so *became a curse for us, to redeem us from the curse of the law,*[399] or Covenant of Works, by satisfying divine justice to the full for our breach of covenant in Adam.

Actively, whilst Christ as our mediator actually kept and fulfilled the whole law, or Covenant of Works in every kind, degree, and circumstance of duty for us, who of our selves are no way able to keep it.[400] That so the whole obedience and righteousness of Christ may be through faith imputed to us:[401] that the *righteousness of the law might be fulfilled in us, who walk not after the flesh, but after the Spirit;*[402] so then, the Covenant of Works must be fulfilled and made good. The first Adam could not do it because he had broken it; the last Adam is therefore brought in, to fulfill all righteousness, and make satisfaction for all our unrighteousness. If then the breach of the covenant was made up again by the last Adam's perfect and constant personal obedience, then surely that breach was made by the first Adam's failing in such obedience. Therefore, perfect and constant personal obedience was required of the first Adam therein.

Question 2: What was the law, rule, or measure of Adam's obedience?

Answer: The law or rule for Adam's obedience was: (1) more generally, the whole Covenant of Works, and (2) more particularly, the two sorts of laws comprehended in the Covenant of Works, namely:

(1) The moral law written in Adam's heart. For why was it written there but to be an inward rule and principle of his obedience? And that it was

---

[398] Philippians 2:8
[399] Galatians 3:10, 13
[400] Galatians 4:4-5, Matthew 3:15
[401] Romans 3:18-19 & 10:4
[402] Romans 8:3-4

written in Adam's heart before the fall, is evident, because even pagans *which have not the written law, yet have the work of the law written in their hearts, doing by nature the things contained in the law*, after the fall.[403]

(2) The positive law of not eating of the tree of knowledge under pain of death.[404] I call it a positive law, because it merely depended upon the will of the imposer. The not eating of that tree was not engraven in nature, but merely imposed at the pleasure of the lawgiver. The subject matter of the law – namely: the eating or not eating of the tree of knowledge – was not bad or good in itself, more than of other trees; but only in respect of God's prohibition, it became bad and unlawful to eat of it. This positive law, some call a *symbolical precept*, because Adam's obedience thereto was to have been a symbol or outward testimony of his obedience and service to God; his homage-penny, etc. Some call it a precept of exploration, because it was given as a special law for trial and discovery of Adam's obedience.

Doubt 1. But why is this forbidden tree called the tree of knowledge of good and evil?

Answer: This tree was so called:

(1) Not from any inward virtue in it, to confer the use of reason to our first parents, who are imagined to be created like infants without the use of reason, as some Hebrews think, but erroneously.[405] For, [1] Why should God prescribe to them such a law with a capital penalty, who had not the use of reason? [2] Adam had such use of reason, that upon first sight he could name the creatures according to their natures.[406] And understood that the woman brought to him was *bone of his bone, and flesh of his flesh*,[407] etc.

(2) Not from any effect or physical efficacy of it, for increasing of knowledge either by working it immediately upon the soul; or immediately upon the animal spirits, refreshing and awakening them, and so mediately

---

[403] Romans 2:14-15
[404] Genesis 2:17
[405] Andre Rivet in Genesis 2, Exercitation 18
[406] Genesis 2:19-20
[407] Genesis 2:22-24

upon the soul, as some think, but falsely.[408] For, [1] the material fruit could not immediately act upon the immaterial soul, to improve knowledge. [2] All the trees of the garden tended to refresh and enliven the spirits, being good for food – and upon that account should all of them be called trees of knowledge. [3] Could this tree have increased Adam's knowledge, can it be imagined God would have forbidden him a tree so advantageous, and envied him so much good? [4] Then Adam's eating of that tree was not such an aggravation of his sin, the matter of the prohibition being not small – as learned writers unanimously judge, and aggravate his sin thereby – but great, and that tree of more consequence than all the other trees of the garden for improvement of knowledge. Consequently, Adam's strength in abstinence from it must needs be the more.

(3) Nor finally was this tree called {*the tree of knowledge*} from the serpent's suggestion in his temptation, *ye shall be as gods, knowing good and evil*,[409] as popish writers fancy.[410] For, can we probably imagine that God would denominate this the tree of knowledge from the devil's impudent lie in the serpent?

(4) But it was called {*the tree of knowledge*}, that is, of experimental knowledge, by way of prolepsis, from the event that would ensue upon eating thereon. For then Adam should experimentally know, to his sorrow, from how much good he had lapsed, and how much evil he had contracted upon himself – as it's usual in Scripture by way of prolepsis or anticipation to give denominations unto things.[411] And this the best, and most received opinion about this denomination.[412]

---

[408] Joseph, Jewish Antiquities, Book 1
[409] Genesis 3:5
[410] Rupert, Tostatus, Pererius on Genesis
[411] As in Genesis 21:14, 31; Numbers 13:23
[412] Arbor illa apellata est scientia dignoscendi boni & malis, non quia inde talia quasi poma pendebant, sed quicquid esset arbor illa, cujus libet pomi, cujus libet fructus esset, ideo sic vocata est; Quia bomo qui nollet bonum à malo discernere per praeceptum, discreturus erat per experimentum, ut tangendo vetitum inveniret supplicium. Aug. de Verb. Dom. Serm. 34. Tom. 10. Andr. Rivet. in Gen. 2. Exercitat. 18. D. Pareus in Genesis 2:9.

Doubt 2: But why did God, besides the natural law engraven in Adam's heart, impose this positive law, forbidding that which was not in itself morally and intrinsically evil?

Answer: The Lord seems to have done this,

(1) *For the more clear discovery of his own absolute power and dominion over man.* Whilst God commands or forbids things which in themselves are consonant or dissonant to human reason as good or bad, God's supremacy over man is not so evident: such commands leaning and being founded upon man's reason and conscience. But when God commands or forbids that which in its own nature is morally neither good nor bad, but only becomes good or bad from the mere will of God commanding or forbidding, nor can any other reason thereof be given but God's will and pleasure; then the absolute supremacy and sovereignty of God is notably manifested, as in this positive law.

(2) *For the more evident trial and manifestation of man's subjection and obedience to God.* For this is pure obedience and subjection indeed, when a man is subject and obedient merely to the will of the lawgiver, though the matter required or forbidden, be in itself neither morally good nor evil. I like Augustine's illustration well: "If a man be charged not to touch a poisonous herb, because it will be hurtful to him that touches it – or not to touch another man's money, because it will be evil to the owner – this is no such trial of obedience, because the evil of the thing forbidden restrains, and not only the authority of him that commands or forbids. But when a man forebears what is forbidden, which, had it not been forbidden, he needed not at all to have forborn."[413] God therefore forbids a tree in itself lawful and good for

---

[413] "Si aliquid mali effet tignum vitud unde probibun hominem Deus, ejus ipsius malnia tura venenatus videretur ad mortem. Quia vero ligna omnia in Paradiso bona plantaverat, qui fecit omnia bona valde, nec ulla ibi natura mali erat: quia nusquam est mali natura: – Ab eo ligno quod malum non erat prohibitus est, ut ipsa per se praecepti conservatio bonum illi esset, & transgressio malum. Nec potuit melius & diligentius commendari, quantum malum fit, sela inobedientia, cum ideo reus iniquitatis factus est homo, quia cam rem tetigit, contra prohibitionem quam si non probibitus tetigit, non utiq peccasset. Nam qui dicit, verbi gratia, noli sangere banc herbam, si forte venenosa est, mortemq: pronunciat, fitetigerit, sequitur quidem mors contemptorem praecepti, sed etiam si nomo

food, thereby to try how purely Adam would obey his mere command without any other motive or consideration. It was expedient that Adam should know himself to be under God. And (as the same Augustine)[414] how shall he be under God, if not under his command?

(3) For the greater aggravation of Adam's sin, in case he should disobey. Partly in that, if he offended, he should offend in so small a matter and so easy to be observed, especially God having granted him liberty to eat of all the trees in the garden besides. Partly in that he by disobeying should so directly reject God's dominion and authority by doing that which merely was to be forborne, because God had forbidden it, which were mere disobedience, mere rebellion against God's dominion. Hence the apostle charges disobedience upon Adam as his proper sin, Romans 5:19.

---

prohibuisset, atq: itte tetigisset, nibilominus utiq., moreretur. Illa quippe res contraria saluti vitaq; ejus esset, sive inde vetaretur, sive non veteratur. Item cum quisq; prohibet tam rem tangi, qua non quidem tangenti, sed illi qui prohibuit obesset: velut si quisquom in alienam preuniom mifesset manum, prohibitus abreo cujus erat pecunia illa: ideo esset prohibito peccatum, quia prohibenti poterat esse damnosum. Cum vero illud tangitur, quod nec tangfenti obesset si non prohiberetur, nec cuiquam alteri quamlibet tangeretur, quare prohibitum est, nisi ut ipsius per se bonum obedientiae, & ipsius per semantum inobedientiae monstraretur?" Augustine, On The Literal Meaning of Genesis, 8.13.3

[414] "Quid est illa Arbor? Si bona est, quare non tango? Si mala est, quid fecit in Paradiso? Prorsus ideo est in Paradiso quia bona est, sed nolo eam tangas: Quare non tango? Quia obedientem te volo, non contradicentem. Serve audi, adhuc serve: sed noli male serve. Serve audi prius Domini jussum, & tunc jubentis disce consilium. Bona est arbor, nolo tangos. Quare? Quia dominus sum, & tu servus. Haec tota causa est. Si parva est dedignaris esse servus? Quid autem tibi expédit nisi esse sub Domino? Quomodo eris sub Domino, nisi fueris sub Praecepto?" August. de verb. Dom. Serm. 34. Tom. 10.

Aphorism 5

When God entered into this Covenant of Works with the first Adam, he was completely able in his own person to keep this Covenant in every point.

Herein God required nothing, but Adam was able to perform it; God forbade nothing, but Adam was able to forbear it.

(1) That Adam had complete ability to keep this Covenant of Works, is evident:

[1] From removal of all causes of disability from Adam at that time. Then there was nothing in Adam that might impede or disable Adam from completely keeping the Covenant of Works. The only disabling impediment is sin. The only cause why Adam's posterity since the fall cannot keep the Covenant of Works, nor consequently be justified thereby, is their sin. *The law is weak through the flesh.*[415] Now Adam had no sin in him at all, neither original nor actual, when God entered into covenant with him. Sin entered afterwards, by his disobedience in eating the forbidden fruit[416] – and with sin, shame and death, the inseparable attendants upon sin.[417]

[2] From the position and presence of all necessary and sufficient causes of ability in Adam: at that time Adam had the perfection of God's image in him. *God created man in his own image, in the image of God created he him*,[418] wherein this image consisted, I now dispute not. But this is clear, *Adam was made upright,*[419] יָשָׁר *yashar*, there rendered {*upright*} signifies one *right, equal, and who bends to neither part*: as Mercerus has observed.[420] So that Adam was even, equal, declining to no part or extreme: thus he was created.

---

[415] Romans 8:3
[416] Romans 5:12, 19; Genesis 3
[417] Genesis 2:25 & 3:7, 10-11; Romans 6:21
[418] Genesis 1:26-27
[419] Ecclesiastes 7:29
[420] In Pagn. Lexico ad verb יָשָׁר

Hence he had all necessary inward ability to perform God's will: {1} a knowing mind, a pure conscience, an obedient and dutiful will, a loving heart, a tractable and obsequious body, all upright. {2} The inscription of God's Covenant in his heart, the moral law, this he had engraven upon his heart, (as formerly was shown).[421] {3} The expression of the positive law, about the tree of knowledge. This was made known to him by word of mouth. Hence Adam had a perfect rule both inward and outward for steering his obedience. Adam therefore having so perfect a principle, and so exact a rule for obedience, must needs be completely able to fulfill this Covenant of Works with God.

[3] From absurdities that otherwise upon denial of Adam's ability would ensue. For: {1} Then God should have required impossibilities of Adam. {2} Then the penalty of death in case of disobedience, should have been unjust: because God never gave Adam complete ability for obedience.

Corollaries

Hence these things result by way of corollary,

(1) ***That Adam, before he broke this Covenant of Works, neither had, nor needed a mediator of reconciliation.*** He needed not the mediation of Jesus Christ the second or last Adam: either for satisfaction, for he had no way sinned; or for intercession, for Adam wanted nothing, and was completely acceptable to God in his person; or for imputation of Christ's righteousness and obedience to him, for Adam was perfectly upright and obedient in himself. O what a difference between Adam then, and Adam's posterity now! He needed no Christ, we need nothing more, etc.

Objection: But the tree of life seems to be a type of Christ, especially if we consider that passage in Revelation.[422]

Answer: The tree of life in Eden was sacramental, but not typical. Sacramental, to assure Adam of the continuance of his life, if he had continued his obedience and eaten thereof – but not typical, to set out a mediator. That

---

[421] See before, in Aphorism 3 of this chapter
[422] Revelation 22:2

passage in Revelation alludes to this tree of life in Eden[423] – an allusion is one thing, an interpretation another. And some have turned it into an allegory,[424] interpreting paradise to be the church, the four rivers therein to be the four gospels, the fruit trees to be the saints, their fruits to be good works, the tree of life to be the holy of holies – even Christ – and the tree of knowledge of good and evil to be the proper freedom of will. This is devised wittily, not solidly.

(2) *That Adam, before breach of covenant, as he neither had, nor needed a mediator, so he neither had, nor needed faith in a mediator.* Adam had a faith in God, whereby he was able, both to believe whatsoever God revealed, and to depend upon God and his promises, as also to perform in love whatsoever God prescribed. And so in Adam's faith, there was a remote capacity of believing any particular revelation God should make touching a mediator, but no particular acting of faith on a mediator. Adam's faith under the Covenant of Works, differs much from ours under the Covenant of Faith: [1] in respect of their rise and manner of conveyance. Adam's faith was naturally implanted in him by God, ours supernaturally. [2] In respect of their foundation wherein they lean. Adam's faith leaned on the title of perfect, upright nature: ours upon the faithful and free promises of God in Christ. [3] In respect of their fruit. Adam's faith produced a changeable righteousness in himself a mutable person: ours an unchangeable righteousness from Christ and the Spirit which are unchangeable. [4] In respect of their actings. Adam's faith acted towards God without any consideration of a mediator: ours acts towards God by Christ the mediator. [5] In respect of their associates, or

---

[423] Revelation 22:2

[424] "This account can be even better read as an allegory of the Church, prophetical of what was to happen in the future. Thus, the Garden is the Church itself, as we can see from the Canticle of Canticles; the four rivers are the four Gospels; the fruit-bearing trees are the saints, as the fruits are their works; and the tree of life is, of course, the Saint of saints, Christ; and the tree of the knowledge of good and evil is the free choice of our own will." Augustine, City of God, edited and abridged by Vernon J. Bourke from the translation by Walsh, Zema, Monahan and Honan, Image Books, 2014, p.270

companions. Faith in Adam was without repentance, because he was sinless; faith in us is always accompanied with repentance, because we are sinful.

(3) That, Adam's breach of covenant is without any excuse. Adam was fully able to keep covenant: therefore Adam is left without all apology for his breach of covenant. He must needs justify God, and condemn himself under the severest penalties for breach of covenant: for God gave him power completely to keep it. And what is here said of Adam is to be understood also of all Adam's posterity in him.

Aphorism 6

This Covenant of Works, Adam utterly broke by disobedience.

For clearing of this, consider: (1) that Adam thus broke the Covenant of Works, (2) how Adam broke this covenant, (3) when and how soon he broke it, (4) how grievous and heinous this breach, and (5) corollaries.

(1) **That Adam utterly broke the Covenant of Works by disobedience, is evident.**
[1] By Scripture-testimonies both of Old and New Testament. In the Old Testament is the narration of this covenant-breach, how the woman seduced by the devil in the serpent, did eat of the tree of knowledge, and how she gave unto Adam her husband, and he did eat.[425] And what sad effects followed thereupon to them both,[426] namely: shame, fear, hiding themselves from God, translation of their fault – the man to his wife, and she to the serpent – enmity between the seed of the woman and serpent, the multiplication of the woman's sorrows, and aggravation of her subjection to her husband, the curse upon the earth; the toil, sorrows, and mortality of Adam, the expulsion of Adam out of Eden, and the effectual abstention of Adam – by cherubims and a flaming sword turning every way – from the tree of life. In the New Testament is an explication of Adam's breach of covenant, how all his posterity sinned and broke covenant in him. *By one man sin entered into the world, in whom all have sinned*,[427] *by one man's disobedience many were made sinners*.[428] And this breach of covenant is set forth by various denominations, namely: sin, Adam's transgression, the offense of one, one man's disobedience: all tending to describe the nature of it.[429]

---

[425] Genesis 3:1-7
[426] Genesis 3:7 to the end of the chapter
[427] Romans 5:12
[428] Romans 5:19
[429] Romans 5:12, 14, 18, 19

[2] By the sad experience which all Adam's posterity have had of the woeful effect of Adam's breach of covenant to this day – all being thereby involved in sin, death, and condemnation.[430] Therefore all Adam's ordinary seed were in covenant with him, broke covenant in him, and smart under covenant-breach by him.

[3] By the manner of God's administration. After Adam's disobedience God utterly laid aside the Covenant of Works, and never set it on foot more, but instead thereof advanced the Covenant of Faith in Christ the second Adam. Thereby notifying to us that, the Covenant of Works was utterly broken and dissolved by the first Adam's sin.

(2) *How did Adam break this Covenant of Works?*

Answer: [1] Adam broke the Covenant of Works by eating of the tree of knowledge, contrary to God's positive symbolic precept imposed upon Adam for trial of his obedience.[431] This act of Adam did complete his fall, and covenant-breach.

[2] This covenant-breach was brought on, not all at once, but by certain steps and degrees: {1} The woman hearkens to the serpent, that is, to the devil in the serpent tempting.[432] {2} She mis-reports God's command, partly adding thereto; *neither shall ye touch it*.[433] For God had not forbidden the touching of it but only the eating of it. Partly taking thence from, detracting from the fidelity of it. For what God spoke peremptorily, *in the day thou eatest thereof, dying thou shalt die*:[434] she alleges doubtfully, *lest peradventure ye die*;[435] as the Hebrew phrase properly signifies.

[3] She so far credits the serpent, as to behold, or eye the tree of knowledge with desire and affectation,[436] conceiving the tree to be: {1} good

---

[430] Romans 5:12, 18, 19
[431] Genesis 2:17 with Genesis 3:6-7
[432] Genesis 3:1-2
[433] Genesis 3:3 with 2:16-17
[434] Genesis 2:17
[435] Genesis 3:3
[436] Genesis 3:6

for food, {2} pleasant to the eye, {3} and desirable to make one wise. As John ranks all that is in and of the world, and not of the Father, under these three heads, the lust of the flesh, the lust of the eye, and the pride of life.[437] {4} She took of the fruit of the tree and did eat.[438] {5} She gave unto her husband, and he did eat.[439] Hence we may understand that of the apostle, Adam was not deceived (that is, not by the serpent), but the woman being deceived was in the transgression (that is, was first in the transgression before Adam).[440] This sin was brought upon Adam by degrees: (i) suggestion, (ii) aversion from good, (iii) delightful inclination to evil and (iv) to execution or acting of sin inclined and consented to, and (v) propagation or derivation of sin to others. Thus Adam sinned, and broke covenant with God.

(3) *The causes of Adam's sin and covenant-breach, thus brought to pass, were several.* The instrumental cause *remote* was the serpent and the devil in him; *immediate* was the woman, Adam's wife. The efficient cause of Adam's sin is hard to be found out. Properly, Adam's sin had no efficient cause at all, but rather a deficient cause. God neither directly nor indirectly could be any cause of it at all, for *God made man upright,*[441] and God, as *he cannot be tempted with evil, so he tempteth no man to evil.*[442] But Adam – being created mutable, though upright, and having a will flexible to good or to evil, and not being confirmed and established immovably in good, but left to his own power and liberty (for God was not bound to confirm, and uphold him) – he declined unto evil, and became like the beasts that perish.

Question: When, and how soon did Adam break this Covenant of Works?

Answer: In the history of Adam's fall, the circumstance of time is not expressly described, and other Scriptures are very silent. Hence, those that have written about this question, both Jewish doctors, ancient fathers, Schoolmen,

---

[437] 1 John 2:16
[438] Genesis 3:6
[439] Genesis 3:6
[440] 1 Timothy 2:14
[441] Ecclesiastes 7:29
[442] James 1:13

and modern authors, have been of various opinions herein, and somewhat unsatisfied. Omitting the diversity of others' opinions, I shall briefly declare herein what to me seems most probable and consentaneous to Scripture without prejudice to others' judgements.

[1] *It is evident that Adam continued in paradise in his concreted integrity for a certain considerable season, before he fell.* For, before the fall: {1} Adam gave names to all living creatures which God brought before him.[443] {2} The woman was made of one of Adam's ribs, taken out of his side, Adam, meanwhile being cast into a deep sleep.[444] {3} God brought the woman to Adam, gave her to him to wife, and Adam so accepted her.[445] {4} God blessed them with the blessing of fruitfulness, and dominion over the earth, and over all the creatures therein.[446] {5} God gave them every herb and every fruit-bearing tree for food.[447] {6} Adam was placed in the garden of Eden to dress it, and to keep it.[448] {7} God – permitting them to eat of all the other trees of the garden – gave command under pain of present death not to eat of the tree of knowledge.[449] All this was orderly done before Adam's fall. And all this required some considerable time.

[2] *It is not likely that Adam continued any long time in his innocency before his fall.* For: {1} Then Adam in all probability would have eaten of the tree of life, and have been confirmed in life against falling, as that phrase intimates, Genesis 3:23, which he did not. {2} Then probably, Eve should have conceived a pure and spotless seed from Adam. The blessing of generation and fruitfulness being already bestowed upon them: and no curse of barrenness inflicted.[450] That was the fruit of the fall. And consequently such seed should not have been begotten in Adam's own likeness, sinful. {3} After the historical narration of these seven particulars aforementioned (which would not require

---

[443] Genesis 2:20
[444] Genesis 2:21-22
[445] Genesis 2:22-24
[446] Genesis 1:28
[447] Genesis 1:29
[448] Genesis 2:8-16
[449] Genesis 2:16-17
[450] Genesis 1:28

any long time to be effected in) presently the story of Adam's fall is related, which seems to intimate, that the fall was not long after Adam's creation.[451] Hence Calvin modestly, "As I have not what to assert touching the time, so I think it may be gathered from Moses his narration, that they did not long retain the integrity which they had; for as soon as he had spoke of their creation, without mention of any other thing, he passes to their defection, etc."[452] And Augustine thinks the transgression presently followed the creation.[453]

[3] *It is probable that Adam continued in paradise neither years, months, weeks, nor days: but sinned and lost paradise in the self-same day in which he was created.* That he was created and corrupted, formed and deformed, made and marred, alive and dead, an inhabitant in and an exile from paradise, in one and the self-same day. For,

{1} There is nothing in the text intimating that Adam stood longer than that one in which he was created, but rather that he fell on the same day. We find not that he kept one sabbath in paradise. We find that Adam and his wife

---

[451] Compare Genesis 1 & 2 with Genesis 3:1, etc.

[452] Calvin's commentary on Genesis 3:6: "A question is mooted by some, concerning the time of this fall, or rather ruin. The opinion has been pretty generally received, that they fell on the day they were created; and, therefore Augustine writes, that they stood only for six hours. The conjecture of others, that the temptation was delayed by Satan till the Sabbath, in order to profane that sacred day, is but weak. And certainly, by instances like these, all pious persons are admonished sparingly to indulge themselves in doubtful speculations. As for myself, since I have nothing to assert positively respecting the time, so I think it may be gathered from the narration of Moses, that they did not long retain the dignity they had received; for as soon as he has said they were created, he passes, without the mention of any other thing, to their fall. If Adam had lived but a moderate space of time with his wife, the blessing of God would not have been unfruitful in the production of offspring; but Moses intimates that they were deprived of God's benefits before they had become accustomed to use them. I therefore readily subscribe to the exclamation of Augustine, O wretched freewill, which, while yet entire, had so little stability!' And, to say no more respecting the shortness of the time, the admonition of Bernard is worthy of remembrance: Since we read that a fall so dreadful took place in Paradise, what shall we do on the dunghill?'" Calvin's Commentaries, Baker, Volume 1, 2005, pp. 156-157

[453] "Cur ergo non corerunt nisi cum exitant de Paradiso. Cito responderi potest, quia mox creata muliere priusquam coierunt, facta est illa transgressio, cujus merito in mortem definati, etiam de loco illius foelicitatis exierunt." Augustine, On The Literal Meaning of Genesis, 9.4.3

were created on the sixth day, after the beast of the earth, cattle and creeping things had been created on the same day.[454] So that Adam was not created in the beginning of the sixth day. And those seven particular occurrences ensuing Adam's creation, which were forementioned, might all of them easily be dispatched in a few hours of the same sixth day. Besides, the serpent's temptation and seducing of the woman, the woman's eating of the tree of knowledge, and giving thereof to her husband, their shame upon their fall, and sewing fig-leaves to cover their shame, might all without difficulty be effected on the same day.[455] And after this the very next thing mentioned, is the voice of God (whereby Adam was called to account for his sin) walking in the garden in the cool of the day. Hebrew: *in the wind of the day*. Jerome renders it, *in the wind after midday*. The Greek, *in the evening*. Chrysostom, *afternoon*;[456] Irenaeus, *in the eventide*.[457] Hence, says Calvin, "That opinion has prevailed, that Adam sinned about noon, and was brought into judgment for it about sunset."[458] Now it's very observable that this is the first evening mentioned after Adam's creation, and the covenant made with him. And the phrase of God's voice walking in the garden in the cool of the day, seems so to be brought in, the context being well considered, as if it related to the close of the day of Adam's creation.

{2} When the serpent began to tempt the woman, the words of the serpent and woman to one another are such, and in the future tenses, as they imply that as yet Adam and his wife had not eaten of any tree at all in the garden.[459] And it is very improbable they would have continued a whole day in the garden in the midst of all that delicious fruit and not have eaten some. And if of any, then of that which was most excellent and desirable, the tree of life. But they tasted not of the tree of life, for then they had been confirmed in

---

[454] Genesis 1:24 to the end of the chapter
[455] Genesis 3:1-8
[456] John Chrysostom on Genesis 3, Homily 17, Tom. 2
[457] Irenaeus, Against Heresies, Book 5, chapter 15 ad fin.
[458] John Calvin on Genesis 3:8
[459] Genesis 3:1-2

eternal life; and had not fallen.⁴⁶⁰ Therefore eating none at all, they seem not to have continued one day in their innocent state.

{3} Christ says the devil was a murderer from the beginning, and abode not in the truth: *a liar, and the father of it.*⁴⁶¹ A murderer of whom? Of our first parents and their posterity. From what beginning? Not from the beginning of the world's creation, which at the least was six days before Adam was murdered by him, but from the beginning of man's creation and being, which most properly and precisely implies the sixth day wherein man was made. Then it was that the devil deceived our first parents by lying, and murdered them. Consequently they fell on the first day of their creation.

{4} Christ the second Adam, incarnate in fullness of time, was put to death for man's sin on the sixth day of the week, which was the preparation before the passover or sabbath.⁴⁶² He was crucified about the sixth hour, that is, our twelve o'clock; and he yielded up the ghost about the ninth hour, that is, about our three of the clock afternoon.⁴⁶³ Probably therefore the first Adam (the figure of him that was to come, and that in respect of this point)⁴⁶⁴ fell into his sin on the sixth day in the afternoon. And so God's threatening to Adam *in the day thou eatest thereof thou shalt surely die*, was most notably fulfilled in Adam's surety Christ, then dying corporally, and tasting of the second death remarkably, for sin.

{5} That passage of the Psalmist is observable to this purpose. Namely, Adam being in honor, lodged-not-a-night, but is likened to beasts that are silenced.⁴⁶⁵ That which in our translation is *man* in the Hebrew is *Adam* and Ainsworth says well, this may be minded both for the first man Adam, who continued not in his dignity, and so for all his children.

And the word {בַּל־יָלִין *bal-jalin*} which we render, {*abideth-not*} most properly signifies {*lodgeth-not-a-night*} as in Genesis 28:11, Exodus 23:18,

---

⁴⁶⁰ Genesis 3:22
⁴⁶¹ John 8:44
⁴⁶² John 19;31, 42
⁴⁶³ Compare John 19:14-16 with Matthew 27:46, 50
⁴⁶⁴ Romans 5:14
⁴⁶⁵ Psalm 49:12

34:25, Deuteronomy 16:4, 2 Samuel 17:8, 19:8, Psalm 30:5, Joshua 8:9. And this the learned in the Hebrew tongue acknowledge. Though therefore I will not restrain the sense of this place only to the first Adam, but extend it also to his posterity for denoting the mutability and momentariness of their honor. Yet it seems singularly to point out Adam's sudden fall from the top-excellency of his dignity, not enjoying it one night.

{6} Learned men both ancient and modern have much inclined upon former considerations to this opinion of Adam's fall in the same day he was framed. Augustine thinks Adam stood only six hours, as Calvin and Mercerus vouch him.[466] Jedudus inclines to Adam's fall in the afternoon.[467] And the annotations there upon Irenaeus allege Cyril, Epiphanius, Diodorus Tresensis, and others, who held that Adam was cast out of paradise on the same day in which he was created. Rashi says that Adam and Eve rebelled about the tenth hour, that is, two hours before sunset, as Louis De Dieu has noted.[468]

Later writers also hold it to be accurate that in one and the same day, Adam was formed and deformed. Broughton in his consent of Scripture shows upon several grounds,[469] as also in his general view of Scriptures (for that book published again with enlargements by Tomas Hayne, was at first penned by H. Broughton, as one of his hearers informed me, and as the book itself seems plainly to witness),[470] and as that learned Mr. G. Walker in his *Doctrine of the Sabbath*,[471] insisting in Broughton's steps, more fully declares. Hence then: (i) Adam kept not one sabbath in paradise, nor did he see one sabbath in his innocency. (ii) The happiness of Adam and of all his posterity whilst it was in their own keeping, and bottomed upon mutable nature, though upright, stood upon a very fickle foundation. It's well for Christians that now their happiness is in Christ's keeping, not in their own: grounded not upon mutable nature, but immutable grace. (iii) Man's corruption is almost as ancient as

---

[466] John Calvin in Genesis 3:6 ut supra Mercer in Genesis 6:8
[467] Iedu. Against Heresies, Book 5 chapter 15
[468] Lud. de Dieu Animadvers. in Genesis 3:8
[469] The General View of Scripture, pp.24-26, Edit. 2, London, 1640.
[470] Hugh Broughton Con. of Script. At the beginning
[471] Mr. G. Walker in his *Doctrine of the sabbath*, chapter 1

man's creation. How soon was God dishonored: and how long has God been provoked by mankind! (iv) Adam's sin must needs be the greater, that he so speedily forgot and forfeited all God's greatest favors. (v) Satan is deservedly branded for *a murderer from the beginning*,[472] and styled *that old serpent the devil*:[473] his subtilty deceiving, and his cruelty murdering mankind from the first day of their being.

(4) *How grievous and heinous was Adam's breach of covenant?*

Answer: Adam's sin and breach of covenant with God was heinous beyond our expression or conception. Who can sufficiently enumerate or aggravate the aggravations thereof? Some few exaggerations I shall touch upon, namely: in respect of the [1] person who sinned, [2] condition and state wherein, [3] place where; [4] time when, [5] law against which, [6] objects against whom, and [7] the many and great evils of sin and punishment attending upon Adam's sin.

[1] **The person who sinned was Adam.** Not an ordinary, but an extraordinary person: consequently his, not an ordinary but an extraordinary sin. For,

{1} Adam was an innocent person, without all sin, perfect and upright in the image of God without any defect.[474] Therefore his mind was most clear, bright, and apprehensive, to have detected the darkness and evil both of sin and of the temptation thereunto. His conscience also was pure and active, under God, to warn him against sin, and all occasions thereof. His will free, and able to have withstood all sin, and all seducements thereunto, most easily. Never mere man since Adam, had such perfection of mind, conscience, will, and of the whole man – being habitually prone to no evil, but propense to all good. Now that Adam – every way able not to sin – should have this mind blinded, this conscience corrupted, this free-will enslaved by sin, how grievous

---

[472] John 8:44
[473] Revelation 20:2
[474] Genesis 1:26-27, Ecclesiastes 7:29

was his sinning! He sinned knowingly and he sinned willingly, therefore he sinned more heinously. Sin the more willingly it is admitted, the more wickedly it is committed. No wonder if a carnal man who has nothing but sin in him can act nothing but sin, or if a Christian that has much corruption mingled with his grace mixes also infirmities with best performances – but for Adam to sin, who had no sinful inclination in him, how strange is it and inexcusable!

{2} Adam was a public person, a complexive person; all mankind were in him, and all in covenant with God with him. He standing, all stood; he falling, all fell. Never man by one sin made so many sinners. By one sin, he made himself and all his posterity sinners from the beginning to the end of the world.[475] Hence learned Augustine well observes that though some other sins such as the unpardonable sin against the Holy Ghost may be greater than this sin of Adam *intensively*, yet Adam's sin is the very greatest and most grievous sin in the world, *extensively* considered.[476]

[2] **The condition and state wherein he sinned, was most happy.** For God's image was his beauty, God's Covenant of Works was his charter for eternal life, all God's creatures on earth were his servants and under his dominion, the whole earth his possession, paradise his habitation, all the fruits of paradise except of the tree of knowledge were his food, and familiar communion with God there – the paradise of paradise. In a word, so blissful his condition as the absence of all evil and presence of all good could render it. We may therefore with the Psalmist burst out into admiration: *Lord, what is man, that thou art mindful of him? And the son of man that thou visitest him? For thou hast made him a little lower than the angels; and hast crowned him with glory and honor. Thou madest him to have dominion over the works of thy hands: thou hast put all things under his feet.*[477] Elegantly, Augustine delineates Adam's paradise-felicity: "Man in paradise lived as he lifted, as long

---

[475] Romans 5:12, 19
[476] Andre Rivet in Genesis 3, exercitation 31
[477] Psalm 8:4-6

as he willed what God had commanded: he lived enjoying God, from whom most good he was good. He lived without any penury, having power so to live perpetually. Meat was at hand lest he should hunger, drink lest he should thirst, the tree of life lest age should dissolve him, and no corruption in his body or out of his body, brought any trouble to any of his senses. No disease was within, and no blow was feared from without. In his flesh greatest soundness; in his spirit entire calmness. As in paradise was neither heat nor cold, so in its inhabitant there was no offense to his good will, by desire or fear."[478]

There was nothing at all grievous, nothing vainly joyous: true joy was perpetuated from God, towards whom love did flame out of a pure heart and a good conscience, and faith unfeigned. And a faithful conjugal society from an honest love, an harmonious vigilance of mind and body, and an unlaborious custody of the command, etc.

Thus and thus happy was Adam's state in which he sinned. Therefore he offended against all God's benefits wherewith he had loaded him: against all the bonds of love, wherewith God had obliged him: against all the dignities and privileges wherewith God had crowned him, when he broke God's command in such condition. The greater God's lovingkindness to Adam: the deeper Adam's unkindness to God. Did God's favors to David so aggravate David's sin?[479] And God's mercies to Israel so heighten Israel's offenses?[480] How much more did God's superabounding blessings to Adam, beyond measure exaggerate Adam's disobedience? Hear O heavens, and give ear O earth! God on every side surrounded Adam with happiness – and this Adam rebelled against the Lord.

[3] The place where Adam sinned was paradise: a place most unfit for sinning in. There God familiarly conversed with Adam.[481] To sin there, was to

---

[478] Augustine, City of God, 14.26.5
[479] 2 Samuel 12:7-9
[480] Isaiah 1:2-3
[481] Genesis 2:15-17

sin in the presence of God. There God entered into the Covenant of Works with Adam:[482] to sin there, was to be extremely unmindful of, and unfaithful in God's Covenant. There was the tree of life,[483] to confirm him in obedience, and the tree of knowledge to caution him against disobedience.[484] To sin there, was to sin against God's antidotes and preservatives. There *grew every tree pleasant to the sight, and good for food*,[485] all pointing at their maker, and inciting Adam to admire his wisdom, adore his power, and extol his goodness; to sin there, was to sin against multitudes of mercies. All the trees and fruits of paradise would aggravate that ingratitude. In a word, paradise was a place wherein was no sin, nor sorrow, therefore to sin there was to pollute paradise, and to transform the Eden of pleasure into an anchor of trouble and perplexity.

[4] **The time when Adam sinned was quickly after his creation.** Probably he was corrupted (as I have shown) the self-same day he was created. What? Was Adam created such a complete soldier, and armed so perfectly with God's image, that he had power to conquer all his spiritual enemies, and that continually, and is he utterly foiled at the very first onset? Was he made so skilful a pilot, able to cross all seas of danger in safety, and is he shipwrecked in the very harbor? Was he able to persevere forever in obedience, and is he turned aside the very first day to disobedience? Was he created and corrupted, formed and deformed, alive and dead, blessed and cursed, happy and miserable, God's freeman and Satan's bond-man, the child of God and the child of the devil, etc., all in one day? This renders Adam's sin exceedingly grievous. If this aggravated Israel's sin that after God's Covenant renewed in Mount Sinai, *they turned aside quickly out of the way* which God commanded them;[486] much more must it aggravate Adam's sin that he turned aside more quickly from God's way – they being corrupt, Adam innocent; they being of

---

[482] Genesis 2:16-17
[483] Genesis 2:9 & 3:22
[484] Genesis 2:9, 17
[485] Genesis 2:9
[486] Exodus 32:7-8, Deuteronomy 9:12

themselves unable to persevere, Adam fully able; they turning aside after almost forty days, Adam the very first day.

[5] **The law against which Adam sinned, was such, that it notably greatened Adam's sin.** *And the Lord God commanded the man, saying, of every tree of the garden thou mayest freely eat: but of the tree of the knowledge of good and evil, thou shalt not eat of it: for in the day that thou eatest thereof, thou shalt surely die.*[487] Here consider:

{1} *The greatness of the lawgiver, the Lord God.* He who created Adam, and all the world by his word: whose dominion is absolute. Of whom alone Adam had his being, well-being and whole dependance. Was it a small thing to sin against so great a God?

{2} *The meanness of him on whom the law was imposed.* The man. Our first parent, a finite creature: in his original despicable dust and ashes.[488] *Adam*, red-earth. And shall dust and ashes rebel against the command of the mighty God?

{3} The weight and importance of the command. It was of greatest importance and concernment, both as an original covenant, and as an original law. (i) *As an original covenant.* This, although it had not the *name*, yet had the *nature* of a covenant, as has been shown. It was a Covenant of Works. The first covenant that ever was in the world. Wherein God and all mankind in Adam were parties. To sin against this command then was to break covenant, and to make himself and all mankind as covenant-breakers guilty of death. (ii) *As an original law.* For as Tertullian well observes, "This law being given, all laws were given which were afterwards published by Moses." That is, *Thou shalt love the LORD thy God with all thine heart, and with all thy soul, and thou shalt love thy neighbor as thyself*, etc. For it was an original law which was given to Adam and Eve in paradise, as it were **the womb of all God's precepts.** If they had loved the Lord their God, they would not have done against his precept; if they had loved their neighbor and themselves, they would not have

---
[487] Genesis 2:16-17
[488] Genesis 2:7 & 3:19

believed the serpent's persuasion, nor had committed murder against themselves, by falling from immortality," etc.[489]

Now to transgress a law of such consequence, which was God's federal law with mankind, and so comprehensive a law containing as it were all other laws in its fruitful womb, must needs be the deeper transgression. (iii) *The penalty of the breach of this law was dreadful*, namely, present death; and that both spiritual, corporal, and eternal, as has been explained. Death (said the heathen) is of terribles, the most terrible. Death (says the Scripture) is the *king of terrors*,[490] and therefore (as Augustine well notes)[491] how great an evil was this, to sin against such a terrifying punishment!

{4} The promise implied consequently to the keeping of this law, was most sweet and desirable, namely: perpetual life, and that in paradise or in a paradise-condition, or in heaven which is best of all. Who would not have obeyed to the utmost ability for the eternizing of such a life? Life is most precious; *all that a man hath, will he give for his life*.[492] And eternal life in paradise would have been a double life: the life of life. Oh how deeply did Adam – and we in him – sin against our own life by violating this law of life! And it's most unnatural to sin against a man's own life.

{5} Finally, consider with what great ease and facility Adam – and we in him – might have kept this command. Might not Adam easily have forborn one tree, when all other trees in Eden besides were allowed him? And the more easy it was to keep it, the more heinous it was to break it. Augustine said excellently, "This of not eating one sort of meat when of others there was such plenty, was so light a precept for observance, so short for remembrance (especially where concupiscence did not as yet resist the will, which afterwards ensued as a punishment), that it was with so much greater injustice violated, by how much more easy observance it might have been performed."[493] And yet elsewhere more excellently: "The forsaker of eternal life, if grace had not

---

[489] Tertullian, Against the Jews, Chapter 2
[490] Job 18:14
[491] Augustine, City of God, 14.15.5
[492] Job 2:4
[493] Augustine, City of God 14.12.5

delivered, was damned with eternal death. If any think this judgment to be too much or unjust, surely he knows not how to measure, how great the iniquity was in sinning, where there was so great a facility of not sinning. For as Abraham's obedience was deservedly proclaimed great because the thing commanded was most difficult to kill his son, so in paradise the disobedience was so much greater because that which was commanded was of no difficulty. And as the obedience of the second man was therein the more honorable in that he was obedient even to death, so the disobedience of the first man was therein the more detestable in that he became disobedient even to death."[494]

[6] **The objects against whom Adam sinned, do also render Adam's sin more grievous.** He sinned against God, himself, and all mankind.

{1} Against God, rebelliously breaking his command, perfidiously violating his Covenant, ungratefully rendering evil unto God for all the multitudes of blessings showered upon him, and most abominably believing the lying suggestions of Satan the father of lies,[495] rather than the infallible word of the God of truth,[496] the God that cannot lie,[497] either in his promise or threatening. Now thus to sin against God is to sin against an infinite majesty, against an infinite glory. And what finite creature can sufficiently comprehend how infinitely it aggravates sin to sin against such infiniteness!

{2} Against himself. Adam sinned against himself many ways, namely: against his *soul*, in disrobing it of God's image in which it was created, and defiling it with Satan's image wherewith it was corrupted. Against his *body*, in embasing it in the service of sin and Satan that which should have been only employed in uprightness and purity; in clothing it with confusion and shame,[498] that which before was adorned with nothing but beauty and honor; and in exposing it to sorrows, wearisomeness, toilsomeness, and thousands of

---

[494] Augustine, City of God 14.5.15
[495] John 8:44
[496] Deuteronomy 32:4
[497] Titus 1:2
[498] Genesis 3:7 with 2:25

infirmities and miseries,[499] which before was utterly unacquainted with all misery and sorrow. Against his *person*, in involving himself in mortality and death, in depriving himself of all his paradise felicities of his primitive integrity, of his dominion over the creatures, and of his communion with the blessed God transcending all. Against his *name*, filling it with ignominy and reproach, that was crowned with glory and honor:[500] for *sin is a reproach to any people*,[501] most of all to him that was totally free from sin, and fully able so to keep himself free. Finally, against his outward estate, in forfeiting both paradise and all the possessions, comforts and privileges which he had on earth,[502] and bringing a curse[503] and a bondage of corruption[504] upon the whole creature, under which it even groans and travails in pain together until now. Thus Adam sinned against himself in respect of soul, body, person, name, and state. How unnatural, horrid, and cruel was it for Adam so to sin against himself!

{3} Against all mankind, even his whole ordinary posterity from the beginning to the end of the world, who all were stained in him, in respect of soul, body, person, name and state, as Adam was.[505] At once, all mankind was polluted and defiled by sin; spoiled and robbed of all their happiness; plunged and drowned in all sorts of misery; murdered and swallowed up by death. Extensively considered, there was never such a sin, such a contagion, such a spoil, such a murder since the world stood; nor can be until the world's end.

[7] **The manifold and great evils both of sin and punishment attending upon Adam's eating of the tree of knowledge, extremely aggravate his sin, and manifest it to be out of measure sinful.**

---

[499] Genesis 3:17-19
[500] Psalm 8:5
[501] Proverbs 14:34
[502] Genesis 3:23-24
[503] Genesis 3:17-18
[504] Romans 8:20-22
[505] Romans 5:12 to the end

{1} **Evil of sin** attending upon Adam's eating of this forbidden tree, is manifold. It is especially antecedent, concomitant, or consequent thereunto.

(i) *Antecedent evils of sin* – repugnant, partly to the moral law, written in Adam's heart; partly to the positive law, given for his trial: gradually foregoing his and Eve's eating of the forbidden fruit – were several, namely,

(a) *Idleness*. In that the woman seems not to be so diligently employed about the dressing and keeping of the garden, in assistance of her husband as she ought, according to God's appointment: when Satan came to tempt.[506] Idleness is a temptation to Satan to tempt us; whereas it is the devil's work to tempt others, it's the idle-man's business to tempt the devil. (b) *Presumptuous curiosity*, or *curious presumption*. In that the woman, being the weaker vessel,[507] dared to entertain so dangerous a conflict with the serpent in her husband's absence. For it's most likely that at the beginning of the serpent's onset, Adam was at some distance from Eve: and the subtle serpent took that advantage. (c) *Inconsiderateness*, and heedless forgetfulness of God's most strict command, which appears in her mis-recital of it two ways. Partly, in adding to it, *neither shall ye touch it*:[508] whereas the command only forbade the eating, not at all the touching of the tree of knowledge. Partly by detracting from it. For God said, *in the day thou eatest thereof, dying thou shalt die*,[509] i.e., Thou shalt surely die, and that presently *ipso facto*. But she omits both the peremptoriness of the threatening, and says, *lest ye die*;[510] or, *lest perhaps ye die*, as the Hebrew word intimates. What God threatened peremptorily, she recites with a perhaps or a peradventure: and she also omits the present suddenness of death threatened in the day of sinning, *for in the day that thou eatest thereof*, etc.[511] And by this forgetful mis-recital of God's command, she gives Satan advantage against herself both to persuade her they should not die,

---

[506] Genesis 2:15
[507] 1 Peter 3:7
[508] Genesis 3:3
[509] Genesis 2:17
[510] Genesis 3:3 פֶּן ne forte Pagnin
[511] Genesis 2:17 with 3:3

and to accuse God of a kind of envy at their happiness.[512] (d) *Unbelief towards God.* In that she did not so fully as she ought to credit God's peremptory threatening of death expressed in case of disobedience, nor his contrary promise of life implied in case of obedience. (e) *Rash and headlong credulity of the serpent, and of Satan in him*; though he both contradicted God's command, and accused God of envy at their happy state, and falsely suggested that by eating they should become as gods, knowing good and evil.[513] How abominable and idolatrous to believe Satan the father of lies:[514] before the God of truth, who cannot lie![515] (f) *Discontenting dislike* with their present condition wherein God had so happily set them. (g) *Ambitious, proud, aspiring above their pitch* to be as gods, knowing good and evil.[516] (h) *Inordinate affection and evil concupiscence.* In desiring an object unlawful, the fruit prohibited.[517] (i) *Irregularity of will.* In choosing rather to harken to the serpent's suggestion, then to God's command. (j) *Lust of the eyes.* In that she fixed a longing look upon the forbidden fruit; and by looking on it, liked it, and designed to eat it.[518] (k) *Incontinence of hands.* In that she refrains not from taking the forbidden fruit.[519] (l) *Intemperance of taste and palate*: in that she eats the fruit, taken; and so her son was completed and finished.[520]

(ii) **Concomitant evils of sin**, accompanying the eating of the forbidden fruit, are also several. Namely, (a) Eve's tempting her husband, both by word and action,[521] to eat of the tree of knowledge: thereby, with herself undoing her husband, to whom she was given for a meet help.[522] (b) Adam's inconsiderate harkening to the voice of his wife who was made for him, rather than to the voice of God for whom he himself was made. (c) Deep ingratitude

---

[512] Genesis 3:4-5
[513] Genesis 3:4-5
[514] John 8:44
[515] Deuteronomy 32:4, Titus 1:2
[516] Genesis 3:5-6
[517] Genesis 3:6
[518] Genesis 3:6
[519] Genesis 3:6
[520] Genesis 3
[521] Genesis 3:17, 3:6
[522] Genesis 2:20

against God, who had crowned Adam with so many and excellent privileges in paradise. *Ingratum dixeris, omnia dixeris*. What worse than to be challenged for ingratitude? How was God displeased with Hezekiah, Judah, and Jerusalem, for not rendering again according to the benefits done unto him?[523] But Adam had benefits done to him, incomparably transcending those of Hezekiah, yet he was so far from rendering according to the benefit done to him, that he rendered evil for good, which is the worst point of ingratitude. To render good for good is man-like, to render good for evil, is God-like, but to render evil for good is devil-like.[524] (d) Direct disobedience to God's express command.[525] And it's no small crime to be disobedient, as we may see in the aggravations of King Saul's disobedience.[526] Disobedience is a rejecting of the word of the Lord – yea it is stubborness, which is as iniquity and idolatry; yea it is rebellion, which is as the sin of witchcraft. (e) Covenant-breaking with God most perfidiously, being able to keep it. (f) Woeful apostasy from a sinless and happy state to a sinful and miserable condition: from God blessed forever and his *blissful service* to the devil damned forever and his *cursed slavery*. None of the sons of men ever apostatized from such eminency, to such extremity.

(iii) **Consequent evils of sin**, ensuing upon the eating of the forbidden fruit; were finally various and grievous. As, (a) An evil conscience filled with guilt, and filling them with shame and terror in respect of God.[527] (b) Flight from God and his presence, which before were so sweet and comfortable.[528] (c) Hypocrisy in hiding their nakedness with figleaves, and in extenuating their sin by translating it from themselves, the man to the woman, and the woman to the serpent.[529] (d) Most cruel murder both of themselves, and of all mankind at once, both in body and soul from the beginning to the end of the

---

[523] 2 Chronicles 32:24-25
[524] Reddere bonum pro bono, humanum; reddere bonum pro malo, Divinum: sed reddere malum pro bono, Diabolicum.
[525] Romans 5:19, Genesis 2:17
[526] 1 Samuel 15:19, 22-23
[527] Genesis 3:7, 10
[528] Genesis 3:8-10
[529] Genesis 3:7, 12-13

world; and of the son of God, Jesus Christ, in some respect also.[530] Themselves they murdered actually, in themselves all mankind virtually and interpretatively, and Jesus Christ himself the Lord of glory occasionally: the first Adam's sin occasioning the second Adam's death.[531] There was never such a heinous horrid cruel murder as this committed in the world by any of the sons of men. (e) The universal corruption of the whole nature of mankind,[532] whereby every person descending from Adam by ordinary propagation, is in soul and body utterly unable[533], indisposed, yea opposite to all spiritual good;[534] and totally evil, and only inclined to evil, and that continually.[535] Which corruption of nature is commonly called {*original sin*}, as being the original spawn and springhead of all actual sins: and it is propagated by natural generation from our first parents to all their ordinary posterity.[536] (f) All the actual sins that have been, are, or shall be in this world from the first Adam's fall, until the second Adam's coming to judgment; together with all the kinds, degrees, sinful circumstances and horrid aggravations thereof, which are utterly beyond man's numbering, measuring or comprehending: all these have taken their rise from Adam's disobedience in eating the forbidden fruit. For all actual sins flow immediately from original, and original sin from Adam's sin.[537] Hence is that scholastic distinction of original sin, into original sin *originated*, and original sin *originating*. That is the corruption of nature, the immediate original of all actuals; this is Adam's sin, the immediate original of the corruption of nature.

Never sin in this world had such a black train of innumerable and intolerable sins following it at the heels, as this sin of Adam had. They seem to parallel the stars of heaven, the sands of the seashore, the dust of the earth, the grass piles upon the ground, and the motes in the sun for multitude. Oh how

---

[530] Genesis 2:16-17, Romans 5:12 to the end, Ephesians 2:1, etc.
[531] Romans 5:19
[532] Romans 3:9, 10-20, Ephesians 2:1-3
[533] Romans 5:6, 8:8, 2 Corinthians 3:5, Philippians 2:13
[534] Romans 8:7, Galatians 5:17
[535] Genesis 6:5, Romans 7:18
[536] John 3:6, Psalm 51:5, Job 14:4, 15:14
[537] James 1:14-15, Romans 7:17, Matthew 15:19

grievous was Adam's sin that was attended with such antecedent, concomitant, and consequent evils of sin! A horrid hydra of many monstrous heads. A complexive, complicated sin indeed. At this, heaven and earth might stand astonished. O ye holy angels, how were ye offended, to see Adam and all the elect in him (of whom ye had such special charge: Psalm 91:11-12, Hebrews 1:14) so quickly transformed into such transgressors! O ye celestial lights, sun, moon and stars, did not ye blush, and veil your brightest faces with sables, beholding Adam such a sinner? O ye fowls of the air, and ye beasts of the field, were not ye filled with horror, when man, your earthly Lord, disrobed himself of his honor by disobedience, and became like the beasts that perish (Psalm 49:12). O ye streams of paradise, were not ye congealed within your banks, when such a deluge of sin overflowed mankind? O ye trees of Eden, did not ye sweat out your moisture? And ye pleasant fruits of the garden, did not ye all presently fade and fall to the earth, when Adam the dresser of the garden, by disobedient tasting of the tree of knowledge, fell so foully from uprightness to unrighteousness (Ecclesiastes 7:29) from God to the devil, from heaven to hell? Surely the whole creation groans and travails in pain together until now under the tedious bondage of this corruption, most earnestly longing for complete deliverance (Romans 8:19, 23).

{2} **Evil of punishment** ensuing upon Adam's disobedience was also various and grievous. And this both in respect of himself, of his wife, and of all their common posterity. As,

(i) *The obliteration and defacing of God's image.*[538] God made man upright; but they have sought out many inventions. No sooner did Adam sin, but he blotted out of his soul thereby the beauteous image of God, and thereon Satan stamped his own odious image instead thereof: so that naturally all are the children of the devil.

(ii) *Shame.* Before they sinned, Adam and his wife (though naked) were not ashamed.[539] But as soon as they had defiled themselves with sin, they were

---

[538] Ecclesiastes 7:29 compared with Colossians 3:9-10 and Ephesians 4:22-24
[539] Genesis 2:25

covered with shame: and *they sewed fig leaves together, and made themselves aprons*, to hide their shame.[540] Shame attends upon sin, as inseparably as the shadow upon the body.[541]

(iii) *Horror of a guilty self-accusing and self-condemning conscience.* Therefore after their fall, they presently were afraid at the presence of God; and hid themselves, because they were naked.[542] And being examined of God, they confess not, but excuse their sin, as Augustine notes: "Did Adam say I have sinned? No; his pride had the deformity of confusion, not the humility of confession."[543]

(iv) *Inability to stand in judgment, when God arraigned them at his bar.* And therefore both of them labor to excuse and translate their fault: Adam to his wife, and she to the serpent.[544] It is the misery of unrighteous persons, that they are snot able to stand, but fall in judgment.[545]

(v) *The peculiar punishments of the female sex.* The Hebrews observe, as Mercerus notes,[546] five degrees of Eve's sin, and answerably, five degrees of her and women's punishment. She sinned, (a) by entertaining the serpent's temptation, believing him rather than God, contrary to God, (b) by being lifted up with ambitious desire to be as God, (c) by beholding the tree of knowledge with a longing look, (d) by taking and eating of it, and (e) by giving also to her husband, so that he did eat.

So she, and women in her, were punished five ways: namely: (a) by their many sorrows in general, (b) by their sorrows in conception, (c) by their sorrows and pains in bringing forth children, (d) by their ardent desires after their husbands notwithstanding, and (e) by their subjection to their husbands.

But the text seems to refer the punishments of the female sex to two heads,[547] namely: (a) multiplied sorrows, and (b) aggravated subjection. (a)

---

[540] Genesis 3:6-7
[541] Romans 6:21
[542] Genesis 3:8-10
[543] Augustine, On the Literal Meaning of Genesis, 11.35.3
[544] Genesis 3:11-13
[545] Psalm 1:5
[546] Joan Mercer in Praelection in Genesis 3:16
[547] Genesis 3:16 vid. John Calvin, commentary

Multiplied sorrows: Partly, in the woman's conceiving with child. Wherein understand all her sorrows, during the time she is with child, till she be delivered: namely, her weakness and nauseousness of stomach, rejection of food, distempered appetite after unwholesome and unfit nourishment, weakness, dullness, wearisomeness, frowardness, longings, faintings, swoonings, and much sickliness, with manifold fears. Partly, in the woman's bringing forth of children, which usually is with such exquisite pains and sharp tortures, as that Scripture is wont thereby to represent the church's extreme afflictions;[548] the pangs of death;[549] the terrors of the day of judgment; and the very torments of hell;[550] the same word for substance being used to signify all these. And sometimes these pains of childbearing prove mortal. Now under bringing forth, we may understand also the bringing up of children, as the phrase is elsewhere used.[551] And in both, what multitudes of cares, fears, griefs, watchings, toilsome troubles, torments, vexations, etc., flow in upon them! (b) An aggravated subjection to their husbands: *their desire must be subject to their husbands, and they must rule over them*.[552] By the law of nature and creation, the woman being made after and for the man, was to be subject unto man, though they had never sinned. But that subjection would have been sweet, pleasant and delightful, and the husband's rule loving, as over a second-self; whereas now since the fall, the husband's rule over his wife seems to be somewhat augmented, and her subjection is become painful, tedious, irksome, and grievous to her. These the punishments peculiar to womankind.

(vi) *God's curse upon the earth*.[553] By {*earth*} seems to be implied the whole visible world,[554] made for man's use and comfort: in the curse whereof, man (whose subsistence was to be on and from the earth) is cursed and punished. By God's curse, the earth, and visible world proportionally, are smitten with

---

[548] Isaiah 26:17:18, Jeremiah 4:31
[549] Psalm 116:3, Acts 2:29
[550] Luke 16:23-25
[551] Genesis 50:23
[552] Genesis 3:16
[553] Genesis 3:17-19
[554] Psalm 115:16, 2 Peter 3:7

barrenness, *toilsomeness*, and *vanity*. (a) *With barrenness*; partly in not yielding their strength of influence and fruitfulness, as before the fall they did abundantly and freely.[555] Partly in bringing forth weeds, thorns and thistles, instead of good fruits; which before the fall it did not bring forth.[556] (b) *With toilsomeness*.[557] The curse and barrenness of the earth being in toilsomeness and laborious wearisome travel with the earth, to improve it unto fruitfulness. *All things are full of labor, man cannot utter it.*[558] (c) *With vanity. Vanity of vanities, saith the preacher, vanity of vanities, all is vanity.*[559] All sublunaries are vanity; partly in respect of their emptiness. There's no satisfaction in any sublunary enjoyment. *The eye is not satisfied with seeing: nor the ear filled with hearing.*[560] *He that loves silver shall not be satisfied with silver; nor he that loves abundance, with increase; this is also vanity.*[561] Partly in respect of their perishableness. *Of old hath God laid the foundation of the earth: and the heavens are the works of thy hands. They shall perish, but thou shalt endure; yea all of them shall wax old like a garment: as a vesture shalt thou change them, and they shall be changed.*[562] Hence Paul says that the creation is made subject to vanity, and is under the bondage of corruption, as it were waiting for a state of glorious liberty. Therefore *the whole creation groaneth, and travels in pain together until now.*[563] And Peter tells us expressly, that *in the day of the Lord, the heavens shall pass away with a great noise, and the elements shall melt with fervent heat, the earth also and the works that are therein shall be burnt up. Nevertheless we look for new heavens and new earth.*[564] Oh, man's sin has in a sort so deeply stained the beauty and glory of this visible world, that the old universal deluge of waters could not wash it, but the fire of the last day must

---

[555] Genesis 3:17 & 4:12
[556] Genesis 3:17-18
[557] Genesis 3:17-19
[558] Ecclesiastes 1:8
[559] Ecclesiastes 1:2
[560] Ecclesiastes 1:8
[561] Ecclesiastes 5:10
[562] Psalm 102:25-26
[563] Romans 8:21-22
[564] 2 Peter 3:10, 13

purify it. Heaven and earth groan and travail in pangs under the curse of man's sin: and shall not man much more groan and be in pain for his own sin? This is the curse upon the creature.

(vii) *God's actual dooming of Adam, and of mankind in him, to an ignominious provision, miserable life, and certain death after all.* (a) His ignominious provision of sustenance in that he must eat the herb of the field.[565] Before the fall he had for food the liberal and delicate fruits of Eden, but since then, his allowance has been both shorter and coarser. As he made himself like the beasts that perish, so he must as well as the beasts eat the herb of the field, a more ignoble nourishment.[566] (b) His miserable life: in regard to the continual sorrows, and laborious painful wearisome toil in providing food and other necessaries all the days of his life. *In sorrow shalt thou eat all the days of thy life. In the sweat of thy face shalt thou eat bread, till thou return unto the ground.*[567] Hence man is necessitated *to rise up early, to set up late, to eat the bread of sorrows.*[568] This *sweat*, the Hebrews refer to the many laborious works and ways of preparing bread; as manuring the ground, plowing it, sowing it, harrowing it, breaking the clods, weeding the corn, reaping it, in-gathering it, thrashing it, winnowing it, grinding it, dressing it, kneading it, baking it in the oven.[569] O how many toilsome tiring imployments is man obnoxious to in providing food and raiment for himself and family! (c) His certain death as the period of all. *Till thou return unto the ground: for out of it wast thou taken: for dust thou art, and unto dust thou shalt return.*[570] Here man is not only sentenced to death, but also to the grave. Under which, understand all sicknesses, diseases, causes, occasions, harbingers or inlets to death, as harmful influence of the heavens, infectiousness of the air, unwholesomeness of the earth, etc.

---

[565] Genesis 3:18
[566] Psalm 49:12
[567] Genesis 3:17, 19
[568] Psalm 127:2
[569] Vid. Joaan. Mercer Praelect. in Genesis 3:19
[570] Genesis 3:19

(viii) *Expulsion of man out of paradise*, and guarding it and the tree of life, with cherubims and a flaming sword turning every way to keep the way of the tree of life,[571] so that Adam might not fondly delude himself with vain hopes of life by the sacrament of the Covenant of Works when he had broken the covenant itself. These, these were the woeful evils of punishment, that like a torrent burst in upon our first parents presently upon their fall, and in them upon all mankind. To speak nothing of the miseries of man in this world in respect of his goods, relations, name, body, and soul, which are innumerable; nor of his endless calamities in the world to come, which (without Christ) are inevitable and intolerable.

Hitherto has been evidenced at large, 1. That Adam broke the Covenant of Works. 2. How Adam broke this covenant by disobedience. 3. When and how soon he broke it. 4. How grievous and heinous this his breach of covenant was. Now in the last place, 5. Certain corollaries, flowing from all are to be considered.

(5) **Corollaries resulting from this aphorism and the explanation of it are several.** As:

[1] **Hence not only Adam, but all mankind in Adam were covenant-breakers with God.** It has formerly been cleared that not only Adam but all his posterity were parties to this covenant with God.[572] Consequently, in Adam's covenant-breaking, they all became covenant-breakers with God. It's dangerous to be covenant-breakers with man; dreadful to be covenant-breakers with God. Here seriously consider:

{1} *That covenant-keeping is most acceptable to God.* For, (i) God commands us to keep covenant with himself.[573] (ii) God's promises are to them that keep covenant with him. To David, that *if his children would keep his covenant, they should sit upon his throne forevermore.*[574] To all the godly, *that*

---

[571] Genesis 3:22-24
[572] See Aphorism 3 of this chapter
[573] Genesis 17:9-10, Deuteronomy 29:9
[574] Psalm 132:12

the mercy of the LORD is from everlasting to everlasting upon them that fear him; and his righteousness unto children's children: to such as keep his covenant, and to those that remember his commandments to do them.[575] (iii) Covenant-keeping makes us like God, and notably resemble him, who is the faithful God, *which keeps covenant and mercy with those that love him, and keep his commandments to a thousand generations.*[576] And the more we resemble God, the more acceptable we are unto God. (iv) Covenant-keeping with God, obtains rich recompense from God. Levi, for observing God's word and keeping his covenant, is established and accepted in his office and divinely blessed.[577] Yea *all the paths of the LORD are mercy and truth unto such as keep his covenant and his testimonies.*[578]

{2} *That contrariwise, covenant-breaking is most abominable to God.* For: (i) Covenant-breaking is ranked by the Holy Ghost amongst the worst of sins, and covenant-breakers among the vilest of sinners.[579] And God cannot abide that such should any way so much as profess, name, or meddle with his covenant.[580] (ii) Covenant-breaking is exposed to many threatenings.[581] (iii) Covenant-breaking pulls down upon men's heads many severe and heavy judgments. How was Israel plagued for dealing falsely in God's Covenant again and again?[582] Yea how has God taken vengeance even upon them that have broken their covenants with men! Joshua and Israel made a covenant with the Gibeonites, that they should live peaceably with them:[583] King Saul contrary thereunto slew some of them, whereupon the Philistines slew him and his sons and many of the Israelites, and the whole land was plagued with a three years famine, till seven of Saul's sons were hanged at the request of the Gibeonites. Zedekiah broke covenant with Nebuchadnezzar, and God delivered him into

---

[575] Psalm 103:17-18
[576] Deuteronomy 7:9, 1 Kings 8:23, Nehemiah 1:5, 9:32
[577] Deuteronomy 33:9-11
[578] Psalm 25:10
[579] Compare Romans 1:31 with 2 Timothy 3:3
[580] Psalm 50:16-17, etc
[581] Genesis 17:14, Jeremiah 22:7-9, Hosea 8:1
[582] Hosea 10:4, etc., Jeremiah 34:18, etc.
[583] Compare Joshua 9:3 with 1 Samuel 13; 2 Samuel 21:1-10

the hands of his enemies, who slew his sons before his eyes, and then put out his eyes.[584] Now if those who broke covenant with man are thus plagued, where shall they appear that have broken covenant with the living God – and that in paradise?

[2] Hence, *Adam's first sin, his covenant-breaking sin, and ours in him, was not small, but extremely sinful.* The act of eating of the fruit of the tree of knowledge, seems to be a small matter: whereupon some have seemed to excuse and extenuate his sin. But how ignorantly, how inconsiderately! Can that sin be small that's clothed with such and so many unparalleled aggravations, as have been already unfolded?

[3] *Hence the Covenant of Works being broken by the first Adam, and by all mankind in him: he and all his posterity lie woefully involved under the curse and penalty of it, even death itself.* This corollary is of great importance, and most seriously to be considered. For the opening of it, note: {1} why Adam and all his posterity, upon breach of the Covenant of Works lie involved under the curse and penalty of it, death, {2} what death it is under which they lie involved, and how they are so involved, and {3} what are the aggravations of this their sad condition under death for sin.

{1} *Adam and all his posterity upon breach of the Covenant of Works lie involved under the curse and penalty of it, death itself.*

(i) Because God in making covenant with Adam and his posterity threatened present and certain death, in case of breach thereof by disobedience in eating the forbidden fruit.[585] The covenant therefore being broken, it concerned God in point both of justice and truth, wherein he is incomparable, to inflict upon them the punishment threatened. Otherwise God would not have been true and just in his words and ways.

---

[584] 2 Chronicles 36:13, etc., 2 Kings 25:4-7, Ezekiel 17:12-22
[585] Genesis 2:16-17

(ii) Because death is the proper wages of sin,[586] and eternal death the most adequate and proportional recompense thereof. Hence the apostle says *by one man sin entered into the world, and death by sin: and so death passed upon all men by that one man, in whom all have sinned.*[587] And again, *by the offense of one, judgment came upon all men to condemnation.*[588]

(iii) Because God made his Covenant not only with Adam, but with all his posterity in him, as has been already shown,[589] and therefore when Adam fell from his integrity, he fell not alone, nor brought the curse and penalty of the Covenant upon himself alone, but all his ordinary posterity fell in him, were involved under the penalty of death with him.

(iv) Because the Covenant of Works in the nature of it, under pain of the curse and death, requires perfect and perpetual personal obedience: according to that of the apostle, *As many as are of the works of the law, are under the curse* (presupposing man's fall, and consequently his inability to keep it), *for it is written, cursed is every one that that continues not in all things which are written in the book of the law to do them.*[590] The Covenant of Works therefore affords no mercy to the transgressors thereof, but inflicts death and the curse for the least delinquency. *For whosoever shall keep the whole law, and yet offend in one point, he is guilty of all.*[591]

{2} **What death it is under which Adam and all his posterity lie involved** – and how they are so involved under death, though Adam did not presently die – has before been declared.[592] Only here I add, touching corporal death, that we may consider three things, namely, the commination, sentence, and execution of it.

---

[586] Romans 6:23
[587] Romans 5:12
[588] Romans 5:18
[589] See before in this first chapter, Aphorism 3
[590] Galatians 3:10, Deuteronomy 27:26
[591] James 2:10
[592] In Book 2, Chapter 1, Aphorism 4, Questions 3 & 4

(i) The commination or threatening of death corporal, as well as spiritual or eternal, in case of disobedience, was propounded to Adam in innocency, to keep him in due obedience.[593]

(ii) The sentence of corporal death was pronounced upon Adam presently upon his disobedience in the same day that he did eat of the forbidden fruit, in these words: *Dust thou art, and unto dust shalt thou return.*[594] So that Adam was now as a condemned malefactor: dead in law, civilly dead, to be executed at the judge's pleasure.

(iii) The execution of corporal death upon Adam and his posterity was respited a while. The death of Adam, and so of the fathers before the flood was respited for about 900 years: so long God reprieved them in the first world, from Adam until Noah.[595] In the second world from Noah until Abraham, man's life, or man's reprieve from death, is shortened in half and brought to about 450 years. In the third world from Abraham until Moses, man's life was contracted to 100 and some odd years. Yea Moses himself says, *The days of our years are threescore years and ten, and if by reason of strength they be fourscore years, yet is their strength labor and sorrow: for it is soon cut off and we fly away.*[596] To this short scantling of 70 or 80 years, are our lives reduced, few reach to 100. Thus the sentence of death corporal is executed upon all mankind, by degrees, until this day, and so will be until the end of the world.

{3} **The aggravations of this sad condition of Adam and his posterity under the penalty of the Covenant of Works broken, are dreadful.** For clearing hereof we are to consider Adam and his posterity after breach of the Covenant of Works, as in a fourfold estate, namely: (i) as covenant-less, (ii) as carnal, (iii) as gracious, and (iv) as glorious.

(i) In a *covenant-less estate*, were Adam and all his posterity in the interval of space between the breach of the Covenant of Works and the making known the Covenant of Faith in Christ. From the fall until the promise of the seed of

---

[593] Genesis 2:17
[594] Genesis 3:6-8, 19
[595] See the history of Genesis throughout
[596] Psalm 90:1, 10

the woman, Adam and all his posterity were covenant-less, without all covenant with God.[597] They had not the Covenant of Works for that was broken, nor the Covenant of Faith in Christ for that was not yet revealed. Hence, in this covenant-less condition, Adam and all his posterity were involved under the penalty of death, (a) *Without all remedy*. For Christ, the only remedy against sin and death, was not as yet promised or revealed at all.[598] (b) *Without all hope*. For whence could Adam have any hope of life? Not from his own fulfilling of the Covenant of Works, for that he had utterly broken; not from faith in Christ fulfilling it for him and satisfying for his breach thereof, for the mystery of Christ and of the Covenant of Faith in him was not as yet made known to Adam, nor could such a remedy ever have come into Adam's thoughts. Therefore in this interval of time between the fall, and the promise of Christ, Adam and all mankind in him were in the most remediless, hopeless, darksome valley of the shadow of death that ever was or shall be on earth from the creation until the judgment day.

(ii) In a *carnal fleshly sinful state*, are all Adam's posterity by nature since the fall and promise of Christ, from their conception until their actual receiving of Christ by faith for life.[599] During this carnal condition, mankind are not so remedilessly and hopelessly miserable as in the former covenantless state, because Jesus Christ the remedy against sin and death and the fundamental hope of life is already revealed to the world, which was not then, yet notwithstanding herein all mankind are woefully miserable in several regards. (a) *In that during this carnal state they are wholly under the curse and penalty of the Covenant of Works, namely, death*. Every carnal man is spiritually dead in sin,[600] yea death itself:[601] corporally dying every day by gradual decays of life, and by afflictions which are petty deaths, and as children of wrath every moment liable to eternal death,[602] being condemned already,

---

[597] Genesis 3:6-7, 15
[598] Acts 4:12, Romans 8:2-3, 1 Corinthians 15:55-57
[599] John 3:5-6, Romans 8:7-8, Psalm 51:4
[600] Ephesians 2:1, 5
[601] Romans 8:6
[602] Ephesians 2:3, Romans 9:22

and having the wrath of God abiding on them.[603] (b) *In that, during their carnal state, they are extreamly insensible of this their dead and cursed condition: and vainly flatter themselves therein with imaginations and dreams that they are alive and in a good spiritual condition towards God.* As the Pharisee, that went into the temple to pray:[604] Paul before conviction and conversion,[605] and the Laodicean angel.[606] Now physicians say that "they are more dangerously sick, that being diseased are insensible of their disease." They are doubly miserable, that being in their carnal condition are not sensible of their misery, but rather count their misery happiness. (c) *In that, during their carnal state, they are utterly unable to help themselves in any degree out of their miserable thraldom of sin and death, without God's supernatural grace.*[607] So that in the first part of conversion, namely, the infusing of principles and habits of grace into the heart, they are merely passive. (d) Finally in that during their carnal condition, they are not only extremely miserable, senseless of their misery, and in respect of themselves utterly helpless under their misery, but also they are most prone to neglect,[608] despise and hate Jesus Christ the only remedy.[609] These are the aggravations of a carnal man's misery.

(iii) In a gracious state are all they that are by effectual calling transplanted out of the first Adam into Jesus Christ the second Adam. During this their gracious state, though they are not totally freed from death, yet they are wholly delivered from the curse of it, through Christ.[610] From death eternal they are fully delivered that, although they deserve it, yet it shall never befall them.[611] From death spiritual they are inchoatively and gradually delivered by the power of the Spirit of life in Christ, and shall be so completely when neither spot nor wrinkle, nor any such thing shall remain upon them. From

---

[603] John 3:18, 36
[604] Luke 18:9-11
[605] Romans 7:9-10
[606] Revelation 3:17
[607] Romans 5:6, 8:8, John 1:12-13, 3:3, 5-6, 8 & 6:44 & 15:5
[608] John 1:11, Hebrews 2:2-3
[609] Luke 19:14, John 15:18, 24-25 & 7:7
[610] Galatians 3:13
[611] John 11:26 & 6:50-51, Romans 8:1

death corporal, together with all the inlets and harbingers thereof, they are delivered in respect of the sting, terror, and curse thereof,[612] though not in respect of the state thereof.[613]

The saints are afflicted and die as well as carnal men – but to the saints, afflictions and death are not enemies but friends,[614] not losses but gains,[615] not miseries but mercies,[616] not punishments but fatherly chastisements,[617] not curses, but blessings,[618] whilst unto carnal men they are altogether contrary.

(iv) In a glorious state, are the spirits of just men made perfect,[619] and shall be both spirits and bodies of all the elect after the Judgment Day.[620] And then no sin, death, curse, affliction, sorrow, or any shadow thereof shall ever trouble them or come near them any more to all eternity: but *all shall be swallowed up in victory*.[621] And thus we are to conceive of the penalty of the Covenant of Works, death: and how Adam and all his posterity are, by their first sin, therein involved.

[4] *Hence, all Adam's posterity from the beginning to the end of the world, have great cause deeply to lament and be humbled for Adam's first sin.* For, not only Adam, but all his posterity sinned in Adam's first sin.[622] That first sin was extremely sinful. That first sin involved not only Adam but all his posterity also under the curse and penalty of death. Was ever sin, all things considered, parallel to this sin? Was ever sin such matter of lamentation and humiliation? If Adam's posterity had no other sin, original or actual, to mourn for, but this one sin alone, they had cause enough to lament it while this world continues, if it were possible, with rivers of tears, and those tears of

---

[612] 1 Corinthians 15:55-57, Hebrews 2:14-15, Galatians 3:13
[613] 1 Thessalonians 4:14
[614] 1 Corinthians 3:22
[615] Philippians 1:21, 23
[616] Psalm 119:75, Hebrews 12:6
[617] Hebrews 12:5-12
[618] Luke 6:22-23, James 1:2
[619] Hebrews 12:23
[620] 1 Thessalonians 4:16-17
[621] 1 Corinthians 15:25-26, 54, etc.
[622] Romans 5:12

blood. How comes it to pass then that we can mourn for actuals, and originals; but mourn least of all, for Adam's and our first sin to be bewailed most of all! When we mourn for actuals, let's, with David, also mourn for original sin, the nursery of actuals:[623] and when we mourn for them, let's mourn likewise for Adam's first sin, the mother of them all.

[5] *Hence, we may see how unsafe it is for mutable man to have his life and happiness in his own keeping.* Adam was made upright, and that in the image of God, but mutable.[624] His life and happiness was put into his own keeping, and depended upon his own personal performance of the Covenant of Works, which he had full power to keep; but being left to the liberty of his own will, temptation alluring, how quickly did he and we in him lose all! How much better has the Lord provided for his elect in Christ the second Adam! Not they, but Christ is entrusted with their life and happiness. *My sheep hear my voice* (says Christ) *and I know them, and they follow me. And I give unto them eternal life, and they shall never perish, neither shall any man pluck them out of my hand.*[625] They are kept as in garrison by the power of God through faith unto salvation.[626] {1} The love of God in Jesus Christ clasps and embraces them inseparably;[627] {2} the faithful constancy of Christ retains them immovably;[628] {3} the incorruptible seed of Christ's word and grace abides in them, and makes them abide in Christ perpetually;[629] and {4} the omnipotent hand of God and Christ, who are stronger than all, protect, preserve and hold them inviolably.[630] Therefore they can never totally nor finally fall.

[6] *Hence seeing as Adam utterly broke the Covenant of Works by disobedience, this covenant-breach is absolutely irreparable by the first*

---

[623] Psalm 51
[624] Ecclesiastes 7:29, Genesis 1:27
[625] John 10:28-29
[626] 1 Peter 1:5
[627] Romans 8:35 to the end
[628] John 6:37
[629] 1 Peter 1:23, 1 John 3:9
[630] John 10:28-29

Adam, and by all his ordinary posterity. It is so wide and desperate a breach, that it's absolutely past all the power and skill of mere mankind, or creature, to close up and repair the same. This is evident,

{1} *From the nature and tenor of the Covenant of Works.* It gives life upon no other terms than upon perfect and perpetual personal obedience, and inflicts death upon the least failing in any one particular. This the tenor and current of the Covenant. Adam failed in one particular: not obeying the symbolic law about the tree of knowledge. By this one failing, the tenor of the Covenant is utterly overthrown, it being impossible that Adam should yield continual obedience, his obedience being discontinued and broken off by his disobedience. Therefore, as virginity once lost can never be recovered, so the Covenant of Works once violated can never be repaired.

{2} *From the requisites, necessary to complete reparation of the broken Covenant of Works.* There are three things principally requisite to such a reparation, namely: (i) full satisfaction of the breach past, (ii) full personal conformity to the Covenant for the present, and (iii) complete fulfilling of the covenant, for the future. (i) There must be full satisfaction of divine justice and truth for the breach of covenant already past, by undergoing the death threatened, and deserved. Now no mere finite creature is able to undergo death corporal, spiritual and eternal, so as fully to satisfy God's infinite justice, but would be utterly and eternally lost and swallowed up therein. And infinite justice offended, requires infinite satisfaction, which finite beings can never perform. (ii) There must be a full personal conformity to the covenant for the present. Otherwise it were absolutely impossible either passively to satisfy for breaches past, or actively to keep the covenant perfectly for time to come. Adam in integrity had not been able to keep the covenant: had not his person then been fully conform to the covenant. Now since Adam's breach of the Covenant of Works, neither he nor any of his ordinary posterity are fully conformed to the Covenant, but naturally all are most contrary thereunto.[631] (iii) There must be, finally, a complete fulfilling of the Covenant of Works for

---

[631] Romans 8:7

the future. But that none of the ordinary posterity of lapsed Adam can perform, because the Scripture hath concluded all under sin.[632] From the utter inability of Adam and all mankind since the fall to fulfill the Covenant of Works. All being dead in sin;[633] without strength,[634] and so the law weak through the flesh;[635] enmity against God and the law of God;[636] and every imagination of the thoughts of man's heart being only evil continually.[637]

[7] ***Finally, hence; the Covenant of Works being utterly broken by Adam's disobedience, nor Adam nor any of his posterity, since the fall can ever be justified before God by the Covenant of Works, or by the works of the law.*** Why?

{1} Because Adam, and all mankind in him, are under sin, by reason of Adam's disobedience.[638] And therefore being wholly unable to all good works, they cannot be justified by good works. Yea are so far from any possibility of being justified by good works: that, without pardoning mercy, they are liable to be condemned eternally for their sins. And this is the apostle's grand argument against justification by the works of the law, where he purposely treats of this subject of justification, namely: neither Jew nor Gentile can be justified by the works of the law, because all of them are under sin. The series of his argumentation,[639] see in Romans 1:17-3:21. And observe it accurately,

{2} Because, as by Adam's disobedience all are concluded under sin: so by the law of works comes the knowledge of sin. How? Chiefly two ways, namely: (i) directly, by discovering what is sin, not only in deeds and words, but in thoughts and imaginations. *I had not known sin* (says Paul*) but by the law: for I had not known lust, except the law had said, thou shalt not covet.*[640] Hence

---

[632] Galatians 3:22
[633] Ephesians 2:1
[634] Romans 5:6
[635] Romans 8:3
[636] Romans 8:7
[637] Genesis 6:5
[638] Compare Galatians 3:22, Romans 5:12, 19, with Romans 8:3 & Titus 1:15-16
[639] See for clearing this, my Key of the Bible, on Romans 4
[640] Romans 7:7

Christ shows in his commentary upon the law, that the law discovers and condemns, not only outward gross sins of life, but also inward close sins of the heart.[641] (ii) Indirectly and occasionally, by irritating and provoking sin through the prohibition and restraint of it, to appear more extremely sinful, as a fierce torrent dammed up swells and ranges more furiously. So Paul, *sin taking occasion by the commandment, wrought in me all manner of concupiscence. For without the law sin was dead.*—thus, *sin by the commandment became exceeding sinful.*[642] Now the Covenant or Law of Works, thus bringing in the knowledge of sin, since the fall, and not the knowledge of any our righteousness at all, is altogether unable to justify us. Hence the apostle thus concludes: *Therefore by the deeds of the law, there shall no flesh be justified in his sight: for by the law is the knowledge of sin.*[643]

{3} Because, since the fall, the law of works curses and condemns all for not continuing in obedience: and therefore it can justify none. *For as many as are of the works of the law, are under the curse: for it is written, cursed is every one that continues not in all things which are written in the book of the law to do them.*[644] Now the same law cannot both bless and curse at once, both justify and condemn at once, all mankind.

---

[641] Matthew 5:21-22, 27-29, 38-40, 43-44
[642] Romans 7:6-14
[643] Romans 3:20
[644] Galatians 3:10

Aphorism 7

Finally, the breach of the Covenant of Works by the disobedience of the first Adam, did wonderfully make way for the establishment of the Covenant of Faith by the obedience of the second Adam.

For it's very observable that Adam had no sooner broken the Covenant of Works, but presently on the selfsame-day, God promises Christ the seed of the woman to heal this breach, and so sets on foot the Covenant of Faith in Christ.[645] Adam, almost as soon as he was made, made haste to destroy mankind, by his sin; God, almost as soon as they were ruined, made haste to save mankind by his Son. Here's no small mystery in this divine dispensation. For unfolding it, consider briefly these two particulars, namely:

(1) God before the foundation of the world, purposing to glorify himself more peculiarly, by mankind, elected some out of mankind *unto the adoption of children in Jesus Christ, according to the good pleasure of his will.*[646]

(2) God, in the beginning of the world, [1] created man in his own image, wholly upright, but mutable; [2] brings man into a Covenant of Works with himself, promising continuance of life upon condition of continued obedience, but threatening present death to disobedience; [3] leaves man to himself and permits him to fall from his integrity, by breaking this covenant, into a miserable state of sin and death. And all this in order to the accomplishment and execution of his eternal decree.

(3) God takes occasion, upon man's miserable state of sin and death through breach of the Covenant of Works, to open to him a door of hope for life and happiness in Christ Jesus by the Covenant of Faith, the breach of the Covenant of Works wonderfully making way for the erecting of the Covenant of Faith, and this in various respects, namely: [1] in respect of God: the breach of covenant giving him the clearest and fittest opportunity in the world, of

---

[645] Compare Genesis 3:6-8 with verse 15
[646] Ephesians 1:4-6

manifesting the infinite riches of his free-grace, love, mercy, etc., in Jesus Christ to mankind now in deepest misery. Man's extremity is God's opportunity. Now was God's only time to exalt himself and his grace on high, when man had debased himself so low. In extremity of misery, to show mercy is double mercy. [2] In respect of man: the breach of covenant bringing him into the greatest necessity of a mediator of divine grace and pardoning mercy in him, and of a Covenant of Faith revealing this mediator and this grace unto him. Until the fall, Adam needed neither Covenant of Faith nor pardoning mercy nor mediator, but after his fall he so needs them all, that without them he dies eternally. This extreme necessity and undone state of man made an excellent way for the replenishing bounty of God. When pain is bitterest, ease is sweetest; when the heart is most sick, reviving cordials are most welcome. [3] In respect of the Covenant of Faith itself, the breach of the Covenant of Works represents to the covenant-breaker nothing but death; the Covenant of Faith is brought in, proclaims a reprieve, yea a free pardon, in the seed of the woman, Christ, to all that by faith will accept him. O sweet Covenant of Faith, that opens a door of hope and mercy, even then when the broken Covenant of Works knows no mercy! O blessed tidings, that an apostate sinner may have an all-sufficient savior! That the breach of the Covenant of Works grounded on mutable nature, should be repaired by the Covenant of Faith in Christ, founded upon immutable grace!

Come and see, see and admire, admire and adore the severity, the goodness, and the wisdom of God. [1] *His severity*, in that sin shall be rewarded with death, at least in the sinner's surety and mediator promised. [2] *His goodness*, in that the condemned sinner shall be restored to life, by a Covenant of Reconciliation. [3] *His wisdom*, in that he could improve, reduce and dispose man's sinful fall to such great advantage both for his own glory, and man's good. Who but the most high God could have extracted such a reviving medicine, out of such a deadly poison? Who but he could have brought such clear light out of such extreme darkness; such supernatural life out of such preternatural death; such celestial good out of such infernal evil?

As Augustine, excellently: "The omnipotent God, who is chiefly good, would by no means suffer any evil to be among his works, were he not so omnipotent and good, that he could bring good even out of evil. If the first covenant had not been marred, the second and more excellent covenant would not have been made."[647]

If the first earthly Adam had not been ruined, the second heavenly Adam Christ would not have been promised. If one sin in Adam had not been so grievous, God's superabounding grace in Christ had not appeared so glorious. "Oh my happy fault," (said Augustine) "to wipe away, that love of his also is opened unto me, desiring and coveting it from my heart root! I could never so well have acknowledged his love unless I had tried it in such great perils. Oh how happily did I fall, that after my fall did more happily rise again!"[648]

Hitherto of God's Covenant of Works with and in the first Adam before the fall. Next of God's Covenant of Faith with and in the last Adam after the fall.

---

[647] Enchiridion, 11.3
[648] Augustine, Meditations, 6.9

Chapter 2

Of God's Covenant of Faith with the last Adam and his seed after the fall, more generally considered.

The Covenant of Faith, that sweet and admirable mystery of divine dispensation, comes next to be unfolded. Though usually it is called the Covenant of Grace, yet I choose rather to style it the Covenant of Faith: (1) because the Covenant of Works and the Covenant of Faith are denominations nearest to the Scripture's own expressions, namely, the law of works, and the law of faith (Romans 3:27). Which for sense and substance, what else are they but the Covenant of Works, and the Covenant of Faith? (2) Because the distribution of God's Covenant into the Covenant of Works and the Covenant of Faith, seems most proper, these being most distinct and opposite members: works being the condition of that, faith the condition of this covenant, and both on man's part. (3) Because that denomination of the Covenant of Grace, is rather coincident with the Covenant of Works, which (as has been shown) was a covenant made with Adam of mere grace and favor, as well as this; God being no way obliged, debt-bound or necessitated to either: this is noted once for all, that none be offended at the phrase of the Covenant of Faith here used.

Now in the unfolding of this Covenant of Faith, I shall, for the greater perspicuity, treat of it, (1) *more generally*, showing, [1] that the Covenant of Works being broken in the first Adam, the Lord pleased to reveal a Covenant of Faith in Christ the last Adam. [2] What this Covenant of Faith is. [3] How this Covenant of Faith is to be distinguished and distributed into its several sorts and branches. (2) *More particularly*, descending to the particular opening of it, in the several periods of its discovery and the forms of its administration.

Aphorism 1

The Covenant of Works being broken in the first Adam, the Lord God was pleased to reveal a Covenant of Faith in Jesus Christ the last Adam.

For more clear unfolding hereof, these things are to be evidenced. namely: (1) that God, upon Adam's breach of the Covenant of Works, revealed the Covenant of Faith, (2) when God revealed this Covenant of Faith, and (3) why he revealed the Covenant of Faith.

(1) That *upon breach of the Covenant of Works in the first Adam, God was pleased to reveal a Covenant of Faith in Jesus Christ: the last Adam*, will appear by conferring some few Scriptures together. For,

[1] One Scripture testifies that Jesus Christ is the last Adam; *the first man Adam was made a living soul: the last Adam was made a quickening spirit.* Again, *the first man is of the earth earthy: the second man is the Lord from heaven.*[649] Here are two Adams opposite one to the other, and the Lord Christ is the second or last of these two Adams.

[2] Another Scripture witnesses that the first Adam in respect of the effect of his disobedience, was *the figure or type of him that was to come,*[650] namely, of Christ, in respect to the effect of his obedience. For, as by the first Adam's disobedience, all his posterity were brought into a state of sin and death; so by the last Adam's obedience, all his posterity (which are many, even all the elect) shall be most freely restored to a state of righteousness and eternal life. Hence it's evident that these two Adams in this parallel stand in reference to their respective posterities not only as two roots whence their posterities flow, but also as two representatives or two universal and public persons representing their several seeds. Adam represented and sustained the person of his seed, all

---

[649] 1 Corinthians 15:45, 47
[650] Consider well that whole context, namely Romans 5:12 to the end of the chapter

mankind, in his disobedience all mankind disobeyed, in his death for disobedience all mankind died also; in like manner, Christ represented and sustained the person of his seed, all the elect; in his obedience all the elect obeyed, and in his justification upon his obedience, all the elect partake in justification of life. So then the first Adam disobeyed what? The Covenant of Works, and so condemned all mankind. Christ the last Adam obeyed what? The same Covenant of Works, the law, and so saved all the elect. How? According to the tenor of the Covenant of Faith, making him a representative surety for all his elect.

[3] Finally another Scripture shows that all mankind being concluded under sin (namely, by reason of Adam's breach of the Covenant of Works) they could not have life by the law or Covenant of Works, sin disabling them to keep it: and thereupon God has given a Covenant of Faith in Christ, to them that believe, namely, to all his elect, they alone being able truly to believe.[651] *If there had been a law given which could have given life, verily righteousness should have been by the law. But the Scripture hath concluded all under sin, that the promise by faith of Jesus Christ might be given to them that believe.*[652]

Now lay all this together: [1] Jesus Christ is the last Adam. [2] The first Adam having condemned all his seed under sin and death by his disobedience, the last Adam restores all his elect unto justification of life by his obedience. [3] The law being unable by reason of sin to give righteousness and life, the covenant or promise by faith in Christ is given instead thereof, and it is clear that the Covenant of Works having been broken by the first Adam, the Lord has revealed a Covenant of Faith in Christ the last Adam.

(2) **When did God reveal the Covenant of Faith in Christ the last Adam?**

---

[651] John 10:26
[652] Galatians 3:21-22

Answer: God was pleased to reveal the Covenant of Faith in Christ, not only under the New Testament since Christ,[653] but also under the Old Testament long before Christ. And that not only to the Jews about the time of their return from the Babylonian captivity,[654] but also to David long before that time,[655] and to Moses and Israel at Sinai long before David's time,[656] and to Abraham long before the days of Moses,[657] and to Noah long before the days of Abraham,[658] yea and to Adam himself long before the days of Noah. For in the self-same day wherein Adam by disobedience broke the Covenant of Works, in that very day, before God either drove the man out of paradise, or pronounced sentence upon him or the woman for their sin, even whilst he was passing sentence upon the serpent (which probably was not many hours after the fall), God revealed this Covenant of Faith in Christ, the seed of the woman, that should bruise the serpent's head.[659]

Notably to this effect said Jerome, "Our God – against all hope, almost against all faith, having out of the riches of his mercy found good in evil, begetting and confirming kindness in wrath – would have the seed of sinning to pass on into the fruit of commiserating, and he who should have destroyed us for our transgression, promised to repair us for his own mercy and at that time wherein we deserved punishments, he shows matter of salvation: that we might understand, how much he was able to perform, being un-offended, that would bestow so much while he was displeased. Therefore in the first man he presently promised us judiciary help, he presently brought forth good things out of his good treasury, he presently published the mysteries unknown to angels themselves, which was to be fulfilled in the last time; and unto the Adam on earth, he promised an Adam from heaven."[660] Thus he, elegantly.

---

[653] Hebrews 8:8, etc., Jeremiah 31:31-35
[654] Jeremiah 32:37 to the end
[655] 2 Samuel 23:5 & 7:5-17, with Psalm 89 throughout
[656] Deuteronomy 5:2-6, Jeremiah 31:32
[657] Genesis 17:7-8, 10-11
[658] Genesis 6:18
[659] Genesis 3:6 to the end of the chapter
[660] Jerome. ad Amic. aegrot. de viro perfect. Tom. 4, Basil 1563

(3) *Why did God reveal the Covenant of Faith in Christ the last Adam, the Covenant of Works being broken by the first Adam?*

Answer: We may conceive that the Lord did this, [1] out of mere grace, love and mercy to mankind. [2] That God's purpose according to election might stand. [3] That God's Covenant and promise might be sure to all the elect. [4] To advance the glory of his goodness and severity in Jesus Christ.

[1] Out of the superabounding riches of his mere grace, love and mercy to mankind. These were the only inward impulsives, or moving causes, whereupon the Lord inclined to reveal a Covenant of Faith in Christ, after the Covenant of Works was broken by Adam, and not anything at all in man. Namely:

{1} His mere grace or free favor to man in lapsed state. What the apostle says of God's Covenant and promise to Abraham – it is of faith, *that it might be by grace*[661] – holds also in all the periods and administrations of the Covenant of Faith; after Adam's fall. *To him that worketh, the reward is not reckoned of grace, but of debt*, says the apostle.[662] But lapsed man could not work, could not fulfill the works of the law, and so have the reward of life as a debt due by God's promise in the Covenant of Works – therefore this Covenant of Faith, God made with him of the riches of his mere grace.

{2} His mere love moved him to make this Covenant of Faith – and that not only without, but contrary to all grounds of love in lapsed man. For man, having broken the Covenant of Works, became a most wretched sinner.[663] As a sinner, he had lost the image of God, and all his beauty, amiableness, loveliness, etc., being wholly deformed, defiled, and unlovely through the image of Satan. Therefore, as God singularly *commended his love to us, in that whilst we were yet sinners, Christ died for us*:[664] so he singularly commended the same love to us, in that whilst we were yet sinners, Christ was freely promised to us.[665]

---

[661] Romans 4:16
[662] Romans 4:4
[663] Romans 5:12, 19
[664] Romans 5:8
[665] Genesis 3:15

{3} His mere mercy. By mercy God is disposed to favor his creatures in misery. Man, having broken the Covenant of Works, was a mere map of misery. And, all things considered, mankind was never so extremely and hopelessly miserable in this world since the creation, as between his breach of the Covenant of Works and God's revealing of the Covenant of Faith. For at that time he had no foundation of hope nor shadow thereof left him. He had no covenant or promise to lean upon: the Covenant of Works being broken, and the Covenant of Faith not revealed. He had no righteousness to depend upon: not his own, for he had lost it; not Christ's, for it was not yet made known. He had no attribute of God to comfort himself with, for he had made himself an utter enemy to God. No creature would relieve him because no mere creature could reconcile him to God. Only death was before him ready to swallow him up. Now in this utmost extremity of man's misery on earth, God proclaims a Covenant of Faith in Christ. Here was a miracle of mercy indeed; mere misery is embraced in the arms of mere mercy.[666]

[2] That God's gracious purpose according to election might stand firm and not be overthrown; all mankind, in Adam's breach of the Covenant of Works being plunged into a state of sin and death, God revealed a Covenant of Faith for recovery of his elect among mankind out of that lost estate. Here note, {1} that God has elected or *chosen some out of mankind, in Jesus Christ before the foundation of the world, to be holy and without blame before him in love, having predestinated them unto the adoption of children by Jesus Christ to himself, according to the good pleasure of his will.*[667] These are called *vessels of mercy, afore prepared unto glory*: all others, *vessels of wrath fitted to destruction.*[668] These are called Christ's sheep, given him of the Father: others, not of his sheep, but goats.[669] {2} That God's counsel according to election is most sure, unalterable, unchangeable. *The foundation of God stands sure, having this seal, the Lord knows them that are his.*[670] And every one that God

---

[666] Titus 3:4-6
[667] Ephesians 1:4-6
[668] Romans 9:22-23
[669] John 10:26-30, Matthew 25:32, 34
[670] 2 Timothy 2:19 with Romans 9:11

predestines, he glorifies.[671] {3} That Adam's breach of the Covenant of Works, involved all mankind, elect as well as reprobates, in a state of sin and death.[672] By which state of sin and death, God's election seems wholly to be crossed and overthrown. {4} That God's revealing his Covenant of Faith in Christ for restoring his elect out of this lapsed state, removes that grand obstruction and impediment to the execution and fulfilling of God's election. For by this Covenant of Faith, the predestined in Christ, are called to him, that they may be justified and glorified by him, according to the election.[673]

[3] That God's Covenant and promise might be sure to all God's elect. The Covenant of Works, founded upon Adam's perfect and perpetual personal obedience, though sure in respect of God, *who cannot lie;*[674] yet was not sure in respect of Adam, who (though upright),[675] was but a mutable creature, and so utterly broke it. Therefore God revealed a Covenant of Faith, founded upon Christ and his perfect obedience, who is perfectly unchangeable, *the same yesterday, and to day, and forever:*[676] that so the covenant might be inviolably sure to all that will believe in him. Hence the apostle says of the promise of the inheritance to Abraham, *therefore it is of faith, that it might be by grace, to the end the promise might be sure to all the seed.*[677]

[4] Finally, the Covenant of Works being broken by the first Adam, God revealed the Covenant of Faith in Christ the last Adam, that thereby he might wonderfully advance the glory of his goodness, and severity, in Jesus Christ.

{1} The glory of his goodness towards his elect. In devising life for them when dead, righteousness for them when sinners, and a sure Covenant of Faith for them when covenant-breakers of the Covenant of Works. Here's the valley of Achor – of trouble – turned into a door of hope; the midnight of misery,

---

[671] Romans 8:29-30
[672] Romans 5:12, 18
[673] Romans 8:29-30
[674] Titus 1:2
[675] Ecclesiastes 7:29
[676] Hebrews 13:8
[677] Romans 4:16

into the day-break of mercy. Oh how glorious is this divine goodness in the eyes of all the elect! They shall ever extol, admire and adore it, both in this and the world to come.

{2} The glory of his severity, both to Satan, and to all reprobates. (i) *To Satan*, that old serpent the devil, God's severity is published in the Covenant of Faith, which brings tidings of Christ the seed of the woman that should bruise the serpent's head, utterly conquer the devil, and destroy his works.[678] Satan in the serpent had ruined man by the woman.[679] And therefore God has devised to ruin Satan and the serpent by the promised seed of the woman.[680] Man fell through Satan's temptation from without himself and found mercy; Satan fell, having no temptation but from within himself, and being fallen, maliciously overthrows mankind, and therefore finds no mercy. Man is pushed down by Satan, and mercy promises him a Christ to save him: Satan pushed down himself and mankind with himself, and severity threatens him the same Christ to damn him. How severely! How mysteriously! (ii) *To reprobates*, the seed of the serpent, God magnifies also his justice and severity, by the Covenant of Faith. For, this covenant establishes an enmity between the seed of the woman, Christ; and the seed of the serpent, reprobates.[681] And shows that Christ shall bruise the head both of the serpent, and of his seed. O how terrible is this severity! If Christ be an enemy to reprobates, who shall be their friend? If Christ bruise them, who shall heal them? If Christ damn them, who shall save them?

What this Covenant of Faith in Christ the last Adam is, and how it is to be distributed, shall be declared in the two next aphorisms. Meanwhile consider these corollaries resulting from this aphorism.

---

[678] Genesis 3:15 with Hebrews 2:14-15, Colossians 2:15 & 1 John 3:8
[679] Genesis 3:12-13
[680] Genesis 3:14-15
[681] Genesis 3:15

Corollaries

Seeing upon breach of the Covenant of Works by the first Adam, God was pleased to reveal a Covenant of Faith in Christ the last Adam: hence note,

[1] ***That God's covenant-administrations are most wisely contrived for the greatest advantage of his own glory.*** God has *made all things for himself*:[682] and orders *all things to himself*.[683] Especially his covenant-administrations render him eminently glorious. He gives Adam a Covenant of Works, which he was able to keep, and so glorifies his goodness and power. He leaves Adam to himself, being mutable, permitting him to fall, and so glorifies his freedom. Adam having broken the Covenant of Works, he reveals a Covenant of Faith in Christ: and so glorifies his goodness and severity, as has been shown. He permits man to become a sinner: that he may proclaim Christ to be a savior. He permits man to lose his own righteousness, which was mutable, so that he may be clothed with God's righteousness which is immutable. He permits man to be involved in misery so that he may be embraced with the greater mercy. He permits man to be deceived by the serpent so that the seed of the woman may destroy the serpent. He permits man to be wounded to the death so that he may more illustriously discover the necessity and efficacy of Jesus Christ for healing and for life. He permits man to lose Eden so that in Christ he may gain heaven. Thus the Almighty brings light out of darkness, strength out of weakness, gains out of losses, health out of sickness, victory out of captivity, liberty out of bondage, happiness out of misery, life out of death, good out of evil, and heaven out of hell. *Oh the depth of the riches both of the wisdom and knowledge of God!*[684] How has he out-shot Satan in his own bow! How has he raised his glory over all, by that which seemed to debase his glory most of all!

[2] ***That God has from the beginning been infinitely more careful of man's happiness, than man of his own happiness.*** God makes man happy,

---

[682] Proverbs 16:4
[683] Romans 11:36
[684] Romans 11:33

places this happiness in his own keeping, gives him ability to keep it, and covenants to continue it to him upon his perfect obedience, but man breaks the covenant, and disrobes himself of all his happiness, regardless of his felicity. Hereupon God establishes a Covenant of Faith, opens a door of hope touching a greater happiness, places it in Christ's keeping, offers it to all that will accept Christ by believing. Here's God's double care of man's happiness: that bestowed not a single care upon his own happiness. O how God thirsts after man's felicity! He is more willing to save man, then man is willing to be saved by him, otherwise man should never have been saved.

[3] *That the revelation of the mystery of the gospel is of great antiquity, having been even from the beginning of the world.* Those who think there is no gospel but in the New Testament, and that no gospel was revealed until Christ's incarnation, do greatly err because they know not the Scriptures nor the grace of God. For what is the gospel but the glad tidings of God's gracious pleasure to save lapsed sinners by Christ? This gospel is preached by the law and the prophets. This gospel was preached unto Abraham 430 years before the law was given,[685] and to Adam presently after the fall in the very beginning of the world in that promise of the *seed of the woman to bruise the serpent's head*.[686] And since that promise, it is evident that the whole Scripture scopes at the proclaiming and displaying of this gospel in one respect or another.

[4] *That all the godly under the Old Testament from the Fall of the first Adam till the incarnation of the last Adam, were saved in the selfsame way for substance, that the faithful are under the New Testament since Christ's coming in the flesh.* For they had for substance the same Covenant of Faith as we do, though more imperfectly and obscurely revealed. The same God, the same mediator Jesus Christ, the same *yesterday, and today, and forever*,[687] though then revealed under types, shadows and promises, now exhibited with open face. They had the same Spirit of Christ as

---

[685] Galatians 3:8, 17
[686] Genesis 3:15
[687] Hebrews 13:8, Genesis 3:15

we do, they lived by the same justifying faith that we do,[688] the same religion and sacraments for substance that we have, and expected the same glorious reward eternally in heaven, that we expect.[689] But here is the eminent difference: the church and people of God under the Old Testament were in their spiritual infancy, and as a child under age, were put under tutors and governors, namely, under a more servile manner of the covenant's administration, but now under the New Testament they are come to their spiritual maturity, like an heir come to age, and are spiritually a more free and willing people under a more free covenant-dispensation.

[5] *That God, having revealed a Covenant of Faith, upon breach of the Covenant of Works, has antiquated, and in some sort abolished the Covenant of Works.* If in the same Covenant of Faith, God's establishing of a new covenant[690] (new not for substance, but for administration) makes the former administration of the covenant old, then much more God's publishing of a new kind of covenant, makes the former kind old. I say, God by setting up a Covenant of Faith, has in some sort abolished the Covenant of Works, namely: {1} in respect of affording life, righteousness and justification, as a covenant. Thus it is abolished generally unto all; for as much as no man since the Fall can be justified by works, but only by faith in Christ.[691] {2} In respect of inflicting condemnation for the breach of the Covenant of Works. So it is abolished to all true believers, that accept the Covenant of Faith and Christ therein: for *there's no condemnation to them that are in Christ Jesus.*[692] Whether in other respects the Covenant of Works be abolished, how far, how far not, and of what use it may still be in the church of God, may be more opportunely considered in treating of the Sinai Covenant.

[6] *That if any persons in the church perish since Adam's fall, under the curse and penalty of the Covenant of Works, they perish because they accept not God's Covenant of Faith.* As the Covenant of Works is unable to

---

[688] Hebrews 11 throughout
[689] 1 Corinthians 10:1-3, etc., Colossians 2:11-12
[690] Hebrews 8:13
[691] Compare Romans 3:20-22, 27-28 with Romans 10:3-4, Galatians 3:11, 21-22
[692] Romans 8:1

give life to anyone after the fall because none can keep it in their own persons, God has published his Covenant of Faith so that they might have life in another: even in Jesus Christ, who should fully keep it. So that faith in Christ according to the second covenant is a remedy against disobedience to the first covenant. To all in the church, this Covenant of Faith is tendered. They therefore shall not so much be condemned for disobedience as for unbelief – the great sin of sins – and may thank themselves, not at all blame God, for their own destruction.[693]

---

[693] John 16:9-11

Aphorism 2

The Covenant of Faith is God's gracious compact or agreement with Jesus Christ the last Adam, and in him with all his seed, after the fall, touching their recovery out of the state of sin and death, into a state of righteousness and eternal life by Christ, that in him the Lord may be their God, and they his people: they accepting Christ and these covenanted mercies by true faith, and walking worthy of them according to the gospel.

For the sake of plainness, I express the nature of the Covenant of Faith thus largely: and it may be farther opened and confirmed, as followeth. In this description note, (1) the genus, or general nature of it. (2) The *differentiam specificam*, or special difference of it.

(1) The general nature of the Covenant of Faith is contained in these words: it is a compact or agreement. Herein generally all covenants divine and human, and amongst divine, both of works and faith do concur, that they are compacts or agreements. Of which has been spoken sufficiently heretofore.[694]

(2) The special difference of this Covenant of Faith, distinguishing it not only from human covenants, but even from God's Covenant of Works, formerly laid open, is comprised in the rest of the description. And more particularly in the [1] efficient, [2] parties, [3] matter, and [4] form of this covenant. These shall be unfolded in four particular sections, to which a fifth section may be added, comprising certain corollaries resulting from the whole.

---

[694] See in Book 1 Chapter 2 Aphorism 2

Section 1

The efficient cause, or author of the Covenant of Faith is God. It is God's gracious compact or agreement.

Here is to be shown: (1) that God is the efficient cause of this Covenant of Faith. (2) How, and in what different notion God is the author of it, so as he was not of the Covenant of Works. (3) What impulsive or moving cause inclined God to devise and set up this Covenant.

(1) ***That God is the efficient cause, or author of this Covenant of Faith***, is most clear. For, [1] the Scriptures speaking of this covenant, and of the gradual discoveries of it, do still ascribe it to God alone, as his covenant, as devised and made by him with his people.[695] [2] Only God could dispense with the penalty of that Covenant of Works – death – which Adam, and in him all mankind had to themselves. And consequently none but God could establish the Covenant of Faith; which by way of remedy against the breach of the Covenant of Works, both relieves the sinner that he should not be condemned, and provides for God's justice, truth and glory, that they should not be impeached. [3] The Lord God, and he alone could devise and contrive this Covenant of Faith – and having devised it, bring it into actual execution. All the angels in heaven, and men on earth could not have invented the mystery of this covenant, had not God – infinitely and unsearchably wise – invented it and revealed it to them. For it is evident that after God had revealed this covenant in many degrees under the Old Testament, yet angels themselves did not so fully understand it till the times of the New Testament, *the manifold wisdom of God being made known by the church unto principalities and powers in heavenly places.*[696] And these are such abstruse things, that (as Peter intimates) the angels still desire to look and pry into for further satisfaction.[697]

---

[695] Genesis 3:14-15 & 6:18 & 17:1-2, 4, 7, 9-10, 13-14, 19, 21; Exodus 24:8; Deuteronomy 5:2-3 & 4:13; 2 Samuel 23:5, Psalm 89:3, 34; Jeremiah 32:40; Hebrews 8:8-10, 10:16
[696] Ephesians 3:10
[697] 1 Peter 1:12

And if angels do not so fully comprehend the mysteries of this covenant, being already devised and revealed, how much less can man fathom it? *Eye hath not seen, ear hath not heard, nor have entered into the heart of man; the things which God hath prepared for them that love him.*[698] And *the love of Christ passes knowledge.*[699] Now if neither men, nor angels can fully comprehend this mystery, much less could they have contrived it, but least of all have brought it to actual execution. How could they have brought the Son of God to be mediator of this covenant, and to that end to become man, to die, etc?

(2) **How and in what sense, God is the author of the Covenant of Faith.** *Answer*: God was the author of both Covenant of Works and of Faith, and herein they agree. But he is author of these two covenants in a far different sense and notion, and herein they disagree. Of the Covenant of Works, God was author, as a loving well-pleased creator, dealing immediately without a mediator with man his perfect and upright creature; but of the Covenant of Faith, God is author as a most gracious and merciful redeemer, dealing mediately in and by a mediator Jesus Christ, with lapsed man, a miserable sinner. Hence the Covenant of Works is deservedly styled {*faedus amicitiae*}, a covenant of amity or friendship, because God and man, at the making thereof were upon terms of perfect friendship with each other; but the Covenant of Faith is called {*faedus reconciliationis*}, a covenant of reconcilement, because at making thereof, God and man were upon terms of enmity against each other by reason of the fall, and now to be reconciled.

(3) **The impulsive, or moving cause, inclining God to contrive and erect this Covenant of Faith; nor was, nor could be anything at all in man, without God.** Neither man's merit, nor his misery; neither man's goodness nor his badness could move God hereunto. Not man's merit or goodness, for whilst man was innocent, he could merit nothing from God, much less after he became nocent and sinful. Sinful man could merit nothing from God, but death due to sin.[700] Nor man's misery or badness, for then, why

---

[698] 1 Corinthians 2:9
[699] Ephesians 3:18-19
[700] Romans 6:23

should not the misery and badness of lapsed angels (which was as great as man's) have moved God to have covenanted with angels? What then? The only moving cause hereof was in God himself, namely: the mere riches of his free-grace and compassionate yearnings of his bowels of mercies moved him. Hereupon the Spirit of God, by the virgin Mary and Zacharias, speaking of the accomplishment of this Covenant of Faith to Abraham and his seed, declares the rise and ground of this Covenant and promise to have been *divine mercy, and bowels of mercy of our God.*[701] And Moses, having recited God's Covenant with Israel in Horeb and the many covenanted blessings bestowed upon them by God, intimates that God's mere love, not anything at all in them, was the moving cause of all. *The LORD did not set his love upon you, nor choose you, because ye were more in number then any people (for ye were the fewest of any people) but because the LORD loved you.—only the LORD had a delight in thy fathers to love them, and he chose their seed after them, even you above all people.*[702] Yea the Lord by Ezekiel, having respect to his covenant with them in Horeb, tells them (under the allegory of a newborn infant, wretched and un-pitied) that *When their navel was not cut, nor they washed with water, nor salted at all, nor swaddled at all, none eye pitying them, when God saw them cast out, loathed and polluted in their own blood,*[703] when they were utterly without merit or amiableness: even then God said unto them *live, and their time was as the time of love, he spread his skirt over her, covered her nakedness, sware unto her, entered into a covenant with her, and she became his.* Now unto this Covenant nothing could move or incline God but riches of mere grace. Finally, when God renewed his covenant promises to the Jews in Babylon, he tells them plainly, *I do not this for your sakes, O house of Israel, but for mine holy name's sake.—not for your sakes do I this, saith the LORD God, be it known unto you: be ashamed and confounded for your own ways, O house of Israel.*[704]

---

[701] Luke 1:54-55, 72-73, 77-78

[702] Deuteronomy 7:7-8 & 10:15, well compared with the series of the context from Deuteronomy 5:1-2, etc.

[703] Ezekiel 16:4-9

[704] Ezekiel 36:22, 32, compared with the context

Section 2

The parties to this Covenant of Faith are two, namely: (1) God, on the one hand. (2) Christ the last Adam, and in him all his seed, on the other hand.

Here will arise farther difference between this and the Covenant of Works in regard to the parties covenanting. For God is here one party to this covenant, not as a bountiful creator, covenanting with his innocent and upright creature as in the Covenant of Works, but as a most merciful restorer of his lapsed and miserable creature. This is so clear that it needs no demonstration or illustration.

Christ the last Adam, and in him all his seed, are the other party. The first Adam, and in him his seed or posterity, were the party with whom God covenanted in the Covenant of Works: but Christ the last Adam, and in him all his seed, are the party with whom God covenants in the Covenant of Faith. This discovers a vast difference between these covenants. And this leads us to consider an excellent mystery, and of singular importance for the comfort of all believers, namely: how Christ the last Adam and his seed are a joint-party to this Covenant of Faith. Very few that treat of the covenant speak to this point, and those who do speak of it rather point at it obscurely than handle it distinctly. That therefore we may have a more clear notion and apprehension of this mystery, let us diligently consider the ensuing parallel between God's dealing with the first Adam – and in him with his seed – in the Covenant of Works, and his dealing with the last Adam, Christ, and his seed in the Covenant of Faith, together with the grounds thereof. The parallel stands chiefly in these four branches, namely,

(1) *As the first man of the earth earthy, is called the first Adam: so the second man, Jesus Christ, the Lord from heaven, is styled the last Adam. The first man Adam was made a living soul: the last Adam was made*

a quickening spirit.—the first man is of the earth, earthy: the second man is the Lord from heaven.[705] Christ is styled the second man, not because he was the second man that was brought into the world – that was Cain[706] – but because he was the second public man, the root and representative of his posterity, as the first man of his. And he is styled the last Adam, partly because as there was no other such public person from the first Adam before Christ, so there should be no other such public person after Christ. Partly, because the first Adam was a figure or type of Christ,[707] and that in several respects, as Paul shows to the Romans and Corinthians.[708]

(2) **As the first Adam had his natural seed and posterity: all mankind; so the last Adam Jesus Christ has his supernatural seed, and spiritual posterity: all the elect.**

[1] That the first Adam had all mankind for his natural seed, is evident: partly in that all mankind originally descended from him, God having *made of one blood all nations of men:*[709] yea even Eve herself being taken out of Adam.[710] Partly in that all mankind sinned in him and died in him in his fall.[711]

[2] That the last Adam also has his supernatural seed, and spiritual posterity, even all the elect, is as evident. For Isaiah, prophesying of Christ's passion, says: *It pleased the Lord to bruise him, he hath put him to grief; when thou shalt make his soul an offering for sin, he shall see his seed.*[712] And David long before him, prophesying of Christ's kingdom and dominion, said, *A seed shall serve him: it shall be accounted to the LORD for a generation.*[713] And again elsewhere; *Thy people shall be willing in the day of thy power, in the beauties of holiness, from the womb of the morning, thou hast the dew of thy*

---

[705] 1 Corinthians 15:45, 47
[706] Genesis 4:1
[707] Romans 5:14 ος εστιν τυπος του μελλοντος ["the figure of him that was to come", KJV]
[708] Compare Romans 5:14 to the end with 1 Corinthians 15:21-22, 45-47
[709] Acts 17:26
[710] Genesis 2
[711] Romans 5:12, etc.
[712] Isaiah 53:10-11
[713] Psalm 22:30

youth.⁷¹⁴ That is, *thy youth* (thy young, or newborn people) *shall be to thee as the morning dew, which falls secretly and plentifully from heaven, and abundantly covers the earth*.⁷¹⁵ So that as the dew is born out of the cool morning air, as out of a womb, distilling thence in innumerable drops upon the earth: so thine elect shall be born unto thee, by the preaching of thy word and first approach of thy heavenly light, in innumerable armies.

Now, who are this seed of Christ? All those that the Father has given Christ by his decree of eternal election,⁷¹⁶ even all his sheep given him by the Father, for whom Christ the good shepherd laid down his life, who hear the shepherd's voice, and believe in him, whether they be Jews or Gentiles.⁷¹⁷ These alone are Christ's spiritual seed; and that, {1} *by decree*, being elected in Christ.⁷¹⁸ {2} *By generation*, being begotten again by Christ the everlasting father.⁷¹⁹ Namely, *meritoriously*, by his death⁷²⁰ and resurrection;⁷²¹ *efficaciously*, by his word⁷²² and Spirit.⁷²³ So that they become his children, and are counted to him for a generation. {3} *By conformity to Christ*, as children to a father. They bear his image, and go like him: especially, in grace;⁷²⁴ in godly life;⁷²⁵ in sufferings;⁷²⁶ and in glory.⁷²⁷ {4} *By filial affection and service to him*:⁷²⁸ as children love and serve their parents. And all Christ's posterity shall be most cheerful volunteers herein. {5} *By participation with Christ in his spirituals and eternals*. Men's posterity share with them in their states and

---

[714] Psalm 110:3
[715] Thus Ainsworth in annotations and Mr. Ed Reynolds in exposition upon Psalm 110
[716] John 17:2, 6, 24
[717] John 10:15-16, 27-29 with 17:20 & Isaiah 49:6
[718] Ephesians 1:4-5
[719] Isaiah 9:6
[720] Isaiah 53:10-11
[721] 1 Peter 1:3
[722] 1 Peter 1:23
[723] John 3:3, 5; Romans 8:2, 11
[724] John 1:14, 16
[725] 1 John 2:6
[726] Romans 8:15-17, 29
[727] Philippians 3:20-21, 1 Corinthians 15:48-49
[728] Psalm 22:30 & 110:3

inheritances, and Christ's seed partake with him in his spiritual privileges and eternal enjoyments.[729]

(3) *As God made the Covenant of Works with the first Adam, and in him (as has been shown) with all his natural seed, so God made the Covenant of Faith with Christ the last Adam, and in him with all his supernatural seed.* And if God made the Covenant of Faith with Christ the last Adam, and in him with all his supernatural seed, then as God is one party to this covenant, Christ his seed must needs be the other. Let us see therefore how this may be cleared, that God made the Covenant of Faith with Christ the last Adam, and in him with all his supernatural seed. In this branch of the parallel consists the greatest difficulty: which may be facilitated by these positions following, namely: [1] Christ-less persons are mere strangers to the Covenant of Faith, and to all the promises thereof. [2] They that are Christ's have the Covenant of Faith, and all the promises thereof as theirs. [3] They that are Christ's have the Covenant of Faith, and the promises thereof theirs only in Christ. [4] God's Covenant of Faith and promises thereof, are first made to Christ and then to his seed, to them that are Christ's, in him.

[1] *Christless persons are mere strangers to God's Covenant of Faith and to all the promises thereof.* This may be proved in several ways, as:

{1} From *testimony of Scripture*. Paul describing to the Ephesians their carnal state before they believed the gospel, says: *At that time ye were without Christ; aliens from the common-wealth of Israel, and strangers from the covenants of promise, having no hope, and without God in the world.*[730] Mark the connection and consequence in these particulars. First they were without Christ. This is the foundation of all their ensuing misery: Christ being (as Zanchi well notes)[731] the gate and door to the possession of all good things, of the present and future life. Then they were *aliens to the commonwealth of Israel.* Having no union to Christ the head, they consequently had no

---

[729] John 1:16 & 17:2, 24
[730] Ephesians 2:12
[731] Zanchi, commentary in Common Places

communion with the church, his mystical body. Thirdly, from both the former, they were strangers from the Covenants of Promise. Why? Because Christ is the foundation of the Covenant and promises:[732] and his church *the pillar and ground of truth*,[733] the recipient and keeper of God's Covenants, wherein they were published and tendered. Therefore, having no union to Christ the head, nor communion with the church his body, they had no part in the Covenants of Promise, appertaining to both. Hence it's evident that Christ-less persons are covenantless and promiseless persons.

{2} *From the nature of a Christ-less state.* A Christ-less state, is a condition of mere sinfulness[734] and utter enmity[735] against God, wholly under the curse[736] and wrath[737] of God: and this without God's remedy, Christ. And therefore it cannot stand with the truth and exact justice of God, to spare such persons from death (much less to give them life by covenant or promise) without full satisfaction. So that Christ-less persons as such have neither actual interest in God's Covenant of Faith and the promises thereof, nor can make any good claim or title thereunto, nor have any immediate capacity thereof, lacking both Christ the foundation of them, and faith for application of them.

{3} *From the nature of the Covenant of Faith and of the promises thereof.* They are peculiar indications of God's fatherly love and favor to us in Christ. For, as Calvin well observes, "God is not a propitious father to us, but only in Christ, and his promises are testimonies of his paternal benevolence towards us. Consequently, they are fulfilled through him alone. The promises, I say, are testimonies of divine grace: for though God be beneficent even to the unworthy, yet when promises are added to his benefits, it is a special reason that there he declares himself a father."[738] So he. Now God's fatherly love, the

---

[732] 2 Corinthians 1:20
[733] 1 Timothy 3:15
[734] Romans 8:8, Genesis 6:5, Ephesians 2:1
[735] Colossians 1:21, Romans 8:7
[736] Galatians 3:10, Genesis 2:17
[737] Ephesians 2:3
[738] John Calvin commentary in 2 Corinthians 1:20

acts and testification thereof, are peculiar to God's own people. *Remember me O LORD* (says David) *with the favor (or, favorable-acceptance) of thy people*.[739] That is, with the special love and free favor wherewith God embraces the elect alone, above all other people. Therefore God's Covenant and promises cannot belong to such as are without the bounds of God's peculiar fatherly love.

[2] **They that are Christ's have the Covenant of Faith, and all the promises thereof, as theirs.** This is evident by various Scriptures. *If ye be Christ's, then are ye Abraham's seed, and heirs according to the promise.*[740] Then, the promise of heirship, not of Canaan, but of this world, and of heaven, is theirs, that are Christ's. Peter, writing to them that had obtained like precious faith with the apostles, says: *exceeding great and precious promises are given to us.*[741] Not to all, but to us: to the faithful. But Paul more fully: *Godliness is profitable unto all things, having promise of the life that now is, and of that which is to come.*[742] That is, all the promises are peculiarly annexed to, and entailed upon godliness: for there is no promise, but either of the life present or future.

[3] **They that are Christ's have the Covenant of Faith, and promises thereof theirs, only in Christ.** Of the covenant, as it was renewed to Abraham, Paul says that it was confirmed of God in Christ.[743] How confirmed in Christ? Answer: in several ways, especially three ways (as Pareus well expounds it)[744] namely: {1} in that it should at last be ratified by the death of Christ as testator (Hebrews 9:15). {2} In that the blessings promised to Abraham and his seed could not be obtained without the merit of Christ's death intervening, by reason of God's justice that admits not of a Covenant of Grace with sinners without satisfaction first for sin. (iii) In that the benefits promised – adoption, justification, sanctification, the inheritance of eternal

---

[739] Psalm 106:4 "the phrase *good will towards thy people,* is to be understood passively of that love which God graciously bears to his elect." John Calvin, commentary on Psalm 106:4
[740] Galatians 3:29
[741] 2 Peter 1:4 with Galatians 3:22 & Hebrews 9:15
[742] 1 Timothy 4:8
[743] Galatians 3:17
[744] David Pareus, Commentary on Galatians 3:17

life – should not be given to Abraham and his seed, but by faith in Christ; then to be exhibited afterwards, now exhibited already. And of the promises, the same Paul elsewhere affirms, that *all the promises of God, in him are yea, and in him amen.*[745] God's promises are all yea and amen: that is, not yea and nay; not one while true, and another while false: but yea and amen, always true. In whom? In him: that is, in Christ Jesus, as the series of the context carries it. How are all the promises yea and amen in Christ?

Calvin thus resolves: "(i) Promises are testimonies of fatherly love. Now, God is not a gracious father to us but in Christ. (ii) We are not fit to partake in God's promises until we obtain remission of sins, which we compass only by Christ. (iii) The promise of adoption, which is the greatest of all, is only made in Christ the root of our adoption."[746] So he.

I add further: what if we say all God's promises are yea and amen, certainty and truth in Christ, forasmuch as they are, (i) *accomplished principally in Christ's person*, the chief center of them all? For all the promises are like the wise-men's star, that one way or another lead to Christ. (ii) *Established by his passion*, Christ as testator confirming his will and testament together with all the promises and bequests thereof by his blood.[747] (iii) *Communicated only to persons in union to Christ.* For as all mankind were united in Adam, when God made the Covenant of Works with them; so all the elect – broken and scattered by Adam's fall – are looked upon as reunited and gathered together again in one in Christ the last Adam when God makes his Covenant of Faith with them.

(i) That in Christ all are gathered together in one, is evident: *That in the dispensation of the fulness of times, he might gather together in one, all things in Christ, both which are in heaven, and which are on earth, even in him.*[748] To this effect, it is said again: *There is neither Jew nor Greek, there is neither bond nor free, there is neither male nor female: for ye are all one in Christ Jesus.*[749]

---

[745] 2 Corinthians 1:20
[746] John Calvin, Commentary on 2 Corinthians 1:20
[747] Hebrews 9:16-17, etc.
[748] Ephesians 1:10
[749] Galatians 3:26

Yea such is this union or oneness that Christ's church and body mystical is called Christ: head and members but one Christ, for *as the body is one, and has many members; and all the members of that one body, being many, are one body: so also is Christ.*[750] That is, Christ mystical, not Christ personal.

(ii) And that when God makes his Covenant of Faith and his promises with his people, he looks upon them all as one in Christ, either intentionally by election, or actually by vocation, and so covenants with them, as is evident: *Now to Abraham and his seed were the promises made. He saith not, and to seeds as of many; but as of one, and to thy seed, which is Christ. And this I say, that the covenant that was confirmed before of God in Christ,*[751] etc. Here the apostle shows that the covenant and promises were made, not to many, but only to one seed: and that this one seed, is Christ. Understand here the word {*Christ*} not *distributively*, as intending only Christ's person; but *collectively*, as comprehending Christ's mystical body, head, and members. Eminently and primarily, Christ the head; secondarily, his church the body. Thus, they that are Christ's have the Covenant of Faith, and promises thereof theirs, only in Christ.

(iii) *God's Covenant of Faith and promises thereof are first made to Christ, and then to his seed in him.* This must needs be so, for: {1} seeing the covenant and promises are made to them that are Christ's – only in Christ, and for his sake – consequently they are first made to Christ, and that both in respect of order, nature, and causality, and then afterwards unto them. For, the effect must succeed the cause in these respects. {2} God's decree of election, and his execution of that decree in all the branches of it, have first respect to Christ, and then secondarily in him to all his seed: and therefore proportionably God's Covenant and promises, being one branch of this execution of God's decree, must first respect Christ, then Christ's seed. Consider well: if we look at God's decree, is not Christ as head and mediator, first of all elected, and then his seed in him?[752] If we look at the execution of God's decree, is not Christ first

---

[750] 1 Corinthians 12:12
[751] Galatians 3:16-17
[752] 1 Peter 1:20 with Ephesians 1:4-5

accepted as God's only beloved Son, and then his seed adopted in him?[753] Is not Christ first justified, that is, acquitted from the guilt of all the sins of his people imputed to him, and then they justified by faith in him?[754] Is not Christ first sanctified, filled with the Spirit, made full of grace and truth, having all fullness dwelling in him: and then all his seed sanctified in him, receiving of his spirit, and of his fullness, even grace for grace?[755] Is not Christ first made heir of all things; and then his seed coheirs with him?[756] Did not Christ as a public person first die, and then all his seed die and suffer in him?[757] Did not Christ first rise from the dead, ascend into heaven, and sit on God's right hand, and then afterwards all that are Christ's rise again, ascend into heaven, and sit on God's right hand, in and with Christ?[758] Shall not Christ first come to judge the world, and then they that are Christ's shall judge the world with him?[759] Why then should it be thought strange that the covenant and promises should first be made to Christ, and then in Christ to all his seed?

(3) **The Scriptures plainly testify that the Covenant of Faith and promises are made unto Christ, as well as to his seed.** This is evident in several periods of this federal administration. As:

[1] In that grandmother-promise, that first promise after Adam's fall *I will put enmity between thee and the woman, and between thy seed and her seed: it shall bruise thy head, and thou shalt bruise his heel.*[760] Here the woman's seed collectively comprehends Christ and all his elect; the serpent's seed, all the children of Satan. But to whom was this first promise made? Not to the serpent or Satan, for though it was immediately spoken to the serpent, yet it was directed to him as a threatening not as a promise. Not to Adam nor to his wife, for herein God directs not his speech to them at all, but only to the

---

[753] Matthew 3:17 with Ephesians 1:5-6
[754] John 16:10, 1 Timothy 3:16, Romans 8:3-4; 4:25; 5:1
[755] John 10:36, 3-4; 1:14, 16; 1 Corinthians 1:30
[756] Hebrews 1:2, Galatians 4:7, Romans 8:16-17, 29
[757] Isaiah 53:4-6, etc., Hebrews 9:12-16, 26, 28
[758] 1 Corinthians 15:20-23, John 14:2-3, 17:24, Hebrews 8:1 with Revelation 3:21
[759] Matthew 25:31-32, etc., Jude 14-15, 1 Corinthians 6:2-4, Revelation 2:26-27
[760] Genesis 3:15

serpent; they are variously spoken to afterwards, as is clear to him that heedfully observes the text[761] – and as yet they were incapable of the promise of grace, no course being taken as yet for satisfaction of divine justice for their sins, to whom then could this promise be made but unto Christ, and to his elect in him?

[2] In the Lord's renewing of covenant with Abraham, the covenant and promises were made to Christ, as the apostle testifies plainly, *Now to Abraham and his seed were the promises made. He saith not, and to seeds, as of many; but as of one, and to thy seed, which is Christ. And this I say, that, the covenant which was confirmed before of God in Christ.*[762] The Greek has it {εις χριστον}, namely, {*unto Christ*} or {*towards Christ*}, which we translate {*in Christ*}. That is, the covenant made with Abraham, tends to Christ, carries and leads us to Christ alone, as in whom the spiritual seed of Abraham should be gathered into one, both out of Jews and Gentiles; as Beza excellently interprets it,[763] And Paul says further: *The law was added because of transgressions, till the seed should come, to whom the promise was made.*[764]

[3] In the days of David and the prophets, many eminent promises of the Covenant of Faith are made and directed by God to Christ so personally, and individually, and that in the second person, that it puts this whole matter quite out of question. As, promises touching Christ's priesthood: *The Lord hath sworn, and will not repent, thou art a priest forever after the order of Melchizedek.*[765] Promises touching his kingship, *The LORD said unto my LORD, sit thou at my right hand, till I make thine enemies thy footstool. The LORD shall send the rod of thy strength out of Sion: rule thou in the midst of thine enemies. Thy people shall be willing in the day of thy power, in the beauties of holiness, from the womb of the morning: thou hast the dew of thy youth.*[766] Promises touching the calling of the Gentiles, etc. *I will declare the*

---

[761] Genesis 3:16-20
[762] Galatians 3:16-17
[763] Beza's Annotations on Galatians 3:17
[764] Galatians 3:19
[765] Psalm 110:4
[766] Psalm 110:1-3

decree, the LORD hath said unto me, thou art my son, this day have I begotten thee. Ask of me, and I shall give thee the heathen for thine inheritance, and the uttermost parts of the earth for thy possession,[767] *etc. I the LORD have called thee in righteousness, and will hold thine hand, and will keep thee, and will give thee for a covenant of the people, for a light of the Gentiles: to open the blind eyes, to bring out the prisoners from the prison, and them that sit in darkness out of the prison house.*[768] *And he said, it is a light thing that thou shouldst be my servant to raise up the tribes of Jacob, and to restore the preserved of Israel: I will also give thee for a light to the Gentiles, that thou mayest be my salvation to the end of the earth; In an acceptable time have I heard thee, and in a day of salvation have I helped thee: and I will preserve thee, and give thee for a covenant of the people, to establish the earth, to cause to inherit the desolate heritages.*[769]

By these and like particulars, it is evident that the Covenant of Faith and promises are personally directed and made to Christ himself as well as to his seed. How then are they made unto Christ? They are either made to him primarily before them, or secondarily after them, or equally with them. Not secondarily after them, for that were to prefer the body before the head. Not equally with them, for that would be to equalize the body to the head. Both of which are extremely absurd: the head Christ so incomparably transcending his mystical body. Therefore it remains clear that the Covenant of Faith and promises thereof are made primarily to Christ, and secondarily to his seed in him.

[4] Finally, to this truth – that the covenant and promises are first made to Christ, and then to his seed in him – the judgments of pious and learned men subscribe. And though this be not so generally spoken to, yet so many and considerable authors express themselves clearly in it, that we are not to look

---

[767] Psalm 2:7-9
[768] Isaiah 42:6-7
[769] Isaiah 49:6-9

upon it as an odd, singular, novel opinion. As {1} particular writers, and {2} the whole national assembly of divines.[770]

{1} Perkins writes, "It is here to be observed, that the promises made to Abraham, are first made to Christ, and then in Christ to all that believe in him, be they Jews or Gentiles." This conclusion is of great use.

(i) First, by it we learn the difference between the promises of the Law and the Gospel. The promises of the law are directed and made to the person of every man particularly; the promises of the gospel are first directed and made to Christ, and then by consequence unto them that are by faith engrafted into Christ.

(ii) Secondly, by this we learn to acknowledge the communion that is between Christ and us. Christ as mediator is first of all elected, and we in him: Christ is first justified, that is, acquitted of our sins, and we justified in him. He is heir of the world, and we heirs in him. He died upon the cross not as a private person but as a public person representing all the elect, and all the elect died in him and with him. In the same manner, they rise with him to life and sit at the right hand of God with him in glory.

(iii) Thirdly, here we see the ground of the certainty of perseverance of all them that are the true children of God. For the office of Christ, to which he is set apart, is to receive the promise of God for us and to apply it unto us. And this work is done by Christ without impediment and without repentance on his part.

(iv) Lastly, here is comfort against the consideration of our unworthiness. "Thou sayest, thou art unworthy of the mercy of God, and therefore hast no hope. And I say again, Lost thou truly exercise thyself in the spiritual exercises of faith, invocation, repentance? Be not discouraged; Thou must not receive the promise immediately of God, but Christ must do it for thee," etc.[771]

---

[770] "Q. With whom was the covenant of grace made? A. The covenant of grace was made with Christ as the second Adam, and in him with all the elect as his seed." Galatians 3:16, Romans 5:15 to the end, Isaiah 50:10-11. So the Assembly, in the Larger Catechism, Question 31.
[771] Mr. William Perkins on Galatians 3:16

Preston writes: "It is said, the promise is made to the seed, yet the promise is made to us; and yet again, the Covenant is made with Abraham. How can all these stand together?

Answer: The promises that are made to the seed, that is, to Christ himself, those are these promises: *Thou shall be a priest for ever; And I will give thee the kingdom of David; thou shalt sit on that throne; thou shalt be a prince of peace, and the government shall be upon thy shoulders.* Likewise, *Thou shalt be a prophet to my people, thou shalt open the prison to the Captive, Thou shalt be anointed*, etc., and, *Thou shalt go and preach to them.* These are the promises that are made unto the seed. The promises that are made to us, though they be of the same covenant, yet they differ in this: the active part is committed to the Messiah, to the seed itself; but the passive part, those are promises that are made to us: *you shall be taught, you shall be made prophets; likewise, you shall have your sins forgiven, you shall have the effect of his priesthood made good unto you; you shall be subject to his government by an inherent righteousness that he shall work in you, for you shall be made kings.* So the promise is made to us. How is the promise made to Abraham? For it is said, *In thee all the nations of the earth shall be blessed.* The meaning of it is that they are derivative promises. The primitive and original was made to Jesus Christ. There was none that ever was partaker of the promises, but the children of Abraham; and therefore they were derived from Abraham to all the men in the world besides, that ever have been since."[772]

Edward Reynolds writes: "Promises are the efficient causes of our purification as they are the rays and beams of Christ the Sun of Righteousness, in whom they are all founded and established. *They are all in him yea, and in him amen* (2 Corinthians 1:20). Every promise by faith apprehended carries a man to Christ, and to the consideration of our unity with him, in the right whereof we have claim to the promises, even as every line in a circumference, though there never so distant from others, does, being pursued, carry a man at last to one and the same center, common unto them all. For the promises are

---

[772] D. Preston of the New Covenant. p. 387, 388. Lond. 1634

not made for any thing in us, nor have their stability in us; but they are made in and for Christ unto us; unto Christ on our behalf, and unto us only so far forth as we are members of Christ. For they were not made to *seeds*, as many; but to *seed*, namely, to Christ, in aggregate, as comprehending the head and the members in the unity of one Body (Galatians 3:16)."[773]

{2} The national assembly of divines: "Q. With whom was the covenant of grace made? A. The covenant of grace was made with Christ as the second Adam, and in him with all the elect as his seed (Galatians 3:16, Romans 5:15 to the end, Isaiah 50:10-11)."[774]

(4) *As the covenant-breaking disobedience of the first Adam involved all his seed with himself in sin and death: so the covenant-keeping obedience of the last Adam, restored all his seed with himself to righteousness and life.*

This the apostle demonstrates at large in Romans 5. Especially in these words: *As by the offense of one judgment came upon all men to condemnation: even so by the righteousness of one, the free gift came upon all men to justification of life. For, as by one man's disobedience many were made sinners: so by the obedience of one shall many be made righteous.*[775] Here Adam's *all* are called his *many*, and Christ's *many* are called his *all*. And though there be some similitude between the event and efficacy of Adam's disobedience, unto his seed; and of Christ's obedience, unto his: yet there is also much dissimilitude. For the efficacy of Christ's obedience incomparably transcends and surpasses the efficacy of Adam's disobedience.[776] Partly in that Christ's obedience saves; Adam's disobedience condemns. Now a thousand fold more efficacy is required to saving, than to damning. Partly in that the sin of Adam condemning his posterity was but one, but the free gift of righteousness by

---

[773] Caput & Corpus Unus est Christus. Aug; Mr. Reynolds in his *Sinfulness of Sin. pag. 345. Lond. 1631.*
[774] Westminster Larger Catechism, Question 31
[775] Romans 5:18-19
[776] Weigh well Romans 5:15-17

Christ justifying his posterity absolves them from many offenses, and not only from that one sin of Adam. And this is much more.

Thus it is evident that: **as Adam – and in him all his natural seed – were a joint-party to the Covenant of Works, before the fall, so Jesus Christ – and in him all his supernatural seed – are a joint-party to the Covenant of Faith, after the fall.**

Section 3

The matter of this Covenant of Faith, comes next to be considered. Which is: the recovery of Christ's seed from the state of sin and death into the state of righteousness and eternal life by Christ, that in him the Lord may be their God, and they his people; they accepting him and these covenanted mercies by true faith, and walking worthy of them according to the gospel. This is the substance and matter of this Covenant, touching which God makes agreement with Christ the last Adam, and in him with all his seed.

For the more distinct unfolding of this excellent mystery, observe, {1} that *in general*, the matter of this Covenant, is the recovery or restoration of Christ's seed, the elect, after their fall in Adam. {2} That *in particular*, touching this recovery and in order to the effecting thereof, the matters agreed upon and covenanted are of two sorts, namely: (i) matters agreed upon and covenanted between God and Jesus Christ the last Adam; (ii) matters agreed upon and covenanted between God and the seed of Christ in him; (iii) matters covenanted and agreed upon in that blessed and heavenly transaction between God the Father, and Jesus Christ the last Adam, touching the recovery of his seed, are in order of nature antecedaneous to the other between God and his seed, as the foundation thereof, and therefore are first to be cleared. And they are either, (a) matters covenanted and promised to Christ, on the part of God the Father, or (b) matters restipulated to God the Father, on the part of Jesus Christ. Formerly, it has been shown that God covenants with Christ, and in him only with his seed, as a joint-party; now is to be declared, *what God covenants with Christ, as well as with his seed; and Christ with God*. Writers are generally silent about this mysterious transaction: but Scriptures are very pregnant and evident.

(i) Matters agreed upon and covenanted between God and Jesus Christ the last Adam

(1) God the Father, on his part, covenants and promises to Jesus Christ the last Adam, in order to the recovery of his seed, many things, yea all things requisite thereunto.

To enumerate all, how impossible! Yet take a taste in these five particulars following, namely, God the Father promises to Christ the last Adam, in order to the recovery of his seed: [1] to invest him with a mediatory office to that end, [2] to accept him in his office, [3] to assist, support, encourage and protect him in the execution of his office, [4] to exalt him most gloriously, after all his abasement undergone by reason of his office, and [5] to prosper and crown him with full success in recovering all his seed.

[1] God promises to invest Christ with a mediatory office

To invest Christ with a mediatory office, whereby he should mediate with God for his seed and their recovery: {1} as a priest, {2} as a prophet, and {3} as a king.

{1} *As a priest.* For, God says to Christ: *The LORD hath sworn, and will not repent; thou art a priest forever after the order of Melchizedek.*[777] Here God promises to Christ an excellent and eternal priesthood.

Objection: The word {*art*} is of the present, not future tense; and therefore promises not what Christ should be for future, but onely declares what Christ is for present.

Answer: This objection in no way evinces this to be no promise. For,

---

[777] Psalm 110:4

(i) This word {*art*} is not in the Hebrew original, and therefore it is printed in a distinct character. The Hebrew is, *Thou a priest*, etc. That is, *Thou shalt be a priest forever* - it being the manner of the Hebrew tongue, sometimes for brevity's sake to leave out a word, which is to be understood, and supplied.

(ii) Though the word {*art*} were in the original, yet this passage were a promise; because the matter spoken of, was (*de bono futuro*) not fulfilled then at present, but to be fulfilled for future. And, when future good is assured though in words of the present tense, it is a promise. This then is God's sure and irrevocable promise to Christ touching that excellent and eternal priesthood, whereby the recovery of his seed was to be meritoriously obtained. The chief acts of the priest's office, and so of Christ's function as priest, are, (a) oblation, and (b) intercession.

Christ offered himself without spot to God, for purging away the sins of his elect once for all: obtaining perfect remission of them forever.[778] And as he prayed for his seed while he was on earth,[779] so *he ever liveth to make intercession for them in heaven*[780] (appearing in the presence of God for them, as their advocate with the Father).[781] This priestly office of Christ is (a) *sure*: because confirmed with God's oath as well as his promise.[782] The promise makes it sure: the oath double sure.[783] (b) *Irrevocable*: the Lord will never repent of this promise and oath. (c) *Excellent*: far surpassing Aaron's order, even of Melchizedek's order, who being King of Righteousness, and then king of Salem, that is, King of Peace, was also priest of the most high God, and so had a royal priesthood.[784] (d) *Everlasting*: a priest forever having (as Melchizedek) an everlasting and unchangeable priesthood: and therefore *being able to save to the uttermost them that come unto God by* him.[785]

---

[778] Hebrews 9:14 & 10:12-19
[779] John 17:20 to the end
[780] Hebrews 7:25
[781] John 17:20 to the end
[782] Hebrews 7:20-21
[783] Hebrews 6:17
[784] Hebrews 7:1-3, etc.
[785] Hebrews 7:16-17, 24-25

{2} *As a prophet*. For the Lord promises thus to Christ; *I the LORD have called thee in righteousness, and will hold thine hand, and will keep thee, and will give thee for a covenant of the people, for a light of the Gentiles: to open the blind eyes, to bring out the prisoners from the prison, and them that sit in darkness out of the prison-house.*[786] Thus God promises to invest him with a prophetic office for opening the eyes of the blind. Christ as a priest purchases and obtains for his seed the recovery that they lacked; Christ as prophet reveals to his seed recovery purchased. This he does, (i) *instrumentally* by his word proclaiming this mystery to them, and (ii) *efficaciously* by his Spirit opening and enlightening their minds and hearts to comprehend it. And Christ by the prophet acknowledges this, *The Lord God hath given me the tongue of the learned, that I should know how to speak a word in season to him that is weary, he wakens morning by morning: he awakens mine ear to hear as the learned.*[787]

{3} *As a king*. For, thus the Father promises to Christ: *Yet have I set my king upon my holy hill of Zion. I will declare the decree: the Lord hath said unto me, thou art my Son, this day have I begotten thee. Ask of me, and I shall give thee the heathen for thine inheritance, and the uttermost parts of the earth for thy possession. Thou shalt break them with a rod of iron, thou shalt dash them in pieces like a potter's vessel.*[788] In these words see, how the Lord in a promissory way, (i) anoints Christ as Zion's king, his church's king, in spite of all his enemies' rage and opposition; (ii) approves and establishes this king by firm decree; (iii) extends his dominion to the Gentiles; and (iv) declares the power of this government against his enemies, whom his iron rod shall incurably break and dash in pieces like a potter's vessel. And elsewhere: *The LORD said unto my LORD, sit thou at my right hand, until I make thine enemies thy footstool. The LORD shall send the rod of thy strength out of Zion: rule thou in the midst of thine enemies. Thy people shall be willing in the day of*

---

[786] Isaiah 42:6-7
[787] Isaiah 50:4
[788] Psalm 2:6-9 with Revelation 2:26-27 & 19:15

thy power.—The LORD at thy right hand shall strike through kings in the day of his wrath. He shall judge among the heathen, he shall fill the places with dead bodies: he shall wound the heads over many countries.[789] Here the Father promises to Christ, in reference to his kingly office: (i) most glorious enthronement (namely, after his resurrection) at his right hand. (ii) Continued reign there until all his enemies be utterly subdued. (iii) A strong scepter, to be sent out of Zion, namely, Christ's powerful word and Spirit, wherewith he shall exercise his regal dominion. (iv) The effect of this his kingly rule, subduing his own to willing obedience, but crushing his enemies, even the greatest heads and rulers in the world that oppose him, with utter destruction.

Thus Christ meritoriously purchases recovery for his seed as a *priest*, clearly reveals this recovery purchased as a *prophet*, and effectually applies to his seed this recovery purchased and revealed as a *king*. Thus the Father covenants with Christ to invest him with a mediatory office of priest, prophet, and king, for the recovery of his seed.

[2] God promises to accept Christ in this his mediatory office

To accept Christ in this his mediatory office: according to that of Isaiah. *Thus saith the LORD, the redeemer of Israel, and his holy one, to him whom man despises, to him whom the nation abhorreth, to a servant of rulers, kings shall see and arise, princes also shall worship, because of the LORD that is faithful, and the holy one of Israel, and he shall choose thee. Thus saith the LORD, in an acceptable time have I heard thee, and in a day of salvation have I helped thee; and I will preserve thee and give thee for a covenant of the people, to establish the earth, and to cause to inherit the desolate heritages.*[790] Yea, Christ in his office is so acceptable to God, that he promises his soul shall delight in him, and consequently in his seed for his sake: *Behold my servant whom I uphold, mine elect in whom my soul delighteth: I have put my Spirit*

---

[789] Psalm 110:1-3, 5-6
[790] Isaiah 49:7-8

upon him, he shall bring forth judgment to the Gentiles.[791] *It came to pass, that Jesus being baptized, and praying, the heaven was opened; and the Holy Ghost descended in a bodily shape like a dove upon him; and a voice came from heaven, which said, Thou art my beloved Son, in thee I am well pleased.*[792]

[3] God promises to assist, support, comfort and protect Jesus Christ in the execution and fulfilling of his office, for the recovery of his seed.

And that especially in three ways, namely:

{1} *Against the utmost extremity of all his sufferings,* that should be inflicted upon him for all the sins of his seed, which sufferings were most numerous and grievous. *Thus saith God the LORD, he that created the heavens, and stretched them out; he that spread forth the earth, and that which comes out of it; he that gives breath unto the people upon it, and spirit to them that walk therein: I the Lord have called thee in righteousness, and will hold thine hand, and will keep thee, and will give thee for a covenant of the people, for a light of the Gentiles,*[793] etc. Here God assures Christ, from his wonderful creation, preservation and government of all things, that he will strengthen, preserve and stand by him in all his mediatory administrations, for recovery of his seed, whether Jews or Gentiles, from the darkness and bondage of sin and death. And Christ himself is brought in, by the prophet, acknowledging thus much, saying; *Listen O isles unto me, and hearken ye people from far; the LORD hath called me from the womb, from the bowels of my mother hath he made mention of my name. And he hath made my mouth like a sharp sword. In the shadow of his hand hath he hid me, and made me a polished shaft, in his quiver hath he hid me; and said unto me, thou art my servant O Israel, in whom I will be glorified.*[794]

---

[791] Isaiah 42:1
[792] Luke 3:21-22
[793] Isaiah 42:5-7
[794] Isaiah 49:1-3

{2} *Against all oppositions and enemies.* To this effect God promises to Christ that he will set up his kingdom in Zion, and extend it even to the Gentiles, notwithstanding all the rage, plots, insurrections, and combinations of Gentiles, Jews, kings of the earth and rulers against him. The Lord meanwhile deriding them, and threatening to destroy them.

{3} *Against all his deepest discouragements,* which he should meet with in the discharge of his function. As, *Then I said, I have labored in vain, I have spent my strength for nought, and in vain: yet surely my judgment is with the LORD, and my work with my God. And now saith the LORD that formed me from the womb to be his servant, to bring Jacob again to him, though Israel be not gathered, yet shall I be glorious in the eyes of the LORD, and my God shall be my strength. And he said, it is a light thing that thou shouldst be my servant to raise up the tribes of Jacob, and to restore the preserved of Israel: I will also give thee for a light to the Gentiles, that thou mayest be my salvation to the end of the earth.*[795] Here Christ is brought in lamenting and complaining of the Jews' contumacy and obstinacy, refusing to be gathered, and as it were rendering his office vain. And against this great discouragement, he is supported: (i) from the testimony of his own conscience in the sight of God, that he has faithfully discharged his office; (ii) from God's acceptance promised him notwithstanding; whatever the world may judge, he should be glorious in the eyes of the Lord; (iii) from God's power and virtue which notwithstanding should be manifest in him, and (iv) from the surpassing success of his office promised for gathering and gaining even of the Gentiles.

---

[795] Isaiah 49:4-6

[4] God promises to exalt Christ gloriously, after he had been debased ignominiously: his mediatory office being put in execution both in his humiliation and exaltation.

Now God the Father covenants with Christ, to exalt him gloriously in his, {1} resurrection from the dead; {2} ascension into heaven; {3} session at God's right hand.

{1} In his resurrection from the dead: *I will declare the decree, the LORD hath said unto me; Thou art my son, this day have I begotten thee.*[796] Which Scripture the apostle Paul interprets as a promise of Christ's resurrection, saying; *God hath fulfilled the same unto us their children, in that he hath raised up Jesus again, as it is also written in the second psalm, thou art my son, this day have I begotten thee.*[797] Christ in his resurrection was begotten and brought forth of the womb of the earth. And Christ elsewhere singularly comforts himself against death and grave, by God's promise of his resurrection.[798]

{2} In his ascension into heaven after his resurrection. For thus God speaks to Christ by his spirit, touching his ascension: *Thou hast ascended up on high; thou hast led captivity captive; thou hast received gifts for men; yea for the rebellious also, that the LORD God might dwell among them.*[799] This the apostle Paul expounds peculiarly of Christ's ascension into heaven, and of the benefits of that his ascension to his church.[800]

{3} In his session or sitting on God's right hand in the highest heavens, after his ascension. For thus the Father promises to Christ: *The LORD said unto my Lord, sit thou at my right hand, until I make thine enemies thy footstool.*[801] That is, *thou shalt sit on my right hand till then.* It is God's promise, not to David, but to Christ, David's Lord, as Peter in his sermon on

---

[796] Psalm 2:7
[797] Acts 13:32-33
[798] Psalm 16:8-11, compared with Acts 2:25-32, 13:35-37
[799] Psalm 68:18
[800] Ephesians 4:7-12, etc.
[801] Psalm 110:1

the day of Pentecost testifies.⁸⁰² Thus God promised to Christ, glorious exaltation in these three eminent degrees of his *resurrection, ascension,* and *sitting at God's right hand*: all which tended much to the completing of his elect's recovery: for as Christ *died for their sins; so he rose again for their justification*;⁸⁰³ ascended that he might *captivate captivity, give gifts to men,*⁸⁰⁴ pour forth his Spirit upon them, and *prepare a place for them*:⁸⁰⁵ and he sits at God's right hand that he may continually intercede and appear for his people,⁸⁰⁶ gather and govern all his seed,⁸⁰⁷ and utterly destroy all his and their enemies.⁸⁰⁸

[5] <u>*God promises to prosper Christ in his office, and crown him with full success therein, for the recovering of all his seed, whether among Jews or Gentiles.*</u>

The LORD shall send the rod of thy strength out of Zion; (here's his office, exercised by the powerful scepter of his word and Spirit sent from Zion, abroad into the world) *rule thou in the midst of thine enemies. Thy people shall be willing in the day of thy power, in the beauties of holiness, from the womb of the morning: thou hast the dew of thy youth.*⁸⁰⁹ Here's the success of his office promised, both in his victorious subduing of his enemies, in the cheerful willingness of his subjects, and in the wonderful numerousness of his people won unto him, even like the innumerable drops of the morning dew. Again, the Lord said to him: *Thou art my son, this day have I begotten thee. Ask of me, and I shall give thee the heathen for thine inheritance, and the uttermost parts of the earth for thy possession. Thou shalt break them with a rod of iron, thou*

---

[802] Acts 2:34-35
[803] Romans 4:25
[804] Ephesians 4:7-9
[805] John 14:2-3
[806] Hebrews 7:25 & 9:24
[807] Psalm 110:1-3
[808] Psalm 110:1, 1 Corinthians 15:24-26
[809] Psalm 110:2-3

shalt dash them in pieces like a potter's vessel.[810] Here the Father promises to the Son upon his resurrection and intercession the Gentiles for his spiritual inheritance and possession, and that his enemies amongst them shall be broken and destroyed by him. And yet more fully: *I the LORD have called thee in righteousness, and will hold thine hand and keep thee, and give thee for a covenant of the people, for a light of the Gentiles. To open the blind eyes, to bring out the prisoners from the prison, and them that sit in darkness out of the prison-house.*[811] *And he said, it is a light thing that thou shouldst be my servant to raise up the tribes of Jacob, and to restore the preserved of Israel: I will also give thee for a light to the Gentiles, that thou mayest be my salvation to the end of the earth. Thus saith the LORD, the redeèmer of Israel, and his holy one, to him whom man despiseth, to him whom the nation abhorreth, to a servant of rulers, kings shall see and arise, princes also shall worship, because of the LORD that is faithful, and the holy one of Israel, and he shall choose thee. Thus saith the LORD, in an acceptable time have I heard thee, and in the day of salvation have I helped thee; and I will preserve thee, and give thee for a covenant of the people, to establish the earth, to cause to inherit the desolate heritages; that thou mayest say to the prisoners, go forth: to them that are in darkness, shew yourselves: they shall feed in the ways, and their pastures shall be in all high places: they shall not hunger nor thirst, neither shall the heat nor sun smite them: for he that hath mercy on them shall lead them, even by the springs of water shall he guide them. And I will make all my mountains a way, and my high-ways shall be exalted. Behold these shall come from far: and lo, these from the north and from the west: and these from the land of Sinim. Sing O heavens, and be joyful O earth, and break forth into singing o mountains: for God hath*

---

[810] Psalm 2:7-9
[811] Isaiah 42:5-8

comforted his people, and will have mercy upon his afflicted.[812] Thus the Father promised complete success to Christ in his mediatory office for recovery of his seed, according to that, *When thou shalt make his soul an offering for sin, he shall see his seed, he shall prolong his days, and the pleasure of the Lord shall prosper in his hand. He shall see of the travel of his soul, and shall be satisfied: by his knowledge shall my righteous servant justify many: for he shall bear their iniquities.*[813]

These things God the Father covenants and promises on his part to Jesus Christ the last Adam.

(2) *Jesus Christ the last Adam restipulates and re-promises on his part to God the Father several things.*

Especially these two, namely: [1] cheerfully and faithfully to accept, undertake and discharge this mediatory office imposed upon him by the Father, in order to the recovery of his seed, the elect. *Wherefore, when he comes into the world he saith; sacrifice and offering thou didst not desire, mine ears hast thou opened: (or as the apostle; but a body hast thou prepared me:) burnt-offering and sin-offering hast thou not required. Then said I, lo, I come: in the volume of the book it is written of me: I delight to do thy will O my God: yea, thy law is within my heart. I have preached righteousness in the great congregation: lo, I have not refrained my lips, O LORD, thou knowest. I have not hid thy righteousness within mine heart, I have declared thy faithfulness*

---

[812] Isaiah 49:6-14. Upon this text Calvin speaks excellently: "[W]hat the Prophet adds, I will give thee to be a covenant, is applicable to no other than Christ. How shall we reconcile these statements? By considering that Christ is not so much his own as ours; for he neither came, nor died, nor rose again for himself. He was sent for the salvation of the Church, and seeks nothing as his own; for he has no want of anything. Accordingly, God makes promises to the whole body of the Church. Christ, who occupies the place of Mediator, receives these promises, and does not plead on behalf of himself as an individual, but of the whole Church, for whose salvation he was sent."

[813] Isaiah 53:10-12

and thy salvation: I have not concealed thy loving kindness and thy truth from the great congregation.[814]

Here Christ restipulates cheerfully to accept and execute his priestly office, in offering himself up a sacrifice once for all to take away his people's sins, as the apostle plainly expounds it, and his prophetic office in preaching God's righteousness, faithfulness, salvation, loving-kindness and truth to his church. And elsewhere, Christ declares this his acceptance of his office, saying; *The Spirit of the LORD God is upon me, because the LORD hath anointed me to preach good tidings unto the meek, he hath sent me to bind up the broken-hearted, to proclaim liberty to the captives, and the opening of the prison to them that are bound: to proclaim the acceptable year of the LORD, and the day of vengeance of our God, to comfort all that mourn: to appoint unto them that mourn in Sion, to give unto them beauty for ashes, the oil of joy for mourning, the garment of praise for the spirit of heaviness, that they might be called the trees of righteousness, the planting of the LORD, that he might be glorified.* Jesus Christ, reading this Scripture on a sabbath-day in the synagogue of Nazareth, when he had closed the book, *began to say unto them, This day is this Scripture fulfilled in your ears.*[815]

[2] Fully to depend and rely upon his heavenly Father for acceptance, assistance and protection in the execution of his office, notwithstanding extremist oppositions, deepest difficulties and distresses. To this effect, Christ, in the prophet, says: *The LORD God hath opened mine ear, and I was not rebellious, neither turned away back. I gave my back to the smiters, and my cheeks to them that plucked off the hair: I hid not my face from shame and spitting. For the LORD God will help me, therefore shall I not be confounded: therefore have I set my face like a flint, and I know that I shall not be ashamed. He is near that justifies me, who will contend with me? Let us stand together; who is mine adversary? Let him come near to me. Behold the LORD God will help me, who is he that shall condemn me? Lo they all shall wax old as a*

---

[814] Compare Psalm 40:6-11 with Hebrews 10:5-11
[815] Isaiah 61:1-3 with Luke 4:18-21

garment: the moth shall eat them up.[816] Thus Christ declares his confidence in God's assistance and acceptance even in his sharpest sufferings. And elsewhere, he is brought in as it were victoriously triumphing against death itself, through his hope of resurrection and glory. *I have set the LORD always before me: because he is at my right hand, I shall not be moved. Therefore my heart is glad, and my glory rejoiceth: my flesh also shall rest in hope. For thou wilt not leave my soul in hell; neither wilt thou suffer thine holy one to see corruption. Thou wilt shew me the path of life: in thy presence is fullness of joy, at thy right hand are pleasures forevermore.*[817]

This is that blessed transaction between God the Father and Jesus Christ, and these are a taste of those precious matters covenanted and agreed upon between them, in order to the recovery of Christ's seed.

(ii) **Matters covenanted and agreed upon, between God and Christ's seed in Christ the last Adam, fall next into consideration.**

And they are either, (1) covenanted and promised by God, or (2) required of and restipulated by Christ's seed in him.

God on his part covenants and promises to Christ's seed in him, several admirable sublime and transcendent benefits. But especially, [1] what God will do in Christ, for Christ's seed, namely: recover them out of a state of sin and death, into a state of righteousness and eternal life. [2] What God will be in Christ, to Christ's seed, namely: he will be to them a God.

[1] *The Lord covenants what he will do for Christ's seed.* He will recover them, etc. Herein note: {1} the benefit or mercy promised, and {2} the object to whom this mercy is peculiarly intended.

---

[816] Isaiah 50:5-9
[817] Psalm 16:8-11 compared with Acts 2:25-28, etc.

{1} **The mercy itself promised**, recovery, etc., may be considered: (i) *more generally*, and (ii) *more particularly*.

(i) More generally, thus conceive of God's recovery of Christ's seed from sin and death to righteousness and life. The elect of Christ, through Adam's disobedience and breach of the Covenant of Works, are plunged into a state of sin and death, as well as others, as has been shown. But God, that his election might stand inviolably, upon Adam's fall, publishes his Covenant of Faith, wherein he declares his gracious will and pleasure, to restore his elect from sin and death, to righteousness and eternal life. Sin and death comprehend in them man's whole natural misery, and are the term from which righteousness and life eternal comprise in them man's whole supernatural remedy, and are the term to which God will restore his elect, Christ's seed.

(a) That God covenants to recover them from sin to righteousness, is clear. For, *This is the covenant that I will make with them after those days, saith the Lord: I will put my laws into their hearts, and in their minds will I write them: and their sins and iniquities will I remember no more. Now where remission of these is, there is no more offering for sin* (Hebrews 10:16-18). So that, when God remembers sins no more, he remits them. Where God remits sins, there needs no more offerings to expiate and purge them away; God is fully satisfied for such, and so accepts and justifies them. And again it is promised, that: *As by one man's disobedience many were made sinners: so by the obedience of one shall many be made righteous*, (Romans 5:10). Here's recovery promised from guilt of sin, to imputed righteousness by justification. God further covenants: *I will give them one heart, and I will put a new spirit within you: and I will take the stony heart out of their flesh, and will give them an heart of flesh; that they may walk in my statutes, and keep mine ordinances, and do them* (Ezekiel 11:19-20 & 36:25-27). Here's recovery promised from the filth and power of sin to inherent righteousness, by sanctification.

(b) That God also covenants to recover Christ's seed from death to eternal life, is as clear. For he says: *If by one man's offense, death reigned by one: much more they which receive abundance of grace, and of the gift of righteousness, shall reign in life by one, Jesus Christ.* (Romans 5:17, 21)—*that as sin hath reigned unto death; even so might grace reign through righteousness unto eternal life, by Jesus Christ our Lord.* This recovery of Christ's seed from the miserable state of sin and death to the happy state of righteousness and eternal life, seems as it were typically to be shadowed out and promised under Israel's recovery from Egypt's miserable bondage, to Canaan (Genesis 15:13-14, 18, Deuteronomy 5:2-3, 6), and the Jews' return from their woeful captivity in Babylon, unto Zion (Jeremiah 24:5-7).

(ii) *More particularly*, God's recovery of Christ's seed from sin and death to righteousness and life being a most large comprehensive benefit, comprises in it many excellent spiritual blessings. (a) Partly in respect of the impetration of it, for Christ's seed; (b) partly in regard of the application of it, to Christ's seed.

(a) The impetration or obtaining of this recovery for Christ's seed was by redemption. *Redemption* is a recovery of Christ's seed from the bondage of sin, Satan, death and the wrath of God, into the contrary spiritual liberty, by the payment of a just and satisfactory price. Hence those phrases: ye are bought with a price (1 Corinthians 6:20). *Ye were not redeemed with corruptible things, as silver and gold from your vain conversation, but with the precious blood of Christ.*[818] *Who gave himself for us, that he might redeem us from all iniquity.*[819] *Christ hath redeemed us from the curse of the law, being made a curse for us.*[820] In this work of redemption, these matters are worthy of consideration, namely: (1) the mediation of the redeemer Christ, between God and his seed;[821] (2) the satisfaction of this mediator, made to God's justice, by his death, for the sins of all his seed;[822] (3) the meritorious reconciliation of all his seed unto God by this full satisfaction.[823]

(b) *The application of this recovery thus obtained to Christ's seed*, is effected especially by these several steps, or degrees, namely:

---

[818] 1 Peter 1:18-19
[819] Titus 2:14
[820] Galatians 3:13
[821] 1 Timothy 2:5
[822] Romans 3:25, Ephesians 5:2, Hebrews 9:13-14 & 10:11-15
[823] 2 Corinthians 5:19-20, Romans 5:10, Daniel 9:24

(1) *By conviction.* Christ's seed being thoroughly convinced both of their own sin and misery, by nature: and of the sufficient remedy thereof in Christ by grace.[824]

(2) *By conversion.* When they are turned from darkness to light, and from the power of Satan unto God.[825] This conversion, in respect of several notions and considerations, is expressed in Scripture by several names, which for substance import one and the same thing. It is styled: [1] in regard to the newness of condition into which they are brought, *renovation* or *renewing*.[826] [2] In regard to nature's inability, and of the necessity of divine power, to bring them unto this new condition, *new-creation*.[827] [3] In regard to God's way of bringing them into this new state, outwardly by the call of his word as the instrument: inwardly by the call of his spirit as the efficient thereof, *vocation*, or *calling*.[828] [4] In regard to the resemblance that this conversion has with man's natural generation and birth, it's styled *regeneration, new-birth*, or *being born from above*.[829] [5] In respect of their separation from sin, unto holiness of person and conversation, *sanctification*.[830] [6] In regard to divine principles, habits and gracious qualifications infused, the *participation of the divine nature*.[831] [7] Finally to mention no more in regard to their spiritual motion from misery to happiness, it's styled a *transition*, or *passing from death to life*.[832] All these for substance being but conversion.

(3) By *adoption.* Christ's convert seed being admitted and accepted as the adopted sons of God by grace, through Christ the only Son of God by nature.[833] In and with which adoption they receive the privileges of sons, namely: [1] the Spirit of adoption, both crying *Abba Father*, and attesting

---

[824] John 16:8-11
[825] Acts 26:18, Matthew 18:3
[826] Titus 3:5, Romans 12:2
[827] 2 Corinthians 5:17, Ephesians 2:10
[828] Romans 8:30, 1 Corinthians 1:2, 26
[829] Titus 3:5, John 3:3, 5-8 & 1:13
[830] 1 Peter 1:2, 1 Corinthians 6:11, 1 Thessalonians 5:23
[831] 2 Peter 1:4
[832] 1 John 3:14
[833] Galatians 4:4-5, John 1:12, Romans 8:15, Ephesians 1:5

their sonship;[834] [2] son-like liberty and freedom;[835] and [3] heirship to God, co-heirship to Christ.[836]

(4) By *justification*, when God freely remits all their unrighteousness, and accounts their persons righteous, merely for the meritorious and satisfactory obedience of Christ, imputed to them of mere grace, through faith only.[837]

(5) By *donation* of various spiritual privileges, as consequential fruits of conversion, adoption and justification, especially these, namely: [1] peace with God in Christ,[838] [2] joy in the Holy Ghost,[839] [3] diffusion or shedding abroad of God's love in the heart,[840] [4] assurance of a good spiritual state towards God, in Christ,[841] [5] progress and growth in grace,[842] and faithful perseverance,[843] or final constancy in this gracious Christian state unto the death.

(6) Finally, by *glorification*, God completes this recovery of his elect from sin and death to righteousness and life; receiving their *spirits made perfect*,[844] into glory, immediately upon death – and at the last day, raising up their bodies in glorious state to be reunited with their spirits,[845] that so both bodies and souls may meet the Lord coming to judgment,[846] may be openly acquitted when the whole world besides shall be condemned,[847] may with Christ judge both men and angels, and afterwards may ascend with Christ into the highest

---

[834] Galatians 4:6, Romans 8:15-16
[835] Galatians 4:7 & 5:1; John 8:36
[836] Galatians 4:7, Romans 8:17
[837] Romans 3:24-26 & 4-8; 2 Corinthians 5:20-21; Romans 5:16-19 & 4:5-8, 24-25
[838] Romans 5:1
[839] Romans 14:17
[840] Romans 5:5
[841] Romans 8:16, Ephesians 1:13-14, 2 Corinthians 13:5, 1 John 3:24, Hebrews 6:10 & 10:22
[842] 2 Peter 3:18, 2 Thessalonians 1:3, Ephesians 4:15-16
[843] Revelation 2:10, 1 Peter 1:5, John 10:27-29, Romans 8:38-39
[844] Acts 7:59, Hebrews 12:23, Luke 2:3, 43; Philippians 1:23
[845] 1 Thessalonians 4:16, 1 Corinthians 15:42-44
[846] 1 Thessalonians 4:7
[847] Matthew 25:32 to the end

heavens,[848] there to have full immediate uninterrupted vision and fruition of God in Christ face to face unto all eternity.[849]

Thus of the benefits covenanted which God will do for Christ's seed: he will recover them, etc.

{2} **The object to whom these grand benefits are intended in Christ, is only *Christ's seed, the elect*.** For, (i) they, and they alone were before the foundation of the world, in Christ eternally elected and predestined to these benefits.[850] (ii) They, and they alone are the persons for whom Christ in fullness of time intentionally shed his blood and laid down his life, that he might purchase and procure these mercies for them. Even for *God's elect*:[851] for *the children of God*.[852] For *the children which God had given him*:[853] for *his church*,[854] for *his people*,[855] *for his sheep*.[856] (iii) They and they alone are the persons to whom these benefits and mercies are in due time actually and effectually applied and bestowed in Jesus Christ through the operation of the Spirit.[857] Consequently they alone that are Christ's seed, the elect, are the object to whom these benefits and mercies are intended in Christ.

[2] <u>*The Lord covenants, what he will be to Christ's seed, namely: he will be to them a God*</u>.

That thus God covenants, is clear in the tenor of the Covenant of Faith, as renewed to Abraham, Israel, David, the Jews, and in the New Covenant. {1} To Abraham, God says: *I will establish my covenant between me and thee, and thy seed after thee, in their generations, for an everlasting covenant: to be a God unto thee, and to thy seed after thee. And I will give unto thee, and to thy seed*

---

[848] 1 Corinthians 6:2-3
[849] 1 Corinthians 13:12, Matthew 5:8, 1 John 3:2, 1 Corinthians 15:28, 1 Thessalonians 4:17
[850] Ephesians 1:4-5, Romans 8:29
[851] Romans 8:33-34
[852] John 11:51-52
[853] Hebrews 2:13-15
[854] Ephesians 5:25, Acts 20:28
[855] Matthew 1:21
[856] John 10:11; 15
[857] Romans 8:29-30; Ephesians 1:3-5; John 10:26 & 17:2 & 6:37, 39; Acts 13:48

*after thee, the land wherein thou art a stranger, all the land of Canaan, for an everlasting possession: and I will be their God.*⁸⁵⁸ {2} To Israel at Horeb, *I am the LORD thy God,*⁸⁵⁹ etc. {3} To David God promises, in reference to his seed; *He shall cry unto me, thou art my father, my God, and the rock of my salvation.*⁸⁶⁰ {4} To the Jews, captivated in Chaldea, the Lord promises frequently by his prophets: *They shall be my people, and I will be their God.*⁸⁶¹ {5} Finally, this is the grand blessing promised under the New Covenant: *I will put my laws into their mind, and write them in their hearts: and I will be to them a God, and they shall be to me a people.*⁸⁶² Thus the Lord covenants what he will be to his people, to the seed of Christ: he will be to them a God. And what could God say more? For, of all federal clauses and promises in God's book, this is the (i) *highest*, (ii) *fullest*, (iii) *surest*, and (iv) *sweetest*.

(i) The *highest*. For the blessing herein promised is the Most-High God,⁸⁶³ the supreme good, the only good: from whose goodness every good thing flows.⁸⁶⁴ It was much that God said to Abraham, being about to enter into covenant with him; *Fear not, Abraham: I am thy shield, and thy exceeding great reward.*⁸⁶⁵ A shield, a reward, a great reward, an exceedingly great reward – and all this to Abraham. What security, what sufficiency is here for Abraham? It was much more, that God, covenanting with David, promised to his seed: *I will be his father, and he shall be my son.*⁸⁶⁶ But it is most of all that the Lord says: *I will be to them a God*. God is higher than heaven or earth, than grace or glory, than things present or to come, than men, angels, or seraphims – and therefore when God promises himself, he promises the highest good promiseable. The whole covenant is a rich ring of gold, or chain of pearl; but

---

[858] Genesis 17:7-8
[859] Deuteronomy 5:2-3, 6; Exodus 29:45
[860] Psalm 89:26, 33-34
[861] Jeremiah 24:7, 30:22, 32:38, 40; Ezekiel 11:20, 36:28
[862] Hebrews 8:10, Jeremiah 31:33
[863] Genesis 14:18-22
[864] Luke 18:19
[865] Genesis 15:1, 18
[866] 2 Samuel 7:14

this promise is as the highest diamond in the ring, and most precious jewel in the chain. It is the very crown and top-excellency of all the promises.

(ii) The *fullest*. No promise in Scripture is so complete and comprehensive as this promise. When God is promised, what is not promised? (a) All that's in God is promised: his wisdom for direction, his power for protection, his grace for acceptation, his mercy for commiseration, his justice for remuneration, etc. (b) All that is God's is promised: his creatures on earth to serve us, his angels in heaven to guard us, his ordinances in this world to make us holy, his recompenses in the world to come to make us happy, his comforts to support us, his graces to adorn us, his glory to crown us, etc. All these are promised – yea all things are promised, when God is promised. God is all in all. Therefore this promise of God is the center where all the promises meet; the sea whereinto all the promises empty themselves.

(iii) The *surest*. For, when God has made several other promises to his people, he is wont to close them up with this: *And I will be your God*. This he adds as a strong bond,[867] or firm seal unto his other promises. And no wonder, for if God will perform this greatest of all blessings, he will never deny or withhold any lesser inferior blessing. If he gives that which implies all good, which is the fountain of all good, then surely he can count no good thing too dear for us. He that spares not his own dearest self, how shall he not with himself freely give us all things?

(iv) Finally, this is the sweetest of all God's promises and of all his covenant-agreements. Namely, I will be to them a God. For, (a) this gives the sweetest right and property. It gives us right to, and property in the sweetest God. God is light without obscurity:[868] how sweet is such light to the mind! God is life without mortality:[869] how sweet is such life unto the soul! God is peace without perplexity:[870] how sweet is such peace unto the conscience! God is love without mutability:[871] how sweet is such love unto the heart! Yea God is

---

[867] Leviticus 26:3-13: particularly see verse 12; Ezekiel 11:16-19
[868] 1 John 1:5
[869] 1 Timothy 6:17
[870] Romans 16:20
[871] 1 John 4:16, Romans 8:38-39

all sweetnesses. And whatsoever sweetness is among the creatures, it originally flows from this uncreated sweetness of God. Oh therefore how incomparable sweet is it to have property in this God, to have this God for our God! (b) This establishes the sweetest relation between God and us: that he should be ours and we his. No relation on earth, of master and servant, of parent and child, or of husband and wife, can be in any degree compared to this relation. They are but shadows, but bitterness, in comparison of this sweetness.[872] (c) This yields the fullest and sweetest satisfaction. No creature can satisfy, or fill the soul; but God fills the soul, satisfies the heart abundantly. Man's heart is made capable of God, and therefore is restless until it centers itself in God. Beyond God, the heart can desire nothing: therefore to have God must needs be sweetest of all. (d) Finally, this promise is an antidote against all gall and bitterness, bringing God to be thine. For then the bitterness of wrath is past, for God is thine to love thee. The bitterness of sin is past, for God is thine freely to pardon and justify thee, fully to purge and sanctify thee from all sin. The bitterness of death is past, for God is thine, to arm thee against death, to pluck out the sting of death, and at last totally to redeem thee from the state of death and from all possibility of dying any more. Oh how infinitely sweet is that God, that thus sweetens all our bitterness! How sweet that promise, that makes this God ours! Thus God covenants what he will be to Christ's seed; he will be their God. And these are the benefits and mercies which God on his part covenants and promises in Christ to his seed.

(2) *Christ's seed on their part, do in like sort reciprocally promise, restipulate and covenant with God in Christ, the performance of various federal duties. namely,*

[1] What they will do. {1} They will accept Christ by true faith; and in Christ, all God's covenanted mercies, and {2} they will walk worthy of him

---

[872] "For Thou alone art gladness: the whole world is full of bitterness." Augustine on Psalm 85 [https://www.bible.ca/history/fathers/NPNF1-08/npnf1-08-93.htm] <Accessed 06/03/2023>

and them, according to the gospel. [2] What they will be. They will become God's people, in Christ. Oh how much is implied here in a few words!

[1] **What they will do.** And here they restipulate two things especially; namely,

{1} *To accept Christ by faith unfeigned, and in him all God's covenanted benefits and mercies.* That they restipulate thus to accept Christ and the covenanted mercies by true faith, will appear upon due consideration of these particulars, namely:

(i) That acceptance of Christ by true faith is required in order to the actual participation of these covenanted mercies: recovery from sin to righteousness from death to life, and having God to be their God. Christ says, *This is the work of God, that ye believe on him whom he hath sent*[873]. John says, *This is his commandment, that we should believe on the name of his son Jesus Christ, and love one another, as he gave us commandment. And he that keeps his commandments,* (whereof this believing in Christ is the chief) *dwells in him and he in him.*[874] And therefore has God to be his God, and has righteousness and life from God in Christ. Thus Paul and Silas command the jailor to believe in order to his salvation; *Believe on the Lord Jesus Christ, and thou shalt be saved, and thine house.*[875]

(ii) That, the not-believing in Christ, is condemned, and threatened with death and damnation. Condemned, as that sin of sins, whereof the spirit of Christ chiefly convinces and reproves the world.[876] Threatened: *he that believeth not shall be damned.*[877] *He that believeth not, is condemned already, because he hath not believed on the name of the only begotten Son of God.—he that believes not the Son, shall not see life: but the wrath of God abides on him.*[878] *This is the record, that God hath given to us eternal life; and this life is*

---

[873] John 6:28-29
[874] 1 John 3:23-24
[875] Acts 16:31
[876] John 16:8-9
[877] Mark 16:16
[878] John 3:18, 36

in his Son. He that hath the Son hath life: and he hath not the Son of God hath not life.[879]

(iii) That, the covenanted benefits are promised peculiarly to believing in Christ, and accepting of him by faith, as: (a) Recovery from sin to righteousness; *to him give all the prophets witness, that through his name whosoever believes in him, shall receive remission of sins.*[880] *By his knowledge* (namely, the knowledge of Christ by faith) *shall my righteous servant justify many; for he shall bear their iniquities.*[881] (b) Recovery also from death to eternal life; *whosoever believes on him shall not be ashamed*: or, as Peter has it, *shall not be confounded.*[882] *Yea, he that believes shall be saved.*[883] *God so loved the world, that he gave his only begotten son: that whosoever believes in him, should not perish, but have everlasting life.*[884] *And Jesus said unto them: I am the bread of life: he that comes to me shall never hunger; and he that believes on me shall never thirst.*[885] *Jesus said unto her; I am the resurrection, and the life: he that believes in me, though he were dead, yet shall he live; and whosoever lives and believes in me shall never die.*[886]

(iv) Finally, that the covenant mercies are actually bestowed upon them that accept Jesus Christ by faith unfeigned. Abraham believed, and is justified with the righteousness of faith, and thereby is made also heir of the world:[887] and this is written, to let us know, that in like manner we shall be justified, and be made heirs, if we believe as Abraham did. *As many as received him*, (that is, Christ,) *to them he gave power to become the sons of God, even to them that believe on his name.*[888] And the apostle declares, that *they which are of the seed of Abraham, are blessed with faithful Abraham,*[889] and that *if there had been a*

---

[879] 1 John 5:11-12
[880] Acts 10:43 with 13:39 and Romans 10:4 & 4:5
[881] Isaiah 53:11
[882] Romans 10:11, 1 Peter 2:6 with Isaiah 28:16
[883] Mark 16:16
[884] John 3:16
[885] John 6:35
[886] John 11:25-26
[887] Romans 4 throughout
[888] John 1:12
[889] Galatians 3:6-9

law given which could have given life, verily righteousness should have been by the law. But the Scripture hath concluded all under sin, that the promise by faith of Jesus Christ might be given to them that believe.[890] And that *by Christ, we have access by faith into this grace, wherein we stand.*[891] Now lay all this together and it is evident that it is required of Christ's seed that they accept Christ by true faith; and in Christ, righteousness, eternal life, and God to be their God. And when they close with God in this covenant, thus they promise to accept him.

{2} *To walk worthy of Christ, and of all these covenanted mercies, according to the gospel.* This worthy-walking is frequently pressed in the gospel: not as implying any meritoriousness therein, but only an harmonious suitableness of course and life becoming them that partake of such a high favor from God in Christ.[892] Especially, Paul, *Giving thanks unto the Father, which hath made us meet to be made partakers of the inheritance of the saints in light: who hath delivered us from the power of darkness, and hath translated us into the kingdom of the son of his love: prays for the Colossians, that they might walk worthy of the Lord unto all pleasing, being fruitful in every good work, and increasing in the knowledge of God; strengthened with all might according to his glorious power, unto all patience and long-suffering with joyfulness.*[893] And herein it is that the gospel places walking worthy of the Lord. This walking worthy of Christ, and of covenant-mercies in him, the tenor of the covenant itself requires, and reduces chiefly to two heads, namely: true repentance, and new obedience.

(i) *True repentance* (which is a sanctified change of the person, and conversation, from sin to righteousness), the Covenant of Faith requires, saying: *When will I sprinkle clean water upon you, and you shall be clean: from all your filthiness, and from all your idols will I cleanse you. A new heart also will I give you, and a new spirit will I put within you, and I will take away the*

---

[890] Galatians 3:21-22
[891] Romans 5:1-2
[892] Ephesians 4:1, 1 Thessalonians 2:12, 2 Thessalonians 1:5, 11
[893] Colossians 1:9-14

stony heart out of your flesh, and I will give you an heart of flesh.—I will also save you from all your uncleanesses.—then shall ye remember your own evil ways, and your doings that were not good, and shall loathe yourselves in your own sight, for your iniquities, and for your abominations.[894] Here's true repentance comprising the holy change both of person and conversation.

(ii) New obedience also, evangelically (which the apostle calls walking in newness of life, Romans 6:4). The Covenant of Faith calls for all of Christ's seed accepting this Covenant. As: (a) from Abraham: *I am the almighty God, walk before me and be thou perfect: and I will make my covenant between me and thee,*[895] etc. (b) From Israel entering into covenant with God in Horeb; unto whom God said; *oh that there were such a heart in them, that they would fear me, and keep all my commandments always! Ye shall observe therefore to do all that the Lord your God hath commanded you: you shall not turn aside to the right hand or to the left.*[896] And Israel said: *All that the Lord hath said will we do, and be obedient.*[897] (c) From David and his seed.[898] And, (d) From the captive Jews, the Lord in his covenant required obedience, saying: *And I will put my spirit within you, and cause you to walk in my statutes, and ye shall keep my judgements, and do them.*[899] And when God's people upon several occasions renewed their covenant with God, they were wont to renew their restipulation of sincere, cordial, universal and constant obedience unto the Lord, as holding themselves by virtue of God's Covenant, obliged so to do.[900] Thus Christ's seed to in him restipulate, what they will do.

[2] **What they will be, namely: they will become God's people in Christ.** This stipulation God eminently requires of them in the tenor of this covenant, that *they shall be his people*.[901] And this which they covenant to be, is

---

[894] Ezekiel 36:25-26, 29, 31
[895] Genesis 17:1-2
[896] Deuteronomy 5:2, etc, with 29:32
[897] Exodus 24:3, 7, Deuteronomy 5:27
[898] Psalm 89:30-32 & 132:12
[899] Ezekiel 36:27
[900] Joshua 24:24-25; 2 Chronicles 15:12-14, 2 Kings 23:3 with 2 Chronicles 34:31-32, Nehemiah 9:38 with 10:28-29, etc.
[901] Jeremiah 24:7, 30:22, 31:33, 32:38; Ezekiel 11:20, 14:11, 36:28, 37:27; Hebrews 8:10

beyond all that they covenant to do. For, as when God promises to be their God, he promises the highest of all mercies, so when they promise to be God's people, they promise the greatest of all duties. What could God say more to them? What could they say more to God? By this restipulation, {1} all they are, {2} all they have, {3} all they can do, {4} and, all they can endure, are promised unto God.

{1} *All they are, is hereby promised to God*. When Christ's seed truly strike covenant with God in Christ, they remain no longer sin's, nor Satan's, nor the world's – no, nor their own, but they become God's. *What, know ye not that your body is the temple of the Holy Ghost in you, which ye have of God, and ye are not your own? For ye are bought with a price. Therefore glorify God in your body, and in your spirit, which are God's.*[902] *For none of us lives to himself, and no man dies to himself. For whether we live, we live unto the Lord: and whether we die, we die unto the Lord: whether we live therefore or die, we are the Lord's.*[903] Their souls and bodies are spiritual temples[904] and sacrifices.[905] Their minds his to know him and his will and to meditate sweetly upon him; their consciences his to accuse or excuse them according to his pleasure in all their well or ill-doings; their memories his to retain him, his counsels, his promises, his comforts, and all the dear experiments of his love and grace, in continual remembrance; their wills his self-denyingly to conform, subscribe, and submit unto his will in all things; their hearts and affections his to love him entirely above all amiables, to hate sin extremely, being most contrary to him, as most detestable, to desire him intensively, above all desirables, to fly from sin exceedingly, as most abominable to joy and delight in him most contentedly, above all delectables, and to grieve most mournfully at that which displeases him, or divides from him, as most lamentable; their eyes his to behold the beauty of his works; their ears, his, to hear the melody of his word; their senses his to be casements and inlets to his goodness; their tongues his, to trumpet

---

[902] 1 Corinthians 6:19-20 & 3:16-17
[903] Romans 14:7-9
[904] 1 Corinthians 3:16-17
[905] Romans 12:1

out his glory; their members his to be weapons of righteousness unto holiness; their breath his melodiously to warble out his praises; their being his to be only for him; and their well-being his, as only from him and in him, and to him.

{2} *All they have, is herein consequently promised to God.* All their honors, pleasures, riches and earthly possessions, liberties, privileges, times, opportunities, artificial habits, natural relations, and supernatural qualifications, they are all homagers unto God, and must be prostrated to his service.

{3} *All they can do for God, is also promised to God.* As, publishing and maintaining his truth: promoting his worship, propagating his gospel, protecting his church, defending his cause, supporting his people, maintaining his ordinances, advancing his kingdom and glory, and fulfilling his will in all the evangelical acts of faith and love.

{4} *Finally, all they can endure for him and his truth, must be duly undergone and devoted to his glory.* They must be *shod with the preparation of the gospel of peace*;[906] that they may *bear Christ's reproach, and persecution for righteousness' sake*;[907] that they may undergo *trials of cruel mockings and scourgings, of bonds and imprisonment*; that if need be they may endure, *to be stoned, sawn asunder, tempted, slain with the sword. To wander about in sheep-skins and goat-skins, in deserts and in mountains, and in dens and caves of the earth, being destitute, afflicted and tormented*;[908] that they may *resist even unto blood, striving against sin*:[909] and that they may *take up their cross daily, following Christ*,[910] not counting their blood or lives precious for his sake,[911] who so loved them as to wash them from their sins in his own blood.[912]

---

[906] Ephesians 6:15
[907] Hebrews 13:13
[908] Hebrews 13:36-38
[909] Hebrews 12:4
[910] Luke 9:23
[911] Acts 20:24
[912] Revelation 1:5, Galatians 5:20

O how great a task do Christ's elect undertake, when they restipulate with God to be his people! And without his singular assistance, who can be sufficient for these things! Thus Christ's seed in covenant: what they will be.

Doubt: *But these conditions required on the part of Christ's seed in this covenant (namely, of unfeigned faith, worthy walking, especially by repentance and new obedience, and of becoming God's people) seem repugnant to that free grace whereupon this covenant is founded, and consequently eclipse the glory of this covenant, rendering it herein like the Covenant of Works, which conditioned for perfect personal obedience.*

Answer: Not so. For resolving of this doubt therefore consider:

(1) That in this Covenant of Faith, as well as in the Covenant of Works, God requires conditions to be restipulated to him by them that are federates with him. This has been cleared by evident testimonies. And it is not formally and properly a covenant, but rather a bare promise, where there is not a mutual agreement and stipulation between parties covenanting for performance of certain terms or conditions to each other reciprocally.

(2) That the conditions required of Christ's seed in the Covenant of Faith, are quite different from the conditions required of Adam and his seed in the Covenant of Works. They differ especially in their matter, original, and end.

[1] *In their matter*. The matter conditioned in the Covenant of Works, was perfect and perpetual personal obedience. But the matter conditioned in the Covenant of Faith, is faith in Christ, repentance, new-obedience, and becoming God's people in Christ. None of these were or could be conditions of the Covenant of Works. Not faith in Christ, because man in innocency needed not Christ, nor faith in him; nor did the Covenant of Works reveal or admit of a mediator. Adam had faith in God the creator, not in God the redeemer. Not repentance, for before the fall there was no sin, and therefore no need of repentance. And after the fall the Covenant of Works leaves no place for repentance, but denounces death without mercy. Not new-obedience, or newness of life, for newness of life, or new-obedience presupposes the old

man, and oldness of disobedience and sin.[913] But Adam had neither old man, nor old sins in him, or in his life, when God entered into covenant with him. Nor becoming God's people in Christ, for Adam – and in him his posterity – were God's people immediately by their own concreted personal integrity, and perfect conformity to God and his will, when God made the Covenant of Works with them, not needing Jesus Christ as a mediator of reconciliation to make them God's people. So that the conditions of this Covenant of Faith wholly differ from those of the Covenant of Works, in their matter.

[2] *In their origin and foundation.* The origin of Adam's obedience conditioned in the Covenant of Works, was within himself, even his natural concreated uprightness in God's image:[914] but the original of these conditions required of Christ's seed in the Covenant of Faith, is without them, above them, namely: not any natural principle, but mere supernatural grace and mercy. Faith and repentance are not of themselves, but are the gift of God:[915] new-obedience, not of themselves, but they are created thereunto in Christ.[916] Nor become they God's people of themselves, but God of mere grace promises to make them such,[917] and makes them such according to his promise.[918]

[3] Finally, the conditions of these two Covenants differ exceedingly in their end, why they are required in them respectively. For, personal obedience – perfect and perpetual – was required as the very matter of Adam's righteousness and justification,[919] and as the only procuring cause of his life, under the Covenant of Works. But the case is far otherwise in the Covenant of Faith: here the very matter of our righteousness is Christ and his perfect obedience, and he thereby is the only meritorious procuring cause of our eternal life.[920] Faith is not the *efficient*, nor *material*, but only the *instrumental* cause of our righteousness and life, as it accepts and receives

---

[913] Romans 6:3-8 with 2 Peter 1:9
[914] Ecclesiastes 7:29, Genesis 1:26-27
[915] Ephesians 2:8, 2 Timothy 2:25
[916] Ephesians 2:10, Ezekiel 36:27
[917] Ezekiel 36:26-28, Hebrews 8:10
[918] 1 Peter 2:3-4; 7, 9-10
[919] Genesis 2:17 with Galatians 3:12
[920] Jeremiah 23:6; 1 Corinthians 1:30, Romans 5:12 to the end

Christ to that end.[921] *Repentance* and *new-obedience* are required as conditions of true justifying faith: true justifying faith must be both *penitential* and *obediential*. *Penitential*, purifying our persons and lives from sin and impurity;[922] *obediential*, working by love, which fulfills the law, and showing itself by good works, and so justifying us declaratively before men – and yet this faith justifies us not, as it is penitential, or as it is obediential, in the court of God, but only as it is instrumental to apply Christ for righteousness.[923] Faith is the instrumental cause of justification covenanted, repentance is the qualification of the person capable of life and salvation, and new obedience is the *way to, not the cause of glorification*.[924]

(3) That consequently, these conditions required in the Covenant of Faith: [1] are so far from rendering the Covenant of Faith like the Covenant of Works that they contrariwise notably increase and evidence the difference between them. [2] They are so far from opposing the free grace of this Covenant of Faith that they heighten and illustrate the free-grace of the covenant so much the more: all these conditions originally springing merely from the riches of free-grace. [3] And finally, these conditions are so far from eclipsing the glory of this covenant, that they contribute much to the splendor of its glory.

Hitherto of the matters covenanted, both between God and Christ the last Adam; as also between God and Christ's seed in him, reciprocally, and respectively.

---

[921] Compare John 1:12 with Romans 3:22, 25-28
[922] Acts 15:9, 1 John 3:3
[923] Galatians 5:6, Romans 13:8-10, James 2:14 to the end
[924] Via ad regnum, non causa regnandi.

Section 4

The form of this Covenant of Faith comes now in the last place briefly to be inquired into. And it is twofold, namely, 1. Inward, and more essential. 2. Outward, and more accidental.

(1) The inward and essential form of this covenant is that mutual stipulation herein between the parties covenanting, namely: both between God and Christ the last Adam, and also between God and all Christ's spiritual seed in him. This reciprocal stipulation, either explicit or at least implicit, is so necessary to the constitution and making up of the essence and being of this covenant, that properly, formally and completely it cannot be a covenant without it. For, otherwise there's no mutual engaging and obliging of the federates one to another: which the proper nature of a covenant requires:

(2) The outward and accidental form of this covenant consists especially in its [1] gradual discoveries, [2] various administrations, [3] testamentary disposition, [4] large and liberal tender, and [5] visible advantages, though it be but outwardly embraced.

[1] *The discoveries of this Covenant of Faith were gradual.* The Covenant of Works seems to be discovered all at once to Adam in the self-same day in which he was created, but this Covenant of Faith was not unfolded all at once, but at sundry times, and by several steps and degrees. As the beauty of the year increases to perfection by degrees, namely: from winter's nakedness and deformity to the buds of herbs and trees, from buds to fragrant flowers and blossoms, from flowers and blossoms to green growing and ripe fruit. Or, as the light of the day grows by degrees to its perfect glory: first, it is daybreak, day dawning, or the peering of the morning: then it is clear daylight, then sunrise, then brighter and brighter day, and at last, brightest noon-day.

Thus God's Covenant of Faith was:

{1} Most obscurely and imperfectly discovered presently after the fall, in the promise of the seed of the woman that should bruise the serpent's head, which is not so much as called a covenant.[925] This was the covenant's daybreak, or first dawning of it to mankind.

{2} Then somewhat more clearly to Noah, where it's first styled a {*covenant*},[926] and under Noah's deliverance in the ark by waters from the general deluge that drowned the whole world is represented the church's deliverance and salvation by Christ from the general deluge of sin and wrath that had overwhelmed all mankind. This was as the covenant's daylight.

{3} More clearly and fully after this, to Abraham – God covenanting to be his God, and the God of his seed,[927] to deliver his seed out of Egypt and bring them to Canaan, a type of heaven, to make him heir of the world,[928] and that *in his seed all the nations of the earth should be blessed*, annexing circumcision for confirmation of the covenant to him.[929] This was as the covenant's orient sunrise: now it began to shine out with bright and beauteous rays of grace.

{4} *More fully and perfectly* after this at Mount Sinai: there God covenants with Israel,[930] and Israel restipulates with God[931] – Moses himself coming between them as a typical mediator.[932] There, the Lord so dispensed his covenant to Israel as to convince, terrify, and direct them thereby. To convince them of their sin and misery in themselves by the moral law, that they might despair of justification by any self-righteousness;[933] to terrify them and frighten them out of themselves and their carnal state by the terror of the Lord in most dreadful manner promulgating this covenant;[934] and to direct them to

---

[925] Genesis 3:15
[926] Genesis 6:18
[927] Genesis 17:7
[928] Genesis 15:13 to the end of the chapter, and 17:8 with Romans 4:13
[929] Genesis 22:18, Acts 3:25, Galatians 3:8
[930] Deuteronomy 5:2-3, 5-6
[931] Exodus 24:3-9
[932] Deuteronomy 5:5, 27-29, etc., Exodus 20:19
[933] Galatians 3:19
[934] Hebrews 12:18-21, Exodus 20:18, etc.

Christ and his righteousness as the only remedy against sin and misery[935] – and this by the ceremonies and types of Christ, annexed.[936]

{5} More clearly and fully after this, to King David, with whom God made an everlasting covenant,[937] ordered in all things, and sure: confirmed by God's sacred oath.[938] Wherein, amongst other things, God covenanted to set up his seed after him, which should build a house to God's name,[939] and to establish his kingdom forever. Which was notably fulfilled both in King Solomon, who built God's material temple, and therein was a type of Christ: and especially in Jesus Christ the anti-type, of the fruit of his loins according to the flesh, raised up to sit upon David's throne spiritually,[940] who builds God's spiritual temple, his church, therein to reign forevermore *till he has put all his enemies under his feet.*[941]

{6} More clearly and fully after this, to the Jews in the Babylonian captivity, with whom God covenanted, *to open their graves, and bring them out of their graves,*[942] even out of their desperate Babylonian captivity into their own land; *to cleanse them thoroughly from all their idols and detestable things;*[943] *to take away their stony hearts and give them hearts of flesh;*[944] *to put his Spirit within them, and cause them to walk in his statutes;*[945] to unite them so sweetly, *that they shall no more be two nations, or two kingdoms,* but be closely conjoined in one under David their king, namely, Jesus Christ the spiritual David,[946] and *to set his tabernacle and sanctuary in the midst of them forevermore, he being their God, and they his people.*[947] These gradual

---

[935] Galatians 3:24
[936] Exodus 24 & 25, etc., being well considered
[937] 2 Samuel 23:5
[938] Acts 2:30, Psalm 132:11 & 89:3-4, etc.
[939] 2 Samuel 7:12-13, 16, with Psalm 89 throughout
[940] Psalm 132:11 with Acts 2:30-31
[941] Psalm 110:1, 1 Corinthians 15:24-26
[942] Ezekiel 37:12-14 & 11:17
[943] Ezekiel 36:25, etc., & 37:23 & 11:18
[944] Ezekiel 36:26 & 11:29
[945] Ezekiel 36:27
[946] Ezekiel 37:19, 21-22, 24-25
[947] Ezekiel 37:26-27

discoveries of God's Covenant at Mount Sinai, to David, and to the captive Jews, were as the brighter and brighter day. Finally,

{7} After all these the New Covenant breaks forth most clearly and completely, being founded upon Christ already exhibited and incarnate, and upon far better promises in Christ, etc.[948] And this was the covenant's noontide brightness, or perfect day.

But why was the Covenant of Faith in Christ discovered gradually, by these steps and degrees, and not fully all at once?

Answer: The Lord seems to have taken this gradual course of discovering his covenant,

{1} Because of the surpassing greatness of this mystery of saving lapsed sinners by Jesus Christ through faith; revealed in this Covenant of Faith, both under the Old and New Testament. This is a mystery of mysteries, wherein many abstruse secrets and mysteries meet, as is declared in the Scriptures.[949] And therefore it was a matter too high and transcendent to be revealed all at once unto the world.

{2} Because of the incapacity and weakness of the church in her primordial state. The church and people of God under the Old Testament until Christ's coming were as a child under age, in minority: too weak and rude to fathom and comprehend the full discoveries of divine grace and wisdom in the covenant; God therefore according to their capacity made known his covenant; not according to what he was able to reveal, but according to what they were able to receive.[950] At first in their infancy he disclosed but the ABC of the covenant until the time of Abraham, then he teaches them to spell it from Abraham until Moses, afterwards he taught them to read it more perfectly from Moses until Christ, and lastly he makes them

---

[948] Jeremiah 31:31-35, Hebrews 8:6, 8, etc.
[949] Matthew 13:11, 1 Corinthians 4:1, 1 Timothy 3:9, 16, Ephesians 6:19 & 3:4, Colossians 4:3, 1 Corinthians 2:7, Ephesians 5:32 & 1:9 & 3:3, 9; Colossians 1:26-27 & 2:2
[950] Galatians 4:1-4

fully to understand it since the incarnation of Christ. Thus as the church grew riper and riper, the Covenant of Faith shined forth clearer and clearer.

{3} That the graces of the church – faith, hope, patience, etc. – might be gradually exercised and improved more and more in waiting and longing for the accomplishment of this covenant in the exhibition of Christ. Hence, *Abraham rejoiced to see Christ's day; and he saw it, and was glad.*[951] Jacob expected the coming of Shiloh, *to whom the gathering of the people should be*: and says, *I have waited for thy salvation, O Lord.*[952] Moses said to Israel, *a prophet shall the LORD your God raise up unto you of your brethren, like unto me, him shall ye hear.*[953] The church breathes out her longing desires after Christ in the flesh, saying, *Let him kiss me with the kisses of his mouth, for thy love is better than wine.*[954] The patriarchs of old, *not having received the promises, saw them afar off, were persuaded of them, and embraced them.*[955] And how were they that waited for the consolation of Israel, ravished and transported with joy when Christ, the kernel of the covenant, was exhibited![956]

{4} Finally, that by these gradual discoveries of the covenant, God might gradually advance the excellency of his glory to the very highest: every additional discovery of his covenant, proportionably augmenting the glory of his free grace, love, mercy and goodness to his elect.

[2] **The administrations of this Covenant of Faith were various, as the discoveries of it were gradual.** The administration was different, but the substance thereof still the same.[957] The various conditions and capacity of the church occasioned this variety. Before Christ, the administration of this covenant was more obscure, carnal and servile, by promises, prophecies, sacrifices, circumcision, Passover, priesthood, a worldly sanctuary, with other

---

[951] John 8:56
[952] Genesis 49:10, 18
[953] Acts 7:37, Deuteronomy 18:15
[954] Song of Solomon 1:2
[955] Hebrews 11:13
[956] Luke 2:25-33, 36-38 & 1:42-45, 46-56, 68-80
[957] 2 Corinthians 3:7-9

ceremonial and typical ordinances of divine service, all shadowing out Christ which was tò come afterwards[958] – the church at that time being as an heir in minority, under tutors and governors. But since Christ, the church being as an heir come to age, the ministration of the covenant was more clear, spiritual, filial, and effectual, by preaching the word to all nations, Gentiles as well as Jews; baptism, the Lord's Supper, and other spiritual sacrifices, ordinances and acts of worship: all representing Christ as come already.[959]

[3] *The disposition or disposal of this Covenant of Faith is testamentary, as well as federal.* It is a *federal testament* or a *testamentary covenant*, as was formerly observed.[960] As a covenant, it is a convention, or an agreement between various parties living, as a testament it is the last will or disposal of one dying, or dead. It is often styled a *testament* in Scripture:[961] the *first testament* or *Old Testament*, and the *New Testament*. And both in reference to Christ and his death, typically represented by the death and blood of sacrifices under the Old: truly exhibited under the New.

The testamentary nature of this Covenant of Faith will best appear in the resemblance that it has to a man's last will or testament, wherein he disposes of his estate – real or personal – to his posterity. In a man's testament are considerable: {1} a testator, {2} a final and unalterable disposal of some estate or inheritance, {3} posterity or friends to whom such estate or inheritance is bequeathed, {4} publication of the testament by word or writing, and {5} ratification of it by the testator's seal annexed, especially by his death ensuing.

Such things proportionably are to be found in this testamentary Covenant of Faith, namely: {1} a testator, Jesus Christ,[962] who also is mediator[963] and

---

[958] Hebrews 12:18-21 compared with 2 Corinthians 3, Hebrews chapters 8-10, 1 Corinthians 10:1, etc., Colossians 2:11-12, Romans 4:11
[959] Hebrews 12:22-25, 2 Corinthians 3, Matthew 28:18-20 & 1 Corinthians 11:20, 23-25, 1 Peter 2:5, John 4:23
[960] See Book 1 Chapter 2 Aphorism 1
[961] Hebrews 7:22, 2 Corinthians 3:14, Luke 22:20, 1 Corinthians 11:25, Hebrews 9:15-20
[962] Hebrews 9:14-18
[963] Hebrews 8:6 & 9:15

surety[964] of the testament, {2} a final and unalterable disposal of the everlasting inheritance, together with all that belongs unto it. The legacies and estate bequeathed is the eternal inheritance, and all things thereunto belonging. The disposal of this inheritance is final and unalterable:[965] this being Christ's last and everlasting will,[966] which is still to stand in force, without addition thereto, detraction thencefrom, or alteration thereof. {3} A posterity to whom this eternal inheritance, etc., is bequeathed, even the elect of God, Christ's spiritual seed, who are made heirs and co-heirs in Christ,[967] the grand heir of all things for their good.[968] {4} Publication of this testament, by written word, the holy Scriptures, given to the church for this end.[969] Scriptures are God's testamentary rolls: his book of the covenant. {5} Ratification of this testament; *instrumentally*, by the sacraments – baptism[970] and the Lord's supper[971] – and *fundamentally*, by the death of Jesus Christ the testator.[972]

[4] **The tender of this Covenant of Faith is very large and liberal.** The covenant and the grace thereof, is not only tendered, published and offered to Christ's seed, by election given to him: but also to the whole visible church, wherein are more tares than wheat; yea even unto them that are out of the visible church, namely: pagans, and infidels.[973] For the Jews rejecting the tender of the gospel and covenant – and thereby counting themselves unworthy of eternal life – the apostles turned to the Gentiles, to preach to them.[974] And so *God was found of them that sought him not: he was made manifest to them that asked not after him.*[975]

---

[964] Hebrews 7:22
[965] Galatians 3:15
[966] Hebrews 13:20
[967] Romans 8:17, Galatians 4:7, 1 Corinthians 3:22-23
[968] Hebrews 1:2
[969] Romans 15:4, 1 Timothy 3:15, 2 Timothy 3:16-17, John 5:39
[970] Matthew 28:19
[971] Luke 22:20, 1 Corinthians 11:25
[972] Hebrews 9:15-18
[973] Romans 10:8, etc. 16-18, etc.
[974] Acts 13:46-48
[975] Romans 10:20

But why is this Covenant of Faith so largely tendered?

Answer: {1} That the elect seed of Christ may be effectually called and gathered, from among the corrupt mass of mankind.[976] For both among Jews and Gentiles, both within and without the church, God's elect are mingled among reprobates as sheep among goats, wheat among tares, good among bad fish; now the covenant tender does segregate and call them out from among them.[977] {2} That reprobates, who neglect so great salvation tendered, may be left without excuse, and their condemnation more justly aggravated. {3} That God and the free tender of the riches of his grace so largely in his covenant may be magnified and glorified, as it fell out among the Gentiles, who perceiving that the gospel should be offered to them as well as to the Jews, *were glad, and glorified the word of the Lord: and as many as were ordained to eternal life believed.*[978]

[5] Finally, *the visible advantages attending upon this tender of God's covenant, though it be but outwardly embraced*, are various and very considerable. As {1} a holy vocation and profession. They are *called with a holy calling*,[979] whereby they are outwardly separated from infidels, and make a holy profession of Christ and of faith in him.[980] Upon which outward calling and profession, the Scripture styles them believers;[981] sanctified,[982] saints by calling:[983] the people of God,[984] etc. {2} Implantation, not only of themselves, but also of their children and seed after them into the visible body of Christ. So that they and theirs become visible members of Christ's mystical body, and are federally holy and externally within covenant, till they break themselves off

---

[976] Romans 8:30
[977] Romans 9:6, 27, Matthew 25:1-13, 32-33, etc., 13:24-25, etc., 47-48; 2 Corinthians 6:16-18 & 7:1
[978] Acts 13:47-48
[979] 2 Timothy 1:9
[980] 2 Corinthians 6:17
[981] Acts 8:13, Luke 8:13
[982] 1 Corinthians 1:2, Hebrews 10:29
[983] Romans 1:7, 1 Corinthians 1:2
[984] Deuteronomy 7:6

again. True faith makes men members of Christ's invisible body: profession of true faith makes them members of his visible. {3} Participation of God's precious ordinances and means of grace, which may prove through God's Spirit effectual to their eternal glory, wherein however they are highly preferred and privileged before all heathens and infidels, to whom salvation of sinners by Christ is not so much as tendered by the glorious Covenant of Faith.

Thus of the nature of the Covenant of Faith described and unfolded in respect of the author of it, parties to it, matters covenanted, and form of the covenant.

Section 5

Of certain corollaries, or consectaries, resulting from the nature of the Covenant of Faith, generally considered.

From the nature of the Covenant of Faith, generally thus described and considered in the last aphorism of the foregoing chapter, these corollaries or consectaries seem naturally to result by way of application (every corollary being as a consequential aphorism, from the general description of the covenant), namely:

Corollary 1

Hence, the Covenant of Faith is a most profound supernatural mystery.

It is (1) a mystery, (2) a profound mystery, and (3) a supernatural mystery.

(1) *The Covenant of Faith is a mystery.* A mystery (in Scripture sense) is a sacred secret, having a hidden understanding. Such a mystery is not obvious to vulgar capacities: but a divine secret, wonderfully hidden from them. It is a comprehensive mystery, a mystery of mysteries, containing many mysteries folded together in it. For,

[1] Here in this covenant is set forth the doctrine and way of sinners' salvation by Christ, and this is called the *mystery of the gospel*;[985] *the mystery of faith*;[986] *the mystery of God, and of the Father, and of Christ.*[987]

[2] Here is described to us the person and office of Jesus Christ, mediator of this covenant, and a joint-party with his seed to this covenant. And this is called *the great mystery of Godliness, God manifest in the flesh, justified in the*

---

[985] Ephesians 6:19
[986] 1 Timothy 3:9
[987] Colossians 2:2

Spirit, seen of angels, preached unto the Gentiles, believed on in the world, received up into glory.[988] In one Christ are many mysteries: and Christ is the kernel of this covenant.

[3] Here it is discovered how Christ's seed, the church, are united closely to Christ by covenant through faith, and in Christ unto God. And this intimate union of the church, Christ's seed, unto Christ, as members of his body, of his flesh, and of his bones (adumbrated in marriage-union between man and wife), is styled a great mystery.[989] [4] Here it is revealed God's singular goodwill unto the Gentiles touching their conversion and incorporation into his church: that the Gentiles should be fellow-heirs, and of the same body, and partakers of his promise in Christ, by the gospel. And this was so great a secret, and so hidden from the church of the Jews, that the apostle calls it, not only, *the mystery*: and *the mystery of Christ, which in other ages was not made known to the sons of men, as it is now revealed unto his holy apostles and prophets by the Spirit*: but also, *the fellowship of the mystery, which from the beginning of the world hath been hid in God.*[990]

[5] Here is disclosed God's most wise and gracious contrivance, for re-collecting and reuniting all things both in heaven and earth, gathering them together in one in Christ the last Adam, as they were shattered, broken, and dissipated in the first Adam. And this is called, *The mystery of God's will, according to his good pleasure which he hath purposed in himself.*[991]

[6] Here is declared, in and with what ordinances this Covenant of Faith is administered from time to time. And these ordinances are called *the mysteries of God*:[992] and the ministers of Christ entrusted with the dispensation of these ordinances, are styled stewards of these mysteries.

[7] Finally, here is promissorily and prophetically foretold how at the great day Christ will deal with all the saints that shall be found alive at his second coming, namely, *They shall be changed in a moment, in the twinkling*

---

[988] 1 Timothy 3:16
[989] Ephesians 5:29-33
[990] Ephesians 3:3-10, Romans 16:25-26
[991] Ephesians 1:9-10
[992] 1 Corinthians 4:1

of an eye, at the last trump. And of this change the apostle says, *Behold, I show you a mystery*.[993] And by this mysterious change, the surviving saints shall be throughly fitted for their covenanted glory.

(2) *The Covenant of Faith is a profound mystery, a great deep*. For, behold herein:

[1] *What a depth of free-grace*! That when all mankind were by the first Adam's disobedience plunged in a state of sin and death, yea and Christ's seed according to election, as sinful dead and worthless as any of the rest: yet these alone out of the common corrupt mass of mankind should be recovered by the obedience of Christ the last Adam to righteousness and life, all the rest being passed by and neglected in their misery.

[2] *What a depth of mercy and loving-kindness*! That wretched worthless loveless sinners who had not obtained mercy, who were not a people, should be so embraced in arms of divine love and mercy as to obtain Christ the mercy of mercies, and in Christ to obtain righteousness against sin, life against death, freedom against bondage, happiness against misery, salvation against condemnation, yea the most high God to be their God, and themselves to be his people.

[3] *What a depth of power*! That sinners should be justified, that dead creatures should be quickened, that enmity against God should be reconciled, and that most extreme baseness should be so highly exalted.

[4] *What a depth of justice*! That sin should be ruined, and yet the sinner be recovered. That *he who knew no sin, should be made sin*,[994] and condemned, and they who knew nothing but sin, should be made the righteousness of God and eternally saved.

[5] Finally, *what a depth of wisdom*! That in this recovery of Christ's seed, innocency should be condemned and the sinner justified, liberty should be imprisoned and captivity released, light should be eclipsed and obscurity enlightened, strength should be weakened and weakness strengthened, peace

---

[993] 1 Corinthians 15:51-52 with 1 Thessalonians 4:16-17
[994] 2 Corinthians 5:21

should be perplexed and perplexity pacified, love should be hated and enmity should be loved, that life should die and death should live. And all this was fulfilled when Christ became a surety and sacrifice for his seed according to this covenant. Yea how profound this mystery of God's wisdom, contriving that the same sinners, should at once both die the death threatened in the Covenant of Works, and so God's truth and justice be fulfilled; and yet not die but live, according to the Covenant of Faith, and so God's election, love and mercy be expressed.

Oh how has God abounded towards us in all wisdom and prudence in these mysterious dispensations![995] To this effect, Luther says most elegantly and spiritually: "Christ, with most sweet names, is called my law, my sin, my death – against the law, against sin, against death – whereas in very deed he is nothing else but mere liberty, righteousness, life and everlasting salvation. And for this cause he is made the law of the law, the sin of sin, the death of death: that he might redeem me from the curse of the law, justify me, and quicken me. So then while Christ is the law, he is also liberty; while he is sin, he is righteousness; and while he is death, he is life. For in that he suffered the law to accuse him, sin to condemn him, and death to devour him, he abolished the law, he condemned sin, he destroyed death, he justified and saved me. So is Christ the poison of the law, sin and death: and the remedy for obtaining liberty, righteousness and everlasting life. Thus in Christ we may behold this joyful conflict: to wit, the law fighting against the law, that it may be to me liberty, sin against sin, that it may be to me righteousness; death against death, that I may obtain life; Christ fighting against the devil, that I may be the child of God: and destroying hell; that I may enjoy the kingdom of heaven."[996]

(3) ***The Covenant of Faith is a supernatural mystery.*** There are mysteries in the creatures in heaven and earth, which natural understanding may discover and comprehend. And there are mysteries in God the creator and governor of all in heaven and earth, namely, his invisible Godhead, power,

---

[995] Ephesians 1:7-8
[996] Martin Luther in his commentary on Galatians 2:19

wisdom, with other attributes, etc., which angels and men by mere natural light may find out and wade into.[997] But this mystery of the Covenant of Faith, namely, that sinners in state of death should be restored to righteousness and life; and that by a surety, to whom their sins should be imputed, and on whom their death should be inflicted; and this surety Jesus Christ, God-man descending from the Father's bosom, who knew no sin, deserved no death; that as sinners' sins are imputed to, and their death inflicted on Christ, so Christ's righteousness through faith, should be imputed to, and his life bestowed upon sinners – and that all this should be revealed in a Covenant of Faith of mere grace when the broken Covenant of Works knew no place for lapsed sinners' recovery – this mystery, I say, is wholly supernatural. No natural light of reason and understanding of men and angels could have devised or imagined such a recovery of sinners as this, from sin and death, to righteousness and life; such a recoverer as this, Jesus Christ God-man in person, reconciling God and man by his office, and such a covenant as this between God and man revealing this recovery, had not God infinitely wise pleased, as to devise, so to disclose and reveal these mysteries unto us. This is *not the wisdom of this world, but the wisdom of God in a mystery, even the hidden wisdom which God ordained before the world unto our glory. Which none of the princes of this world knew: for had they known it, they would not have crucified the Lord of glory. But as it is written, eye hath not seen, nor ear heard, neither have entered into the heart of man, the things which God hath prepared for them that love him. But God hath revealed them unto us by his Spirit.*[998]

And by this divine revelation we become *able to comprehend with all saints, what is the breadth, and length, and depth, and height: and to know the love of Christ, which passes knowledge, that we may be filled with all the fullness of God.*[999]

---

[997] Romans 1:18-21
[998] 1 Corinthians 2:6-10
[999] Ephesisans 3:18-19

Corollary 2

Hence the Covenant of Faith is a wonderful compound and contrivance of mere grace.

Let us understand, (1) what {*grace*} in Scripture-language implies, and (2) what a composition of grace this Covenant of Faith is.

(1) {*Grace*} in Scripture-phrase has manifold acceptations. It's needless here to touch upon all, but only upon such as are pertinent to the present purpose. {*Grace*} therefore imports,

[1] Primarily and most frequently, God's free favor wherewith he respects his creatures, and whence all blessings and benefits originally flow to his creatures. *There is a remnant according to the election of grace.*[1000]

Now this fountain grace, this springhead of all good to the creatures, looks upon the creatures two ways as Cameron well notes, namely: "{1} As creatures no way deserving God's favor, or any fruits thereof. For, creatures, as creatures, can deserve nothing from the creator, having nothing but what they had from him. {2} As creatures miserable through sin; deserving the contrary, nothing but ill from the creator."[1001] The former is the grace of benevolence or goodwill:[1002] the latter the grace of commiseration or bowels of mercy.[1003] According to the former, Adam and we in him had paradise, communion with God, Covenant of Works,[1004] etc., before the fall: according to the latter, the elect obtain redemption,[1005] justification, etc., after the fall.[1006]

[2] Secondarily and less principally, grace imports the fruits and effects of God's favor. These are called grace, because originally they flow only from divine grace. As the doctrine of the gospel and covenant, is called grace; *the*

[1000] Romans 11:5
[1001] John Cameron in Praelect. De Ecclesia p.240 in fol. Geneva 1642
[1002] Ephesians 1:5-6
[1003] Luke 1:78, Psalm 51:1, Exodus 34:6
[1004] See before in Book 1 Chapter 2 Aphorism 3
[1005] Romans 3:24
[1006] Ephesians 1:7

grace of God which bringeth salvation.[1007] Habits of sanctification are styled grace, but *grow in grace.*[1008] Exercise of these habits, as distribution to the saints' necessities is styled grace; *so he would finish in you the same grace also,*[1009] etc.

(2) *The Covenant of Faith now, is a compound of mere grace.* Namely, it is an effect of divine grace and favor, wholly and merely gratuitous: man not only, not deserving anything at all therein, but most justly and altogether deserving the contrary. The Covenant of Works, with the first Adam, as his creature, was gratuitous, Adam not deserving it from God; but the Covenant of Faith with us as sinful creatures, in Christ the last Adam, is double gratuitous, we deserving the contrary evil of punishments from God. And in this sense probably, some style this {*the Covenant of Grace*}, not so much by way of contrariety to the Covenant of Works, which also is gratuitous, namely: in respect of the grace of benevolence; but rather by way of supereminence, this covenant being gratuitous both according to the grace of benevolence, and of commiseration. More particularly:

[1] God's making of this Covenant of Faith with man since the fall, is of mere grace. Grace the only impulsive or moving cause inclining God thereunto, as has been shown.[1010]

[2] Jesus Christ, the surety[1011] and mediator[1012] of this Covenant of Faith, is only of mere grace. {1} Of mere grace he was eternally elected for his seed, and they elected in him.[1013] {2} Of mere grace he was promised to his seed from the beginning of the world. He is the *mercy promised* to our fathers.[1014] All the promises both of Christ, and in Christ, which are *exceeding great and precious*, are *given to us*.[1015] And the gift is free. {3} Of mere grace he in fullness

---

[1007] Titus 2:11
[1008] 2 Peter 3:18
[1009] 2 Corinthians 8:6
[1010] In Book 2 Chapter 2 Aphorism 2 Section 1
[1011] Hebrews 7:22
[1012] Hebrews 8:6
[1013] Ephesians 1:5-6
[1014] Luke 1:72
[1015] 2 Peter 1:4

of time was exhibited and delivered for his seed. Hence he is styled, *the gift of God*.[1016] *A son given to us. God so loved the world, that he gave his only begotten son.*[1017] He is also said *to taste death by the grace of God*, etc.[1018] {4} Of mere grace, Christ and his benefits are tendered and offered unto his seed. *Ho every one that thirsteth, come ye to the waters, and he that hath no money; come ye, buy and eat, yea come, buy wine and milk without money, and without price.*[1019] And again; *Let him that is athirst, come. And whosoever will, let him take the water of life freely.*[1020]

[3] *The matters covenanted are of mere grace; whether on God's part promised, or on our part restipulated.* On God's part, the recovery of Christ's seed from the state of sin and death to a state of righteousness and life, is of mere grace. *By grace ye are saved: not of works, lest any man should boast.*[1021] {1} The impetration or obtaining of this recovery by redemption is of mere grace; *in whom we have redemption through his blood the forgiveness of sins: according to the riches of his grace.*[1022] {2} The application of this recovery gradually, is of mere grace, namely: (i) Conviction effectual of our misery, and the remedy thereof is of grace; *the grace of God which bringeth salvation hath appeared to all men,*[1023] etc: *To you it's given to know the mysteries of the kingdom.*[1024] (ii) Conversion is of mere grace, whether it be styled {regeneration} or {renewing}: *not by works of righteousness which we have done, but according to his mercy he saved us, by the washing of regeneration, and renewing of the Holy Ghost.*[1025] Or {repentance}: *if God peradventure will give them repentance.*[1026] *Him hath God exalted with his right hand, to be a*

[1016] John 4:10
[1017] Isaiah 9:6 with John 3:16
[1018] Hebrews 2:9
[1019] Isaiah 55:1
[1020] Revelation 22:17
[1021] Ephesians 2:5, 8
[1022] Ephesians 1:7
[1023] Titus 2:11
[1024] Matthew 13:11, Luke 8:10
[1025] Titus 3:5
[1026] 2 Timothy 2:25

prince and a savior, for to give repentance to Israel.[1027] Or {calling}: *who hath saved us, and called us with a holy calling, not according to our works, but according to his own purpose and grace which was given us in Christ Jesus before the world began.*[1028] (iii) Adoption is of mere grace: *Having predestinated us unto the adoption of children by Jesus Christ to himself, according to the good pleasure of his will: to the praise of the glory of his grace.*[1029] (iv) Justification is of mere grace: *all have sinned and come short of the glory of God, being justified freely by his grace.*[1030] (v) Sanctification is of mere grace: *But God who is rich in mercy, for his great love wherewith he loved us, even when we were dead in sins, hath quickened us together with Christ, (by grace ye are saved) and hath raised us up together, and made us sit together in heavenly places in Christ Jesus. That in the ages to come he might shew the exceeding riches of his grace, in his kindness towards us, through Christ Jesus.*[1031] (vi) Finally, glorification is of mere grace also; *but the gift of God is eternal life through Jesus Christ our Lord.*[1032] *That as sin hath reigned unto death, even so might grace reign through righteousness unto eternal life by Jesus Christ our Lord.*[1033]

On the part of Christ's seed, the conditions required and restipulated, are in like sort of mere grace, namely: (i) faith: *unto you it is given, in the behalf of Christ, not only to believe on him.*[1034] And again: *by grace are ye saved through faith, and that not of yourselves, it is the gift of God.*[1035] So that, though God in this covenant condition with Christ's seed for believing, yet God freely enables them to perform this condition, giving them faith whereby they do believe. (ii) Walking worthy of Christ and covenanted mercies, is also of mere grace: *For we are his workmanship, created in Christ Jesus unto good works, which God hath before ordained that we should walk in them.—not that we are sufficient of*

[1027] Acts 5:31
[1028] 2 Timothy 1:9, 1 Corinthians 1:26-29
[1029] Ephesians 1:5-6
[1030] Romans 3:23-24, Titus 3:7
[1031] Ephesians 2:4-7
[1032] Romans 6:23
[1033] Romans 5:21
[1034] Philippians 1:29
[1035] Ephesians 2:8

ourselves to think anything as of ourselves: but our sufficiency is of God.—who works in us both to will, and to do, of his good pleasure.[1036]

Thus this Covenant of Faith is a mere compound of free-grace, wherein the exceeding riches of the glory of divine grace are displayed, that no flesh in the point of salvation and recovery by Jesus Christ may have the least color or shadow of boasting and glorying in itself; but that he that glories, might only glory in the Lord, and in the transcendent treasures of his loving-kindnesses, tender mercies, and free grace.

[1036] Ephesians 2:10 with 2 Corinthians 3:15 & Philippians 2:13

Corollary 3

Hence Jesus Christ is the very marrow and kernel of the Covenant of Faith.

This covenant is as a celestial orb, and Christ is as the radiant sun in this orb. This covenant is a blessed circle and circumference of grace, and Christ the very center of this circle. This covenant is as a golden cabinet: Christ as the most precious diamond or jewel in this cabinet, and all other the rich treasures of righteousness, life, etc., therein, as the appendants, ornaments and garnish of this jewel. Amongst them, Christ stands as once the tree of life among the trees in the midst of Eden. How can we cast our eyes upon this covenant, which is so full of Christ, and not observe therein much of Christ? Did the wise men *so rejoice with exceeding great joy, when they saw the star* that conducted them to Christ on earth?[1037] How much more should Christians rejoice when they look into this covenant which conducts them to the same Christ, not only as heretofore on earth, but as now also in heaven!

The angel after Christ's resurrection said of his sepulcher, *He is not here, behold the place where they laid him.*[1038] But of this covenant we may say: "Christ is here, come see the place where the Lord lies." For, (1) Christ is the ancient, yea the eternal foundation of this covenant. (2) Christ is the chief party to this covenant with God. (3) Christ is the only mediator of this covenant. (4) Christ is the precious matter of this covenant. Come and see.

(1) *Christ is the ancient, yea the eternal foundation of this covenant.*

[1] Christ is the *ancient foundation of this covenant.* For God, revealing this covenant at Mount Sinai, founded it upon Christ the substance of those types and ceremonies digested into that federal administration.[1039] And before that, God, revealing this covenant to Abraham, grounded it upon Christ

---

[1037] Matthew 2:9-10
[1038] Mark 16:6
[1039] Deuteronomy 5:2, etc.

Abraham's seed, in whom *all the families of the earth should be blessed*.[1040] And before both, God revealing this Covenant even in paradise presently after the fall, bottomed it upon Christ the seed of the woman.[1041] And this is very ancient indeed, almost as ancient as the world itself, probably within a few days.

[2] Yea Christ is the eternal foundation of this covenant. For God covenanted and promised nothing in Christ in time but what he had decreed and purposed in Christ before all time. God *hath chosen us in Christ before the foundation of the world, that we should be holy and without blame before him in love*.[1042] Consequently God (foreseeing our fall in Adam) decreed to recover us by Christ, that we might be thus holy and blameless, and to make known this his purpose to us in this Covenant. Hence our salvation and vocation are said to be given us of God in Christ before the world began; *who hath saved us, and called us with a holy calling, not according to our works, but according to his own purpose and grace which was given us in Christ Jesus before the world began*.[1043]

Yea, eternal life is said to be promised before the world began: *in hope of eternal life, which God, that cannot lie, promised before the world began*.[1044] How could salvation and vocation be given us, and eternal life be promised before the world began? Namely, they were given and promised in God's decree in Christ, that is, decreed eternally to be given, and to be promised in him. For all things and times are always present with God, as Beza well observes.[1045] Unless we may say that God before the foundation of the world promised to Christ (in his eternal counsel and transaction with him) eternal life for his seed. In some sense therefore, God's promise and Covenant in Christ was before the world began. Therefore this Covenant, in reference to

---

[1040] Genesis 17:1-2, etc. & 12:3, Acts 3:25-26
[1041] Genesis 3:15
[1042] Ephesians 1:4, etc.
[1043] 2 Timothy 1:9
[1044] Titus 1:2
[1045] Beza, Annotations on Titus 1:2 & 2 Timothy 1:9

the foundation of it, is free, sure, and everlasting. *Free*, because it is before all works; *sure*, because it is before all sin; *everlasting*, because it is before all time.

(2) ***Christ is chief party to this covenant, with God.*** For as God is a party on the one hand, so Christ and his seed are a joint party on the other. God deals not with Christ's seed separately and distinctly by themselves alone, for so they are not capable of confederation with God: but he deals with them jointly with Christ and in Christ. As he dealt with the first Adam and his seed in the Covenant of Works, so he deals with Christ the last Adam and his seed in the Covenant of Faith. Now this is our great advantage. For as the disciples were safe at sea against greatest storms and tempests, when Christ was in the ship,[1046] so Christ's seed are safe spiritually against greatest tempests of sin, wrath, death, and temptation, when Christ is embarked in the same Covenant with them. Though they be foolish, Christ is wise; though they be weak, Christ is strong; though they be faithless, Christ is faithful; though they be sinners, Christ is righteous and separate from sinners; though they be enemies, Christ is their reconciler; though they be cursed, Christ is blessed, and the blesser of all his seed; though they be death, Christ is life; though they be condemnation, Christ is salvation; though they be nothing, Christ is all. Whatsoever therefore is wanting in Christ's seed, is abounding in Christ completely to bear up one side of this Covenant with and for his seed: as the blessed God the other for himself.

(3) ***Christ is the only mediator of this Covenant of Faith.***[1047] For:

[1] Christ alone is the mediator of reconciliation, recovering his seed meritoriously by his blood from sin and death to righteousness and life, and reconciling them to God.[1048] Hence he is called the surety, and the testator of

---

[1046] Matthew 8:23-28
[1047] Hebrews 8:6 & 9:15; 1 Timothy 2:5
[1048] Hebrews 9:14-15, etc., 2 Corinthians 5:19-21, Romans 5:10

this Covenant,[1049] engaging himself under our debt, and ratifying this testament by his death.

[2] Christ alone is the meritorious mediator of intercession,[1050] by whom we have access unto God with boldness,[1051] and acceptance with God in all our prayers and suits made according to his will.[1052]

[3] Christ alone is the mediator of all revelation, instruction and doctrine: he being that eternal wisdom and word of God by whom the Father still made known himself and his will to mankind from the beginning of the world since the fall.[1053] Hence, it's observable that when God spoke of old to the fathers, he spoke by Christ; yea, when God gave the law, the Covenant on Sinai, *it was ordained by angels in the hand of a mediator*.[1054] That is, God dispensed it not only by the ministry of angels, but also of the mediator. What mediator? Not Moses, as Beza,[1055] and others after him interpret:[1056] but Christ, as Jerome, Ambrose, Chrysostom, Oecumen, Calvin, Pareus, and others do well expound it.[1057]

(4) *Finally, Christ is the precious matter of this covenant*. All the matters covenanted from God to Christ's seed, or restipulated from them to God, are either Christ himself, or mysteries in Christ. [1] The recoverer and restorer of Christ's seed is Christ.[1058] [2] The righteousness and eternal life whereunto they are recovered is the righteousness and life of Christ.[1059] [3] The covenant-relation between God and them – he being their God, and they his people – is founded in Christ.[1060] [4] The faith accepting those benefits is

---

[1049] Hebrews 7:22 & 9:16, etc.
[1050] 1 John 2:1-2, Hebrews 7:25 & 9:24
[1051] Hebrews 4:15, 26
[1052] Revelation 8:3-4; John 14:13-14
[1053] John 1:1-2, 4, 18; Proverbs 8 throughout, 1 Corinthians 1:30
[1054] Galatians 3:19
[1055] Beza on Galatians 3:19
[1056] Piscator in Schol. Ad Gal 3:19; John Diodati in his Annotations on Galatians 3:19
[1057] See their commentaries on Galatians 3, especially verse 19
[1058] Matthew 1:21, Titus 2:13-14
[1059] Matthew 6:33, 2 Corinthians 5:21, 1 Corinthians 1:30, 1 John 5:11-12
[1060] Galatians 3:26

the *faith of the Son of God, Jesus Christ*.[1061] [5] The worthy walking consequentially required is that whereunto they are created in Christ.[1062] Thus Christ, one way or another, is the very matter of the Covenant. We cannot intentively behold the Covenant, but there we may discern Jesus Christ engraven upon every *promise*, every *benefit*, and upon every *duty* of the covenant.

Thus Christ is the *foundation, party, mediator*, and *matter* of this Covenant of Faith. How excellently! The Covenant of Faith is the marrow of the whole Scriptures, the whole Bible since the fall tending to reveal this mystery, and Christ is the marrow of the Covenant of Faith, the whole covenant being as a heavenly womb full of this blessed babe.

"My eyes," (said Luther) "shall behold nothing else but this inestimable prize, my Lord and Savior Christ. He ought to be such a treasure unto me, that all other things should be but dung in comparison to him. He ought to be such a light to me, that when I have apprehended him by faith, I should not know whether there be any law, any sin, any righteousness, or any unrighteousness in the world. For what are all things which are in heaven and earth in comparison to the Son of God, Jesus Christ, my Lord and Savior, who loved me, and gave himself for me?"[1063]

[1061] Galatians 2:20
[1062] Ephesians 2:10
[1063] Martin Luther, commentary on Galatians 2:21

Corollary 4

Hence the Covenant of Faith may in a right and sound sense be acknowledged conditional.

It is not repugnant to, or inconsistent with, the nature of the Covenant of Faith to be conditional, as God on his part promises: (1) what he will do for Christ's seed, and (2) what he will be to Christ's seed: so Christ's seed on their part repromise, restipulate and re-oblige themselves. (1) What they will do, namely: they will accept Christ and all covenanted mercies in him by faith, and they will walk worthy of him and them in all well-pleasing, according to the gospel; (2) what they will be, namely, they will become God's covenant-people in Jesus Christ. And all this God conditions with them and requires from them. So that this Covenant is conditional, God therein imposing terms and conditions upon Christ's seed.

And here it may be opportune and useful, to take a little into consideration that troublesome question: *Whether the Covenant of Faith (or grace) be conditional or not?* Whether God makes it *absolutely* without all conditions on man's part,[1064] as some are of opinion; or *conditionally* upon certain terms and conditions required from him, as others judge.[1065] For more clear resolution and satisfaction to this question, I shall do three things, namely: (1) lay down the true state of the question, (2) assert and confirm that which shall be resolved upon as truth by sundry arguments, and (3) refute and answer such objections as are made, with any color of strength, to the contrary.

And all this I shall endeavor with what brevity and perspicuity I can, as being more desirous to treat this subject of the Covenant doctrinally and practically, then polemically or controversially.

(1) **As for the true state of the question, namely: whether the Covenant of Faith (usually styled the Covenant of Grace) be conditional, or not?** I offer these three things briefly to be considered for clearing of it, so that we may see wherein the very knot and point of difference lies, namely: [1] the notation of the word {*conditional*} or {*condition*}, [2] the distinction or distribution of *conditions* into several sorts, and [3] the particular declaration and signification thereupon in certain distinct positions or conclusions,

---

[1064] The absoluteness of the Covenant of Grace, without condition, is asserted by D. Crisp: "In this Covenant of Grace to wit the New Covenant, it is far otherwise; There is not any condition in this covenant.—I say the New Covenant is without any conditions whatsoever on man's part. Man is tied to no condition that he must perform, that if he do not perform, the covenant is made void by him." Christ alone exalted, *Christ Alone Exalted*, Sermon 6, p. 159. "The whole performance of the covenant lies only upon God himself, and that there is not one bond or obligation upon man to the fulfilling of the covenant, or partaking in the benefits of the covenant." Page 161, 162. Again: "All the tie lies upon God's part, to do everything that is mentioned in the covenant.—I say only in way of condition of the covenant you must do nothing." p. 164, 165. *And afterwards*: "I must needs tell you directly and according to the truth, That faith is not the condition of the covenant." *Same Sermon, p. 166*. By M. Saltmarsh, "Whatsoever promise has a condition in it, is ours in Christ, who only is the conditioned person for all promises." Free Grace, page 105.— "All the conditions were on Christ's part, none on ours." There, p. 126.— "In the New-Covenant God gives himself freely in Christ, undertaking all both with the Father and the soul, nothing being required on man's part." There. p. 153. "Those ministers who press repentance and faith, do over-heat the wine of the gospel with conditions and qualifications; So the poor souls cannot taste it." *In his Occasional word. By sundry others also, who incline in whole or in part to the Antinomian misapprehensions.*

[1065] The conditionality of the Covenant of Faith (or Grace) is on the contrary maintained by very many eminently godly, learned, and judicious; yea the general current of sound Writers, both ancient and modern, and these both foreign and domestic, runs this way most unanimously: As shall hereafter particularly appear.

wherein the true state of the question consists. Hereby the truth shall be more distinctively manifested, and more easily confirmed; as also all objections to the contrary more readily and satisfactorily answered.

[1] First, as for the notation of the word {*conditional*} or {*condition*}, I shall not stay much upon it. {*Conditional*}, is that which has some condition annexed or adjoined to it. {*Condition*} is a Latin word, derived from {*condo*},[1066] to lay up safe, to build, to found, to compose, to make up, to prescribe, etc. Hence {*condition*} notes, {1} properly, the action of making, framing or composing anything. {2} Then the passion in being made or composed, etc. {3} The quality by which one frames any thing, or whereby any thing is framed, etc. {4} Hence, it's used for the state which is made by framing anything. And hereupon for any state which any person or thing or cause has or receives in any way. As a man abounding with honor, wealth, etc., is said to be a man of a good condition, namely: in respect of his outward state. So a house well-built, a castle well-defended, victualled, etc., a cause well set forth and managed, etc., are said to be in a good condition. But none of these notions or significations of a condition so fitly agree to this present question. {5} {*Condition*} is in a peculiar manner used to note the moderation, circumscription, limitation or restriction of anything: as by certain exceptions, provisoes, terms, qualifications, etc. Propounded or imposed. Hence, {*conditional*} is opposed to absolute, simple, etc., because a condition is accounted amongst the ways, manners, or means, whereby any thing may be framed, obtained or compassed. And in this last sense chiefly, the term {*condition*} is to be understood in the question in hand: whether the Covenant of Faith be conditional, or not? That is, whether God has so framed and propounded in his word the Covenant of Faith to man, in and through Christ, as that he has moderated, circumscribed, limited, restrained it with certain terms, provisos, obligations, qualifications, yes, and duties imposed and required of them that shall join in this Covenant with God, or whether this

---

[1066] Condere proprie est in tenum & interiorem locum dare ad custodian faciliorem: conscribere, facere, componere & struere. Fest. Fran. Holy-Okes Dictionary in verb. *Conda & conditio*

covenant be not laid down absolutely and simply, without any limitation or imposition of qualifications, terms, tithes or duties at all upon those that enter into this Covenant with God? But enough touching the notation of the word {*conditional*} or {*condition*}.

[2] Secondly, we come to the distribution or distinguishing of conditions thus taken, into their several sorts: and all with special reference had therein to God's Covenant's conditions, in reference to God's Covenants, may be considered, {1} most largely, {2} more restrictively, and {3} most strictly.

{1} *Most largely*. So, conditions imply to us, any qualifications, dispositions, terms, ties, duties or performances whatsoever, in any sort imposed upon us, or required from us by God, in reference to his covenant: whether these conditions be, (i) *antecedent*, or going before; (ii) *concomitant*, or accompanying; (iii) *consequent*, or following our entering into, or joining in covenant with God, in order to justification, or salvation.

(i) *Conditions antecedent*, or going before God's covenanting with man, especially before his conversion, regeneration and justification wherein the covenant is effectually and savingly struck between God and man, are asserted variously. And such conditions may be referred chiefly to these three heads, namely: (a) *Meritorious*. (b) *Impulsive*. (c) *Preparatory*.

(a) *Meritorious conditions* the papists in effect assert. As Bellarmine their grand champion says, "A man not reconciled may by works of repentance, impetrate, and of congruity merit, the grace of justification, as was demonstrated in the first book; why may not therefore the self-same man, when he is just and the friend of God, impetrate, and of congruity merit reparation, if perhaps he shall fall?"[1067] This his congruous merit by works of repentance in a person unreconciled, he makes an *antecedent meritorious cause* or *condition* of justification, and consequently of covenanting with God whereby justification is actually applied. But we deny all merit in man; much

---

[1067] Bellarmine, Tome 4.1.5, on Justification, chapter 22

more all meritorious conditions or dispositions in unreconciled man to God's Covenant of Faith or justification. Acknowledging only Christ's pre-ordained merit, to be the sole antecedent meritorious cause or condition of our covenanting with God, justification and salvation.

(b) *Impulsive conditions* moving and inclining God to work faith in one rather than in another, and to regenerate one rather than another (and consequently to bring one into covenant with God effectually rather than another) the Arminians seem to maintain. One said: "Littleness and humility are pre-required of God as a condition, unto this, that he will beget faith in Paul rather in Caiaphas."[1068] Another said that, "Repentance, faith, and even the performance of the commandments are pre-required, unto this, that any one become partaker of the promises of the New Covenant, among which is regeneration."[1069] But all such impulsive or moving causes or conditions in the creature, inclining God to bring man into Covenant of Faith with himself, or to give him the justifying or saving graces of the covenant, we utterly reject and deny, as having no ground in Scripture, knowing that God's mere grace and εὐδοκίαν θελήματος, is the sole antecedent impulsive or moving cause of his bringing one man rather than another into covenant with himself, and into the grace of the Covenant, Romans 3:24. & 4:16. & 5:15-18; 20-21, and 9:15-16, 18. Ephesians. 1: 4-5, 7, 9, 11.

(c) *Preparatory* conditions fitting and disposing, both for entering into the Covenant of Faith with God, and for regeneration and justification, the benefits of that covenant, are diverse: yet all given of God to us as well as required by God from us. As, (1) *hearing God's covenant promulged, or preached*. Thus Noah,[1070] Abraham,[1071] Israel at Mount Sinai,[1072] and men now under the New Testament,[1073] first heard, and hear the covenant published to

---

[1068] Nicol Grevinch
[1069] Episcop. in Thes. privat. Disp. 3 & 40. Vid. etiam D. Ames. Coron. in Artic. 3. de Causa fidei, Thes. 3. Videatur etiam Armin. in Articul nonnul
[1070] Genesis 6:18, etc.
[1071] Genesis 12:1-3 & 15:1, 5-6, 18, etc., & 17:2, etc.
[1072] Exodus 19 & 20 with 24
[1073] Romans 10:6-18

them, before they actually join with God in that Covenant. Until they hear it, they cannot know it; until they know it, they cannot actually and expressly consent to it. (2) *Conviction of the necessity of such a covenant-state*, for remedy of their sin and misery. As Israel, terrified by promulgation of the Sinai Covenant, discovering so much sin and wrath, were convinced of the necessity of a mediator in whom they might enter into covenant with God.[1074] Peter's hearers were for their sins first pricked in their hearts, and then they came to close with the covenant and promises by believing.[1075] (3) *Effectual calling* is (in order of nature, if not in time):[1076] an *antecedent preparatory condition* which God works in men in order to their closing with him in his covenant. Not only the outward call by the word, but also the inward call by the Spirit, principling the heart with supernatural habits of grace, as self-denial, faith, repentance, etc. (in which work the heart is merely passive) is a necessary preparation to actual entering into covenant with God. For by the actual exercise of true faith, assenting and applying, we actually accept God's Covenant and justification. Now the habit in order of nature and causality, must go before the act: we must have faith, self-denial, repentance, etc., before we can use or exercise faith, or any of them Paul makes vocation preparatory to justification; *whom he predestinated them he called: whom he called them he justified.*[1077] First called, then justified. Thus God first called Abraham from his idolatrous and ungodly condition, and then brought him into covenant with himself and justified him.[1078] His calling was a preparatory condition or qualification in order to his covenanting with God and justification. These and like antecedent preparatory conditions or qualifications, rendering the subject capable and more immediately fit for entering into covenant with God in Christ, God requires of us, and works in us. But as for any antecedent preparatories – as in and from ourselves, by any power of free-will, disposing to accept grace tendered, or to persevere in grace received, or to merit grace or

---

[1074] Exodus 20:18-19 with Deuteronomy 5:22-30
[1075] Acts 2:37-42
[1076] Acts 2:38-39
[1077] Romans 8:30
[1078] Genesis 12:1-3 & 15:5-6, 18, etc., & 17:2, etc., Romans 4

glory – such preparations we utterly deny and disallow, as impossible to the corrupt state of man, and as utterly inconsistent with the riches of the grace of God.

Here also it may be noted, how some distinguish (and not amiss) of the promises of the Covenant of Grace; that some of them are conditional, namely: those that concern the end itself, enjoyment of God in heaven, salvation, etc.; that others are absolute, namely: those that concern the way and means, to the end, which God promises absolutely to give.[1079]

(ii) *Conditions concomitant*, or accompanying God's entering into covenant with man, are: the acting, actual exercising, using or putting forth of such preparatory habits of grace as are already received in order to close with God actually in his Covenant accordingly, as the nature of his Covenant requires. Thus God requires of them that join in covenant with him:

The act of self-denial by an holy self-resignation and self-renouncing: as in Abraham; when God covenanted with him, he must actually deny, and depart from his country, kindred and father's house.[1080] Paul actually denied all self-righteousness, and self-excellencies, as loss and dung, for the excellency of the knowledge of Christ, and for Christ's righteousness by faith.[1081] Christ requires all that come to him to *deny themselves*.[1082] The grace of God, the gospel, teaches all that would walk with God according to his Covenant, to deny all ungodliness and worldly lusts.[1083]

[1079] *Intelligere te oportet*, etc. Thou must understand that the promises of God are, either concerning the end itself, namely man's enjoyment of God in eternal happiness, and the salvation of our souls; or such as concern the way and means unto that end. Now those which do concern the end, are indeed conditional, that no profane person should dare to stretch forth his hand to the Tree of Life. But lest there should be none to whom these promises may appertain, for we all come short of the condition, he hath made promises of the conditions themselves, and made them pure, free, simple, absolute, *nullis conditionum articula circumscriptas*, not circumscribed with any articles of conditions at all. *Abbots in Thoms. Diat. page 148.*
[1080] Genesis 12:1-4 with Galatians 3:16-17
[1081] Philippians 3:4-12
[1082] Luke 9:23
[1083] Titus 2:11-12

The *acting of repentance*. Thus Christ began to preach the gospel, or covenant of God: *Repent ye, and believe the gospel*.[1084] Thus Peter directs his heart-wounded hearers: *Repent, for the promise is to you and to your children, and to all that are afar off, even as many as the Lord our God shall call*.[1085]

The *acting of faith*: taking the Lord for their God, and consenting thereby to be his people. In the Sinai Covenant's solemn sanction, Moses with a bunch of hyssop actually sprinkled one half of the blood of the sacrifices on the people, as the other half on the altar: hereby teaching them actually to apply by faith the blood of Christ to themselves in whom God accepted them as his covenant-people.[1086] Christ preached: *believe the gospel*.[1087] The apostle Paul and Silas preached the New Covenant thus to the jailor *trembling, and saying, Sirs, what must I do to be saved? Believe on the Lord Jesus Christ, and thou shalt be saved, and thy house*.[1088] No one duty is more pressed than actually believing, to those who would close actually in covenant with God.[1089]

The *acting of love*. The Sinai Covenant, the Old Testament, was a marriage covenant between God and Israel.[1090] And this marriage covenant in the nature of it required the mutual acting and exercising of their love to God. This therefore was the great commandment conditioned in the Sinai Covenant: *Thou shalt love the LORD thy God with all thine heart, with all thy soul, and with all thy might*.[1091]

(iii) *Conditions consequent*, or following God's taking man into covenant with himself, are such duties or performances as God requires from a people in covenant with him, and which flow from a true covenant-state as the proper fruits, effects and consequents thereof. As,

---

[1084] Mark 1:15
[1085] Acts 2:38-39
[1086] Exodus 24:6-8 with Hebrews 9:18-20
[1087] Mark 1:15
[1088] Acts 16:29-32
[1089] Romans 10;6-18
[1090] Jeremiah 31:31-32, Ezekiel 16:8
[1091] Deuteronomy 5:6-7 & 6:4-5, Matthew 22:37

Sincere universal and constant evangelical obedience to God according to the mandatory part of his covenant. Thus, God covenants with Noah to save him and his family in an ark by water from the general deluge, but Noah after this covenant must be obedient fully to God in making, entering into, and continuing in the ark.[1092] God covenants with Abraham that *in his seed all the families of the earth should be blessed*, etc.[1093] But after this, Abraham must walk before God (namely, in all true faith and obedience) and be perfect. And particularly, himself and all his males must be circumcised throughout their generations in token of this covenant. God covenants with Israel at Mount Sinai, *to be their God, to raise them up Christ a prophet and mediator from among themselves*, etc.[1094] But after this, Israel must walk in all upright obedience to all God's laws and commandments in an evangelical sense. *O that there were such a heart in them, that they would fear me, and keep all my commandments always, that it might be well with them and their children forever*[1095]. God covenants with the Babylonian captives to give them a new heart and spirit, etc., but after this they must walk in his statutes, and keep his judgements, and do them.[1096] The like may be said of all expressions of the Covenant of Faith.

Renewing covenant with God by renewed repentance, in case of covenant-breaches or backslidings. Thus God tells Israel; *if they shall forsake the covenant of the Lord God*, to serve other gods, so that the Lord thereupon shall root them out of Canaan, and disperse them into strange countries, yet if they shall return unto the Lord their God and obey his voice according to all that he commanded them, then he would gather them again, etc., promising to *circumcise their heart to this effect.—and thou shalt return and obey the voice of*

[1092] Genesis 6:17-18, etc.
[1093] Genesis 12:2-3 & 15:18 with 17:1-2, 9-15
[1094] Exodus 20:2-3, Deuteronomy 5:6-7
[1095] Deuteronomy 5:29, 32-33 & 6:1-4 to 10:17-18 & 8:1, 6, and often
[1096] Ezekiel 37:24-27

the Lord.[1097] God commands renewing of repentance in case of all failings against the covenant, promising re-acceptance of his people thereupon.[1098]

Thus of conditions in reference to God's covenant, considered most largely.

{2} *More restrictively*, so, the condition of the Covenant of Faith does more peculiarly and singularly import to us that special instrumental cause, or means whereby we accept or receive the federal benefits promised, which is only true faith. And by this condition of faith,[1099] the Covenant of Faith or Grace is most directly opposed and contradistinguished from the Covenant of Works, the special condition whereof was works, done by a man's own ability. This faith is so singular and eminent a condition of this covenant, that both covenant, federal benefits, and federal parties in covenant with God, receive their denominations from faith. The covenant is styled the law of faith[1100] – the federal righteousness of it, the righteousness of faith[1101] – and the federates with God, those who are of faith.[1102] In this sense, one said well: "Faith has the greatest honor above all other graces, to be the condition of the covenant."[1103]

[1097] Deuteronomy 30:1-9 with 29:24 to the end

[1098] "Of them that slip aside and transgress the covenant, God calls for and commands repentance, that is, it is his will and command, that they bethink themselves of their evil-doings, confess their iniquities, and turn unto the Lord. The frequent and earnest exhortations of the prophets made to backsliding and rebellious Israel, that she should acknowledge her wickedness and return unto the Lord (Jeremiah 3:7, 22 & 4:1-2) is a full commentary of that which God required of them in this covenant, in case they should turn away from the holy commandment. The Lord protests by his prophet Ezekiel, That he has no pleasure in the death of him that dieth, but rather that he should repent and live. Ezekiel 18:27-28, 31-32. & 33:11-12. And the same for substance he made known to Israel in the covenant which he stroke with them, namely: that if they transgress and go astray, he does admit, will accept and approve, nay command their unfeigned repentance, and coming home unto the Lord. that they might live." *Mr. John Ball, Treatise of the Covenant, chap. 8. page 133. Lord. 1645.*

[1099] Romans 3:27 & 10:5-14

[1100] Romans 3:27

[1101] Romans 10:6, Philippians 3:9, Hebrews 11:7

[1102] Galatians 3:9

[1103] Mr. Jeremiah Burroughs in *Moses' Self-Denial*

And to this effect another said much better than he: "The stipulation required, is, that we take God to be our God: that is, that we repent of our iniquities, believe the promises of mercy and embrace them with the whole heart, and yield love, fear,[1104] reverence, worship and obedience unto him according to the prescript rule of his word. Repentance is called for in this covenant, as it sets forth the subject capable of salvation by faith; but is itself only an acknowledgement of sin, no healing of our wound or cause of our acquittance. By repentance we know ourselves, we feel our sickness, we hunger and thirst after grace, but the hand which we stretch forth to receive it, is faith alone, without which repentance is nothing but darkness and despair. Repentance is the condition of faith, and the qualification of a person capable of salvation: but faith alone is the cause of justification and salvation on our part required: it is a penitent and petitioning faith whereby we receive the promises of mercy, but we are not justified partly by prayer, partly by repentance, and partly by faith, but by that faith which stirs up godly sorrow for sin, and enforces us to pray for pardon and salvation. Faith is a necessary and lively instrument of justification, which is amongst the number of true causes, not being a cause without which the thing is not done, but a cause whereby it is done," etc.[1105] After which discourse he thus winds it up towards a conclusion: "If then, when we speak of the conditions of the Covenant of Grace, by {*conditions*}, we understand what is required on our part, as precedent, concomitant, or subsequent to justification, repentance, faith and obedience are all conditions: but if by {*condition*} we understand what is required on our part, as the cause of the good promised, though only instrumental, faith or belief in the promises of free mercy is the only condition."

{3} ***Most strictly***, a *condition* of a covenant may import such a restipulation from man to God, as God requires to be perfectly in all parts and degrees, and constantly performed by him in his own person, without the least

---

[1104] This reads {*fea*} in the original text.
[1105] Mr. John Ball in his *Treatise of the Covenant*, chapter 3, p.17-20, London, 1645

failure or default, otherwise the covenant will be broken. Now {*condition*} taken in this extremity of strictness and rigor, without any terms of moderation or mercy at all, in case of the least default, was the condition of the Covenant of Works. According to that; *Cursed is everyone that continues not in all things which are written in the book of the law to do them.*[1106] Wherein, (i) perfect, and (ii) perpetual, (iii) personal obedience, is the rigorous condition required: without which the curse could not be avoided.

Thirdly, these things thus premised, the true state of the question may be declared in these few positions following, touching the conditionality of the Covenant of Faith, namely:

(i) *No condition (taken in the most strict and rigorous sense) is imposed or required by God upon, or from his people in any dispensation of the Covenant of Faith, so as the least gradual failing of that complete exactness should utterly dissolve and break the covenant.* Such an exact rigorous obedience was the condition of the Covenant of Works, imposed on Adam in innocency, whose failing in one act utterly broke and dissolved the Covenant of Works so that it became totally impossible both for him and all his sinful posterity ever to keep or to be justified by the Covenant of Works any more. But no condition – neither of faith, nor of repentance, nor of obedience, etc. – is in such a rigorous sense required or imposed in the Covenant of Faith, in any expression of it, but every condition is evangelically leanified and sweetened with the adjunct of integrity and sincerity. Unfeigned faith is accepted, though attended with some gradual weakness and imperfection;[1107] sincere, upright uniform obedience is accepted, though accompanied with sundry defects and infirmities.[1108] In this Covenant, God requires strict, exact and perfect obedience, but accepts sincere, uniform, impartial obedience. He calls for exactness and accepts uprightness. If exactness were not required, gradual failings and other infirmities would not be reputed sins, mourned for, and

---

[1106] Galatians 3:10, Deuteronomy 27:26
[1107] 1 Timothy 1:5
[1108] Psalm 19:12-13 & 119:6

strived against. If uprightness were not accepted, no flesh could be justified or saved.

(ii) *No conditions, in, or from man, as impulsive or meritorious to his covenant-state, are required or admitted at all in this Covenant of Faith.* In man out of covenant with God, there can be no antecedent cause or condition either meriting from God – of condignity or of congruity – to be brought into covenant with him, or to be a partaker of justification, or any other saving benefit of the covenant from him, or moving and inclining God to bring him into covenant with himself. All such antecedent conditions we utterly disclaim as wholly inconsistent with this gratuitous gospel Covenant of Faith.[1109] *Antecedent impulsives* or *motives* in man, we leave to the Remonstrants and papists; *antecedent merits* to the papists. The most perfect believers cannot properly merit, at all – much less unbelievers. See Romans 11:35-36, Job 22:2 & 35:4-5, Romans 3:12, Luke 17:10. .

(iii) In the *restrictive sense, unfeigned faith, and that alone, is the condition of the Covenant of Faith.* Faith alone being that supernatural instrument whereby a man actually on his part (through the grace of God) accepts the covenant, and the promised mercies of the covenant.

(iv) *If we understand conditions most largely. So the Covenant of Faith admits of, and requires many supernatural conditions, both antecedent, for preparing supernaturally for the covenant; and concomitant, for closing with the covenant; and consequent, for suitable walking according to the covenant afterwards.* As has been explained.

[1109] True it is the promises run upon this condition: *If ye obey my voice, and do my commandments*; But conditions are of two sorts, antecedent or consequent. antecedent, when the condition is the cause of the thing promised or given, as in all civil contracts of justice, where one thing is given for another. Consequent, when the condition is annexed to the promise, as a qualification in the subject, or an adjunct that must attend the thing promised. And in this later sense, obedience to the commandments, was a condition of the promise: Not a cause why the thing promised was vouchsafed; but a qualification of the subject capable, or a consequence of such great mercy freely conferred. Mr. John Ball in his Treatise of the Covenant, chap. 8. pag. 132, 133. Lond. 1645.

And according to these two last positions only, we assert and maintain that the Covenant of Faith, or Grace is *conditional*.

(2) **For confirmation of this assertion of the conditionality of the Covenant of Faith**, thus stated (as the plain and evident truth), I offer these few arguments or reasons briefly.

[1] The very nature of all God's covenants with man necessarily implies and requires therein conditions, terms, restipulations, re-promissions, re-engagements from man to God: without which, nothing can properly and exactly be called a covenant. God (among other ways) expresses his will to man, by promise, by threats, by command, by covenant. Each of these, in the nature of the thing, have a precise and peculiar propriety of essence, differencing and distinguishing them one from another. By *promise*, God declares what good he will do for man; by *threatening*, he declares what evil he will inflict upon man; by command, he declares what duty and performance he expects from man; but by *covenant*, he declares both what mercies and blessings he will on his part perform to man, and what duties man should on his part perform reflexively towards God. This is the proper nature of a *covenant*. It comprises *mutual consent and agreement of the federates about some mutual performances, and reciprocal obligations.*

A bare naked promise holds forth mercy from God, but not any duty from man; a bare naked command holds forth duty from man, but not any mercy or blessing from God. But a covenant wherein God and man convene and agree, holds forth both mercy from God and duty from man. So that a promise or a command in the precise nature thereof may be without mutual obligation, but a covenant has in it always a mutual obligation between God and man, the federal parties. To speak therefore of a covenant of God with man without conditions required on man's part, is a contradiction in the adject. Whatsoever promise has in it the proper nature of a covenant is conditional – expressly or implicitly – and whatsoever promise is conditional, has in it the nature of a covenant. All God's Covenants with man are either of works or of faith. In the Covenant of Works before the fall, God promised perpetual life to man in paradise, but conditioned with man to perform perfect and perpetual obedience to God in his own person, otherwise he should die the death.[1110] In the Covenant of Faith since the fall, God promises lapsed man's restoration by Jesus Christ, but conditions with man to believe in Jesus Christ, otherwise he should not share in that restoration.[1111]

[2] God has – expressly or implicitly – imposed upon his covenant-people such conditions and terms as these, by the Covenant of Faith in all the observable expressures, and discoveries thereof. Such re-stipulations, re-performances, re-promissions, etc. God still requires and conditions from those who will lay hold of his covenant and mean to approve themselves his true covenant-people. And therefore his Covenant of Faith must needs be conditional. The consequence is undeniable. The antecedent also is easily cleared by induction of particulars. For,

{1} In the first expressure of the Covenant of Faith from Adam until Noah, God promised explicitly to put an enmity between the seed of the woman (namely: primarily Christ and secondarily his members) and the serpent and his seed, that is: Satan and the wicked, and that the woman's seed should bruise the serpent's head.[1112] But withal God conditioned implicitly with the woman's seed Christ and his members that Christ should fight against and subdue the devil and his seed efficaciously and meritoriously, and that all his members should renounce the serpent and his seed and fight against them by gospel-faith and obedience in Christ that they might bruise his head.

{2} In the second expressure of the Covenant from Noah until Abraham, God promised to save Noah and his family in the ark by water from the general flood, but yet God conditioned with Noah that he should believe this his salvation by such means, and that he should obey God in preparing an ark,

---

[1110] Genesis 2:9, 16-17
[1111] Romans 10:6 etc., John 3:15-16, 18, 36; Mark 16:16
[1112] Genesis 3:15

in laying up necessary provision in it, in entering into it, and continuing in it till the flood should be abated.[1113]

{3} In the third Covenant expressure from Abraham until Moses, God promised to Abraham to be a God to him and his seed, to make all the nations of the earth blessed in his seed, to give them the land of Canaan, etc;[1114] but yet indented and conditioned with Abraham to deny his country, kindred, and father's house, to believe in the Lord, to walk before him and be perfect, and to submit himself and all his male seed to the token of the covenant circumcision.[1115]

{4} In the fourth Covenant expressure from Moses until David, God promised to be a God to Israel,[1116] to raise them up Christ a prophet and mediator like Moses from among themselves,[1117] to give them his sanctifying Spirit, and many spiritual blessings,[1118] to superadd to them Canaan, and many temporals, and at last to crown them with eternal life;[1119] but withal God conditioned and articled with them, that they should be his covenant-people,[1120] that they should keep his Covenant by true faith and sincere impartial obedience to all his commandments: *and he declared unto them his covenant which he commanded them to perform, even ten commandments.*[1121] And that in case of any contrary failings, they should bethink themselves, repent, and return to God.[1122]

{5} In the fifth Covenant expressure from David until the Babylonian captivity, God promised: *to establish David's seed forever, to set up the fruit of his body upon his throne, to build up his throne to all generations*, etc.[1123] But withal conditioned with David, *if thy children will keep my covenant and my*

[1113] Genesis 6:18, compared with 1 Peter 3:21
[1114] Genesis 17:7-8; 12:2-3 & 15:18, etc.
[1115] Genesis 12:1-3, 15:6, 17:1-2, 9-15
[1116] Exodus 20:2-3, Deuteronomy 26:12
[1117] Leviticus 18:15-20
[1118] Deuteronomy 30:6, 8
[1119] Exodus 20:12, Ephesians 6:2, Deuteronomy 28:1-15, Leviticus 26:3-14
[1120] Exodus 20:2-3, Leviticus 26:12
[1121] Exodus 19:5, Deuteronomy 4:13 & 5:29
[1122] Deuteronomy 30:1-2, Leviticus 26:40-42, 1 Kings 8:46-54
[1123] Psalm 132:11 & 89:3-4, 19-38

testimony, that I shall teach them; otherwise, *he would visit their transgression with the rod, and their iniquity with stripes,* etc.[1124]

{6} In the sixth Covenant expressure from the Babylonian captivity until Christ, God promised to his people: to gather them out of all countries whither he had driven them, to bring them back to their own land and cause them to dwell safely, to be their God, not to turn away from them to do them good, etc.[1125] But withal he conditioned with them, that they should be his people, that they should not depart away from him, but fear him forever, etc.[1126]

{7} Finally, in the seventh and last covenant-expressure, the New Covenant, God promises to his people, to put and write his law in their hearts and minds, to be their God, to make them all know the Lord, to be merciful to their unrighteousnesses, to remember their sins and their iniquities no more:[1127] but withal agrees and conditions with them; to be his people (which one condition has all other conditions in it),[1128] to draw near with a true heart, with full assurance of faith, etc.[1129] To hold fast the profession of our faith without wavering, to consider one another, to provoke unto love and good works, etc. And elsewhere, from the covenant promises, we are pressed to perfect sanctification.[1130] Thus the whole series of the Covenant of Faith from first to last is propounded in all the noted discoveries of it, with conditions and duties required from God's covenant people: and therefore it is conditional throughout all ages. He that does not see this, is either a great stranger to the Scriptures, or he wilfully shuts his eyes against the light thereof.

[3] The many cautions, warnings, and threatenings annexed to the Covenant of Faith in all the several discoveries thereof – against breaking,

---

[1124] Psalm 132:12 & 89:30-33
[1125] Jeremiah 32:37 to the end
[1126] Jeremiah 32:38-40
[1127] Hebrews 8:8 to the end
[1128] Hebrews 8:10
[1129] Hebrews 10:16-26
[1130] 2 Corinthians 6:17-18 & 7:1

violating or transgressing God's Covenant, by unbelief or disobedience – do eminently imply that the contrary duties, or keeping of that covenant, are required and conditioned in the Covenant of Faith,[1131] and consequently that it is conditional.

[4] Without such federal conditions, terms or qualifications as these, none can be duly prepared for the Covenant of Faith or be actually stated in and partakers of the Covenant of Faith and the federal benefits thereof, nor can converse and walk suitably and agreeably to the Covenant of Faith. Therefore such conditions are, in their place and kind, necessary to the effectual application of the Covenant, and of covenant benefits unto us, for our covenant preparation, our covenant participation, and our covenant conversation. {1} How should we be prepared for entering into covenant with God, without some such antecedent preparatory conditions as these, namely: (i) hearing God's covenant preached, (ii) conviction of the necessity of a true covenant-state in Christ, (iii) and effectual calling, instilling supernatural abilities and principles for closing actually with the covenant? {2} How should we actually close with God in this covenant, without the acting or actual exerting and exercising of (i) self-denial, (ii) repentance, (iii) faith, (iv) love, and such like concomitant conditions? {3} How should we walk answerably to such a covenant-state afterwards, without (i) sincere, impartial, and constant gospel-obedience to God in Christ according to covenant-commands; (ii) renewing of repentance in case of failings and backslidings; or such consequent covenant-conditions? All which I have already proved to be necessary covenant

---

[1131] As, {1} Under the first covenant-discovery (Genesis 4:7, 1:6, 3:7, 13). {2} Under the second covenant-discovery from Noah until Abraham (Genesis 6:17-18. & 7:4. & 9:5-6, 25-26). {3} Under the third Covenant-discovery from Abraham until Moses (Genesis 17:14). {4} Under the fourth Covenant-discovery from Moses until David (Exodus 20:6-7. & 31:14-15. & 33:3, 5 & 34:7, Leviticus 26:14-40, Deuteronomy 28:16. to the end, etc). {5} Under the fifth covenant-dispensation from David until the captivity (Psalm 89:30-33, 2 Samuel 7:14). {6} Under the sixth covenant-dispensation, from the captivity until Christ. (Ezekiel 11:19-21, Malachi 2:11-13 & 3:5, 8-10. & 4:1). {7} Lastly, under the New Testament (Mark 16:16, John 3:18, 36, 1 Corinthians 6:9-10, Revelation 21:8).

conditions, in opening the state of the question. And if these be so requisite to our covenant state, how can they be anything other than covenant conditions?

[5] Such conditions as these, do in no regard eclipse, but rather, much advance both the glory of God's free grace and the sweetness of our consolation. Why then should it be thought harsh, strange, inconvenient, or any way prejudicial, to assert the conditionality of this Covenant of Faith?

{1} *These conditions do not eclipse, but advance the riches and glory of God's free grace.* For, (i) All antecedent conditions that might be imagined or pretended – either to merit any covenant-blessing from God, or as any impulsive cause to move or incline God to admit us into covenant with himself – are hereby utterly disclaimed and disavowed. (ii) All these covenant conditions allowed and asserted – antecedent, concomitant and consequent – are avowed by us to be wholly supernatural: the mere fruits and effects of divine grace, not at all of human nature; wholly of God, and not of ourselves at all. Of mere grace, God contrived his Covenant for us, God revealed his Covenant to us, God prepares us for his Covenant, God instates us in his covenant, and of the same mere grace he enables us to walk according to his Covenant proportionably: all is entirely of his mere grace. Therefore herein we take no glory at all to ourselves, but return the whole glory entirely to God alone. For *what have we, but we have received it from him?*[1132] *He works in us both to will and to do, of his good pleasure.*[1133] *He draws, and we come.*[1134] *He quickens us*: and then *lives in us, and we by him.*[1135] He works all in us, and for us without whom *we can do nothing.*[1136] To him we herein ascribe, the first grace, principling us; and the second grace, actuating those principles: preventing grace, and subsequent grace: operating grace, and cooperating grace, knocking grace, opening grace, entering grace: we ascribe all to him, and

---

[1132] 1 Corinthians 4:7
[1133] Philippians 2:13
[1134] John 6:44, Song of Solomon 1:4
[1135] Ephesians 1, etc., Galatians 2:20, John 6:57
[1136] John 15:5

to his grace.[1137] *For of him, and through him, and to him, are all things.*[1138] (iii) The apostle tells us that the special condition of faith whereby we receive the covenant and covenanted inheritance is most subservient to grace, saying, *therefore it is of faith, that it might be by grace.*[1139] If the inheritance were by works, it should be of debt; but being by faith, it is of grace. Faith and grace go together. Grace freely gives; faith alone receives. Grace is the fountain; faith the cistern.

{2} *These and like conditions do not eclipse but augment the sweetness of our consolations also.* For, (i) by these *preparatory conditions*, we are comfortably qualified to be subjects capable of the covenant. (ii) By these *concomitant conditions*, we are comfortably enabled to accept and lay hold upon God's Covenant, who by nature are strangers to the saving benefits of his covenant. And the *promise is made sure to all the believing seed.*[1140] (iii) By these *consequent conditions*, we are comfortably conformed in our conversation to the tenor of God's Covenant which we have accepted. (iv) By all these *conditions*, we are comfortably distinguished from all people that are strangers to God's Covenants, and we may comfortably try ourselves and discover whether we be in a good covenant state or not.

[6] Many and great absurdities, inconveniencies, paradoxes, and incongruities must needs inevitably follow, upon denial of conditionality to the Covenant of Faith. For if in the Covenant of Faith, or in any one expressure thereof, there be no terms, ties, restipulations, re-obligations, conditions, etc., imposed upon man, or expected from man, but all the ties and obligations are only on God's part:

{1} Then the Covenant of Faith binds only one, not both the federates. While God is bound by his *stipulation*, man is not bound by any *restipulation*. Now how absurd and contrary to the nature of a covenant is it to think God

---

[1137] Revelation 3:20, Song of Solomon 5:4, etc.
[1138] Romans 11:36
[1139] Romans 4:16
[1140] Romans 4:16

to be under obligation to man, and yet man to be at liberty from God? Covenants imply reciprocal obligations between federates.

{2} Then God and man may agree in one and the same Covenant of Faith as federates, and yet man on his part never consent to the covenant. For consent to the covenant by faith is one of the conditions asserted on our part, but if there be no conditions at all on our part, then there is no consent. How gross and absurd a paradox is this, to imagine man's covenant agreement with God, yet without consent?

{3} Then those that become federates with God in the Covenant of Faith, have no more covenant obligation, bond, tie, or duty lying upon them, after their closing in covenant with God than before. They are no more bound to fear, love, obey, serve, walk with God, after covenanting with him in Christ than before. For, the covenant brings no tie or condition upon them, but leaves them loose. How absurd! This makes God's Covenant a very loose covenant, a very licentious covenant, and therein God to have very ill provided for his own worship and service.

{4} Then a man may be in covenant with God, and yet not differ at all by any inward covenant-qualification, or outward covenant-conversation from them that are out of covenant. For, they that are out of covenant with God, are destitute wholly of all salvific covenant conditions: and (according to this opinion) so is he. So that in this regard, it had been as good for him to have been still without, as within a covenant-state.

{5} Then God's covenant-people have no gospel-rule written for their faith and obedience. For they (according to this fond opinion) have no tie or condition at all imposed upon them in this Covenant of Faith, therefore the condition of faith and the condition of obedience is not thereby enjoined upon them. Consequently, if it be not required by the Covenant of Faith, it is not required in all the Scripture. For since the fall, the whole Scripture, which is gospel, is taken up with propounding or expounding the Covenant of Faith in Christ in one respect or another, throughout all the various dispensations thereof.

{6} Then neglect of those grand comprehensive Christian duties – faith and obedience to God in Christ – is no sin. For the Covenant of Faith (think they) does not impose or require these conditions and duties, and consequently, no Scripture requires them. How can it be then any sin to neglect them? For *where there's no law, there's no transgression.*[1141] And what is sin, if this be not sin?

{7} Then the having, and using of faith and obedience towards God in Jesus Christ, is not the way to heaven and eternal salvation. Why? Because (according to this opinion) the Covenant of Faith, which peculiarly chalks out to us the true way to heaven and salvation, yet requires no such conditions at all from us, as faith and obedience, in order to eternal salvation. But this is notoriously contrary to the covenant and Scriptures, teaching that without them there's no salvation.[1142]

{8} Then faith and obedience to God in Jesus Christ were will-worship, un-instituted, un-required of God. For, if the Covenant of Faith do not require them, do not indent and condition for them, no Scripture since the Fall requires them: all Scripture being wholly taken up one way or other about this Covenant of Faith. And if they be not required from us, how shall they be excused from will-worship, and being inventions of man?[1143] God then may say, *who required these things at your hands?*[1144]

{9} Then the pagans that are utter aliens to God's Covenant of Faith, are as much tied to duties of religion, as true Christians that are federates with God in Christ. For these are (after this opinion) tied to no duties, terms or conditions, by covenant, and those, as well as Christians, are tied by the law and light of nature in the natural conscience to believe, obey, worship and serve the true God, that has made heaven and earth.[1145]

[1141] Romans 4:15 & 5:13
[1142] Mark 16:16, John 3:18, 36, Hebrews 11:6, 2 Thessalonians 1:8, Hebrews 12:14, James 2:14 to the end
[1143] Jeremiah 7:31 & 32:35
[1144] Isaiah 1:12
[1145] Romans 1:18 to the end & 2:14-16

{10} Then finally, the gospel ministry and ordinances of Christ both under Old and New Testament, intended and given of God to his church for preparing man for Christ, for espousing man savingly to Christ, and for guiding men conscientiously in Christ unto perfection, are altogether vain and useless.[1146] For (according to this opinion) all conditions tending to prepare for Christ, unite to him, or to give communion with him, are denied. But the Scriptures abundantly testify that God's Covenant of Faith appoints a gospel-ministry and ordinances for the said end, to continue in his church till the world's end.

From all this, it's plain that to deny the *conditionality* of the Covenant of Faith is an absurd opinion with a witness that dashes upon so many notorious and intolerable absurdities.

[7] The judgments of sound writers, godly and learned, ancient and modern, foreign and domestic, do unanimously subscribe to the conditionality of the Covenant of Faith or grace, in the sense before stated and explained. And we are to walk in the way of good men, and keep the paths of the righteous:[1147] and to follow them that are of the truth, as they follow Christ and his truth.[1148] Ancient writers (I confess) speak more sparingly of God's Covenant of Grace, and so consequently of the conditions therein required on our part: notwithstanding they frequently urge the necessity and use of repentance, faith, obedience, etc., in order to the attainment of the respective blessings spiritual and eternally promised, which is as much for substance. But modern writers proceed to more exact consideration of God's Covenant and plainly assert the conditionality thereof in express terms. I offer here a brief taste of their sense in this point to the reader, whereby he may see that this conditionality of the covenant is not any odd opinion of singularity, but a truth very generally received.

[1146] Matthew 28:18-20, Acts 26:18, Ephesians 4:8-14, 2 Corinthians 5:19-20, 2 Corinthians 11:2, 1 Corinthians 11:26
[1147] Proverbs 2:20
[1148] 1 Corinthians 11:1

Clement of Rome, who lived in the apostles' times, thus speaks of God's expectation of repentance in all that convert to him, i.e., "Let us consider all generations, and we may learn that in every generation the Lord has given place of repentance to them that were willing to convert unto him. Noah preached repentance, and those that obeyed him were saved. Jonah preached destruction to the Ninevites, but they that repented of their sins, pacified God with their prayers, and obtained salvation, although they were aliens to God, etc. (Ezekiel 23:11. etc., Isaiah 1:16. etc.) Therefore he, willing that all his beloved ones should be partakers of repentance, has established it by his omnipotent will."[1149] Thus he speaks of our justification by faith alone, and not by good works; yet exhorts upon other grounds unto good-works, etc. "And we being called by his will in Christ Jesus, are not justified by ourselves, nor by our own wisdom, or understanding, or godliness, or works which we have wrought in holiness of heart: but by faith, by which the almighty God has justified all from the beginning. To whom be glory unto ages of ages, amen. What then shall we do, brethren? Shall we cease from well-doing, and relinquish charity? The Lord does by no means suffer this to be done of us, but let us hasten with all diligence and readiness of mind to finish every good work. We see all the just were adorned with good works, and even the Lord himself adorning himself with works rejoiced," etc.[1150]

And elsewhere he thus incites to obedience: "Take we Enoch, who being found righteous in obedience, was translated, nor was his death found. Noah being found faithful, by his ministry he preached regeneration to the world; and by him the Lord saved the creatures which with consent entered into the ark. Abraham, called the friend of God, was found faithful in that he became obedient to the words of God. He, by obedience came out from his country, and from his kindred, and from his father's house, that leaving a little country, and a weak kindred, and a small house, he might inherit the promises of God (Genesis 12:1, etc., 13:14, etc., 15:5, etc.)."[1151]

[1149] Clem. Rom. In 1. Ep. Ad cor. p. 10, 11, 12. Edit. Oxonii. 1633
[1150] Ibid. Pag. 41, 42, 43.
[1151] Ibid. Pag. 12, 13, 14, 15.

And thus he elsewhere directs, in reference to the obtaining of promised gifts, and the finding of Christ, etc., i.e. "Let us therefore earnestly strive to be found in the number of them that wait for him, that we may partake the gifts promised. But how shall this be, beloved? If our mind be established on God by faith, if we seek out things well-pleasing and acceptable to him, if we perform things agreeable to his inculpable will, and if we shall follow the way of truth etc.—this is the way beloved, in which we shall find our savior Jesus Christ, the high-priest of our offerings, the supporter and succourer of our infirmity," etc.[1152]

Justin Martyr, the philosopher, who wrote about 150 years after Christ, thus declares the necessity of faith in Christ and repentance, etc. exhorting the Jews thereunto, etc., i.e., "If there be among you any perjured-person, or thief, let him cease to sin: if any fornicator, let him repent; and keep true and joyful sabbaths to God: if any have impure hands, let him wash them, and become pure. For Isaiah has not sent you into a bath, that there you might wash away murders and other offenses, which even the water of the sea is not sufficient to purge away; but, as is meet, this anciently was that salvifical washing, which was spoken to the penitent – nor are they any more purified with the blood of goats or sheep, or with the ashes of an heifer, or like oblations, but by faith through the blood of Christ, and his death, who died for that very cause, as Isaiah says, etc. Therefore by the laver of repentance, and of the knowledge of God, which was instituted for the sins of God's people, as Isaiah's cries, we believe, and know, and preach; that very washing declared by him, which alone can purify the penitent, to be the water of life."[1153]

And afterwards he says: "Abraham had not from God a testimony of his righteousness, for his circumcision, but for his faith. For before he was circumcised, thus it was said of him: *and Abraham believed God, and that was reckoned to him unto righteousness.* Wherefore we also in the uncircumcision of our flesh, believing God through Christ, and obtaining that circumcision

---

[1152] Ibid. Pag. 45, 46, 47.
[1153] Justin Martyr, Dialogue with Trypho the Jew

which is profitable to the obtainers, namely, circumcision of the heart, we hope we shall appear just and well-pleasing unto God."[1154]

Cyprian, who wrote about 240 years after Christ, singularly commends faith as that whereby we are justified, whereby we receive the plentiful endowments of the Holy Ghost, and whereby we have all our ability.[1155] Ambrose, who flourished in the year 374, etc., after Christ, thus speaks of the necessity of faith to salvation.[1156] Jerome, who flourished in the 385th year after Christ, does plainly assert certain promises (which have special reference to the times of the New Testament) to be upon condition.[1157] Chrysostom, who flourished, in the year 398 after Christ, shows that God requires faith unto justification, i.e., hearing of salvation, he added righteousness and not thy righteousness, but God's subindicating the abundance and facility thereof. "For thou dost not obtain it by sweatings and labors, but receivest it from the gift above, being only one thing from within, to believe."[1158] And afterwards: "How is it excluded, says he? By what law? Of works? Nay, but by the law of faith. Lo, he calls even faith a law, persisting in the names, that he might

---

[1154] Justin Martyr, Dialogue with Trypho the Jew

[1155] Cypr. Testimon. L. 3. S. 42. P 428. Edit. 1593 "Fidem in totum prodesse: & tantum nos posse, quantum credimus. In genesi; et credidit Abraham deo, & deputatum est ei ad justitiam. And elsewhere, non enim, qui beneficiorum terrestrium mos, in capessendo munere coelesti, mensura ulla vel modus est: profluens largiter spiritus nullis finibus premitur, nec coercentibus claustris intra certa metarum spatia fraenatur. Manat jugiter: exuberat affluenter. Nostrum tantum sitiat pectus, & pateat. Quantum illuc fidei capacis afferimus, tantum gratiae inundantis haurimus."

[1156] "Secundum propositum gratiae dei. Sic decretum dicit à Dio ut cessante lege solam fidem gratiae dei posceret ad salutem.—manifestè beati sunt, quibus sine labore vel opere aliquo remittuntur iniquitates & peccata teguntur nullâ ab his requisitâ poenitentiae operâ, nisi tantum ut credant." Ambrose's Commentary on Romans 4. p. 189. Edit. 1567. And elsewhere, speaking of the law of the Spirit, he saith: "Haec lex dat libertatem, solam fidem poscens: ut quia quae non videt credit, de conditione erui mereatur." Com. In ep. 2. Ad corinth. C. 3. Pag. 299.

[1157] illudque dicamus, quod etiamsi carnaliter sunt promissa judaeis, tamen sub conditione sunt promissa, ut si suscepissent lumen suum quod ad eos missum fuerat, tunc etiam ista sequerentur. Quod namely, Per desiderium auri, & opum abundantiam, rerumque carnalium, quarum semper ista gens capiatur illecebris, susciperent ad se missum filium dei: quem quia non susceperunt, universa sublata sunt, & suscipientibus spiritualiter reddita haereditas. Hieronym. Comment. In Isaiam. Cap. 60 pag. 228. A. B. Tom. 5. Edit. 1553.

[1158] Chrys. Homil. 2. In ep. Ad rom. 1. 17 p. 28. A. Edit. Paris. 1633

leanify the seeming newness. But what is the law of faith? To be saved by grace. Hence he shows the power of God, that he not only saves, but also justifies, and leads unto glorying needing nothing of works, but requiring faith alone."[1159]

Augustine, who flourished in the year 420 after Christ, declares faith to be fundamentally necessary, but such a faith as works by love, and produces good works.[1160]

To mention no more ancient writers, come we to the latter writers, foreign and domestic, who speak more punctually and clearly to the matter in hand.

Calvin, that apostolical man, speaking of the covenant mentioned in Hosea 2, thus expresses the reciprocity, and consequently the conditionality thereof: "He then declares by what means he would do this, even in righteousness and judgment, and then in kindness and mercies, and thirdly, in faithfulness. God had indeed from the beginning covenanted with the Israelites in righteousness and judgment; there was nothing disguised or false in his covenant: as then God had in sincerity adopted the people, to what vices does he oppose righteousness and judgment? I answer: these words must be

---

[1159] Ibid. Homil. 7. In epist. Ad rom. 3 27. Pag. 79 a. B.

[1160] fundamentum christus est in structura architecti sapientis 1 Corinthians 3.—si autem Christus, proculdubio fides Christi: per fidem quippe habitat Christus in cordibus sicut idem apostolus dicit. Eph 3. Porro fides Christi illa utique, quam definivit apostolus, quae per dilectionem operatur. Aug. De fide & operih. C. 16 pag. 71. D. Tom. 4 edit. Basil 1569. Again: "Cum ergo dicit apostolus, arbitrari se justificari hominem per fidem sine operibus legis: non hoc agit ut praecepta ac professa fide opera justitiae contemnantur, sed ut sciat se quisque justificari, etiamsi legis opera non praecesserint. Sequuntur enim justificatum: non praecedunt justificandum". Ibid cap. 14. P. 68. C. And elsewhere: "sicut per unius delictum in omnes homines in condemnationem, ut nullus praetermitteretur: sic & in eo quod dictum est, per unius justitiam in omnes homines in justificationem vitae, nullus praetermissus est. Non quia omnes in eum credunt, & baptismo ejus abluuntur: sed quia nemo justificatur, nisi in eum credat, & baptismo ejus abluatur." De natur. & grat. Contra pelagian. Cap. 41. Page 750. D. Tom. 7. And a little after that; ea quippe fides justos sanavit antiquos, quae sanat & nos; id est, mediatoris dei & hominum hominis iesu Christi, fides sanguinis ejus, fides crucis ejus, fides mortis & resurrectionis ejus. Ibid. Cap. 44. Page 751.

applied to both the contracting parties; then, by righteousness God means not only his own, but that also which is, as they say, mutual and reciprocal."[1161]

Luther declares that as God deals with us by way of promise, we deal with him by way of faith.[1162] Peter Martyr, describing the covenant, asserts the mutual stipulation of the federates, namely, of God and his people to one another.[1163]

Cameron describes the Covenant of Grace by the express mention of faith in Christ as the condition thereof, and asserts, that in that covenant, God stipulates and requires faith from us:[1164] Ursinus and Pareus, writing of that common place, of God's Covenant, do often express the conditionality of the

---

[1161] John Calvin, commentary on Hosea 2:19. "And afterwards; et ipsa dicet mihi, tu deus meus. Propheta enim significat deum antevertere nos federe suo, quia alioqui arcemur ab accessu. Deus ergo sponte nos praevenit & corrigit nobis manum, deinde subsequitur consensus fidei nostrae."

[1162] Deus non aliter cum hominibus unquam egit, aut agit, quam verbo promissionis: rursus nec nos cum deo unquam agere aliquid possumus quam fide in verbum promissionis ejus. Opera ille nihil curat, nec eis indiget, quibus potius erga homines & cum hominibus & nobis ipsis agimus. Indiget autem ut verax in suis promissis in no bis habeatur, talisque longanimiter sustineatur, ac sic fide, spe & caritate colatur. Quo fit ut gloriam suam in nobis obtineat, dum non nobis currentibus, sed ipso miserente, promittente, donante, omnia bona accipimus & habemus. *Luth. In tom. 2. Latin. Page 280 a.*

[1163] "And what the promises were, which should be kept of each party, the Scripture oftentimes teaches. For God promised, that he would be the God of his people; namely, that he would be with them, to help them, to deliver them, and by all means (as touching all kinds of good things) to bless them. The people again promised that they would count the Lord Jehovah for their God, in believing, worshiping, and obeying him. And Christ was in the league, as the mediator between each party. This is the exposition and nature of the covenant between God and man." Peter Martyr, *Common Places*, 2.16.1.
<https://quod.lib.umich.edu/e/eebo2/A14350.0001.001/1:8.16?c=eebo;c=eebo2;g=eebogroup;rgn=div2;view=fulltext;xc=1;rgn1=author;q1=vermigli> [Accessed 6/3/2023]

[1164] "Fedus gratiae est illud quo deus, propositâ conditione fidei in Christum, remissionem peccatorum in ejus sanguine, & vitam coelestem pollicetur, idque eo fine, ut ostendat divitias misericordiae suae." John Cameron. De tripl. Dei cum homine federe. Thes. 82. And before: "quomodo differat fides illa quam praesupponit justitia exacta in federe naturae, ab ea fide quam stipulatur deus in federe gratiae." Thes. 11.—"in hoc convenire cum fide quae postulatur in federe gratiae,—at fides quae requiritur in federe gratiae." Thes. 14.

Covenant of Grace.[1165] Wendeline, in his excellent system of Christian theology, describing the Covenant of Grace, still insists upon the conditionality thereof.[1166] The four learned professors of Leiden, namely: Poliander, Rivet, Walaeus, and Thysius, though they deny the New Testament properly so called to require the condition of fulfilling the whole law in Bellarmine's sense, yet in another and sound sense they assert the conditionality of the new covenant.[1167]

Mr. John Ball, in his judicious treatise of the Covenant of Grace, does often mention the conditionality of the covenant, as:

{1} *In the general nature of it*. Chapter 3, pages 17-20. The words I have heretofore expressed in this question.

[1165] "Fedus dei est mutua pactio inter deum & homines, quâ deus confirmat hominibus, se futurum eis propitium, remissurum peccata, etc. Vicissim homines se obligant deo ad fidem & poenitentiam, hoc est, ad recipiendum vera fide hoc tantum beneficium, etc. Fedus dei est unum substantia, duplex circumstantiis: seu, est unum, quod ad conditiones principales, quas deus nobis, & nos deo stipulamur: & sunt duo quod ad conditiones minus principales, vel ut alii loquuntur, quod ad modum administrationis. Zach. Ursin. In explicat. Catechet. Quest. 18. De federe, sect. 1. & 3.

[1166] "Fedus gratiae, est dispositio dei gratuita, quâ per mortem filii sui salutem aeternam promittit hominibus, obedientiam fidei repromittentibus & praestantibus. Materia sunt personae seu partes fedus ineuntes, 1. Deus, promittens vitam sub conditione fidei & cultus sui. 2. Homines, fidem & obedientiam repromittentes. Forma est mutua partium, secundum certas conditiones, obligatio.—et vel maximè huic commendat dei gratiam & misericordiam quod ad praescriptae conditionis impletionem ipse hominem disponit per gratiam non tantum sufficientem quâ possit, sed & efficacem, quâ velit implere conditionem. Hos. 2. 19, 20. Phil, 2. 13. M. *Fred. Wendelin. Christian. Theol. L. 1. Cap. 19. Thes. 9. & expl. C.*

[1167] "But we do deny this, which they hold, that the New Testament strictly speaking, insofar as it is the teaching of the promise of the grace given in Christ, demands the "condition of fulfilling the entire law", as Bellarmine would have it (*On Justification* Book 4 Chapter 2); or that the righteous are not free from observing the divine law insofar as it demands complete obedience, whereby someone is declared righteous as he deserves. [...] the condition of faith and new obedience (which is everywhere impressed on us) is demanded. But God provides these conditions freely, nd their imperfect quality forms no hindrance to salvation (which flows from another source) , so long as they are genuine. But this is not how we should view the condition of fulfilling the entire Law, which they make into a cause of salvation. God does not bestow it in this life on anyone in such a way that they can bear God's judgment." *Synopsis of A Purer Theology*, Volume 1, *Disp. 23. Sect. 27, 28, 29*, Edited by William Den Boer & Riemer a. Faber, translated by Riemer A. Faber, Davenant Institute 2023, pp.255-256

{2} *In the Covenant of Promise with Adam.* Of this Covenant there be two parts: (i) a promise and (ii) a stipulation. The stipulation is that they believe in him that justifies the ungodly and walk before him in all well-pleasing. This may be gathered because the promise of forgiveness cannot be received but by faith, and by faith it is that we overcome the world and vanquish Satan, the enemy of our souls, etc.[1168]

{3} *In the Covenant with Abraham.* This Covenant was made in form of a promise, to be performed according to the purpose of election: *In thy seed shall all nations of the earth be blessed*: and in form of a covenant, consisting of a free promise, and restipulation: *I Am God all-sufficient, walk before me, and be perfect.*[1169]

{4} *In the Covenant with Israel at Mount Sinai*, true it is the promises run upon this condition, etc. (*as I have formerly in this question recited the words*)[1170]. And afterwards he adds, "The condition of this Covenant (in the sense aforesaid) is faith in the promised Messiah, which is implied in the promise, *I will be thy God*; and commanded in the precept built upon it, *Thou shalt have me to be thy God.*"[1171] And again: "These words, *Do this and live*, must not be interpreted, as if they did promise life upon a condition of perfect obedience, and for works done in such exactness as is required; but they must be expounded evangelically, describing the subject capable of life eternal, not the cause why life and salvation is conferred. And by doing, sincere uniform impartial obedience, not exact fulfilling of the law in every tittle, is to be understood."[1172]

{5} *In the Covenant with David*, the condition of this covenant is that they should walk in the ways of the Lord, and keep his watch, etc.[1173]

{6} *In the description of the New Covenant*, the free covenant which God of his rich grace in Jesus Christ incarnate, crucified dead buried, raised up to

---

[1168] Chapter 5. pages 43-44.
[1169] Chapter 6, page 48
[1170] Chapter 8, pages 132-33
[1171] Chapter 8, page 134
[1172] Chapter 8, pages 136-137
[1173] Chapter 9 page 149

life, and ascended up to heaven, has made and plainly revealed unto the world of Jew and Gentile, promising to be their God and father by right of redemption, etc., if they repent of their iniquities, believe in Christ, and through or by Christ in him, and walk before him in sincere constant and conscionable obedience.[1174]

Mr. George Walker in his *Compendious Treatise of Old and New Covenant* thus expresses the nature of a covenant in general, namely: {1} every true covenant presupposes a division or separation. {2} It comprehends in it a mutual promising and binding between two distinct parties. {3} There must be faithful dealing without fraud or dissembling on both sides. {4} This must be between choice persons. {5} It must be about choice matters and upon choice conditions agreed upon by both. {6} It must tend to the well-ordering and composing of things between them.[1175] Now if a covenant in general has in it mutual promising and binding of the federate parties, and choice conditions agreed upon by both: consequently every particular species of a covenant has mutual promising, binding, and conditions. Again, touching the covenant of nature, he says: the condition on man's part, was obedience to God's law, and subjection to God his creator in all things.[1176] And though he say that in the Covenant of Grace there is not any condition or law to be performed on man's part by man himself, as in the Covenant of Nature: yet he grants, that certain gifts, graces, works and fruits of the Spirit: *outward* as the word preached and heard. The sacraments given and received, etc., *inwardly* as faith by which Christ is received and applied: repentance, love, hope, and other saving graces, are required to be in man to make him an actual partaker of Christ, and of life and salvation in him.[1177] And this is as much as we assert, denying all conditions as of and from ourselves, accounting all conditions or terms from us to be mere fruits of God's grace.

[1174] Chapter 1. *Of the new covenant*, page 198
[1175] chapter 4. Page 48, 49. London 1640
[1176] Chapter 5 pages 50-51
[1177] Chapter 5 pages 55-56

Mr. William Pemble, opening the nature of the Covenant of Grace and of works, for clearing the subject of justification, says: "The distinction is this: the law offers life unto man upon condition of perfect obedience cursing the transgressors thereof in the least point with eternal death; whereas the gospel offers life unto man upon another condition, namely, of repentance and faith in Christ, promising remission of sins to such as repent and believe. That this is the main essential and proper difference between the Covenant of Works and of Grace, that is between the law and the gospel, we shall endeavor to make good against those of the Romish apostasy who deny it." And after his proofs for it says: "From whence we conclude firmly, that the difference between the law and the gospel assigned by our divines, is most certain and agreeable to the Scriptures, namely, that the law gives life unto the just, upon condition of perfect obedience in all things; the gospel gives life unto sinners, upon condition they repent and believe in Christ Jesus."[1178]

Mr. John Owen says: "Are we of ourselves any way more able to fulfill the condition of the New Covenant? Is it not as easy for a man by his own strength to fulfill the whole law as to repent and savingly believe the promise of the gospel? This then is one main difference of these two covenants: that the Lord did in the Old only require the condition; now in the New he will also effect it in all the federates, to whom the Covenant is extended."[1179]

Mr. William Perkins, who by his left-handed dexterity stabbed popery to the heart, thus describes the Covenant of Grace: "The Covenant of Grace is that whereby God, freely promising Christ and his benefits, exacts again of man that he would by faith receive Christ and repent of his sins (Hosea 2:18-19, Ezekiel 36:25-27, Malachi 3:1)."[1180] And elsewhere says: "In the Covenant of Grace two things must be considered: the substance thereof and the condition. The substance of the covenant is that righteousness and life everlasting is given to God's church and people by Christ. The condition is

---

[1178] Pemble, Treatise of Justification, Sect. 4. Chap. 1. pp. 214-217. London, 1635.

[1179] John Owen, *Treatise of Redemption*, Book 3 chapter 1, pages 103-104, London, 1648

[1180] William Perkins, *The order of causes of salvation*, chap. 31. Page 70. A. Vol. 1. Lond. 1626.

that we for our part are by faith to receive the aforesaid benefits. And this condition is by grace as well as the substance, etc."[1181]

Mr. Edward Reynolds says: "In the New Covenant, God works first. In the first covenant, man was able by his created and natural strength, to work his own condition, and so to expect God's performance, but in the New, as there is difference in the things covenanted – then only righteousness and salvation; now, remission of sins, and adoption; in the means or intermediate causes, which are now Christ and his righteousness and Spirit; in the stability: that a perishable, this an eternal and final covenant that can never be changed; in the conditions: there legal obedience, here only faith and the certain consequent thereof repentance – so likewise is there difference in the manner of performing these conditions, for now God himself begins first to work upon us and in us, before we move or stir towards him. He does not only command us and leave us to our created strength to obey the command, but he furnishes us with his own grace and Spirit to fulfill the command: and when he bids us come unto him, he does likewise draw us unto him."[1182]

The godly and learned assembly of divines, who have done more faithful service to Jesus Christ and his church then any provincial or national synod or convocation before them since England received the gospel, thus set forth God's covenant: "Man by his fall having made himself incapable of life by that covenant, the Lord was pleased to make a second, commonly called the Covenant of Grace; wherein he freely offered unto sinners life and salvation by Jesus Christ, requiring of them faith in him that they may be saved, and promising to give unto all those that are ordained unto life, his Holy Spirit, to make them willing and able to believe."[1183]

And elsewhere they express themselves yet more fully: "The grace of God is manifested in the second covenant in that he freely provides and offers to sinners a mediator, and life and salvation by him, and requiring faith as the

---

[1181] William Perkins, *A Reformed Catholic*, Of Justification, II, Difference about the manner of justification,.page 571. B. C. Vol. 1.
[1182] Edward Reynolds, *The life of Christ*, Page 512. London 1632.
[1183] Westminster Confession of Faith, Chapter 7.3, 1646

condition to interest them in him, promises and gives his Holy Spirit to all his elect to work in them that faith with all other saving graces, and to enable them unto all holy obedience as the evidence of the truth of their faith and thankfulness to God, and as the way which he hath appointed them to salvation."[1184]

This cloud of witnesses may suffice (though many more might easily be added): {1} to show the consent of writers to the conditionality of the covenant, and {2} to clear yet further the true state of the question. But thus much for confirmation of the covenant's conditionality.

(3) *Lastly, as for refutation of contrary arguments or objections, militating against the conditionality of the covenant, they may be easily answered from due consideration of the premises.* I shall not need therefore to insist much upon them.

[**Argument 1**] *If the covenant stands upon any conditions to be performed on man's part, it cannot be an everlasting covenant, except man were so confirmed in righteousness, that he should never fail in that which is his part. But man is not now so confirmed. Man did fail in the condition, while there were conditions before in the first covenant, and thereby the covenant was frustrated.*[1185]

Answer: {1} True; the Covenant of Faith or Grace is a final and everlasting covenant, never to determine.[1186] {2} It's also true that the conditions which we assert do not in any way prejudice the Covenant's perpetuity, but rather establish it. The condition of faith ensures the promise: *Therefore it is of faith, that it might be by grace: to the end the promise might be sure to all the seed.*[1187] The perpetuity of the Covenant stands not, is not founded or bottomed, upon conditions in us: but upon God's free-grace,

---

[1184] Westminster Larger Catechism, Question 32, 1648
[1185] Tobias Crisp, *Christ Alone Exalted*, Sermon 6, p.160, London, 1643.
[1186] Genesis 17:13, 19; 2 Samuel 23:5, Jeremiah 32:40, Ezekiel 37:26, Hebrews 13:22
[1187] Romans 4:16

inviolable truth and faithfulness, and Christ's all-sufficient everliving merit. {3} The objection holds against *conditions most strictly taken*, such as was Adam's obedience to the first Covenant, but such conditions we disclaim. Against *conditions asserted*, it holds not.

[**Argument 2**] *A man has no tie upon him to perform any thing whatsoever in the Covenant; as a condition that must be observed on his part. The Covenant plainly shows that the whole performance of the covenant lies only upon God himself, and that there is not one bond or obligation upon man to the fulfilling of the Covenant, or partaking in the benefit of the Covenant (Hebrews 8:10, John 6:45, Ezekiel 36:25, 29). If there be a condition, and there should be a failing in the condition, he that undertakes all things in the covenant must needs be in fault. But the truth is, the particulars mentioned in those texts are not conditions of the Covenant, but consequences of the covenant.*[1188]

Answer: {1} If God absolutely and properly does all in the Covenant, then it is not properly a covenant but a promise. {2} If we take conditions most largely, for antecedent preparatory, concomitant, and consequent conditions, or more restrictively, for the instrument of application, faith, as has been explained, then man has many ties, bonds, and obligations upon him, as has been proved. But if we take conditions for *antecedent impulsive* or *meritorious causes*, or most strictly, such bonds we deny in this Covenant as well as Crisp. {3} God as the primary, most free, independent cause and agent, obliged by no superior law, undertakes in the Covenant both to perform his part and to enable us in an evangelical sense to perform our part, giving both to will and to do, both first grace and second grace, infusing habits, and drawing them into act; notwithstanding, *acti agimus*: being acted by him, we act with him. God works not upon us, as men upon stones. He draws, and we come. He is *author and finisher of faith*;[1189] yet we believe. Efficiently God performs all by enabling us to perform, but formally and subjectively we

---

[1188] Tobias Crisp, Ibid., p.161-165
[1189] Hebrews 12:2

perform from him. {4} Hence all our performances are originally to be ascribed to God, and all our failings to ourselves. It's no less than blasphemous to translate our covenant-failings upon God.

[**Argument 3**] *The Covenant in the actual substance of it is made good to a person before he can do anything. The main thing in a covenant is God's being the God of a people, and the model of that is God's love which is cast upon man before he can do anything, Romans 9.:11.*[1190]

Answer: {1} God's love in election is cast upon man before the world was: much more before man can do anything. {2} This love is not God's Covenant; the Covenant is the effect of this love. {3} There are concomitant and consequent, as well as antecedent conditions. Further [resolutions] to objections, see in others.[1191]

[1190] D. T. Crisp, ibid., p.165, etc.
[1191] Mr. Rutherford, *Christ Dying*, pages 471-478, and Mr. John Graile, *Vindication of Conditions in the Covenant*

Corollary 5

Hence, *the Covenant of Faith is a sweet paradise of believers' union to, and communion with God in Jesus Christ.*

We may conceive of a threefold paradise, and a threefold union and communion with God therein. A threefold paradise, namely, *terrestrial*, wherein Adam was placed in innocency;[1192] *spiritual*, wherein believers are placed in grace; and *celestial*, wherein the righteous are placed in glory.[1193] Answerably, a threefold union and communion with God, namely: natural, gracious and glorious. *Natura*, and such union and communion Adam had with God in Eden the earthly paradise before his fall by his natural integrity.[1194] *Gracious*, and such union and communion believers have with God in Jesus Christ through the Spirit by faith in this world.[1195] *Glorious*, and such union and communion just men made perfect shall have with God in Christ fully and immediately face to face forever in the highest heavens.[1196] The natural union and communion with God, in the earthly Eden, Adam enjoyed by the Covenant of Works. The supernatural union and communion with God, whether gracious on earth, or glorious in heaven, Christ's seed enjoy by the Covenant of Faith, initiate here, and consummate hereafter. And so this Covenant of Faith brings believers from paradise, through paradise, to paradise. *From paradise*, even the earthly Eden where this covenant after the fall had its first rise and original,[1197] *through paradise*, even the spiritual Eden of union and communion with God in his church, where this Covenant has its growth and increase, and *to paradise*, even the third heavens, where this covenant shall have its fullness and accomplishment.[1198]

[1192] Genesis 2:8-18
[1193] 2 Corinthians 12:2-4, Luke 23:43, Revelation 2:7
[1194] Ecclesiastes 7:29 with Genesis chapters 1-3
[1195] John 17:20 to the end, 1 John 3:2, 2 Corinthians 13:14
[1196] John 17:24, 1 John 3:2-3, 1 Corinthians 13:12, Matthew 5:8, Hebrews 12:22-23
[1197] Genesis 3
[1198] Hebrews 8:6, 9

Now this union and communion with God (which is the saints' spiritual paradise, and heaven on earth) is grounded upon this Covenant of Faith. How? In this sort. According to this covenant,

(1) We have union unto Christ by faith immediately. For, accepting him by faith as our mediator, root and representative; we actually become his seed, his spouse, his members: who before were only such intentionally by God's decree.[1199]

(2) We thus – united to Christ – are mediately through Christ's mediation brought into union with God, he becoming our God, and we his people.[1200]

(3) Being thus brought into this mystical union to Christ and God, we consequently obtain sweet heavenly communion with them both: *and truly our fellowship is with the Father and his Son Jesus Christ*.[1201] So that righteousness, both imputed to us and inherent in us, eternal life and all things referring and appertaining hereunto, are freely made ours, in God and in Christ. These three things Christ notably expresses in his sweet and heavenly prayer: praying *for all them that should believe on him through his apostles' word, that they all may be one, as thou father art in me, and I in thee, that they also may be one in us. I in them, and thou in me, that they may be made perfect in one*.[1202] Here's their union mystical to the Father and to Christ: but to Christ first, and then in him to the Father. *That the world may know that thou hast sent me; and hast loved them as thou hast loved me. Father, I will that they also whom thou hast given me, may be with me where I am, that they may behold my glory which thou hast given me*. Here's their communion with the Father, in his *love*; and with the Son, in his *glory*, flowing from the former union.

[1199] John 1:11
[1200] John 14:6, Colossians 1:20, Hebrews 8:10
[1201] 1 John 1:3
[1202] John 17:20 to the end of the chapter

Corollary 6

Hence, the substance and matters of this Covenant of Faith are most high and great: far surpassing the matters of all other covenants, whether of God or man.

Man never could covenant with man, what God herein covenants with Christ and his seed: and God never did covenant with man in the Covenant of Works, what he here covenants in this covenant. For,

(1) **How high and great are the mercies here promised on God's part!**

[1] To Christ the last Adam, God (as has been formerly proven) promises: {1} to invest him with a mediatory office, whereby he should prevailingly mediate with God as priest, prophet and king for the recovery of his seed. {2} To assist, comfort and protect Christ in the executing and fulfilling of this his office, against all extremities of sufferings, all oppositions of enemies, and all his deepest discouragements. {3} To exalt Christ gloriously, in his resurrection from the dead, ascension into heaven, and session at God's right hand: after he had been humbled and abased most ignominiously. {4} To accept Christ delightfully and contentedly in this his mediation for his seed. {5} To crown and prosper Christ with complete success in this his office for the recovering of all his seed. These, amongst other excellent blessings, God promises to Christ the last Adam, in order to the recovery of his seed.

[2] To Christ's seed also in him, God covenants and promises these things principally, namely: {1} to restore them from the state of sin, to the state of righteousness both imputed and inherent. {2} To recover them from death, to eternal life by Christ. {3} To be to them a God. Now, how high and transcendent are these blessings promised! No created beings can promise such benefits. God never promised such things in the Covenant of Works to Adam in innocency: there's no promise of any Christ, or to any Christ, or of any righteousness or life by him, or of being Adam's God in him. These are the

greatest mercies that sinners can need, Christ's seed can receive, or God himself can give.

(2) **How high and great the duties restipulated!**

[1] By Christ the last Adam, who re-obliges himself to God, {1} to accept, undertake and discharge this mediatory office cheerfully and faithfully, for the recovery of his seed. {2} To depend and fully rely upon his heavenly father, for assistance, protection and acceptance in the execution of his office, notwithstanding all distresses, oppositions and discouragements.

[2] By Christ's seed, who in Christ restipulate, {1} to accept Jesus Christ, and in him all covenanted mercies by faith unfeigned; {2} to walk worthy of Christ, and all these covenanted mercies, according to the gospel; {3} and in Jesus Christ, to become the people of the living God. Behold, what manner of duties are here! *Never office in this world so weighty and intricate as the mediatory office.* For, hereby in order to the recovery of Christ's seed, God's exact law was in all points to be fulfilled, God's infinite justice offended by their sins was fully to be satisfied and appeased, and sin, death, hell and all the powers of darkness were to be condemned and subdued. What abasement, what temptations, what reproaches and persecutions, what prayers, what tears, what torments of body, what disertions and agonies of soul, and what effusion of his dearest heart's blood, did the effecting of these cost Jesus Christ? Never a creature in this world did or could so depend upon God in such a Red Sea of calamities as Christ did, whose faith failed not in the least degree. And as for Christ's seed, their accepting Christ by faith, walking worthy of him evangelically, and becoming God's people, are comprehensive duties, altogether supernatural and contra-natural, and wholly above and against all corrupted naturals. They wholly debase nature but exalt grace. They all together nullified the sinner, strike him off his base, and strip him of his boasting; but they magnify, yea, omnify the savior, set him upon his throne, and ascribe to him all the glory.

Corollary 7

*Hence, **the properties and perfections of this Covenant of Faith are various and excellent.***

In the nature of this covenant thus described and opened, these are more especially observable, namely, it is, (1) holy, (2) gratuitous, (3) ordered in all things, (4) sure, (5) comfortable, and (6) everlasting.

(1) The Covenant of Faith is Holy

The Covenant of Faith is styled {*holy*},

[1] In the Old Testament by Daniel, describing the wickedness of Antiochus Epiphanes: *His heart shall be against the holy covenant. He shall have indignation against the holy covenant. And have intelligence with them that forsake the holy covenant.*[1203] To this effect the Psalmist, describing Israel's wonderful deliverance out of Egypt, lays down this as the cause thereof: God's faithfulness in his holy promise or covenant – *for he remembered his holy promise, and Abraham his servant*[1204] – {*promise*} here being put for {*covenant*} by a synecdoche.

[2] In the New Testament by Luke; *to perform the mercy promised to our fathers, and to remember his holy covenant.*[1205] The oath which he sware to our father Abraham, etc. Thus, that this covenant is holy, is evident. But what is this holiness ascribed to the covenant? And in what respects is it holy? Answer: A thing may be called *holy*, and so this covenant, *holy*, in five respects, namely: {1} *in respect of its separation from common things: or from common to sacred use and service.* Thus persons and things dedicated and set apart for holy religious use, are frequently in Scripture called holy.[1206] And thus the

---

[1203] Daniel 11:28, 30
[1204] Psalm 105:42-43
[1205] Luke 1:72
[1206] Leviticus 21:6-8, Exodus 3:5 & 16:23, Psalm 46:4; 1 Kings 8:4

Covenant of Faith is holy, being separated, dedicated and set apart to a holy and spiritual use, namely: the uniting of God and sinners in a sacred bond of reconciliation in Christ. {2} *In respect of its perfection.* Holiness implies an absence of imperfection, and a presence of perfection. And this, some think, is especially signified by holiness.[1207] Thus God, being most absolutely perfect without all imperfection, is most absolutely holy.[1208] And God's Covenant, being a perfect covenant in its kind, and wanting no perfection therein for the complete advancement of the sinner's happiness and God's glory thereby, is in this regard proportionably holy. {3} *In respect of its pureness and clearness from all pollution, defilement, spot, or stain of sin: when there's no sinful mixture in it.* As gold is said to be pure, when it is full of itself, all gold, and no mixture of dross in it; honey is said to be pure, when there is no mixture of dregs in it. Thus God, being most pure, having no mixture of sin or darkness at all in him, is most holy.[1209] The godly being washed in Christ's blood, and purified by Christ's sanctifying Spirit,[1210] are above all other people, a holy nation, etc.[1211] And in this sense, God's Covenant is holy, being pure, clean and separate from all sin and sinful defilement, which may be incident to man's covenants.

Everything in and about this covenant being in this sense pure and holy: the covenant itself must needs be pure and holy also. For: (i) the author of this covenant is holy, namely, the Lord God, who is *holy, holy, holy,*[1212] holiness itself.[1213] *Who is like unto thee, glorious in holiness?*[1214] (ii) The mediator of this covenant is holy, namely, Jesus Christ, who is *that holy thing*.[1215] *The Holy One*.[1216] *The Holy One of God*.[1217] (iii) The parties to this Covenant are holy,

---

[1207] Andre Rivet, Commentary on Exodus 15:11
[1208] Job 11:7-9 with Exodus 15:10-11
[1209] Hebrews 1:13, Psalm 92:15, 1 John 1:5, Isaiah 6:3
[1210] Revelation 1:5, Acts 15:9, 1 Corinthians 6:11
[1211] 1 Peter 2:5, 9
[1212] Isaiah 6:3, Revelation 4:8
[1213] Psalm 89:35
[1214] Exodus 15:11
[1215] Luke 1:35
[1216] Acts 2:27 & 13:35 & 3:14, 1 John 2:20
[1217] Mark 1:24, Luke 4:34

namely: on the one hand the most holy God; on the other hand, Jesus Christ the last Adam and his seed. Christ is holy, as has been shown. And Christ's seed are conformable to him in holiness. And thereupon styled *holy brethren*,[1218] *holy men*,[1219] *holy women*,[1220] *a holy temple*,[1221] *a holy priesthood*,[1222] *a holy nation*,[1223] *a holy people*,[1224] etc. (iv) The matters or blessings covenanted on God's part to us are holy, namely: our recovery by Christ, the Holy One of God, from the state of sin unto a state of holiness and righteousness enjoyed in our persons[1225] and expressed in our conversations.[1226] (v) Finally, the matters and conditions restipulated by us unto God, are holy; namely: accepting Christ by believing, believing being called *our most holy faith*.[1227] Walking worthy of Christ, etc., which is in another phrase styled, *walking before God in holiness and righteousness all the days of our life*.[1228] And: *perfecting holiness in the fear of God*,[1229] etc. Oh therefore how holy in these regards is this Covenant of God!

{4} *In respect of its heavenliness*. A thing that is heavenly, sublime, spiritual, abstracted and lifted up from earthliness, is said to be holy. Hence some derive the Greek word for *holy* {ἅγιος}, from ἄ & γη *without the earth*: as it were, *unearthly*.[1230] For, everything that is in heaven, or is heavenly, is holy. Thus this Covenant consequently is holy, for it is a most sublime, spiritual, heavenly mystery. It was contrived in heaven; all the world could not have devised or imagined such a way for recovery of sinners, and it brings all them at last unto heaven that embrace it and close with God in it. {5} Finally, *in*

[1218] Hebrews 3:1, 1 Thessalonians 5:27
[1219] 2 Peter 1:21
[1220] 1 Peter 3:5
[1221] Ephesians 2:21, 1 Corinthians 3:17
[1222] 1 Peter 2:5
[1223] Exodus 19:6, 1 Peter 2:9
[1224] Deuteronomy 7:6 & 28:9; Isaiah 62:12
[1225] Ephesians 4:24, 1 Peter 2:5, 9
[1226] Luke 1:72-75
[1227] Jude 20
[1228] Luke 1:72
[1229] 2 Corinthians 7:1
[1230] Here several words are missing in Greek

respect of its firmness and settled stability a thing is called holy. Hence Augustine thinks the Latin name for {*holy*} is derived from firmness and establishment, *sanctus, quasi sancitus.*[1231] Thus this Covenant is holy, that is, firm, sure established that it cannot be shaken or overthrown, as after will appear in opening the property of its sureness. Now his Covenant of Faith being every way thus sacred and holy: (i) it is highly to be preferred above all common human covenants in this point of holiness. (ii) An unholy sinful state, and inward saving interest in this holy Covenant are inconsistent. He that intends to have a share in this holy Covenant, must himself become holy in person and conversation. (iii) They that are federates with God in Christ according to this Covenant, should in conformity to this Covenant, both think, speak, act and in all points walk holily, heavenly, and unblameably.

(2) The Covenant of Faith is Gratuitous

The Covenant of Faith is wholly and merely of free-grace. For what the apostle said of the inheritance of life and salvation, we may say of this Covenant of Faith promising this inheritance; *Therefore it is of faith, that it might be by grace; to the end the promise might be sure to all the seed.*[1232] Grace and faith are inseparable relatives, which stand or fall together. If it be a Covenant of Faith, for the condition of it; it must consequently be a Covenant of Grace, for the foundation of it: and so on the contrary. For faith has nothing for its object in this Covenant but mere grace, having nothing herein propounded by way of promise from God, or by way of restipulation from Christ's seed, but all of mere grace. And that, not only the grace of favor towards creatures which had place in the Covenant of Works, but also the grace of commiseration towards sinful, lapsed creatures, which only has place

---

[1231] "Ideo Spiritus Sanctus dicitur, quoniam ad permanendum sanciuntur, quicunque sanctificantur; Nec dubium est à Sanciendo sanctitatem vocari" *Aug. de Fld. & Symb. p. 147. D. Tom. 3. Basil. 1569. Ger. Harm. Evan. c. 180. p. 400.*
[1232] Romans 4:16

in this Covenant of Faith – but of the gratuitousness of this Covenant, enough formerly.[1233]

---

(3) The Covenant of Faith is Ordered in All Things

---

(3) Ordered in all things. *Although mine house be not so with God, yet he hath made with me an everlasting covenant, ordered in all things* בְּרִית עֲרוּכָה בַּכֹּל *berith hharoucah baccol,* namely, *a covenant ordered in all.*[1234] Thus David styles God's Covenant, which was made with him: and so proportionably every particular discovery of this Covenant of Faith is ordered in all. The Hebrew word translated {*ordered*} signifies, orderly-disposed, orderly set, or placed by reason and proportion, orderly fitted, furnished, prepared, directed, settled, addressed.[1235] The Septuagint renders it {πεφυλαγμένην}, *ready, prepared.* As a table is prepared and furnished when stored with all manner of provision, or as an army is marshaled, ranked or set in graceful order, when everyone is in his place, so this Covenant is contrived and put in most excellent order, well furnished and prepared with all necessaries to salvation, and which shall be orderly disposed to Christ's seed in due season. *God is the God of order*,[1236] as he most orderly created all things at first, so in most comely and beautiful order he governs all things created ever since; especially the mysteries of grace for the salvation of his elect?[1237] More particularly this Covenant is ordered in all things, in these respects following. Namely:

[1] ***In respect of the inward constitution of the Covenant.*** How excellently and orderly has God composed it and constituted it of matter and form?

{1} The *matter*,

[1233] In Book 2 chapter 2 Aphorism 2 Section 1 & Corollary 2
[1234] 2 Samuel 23:5
[1235] Vid. Pagn in Thesaur. Ad verb ערך
[1236] 1 Corinthians 14:33 & 15:23
[1237] Genesis 1 throughout, Psalm 104 throughout, Ecclesiastes 3:11

(i) On God's part promised, is the recovery of Christ's seed by Jesus Christ from the state of sin and death, to the state of righteousness and life, that so the Lord may be their God. And this matter is admirably well ordered. For, (a) here's the blessings or mercies promised, namely, recovery, etc., God becoming their God, what could be ordered and prepared more suitably and more sufficiently for poor lost sinners' salvation and happiness. Here are fit and full supplies for all their spiritual wants. (b) Here are the parties to whom these covenanted mercies are peculiarly intended; namely, Christ's seed. Not all men, but only God's elect. They alone must share in these special mercies, peculiarly prepared for them. (c) Here is the only mediator by whom these persons shall come to enjoy these promised mercies, namely, Jesus Christ, with whom God had a blessed transaction for effecting thereof.

(ii) On our part, the matter restipulated is: (a) our accepting of Christ and covenanted mercies by true faith. How shall they else be made ours? (b) Our walking worthily of them according to the gospel. How else shall we walk thankfully, and really testify they are ours? (c) Our giving up ourselves to God as his people. How otherwise can we assure ourselves that he is our God?

{2} The *form* of this Covenant is the mutual obligation and reciprocal engagement of the federate parties to each other. Oh how comely and beautifully, with what symmetry and proportion are all things in this Covenant ordered and prepared!

[2] ***In respect of the outward dispensation of the Covenant, it is ordered in all things.*** God observed an order of degrees in revealing it. He made it not known at all, until Adam had quite broken the Covenant of Works.[1238] And then but gradually: first discovering it more darkly, remotely and imperfectly, as we see things a great way off, but afterward more clearly, immediately, and completely, as we discern things at hand. God observed also an order of proportion in dispensing it, having therein respect both to his church's non-age and full age. {1} *In her non-age* dispensing it sparingly, carnally and servilely in certain initial elements and rudiments of ceremonies,

---

[1238] Genesis 2:16-17 with Genesis 3:6, 15

types and carnal observances, as his people's weakness and dullness was able to bear it, but: {2} *In her full age* he dispensed it, more freely, fully and spiritually after the coming of Christ. How orderly was this his proceeding!

[3] ***In respect of the accomplishment of it in Christ, this Covenant is ordered in all things.*** It makes Christ known first dimly, as at a great distance: then clearly, as at hand. This Covenant is a cabinet: Christ is the rich treasure in this covenant-cabinet, but not fully disclosed all at once. {1} At first he was represented as *the seed of the woman bruising the serpent's head*.[1239] {2} Then (under the type of Noah saving his family in the ark by waters)[1240] as a savior of his family and little flock by his blood from perishing in their sins by the deluge of God's wrath overwhelming all the world besides. {3} Then as the seed of Abraham, in whom all the kindreds and families of the earth should be blessed.[1241] {4} Then as the anti-type of the Mosaical sacrifices, purgations and other ceremonies, both expiating the guilt, and purifying the filth of sin, from his seed.[1242] {5} After this, as the seed of David, that as king, should sit upon his throne forever: spiritually reigning and ruling over his church.[1243] {6} Then as the true David, that should reunite his people into one nation; and into one kingdom, not to be divided any more.[1244] {7} After all, as God-man, dwelling with men, full of grace and truth, actually dying for his seed, and discharging all the offices of his mediatourship, so that they have eternal redemption obtained for them, and their sins and iniquities God will remember no more.[1245]

[4] ***Finally, in respect of the application of it to Christ's seed, this Covenant of Faith is ordered in all things.*** Herein God proceeds most orderly with them: though they do not always distinctly observe the order and method of his proceedings. {1} God tenders his Covenant to them. {2} He in

---

[1239] Genesis 3:15
[1240] Genesis 6:18, etc., Hebrews 11:7, 1 Peter 3:20-21
[1241] Genesis 12:3 & 22:18 with Acts 3:25, Galatians 3:8-9
[1242] Exodus 24 & 25, etc., with John 1:17, Colossians 2:17, Hebrews 9:9-15
[1243] Psalm 89:3-4, 29 & 132:11 with Acts 2:30
[1244] Ezekiel 27:21-28 with John 10:16
[1245] John 1:14, 1 Timothy 3:16, John 10:11, 15, Ephesians 5:25-27, Hebrews 9:12 & 8:8-13

his due time convinces them thereby through the operation of his Spirit, that they are naturally in a woeful state of sin and death in the first Adam, and that notwithstanding there is a sufficient remedy, and means of their recovery in Christ the last Adam. {3} He converts and calls them effectually from sin to righteousness, *from darkness to light, and from the power of Satan unto God.* {4} He adopts them into his own family in Jesus Christ as his sons and daughters. {5} He justifies them freely by his grace, imputing Christ's righteousness unto them by faith. {6} He vouchsafes them sweet heavenly communion with himself in Christ by his Spirit, affording all privileges of grace. {7} He glorifies them eternally with himself and Jesus Christ in the highest heavens, vouchsafing immediate vision and full fruition of God, Father, Son, and Holy Spirit forevermore. O how admirable is this order of covenant-application, and how highly estimable by all Christ's seed.

(4) The Covenant of Faith is Sure

The Covenant of Faith is faithful, faithfully kept and performed by God, firm, sure, unbroken, whereof God will always be mindful, whereunto he will still have respect that it may be punctually and accurately performed. In this regard this covenant is in the Old Testament styled וּשְׁמֻרָה *shemurah*,[1246] that is, kept, observed, performed (one translator renders it, *sure*), and as that learned Mercerus notes,[1247] it imports care, diligence, and solicitude, lest any thing be let go, let slip, etc. Such singular care and solicitude God takes, lest his covenant should in any respect fail. Hence it is elsewhere implied to be a covenant that *cannot be broken.*[1248] In the New Testament it is styled a promise firm, or sure to all the seed: βεβαιαν την επαγγελιαν παντι τω σπερματι – *that*

[1246] 2 Samuel 23:5

[1247] Curam, sollicitudinem & diligentiam con..., ne quid emittatur, elabatur aut excutiatur. Mercer. in Pagn. Thesaur. ad verb. שמר. Machine translation: "With care, concern, and diligence, lest anything should be thrown, lifted, or shaken."

[1248] Jeremiah 33:20-21

the promise might be firm to all the seed.[1249] It has respect to God's Covenant with Abraham, to whose spiritual seed, whether Jews or Gentiles, the covenant of the eternal inheritance is firm. And elsewhere God's promise or covenant with Abraham is called {πραγμάτων ἀμεταθέτων}, an immutable thing: *that by two immutable things, in which it was impossible for God to lie,* etc.[1250] God's promise and God's oath annexed thereto, are these two immutable things, as the context there clears it.

Now this sureness of the Covenant is a property most consequential and comfortable to the heirs of the promise, and children of the covenant. Therefore it is said: *God willing more abundantly to shew unto the heirs of promise the immutability of his counsel, confirmed it by an oath. That by two immutable things, in which it was impossible for God to lie, we might have a strong consolation.*[1251]— {ἰσχυρὰν παράκλησιν}, that is a *valiant, strong, prevailing consolation*. Let us therefore a little further enquire into this sureness of God's Covenant, and the grounds thereof (which is incomparably more firm, sure, immutable and irrevocable than all other covenants in the world), that hereby we may lay a surer foundation of affiance and comfort in God's Covenant and promise. We may fail, but God's Covenant will never fail us. This sureness of the Covenant may illustriously be discovered: [1] from the nature, properties and perfections of the covenant-making God; [2] from God's manifold methods for establishment of his Covenant; [3] from God's actual accomplishment of his Covenant most punctually, in the experience of all ages; [4] from removal of all imaginable corrumpent causes that might render this Covenant infirm or unfaithful; [5] from the durable and everlasting nature of the Covenant itself.

[1] **From the nature, properties and essential perfections of the covenant-making God.** These are such, that they proclaim him to be a God

---

[1249] Romans 4:16
[1250] Hebrews 6:18
[1251] Hebrews 6:17-18

keeping covenant and mercy with his servants, with them that love him, etc.,[1252] and, that *there is no God like him, in heaven above, or on earth beneath, keeping covenant and mercy*, etc.[1253] For God that made this Covenant, is: {1} Jehovah, {2} most gracious, {3} true, {4} faithful, {5} wise, {6} powerful, {7} immutable. And therefore his Covenant must needs be unquestionably sure.

{1} *God is Jehovah*. JEHOVAH is God's chief essential name, not only denoting: (i) his eternal independent being in and of himself, (ii) and his giving of being to all created things, but also (iii) his giving being and existence to his covenant and promises. Hereupon when God was now about to bring Israel out of Egypt, and to conduct them to Canaan, as he had covenanted to Abraham, he says: *I appeared unto Abraham, unto Isaac, and unto Jacob by the name of God Almighty: but by my name Jehovah was I not known to them.*[1254] God was *doctrinally* and *in part* known to them by his name Jehovah, for it was revealed to them before.[1255] But he was not *experimentally* and so *plenarily* made known to them by this name, as now he was about to make himself known to Israel in his actual fulfilling and performing of his promise and covenant to them, by bringing them out of Egypt into Canaan. And this is the interpretation plainly given in the following verses, namely, verses 4-9. So then it is most natural to God to fulfill his promise. God can as soon forget his nature, his being, and this his glorious name Jehovah, as forget his Covenant.

{2} *God is most gracious*.[1256] His free grace, both of benevolence and favor to his creatures, and of commiseration to his miserable and sinful creatures, is incomparable. Of mere grace God at first made this Covenant of Faith, lapsed creatures having nothing at all in them, that might in the least degree move or invite the Lord thereunto (as has been shown),[1257] but rather every thing inciting to the contrary: now if God should make this his Covenant, not only without, but even quite contrary to all motives and inducements in the

---

[1252] Daniel 9:4, Nehemiah 1:5 & 9:32
[1253] 1 Kings 3:23; 2 Chronicles 6:14
[1254] Exodus 6:3. This verse is clearly expounded in verses 4-9 following.
[1255] To Abraham, Genesis 22:14; to Isaac, Genesis 26:23-25; and to Jacob, Genesis 27:20.
[1256] רחום וחנון *Commiserating and gracious*, Exodus 34:6, Psalm 103:8
[1257] See Book 2 Chapter 2 Aphorism 2 Sections 1. & [...] .2

creature, of his own mere grace, shall he not of the same mere grace make it good? That which is wholly bottomed upon mere divine grace, without the creature, is founded only upon God, therefore it is, without exception, sure. The eternal inheritance covenanted, *is therefore of faith, that it might be by grace; to the end the promise might be sure to all the seed: not to that only which is of the law, but to that also which is of the faith of Abraham, who is the father of us all.*[1258]

{3} *God is most true*:[1259] yea truth itself, the only supreme truth.[1260] He is plenteous in mercy and truth.[1261] And the truth of the Lord endures forever, to all generations.[1262] Hence therefore God's promises and covenant must needs be sure and true forever, because God, the true God, *which cannot lie*,[1263] promises and covenants. So that God's Covenant and promise is that *immutable thing, wherein it is impossible that God should lie.*[1264] Man may covenant and promise, and yet not perform: all men are liars. The truest men are but mutably true. But *God is not as man, that he should lie.*[1265] Now if it be impossible God should lie in promising, it is impossible his promise should fail until it comes to performing.

{4} *God is most faithful*: therefore in his covenants and promises, he will not, he cannot delude or deceive. *If we believe not, yet he abideth faithful, he cannot deny himself.*[1266] Many Jews did not believe God's Covenant, yet their unfaithfulness did not overthrow God's Covenant, or his faithfulness therein. *For, what if some did not believe? Shall their unbelief make the faith of God of none effect? God forbid: yea let God be true, but every man a liar.*[1267] How notably says the Scripture elsewhere to Israel; *Know therefore that the Lord thy*

[1258] Romans 4:16
[1259] Jeremiah 10:10, Job 17:3, John 5:20
[1260] Deuteronomy 32:4, Psalm 31:5
[1261] Psalm 86:15
[1262] Psalm 117:2 & 100:5
[1263] Titus 1:2
[1264] Hebrews 6:17-18
[1265] 1 Samuel 15:29
[1266] 2 Timothy 2:13
[1267] Romans 3:3-4

God, he is God, the faithful God, which keeps covenant and mercy with them that love him, and keep his commandments to a thousand generations.[1268] So then, because he is a faithful God, he is a covenant-keeping God: his Covenant is sure. Hereupon the apostle exhorts: *Let us hold fast the profession of our faith without wavering.*[1269] Why? For he is faithful that promised. And upon this attribute of God's faithfulness, Sarah raised up her faith to believe God's Covenant and promise against reason and the course of nature: *Through faith also Sarah herself received strength to conceive seed, and was delivered of a child when she was past age, because she judged him faithful that had promised.*[1270]

{5} *God is most wise.* He is *the only wise God*:[1271] *he knoweth all things, and no thought can be withheld from him: he understandeth our thoughts afar off.*[1272] *Known unto God are all his works from the beginning of the world*:[1273] and so even unto the end of the world: yea, *his understanding is infinite.*[1274] And as he *worketh all things*, so he makes, and makes good his covenants and promises, *according to the counsel of his own will.*[1275] Therefore God's Covenants and promises cannot fail and be infringed, as man's may, and oft are, through imprudence, oscitancy, inadvertency, want of foresight, etc. God never promises anything, but he has most wisely contrived and determined aforehand how to bring it to pass.

{6} *God is most powerful.* Not only mighty,[1276] but Almighty:[1277] he can do all things; and all things with ease. He made the world with his word; *he spoke and they were created: he commanded and they stood fast.*[1278] He *is able to do exceeding abundantly above all that we ask or think.*[1279] Therefore, though

---

[1268] Deuteronomy 7:9
[1269] Hebrews 10:23
[1270] Hebrews 11:11
[1271] 1 Timothy 1:17
[1272] John 21:17, Job 42:2
[1273] Acts 15:18
[1274] Psalm 147:5
[1275] Ephesians 1:11
[1276] Job 36:5
[1277] Genesis 17:1; John 21:17; Genesis 18:14
[1278] Psalm 148:5 & 33:9
[1279] Ephesians 3:20

man oft-times promises beyond his ability, yet God nor does nor can promise beyond his power of performance. Though he should covenant and promise things never so great, strange, difficult, improbable, and to flesh and blood, or created power impossible, yet he can easily perform all, above the capacity of our sense, reason and faith itself: *Is anything too hard for the LORD?*[1280] He covenanted to give Abraham seed by Sarah, and that in his seed all the nations of the earth should be blessed, and he was both able to perform this seed, notwithstanding the deadness of Abraham's body and Sarah's womb, and also able to bless all nations in his seed, though Isaac should have been offered up for a burnt-offering. And therefore as to the former, *Abraham against hope believed in hope, and considered not his own body now dead, when he was about an hundred years old, neither yet the deadness of Sarah's womb; neither staggered he at the promise of God through unbelief: being fully persuaded, that what he had promised, he was able also to perform.*[1281] As to the latter, Abraham when he was tried, offered up Isaac: *and he that had received the promises, offered up his only begotten son; of whom it was said, that in Isaac shall thy seed be called. Accounting that God was able to raise him up even from the dead.*[1282] Thus Abraham looks upon God's Covenant, and God's ability fully to perform it; overlooking all contrary difficulties and impossibilities: God's promise resting upon the shoulders of his power, bears up Abraham's faith in the covenant, against all discouragements. Oh this power of God is the pillar of God's promise; and should be the pillar of our faith. We seldom stagger at the hardness and greatness of any promise of God, but we stagger first at the power of God. But God's power makes his Covenant sure.

{7} Finally, God is *immutable*, and unchangeable, still the same. *With him is no variableness, nor shadow of turning.*[1283] *The strength of Israel is not as the son of man that he should repent.*[1284] Consequently his covenant is immutable and unchangeable also. *That by two immutable things* (namely,

---

[1280] Genesis 18:14
[1281] Romans 4:17-22
[1282] Hebrews 11:17-19
[1283] James 1:17
[1284] 1 Samuel 15:29

God's promise and oath) *in which it is impossible that God should lie, we might have strong consolation.*[1285]

[2] ***From God's manifold methods and ways for establishment and confirmation of his Covenant, the sureness of his covenant is more infallibly assured to his people.*** God's Covenant barely delivered by him is sure enough itself, and heaven and earth may sooner pass away than any branch or word of his Covenant should pass away and be unfulfilled, but God has used many other courses besides bare publication for ratifying and ensuring his Covenant to us so that our faith therein might be firm without staggering and that our consolation thence might be strong without fainting. God has especially established his covenant to his people: {1} by writing it, {2} by the surest manner of expressing it, {3} by ratifying promises, {4} by federal solemnities, {5} by covenant seals and tokens, {6} by his own inviolable oath, and {7} by his son Christ's irrevocable death.

{1} *By writing the covenant.* At first, God's Covenant was declared to Adam, Noah, Abraham, etc., until the days of Moses, only by word of mouth: God uttering it to them by audible voice.[1286] But in and after Moses' days, God still committed his Covenant to writing – and this in all the discoveries and dispensations of it, from first to last. Holy Scriptures are his covenant-tables, his federal instruments. Herein we may read, as in a perpetual record, the tenor of God's covenant with his people, and of their restipulation with God, together with all the promises, privileges, conditions and clauses thereof. And all this, that God's Covenant might be made infallibly evident, certain and sure to his people in Christ from age to age. Time might obliterate a vocal covenant only out of memory, but no time shall possibly wipe God's written Covenant out of his book.

{2} *By the surest manner of expressing the Covenant.* God covenanting and promising mercies for time to come, expresses his promise so as if they were performed already for the time past. Hereby denoting the sureness of

---

[1285] Hebrews 6:17-18
[1286] Genesis 3:15 & 6:18 & 17:1-2, etc,

performance, the sureness of the Covenant. As God expressed his Covenant to Abraham: *In that same day the LORD made a covenant with Abraham, saying, unto thy seed have I given this land from the river of Egypt, to the great river the River Euphrates.*[1287] At this time Abraham had no seed at all: *Abraham said, LORD God, what wilt thou give me, seeing I go childless?*[1288] And when Abraham had seed, his seed enjoyed not this covenanted land of Canaan till after their 400 years' affliction in Egypt:[1289] and yet God says, unto thy seed have I given this land. How could this be? Or, why is it thus expressed? That learned Mercerus observes thus, out of Rashi, *I have given, for I will give: because that which the Lord promises for future is as sure, as if it were now done.*[1290] And out of Rambau, he speaks in the preter-tense, I have given: *because of his present covenant.* In two promises before God uses the future tense, *to thy seed I will give this land*:[1291] but now when he strikes a covenant with Abraham, *he declares and fully makes him and his seed lords of that land; and that he may signify this, he uses the preter-tense,* I have given: i.e. I give. *Thou mayest certainly know that this land is thy seed's, by virtue of the covenant I make with thee. Whereupon he prescribes the bounds of the land, which he had not done before.* Another observes that the Hebrew doctors scan the words thus: "He says not, *I will give*; but, *I have given*: and yet Abraham had now begotten no children. But because the word of the holy blessed God is a deed, therefore he so speaks. Mideas Tillim. Psalm 27:2."[1292]

{3} *By ratifying promises super-added.* God not only makes covenant with, and promises to, his people, but he also frequently and in pity promises to make good his covenants and promises. These therefore may well be called {*ratifying promises*}, because annexed for further ratifying, ensuring and peremptory confirming of God's Covenant to us.

[1287] Genesis 15:18
[1288] Genesis 15:2
[1289] Genesis 15:13-16
[1290] Joan Mercer in Praelection in Genesis 15:18
[1291] Genesis 12:7 & 13:15
[1292] Henry Ainsworth in his Annotations on Genesis 15:18

(i) Thus God makes sure his covenant to Israel: *If ye hearken to these judgements, and keep and do them: the LORD thy God shall keep unto thee the covenant and the mercy which he sware unto thy fathers.*[1293] And elsewhere: *I made you to go out of Egypt, and have brought you unto the land which I sware unto your fathers. And I said, I will never break my covenant with you.*[1294]

(ii) Thus God makes sure his Covenant to David: *My covenant will I not break, nor alter the thing that is gone out of my lips. Once have I sworn by mine holiness, that I will not lie unto David.*[1295]

(iii) Thus God makes sure his Covenant to his captive people: *Thus saith the LORD, if you can break my covenant of the day, and my covenant of the night, and that there should not be day and night in their season: then may also my covenant be broken with David my servant, that he should not have a son to reign upon his throne. And with the Levites the priests, my ministers.*[1296] (a) Thus God makes sure his Covenant to the church of the Gentiles: *The mountains shall depart, and the hills be removed, but my kindness shall not depart from thee; neither shall the covenant of my peace be removed, saith the Lord, that hath mercy on thee.*[1297] (b) In a word, thus the Lord makes sure his covenant indefinitely; *The LORD is gracious and full of compassion.—he will ever be mindful of his covenant.*[1298] What? Will the Lord not break nor alter his covenant; never break it? Will he keep it, and be ever mindful of it? Shall God's covenant be as inviolable as the course and revolution of day and night, and more immovable then the very hills and mountains? Why then should we suspect or stagger at the sureness of God's covenant, oh we of little faith?

(iv) *By federal solemnities annexed, God hath further established his covenants to his people.* The usual solemnities in covenant-making of old, was by striking, killing, dividing and offering up of sacrifices with sprinkling of their blood. Hence that phrase of cutting or striking the Covenant: *Gather*

[1293] Deuteronomy 7:12
[1294] Judges 2:1
[1295] Psalm 89:34-35
[1296] Jeremiah 33:20-22
[1297] Isaiah 54:10
[1298] Psalm 111:5

together unto me my saints, striking my covenant with sacrifice, as it is to be rendered out of the Hebrew.[1299] The manner of this solemnity Jeremiah declares, saying:[1300] *I will give the men that have transgressed my covenant, which have not performed the words of the covenant which they had struck before me, when they cut the calf in twain, and passed between the parts thereof.*[1301] Their manner was to kill sacrifices, to cut these sacrifices in twain, to lay the two parts thus divided in the midst, piece against piece, exactly one over against another, to answer each other, and then the parties covenanting passed between the parts of the sacrifices, so slit in twain, and laid answerably to one another. The meaning of which ceremonies and solemnities is conceived to be this, namely: as part answered to part, so there was an harmonious correspondence and answerableness of their minds and hearts that struck covenant. And as part was severed from part, so the covenanters implied (if not expressed) an imprecation or curse, wishing the like dissection and destruction to the parties covenanting as most deserved, if they should break the covenant or deal falsely therein. Whence that phrase of entering into a curse, and into an oath. Nehemiah 10:29. Now the Lord, for further ensuring of his Covenant to his people, has sometimes pleased to use this solemnity, as (a) to Abram, and (b) to Israel.

(a) To Abram, when he desired to have God's promise of Canaan confirmed to him, saying: *LORD God, whereby shall I know that I shall inherit it? And he said unto him, take me a heifer of three years old, and a she-goat of three years old, and a ram of three years old, and a turtle dove, and a young pigeon. And he took unto him all these, and divided them in the midst, and laid each piece one against another; And it came to pass, that when the sun went down, and it was dark, behold a smoking furnace, and a lamp of fire that*

[1299] Psalm 50:5

[1300] Jeremiah 34:18

[1301]This ceremony, or solemnity of covenanting, the heathen used, having borrowed it probably from the Jews. "Et caesa jungebant federa porca" Virgil Aeneid 1.8. See also Homer, Iliad, 1.3, Cicero, de Invent. Lib.2, Liv. Hist.l.x. But especially Virgil describes this ancient custom among the Romans, with others among other nations in their making of covenants. See Polydor. Virgil de Inventione Renum, lib 2, cap. 15.

passed between those pieces. In that same day the Lord made a covenant with Abram, saying, etc.[1302] Thus God confirms Abram by his Covenant, and confirms his Covenant by this solemnity. And why may not we interpret the smoking furnace as representing Abram's posterity that should be deeply afflicted in Egypt before Canaan be given them: and the lamp of fire, as representing God that should at last enlighten their darkness and bring them out of Egypt, etc. God being often in Scripture compared to fire,[1303] and to a lamp?[1304] (b) To Israel when they were brought out of Egypt, God also established his Covenant by sacrifices, and sprinkling of blood.[1305] Of which sacrifices and blood we have the truth in Christ: as after will appear.

(v) *By covenant-seals and tokens*, God has also confirmed and ensured his Covenant to his people. Thus when God made a covenant with Abraham, to be a God to him and to his seed to give them Canaan, etc., he confirmed this covenant by circumcision, as a token of the covenant between God and them. Yea so notably did circumcision ratify this covenant, that (by a *metonymy* of the thing signified put for the sign signifying) it is called {*the covenant of circumcision*},[1306] and God says of it, *My covenant shall be in your flesh for an everlasting covenant.*[1307] So they did indelibly receive this character of God's Covenant into their flesh, and did always carry about with them in their body this sign and mark of the covenant, for their notable confirmation therein. God thereby assuring them, that as certainly as they had this sign in their flesh: so certainly God's Covenant should be made good to them. Nor only was circumcision a sign or token of the covenant to Abraham, but also a seal of the covenant, for *he received the sign of circumcision, a seal of the righteousness of the faith, which he had yet being uncircumcised.*[1308]

[1302] Genesis 15:8-10, 17-18
[1303] Hebrews 12:29, Exodus 3:2, Daniel 10:6, Revelation 1:14
[1304] 2 Samuel 22:29
[1305] Exodus 24:3-9
[1306] Acts 7:8
[1307] Genesis 17:13
[1308] Romans 4:11

Now as the righteousness of works was the matter of the Covenant of Works, so the righteousness of faith is the matter of this Covenant of Faith, as has already been evidenced. If then circumcision was a seal of the righteousness of faith, which is the matter covenanted, consequently it was a seal of the covenant itself: *a seal*: to what end? Not for *impression, distinction,* or *concealment* (though for those uses seals are sometimes used), but for *confirmation.* Hereby God giving Abraham further assurance of his righteousness of faith promised him in the Covenant. Proportionably, all the other sacraments both before, and since Christ, are not only signs and tokens, but also seals of the Covenant: for what belongs to one sacrament as a sacrament belongs also to every sacrament.

And of the cup in the Lord's supper, Christ says: *This cup is the new testament (*or, *new covenant) in my blood.*[1309] That is, this cup is so true and sure a token and seal of the New Covenant, that it may be called the New Covenant itself. Thus, by these outward familiar signs incurring into the senses, the Lord has notably confirmed his Covenant to his people, and their faith therein. Which confirmation is grounded upon that sacramental union or relation between the signs and things signified; the signs truly signifying, sealing and exhibiting the inward covenanted mysteries. And which sacramental union or relation in signifying, sealing and exhibiting is grounded upon Christ's institution thus appointing it.

(vi) *By his own inviolable oath, God makes his covenant sure to his people.* An oath amongst men is the strongest, surest, most sacred, and inviolable bond: *For men verily swear by the greater, and an oath for confirmation is to them an end of all strife: wherein God willing more abundantly to shew unto the heirs of promise the immutability of his counsel, confirmed it by an oath; that by two immutable things,* (namely, God's promise of the inheritance, and his oath) *in which it was impossible for God to lie, we might have a strong consolation,* etc.[1310] God then not only makes his covenant but also swears his

---

[1309] Luke 22:19-20 with 1 Corinthians 11:25
[1310] Hebrews 6:16-18

covenant. *And when he could swear by no greater, he sware by himself.*[1311] Thus God added the solemn sanction and immutable band of an oath to his covenant and promise: and this to Abraham, Israel, and David. (a) To Abraham; *For when God made promise to Abraham, because he could swear by no greater, he sware by himself.*[1312] Hence God's Covenant with Abraham, is so often mentioned with God's oath to him and to his seed.[1313] (b) To Israel, when God besides his Covenant in Horeb, renewed his Covenant with them in the land of Moab peculiarly against the idolatry of the nations, this God confirmed by *oath*.[1314] (c) To David, finally God ratified his Covenant by oath, for his greater security and assurance therein. God said, *I have made a covenant with my chosen, I have sworn unto David my servant. Thy seed will I establish forever, and build up thy throne to all generations.*[1315] And again; *My covenant will I not break, nor alter the thing that is gone out of my lips. Once have I sworn by mine holiness, that I will not lie unto David.*[1316] Which covenant-oath of God to David had its principal accomplishment in Christ, *of the fruit of his loins according to the flesh, raised up to sit on David's throne.*[1317] Now *hath God said it, and will he not do it? Hath he sworn it, and will he not bring it to pass?* Yea the exhibition of Christ in our flesh in fullness of time, was in performance of the mercy promised to our fathers, and in remembrance of his holy covenant: the oath which he sware to our father Abraham, etc.[1318] Dare we trust an honest man upon his bare word? Much more upon his oath? And shall we not much more have strong confidence and consolation upon God's promise and oath?

(vii) Finally, *the Covenant is confirmed and made sure by Christ's irrevocable death.* In which regard, the Covenant is to be considered in the notion of a testament; and Christ as the testator of this will and testament (as

---

[1311] Hebrews 6:13
[1312] Hebrews 6:13
[1313] Genesis 26:3, Psalm 105:8-11, Luke 1:72-73
[1314] Deuteronomy 29:12, 14
[1315] Psalm 89:3-4
[1316] Psalm 89:34-35
[1317] Acts 2:30-31
[1318] Luke 1:72-73

was formerly noted), as therefore a man's will and testament is confirmed by the testator's death irrevocably, so that *no man adds thereto, nor takes thence-from; for where a testament is, there must also of necessity be the death of the testator; for a testament is of force after men are dead, otherwise it is of no strength at all while the testator liveth*: so Jesus Christ has unalterably confirmed his will and testament, the New Covenant by his blood and death: *that by means of death for the redemption of the transgressions that were under the first testament, they which are called, might receive the promise of eternal inheritance.*[1319] Hereupon Christ's blood is called *the blood of the everlasting covenant, or testament.*[1320] And, *his blood of the new testament.*[1321] Also the Covenant itself is styled *the new testament in his blood.*[1322] Because his Covenant and testament is founded, stablished, ratified, and immutably sealed up, in, and by his blood. So then his Covenant is most firm and sure: there can be no addition to it, detraction from it, or alteration of it; unless the death of Jesus Christ, whereby it is confirmed, were frustrated and overthrown. Yea, the covenant is as sure, as Christ's death is sure. The covenant can no more fail or die, than Christ can be brought down from the right hand of the majesty on high to die a second time. Christ being risen, dies no more, returns no more to corruption, and therefore he is the *sure mercies of David*;[1323] consequently, his Covenant in his death, never more to be repeated or reiterated, is become the sure Covenant of God, the sure testament of Jesus Christ.

Thus by all these *methods* for establishing his Covenant, God has made it unquestionably sure to all his people.

[3] *From God's actual accomplishment and most punctual performance of his covenant to his people, in the experience of all ages, God's Covenant will further appear to be most sure.* God has always been most exact in fulfilling his covenant and promise. He never yet failed his

---

[1319] Galatians 3:15 with Hebrews 9:15-18
[1320] Hebrews 13:20
[1321] Matthew 26:28, Mark 14:24
[1322] Luke 22:20, 1 Corinthians 11:25
[1323] Compare Isaiah 55:3 with Acts 13:34

people herein; nor ever will. He ever did, and consequently ever will, make his Covenant and all the promises thereof subsist in their season, for he is a faithful and an unalterable God, still the same.

{1} God covenanted in paradise, *that the seed of the woman should bruise the serpent's head.*[1324] And this Covenant he punctually performed; for, *When the fullness of time was come, God sent his Son made of a woman, made under the law, to redeem them that were under the law. And for this purpose the Son of God was manifested, that he might destroy the works of the devil.*[1325] And this, *As he spoke by the mouth of his holy prophets, which have been since the world began. That we should be saved from our enemies, and from the hand of all that hate us. To perform the mercy promised to our fathers, and to remember his holy covenant.*[1326]

{2} God covenanted with Noah, to save him and his family, and a seed of the creatures in the ark from perishing in that general deluge wherewith the whole world was drowned.[1327] And God exactly performed this his covenant with Noah and his family; they were preserved, when all flesh perished.[1328]

{3} God covenanted with Abraham, (i) to make his seed as numerous as the stars of heaven: when as yet he had no child.[1329] (ii) To bring his seed out of Egypt's affliction, after four hundred and thirty years. (iii) To give the land of Canaan to his seed, from the river of Egypt, to the River Euphrates. And, (iv) that, *in his seed all the nations of the earth should be blessed.*[1330]

And all these covenanted mercies God exactly performed in their season. For, (i) his posterity became wonderfully numerous. *Through faith Sarah herself received strength to conceive seed, and was delivered of a child when she was past age, because she judged him faithful who had promised. Therefore sprang there even of one, and him as good as dead, so many as the stars of the*

[1324] Genesis 3:15
[1325] Galatians 4:4-5 with 1 John 3:8
[1326] Luke 1:70-72
[1327] Genesis 6:17-18, etc.
[1328] Genesis 7:23 & 8 throughout, with Hebrews 11:7
[1329] Genesis 15:5, 13-14, 18, etc.
[1330] Genesis 22:18

sky in multitude, and as the sand which is by the sea-shore innumerable.[1331] (ii) His seed was in Egypt under great affliction. *But when the time of the promise drew nigh, which God had sworn to Abraham, the people grew and multiplied in Egypt.*[1332] — *And the children of Israel signed by reason of their bondage.—And God heard their groaning, and God remembered his covenant with Abraham, with Isaac, and with Jacob.*[1333] And God sent Moses and Aaron to deliver them, with many signs and wonders. Now God began experimentally to make himself known to his people by his name *JEHOVAH*, in giving actual being to his Covenant and promises: in bringing them out of Egypt.[1334] *And it came to pass at the end of the 430 years, even the self same day it came to pass, that all the hosts of the LORD went out from the land of Egypt.*[1335] Thus God kept touch with them in his Covenant, to a very year, yea to a very day. (iii) His seed, the children of Israel, were also brought according to God's Covenant with Abraham into actual possession of Canaan the land of rest, after their deliverance out of Egypt, God conducting them thither by Joshua, the type of Jesus. *And the LORD gave unto Israel all the land which he sware to give unto their fathers: and they possessed it, and dwelt therein: and the LORD gave them rest round about, according to all that he sware unto their fathers: and there stood not a man of all their enemies before them: the LORD delivered all their enemies into their hand. There failed not ought of any good thing which the LORD had spoken unto the house of Israel: all came to pass.*[1336] This the Levites notably confessed and amplified, in their prayer on a solemn day of fasting: saying: *Thou art the LORD the God who didst choose Abram,—and madest a covenant with him to give the land of the Canaanites,—to give it to his seed: and hast performed thy words, for thou art righteous.*[1337] The manner and way of God's performance being largely and

---

[1331] Hebrews 11:11-12
[1332] Acts 7:17
[1333] Exodus 2:23-25 & 3 etc.
[1334] Exodus 3:4, etc.
[1335] Exodus 12:41 with Acts 7:6-7 & Galatians 3:17
[1336] Joshua 21:43-45 & 23:14
[1337] Nehemiah 9:7-8 to 26

emphatically described. And more particularly the Psalmist describes the accurateness of this performance of God's Covenant, beginning his description thus: *He hath remembered his covenant forever: the word which he commanded to a thousand generations: which covenant he made with Abraham, and his oath unto Isaac: and confirmed the same unto Jacob for a law, and to Israel for an everlasting covenant, saying, unto thee will I give the land of Canaan, the lot of your inheritance.*[1338] And closing up his description thus: *For he remembered his holy promise, and Abraham his servant. And he brought forth his people with joy, and his chosen with gladness: and gave them the lands of the heathen: and they inherited the labor of the people; that they might observe his statutes, and keep his laws.*[1339] (iv) Finally, in Abraham's seed (that seed of seeds, Jesus Christ, the son of Abraham, according to the flesh),[1340] God blesses all the families of the earth, as Peter in his sermon testifies to the men of Israel, saying, *Ye are the children of the prophets, and of the covenant which God made with our fathers, saying unto Abraham, and in thy seed shall all the kindreds of the earth be blessed. Unto you first, God having raised up his son Jesus, sent him to bless you, in turning away every one of you from his iniquities.*[1341] Nor were the Jews only, but the Gentiles also blessed in Abraham's seed. For *Christ hath redeemed us from the curse of the law, being made a curse for us.—that the blessing of Abraham might come on the Gentiles through Jesus Christ.—so then they which be of faith (whether Jews or Gentiles,) are blessed with faithful Abraham.*[1342] Thus God performed his covenant to Abraham most punctually, in the several branches and particulars of it.

{4} God covenanted again at Mount Sinai to give Canaan to the children of Israel,[1343] *to bring them to a good land, a land of brooks of water, of fountains, and depths that spring out of valleys and hills. A land of wheat, and barley, and vines, and fig-trees, and pomegranates, a land of oil olive and*

[1338] Psalm 105:8-11 and so on, to verse 42
[1339] Psalm 105:42-45
[1340] Matthew 1:1-2, etc.
[1341] Acts 3:25-26
[1342] Galatians 3:9, 13-14
[1343] Deuteronomy 5:2-3, 16

honey. A land wherein thou shalt eat bread without scarceness, thou shalt not lack any thing in it; a land whose stones are iron, and out of whose hills thou mayest dig brass.[1344] And Solomon before all the congregation of Israel, at the dedication of the temple, confessed God's performance herein, saying: *Blessed be the Lord, that hath given rest unto his people Israel, according to all that he promised: there hath not fallen, (or, failed) one word of all his good promise, which he promised by the hand of Moses his servant.*[1345]

{5} God covenanted and swore to David *to raise up his seed which should build God an house, to establish his seed forever, and build up his throne to all generations*, etc.[1346] This Covenant, God admirably fulfilled both in the type, *Solomon*: and in the anti-type, *Christ*, both of them of the seed of *David*: both of them kings, set upon David's throne: namely, *Solomon temporally*, Christ *spiritually*: and both of them builders of God's house, namely: Solomon of his material temple, Christ of his mystical and spiritual temple the church. Hereupon Solomon confessed: *O LORD God of Israel, there is no God like thee in the heaven, nor in the earth; which keepest covenant and mercy unto thy servants that walk before thee with all their hearts: thou which hast kept with thy servant David my father that which thou hast promised him and spakest with thy mouth, and hast fulfilled with thine hand, as it is this day.*[1347] But this Covenant had its chief accomplishment in Christ, of the fruit of David's loins according to the flesh, whom God raised up to sit upon his throne, and to build his church, as is elsewhere testified.[1348]

{6} God covenanted with his captive-people in Babylon, that after seventy years of captivity, he would visit the king of Babylon, and his land in judgment to destroy them, but would visit his people there in mercy to deliver, them thence: and that though their condition seemed to be dead and desperate, yet he would *open their graves, and bring them out of their graves.*[1349] And God

---

[1344] Deuteronomy 8:7-9
[1345] 1 Kings 8:56
[1346] 2 Samuel 7:11-16; Psalm 89:3-4
[1347] 1 Kings 8:23-24 & 2 Chronicles 6:14-15
[1348] Acts 2:29, 30-37 & 13:32-38, Ephesians 2:20-22 & 4:8-14
[1349] Jeremiah 25:13-14 & 29:10-15, Ezekiel 36:23 to the end, & 37:11-14

punctually performed this covenant and promise to them. For Belshazzar king of Babylon being slain, Darius the Mede with Cyrus the Persian took the kingdom.[1350] *And in the first year of Cyrus king of Persia (that the word of the LORD, by the mouth of Jeremiah might be fulfilled), the LORD stirred up the spirit of Cyrus king of Persia, that he made proclamation, that all the people of the Jews, who were willing, should go up to Jerusalem to build the house of God,* etc.[1351]

{7} Finally, God promised and covenanted to *make a new covenant with the house of Israel, and the house of Judah,* and expressed what should be the tenor of the covenant.[1352] And God, in performance of this covenant and promise, sent Jesus Christ to be *mediator of this better covenant, established upon better promises.*[1353] The other covenant thereby being made old, and vanishing away. For the Scripture says of Christ: *By one offering he hath forever perfected them that are sanctified, whereof the Holy Ghost also is a witness to us. For after that he had said before, this is the covenant that I will make with them after those days, saith the LORD: I will put my laws into their hearts; and in their minds will I write them: and their sins and iniquities will I remember no more. Now where remission of these is, there is no more offering for sin.*[1354] So then the New Covenant promising *to remember their sins and iniquities no more* is only accomplished in Christ, who has so fully satisfied God's justice for the sins of all his seed by the price of his own blood and death, that there needs no more expiatory sacrifice to be offered for their sins forever. *But in those Levitical sacrifices, there is a remembrance again made of sins every year: for it is not possible that the blood of bulls and of goats should take away sins.*[1355] Wherefore Christ came, and by the sacrifice of himself blots out the remembrance of his people's sins with God forever.

[1350] Daniel 5:25 to the end of the chapter
[1351] 2 Chronicles 36:22-23, Nehemiah 1 throughout, and the ensuing chapters
[1352] Jeremiah 31:31-34
[1353] Hebrews 8:6 to the end
[1354] Hebrews 10:13-19
[1355] Hebrews 10:1-15

Thus it's evident in all the grand periods of the covenant's administration that in all ages God has ever been mindful of his Covenant, exactly performing it in its season. The church's continued experience hereof notably demonstrates the unparalleled faithfulness of God and sureness of his covenant. For God is still as true, faithful, unchangeable, all-sufficient, gracious, merciful, and every way as able and willing to perform his Covenant to Christ's seed now as he was of old. And what should I add more? Time would fail me to descend to particular promises, the branches of God's Covenant, and to show how accurately they have been still accomplished – and that not only to Christ's seed but sometimes even to Christ's enemies. But these may more properly be considered of in the handling of the promises.

[4] *From removal of all imaginable corrumpent causes, that might possibly render God's Covenant unfaithful, or unsure.* What can there possibly be imagined by the most trembling scrupling doubting soul that can any way impeach or weaken the sureness of this Covenant of Faith? For, {1} nothing in God can do it. {2} Nothing in Christ. {3} Nothing in Christ's seed. {4} Nothing in the enemies of Christ and his seed, namely, The serpent and his seed. {5} Nothing in the law of God. {6} Nothing in the threatenings of God. {7} Nothing in the covenant itself can possibly overthrow or once shake the stability and sureness of the Covenant of Faith. And besides these, what can be suspected? Wherefore then do we so doubt and stagger at God's Covenant through unbelief, O we of little faith?

{1} **Nothing in God can be imagined against the sureness of his covenant.** (i) Not any falsehood. For, *God that covenants and promises, cannot lie,*[1356] yea, *it's impossible he should lie in his promises.*[1357] (ii) Not any unfaithfulness. For, God *that promises is faithful: he is the faithful God, keeping covenant and mercy.*[1358] (iii) Not any folly or unskillfulness in bringing his covenants to pass. For, *God is only wise: and his understanding is*

[1356] Titus 1:2
[1357] Hebrews 6:17-18
[1358] Hebrews 11:11 with Deuteronomy 7:9

infinite.[1359] He knows how to accomplish every word of his; to that end, both how to remove all obstructions and impediments to their performance, and how to overpower all things that they shall cooperate thereunto. (iv) Not any infirmity or weakness. For, *what God promises he is fully able to perform*.[1360] And *nothing can be too hard for him who can do all things*.[1361] (v) Not any injustice or unrighteousness. For, *is God unrighteous? God forbid: for then how shall God judge the world?*[1362] Yea God is so righteous, that *no unrighteousness is in him*, or can come from him, or can in the least degree be approved by him.[1363] *He made a covenant with Abraham, and performed his words, because he is righteous.*[1364] (vi) Not any inconstancy or variableness. For, *with God is no variableness, nor shadow of turning*.[1365] His promise and oath are *two immutable things, declaring the immutability of his counsel*.[1366] *The Lord hath sworn, and will not repent.*[1367] God says: *Once have I sworn by mine holiness, that I will not lie unto David. My covenant will I not break, nor alter the thing that is gone out of my lips.*[1368] (vii) Finally, not any covenant-breaking disposition or inclination in God. For, God is always a covenant-remembering, and a covenant-keeping God.[1369]

{2} **Nothing in Christ can be imagined as destructive to the Covenant of Faith.** For that must be supposed to be in him, either as *God*; or as *man*; or as *Godman, mediator* between God and man. For, in other notion or respect, how should we consider him? But in none of all these regards or considerations can anything be found in Christ destructive to the sureness of this Covenant of Faith.

[1359] 1 Timothy 1:17 with Psalm 147:5
[1360] Romans 4:21
[1361] Genesis 18:14, Job 42:2
[1362] Romans 3:5-6 & 9:14
[1363] Psalm 92:15, Deuteronomy 32:4, Habakkuk 1:13
[1364] Nehemiah 9:8
[1365] James 1:17
[1366] Hebrews 6:16-18
[1367] Psalm 110:4
[1368] Psalm 89:34-35
[1369] Psalm 11:5 & 105:8, 1 Kings 8:23

(i) *Not anything in him as he is God.* For, it has been cleared already, that nothing can be imagined in God against the sureness of the covenant.

(ii) *Nothing in Christ as he is man, can infringe the Covenant.* For, if anything: doubtless, sin. But sin in Christ cannot do it, for that must be either (a) sin inherent in him, and acted by him, or (b) sin imputed to him, and punished in him: yet neither of these can prevail.

(a) Not sin inherent in him or acted by him, for in this sense *he knew no sin*:[1370] he was *holy, harmless, undefiled, separate from sinners*:[1371] *he was in all points tempted like as we are, yet without sin.*[1372] When Satan had tempted him both before his public ministry, and at his death with all advantageous subtleties and importunities, yet *he left him*, because he could find *nothing in him*;[1373] no tinder of sin to catch fire at any or all the sparks of his temptations. *He did no violence, neither was any deceit in his mouth.*[1374] Though therefore he was by wicked hands condemned and put to death, yet none of his judges or adversaries or their witnesses could find any just cause or matter against him. Yea contrariwise, Pilate his judge professed before the Jews, that *neither he himself, nor yet Herod, found any fault in him*:[1375] the thief on the cross crucified with him, said, *This man hath done nothing amiss*:[1376] *The centurion when he saw what was done, glorified God, saying, certainly this was a righteous man; truly this was the Son of God. And all the people that came together to that sight, beholding the things which were done, smote their breasts and returned.*[1377]

(b) Nor sin imputed to him and punished upon him could prejudice this covenant, but rather established and fulfilled the same. For hereby, he only wrought the recovery of his seed from sin to righteousness, and from death to eternal life. *He who knew no sin, was made sin for us: that we might be made*

[1370] 2 Corinthians 5:21
[1371] Hebrews 7:26
[1372] Hebrews 4:15
[1373] Matthew 4:11, Luke 4:13, John 14:30
[1374] Isaiah 53:9
[1375] Luke 23:14-15, 22
[1376] Luke 23:41
[1377] Matthew 27:5, Luke 23:47-48

the righteousness of God in him.[1378] And *what the law could not do, in that it was weak through the flesh, God sending his own son in the likeness of sinful flesh, and for sin, condemned sin in the flesh: that the righteousness of the law might be fulfilled in us.*[1379] And to this end Christ had covenanted and restipulated with the Father, as has been shown to accept and undergo the mediatory office, and particularly as a priest to offer up himself a sacrifice for the sins of his seed.

(iii) Finally, nothing in Christ as God-man, mediator between God and man, can shake or in the least degree weaken the sureness of this Covenant. For, (a) Christ as mediator builds and ratifies the Covenant by his death, and therefore he cannot destroy it.[1380] (b) Again, *in Christ all God's promises are yea, and amen.*[1381] (c) Furthermore, if anything in Christ as mediator should enervate the Covenant, it must be either some insufficiency or unfaithfulness in his mediation, for what else can be probably imagined? But in Christ neither of these can have place. Not insufficiency: for, *the fullness of the Godhead dwells in him:*[1382] he was *anointed with the oil of gladness above all his fellows;* for *he received not the spirit by measure,* as they did;[1383] *he is full of grace and truth, yea all fullness dwells in him; that of his fullness we may all receive, and grace for grace:*[1384] he is *made of God to us wisdom, righteousness, sanctification and redemption:*[1385] he is *able to save them to the uttermost, that come unto God by him, seeing he ever lives to make intercession for them:*[1386] he is *all and in all,*[1387] and *we are complete in him.*[1388] Not unfaithfulness: for, *as he is a merciful,* so he is *a faithful high-priest in things pertaining to God, to*

[1378] 2 Corinthians 5:21
[1379] Romans 8:3-4
[1380] Hebrews 7:22 & 9:15-18 & 1 Corinthians 11:25
[1381] 2 Corinthians 1:20
[1382] Colossians 2:9
[1383] Psalm 45:7 with John 3:34
[1384] John 1:14, 16, Colossians 1:19
[1385] 1 Corinthians 1:30
[1386] Hebrews 7:25
[1387] Colossians 3:11
[1388] Colossians 2:10

make reconciliation for the sins of the people.[1389] *He was faithful to him that appointed, as also Moses was faithful in all his house: yea more then so; Moses was faithful in all God's house, as a servant, but Christ as a son over his own house, whose house are we:*[1390] he *having loved his own, loved them to the end:*[1391] he *gives eternal life unto his sheep, and they shall never perish, neither shall any pluck them out of his hand.*[1392] And *Jesus Christ is the same yesterday, and today, and forever.*[1393] Thus nothing in Christ can enfeeble God's Covenant.

{3} **Nothing in Christ's seed can dash the sureness of God's Covenant**. For neither their unworthiness, nor their weakness, nor their unfaithfulness, nor their inconstancy shall do it.

(i) Not their unworthiness by reason of sin and corruption. For,

(a) When God first of all revealed this Covenant of Faith in paradise, it was done so in time upon Adam's fall, and at that time, Adam and all mankind in him were in the most wretched, sinful, and unworthy condition that ever they were or shall be in on earth from the creation till the Judgment Day,[1394] as has been manifested.[1395] And when God renewed this covenant to Israel, they were (as God shows)[1396] altogether unworthy of any such federal favor. As therefore their unworthiness hindered not God from making covenant with them: no more can their unworthiness hinder him from keeping it with them, being made.

(b) This is a *Covenant* of *Grace* and *Faith*, as has been demonstrated. *Grace* is the foundation of it, on God's part: *faith* the condition of it, on ours. And yet that *faith not of ourselves: it is the gift of God.*[1397] Therefore God's Covenant, and the sureness thereof, has no dependance at all upon us, or upon any thing that is ours, but only upon God: seeing both the *foundation* and

---

[1389] Hebrews 2:17
[1390] Hebrews 2:1-2, 5-6
[1391] John 13:1
[1392] John 10:28-29
[1393] Hebrews 13:8
[1394] Genesis 3:6-7, 15
[1395] In Book 2 Chapter 1 Aphorism 6 Corollary 2
[1396] Ezekiel 16:2-9 & 36:21-33
[1397] Ephesians 2:8

condition of it are from God. Consequently it must needs be sure, though we be never so unworthy. *Therefore it is of faith, that it might be by grace: to the end the promise might be sure to all the seed*:[1398] whether Jews or Gentiles.

(c) This Covenant of Faith removes and destroys all the sinful unworthiness of Christ's seed: God herein covenanting *to be merciful to their unrighteousness, and to remember their sins and their iniquities no more.*[1399] And therefore their sins and unworthiness removed by the covenant, cannot destroy or shake the sureness of the covenant. The covenant-remedy against their sin and unworthiness, incomparably transcends and surpasses all their sins and unworthiness. Christ and his death are this remedy. Now Christ has more *righteousness* for them than they have *unrighteousness*, Christ has more *pardons* than they have *debts*, Christ has more *healing* than they have *wounds*, Christ has more *justification* than they have *condemnation*, Christ has more *blessings* than they have *curses*, for Christ's worthiness is the worthiness of an infinite God, their unworthiness is but at the utmost the unworthiness of finite creatures.

(ii) *Not their weakness to perform their part of the covenant, which they have conditioned and restipulated*, shall infringe upon the covenant's sureness. For God (whose *strength is perfected* in his people's weakness)[1400] has fully provided against all their weakness in this covenant; saying, *I will make an everlasting covenant with them, that I will not turn away from them, to do them good; but I will put my fear in their hearts, that they shall not depart from me.*[1401] And again: *I will put my laws in their mind, and write them in their hearts: and I will be to them a God, and they shall be to me a people.*[1402] What a full provision is here against all our weakness! And that chiefly two-ways. (a) Partly, by God's principling us; he will put his fear into our hearts, and write his laws in our minds. These shall so strengthen us, that we shall not depart from him. (b) Partly, by God's undertaking for us, as well as

---

[1398] Romans 4:16
[1399] Hebrews 8:12
[1400] 2 Corinthians 12:9
[1401] Jeremiah 32:40
[1402] Hebrews 8:10

for himself. He undertakes for both sides: that he will not turn away from us, and that we shall not depart from him: that he will be our God, and that we shall be his people. When man and wife covenant, or when man and man covenant, each party undertakes only for himself; none undertakes for both parties, nor can. But God undertakes for both: truly he will be, and we shall perform. Here's no place for weakness to harm the Covenant's sureness.

(iii) *Not their unfaithfulness in God's Covenant*, can dash the sureness of the Covenant. For, (a) the Covenant's sureness is based upon the faithfulness of God and not of man.[1403] Therefore if God's faithfulness abide sure and impregnable, his covenant also will abide sure and impregnable man's unfaithfulness cannot overthrow God's faithfulness. (b) God has been wont to have respect to his Covenant and faithfully to perform it to the political body of his people, his visible church, though many therein dealt unfaithfully, perfidiously and rebelliously against him. *Israel departed not from the sins of the house of Jeroboam*, wherefore God gave them to be oppressed by Hazael, king of Syria, but destroyed them not presently, for *The LORD was gracious to them, and had compassion on them, and had respect unto them, because of his covenant with Abraham, Isaac, and Jacob, and would not destroy them, neither cast he them from his presence, as yet.*[1404] How often did they sin against God and provoke him both in the wilderness and in Canaan? For which, how often did God punish them by afflictions and enemies? *Nevertheless he regarded their affliction, when he heard their cry. And he remembered for them his covenant, and repented according to the multitude of his mercies.*[1405] Hereupon says the apostle of the body of the Jewish church, *What if some did not believe? Shall their unbelief make the faith of God (that is, the faithfulness of God in his covenant) of none effect? God forbid, yea, let God be true, but every man a liar.*[1406] (c) Yea God is pleased faithfully to perform his Covenant with every individual person of Christ's true spiritual seed, notwithstanding their

---

[1403] Hebrews 6:17-18, Psalm 89:34-35, Hebrews 11:11-12, Titus 1:2
[1404] 2 Kings 13:6, 22-23
[1405] Psalm 106 throughout, especially verses 44-45
[1406] Romans 3:3-4

manifold failings, and particular unfaithfulnesses that his truth and faithfulness may be the more gloriously commended. Their unfaithfulness (which is never habitual, and reigning) serves rather to illustrate how they overthrow the Lord's fidelity, inasmuch as he performs his Covenant and promise, even to those of his that in some part deal unfaithfully in covenant with him, rather pardoning their iniquities, then suffering his truth to fail. Thus God dealt with David, as he confesses, *Against thee, thee only have I sinned, and done this evil in thy sight: that thou mightest be justified when thou speakest.*[1407] That is, (as some expound it):[1408] *I have fallen through thy just permission, and this thou hast suffered, that thou mightest be justified,* that is, declared and known to be just and faithful in thy promise. Thus God promised also to deal with David's seed in the tenor of his Covenant with him: *My covenant shall stand fast with him. His seed also will I make forever, and his throne as the days of heaven. If his children forsake my law, and walk not in my judgments; if they break my statutes, and keep not my commandments: then will I visit their transgression with the rod, and their iniquity with stripes. Nevertheless my loving-kindness will I not utterly take from him: nor suffer my faithfulness to fail. My covenant will I not break; nor alter the thing that is gone out of my lips. Once I have sworn by mine holiness, that I will not lie unto David*[1409]. So true is that of the apostle's touching Christ, *If we believe not, yet he abides faithful, he cannot deny himself.*[1410]

(iv) Finally, *not the inconstancy of Christ's seed, can render God's Covenant inconstant or unsure.* For, though carnal men and hypocrites be inconstant, unsettled, wavering and tossed to and fro, yet true believers are habitually fixed and unmovable. *They that trust in the LORD shall be as Mount Sion, which cannot be removed, but abideth forever.*[1411] They are built upon a rock, the rock Christ by faith, and *the gates of hell shall not prevail against them.*[1412] The

---

[1407] Psalm 51:4 with Romans 3:3-5, etc.
[1408] D. Will. Sclater in his exposition on Romans 3:3-4
[1409] Psalm 89:28-38
[1410] 2 Timothy 2:13
[1411] Psalm 125:1-2
[1412] Matthew 16:18

Lord himself has in his Covenant engaged for them, to *put his fear in their hearts, that they shall not depart from him.*[1413] Therefore though they may fall, yet shall they never finally and totally fall away. Though they may have relics of inconstancy in them, yet shall not that inconstancy prevail to have dominion over them. The immutable God will not only be constant in his Covenant to them, but also make them constant therein by him.

{4} **Nothing in the enemies of Christ and his seed – namely, in the serpent and his seed – can shake the sureness of God's Covenant.** For what can be supposed in them to do it? (i) *Not their malice.* For God's love and tender dearness to his covenant and people is infinite: and therefore incomparably surpassing the finite malice of the devil and all wicked men against them.[1414] (ii) *Not their policy.* For, though the old serpent the devil and his seed deal extreme subtlety against God's Covenant and people, yet the Lord only wise, infinite in understanding, and unsearchable in counsel, can easily infatuate [make foolish] all their policies. And the counsel of the Lord, that shall stand.[1415] (iii) *Not their power.* For God is stronger than all,[1416] and nothing can either enfeeble his Covenant or pluck his covenant-people out of his hand. (iv) Nor finally anything that can be imagined in them. For in this covenant, God has covenanted and promised to put such *enmity between the two seeds*, namely: of the woman and the serpent, that though the serpent and his seed bruise the heel of Christ and Christians, the woman's seed, to their molestation, yet they shall bruise the head of the serpent and his seed the wicked, to their utter destruction.[1417]

{5} **Nothing in the law of God can dash the sureness of this Covenant.** For, (i) *this Covenant was confirmed and established to Abraham in Christ* (and thereby the earthly Canaan, and heavenly inheritance), *430 years before*

[1413] Jeremiah 32:40
[1414] John 3:16, Isaiah 63:7-9, Deuteronomy 32:10-14, 1 John 3:1-2 compared with Daniel 11:30, 32, 45
[1415] Revelation 20:2, Genesis 3:15 with 2 Corinthians 2:11, Revelation 2:24, Exodus 1:10, Acts 7:19, Psalm 10:2, 7-10, 2 Samuel 15:31 & 17:14, Proverbs 19:21
[1416] John 10:28-29, Romans 16:20, Colossians 2:15
[1417] Genesis 3:15

the law was given: therefore the law cannot disannul it, that it should make the promise of God of none effect.[1418] (ii) The law is not against God's Covenant, therefore it cannot prejudice the sureness thereof at all. *Is the law then against the promises of God? God forbid.*[1419] Why? Partly because the law was not given on Mount Sinai to afford life and justification by it, but rather to seal up condemnation by convincing all of sin, that despairing in themselves they might go to Christ for life. Partly because the law was given to the Jews to be their *schoolmaster to bring them to Christ* (the moral law by convincing and correcting them for sin; the ceremonial law by directing them unto Christ, the remedy against sin) so that they might be justified by faith according to the tenor of this covenant. So that the Law (as published on Sinai) was given as a Covenant of Faith not as a Covenant of Works, as will further appear in the distinct handling of that particular administration of the covenant, and therefore it tends to confirm, settle, and establish the Covenant of Faith, and not in the least degree to weaken it.

{6} **Nothing in the threatenings of God can enfeeble or overthrow this covenant**. For, (i) if the law itself cannot overthrow it, how should the threatenings and curse of the law do it, which are but denunciations of penalties annexed to the law? (ii) *Christ hath redeemed his seed from the curse of the law, by becoming a curse for them.*[1420] Therefore the curse and threatenings of the law can in no degree prejudice their state in this Covenant of Faith. (iii) Of God's threatening there is a double use: condemnatory and cautionary. They are condemnatory to them that lie under the penalty of the broken Covenant of Works, who accept not God's Covenant of Faith and Christ therein: but to none else. They are only cautionary to Christ's seed who are in the Covenant of Faith with God, to prevent them from sinning against God and his covenant. Curses and threatenings as well as blessings and promises are additionals and appendixes to this Covenant. That phrase is

---

[1418] Galatians 3:16-18
[1419] Galatians 3:19-23. Weigh well the apostle's argumentation in this context.
[1420] Galatians 3:13

observable, *according to all the curses of the covenant*[1421]. And therefore being additionals annexed, they cannot weaken but strengthen the Covenant. In God's threatenings are (as of old in God's cloud between the Israelites and Egyptians)[1422] a bright side, and a dark side; the honey and the gall; the good and the evil. The evil, the dark side of the threatenings, namely, the curse, the vengeance of God, the destruction, the damnation, etc., are intended for godless, Christ-less, covenantless persons. But the good, the bright side of the threatenings, as incitements to a holy fear, cautions against sin, inducements unto duty and obedience, indications of divine truth and justice, etc., are peculiarly intended to God's covenant-people. Without promises we would basely despair; without threatenings we would proudly presume. "Between these two milestones," (as Luther well said) "God's people are made sweet meal." God's Covenant is his act or charter of grace to his church; God's promises and threats are his articles of agreement, provisos, and cautions therein. God's Covenant is as the garden of Eden: the promises as the pleasant fruit-trees, especially as the tree of life, and the threatenings as the tree of the knowledge of good and evil. Eden was for delight, the fruit trees for food, the Tree of Life for confirmation in good, the Tree of Knowledge for caution against evil; so here proportionably, God's Covenant is for his people's spiritual delight, his promises for her encouragement and establishment in all goodness and happiness, and his threatnings for her caution and preservation against sin and misery.

{7} Finally, nothing in the covenant itself can overthrow or shake the sureness of it. (i) *Not the foundation of it*; for, that is not weak or movable, but strong and immovable, namely: God's mere grace,[1423] and Christ's meritorious death,[1424] and both according to God's eternal and immutable decree.[1425] (ii) *Not the parties to it*; for, God on his part *cannot lie*,[1426] or suffer

---

[1421] Deuteronomy 29:21
[1422] Exodus 14:19-20
[1423] Romans 4:16, Ezekiel 16:1-9 & 36:32
[1424] Hebrews 9:14-21
[1425] Ephesians 1:4-7
[1426] Titus 1:2

his covenant-faithfulness to fail:[1427] and Christ with his seed on their part, shall not fail, or deal falsely in God's Covenant.[1428] (iii) *Not the greatness of the blessings and mercies covenanted*; for, *what God hath promised, he is fully able to perform*,[1429] and has already performed them in all ages by-past, *being able to do exceeding abundantly above all that we ask or think*; for he can do all things.[1430] (iv) Nor, finally, the difficulty of the conditions restipulated by Christ's seed; for, Christ lives in them, acts in them, works all their works for them.[1431] And therefore they *can do all things through Christ strengthening them*.[1432] Thus, nothing in God, nothing in Christ, nothing in Christ's seed, nothing in the enemies of Christ and his seed, nothing in the law, nothing in God's threatenings, and nothing in God's Covenant itself, can be imagined, as a corrupt cause to dash or shake the sureness of God's Covenant. Now therefore let all the children of the Covenant and promises fix their faith and confidence upon this sure covenant of God, as upon an impregnable rock, that thence they may extract strong consolation in all times of need against all disconsolations whatsoever. (v) Finally, the sureness of the Covenant may be further demonstrated from the durable and everlasting nature of it. That must needs be sure, which is everlasting. Now this Covenant is *everlasting*.[1433] But this everlastingness of it makes a distinct property, particularly to be considered.

[1427] Psalm 89:33-34
[1428] Jeremiah 32:38-40
[1429] Romans 4:21
[1430] Ephesians 3:20, Job 42:2
[1431] Galatians 2:20
[1432] Philippians 4:13
[1433] 2 Samuel 23:5, Hebrews 13:20

(5) The Covenant of Faith is Comfortable

The Covenant of Faith is a most comfortable covenant; it is an exquisite heart-reviving cordial indeed to all the faithful. For clearing of this sweet property, let us see: [1] how it may appear, that it is comfortable, [2] to whom it is comfortable, and [3] in what respect it is comfortable.

[1] *That this Covenant of Faith is a comfortable covenant,* may be evidenced in several ways. For,

{1} The whole Scriptures are comfortable. They are a rich shop or cabinet of cordials for, *Whatsoever things were written aforetime, were written for our learning, that we through patience and comfort of the Scriptures might have hope.*[1434] Consequently, the Covenant of Faith, and the precious promises thereof, being of all other the most eminent, sweet, and evangelical part of Scripture, must needs be comfortable.

{2} God singularly intended his people's comfort, in his making covenant with them. For this very end, amongst others, he revealed his covenant: that he might advance their comforts. Hence the apostle says of God's Covenant with Abraham; that *He confirmed it by an oath. That by two immutable things* (namely: his Covenant and oath), *in which it was impossible for God to lie, we might have a strong consolation.*[1435] So then, God intended our consolation, by his immutable Covenant and promise: and he intended our strong consolation, by his immutable oath strengthening and confirming his Covenant. Now if God intended our comfort by this covenant; doubtless he so fitted and framed the Covenant so that it might be comfortable to us. For whatsoever means he ordains to any end, he makes them sufficient and effectual for attaining such an end.

[1434] Romans 15:4
[1435] Hebrews 6:17-18

{3} God's people have actually supported and comforted themselves by God's Covenant, against saddest objects and occasions of disconsolation. Thus, though David's house was *not like the morning light when the sun rises without clouds, nor like tender grass springing out of the earth by clear shining after rain*,[1436] as is promised to him that rules over men justly in the fear of God, though his house was not clear without clouds of troubles and afflictions, nor did grow at present so prosperously and flourishingly; yet against this saddening discomfort, David stays his heart with the rich cordial of God's Covenant. *Although mine house be not so with God: yet he hath made with me an everlasting covenant, ordered in all things, and sure; therefore this is all my salvation, and all my delight, although he make it not to grow* (thus we may render the Hebrew),[1437] thus also the church of God, in extreme calamities under cruel persecuting enemies, yet comforts and encourages herself in her prayer to the Lord by consideration of God's Covenant (among other grounds of support), saying: *O deliver not the soul of thy turtle-dove unto the multitude of the wicked, forget not the congregation of thy poor forever. Have respect unto the covenant*, etc.[1438] When God's people therefore have been in deepest waters and roughest seas of distress, they have been wont to catch hold of this sure rock of God's Covenant and there to save and repose themselves.

[2] *To whom this Covenant of Faith is comfortable*, may thus be declared.

{1} *First we must distinguish of persons*. All persons may be considered: (i) Either unconverted, and in their mere carnal condition in the first Adam,[1439] or: (ii) *As in the way of conversion* under conviction of their extreme natural misery, without Christ; and of the all-sufficient supernatural remedy in Christ: which conviction is effected in them by the Spirit of Christ.[1440] Or (iii) as

---

[1436] 2 Samuel 23:4
[1437] 2 Samuel 23:3-5
[1438] Psalm 74:19-20
[1439] Romans 8:6-8
[1440] John 16:9-10

effectually converted and actually called from darkness to light and from the power of Satan unto God.[1441]

{2} *Next we must distinguish of comfort.* (i) There's a *carnal comfort*, which even hypocrites, formalists, and carnal persons may receive either from carnal objects, or from spiritual objects carnally apprehended, but which vanishes away.[1442] (ii) There's a spiritual comfort arising from spiritual grounds and objects spiritually apprehended. As from *the Spirit of God*,[1443] *the light of God's countenance lifted up upon us*;[1444] *justification by faith in Jesus Christ*;[1445] *the fear of the Lord*,[1446] etc., which comforts are the peculiar inheritance of God's people: *strangers shall not meddle with their joy*.[1447] Now things may be said to be spiritually comfortable two ways, namely: *potentially* and *actually*. *Potentially* those spiritual things are comfortable, which have in themselves some principle, cause, foundation, ground or matter of comfort; whereby they are disposed and able to comfort, if applied. Thus Christ, the Scriptures, the Covenant, and promises have in them much matter and ground of comfort, if apprehended and applied by faith. *Actually* those spiritual things are comfortable, which upon application do actually and effectually comfort indeed. And this, partly by secret supportment against despair and overwhelming disconsolations. Hereby the heart is sufficiently, though obscurely, *held up* and *stayed* from fainting and sinking.[1448] Partly by sensible refreshment; hereby the heart being evidently enlarged, revived and cheered up against discomforts, even unto joy and delight, etc.[1449] Thus conceive of comfort, and of things comfortable.

{3} *Now these things premised, we may more clearly judge, unto whom this Covenant of Faith is comfortable.* (i) Unto mere carnal unconverted persons,

---

[1441] Matthew 18:3, Romans 8:30, Acts 26:18
[1442] Matthew 13:20-21, Mark 6:20, Hebrews 6:4-6
[1443] Romans 14:17
[1444] Psalm 4:6-7
[1445] Romans 5:1-3
[1446] Acts 9:31
[1447] Proverbs 14:10
[1448] Song of Solomon 2:5, Psalm 27:13, 1 Samuel 30:6
[1449] Psalm 94:17-19, Romans 5:1-3

the Covenant carnally apprehended may be carnally comfortable: as the gospel carnally tasted may bring joy to a carnal apprehension.[1450] To such also it is potentially comfortable, there being such ground and matter of comfort therein, as is able to comfort any persons to whom it is or shall be effectually applied. But actually, and in a true spiritual sense, this covenant is not comfortable, nor can be, to any mere carnal man, so remaining.[1451] (ii) Unto persons under conviction and in the way of conversion, this Covenant of Faith is comfortable: not only *potentially*, as a ground and foundation of possible comfort, but in some sense *actually*, by supporting them secretly against despair, under the terrors of conscience, horror of divine wrath, and dreadful curse of the law, for sin.[1452] For if the Lord did not secretly sustain and bear up a poor soul under such spiritual agonies by his Covenant in Christ, how quickly would he run with Judas into desperate extremities![1453] (iii) Finally, unto persons effectually called and converted, this Covenant is comfortable, not *carnally*, but *spiritually*: and that not only *potentially*, as having in it rich matter of comfort, but also *actually*, as being actually applied unto them for comfort. In which regard, they are *sometimes* secretly supported by it against sinking and fainting: *sometimes* they are sensibly refreshed with evident peace, enlargement and joy. To these the covenant is primarily and especially comfortable. Hence the apostle declaring *God's willingness more abundantly to show the immutability of his counsel in his covenant, saith he, confirmed it by an oath: that by two immutable things, in which it was impossible that God should lie, we might have a strong consolation*: and does also express to whom all this comfort by the covenant was intended, namely, *to the heirs of promise.—who have fled for refuge to lay hold upon the hope set before us.*[1454] That is, to true converts, and believers, who have fled by faith to lay hold of the promised inheritance, as well as Abraham. How eminent then is the privilege of God's people converted, or in converting, beyond all carnal unconverted

---

[1450] Matthew 13:20-21, Mark 6:20, Hebrews 6:4-6
[1451] Proverbs 14:20
[1452] Matthew 11:28-30, Acts 2:36-37, etc.
[1453] Matthew 27:3-5
[1454] Hebrews 6:17-18

ones in the world, in that this covenant of faith is so singularly and peculiarly comfortable unto them! They alone shall eat this hidden manna: they alone shall drink this living water, and lick this refreshing honey out of this heavenly rock.

[3] *How and in what respects the covenant is comfortable.* This Covenant of Faith is comfortable to the faithful heirs of promise: {1} originally, {2} divinely, {3} comprehensively, {4} strongly, {5} gradually, {6} suitably, and {7} continually.

{1} *Originally comfortable.* The Covenant of Faith was the first dawning of comfort and original discovery thereof to lapsed man after the fall. After Adam (and we all in him) had broken the Covenant of Works, nothing but despair, divine wrath, and death could be represented unto him until this Covenant of Faith in Christ, *the seed of the woman*, was revealed.[1455] This was the first peering of the morning and day of salvation. This was God's first overture of peace to poor sinners. This was the first opening of a door of hope to hopeless creatures. And all discoveries of comfort from God do originally flow from this primary and most ancient discovery. God's mere grace and eternal decree in Christ are the very first original of all our comfort: but God's Covenant of Faith in Christ, is the very first and original discovery of all our comfort. And that which is first in any kind, is excellent. Our comfort, if we look at the antiquity of its publication, is as ancient as paradise.

{2} *Divinely comfortable.* The Covenant of Faith – and all the comfortableness thereof – is wholly and only from God in Jesus Christ. The author of it is God himself. The federate parties are divine, namely: God and Christ with his seed. The foundation of it is divine: namely, God's mere grace.[1456] The benefits and matters promised to Christ's seed therein are divine: recovery from sin and death to righteousness and everlasting life by Christ so that the Lord may be our God and we his people. The condition required of and are stipulated by Christ's seed, divine, namely: faith, which is

---

[1455] Genesis 3:15
[1456] Romans 4;16

not of ourselves, but is the gift of God;[1457] and evangelical obedience, whereunto we are created in Christ.[1458] All these are divine, and all these are most comfortable; therefore they are divinely comfortable. Now the Covenant's comfortableness being merely divine, and not human, consequently the comforts of the Covenant are: (i) *cordial indeed*, (ii) *transcendent*, and (iii) *permanent*.

(i) *Cordial indeed*. Not formally and in show, but really and effectually comfortable. Man's comforts may sound in the ear, but never reach the heart: but God's covenant consolations reach to the very heart and soul to strengthen and revive them. Hence God's speaking comfortably, is in the Hebrew phrase styled {*speaking to the heart*}.[1459] God alone (who has all hearts in his hand, and made the heart) knows the heart's bitterness and dejections: and he alone can appropriate to the heart effectual refreshments.

(ii) *Transcendent*. Human and creature comforts may be small, but the divine covenant comforts are not small, but great and transcendent.[1460] They far surpass all created discomforts. If discomforts of God's covenant-people abound, then God's covenant-consolations in Christ do abound and superabound.[1461] The occasions of our discomforts are finite, the foundation of our comforts is infinite, even the *God of all consolation*,[1462] who can create and command all kinds and all degrees of consolation for his people. This is most sweet.

(iii) *Permanent and continuing*: man's comforts are ofttimes but a flash, quickly vanishing and leaving the heart sadder and more disconsolate; as a flash of lightning gone in a moment, and leaving the night darker; but God's comforts are fixed, lasting and *everlasting comforts*;[1463] they minister matter of *everlasting joy* and continual rejoicing.[1464]

[1457] Ephesians 2:8
[1458] Ephesians 2:10
[1459] Hosea 2:14
[1460] Job 15:11
[1461] 2 Corinthians 1:4-5
[1462] 2 Corinthians 1:3
[1463] 2 Thessalonians 2:26
[1464] Isaiah 51:11 with 1 Thessalonians 5:16, Philippians 4:4

{3} *Comprehensively comfortable.* The Covenant of Faith does (if we consider it) comprehend all the Scripture-consolations in it, which have been propounded to mankind since Adam's fall. For, (i) *the matter of all Scripture-comforts,* is Christ with all his benefits. All Scripture consolations are centered in Christ, as the common meeting place. What is there in Scripture any way comfortable indeed, but as it tends to Christ, leads to the enjoyment of Christ in some regard or other? Now Christ and all his benefits are comprised in this covenant, and consequently, all his comforts also. (ii) *The instrumental means,* whereby all Scripture-comforts in Christ are tendered, is the *promises,* which *are all yea and amen in Christ.*[1465] Now these promises are all of them as so many branches, clauses or articles of the Covenant. Whatsoever comfort there is in the promises, it is consequently in the Covenant itself. (iii) The *instrumental mean* whereby all Scripture-comforts in Christ and the promises are actually and effectually applied, is peculiarly *faith.*[1466] Now as faith is the condition of this Covenant, whatsoever comfortableness therefore is in faith, is also comprehended in this Covenant. Hence we may say of this Covenant of Faith, that it is *God's great magazine and rich treasury of comforts; God's general receptacle and storehouse of heavenly refreshment, of spiritual support.* No kind or sort of comfort for any disconsolate condition whatsoever, but may be hence extracted.

{4} *Strongly and prevailingly comfortable.* Human comforts are but weak and feeble, discomforts oftentimes prevailing over them, and leaving the heart fainting, sinking, despairing. But God's covenant comforts are strong and prevailing comforts. Stronger than all their discomforts whatsoever, and prevailing finally over them. To this effect it is said that God confirmed his covenant, etc., to the heirs of promise by an oath. *That by two immutable things in which it was impossible for God to lie, we might have {ἰσχυραν παρακλησιν}, a strong consolation or, a potent, a mighty consolation.*[1467] It is opposed to that which is invalid, infirm. So then, God most strongly

---

[1465] 2 Corinthians 1:20, 2 Peter 1:3-4, 1 Timothy 4;8
[1466] John 1:12-13, Ephesians 3:17, Romans 5:1, etc., Galatians 2:20
[1467] Hebrews 6:17-18

confirmed his Covenant so that his federate people might have strong consolation from his Covenant.

{5} *Gradually comfortable.* The Covenant of Faith was revealed by degrees, the following administrations (as has been already shown) being still more complete and excellent than the foregoing. Proportionably the covenant (though comfortable in every administration, yet) is still more and more comfortable in the succeeding then in the foregoing dispensations: and in the last administration, namely, the New Covenant, most comfortable of all. Christ *hath kept the good wine until now*: his best consolations, until this last administration of the covenant. Christ actually exhibited, being far more comfortable, then Christ merely promised.

{6} *Suitably, sufficiently and completely comfortable.* Christ's elect seed, whether converted already, or in the way of converting to Christ, can have no cause of discomfort and trouble possibly incident unto them, against which they may not furnish themselves with pregnant, suitable, and sufficient consolations from this Covenant of Faith. For,

(i) **How comfortable is this covenant against sin, and all self-unworthiness!** Herein God covenants thus: *I will be merciful to their unrighteousnesses, and their sins and their transgressions I will not remember any more.*[1468] What an admirable cordial is this to poor bruised and heavy-laden souls, pressed down to the earth, yea even to the gates of hell, with the sense of self-sinfulness and self-vileness? These words may even lift up their spirits to heaven, in hope and consolation. For,

(a) Here's the object of discomfort fully expressed, and that in three words, and all in the plural number: *unrighteousnesses, sins, transgressions.*[1469] To intimate to us, that God has mercy and pardon enough for all his covenant-people's sins, of whichever kind: original, actual; against piety, equity, or sobriety, etc; of whatever degrees or aggravations, whether against mercies, judgements, means of grace, etc; and by what names or titles soever

---

[1468] Hebrews 8:12, Jeremiah 31:34
[1469] αδικιαις, αμαρτιων, ανομιων [See Hebrews 8:12]

they be styled and known. Why else does the Lord here use such a heap of words?

(b) Here's God's act of grace for his people's consolation, against the former discomfort, most satisfactorily promised in two phrases: (1) *He will be merciful to their unrighteousnesses.* God's mercy is infinite and their unrighteousnesses are *finite*, therefore his mercies shall utterly swallow up all their sinful miseries. (2) *He will not remember their sins and transgressions anymore.* He will not only forgive, but *forget*. He will cross his debt-book so that they shall never be questioned or called to account for them. He will pass an eternal *act of oblivion* upon them. Their sins shall be utterly buried in oblivion, as if they had never been. Oh sweet refreshment! Then, their sins may be in them but shall not be imputed to them. Their transgressions may burden them but shall not sink them, may press them but shall not oppress them, may exercise them but shall not execute them, and may grieve and afflict them a while but shall not condemn them or separate them at all from God in this or the world to come.

(ii) **How comfortable is this covenant against all spiritual enemies, the flesh, the world and the devil, and their temptations!** These may oppose, tempt, and trouble God's people, yet shall not prevail over God's people, but rather God's people over them, according to the intimation of this covenant.

(a) Over the flesh and sin: partly, in that *God will be merciful to their unrighteousnesses, and their sins and transgressions he will not remember any more*[1470]. Partly in that God *will write his law in their minds, and put his fear in their hearts, that they shall not depart away from him.*[1471] If God then will not remember their sins anymore, here's their justification from sin, so that they shall not be condemned for it. If God will plant his laws and fear in them that they shall not depart from him: here's their sanctification against sin, so that sin shall never separate them from God. In both here's their victory over sin.

[1470] Hebrews 8:12, Jeremiah 31:34
[1471] Hebrews 8:10 with Jeremiah 32:40

(b) Over the world and the things of the world: partly, in that Christ their covenant-mediator has already overcome the world for them. *In the world ye shall have tribulation; but, be of good cheer, I have overcome the world.*[1472] Partly in that our covenant faith is the victory that overcomes the world. *Whatsoever is born of God overcomes the world: and this is the victory that overcomes the world, even our faith. Who is he that overcomes the world, but he that believes that Jesus is the son of God?*[1473]

(c) Over the devil and Satan, this Covenant assures us also of victory in that it promises, (1) that *the seed of the woman* (namely, Christ and his elect) *shall bruise the head of the serpent.*[1474] And in the serpent's head chiefly is his poison, policy, and greatest mischief seated. (2) That God's covenant people shall have God's *fear put into their hearts, so as they shall not depart away from God.*[1475] Consequently, no power or devices of Satan shall ever be able to *separate them from the love of God in Jesus Christ their Lord*, in which regard they are *more than conquerors.*[1476] (3) that *God will be to them a God: and they shall be to him a people.*[1477] And if God be theirs, *if God be for them, what can prevailingly be against them?*[1478] How comfortable these things are! What though we have many enemies, in and for Christ? We have more and stronger consolations in God's Covenant through Christ.

(iii) **How comfortable is this covenant against divine wrath!** God's wrath is most terrible and intolerable to sinful dust and ashes. *In his favor is life*, consequently in his frown is death.[1479] *Who may stand before him when he is angry?*[1480] He but *looks on the earth and it trembleth*: he but *touches the hills, and they smoke.*[1481] Hereupon God's people, above all things, supplicate

---

[1472] John 16:33
[1473] 1 John 5:4-5
[1474] Genesis 3:15
[1475] Jeremiah 32:40 with Romans 8:35 to the end of the chapter
[1476] Romans 8:35, 37
[1477] Jeremiah 31:33, Hebrews 8:10
[1478] Romans 8:31
[1479] Psalm 30:5
[1480] Psalm 76:7
[1481] Psalm 104:32

for his favor: *Many say, who will shew us good? Lord lift thou up the light of thy countenance upon us:*[1482] and deprecate his wrath, *O LORD rebuke me not in thine anger, neither chasten me in thine hot displeasure.*[1483] Now this covenant does sweetly secure and comfort us against divine wrath for sin: (a) by assuring us that the matter, or procuring cause of God's wrath, namely, Our sins, shall be totally and finally removed out of his sight and memory.[1484] Consequently his wrath shall be removed with our sins. (b) By certifying us, that, though *God for our iniquities,* and failings (arising from the reliques of sin in us) *chasten us with stripes and visit us with a rod: yet his lovingkindness he will not utterly take from us, nor suffer his faithfulness to fail.*[1485] Now if God's faithfulness and loving-kindness shall not fail us; God's wrath shall not condemn us. (c) By telling us that *the LORD will be our God, and we shall be his people.*[1486] Now by this blissful covenant-relation between God and us, God's revenging wrath is removed from us forevermore.

(iv) **How comfortable is this covenant against all terrors of conscience!** When conscience is once thoroughly awakened with clear apprehensions of sin, the curse, and wrath of God for sin; oh, how furiously does it sting, gnaw, and tear the very soul in pieces! How restless, how perplexed, how despairing, how dangerous is such a man's condition! *The spirit of a man will sustain his infirmity: but a wounded spirit who can bear?*[1487] Yet in this covenant are excellent antidotes against all these troubles and terrors of conscience. For, (a) herein God promises (as has been shown) recovery from the state of sin and death, to a state of righteousness and eternal life: and this by Christ, through faith. Therefore here is justification and pardon of sin promised: free justification through faith without merit, and full justification by Jesus Christ, God as well as man. And will not this calm the most perplexed and wounded conscience? *Being justified by faith we have peace with God through Jesus*

[1482] Psalm 4:6
[1483] Psalm 6:1
[1484] Jeremiah 31:34, Hebrews 8:12
[1485] Psalm 89:30-35
[1486] Jeremiah 31:33, Hebrews 8:10
[1487] Proverbs 18:14

Christ our Lord.[1488] So that we not only joy in hope of the glory of God, but also we glory in tribulation. Therefore come unto this covenant, and therein unto Christ by faith *all ye that labor and are heavy laden, and he will give you rest. Take his yoke upon you,—and you shall find rest to your souls.*[1489] Christ that by a word made such a perfect calm in the tempestuous sea, can as easily by a word make a perfect calm in a troubled conscience. (b) Herein God covenants to be *our God, and that we shall be his people.*[1490] So that our main and principal happiness is safe and secure. Here's matter of triumph, against all terror and trouble of spirit whatsoever.

(v) **How comfortable is this Covenant against the *wages of sin, death* that *king of terrors*: and all the harbingers of death, afflictions, weaknesses, pains, diseases, etc!**[1491] For,

(a) This Covenant of Faith is a direct and plenary remedy against the breach of the Covenant of Works, and the penalty of that breach, death. According to this Covenant of Works man brought death upon himself by his own *disobedience*;[1492] according to this Covenant of Faith,

God restores lapsed man from sin to righteousness, from death to life, by the obedience of his surety and mediator Jesus Christ.

(b) This covenant leads us to Christ, and to a state of salvation in him: consequently, if once we be in Christ, *there's no condemnation to us.*[1493]

(c) This covenant, embraced by faith, makes God ours, and Jesus Christ ours. Now if God and Jesus Christ be once ours, all things are ours for our good. Poverty as well as riches; wants as well as fullness, sickness as well as health, weakness as well as strength, pains as well as ease, death as well as life. The worst of these are ours, for our benefit as well as the best of these. Death and its harbingers are in their kind through Christ advantageous, amicable and gainful to us, as well as life and its refreshments. *All are yours, whether the*

[1488] Romans 5:1
[1489] Matthew 11:28-30
[1490] Jeremiah 31:33, Hebrews 8:10
[1491] Job 18:14, Romans 6:23
[1492] Romans 5:12 to the end
[1493] Romans 8:1

world, or life, or death, or things present, or things to come: all are yours: and ye are Christ's, and Christ is God's.[1494] (1) By death's harbingers, necessities, distresses, afflictions, etc., God's people are *humbled*, that they wax not proud,[1495] *proved* and tried that they be not dross, but pure gold,[1496] *purged* and refined from their sins and iniquities,[1497] *improved* and advantaged in their graces and spiritual growth,[1498] as the body by a growing ague, or as the grass by an April shower: *experimentally acquainted* with God and his ways in Christ, more than ever,[1499] *reduced* from disobedient wanderings out of Christ's paths,[1500] *incited* to more diligent and vigilant obedience,[1501] *conformed* unto Jesus Christ their elder brother, *assured* more and more of their filial relation to God, and of God's paternal faithfulness to them,[1502] and in a word, hereby they are *wrought, fitted,* and *prepared* for eternal glory.[1503] Our souls are apt to canker and grow rusty by sin; afflictions are God's sharp files that rub off our rust. The strings of a musical instrument when struck make the sweetest melody; so the strokes of afflictions make our souls spiritually melodious. John Bradford in prison said, "God does thus punish me: nay rather in punishing blesses me. And indeed I thank him more of this prison, than of any pasture, yea than of any pleasure that ever I had, for in it I find my most sweet good God always."[1504] Ignatius professed when he began to be a sufferer, he began to be a disciple of Christ indeed.[1505] (2) By death itself, God's people are so delivered from all their sins, sorrows, miseries and enemies,[1506] as Israel once by the Red Sea from the Egyptians, or as Jonah once

---

[1494] 1 Corinthians 3:21-23
[1495] Deuteronomy 8:15-16
[1496] Deuteronomy 8:15-16, James 1:2-3
[1497] Isaiah 27:9
[1498] Romans 5:3-5; James 1:3
[1499] Romans 5:4
[1500] Psalm 119:67
[1501] Psalm 119:67, 71
[1502] Hebrews 12:5-10
[1503] 2 Corinthians 4:17
[1504] John Bradford, Epistle ad matrem
[1505] Ignatius, letters to the Romans
[1506] Romans 6:7, Revelation 14:13

from the sea, waves and storms, by being swallowed up in the fish's belly. They are *laid to sleep* in the bed of the grave perfumed by Christ's own body,[1507] and are let out of an earthly tabernacle into the house not made with hands eternal in the heavens.[1508] It would be ill with Christians if they might not die and so go home to their heavenly Father. Oh blessed Covenant that can thus turn potions into medicines, and worst of evils for sin unto good for the sinner!

(vi) **How comfortable is this Covenant in respect of all our graces!**

(a) *Are we troubled about the truth of grace?* By this Covenant we may resolve ourselves. Covenant grace is true grace. Now covenant grace: (1) *illuminates* the darkest mind in the weakest Christian so as savingly to know the Lord, and principles of godliness. *And they shall no more teach every man his neighbor, and every man his brother, saying, "Know the LORD", for they shall all know me, from the greatest of them unto the least of them, saith the LORD.*[1509] (2) *Mollifies* the hardest heart so as to transform and turn *a heart of stone into a heart of flesh.*[1510] (3) *Renews* the very frame of heart and spirit, that they become new creatures. *A new heart also will I give you, and a new spirit will I put within you.*[1511] (4) *Conforms* the mind and heart sweetly to the laws of God. *I will put my laws into their mind, and write them in their hearts.*[1512] So, there shall be a law within them, answerable and conformed to the law without them. (5) *Purifies* and cleanses them both from guilt and filth of their iniquities.[1513] (6) *Prevails* victoriously over the old serpent and all his subtilties: bruising his head.[1514] (7) (i) Finally, covenant grace makes us effectually and wholly the people of God. *And I will be their God, and they shall be my people.*[1515] If we be furnished with such grace as this: then we may be of good comfort, for we have true covenant grace.

[1507] Isaiah 57:2, 1 Thessalonians 4:13
[1508] Luke 2:29, 2 Corinthians 5:1
[1509] Jeremiah 31:34
[1510] Ezekiel 36:26
[1511] Ezekiel 36:26
[1512] Hebrews 8:10
[1513] Hebrews 8:12, Ezekiel 36:25-27, 29
[1514] Genesis 3:15
[1515] Jeremiah 31:33

(ii) *Are we obstructed in the actings of grace, that they are low, dull, feeble, etc., in their operations: and this discourages us?* Behold this Covenant comforts against all such obstructions and discouragements. Partly promising that *God will put his Spirit within us, and cause us to walk in his statutes, and keep his judgements and do them.*[1516] This is very comfortable. Partly alluring our graces – especially our faith, hope, and love – to act towards God and Jesus Christ with all vivacity and alacrity, who offer themselves in this Covenant of Faith, to do so much for us and to be wholly ours forevermore. What greater and quickening motives could be laid before us?

(iii) *Are we perplexed at defects and weaknesses of grace?* Herein this covenant relieves and comforts us. For, according to this covenant, (1) we have *God's Spirit put within us.*[1517] This is clearly covenanted. Now God's Spirit, being the Spirit of grace, supplies them, in whom he is, with all kinds and degrees of grace necessary unto salvation, and helps their infirmities (Romans 8:26). (2) Be our graces never so weak and feeble, yet they are sufficient to make us God's people, both for present, and forever.[1518] Though weak, yet are they so strong as to bring us at last unto glory.

(iv) Finally, *are we afraid of decays of grace, that our graces will at last wither, and we fall away?* Have we such a covenant as this: and shall we be afraid of apostasy? Consider, (a) this Covenant is *an everlasting covenant.*[1519] Therefore the grace of this covenant must needs be everlasting grace. (b) This Covenant is most sure and faithful: nothing shall overthrow it. Therefore grace begun in us according to this Covenant, cannot fail. (c) God in this covenant expressly promises; *I will not turn away from them, to do them good: but I will put my fear in their hearts, that they shall not depart from me.*[1520] God will not turn from them: they shall not depart from God. Oh how sweet and cordial are these comforts!

[1516] Ezekiel 36:27
[1517] Ezekiel 36:27 with Zechariah 12:10, Galatians 5:22-23
[1518] Jeremiah 31:33 & Hebrews 8:10
[1519] 2 Samuel 23:5, Jeremiah 32:40, Hebrews 13:20
[1520] Jeremiah 32:40

(vii) **How comfortable is this covenant in regard to prayer and all Christian duties!** For,

(a) *This covenant notably encourages unto prayer, and to all duties of Christian obedience, by the many promises of divine audience and acceptance, comprised in the Covenant.*[1521] Hereupon God's people in former ages have so encouraged themselves to prayer, and in prayer by God's Covenant and promises. As the church, in great affliction,[1522] Jacob in great fear of Esau,[1523] David upon God's renewing covenant with him.[1524] King Jehoshaphat, in extreme danger of his enemies,[1525] the Levites, in their solemn day of humiliation for the sins of the people, etc.[1526] In like sort all God's people in all succeeding ages may encourage themselves both unto prayer and in praying, by the Covenant and the promises thereof. As Aaron and Hur held up the hands of Moses praying, so the covenant and promises hold up the hands of faith and fervency in Christians praying. And in like sort God's Covenant and promises encourage unto all Christian duties. Hence God's Covenant and promises, and the performance thereof to Israel most punctually, are remembered and storied, that (from consideration thereof) God's people might *observe his statutes, and keep his laws.*[1527]

(b) This Covenant singularly supports and comforts God's people against all their failings and infirmities discovered in prayer or in any other Christian observance, and this in several ways, as:

(1) Partly, by declaring upon what terms and considerations we are now to perform all Christian duties, *prayer*, etc., not as matters antecedent to our justification and acceptance with God (as once personal obedience was required under the Covenant of Works), but as *matters subsequent to*, and following upon our justification and acceptance with God in Christ. Not as

---

[1521] Zechariah 12:10, Jeremiah 29:12, Psalm 50:15, Matthew 7:7, 11 with Luke 11:13, Matthew 21:22, John 14:23 & 14:13, James 5:15, Romans 10:13
[1522] Psalm 74:19-20
[1523] Genesis 32:9, 12
[1524] 2 Samuel 7:25 to the end of the chapter
[1525] 2 Chronicles 20:7-9, etc.
[1526] Nehemiah 9:7-8, etc.
[1527] Psalm 105:7-9, etc., 42, 45

causes of justification, but as *fruits and effects* of justifying faith, as James implies.[1528] Not as matters of righteousness before God, but as matters of true thankfulness unto God for his righteousness bestowed upon us. As Luther said excellently: "The weak are to be instructed how good works do not justify: how they ought to be done, how not to be done. They ought to be done, not as the cause, but as the fruits of righteousness. And, when we are made righteous, we ought to do them, but not contrariwise, to the end that when we are unrighteous, we may be made righteous. The tree makes the apple, but not the apple the tree."[1529] Thus this Covenant, though it requires faith as the instrumental cause of our justification before God, yet it requires worthy walking in all Christian duties as fruits and effects of a justified state, and as testifications of love and gratitude to God for the same. Now this is comfortable, that our Christian duties are not the cause or matter of our righteousness before God; for then our failings therein would condemn us: but are fruits of a justified state. Therefore God accepting the integrity of them covers their infirmities.

(2) Partly by discovering to them, that seeing God when he brings them first into covenant with himself is *merciful to their unrighteousness, and will remember their sins and transgressions no more*,[1530] which they committed in their carnal state: much more he will be merciful to all the infirmities, failings and weaknesses of their Christian duties, and to all the relics of sin in them, and *will remember them no more*, whereof they become guilty in their covenant-state. If God should remit the ten thousand talents, will he not much more forgive the hundred pence? How comfortable are these considerations! God's people according to this Covenant are not justified for their Christian duties: nor shall they be condemned for their failings and infirmities in their Christian duties. But their infirmities being covered, their evangelical integrity in all their duties and services shall be accepted.

[1528] James 2:14 to the end of the chapter
[1529] Martin Luther on Galatians 2:20
[1530] Jeremiah 31:34, Hebrews 8:12

(viii) **Finally, how comfortable is this covenant against all difficulties or impediments that may arise, and all objections that may possibly be made, contrary to the salvation or happiness of all God's covenant people!** This Covenant removes all impediments, facilitates all difficulties, and answers all objections that may stand in the way or discourage them.

(a) Is it guilt of sin? *God will be merciful to their unrighteousness, and will never remember their sins or transgressions any more.*[1531]

(b) Is it inherent filth and power of sin? *God will sprinkle clean water upon them, and they shall be clean: from all their filthiness, and from all their idols will be cleansed of them. A new heart also will he give them, and a new spirit will he put within them.*[1532]

(c) Is it hardness and impenitence of heart? *God will take away the stony heart out of their flesh, and will give them a heart of flesh. They shall they remember their own evil ways, and their doings that were not good; and shall loathe themselves in their own fight, for their iniquities, and for their abominations.*[1533]

(d) Is it divine wrath, and the extreme distance between God and them? God's wrath is passed away from them, Christ according to this Covenant having fully satisfied divine justice in their behalf: and they are by covenant become *a people near unto God*;[1534] he being *their God, and they his people.*[1535]

(e) Is it the curse and condemnation of the law? *Christ hath redeemed* them (according to this covenant) *from the curse of the law, being made a curse for them.*[1536] So that *now there is no condemnation to them that are in Christ Jesus.*[1537]

(f) Is it infirmity or weakness of graces or duties? Be their graces never so infirm, yet shall they persevere to the end: God having covenanted *to give one*

[1531] Jeremiah 31:34, Hebrews 8:12
[1532] Ezekiel 36:25-26
[1533] Ezekiel 36:26, 31
[1534] Psalm 148:14
[1535] Jeremiah 31:33, Hebrews 8:10
[1536] Galatians 3:13-14
[1537] Romans 8:1

heart and one way, that they may fear him forever (Hebrew: *all days*), and *to put his fear in their hearts, that they shall not depart from him.*[1538] Their weakest graces then, shall be so strong as to last forever, as to keep them close to God forever. And consequently they shall be stronger than all their sins and spiritual enemies. As for infirmities in their duties, God has promised to relieve them by his Spirit: *I will put my spirit within you, and cause you to walk in my statutes, and ye shall keep my judgements and do them.*[1539] And according to this Covenant of Faith, as their *perfections* in duties cannot justify them: so their *imperfections* in duties shall not condemn them. For, *God will be merciful to their unrighteousnesses.*[1540] In a word, God undertakes for both sides: for them and for himself. He will be their God, and they shall be his people.

(g) Finally, is it death, the devil, or anything that can hinder the happiness of God's covenant people? Nothing at all shall do it. Neither death, for this Covenant removes them from death to life. Nor devil; for, this Covenant assures *the old serpent's head shall be bruised by the seed of the woman.*[1541] Nor anything, for: *If God be thus for them; who, or what shall prevailingly be against them?—who shall lay anything to the charge of God's elect? It is God that justifieth: who is he that condemneth?*[1542] Come hither ye children of God's Covenant, and heirs of promise, and comfort one another with these words.

[1538] Jeremiah 32:39-40
[1539] Ezekiel 36:26
[1540] Hebrews 8:12
[1541] Genesis 3:15
[1542] Romans 8:31, 33-34

(6) The Covenant of Faith is Everlasting

God's Covenant of Faith is not only long-lasting, but everlasting. This the last property of this Covenant, which I shall here open, and that briefly, showing: [1] that this Covenant is everlasting, and [2] how, and in what sense, it is everlasting.

[1] *That this covenant is everlasting*, is clear:

{1} From God's denomination, who has often styled it *{an everlasting covenant}*. In the Old Testament he frequently calls it, in Hebrew בְּרִית עוֹלָם *berith olam*: *{a covenant of eternity}*.[1543] In the New Testament he calls it in Greek διαθηκης αιωνιου, *diatheke aionios*: *{the eternal covenant}* or *{the everlasting covenant}*.[1544]

{2} *From the confession of such as be in covenant with God*, acknowledging God's Covenant to be everlasting, as the covenant with Israel touching *Canaan* was an *everlasting covenant*.[1545] And David said of this Covenant renewed with him: *Although mine house be not so with God, yet he hath made with me an everlasting covenant.*[1546]

{3} *From the nature of the Covenant itself*, as formerly opened and confirmed, it is clear the Covenant of Faith must needs be everlasting, whether we take notice of the *order, sureness, matter*, or *mediator* of it.

(i) *The order of it*, is last, the Covenant of Works in innocency was first. That being wholly overthrown by the fall, the Covenant of Faith succeeds and comes in place thereof as a remedy, offering Jesus Christ as a public surety for all God's elect, passively to satisfy divine justice offended to the full by his suffering the curse and penalty of the broken covenant for them, and actively to fulfill all righteousness in his own person completely which the Covenant of

---

[1543] Genesis 17:19, Isaiah 24:5 & 55:3 & 61:8, Jeremiah 32:40, Ezekiel 16:60 & 37:26
[1544] Hebrews 13:20
[1545] 1 Chronicles 16:17-18 & Psalm 105:10-11
[1546] 2 Samuel 23:5

Works required. The Covenant of Faith – and therein Christ – being despised, no other covenant takes place, by way of remedy, but certain perdition follows. This Covenant therefore is everlasting.

(ii) *The sureness of this Covenant* is such that (as has been abundantly cleared), nothing can possibly overthrow it. Now that must needs be *everlasting*, which nothing can overthrow. The Covenant of Works was not everlasting because it was not sure: it was quickly overthrown by Adam's disobedience.

(iii) *The matter of this covenant is everlasting*, namely: righteousness and everlasting life on God's part, and an everlasting covenant relation established between God and his covenant people. *I will not remember their sins and transgressions any more.—I will be to them a God, and they shall be to me a people.*[1547] How long? Forever. No time is limited. Now, the matter covenanted being everlasting, the covenant is so also.

(iv) Finally, the mediator of the Covenant is everlasting, namely: *Jesus Christ yesterday, and today, and forever the same.*[1548] His person is eternal,[1549] his office everlasting;[1550] consequently the covenant – whereof he is mediator – is everlasting.

[2] *How, and in what sense this Covenant is everlasting*: for clearing of this, consider, a thing is said to be eternal or everlasting three ways. namely,

{1} Most properly, perfectly, and absolutely anything is everlasting which never had beginning, never succession of former or latter, or any change, and never shall have end. This (as the Schoolmen phrase it) is: *aeternum & a parte ante, & a parte post: in quo nec est prius, nec posterius*, etc. namely: eternal both in respect of the part before and the part after, wherein is neither former nor latter but all at once. This in the Hebrew phrase is styled, לְעוֹלָם וָעֶד *leolam vaed*;[1551] *ever and yet,* from לְעוֹלָם *leolam, latuit*; which signifies *to lie hid*;

[1547] Hebrews 8:10, 12
[1548] Hebrews 13:8
[1549] John 1:1-2, Isaiah 6:9, Hebrews 1:8, 10-12
[1550] Hebrews 1:8, Isaiah 9:7, Hebrews
[1551] Psalm 9:5-6

because the beginning and end of that which is eternal is hid, past finding out: and in that which is properly eternal, we can never come to a period. There is still עַד; *ed*, a yet: something further and further then we can comprehend. In Greek it is called {*always existing*}, for that which is properly eternal is always existing; still the same. In this sense God and he alone is eternal or everlasting, being absolutely incapable of beginning, succession or end.[1552]

{2} *Improperly*, a thing is styled everlasting or eternal which (though it had a beginning, yet) never shall have end. In this sense, hell's torment is called everlasting punishment and heaven's happiness is called life eternal, for these shall once begin but never end.[1553]

{3} *Most improperly*, a thing is sometimes counted everlasting or eternal which is only diuturnal or long-lasting, which both had a beginning and shall have an end. Thus God covenanted to give Phinehas and his seed, *an everlasting priesthood*,[1554] and yet his priesthood had its beginning and end, as all other ceremonies and types. Thus God promised Canaan, etc. for an *everlasting possession to Jacob's seed*,[1555] and yet as they began, so they ceased to possess that land.

God's Covenant also may be considered: {1} according to the substance of it, as tendering unto sinners righteousness and eternal life by Jesus Christ through faith, the Lord becoming their God and they his people. {2} According to the circumstances of it, or its manner of administration, whith was in one sort before Moses, in another sort under and after Moses until Christ, and in another sort after Christ, as has been abundantly declared.

Now these things premised, it is easy to resolve how *the Covenant of Faith is everlasting*. {1} It is not everlasting either for circumstance, or substance, absolutely, perfectly and most properly. For that is God's sole prerogative. {2} It is everlasting according to the substance of it, improperly. That is, though it had a beginning presently after Adam's fall, yet it shall never have an end: but

---

[1552] Genesis 21:33, Isaiah 5:7, 15, Psalm 90:2 & 102:24-28
[1553] Matthew 25:46 with Daniel 12:2, Luke 16:9
[1554] Numbers 25:12-13
[1555] Genesis 48:4

God's covenant-people shall be his people and he their God both in this and the world to come. {3} It is everlasting according to the circumstance or manner of administration, most improperly, having both beginning and end. That is, being longlasting. So the Mosaical administration continued until Christ. The evangelical administration shall continue from Christ until the end of the world. Then all administrations shall cease, and be swallowed up in immediate vision and full fruition of God in Christ blessed forevermore.

Thus *the Covenant of Faith is everlasting*, that is, *without end*, for the substance of it. Consequently: {1} It is most firm, faithful and sure. That is sure, which is everlasting. {2} All the federates or covenant-people of God shall persevere to the end, and never apostatize. They may fall, yet not totally, nor finally fall away: *nothing shall separate them from God's love in Christ*, whilst the everlasting covenant keeps them still in God's everlasting arms.[1556] {3} This Covenant of Faith is God's last covenant, after which no succeeding covenant is to be expected. What can succeed that has no end? The *Covenant of Faith* succeeded the first covenant, the *Covenant of Works*: and tendered a remedy against that covenant-breach. But if this remedy, this Covenant of Faith, be not accepted but despised, where shall such despises appear?

Hitherto of the properties of this Covenant of Faith.

[1556] Romans 8:35

Corollary 8

Hence finally, the concord and discord, the agreement and difference, between the Covenant of Works, and the Covenant of Faith, is notably conspicuous from the nature of the Covenant of Faith thus unfolded in the general.

If the natures of the Covenant of Works, and of the Covenant of Faith, formerly described, be duly weighed, it will evidently appear, that in some few things they agree, but in many things they disagree.

As a ground for opening of this agreement and difference between these two covenants, those words of the apostle are considerable. *Where is boasting then? It is excluded. By what law? Of works? Nay: but by the law of faith.*[1557] In this accurate epistle, the apostle, treating of our justification before God, having shown at large that neither Jew nor Gentile can be justified by the works of the law (Romans 1:17-3:21). He proves that both Jew and Gentile are justified of mere grace by faith alone in Jesus Christ.

(1) Because God has without the law revealed another way of justifying sinners, namely: by remitting their sins freely through faith in Christ's blood (Romans 3:21-27).

(2) Because justification by faith excludes all boasting from anything at all in the sinner (Romans 3:27). Therefore (God intending to take all the glory of sinners' justification to himself alone) all both Jews and Gentiles must be justified by faith only. God being one, and his way of justifying one also (Romans 3:28-30). And yet this does not make void, but establishes the law in Christ (Romans 3:31).

(3) Because Abraham, the father of the faithful was justified by faith only without the works of the law, and that in his uncircumcised state: consequently so must all his spiritual seed be justified (chapter 4 throughout). Thus stands the context. Romans 3:27 then shows: [1] that's God's way of

---

[1557] Romans 3:27

justifying sinners, which excludes all boasting from sinners. And, [2] not *the law of works*, but *the law of faith* excludes such boasting. By {*law of works*}, understand *the doctrine of works*, namely: that doctrine which prescribes and requires works as the condition and matter of our justification. This is only *the Covenant of Works*. It is said {*works*} not {*work*} because it is not one, but all the works of the law for kind and degree perfectly and perpetually done in man's own person, that will justify according to the Covenant of Works. By {*law of faith*} understand *the doctrine of faith*, namely: that doctrine which prescribes faith only as the instrument and condition of justifying. This is only *the Covenant of Faith*, the gospel between these two laws, these two covenants, this text expresses a *concord* and a *discord*. A concord, in that they are each of them styled a law; a discord, in that the one requires works, the other faith, as the condition: and in that boasting, is excluded by the one but not by the other. Whence it is clear that, *as there is some agreement, so there is some disagreement between the Covenant of Faith and the Covenant of Works*. Note: (1) wherein they agree, (2) wherein they disagree, and (3) results from both.

(1) **The agreement between the Covenant of Works and Covenant of Faith consists chiefly in certain generalities. Namely: they agree in the general notion and consideration.**

[1] *Of their efficient cause*, or *author*. One and the self-same absolute, infinite and eternal God being the prime cause and author both of the Covenant of Works, and of the Covenant of Faith.[1558] For none but God can create and institute a covenant between God and man; which shall be acceptable to God, and advantageous to man.

[2] *Of their impulsive, or inward moving cause; namely, divine grace*. Of mere grace God pleased to admit Adam into covenant with himself in innocency:[1559] for the most perfect creature having nothing but what he received from the creator, can demerit nothing from the creator. And of mere

---

[1558] Genesis 2:16-17 with Genesis 3:15 & 6:18 & 17:2, etc., Exodus 24:8, 1 Samuel 23:5, Jeremiah 32:38-40, etc, Hebrews 8:8, etc.
[1559] Genesis 2:16-17, 1 Corinthians 4:7

grace God admitted man into covenant with himself after the fall: lapsed man being much more unable then man innocent to challenge anything from God by way of merit.[1560]

[3] *Of the federates, or parties covenanting.* To both these covenants, *God and man* are parties.[1561] Not God and angels; not God and inferior creatures. God then is a party on the one hand, and man on the other. Yea man as in an Adam, as in a public person, is a party to the Covenant of Faith, as well as to the Covenant of Works.[1562] As these are two covenants, so there are two Adams and their respective seeds, with these two Adams and their seeds, God contracts in these two covenants respectively: as has been formerly cleared at large.[1563]

[4] *Of the matters covenanted and restipulated.* In both these covenants God propounds a law, and promises life to man upon some condition.[1564] And man restipulates in some sense faith and obedience to God. There is a *faith* required in the Covenant of Works, as well as in the Covenant of Faith, and an *obedience* required and restipulated in the Covenant of Faith, as well as in the Covenant of Works (though of a different nature), as after will appear.

[5] *Of the form of the Covenants.* The general form of both these Covenants is a mutual agreement and reciprocal stipulation between the federates God and man.[1565]

[6] *Of the inward foundation or principle of performance on both God's part, and man's.* On God's part, the inward principle (if we may so speak) inclining him to perform whatsoever he promised in both these Covenants, is his *truth and fidelity.*[1566] *On man's part*, the inward ground and principle disposing and enabling him to keep and perform what he restipulates to God in both these Covenants, is God's writing his law and Covenant *in his mind,*

[1560] Ezekiel 16:1-9 & 36:22, 32
[1561] Genesis 2:16-17 & 17:2
[1562] Compare Genesis 2:16-17 & Romans 5:12, 14, with Genesis 3:15, Romans 5:14 to the end, Galatians 3:16-17
[1563] See in Book 2 Chapter 2 Aphorism 2 Section 3
[1564] Genesis 2:16-17 & 3:15, Deuteronomy 5:2, etc.
[1565] See before in Chapter 2 Aphorism 2 Section 4
[1566] Titus 1:2, Hebrews 10:23 & 11:11, Deuteronomy 7:9

and putting his Spirit and fear into his inward parts. In Adam's heart, the law or Covenant of Works was written *naturally,* and enabled him to observe it.[1567] In every godly man's heart, the law or Covenant of Faith is written in his mind, and God's Spirit and fear put into his heart *supernaturally,* and enables them to keep it.[1568] When this inscription fails or is obliterated, proportionally the federal performance fails and is obstructed.

[7] Finally, *the Covenant of Works and faith do agree in their general scope and end,* namely, God's manifestation of his excellent glory to and in his creature, and man's participation of true and eternal happiness from and in his creator God blessed forevermore. Amen.

Thus these two covenants do well agree in these general respects and considerations. But all this agreement is very imperfect, remote, and at a great distance, being only generic. The difference between them on the other hand is more perfect, immediate, and near at hand, being specific.

(2) **The disagreement, or difference between the Covenant of Works, and the Covenant of Faith, is manifold and very great.** And it consists not in general, but in precise special respects and considerations, as:

[1] ***They differ in the special consideration of their efficient cause, or author.*** One and the same faithful and ever-living God was the author of them both: but in different respects.[1569] He was author of the *Covenant of Works,* as a loving well-pleased and bountiful creator, dealing with his upright, perfect and spotless creature, but he was author of the *Covenant of Faith,* as a most gracious and merciful redeemer in Christ, dealing with his elect lapsed into sin and misery through *Adam's* disobedience. So that God founded the Covenant of Works upon the integrity of man's *creation*; but he grounded the Covenant of Faith upon the perfection of man's *redemption.* Hence, the Covenant of Works is styled by some, *a covenant of amity,* or *friendship*: because when it was made there was perfect amity between God and man.

[1567] Genesis 2:16-17 with Romans 2:14-16
[1568] Jeremiah 31:33 & 32:40, Ezekiel 36:26-27
[1569] Genesis 2:16-17 with Genesis 3:15 & 6:18 & 17:2, etc.

Contrariwise the *Covenant of Faith* is called a {*covenant of reconciliation*}, because when it was first made there was between God and man extreme enmity, needing reconciliation.

[2] ***They differ in the special notion of their impulsive, or inward moving cause.*** God's mere grace was the sole inward cause inclining him to make both these covenants: but differently. *God's grace*, as it is *grace of benevolence*, or *of goodwill* towards his perfect and innocent creatures (yet deserving no good thing at all from their creator, no more then the most curiously fashioned pot can deserve ought from the potter), I say, this grace of goodwill moved God to make his Covenant of Works. But God's grace, as it is grace of commiseration and of bowels of mercy, towards his sinful and miserable creatures, deserving only all evil from their creator, moved him to make the Covenant of Faith, as has formerly been explained more at large.[1570] So that, though in some sense the Covenant of Works was of grace: yet the Covenant of Faith is of grace much more peculiarly and eminently. Hence by way of singular eminency it is called {*the Covenant of Grace*}.

[3] ***They differ in the special consideration of the federates*, or *parties covenanting*.** True, God and man (yea man as in an Adam, as in a public or universal person) are parties to both these Covenants, yet in far different sort. God as a well-pleased, benevolent, and bountiful creator: man as a pure and upright creature in the first Adam, were parties to the Covenant of Works.[1571] On the other hand, God as a gracious, merciful, and compassionate redeemer in Christ: man as a polluted, wretched, undone sinner, yet elected and respected in Christ Jesus the last Adam, are federates or parties to the Covenant of Faith.[1572]

[4] ***They differ in the special notion of the matters covenanted in both these Covenants.*** For though, on God's part there be a law imposed, and a promise of everlasting life propounded and on man's part faith and

---

[1570] See Corollary 2 in this present chapter
[1571] Genesis 2:16-17, Ecclesiastes 7:29
[1572] Genesis 3:15

obedience restipulated, in both these Covenants, yet these matters are set forth herein with great difference.

{1} On God's part, his law and promise, in the Covenant of Works and of Faith differ much.

(i) His law or command imposed in them, may be thus differentiated and distinguished. (a) In that Covenant his law is a law of works, requiring works, as the condition and matter of man's justification; in this Covenant, his law is a law of faith, requiring faith in Christ, as the instrument and condition of justification.[1573] (b) In the Covenant of Works God's law and command is immediately laid upon man's own person only, in its utmost extent, exaction, rigor and curse.[1574] But in the Covenant of Faith, God's law and command is immediately laid upon Christ's person only in its utmost extent, rigor, and curse;[1575] and in Christ upon his covenant-seed with merciful lenity and moderation, God accepting their upright respect to all his commands and covering their infirmities.[1576] This makes Christ's yoke an easy yoke, and his burden a light burden. (c) The law imposed in the Covenant of Works, was only natural: but the law of the Covenant of Faith is also supernatural.

(ii) God's promise in these two Covenants is exceedingly different also. For, (a) the Covenant of Works promises life, yea a blessed and everlasting life, yet only an animate life or natural life on earth in paradise, so far as we can gather from Scripture;[1577] but the Covenant of Faith promises not only a happy everlasting life, but a supernatural and divine life, even a noble translation from sin and death to righteousness and eternal life, inchoate on earth by grace, consummate in heaven by glory.[1578] (b) That Covenant promised everlasting life on earth, as a reward of justice; this Covenant promises eternal life in heaven, as the reward of the riches of mercy and free-grace. *To him that worketh, is the reward not reckoned of grace but of debt:*

[1573] Genesis 2:16-17 with Romans 3:27, Galatians 3:11-12
[1574] Genesis 2:16-17, Galatians 3:10
[1575] Galatians 4:4-5 & 3:13, Romans 8:3
[1576] Romans 8:3-4, 26, Psalm 119:6, 1 Kings 15:5, Matthew 11:30
[1577] Genesis 2:16-17, Galatians 3:12
[1578] Romans 1:17, Galatians 3:11, John 6:35, 53-54 & 11:25

but to him that works not, but believeth on him that justifies the ungodly, is the reward not reckoned of debt but of grace.[1579] (c) That Covenant promises life everlasting to perpetual and perfect personal obedience, but in case of failing though but in the least degree, leaves no place for repentance or remission of sin.[1580] But this Covenant promises eternal life to him that believes;[1581] and withall free remission of sin to him that repents,[1582] yea repentance also to him that sins.[1583] (d) Finally, that Covenant of Works promised life upon condition of perfect personal obedience, but promised not a permanent ability for such obedience;[1584] but this Covenant of Faith not only promises everlasting life unto believing, but also persevering principles of grace enabling them so to believe unto the end.[1585]

{2} *On man's part, faith* and *obedience* restipulated in these two covenants have their respective differences also.

(i) Faith restipulated in the Covenant of Works, though it agree with faith restipulated in the Covenant of Faith, in that: (a) both of them are of God, (b) both of them tend to persuade man of God's love; (c) both of them beget and breed in man love to God (as that learned Cameron has well observed),[1586] yet it differs also from it, in several ways, namely: (a) *in the manner of God's requiring it.* Faith in the Covenant of Works is required, not expressly, but only implicitly and by consequence; because in innocency man had not the least cause to doubt or suspect God's love to him. But faith in the Covenant of Faith is required expressly and directly; because after the fall the conscience of the sinner terrified with the guilt of sin, death, and divine wrath, cannot possibly be raised up to true hope and comfort, but by God's free promises embraced by faith. (b) *In the foundation thereof.* Faith restipulated in the Covenant of Works, as it was bestowed of God (*per modum naturae*, as the

---

[1579] Romans 4:4-5, etc.
[1580] Genesis 2:17, Galatians 3:12
[1581] John 3:16, Mark 10:16
[1582] Hebrews 8:12 with Ezekiel 36:25, 27, 31, Isaiah 1:16-18 & 55:7
[1583] Ezekiel 36:26, 31, Zechariah 12:10, etc.
[1584] Genesis 2:16-17 with Romans 8:3, Galatians 3:21-22
[1585] Jeremiah 32:38-40
[1586] John Cameron, de triplici foedere, Thes. 12, 13, 14

schools speak) in a natural way: so it is grounded and leans upon the title of perfect nature. But the faith of this Covenant of Faith, as it is from God, (*per modum gratiae supernaturalis,*) by way of supernatural grace,[1587] so it is bottomed and leans upon Christ's supernatural righteousness and God's promise in him.[1588] (c) *In the fruit and effect thereof.* The faith of that covenant, having but a changeable principle of nature, produced in Adam only a changeable righteousness, which was finally and totally lost: but the faith of the Covenant of Faith, arising from an eternal and unchangeable principle, the Spirit of grace; breeds a righteousness like itself,[1589] eternal and unchangeable, which can never be lost finally and totally.[1590]

(ii) *Obedience* restipulated in that Covenant remarkably differs from obedience in this. For, (a) obedience in the Covenant of Works, was to be performed to God only as man's creator and preserver: but obedience in the Covenant of Faith is to be performed to God not only as man's creator and preserver; but also as man's restorer and redeemer in Jesus Christ. (b) Obedience according to that Covenant was to be perfect for kinds and degrees, perpetual for continuance without the least omission or intermission, and personal, only performed by a man's own person: that Covenant admitting no mediator, surety or substitute at all, in point of obedience or in case of failing therein.[1591] Obedience according to this Covenant, is to be accurately perfect and perpetual in Christ's person as the sinner's mediator and surety,[1592] and sincerely perfect, upright and constant in the believer's person in and through Christ.[1593] (c) This perfect, perpetual personal obedience according to that Covenant was the very condition of Adam's justification, and the very matter of his righteousness.[1594] But according to this Covenant, Christ's perfect and perpetual *obedience active and passive* in his own person, imputed by faith, is

---

[1587] Ephesians 2:8
[1588] Romans 3:24-26 & 5:18-19
[1589] Galatians 5:22, 2 Corinthians 4:13 with Zechariah 12:10-11
[1590] Daniel 9:24, Hebrews 10:12-14, 14-19
[1591] Genesis 2:16-17, Galatians 3:12
[1592] Galatians 4:4
[1593] Genesis 17:1-2
[1594] Genesis 2:16-17, Galatians 3:12

the only matter of the sinner's righteousness, whereby he is freely and fully justified before God.[1595] The justified person's obedience is not at all the cause or matter of his righteousness, or the condition of his justification before God, but rather the consequent qualification of the person justified, the fruit and effect of justification, the real testification of justified persons' thankfulness unto God, the matter of their righteousness only before men – the *way to reigning, not the cause of reigning* with Christ in heaven.[1596] (d) Finally, according to that Covenant of Works, the least failing in obedience was punishable by death without all hope of mercy on God's part, or possibility of repentance and satisfaction on man's part; but according to this covenant the justified person's upright obedience is in Christ accepted, and all the imperfections, infirmities and failings thereof covered of mere grace and mercy in Christ, through faith and repentance. Thus these two Covenants differ exceedingly in the special and peculiar consideration of the matters covenanted in them respectively, whether on God's part or on man's.

[5] *They differ in their special form or manner,* namely:

{1} In their form of manifestation. For, (i) the Covenant of Works was promised and established both at once.[1597] The Covenant of Faith was promised in the Old Testament a long time before it was established by the blood of Christ in the New Testament.[1598] And it was discovered, not wholly and entirely all at once, but gradually by steps and degrees according to the church's capacity. (ii) The Covenant of Works, the law of God, was in some sort evident to the light of nature and to natural conscience, at least in respect of the outward acts of duty required, and gross acts of sin prohibited. For, *even the Gentiles, who have not the law, do by nature the things contained in the law, being therein a law unto themselves, which shows the work of the law in some measure written in their hearts.*[1599] But the Covenant of Faith is not at all evident in the least degree to a natural conscience by any light of nature, but is

---

[1595] Romans 5:18-19 & 3:23-26
[1596] Bona opera sunt via regni, non causa regnandi
[1597] Genesis 2:16-17
[1598] Genesis 3:15 with Hebrews 9:15-17, 1 Corinthians 11:25
[1599] Romans 2:14-15

merely and wholly discovered by divine supernatural revelation. All the men on earth, all the angels in heaven, could not have devised or imagined such a way of justifying and saving of sinners by Jesus Christ. Hence though naturally we are very prone to seek for justification by works, and duties, and with much ado are beaten off from this false way, because somewhat agreeable to nature, yet we are hardly drawn to believe in Jesus Christ for justification; believing being wholly above nature, yea and against nature. Therefore the least degree of true faith is most highly to be valued and is very comfortable.

{2} *In their form, sanction, or establishment.* The Covenant of Works was established by command of duty, a threatening of death in case of disobedience, an implicit promise of life to contrary obedience, and by two sacramental trees: yet all without a mediator.[1600] Nor was there need of any mediator because Adam was perfect. But the Covenant of Faith – together with all the commands, promises, sacraments, etc., thereof – are established in and with a mediator Jesus Christ.[1601]

{3} In their form of administration. For (i) the Covenant of Works was administered by a *natural inscription* of it in the heart.[1602] The Covenant of Faith by a *supernatural inscription* of it in the mind and heart.[1603] (ii) That was administered by divine voice without Scripture;[1604] this both by divine voice and Scripture.[1605] (iii) That was administered *conditionally*, promising life upon condition of obedience, which condition being performed, Adam should have had life as a due debt in some sense, and boasting would not have been then excluded (although Adam even in innocence could not in a strict sense have merited anything from God, he having all of God's mere bounty), but this Covenant of Faith is administered more absolutely. That is, it promises not eternal life to any person for any merit, work, worth, disposition or

---

[1600] Genesis 2:16-17, 9
[1601] Genesis 3:15, Galatians 3:17, Hebrews 8:6, John 14:15, 21, 2 Corinthians 1:20, 1 Corinthians 10:1-3
[1602] Romans 2:14-15
[1603] Hebrews 8:10
[1604] Genesis 2:16-17
[1605] Genesis 3:15 & 6:18 & 17:2 with Exodus 24:7-8, Hebrews 9:19

intention under any sense or notion in him; but only to faith accepting Jesus Christ. Otherwise faith is required herein as a condition. Nor is this covenant so absolute as to exclude all repentance, new obedience, and walking worthily of God: which are herein required under other notions.

[6] *They differ in their respective properties and perfections.* For,

{1} The Covenant of Works was of grace, yet that the grace of benevolence only to an understanding creature; but the Covenant of Faith is of mere grace, and that both the grace of benevolence, and the grace of merciful commiserations; also to ill-deserving sinners.

{2} The Covenant of Works was not sure. For though God's promise in respect of himself was sure and inviolable, yet in respect of Adam and his mutable principles, (he being not confirmed in good immutably), it became mutable also, and was overthrown by his disobedience.[1606] But the Covenant of Faith is so immovably and inviolably sure that (as has been shown) nothing shall be ever able to overthrow it.

{3} The Covenant of Works was comfortable only to a pure and perfect creature, and that only whilst he continued in that purity and perfection; otherwise in case of the least failing, it speaks nothing but death without mercy.[1607] But the Covenant of Faith is most comfortable to an impure, imperfect sinner, tendering to him a most pure, perfect and all-sufficient savior, *able to save him to the uttermost*, and as willing as able.[1608] How much more is it comfortable to an imperfect saint that has already accepted Jesus Christ, and this covenanted salvation in him? So that this covenant speaks nothing but mercy, bowels of mercy, life, peace and salvation to all distressed creatures that will accept it.

{4} The Covenant of Works was no lasting covenant; it continued no longer in its privileges and advantages to man, then Adam continued in his integrity, which probably was not very many hours (as has been shown). Although it continues of force still in its curse and penalty to all Adam's carnal

---

[1606] Genesis 3:6-7
[1607] Genesis 2:16-17, Galatians 3:10
[1608] Hebrews 7:25, Matthew 11:28-29

seed that have not accepted Jesus Christ the last Adam as their savior.[1609] But the Covenant of Faith is a long-lasting, yea an everlasting covenant, as has been explained.[1610] The Covenant of Faith first made in paradise did antiquate and make old the Covenant of Works: but no other covenant shall ever succeed to antiquate or abolish the Covenant of Faith.

[7] *They differ in regard of their peculiar and respective effects.* For,

{1} The Covenant of Works afforded to man communion with God only as a loving and bountiful creator: the Covenant of Faith affords to man communion with God also as with a most faithful, merciful, compassionate redeemer in Christ.

{2} The Covenant of Works lifted innocent Adam up to the dignity of an honorable servant, of a noble creature above all sublunary creatures, so that he became little less than angels;[1611] but the Covenant of Faith surpassingly advances sinful and miserable man, naturally a child of wrath,[1612] to the high and heavenly dignity of membership in Christ, sonship to God, and heirship, yea co-heirship with Christ in respect of eternal glory.[1613] So that now man little lower than the angels according to that covenant, becomes much higher then the angels according to this covenant.

{3} The Covenant of Works excludes not all boasting, man having an inward ability in himself perfectly to perform the condition of that covenant required and restipulated on his part, which performance was the very matter of his righteousness and cause of his justification;[1614] but the Covenant of Faith totally excludes all boasting, the matter of the sinner's righteousness and justification being wholly without himself, namely: the obedience and righteousness of Christ. And the whole mystery of this covenant, being only a contrivance of mere grace.

[1609] Galatians 3:10
[1610] 2 Samuel 23:5, Hebrews 13:20
[1611] Psalm 8
[1612] Ephesians 2:3
[1613] Ephesians 5:30, 1 John 3:1-2, Galatians 4:4-6, Romans 8:16-17
[1614] Romans 3:27

{4} The Covenant of Works, though it would have made man happy in persevering, yet it enabled him not to persevere; but the Covenant of Faith both makes the federates persevere, and happy in persevering.

[8] *Finally, these two covenants differ in regard to the speciality of their end.* For, though both of them tend ultimately to advance God's excellent glory, and secondarily to promote man's happiness, yet they tend hereunto differently.

{1} The Covenant of Works tends peculiarly to display the excellent glory of God's freedom, wisdom, goodness, bountifulness and justice; but the Covenant of Faith much more eminently advances God's glory in all these perfections; and over and above, most singularly proclaims to all the world, the exceeding riches of the glory of God's free-grace, tender-mercies, and long-suffering.

{2} The Covenant of Works tends to advance God's glory, in dealing with his creatures without a mediator, so that by the Covenant of Works no glory at all was intended to God as a redeemer in Christ, or to Christ as a mediator. But the Covenant of Faith tends singularly to magnify God's glory, in dealing with his creatures by a mediator Jesus Christ; so that the glory of the Son of God, Jesus Christ, God-man, as mediator and savior of sinners, is in this covenant eminently provided for: *that all men may honor the Son as they honor the Father.*[1615]

{3} The Covenant of Works tended to promote man's happiness through perfection of nature in an everlasting life on earth. But the Covenant of Faith tends to advance man's happiness, through perfections of Christ's righteousness, grace, and glory in an everlasting life in the highest heavens.

(3) **_Results arising from this agreement and disagreement between the Covenant of Works, and the Covenant of Faith, are several, namely_:**

[1] Hence *the Covenant of Faith being once erected and set on foot by God, the Covenant of Works is abolished and abrogated as to the point of*

[1615] John 5:22-23

justification and happiness by it. Why? Because the Covenant of Faith brings in a quite opposite and contrary way of justification and happiness; not by man's own personal obedience from principles of upright nature; but by Christ's perfect, personal obedience imputed of mere grace, and apprehended by faith. Now we must be justified and saved by righteousness and obedience without us, not within us; by righteousness imputed, not inherent; by faith, not by works; of mere grace, not of debt. Consequently, the Covenant of Faith that brings in this new way of justification and happiness, does antiquate the Covenant of Works wholly as to that old way of justification and happiness by works. *Christ is the end of the law for righteousness to those who believe.*[1616]

[2] Hence *the Covenant of Faith, being truly accepted by us, the Covenant of Works is also abolished and abrogated in respect of us, as to the point of death and condemnation by it*. For, though the broken Covenant of Works pronounces nothing but death and damnation upon Adam and all his posterity whilst under the penalty and forfeiture of that Covenant, yet the Covenant of Faith in Christ, by way of antidote and remedy thereunto, pronounces life and salvation to all that will accept it and believe. The Covenant of Faith then is the poor sinner's sanctuary, and city of refuge to fly unto from the vengeance of the Covenant of Works. They then that truly believe, accept this Covenant of Faith; and accepting it, they embrace Christ, and are implanted into him; and being once *in Christ, there is no condemnation to them*;[1617] in that regard the Covenant of Works hath no more to do with them.

[3] Hence *the self-same persons cannot at one and the same time be under the Covenant of Works, and the Covenant of Faith*. Successively, and at several times, they may be, and all are under them both since the fall. Adam presently upon his disobedience was under the condemnation of the Covenant of Works, until he accepted the Covenant of Faith,[1618] and so all Adam's posterity while carnal are under the curse and condemnation of the Covenant of Works,

---

[1616] Romans 10:4
[1617] Romans 8:1
[1618] Genesis 3:6-7, etc.

til they by true faith accept Christ and the Covenant of Faith.[1619] But none can be under both these covenants at once. For none can be justified by works and faith at once; by inherent, and imputed righteousness at once: none can be happy without a mediator, and by a mediator at once, none can be righteous by nature, and grace at once, none can be under two such contrary and irreconcilable covenants at once. *If by grace, then is it no more of works: otherwise grace is no more grace. But if it be of works, then is it no more grace: otherwise work is no more work.*[1620]

[4] The Covenant of Faith does far surpass and excel the Covenant of Works. Consider well all these special differences between them, and half an eye may see which excels: {1} the Covenant of Works was from God as a liberal creator; the Covenant of Faith from God as a compassionate redeemer. {2} That was of the grace of goodwill; this of the grace of commiseration. {3} That was between God and man as in the first Adam; this between God and man as in Christ the last Adam. {4} That required perfect and perpetual personal obedience, to be performed by natural faith and abilities, promising thereupon everlasting life on earth; this requires perfect and perpetual personal obedience in Christ, as the matter of our righteousness, accepts upright obedience in his seed, to be performed by supernatural faith and abilities, promising everlasting life in heaven. {5} That was established upon the foundation of perfect nature without a mediator; this upon the foundation of most perfect grace in a mediator Jesus Christ. {6} That was mutable, and lasted but a while; this most sure and everlasting. {7} That afforded communion with God as a creator, elevated man to the dignity of an eminent servant, excluded not boasting, nor enabled unto persevering; but this affords communion with God as a savior, elevates man to the honor of sonship, heirship and co-heirship with Christ, excludes all self-boasting, and enables unto final persevering. {8} Finally, that tended to magnify God's wisdom, goodness and bounty, and to advance man's happiness on earth, but both without any honor intended to a mediator; but this tends besides these to extol God's commiserating grace, bowels of mercy

---

[1619] Galatians 3:10
[1620] Romans 11:6

and long-suffering, and to promote man's happiness forever in heaven, in both intending most singular honor to Jesus Christ the mediator. Thus though the glory of the Covenant of Works in itself was great, yet comparatively it was but small, to this glory of the Covenant of Faith which so far excels.

[5] Hence, *to be under the Covenant of Faith, is far better than to be under the Covenant of Works in any regard.* For since the fall, they that are under the Covenant of Works are under the curse and damnation of it, but they that are under and in the Covenant of Faith are in a state of bliss and salvation. Before the fall, Adam – able to keep the Covenant of Words – had a natural and earthly happiness thereby, but those that are in the Covenant of Faith have thereby a spiritual and heavenly happiness. Who would not long to be within this Covenant?

[6] Hence, finally, *though Adam and all mankind in him, under the Covenant of Works were much bound to God before the fall, yet mankind under the Covenant of Faith is much more bound to God since the fall.* For in that covenant, God condescended to a finite creature: in this covenant God descends to a wretched sinner. In that covenant, God showed much bounty to mankind, deserving no good; in this God shows much grace and mercy to mankind, deserving nothing but ill. In that God promised Adam a heaven on earth; in this God promises us a heaven in heaven. God has done more for us by far in the last Adam, then ever he did for us in the first Adam. Then he made us happy; now he makes us double happy. Then he gave us one world; now he gives us two worlds. Oh let us be doubly thankful for this Covenant of Faith: as thankful as is possible now on earth, and hereafter we shall be more thankful than now is either possible or imaginable eternally in heaven.

Hitherto the two first things propounded, for opening the nature of the **Covenant of Faith** *more generally, have been at large cleared, in two distinct aphorisms, namely:*

(1) That, the **Covenant of Works** being broken in the first Adam: the Lord pleased to reveal a **Covenant of Faith** in Jesus Christ the last Adam.

(2) What this **Covenant of Faith** is.

*Next consider we of the third and last thing propounded for clearing of the nature of the **Covenant of Faith** in general, namely:*

(3) How this **Covenant of Faith** is to be distinguished and distributed into its several branches. This shall be very briefly evidenced in this third aphorism ensuing, namely:

Aphorism 3

The Covenant of Faith may be sub-distinguished, or distributed into two branches:
1. God's Covenant of Promise with one peculiar sort of people only before Christ.
2. God's Covenant of Performance, or the New Covenant, with all sorts of people, since Christ.

This is not so much a distribution of a genus into contra-distinct species, or different kinds of covenants: as of a species, or of one kind of covenant, into its individuals, different one from another, not substantially and essentially; but only accidentally and circumstantially, as will afterwards appear. For the better opening of this distinction in this aphorism, I shall endeavor to clear these particulars, namely: (1) that this distinction is agreeable to Scripture. (2) That Jesus Christ, the chief matter of the Covenant of Faith, is the foundation and original ground of this distinction, as he comes under different considerations. (3) What the terms of the distinction – namely: {*Covenants of Promise*} and {*Covenant of Performance*} – do mean. (4) That the Covenants of Promise were before Christ, and limited peculiarly to one sort of people; but the Covenant of Performance since Christ, and extended to all sorts of people. (5) Which are the principal periods and degrees of the Covenants of Promise, and of the administrations thereof.

(1) **That this distinction is agreeable to Scripture** is not obscurely intimated in that passage of the apostle to the Ephesians, *wherefore remember, that ye being in time passed Gentiles in the flesh,—that at that time ye were without Christ, being aliens from the common-wealth of Israel, and strangers from the COVENANTS of PROMISE, having no hope, and without God in the world.*[1621] Here the apostle, that he may make the Ephesians more

---

[1621] Ephesians 2:11-13

abundantly sensible of their spiritual state in Christ, and surpassing happiness thereof, remembers them of their contrary carnal state in Gentilism or paganism, and the manifold miseries thereof. *Contraries compared together do conspicuously illustrate one another.*

Whilst they were *Gentiles in the flesh*: that is, in their paganism, which (for the generality of them) lasted until Christ's coming and death; as they were without Christ the head and *aliens from the common-wealth of Israel*, the church of Christ, so they were strangers to the Covenants of Promise, peculiarly belonging to the church, in Christ: and consequently they were hopeless, and without God in the world.

So then, *without Christ, without the church*, his mystical body; *without the church, without the covenants of promise*, the church's charter of privileges; *without covenants of promise, without hope*, which is immediately grounded upon the promises; and *without hope, without God himself*, who is the prime efficient, principal object, and ultimate end of hope. How elegantly are these things ordered by the apostle! This is the immediate intent of these words. So that this Scripture gives notable light to this distinction. For,

[1] Herein, one member of the distinction is plainly expressed, namely: Covenants of promise. Which covenant is here styled: {*Covenants of Promise*}? Not the Covenant of Works. For in what sense can it be called {*covenants*} in the plural number, seeing it was but only one single covenant, and had but only one single administration? Therefore it must needs be *the Covenant of Faith*, which the apostle here intends by *the Covenants of Promise*, which though it be but one for substance yet it had many several administrations, and hence is called {*covenants*}.

[2] Herein, under this notion of *the Covenants of Promise*, the *Covenant of Faith* is intended, only as it was dispensed in several distinct administrations before Christ's death: and not at all as it was dispensed after his death, for: {1} after Christ's death the administration of the Covenant of Faith is only one; and therefore in that respect it cannot be called covenants, as it may in respect of the many administrations before Christ. {2} To the Covenants of Promise, these Ephesians and so all the Gentiles during their Gentilism were strangers.

How long? Till Christ by his blood brought them nigh and broke down the partition-wall by his death.[1622] So then, these Covenants of Promise are the Covenant of Faith only as dispensed before Christ's death, unto which all the Gentiles were strangers, the Covenants of Promise peculiarly belonging to the commonwealth of Israel only.

[3] Herein finally, the other member of the distinction is consequently implied, namely, God's Covenant of Performance, or his New Covenant. For the apostle says not barely, they were strangers to the covenants, but exegetically and discretively he explains himself saying, *at that time ye were strangers to the covenants of promise*: implying there was now a Covenant of Performance, a new covenant in Christ performed, unto which they were not strangers as formerly they were to the Covenants of Promise. Now Covenants of Promise and of Performance are members directly opposite and contradistinct and mutually implying one another. Thus, this distinction is based upon Scripture.

(2) *That Jesus Christ, the chief matter of the Covenant of Faith, is the foundation and original ground of this distinction, as he comes under different considerations.* Jesus Christ is considered and presented to his church in the Covenant of Faith two ways, namely:

[1] As promised to come afterwards in fullness of time in human flesh, and therein to live, suffer, die, be buried, rise again, ascend into heaven, and to sit at God's right hand, and all for the accomplishment of the redemption and recovery of his elect from sin and death to righteousness and eternal life. In this sense, Christ was tendered to Adam, Noah, Abraham, Isaac, Jacob, Moses, Israel, David, and to all the holy patriarchs, prophets, and people of God under the Old Testament, before Christ's incarnation. Hence Christ is styled by Zacharias *the mercy promised to our fathers*.[1623] Or, *the mercy with our fathers*. The promise. *These all having obtained a good report through faith*

[1622] Ephesians 2:12-13
[1623] ποιησαι ελεος μετα των πατερων ημων i.e. *To perform the Mercy with our Fathers.* See Luke 1:72.

received not the promise:[1624] that is, *Christ incarnate, etc. promised*: Christ being the great promise, and the accomplishment of the promises. Now the Covenant of Faith tendering Christ as promised, is styled {*the Covenants of Promise*}. Covenants in the plural but promise in the singular number because for substance, the principal promised mercy – Christ is but one, though for circumstance and manner of administration the tender of Christ of old was various.

[2] *As performed, and in fullness of time come already in our flesh*, and therein having lived, died, been buried, risen from the dead, ascended, and being sat down on God's right hand, and having done and endured already whatsoever was requisite for his elect's recovery. In this sense and notion, Christ is tendered to his apostles, churches, and people under the New Testament, especially from his ascension until the end of the world. For upon the solemn day of Pentecost when people of all nations were met together at Jerusalem, the evangelical kingdom of Christ began and the New Covenant in him was most solemnly promulgated,[1625] as Cameron also well observes.[1626] Hence the actual performance and exhibition of Christ is called *some better thing provided for us by God*:[1627] that is, for us under the New Testament rather than for them of the Old, namely, Christ exhibited, who is the performance of the types, prophecies, and promises of Old. Of which Zechariah said: *Blessed be the Lord God of Israel; for he hath visited and redeemed his people, and hath raised up an horn of salvation for us in the house of his servant David. As he spake by the mouth of his holy prophets which have been since the world began; to PERFORM the mercy promised to our fathers, and to remember his holy covenant.*[1628] Hereupon the Covenant of Faith tendering Christ as performed and exhibited already, may be called {*the Covenant of Performance*} or {*the New Covenant*}. Thus as this sub-distinction

---

[1624] Hebrews 11:39
[1625] Acts 2
[1626] Iohan Cameron, de triplici Faedere, Thes. 39-40 in Opuscul miscellan.
[1627] Hebrews 11:40
[1628] Luke 1:68-73, etc.

of the covenant is warranted by Scripture: so it is grounded upon Christ as promised and performed, the chief matter and mystery of this Covenant.

(3) *What these terms of this distinction – namely:* {Covenants of Promise} *and* {Covenant of Performance} *– do mean, may be easily collected by what has been said.* Some render it {*strangers from the tables of promise*}.[1629] The Covenant of God being written in tables, and committed as a choice treasure to Israel's custody. But this seems too restrictive: God having made covenants with his people long before any tables thereof were made.[1630] It's better translated {*strangers from the covenants of promise*}.

[1] By {*Covenants of Promise*}, some understand "the covenants of the law and of the gospel; for these two Covenants were well known to Israel."[1631] But this is too narrow; God having made Covenants with them before the law, why should those be here excluded? Besides, it is not so exact and proper to say, *the covenants of the law* and *of the gospel.* For if by {*the covenants of the law*} it is meant the covenant at Horeb, then this, as there made, was gospel; as after in its place, may appear.[1632] Rather, by {*Covenants of Promise*}, understand God's Covenant and promise of Christ in due time to be exhibited, and of life by him to sinners through faith, which from the fall of Adam until Christ's incarnation was but one and the same for substance. Therefore it is said {*promise*} in the singular number, but was manifold and various for circumstance and manner of administration, and thereupon is called {*covenants*} in the plural number. And thus those learned authors Zanchi[1633]

[1629] Calvin on Ephesians 2:12
[1630] Genesis 6:18 & 15 & 17
[1631] Mr. Paul Bayne in his comment on Ephesians 3:12
[1632] Deuteronomy 5:2, etc.
[1633] "Conditiones, qua stipulabatur Deus, ad Summam & in substantia, eaedem fuerunt. Fides scilicet viva cum Dei Dilectione conjuncta, & Obedientia. Sed pro diversitate Temporum, in accidentibus fuerunt varitae. Quia ante Mosen paucas instituit Ceremonias; per Mosen, multas; Per Christum abrogatae istae fuerunt, & pauciores & faciliores substitutae. Atque hoc sibi voluit Apostolus, cum unam Promissionem nominavit, & plura pacta." Zanchi commentary on Ephesians 2:12.

and Beza[1634] do well interpret these words. God made a covenant with Noah, with Abraham, with Israel at Sinai, etc. Yet these were not many covenants really and substantially distinct, but rather, one and the same Covenant in Christ under many several dispensations and administrations. All the covenants and all the promises meet and con-center themselves in that one fundamental and complexive promise of Christ. Now after the fall, whatsoever covenants were made in Christ to come for future and to be exhibited afterwards – from the first Adam's sinning till the last Adam's suffering – are called the Covenants of Promise.

[2] By {*Covenant of Performance*} (which term I use *docendi* & *discendi gratia*, for the more clear expressing myself), understand that dispensation of the same Covenant of Faith in Christ actually performed and exhibited for sinners' salvation, which the Scripture styles {*a new covenant*},[1635] because this dispensation should still continue new, and never wax old or wear away until the world's end, as the former dispensations waxed old and vanished away.[1636]

(4) *The Covenants of Promise were before Christ, and limited peculiarly to one sort of people: but the Covenant of Performance, or the New Covenant, since Christ, and extended to all sorts of people.*

[1] The former, namely, *that the Covenants of Promise were before Christ, and limited peculiarly to one sort of people*, is evident:

{1} Because the Gentiles (the generality, the body of the Gentiles) until Christ's coming to break down the partition-wall, and to incorporate them into the body of his church, were without Christ, the fountain of all happiness; consequently aliens to the church, the commonwealth of Israel,

---

[1634] Et extraneos a faederibus Promissiones. Una fuit Promissio, si rem ipsam spectes: sed saepius Sancita. Ideo διαθηκων scripsit multitudinis numero. Possumus etiam Tabulas Metonymice interpretari? Nomen autem της επαγγελιας, veteres codices secuti, cum praecedentibus conjuximus, quod nonnulli ad ελπιδα, eadem tamen manente sententia, cum nihil sperandum sit nisi quod promissum est, & vicissim nulla sit extra fadus Promissio. Bez. Annotat. In Ephes. 2. 12.

[1635] Jeremiah 31:31, Hebrews 8:8

[1636] Hebrews 8:13

founded upon Christ; and strangers to the covenants of promise, the outward bond of union between Christ and his church.[1637]

{2} Because the Scriptures frequently account God's Covenants and promises to be the peculiar prerogatives and privileges of God's church and people the Jews, wherein no Gentiles (unless some few proselytes to the Jewish religion) had any share. They neither had knowledge of them; nor interest in them. *He sheweth his word unto Jacob, his statute; and judgements unto Israel* (herein his Covenants of Promise are comprehended). *He hath not dealt so with any nation: and as for his judgements they have not known them.*[1638] *What advantage then hath the Jew? Or what profit is there of circumcision? Much every way: chiefly because that unto them were committed the oracles of God.*[1639] *Who are Israelites, to whom pertains the adoption, and the glory, and the covenants, and the giving of the law, and the service of God, and the promises.*[1640]

[2] The latter, namely, *that the Covenant of Performance, or New Covenant is since Christ, and extended to all sorts of people and nations*, is no less evident. For,

{1} Jesus Christ by his death has destroyed the middle wall of partition between Jews and Gentiles, and so has made way for their union, incorporation and consolidation into one mystical body of Christ.[1641]

{2} Since Christ, this great mystery, namely: *that the Gentiles should be fellow-heirs, and of the same body, and partakers of his promise in Christ, by the gospel, is revealed* (so as it was not before) *to his holy apostles and prophets by the Spirit.*[1642] And not only so, but Christ after his resurrection gave his apostles express charge and commission to *go into all the world, to teach all*

[1637] Ephesians 2:11-12
[1638] Psalm 147:19-20
[1639] Romans 3:1-2
[1640] Romans 9:4
[1641] Ephesians 2:13 to the end of the chapter
[1642] Ephesians 3:4-6

nations, and preach the gospel to every creature, promising salvation to every one that should believe in Christ crucified.[1643]

{3} After Christ's ascension into heaven (when he had now fulfillled in his own person all things requisite for the recovery of his elect according to the Covenants of Promise), this Covenant of Performance or New Covenant was solemnly promulgated and published at Jerusalem, before people of all nations, on the day of Pentecost;[1644] as the Covenants of Promise were solemnly promulgated on Mount Sinai, before all Israel. And since that time the new covenant in Christ already crucified, risen again, ascended etc., is preached over all the world with great success to this very day.

Herein therefore is a remarkable difference between the *Covenants of Promise*, and that of *Performance*, the *New Covenant*, namely: in their extensiveness. And there are many other points of difference between them needful to be opened. But it will not be proper nor orderly here to unfold either the agreement or differences between them, until the natures of them both be particularly handled, which will be after the nature of the New Covenant shall be described.

Hence note by way of corollary:

[1] That the Covenants of Promise, and the New Covenant, are really and substantially one and the same, both tendering the same Christ, but they differ circumstantially and accidentally.

[2] The riches of God's grace and covenant mercy are much more diffusive and extensive since Christ than before Christ. And if such tenders of grace be neglected, such neglect will be much more intolerable and inexcusable.

[3] The people of God before Christ were in those times the only happy people on earth: and the Gentiles generally most miserable. Those being in covenant with God; these strangers to the Covenants of Promise, without Christ, church, hope and God in the world.[1645]

[1643] Matthew 28:19-20, Mark 16:15-16
[1644] Acts 2:1-2, etc.
[1645] Ephesians 2:12

[4] Though under the Covenants of Promise the Gentiles were only miserable, whilst the Jews were happy: yet since Christ, the Gentiles are every way equal, yea many ways superior to the Jews in happiness, being as freely and fully admitted into the New Covenant as the Jews, though before they were no covenant-people.

(5) *The principal periods, or chief gradual discoveries of the Covenants of Promise and of the administrations thereof, are represented in this ensuing scheme, namely:*

God's Covenant of Faith with Jesus Christ the last Adam, and in him with all his spiritual seed, has respect to Christ, and their recovery by him from sin and death, to righteousness and life, [1] *as promised*; [2] *as performed*.

[1] *As promised only*, and that from the sin of the first Adam, till the death of Jesus Christ the last Adam, during the time of the Old Testament. And the Covenant of Faith thus respecting Christ and the recovery of his seed, onely as promised, is styled the covenants of promise. These Covenants of Promise in regard to their more remarkable discoveries, repetitions, and administrations, may be principally reduced to these six eminent periods of time, namely, {1} from Adam until Noah, which was the most obscure and imperfect discovery of all. {2} From Noah until Abraham, which was a little more clear then the former. {3} From Abraham until Moses and the Sinai-covenant, which was much more clear, and perfect than both the former. {4} From Moses until David the king, which was a federal discovery and administration more full, perfect and clear then that from Abraham to Moses. {5} From David until about the time of the Jews' captivity in Babylon, which had much additional perfection and clearness beyond that under Moses. {6} Finally, from about the time of the Babylonian captivity until the death of Christ, which discovery and administration of the covenants of promise surpassed all the former in clearness, fullness and perfection, as has formerly

been manifested in brief, and in the opening of these particulars will appear more at large.[1646]

[2] *As performed according to covenant and promise*, and that especially from the death of Jesus Christ the last Adam until the end of the world during the whole time of the New Testament. And the Covenant of Faith thus respecting Christ and the recovery of his seed as actually exhibited, effected and accomplished, may be styled {*the Covenant of Performance*} and is the New Covenant, far surpassing the Covenants of Promise in all its periods, excellencies, and perfections.

Hitherto of God's Covenant of Faith in Christ the last Adam, in general. Next of this selfsame Covenant in particular, according to the particular discoveries, repetitions, administrations and periods thereof.

[1646] See in Book 2 Chapter 2 Aphorism 2 Section 4, The Form of Covenant of Faith

Book III

Of God's Covenant of Faith in Christ, in particular, namely: of the Covenants of Promise before Christ, in six remarkable expressions of it.

400

Chapter 1

Of the discovery and administration of the covenants of promise, in the first period of time remarkable, namely: from Adam until Noah.

Having in the former book treated of the Covenant of Faith, in general, I come now to handle the several discoveries, administrations and periods of the same Covenant of Faith, in particular. And here, according to order of nature, the **Covenants of Promise** come first to be considered: and then in the fourth book, the **Covenant of Performance**, or **New Covenant**. *Those* being before; *this* since Christ's incarnation. The Covenants of Promise consisting of many several discoveries and administrations of one and the same covenant according to several revolutions of times, that discovery and administration of the covenant which was in the first period of time, namely from Adam to Noah, shall first of all be unfolded, and the rest as they follow in order.

Moses (the man of God,[1647] the peerless prophet of the Old Testament, the first and most ancient penman of holy writ),[1648] wrote first of Christ, and of God's gracious promise and covenant in him towards sinners after Adam's fall. Hereupon he, writing the first gospel, may deservedly be styled the first evangelist: and from his writings Christ and his apostles were frequently wont to confirm their evangelical doctrine.[1649]

His first record of God's promise and covenant in Christ for recovery of sinners after the fall of Adam, is in those words which God himself immediately uttered in paradise presently upon Adam's fall, namely: *The LORD God said unto the serpent. Because thou hast done this, thou art cursed*

[1647] Psalm 90:1 - see the title
[1648] Deuteronomy 34:10-12, Numbers 12:6-8
[1649] Luke 24:7, John 5:46

above all cattle and above every beast of the field: upon thy belly shalt thou go, and dust shalt thou eat all the days of thy life. And I will put enmity between thee and the woman, and between thy seed and her seed. It shall bruise thine head, and thou shalt bruise his heel.[1650]

These words are the first and most ancient gospel recorded in the Bible, almost as old as the very foundation of the world: whence the gospel is styled *the everlasting gospel.*[1651] Here God began to lay the first foundation-stone of the Covenants of Promise, and to open his rich cabinet of grace and mercy towards sinners. Here, therefore, let us begin to inquire after his holy pleasure in that regard. And to that end consider we chiefly:

1. The occasion of those words.

2. The sense and meaning of them.

3. Such positions or aphorisms as a result of them touching this first discovery of God's Covenants of Promise, from Adam to Noah.

[1650] Genesis 3:14-15
[1651] Revelation 14:6

Section 1

The occasion of these words stands thus. In this third chapter of Genesis, Moses describes the first rise and origin of man's sin and misery. More particularly he declares:

(1) *The outward impulsive, or moving cause enticing the woman to sin*, namely: [1] the principal cause, Satan. [2] The instrumental cause employed by Satan herein, the serpent. namely. The spiritual serpent, and the sensible serpent (as Chrysostom's phrase is, Gen 3:1-6).[1652]

(2) *The actual perpetration of sin*. [1] By the woman, seduced by the serpent. [2] By Adam, deceived by the woman (Genesis 3:6).

(3) *The effects and consequences of their sin*. Namely: [1] their immediate guilt, shame, and flight from God's presence (v. 7-8). [2] God's conventing, examining and convicting them: who, partly confessed the fact, and partly excused themselves: Adam devolving the fault upon the woman, the woman upon the serpent: verses 9-24. [3] God's proceeding to sentence with the offenders (as Ambrose notes) *according to the order of their offending*.[1653] As the serpent seduced the woman first, then the woman seduced Adam: so the serpent is first doomed, then the woman, and Adam last of all. The serpent is sentenced to a four fold punishment, namely: {1} to the curse above all cattle, {2} to go upon his belly, and to continual eating of dust, {3} to enmity between him and the woman, between his seed and her seed, and {4} finally, to ruin and destruction by the woman's seed, verses 14-15. Thus is the occasion and coherence of these words with the series of the context: so that God, in pronouncing the serpent's ruin, promises man's recovery. And God promised man's recovery presently after his sinning, and before his sentencing for sin. Oh the riches of his mercy!

[1652] John Chrysostom, Homily, l.17 in Genesis 3 Tom. 2
[1653] Secundum erroris Ordinem damnationis quoque or do servatus est. Ambros. de Paradis. lib. cap. 15. To. 4.

Section 2

The sense and meaning of these words is not so obvious as the occasion. Among the learned there are many questions moved, and different opinions about their resolution. Waving curiosities, let us inquire into the sense of such particulars, as more especially tend to clear the words to us, and this first discovery of the Covenants of Promise, namely: (1) What serpent is meant here? (2) What woman is here intended? (3) What is meant by these two seeds: the serpent's seed, and the woman's seed? (4) What are the punishments that are here threatened and pronounced upon the serpent, and his seed? (5) What benefits are consequently implied or promised, for the woman and her seed?

These things being unfolded, the sense will be evident.

(1) **What serpent is meant here**? About this there are three opinions: two extreme, and one middle between both.

[1] Some understand here only the *sensible* and *corporal* serpent: the tenor of the words seeming to carry the sense only that way. This is the opinion of some later Jews, as writers observe.[1654] But this opinion cannot stand. Partly, because if that were the case, then the corporal serpent only (which was but the instrument in seducing Eve) would be punished and the spiritual serpent Satan – the principal agent – would go unpunished. Partly because then our first parents and all their posterity in them should be deprived of that comfortable promise of their recovery from Satan's power and tyranny, by the seed of the woman, bruising the serpent's head. Besides which promise, what had they further with which to comfort themselves for many hundreds of years? This promise alone giving them hope of restoration by Christ.

[2] Some contrariwise understand here only the *spiritual, incorporeal* serpent, that *old serpent the devil and Satan*.[1655] And this seems to be the opinion of various ancient writers, who please themselves here with witty

---

[1654] Andre Rivet in Genesis 3, exercitation 35; David Pareus in his commentary on Genesis 3:14-15, etc.
[1655] Revelation 20:2

allegories, yet differing from one another, such as Ambrose,[1656] Augustine,[1657] Gregory,[1658] etc. But this opinion cannot be admitted. Partly, because of that phrase, *Because thou hast done this, thou art cursed above all cattle, and above every beast of the field*, verse 14, plainly ranks the serpent that was cursed among the cattle and beasts of the field; partly, because then the whole text must be understood only figuratively, and not at all literally, and so be turned into a mere allegory, which is neither safe nor solid.

[3] Some, seeing the inconvenience of both these extremes, understand both the *corporeal* and *incorporeal serpent*, the *sensible*, and the *spiritual serpent*, the serpent which was one beast of the field, and the old serpent the devil and Satan. And that the letter of the text intends both: but the serpent *immediately* and less principally, the devil *mediately* and more principally. Of this opinion is Chrysostom,[1659] (several learned modern writers also subscribing to him),[1660] "If these things (says he of this curse) be spoken of the sensible serpent, much more are they to be taken of the intelligible serpent, etc." And no wonder, for: {1} how absurd and unreasonable it is to think that the righteous God would thus severely curse and punish the *instrument*, and let Satan the *principal agent* escape scot-free. {2} The apostle, alluding plainly to this place, says, *God shall bruise Satan under your feet shortly*.[1661] As the corporal serpent is bruised under foot corporally; so the incorporeal serpent spiritually. He implies that; and expresses this. {3} This whole doom and punishment here denounced is easily applicable to both these serpents, as will afterwards appear in resolving of the fourth particular question.

(2) *What woman is here intended*? Here also I find, among authors, three opinions.

[1656] Ambrose, lib. de suga Seculi. C. 7. circa med & lib. de Paradis. c. 15. Tom. 4.

[1657] Augustine, Against the Manichaens, 1.2.17.1, & On The Literal Meaning of Genesis 11.36.3

[1658] Gregory on Psalm 101

[1659] John Chrysostom on Genesis 3, Homily 17, circ. med. Rom. 2

[1660] Ioan. Mercer. Praelect. in Genesis 3. Andre Rivet in Genesis 3. Exercitation 35.—David Pareus Commentary on Genesis 3:14. etc., John Calvin on Genesis 3:14-15

[1661] Romans 16:20

[1] Some take the word {*woman*} here in a mystical sense, either to signify the church, oppugned by the old serpent the devil. Thus the Anabaptists, as Gomarus notes.[1662] Or to signify, our sense, as Ambrose, who makes the serpent a type of corporal delight, the woman a symbol of our sense, and the man the delight of the mind.[1663] But this is more witty than it is solid. Nor is there here any cause to forsake the plain history and fly to allegories.

[2] Some by {*woman*} understand the virgin Mary, the mother of Christ, and render the following phrase, thus: *She shall bruise thine head*. Ascribing the bruising of the serpent's head to the woman, to the virgin Mary: not to Christ, the principal *seed of the woman*. And this is the interpretation of the popish writers, in their vulgar edition, made authentic by their wicked Trent council, and in their *Mary's Psalter*. And for the better countenancing of this corrupt translation, they have by the perfidiousness of Guy Fabricius corrupted the Hebrew text in the Interlinear Bible printed at Antwerp, putting in היא *she* for הוא *it*, that is, the seed of the woman. But our learned divines justly condemn this notorious corrupting of the text:[1664] {1} as inconsistent with the double syntax of the Hebrew context. {2} As incompatible with the subject matter in hand, namely. The bruising of the serpent's head, which peculiarly belongs to Christ. {3} As repugnant to the testimonies of ancient and modern writers. Yea and the more learned and ingenuous papists themselves confess the corruption.

[3] They think best who here apply this word {*woman*} immediately, and especially to Eve, as then the only woman in the world when this was spoken:[1665] the only woman that was immediately deceived by the serpent and did immediately deceive her husband, but mediately to other women, even the whole sex in some sort, namely: in respect of the enmity with the serpent, but peculiarly in respect of the promised seed, such women of whom Christ lineally descended according to the flesh, among whom the virgin Mary was

---

[1662] Franciscus Gomarus in Appendix to the 2nd Part, p.533, 1644
[1663] Ambrose de Parad. Lib.c.15 Tom. 4
[1664] Andre Rivet in Genesis 3, Exercitation 36, John Calvin on Genesis 3:15, John Mercer, Praelection in Genesis 3:15, Franciscus Gomarus in Appendix to the 2nd Part, p.533, 1644
[1665] Andre Rivet in Genesis 3, exercitation 37, ad initium.

the most eminent, being the immediate mother of Christ. And experience of all ages since the fall testifies this implacable enmity between the serpent and the woman, namely: not only Eve but her whole sex – every woman being presently filled with horror at the very sight of a serpent. And not only the woman, but the man also is at enmity with serpents, for it is added: *and between thy seed, and her seed*. But the woman is chiefly expressed because: {1} the woman was first in the transgression, and had most need of this caution and admonition against the serpent, with whom she had been too familiar.[1666] {2} The woman also, having the greatest cause of humiliation, had most need to be raised up with consolation. {3} Satan should be the more confounded and shamed, the woman the weaker vessel being opposed against him, as one that should subdue him.

(3) ***What is meant by these two seeds, the serpent's seed, and the woman's seed?*** Answer: The word {*seed*} properly denotes that of which some like thing is generated. Thus *grains of corn, kernels of fruit*, etc., are called {*seed*} properly.[1667] But by a metonymy of the effect, {*seed*} sometimes signifies that which is generated of seed. So children are called seed: *the seed of Abraham*, etc.[1668] In this better sense we are to take it here. Again {*seed*} in this latter sense is either *natural*, or *spiritual*.

[1] *Natural*, which is the proper issue of natural parents. And thus the word is used, either *distributively* for one alone. So Seth is called *another seed instead of* Abel.[1669] And of Ishmael, God said, *Of the son of the bond-woman will I make a nation, because he is thy seed*.[1670] Or collectively for many together. So God said to Abram, *I will establish my covenant between me and thee, and thy seed after thee; in their generations*, etc.[1671] Thus it is more frequently used.

[1666] Genesis 3:6, 1 Timothy 2:14
[1667] Genesis 1:11-12
[1668] Genesis 17:7 with Psalm 105:6, Isaiah 41:8, Galatians 3:16, Romans 11:1
[1669] Genesis 4:25
[1670] Genesis 21:13
[1671] Genesis 17:7-10

[2] ***Spiritual***, or *metaphorical seed*, is that which has some analogy or resemblance to natural seed or posterity. Natural children resemble, imitate and obey their parents: so they that resemble, imitate and obey God are counted his children, his seed;[1672] and they that resemble, imitate and obey Satan are called his children, his seed.[1673] Now these things premised, we may thus resolve that by the {*seed of the serpent*} we are to understand {1} the *natural seed* or *brood of the corporeal serpent*, between which and the woman's seed here is settled a perpetual feud, a hereditary and incurable enmity. But we must not limit the interpretation to this seed only, as the Jews do.[1674] We are further to understand {2} the *spiritual* or *metaphorical seed of the incorporeal serpent, Satan*, namely: all reprobates and wicked persons, which he does, as it were, beget by his diabolical instilling of evil into them, whereby he makes them like himself in corruption and destruction. This *seed of the old serpent* will be at perpetual and hereditary enmity with the seed of the woman: and the seed of the woman against it. And this is the seed which is here principally intended: Satan, the father of this seed, being the principal agent in man's ruin.

By {*seed of the woman*} what we are to understand, is a great and famous controversy:[1675] and that not only between the orthodox, and heterodox, but even among the orthodox writers themselves, namely: whether the word {*seed*} here is to be taken, {1} *universally of all the woman's posterity whatsoever*. Or, {2} *individually only of Christ, the principal seed, the seed of the virgin*. Or, {3} *collectively of Christ and all his spiritual seed according to the election*.

{1} *Seed here cannot be taken universally of all and singular the posterity of the woman without exception*. For, (i) many, yea most of the natural seed of the woman do in all ages degenerate into the seed of the serpent, so that Christ's flock is but a *little flock*:[1676] and comparatively *the whole world lies in*

[1672] 1 John 3:1-3, Psalm 22:30, Isaiah 53:10
[1673] John 8:44, 1 John 3:8, 10; John 14:30, Ephesians 2:2
[1674] Vid. Andre Rivet in Genesis 3, Exercitation 37, *ad in it*
[1675] Quid Semen mulieris sit controversia est nobilis. Fran. Gomar. in Append. ad Part. 2. p. 532.
[1676] Luke 12:32

wickedness.[1677] Now those that degenerate into the serpent's seed, cannot be here intended by the *woman's seed*, because these two seeds are set at extreme enmity against one another. (ii) The *woman's seed* here spoken of, shall bruise the *serpent's head*. But all universally shall not bruise the serpent's head, and have full victory over Satan: for then all should be saved, inasmuch as *whosoever overcometh* shall be saved.[1678] Rather, the greatest part is overcome by the *prince of the world that rules in the children of disobedience.*[1679]

{2} *Seed here cannot be taken only individually and singularly of Christ alone, the seed of the virgin, exclusively, so as to exclude all besides himself.* Though some learned writers lean this way,[1680] and Pareus gives some reasons for this opinion, which that learned Rivet answers.[1681] Let the reader consult them.

{3} *But {seed} here is to be taken collectively, as comprehending Christ and all his seed, Christ and all his elect members* (yet Christ as the head, them as the body; Christ principally, them secondarily; Christ by way of eminency, as the seed blessing, them by way of participation with Christ, as the seed blessed), for (i) the antithesis, or opposition of the seeds requires this, namely: as the seed of the serpent is taken collectively for all the wicked and reprobate vassals of Satan, so the seed of the woman is to be taken for all the godly elect born of a woman: first Christ and then all his seed in him. Otherwise the opposition will not be fit. Doubtless if {*seed*} in the one phrase be taken collectively, then in the opposite phrase it must not be taken individually. It must be understood collectively in both, or singularly in both. (ii) By {*the woman*}, Eve is immediately to be understood. Consequently by the {*seed of the woman*}, all Eve's posterity that degenerate not into the seed of the serpent. But first Christ, then they that are Christ's. (iii) That seed of the woman is intended, against which the serpent and his seed are at enmity, but the *serpent*

[1677] 1 John 5:19
[1678] Revelation 2:11, 17, 26-28 & 3:5, 12, 21
[1679] Ephesians 2:2-3
[1680] Franciscus Gomarus in Appendix ad Part 2, p.532 - 10. Mercer. in Praelec. ad Genesis 3:15
[1681] David Pareus in Genesis 3:15 with Andre Rivet in Genesis 3, Excertitation 37

and *his seed* are at enmity not only against Christ but against all that belong to Christ.[1682] (iv) Finally that *seed of the woman* is here meant, which shall victoriously *bruise the serpent's head*, but that shall be done both by Christ and his elect members. By Christ *originally and primitively*, through his own power; by them that are Christ's *derivatively*, through power derived and victory communicated from Christ unto them.

(4) **Which punishments are here pronounced upon the serpent.** For clearing this, consider that, as there was a twofold serpent tempting, namely: the invisible serpent, Satan efficiently, and the visible, corporeal serpent, the beast, instrumentally; so these two serpents had two sorts of punishments inflicted on them respectively: the visible serpent had his corporal punishments laid on him, and proportionably the invisible serpent had his spiritual punishments allotted unto him. Those were grievous; these double grievous. And the punishments of the *visible serpent*, by *analogie indigitate* to us the punishments of the *serpent invisible*. The punishments of the *visible serpent* were especially four. namely:

[1] An extreme curse above all cattle and wild beasts of the field. *And the Lord God said unto the serpent, because thou hast done this, thou art cursed above all cattle, and above every beast of the field.*[1683] Hereupon the serpent becomes the most loathed and abhorred of all these creatures. But this is more general.

[2] An ugly, deformed and debased posture of body. *Upon thy belly shalt thou go, and dust shalt thou eat all the days of thy life.*[1684]

{1} Touching *the serpent's going upon his belly*, (i) some think this was the serpent's natural posture, and that it became penal to him only by divine destination. But (as Rivet notes) this is not sufficiently proved, by them that assert it.[1685] (ii) Some suppose that at first the serpent had legs and feet, as other beasts had, because he seems at diverse times to be reckoned or ranked

---

[1682] Revelation 12 throughout, John 15:18-21
[1683] Genesis 3:14
[1684] Genesis 3:14
[1685] Andre Rivet in Genesis 3 Exercitation 35 p.173 b. Lugdun, 1633.

with cattle and beasts; now beasts are distinguished in kind from creeping things.[1686] And that he was deprived of his feet and cast upon his belly, upon Satan's abusing him to seduce the woman.[1687] This is ascribed to B. Ephraim.[1688] (iii) Others are of opinion that though at first the serpent had no feet, yet he crept more easily upon the hinder part of his body, his head and breast being straight and lifted up from the earth, not as the head and breast of a man, but of a hart, peacock, etc., but after his seducing of the woman, his head and breast also were cast upon the ground. This is ascribed to Luther. Now, though we cannot herein positively determine, the Scripture being so silent, yet forasmuch as the serpent spoke to the woman,[1689] it is very probable his posture was either *naturally erect* in the forepart of his body, or *occasionally lifted up* for that time; otherwise his other ugly posture might have caused the woman to fear and shun him.

{2} Touching his *eating of dust*, it seems not to be a new sort of punishment, that the serpent should eat nothing but dust; for experience tells us the serpent feeds upon herbs and other creatures: but rather it is an additional exposition and aggravation of the former punishment. As if it had been said, *Thou shalt so creep upon thy belly with thy whole body on the earth, that thy mouth and nostrils shall be filled with dust raised up by thy creeping, thy mouth still going so close to the earth, as if thou wert eating and licking up the dust.*

[3] An inveterate hereditary enmity between the serpent and the woman, and between their two seeds. So that the serpent fears and flies the very sight of man and woman, creeping into holes and caverns of the earth from them; and contrariwise, mankind, especially women, fearing, hating and abhorring serpents, even to their destruction.

[4] Finally, an utter destruction of the serpent by the woman's seed: though the serpent may in some strait wound and bruise man's heel, yet man

---

[1686] Genesis 1:14
[1687] Genesis 1:25
[1688] Vid. Moses Bar-Cepha in lib. De Paradiso
[1689] Genesis 3:1, etc.

shall bruise his head, totally destroy him, not contenting himself to crush or wound his body, but his most vital and hurtful part, his head. These are the punishments of the corporal serpent. For these, the letter of the text is clear. And though the serpent was without reason, did not properly sin, nor could understand these judgments pronounced: yet was it according to divine wisdom and justice, thus to denounce these punishments upon the serpent. {1} Partly because the serpent became the instrument to dishonor God and ruin man: which was made in his kind to serve God and man. {2} Partly to testify God's extreme detestation of the fact, who so punishes the very instrument whereby it was effected. As when a man so abhors a murder, that he breaks and burns the very knife or weapon whereby it was committed, etc. {3} Partly, to instruct our first parents how heinous their sin was, and how deeply God displeased thereby, who so plagues the serpent being the occasion thereof. {4} Partly to let Satan the old serpent see what vengeance he was to expect, for seducing mankind. For if this be done to the instrument, what shall be done to the principal agent?

The punishments of Satan the invisible serpent, which are principally here intended under the former literal punishments of the visible serpent, are proportionally four also. namely:

[1] *He is extremely cursed*. As the serpent was cursed above all cattle, so Satan is cursed above all creatures with God's direful curse.

[2] *He is deeply debased, and that forever without all hope or possibility of relief*. For as the serpent was doomed to that basest posture of *creeping upon his belly*, and consequently as it were *eating the dust*, and that *all the days of his life* (by which postures the Scripture is wont to signify deepest abjection and ignominy of a man subdued, prostrate, abased, fearing or feeling the most extreme misery, etc.),[1690] so Satan, that proudest spirit who lifted himself up against God, and disdained to be debased for his sin below man, was therefore for his seducing of man debased to utter ignominy, contempt, baseness, as it were creeping on the earth and licking the very dust under man's feet, and to

---

[1690] Isaiah 29:4 & 49:23, Micah 7:17, Psalm 72:9 & 44:25

be trampled upon by him, and this continually. Not that Satan was not cast down from heaven to hell, before, for leaving his first estate:[1691] but that now he received an additional aggravation of his punishment, for his destroying of mankind. This seems the most sober and sound application of this second punishment to Satan. As for those interpretations of his going upon his belly, and eating the dust, either to intimate the double sin, pride and luxury, whereunto he tempts man; as some.[1692] Or to imply gluttony, lustful thoughts or actions, whereunto he solicits men; as others.[1693] Or to import that Satan should thenceforth have no power over the soul, but only over the body, which is dust: as the Kabbalistic Jews.[1694] Or, that Satan, who delights to feed upon the death of men, shall only eat them that are dust, that is earthly men: as Jerome.[1695] These and like interpretations (though witty glosses, allusions or allegories), seem not so safe and solid to be insisted upon.

[3] *He, and his seed, namely: all wicked angels and reprobate men, (who imitate him, obey him, are acted by him, and become like him in evil), are plagued with a spiritual enmity of the woman and her seed, namely, Christ and all his elect against them*: Michael and his angels and saints, against the dragon and his angels and limbs.[1696] And *greater is he that is in us than he that is in the world.*[1697]

[4] Finally, *Satan shall be utterly crushed and destroyed by the woman's seed*. For, though he may *bruise the heel* (far from head and heart), that is, do some less dangerous hurt to the woman's seed: yet shall his very head (wherein his policy, strength and mischief chiefly lies), be *bruised* by the woman's seed. He may *hurt* the woman's seed, but the woman's seed will totally *destroy* him. For (as one wittily observes) the serpent has but *one head*; when that is bruised, he is ruined: as Luther notes, "The least blow on his head kills him;

[1691] 2 Peter 2:4
[1692] Augustine, On the Literal Meaning of Genesis, chapters 13 & 18
[1693] Gregory, Moral, l.12 c.2
[1694] Ambrose, lib 1. De Poenit c.13
[1695] Jerome on Isaiah 65:25, Tome 5
[1696] Revelation 12:7-8, etc.
[1697] 1 John 4:4

but the woman's seed has two heels. When one is bruised, he can go upon the other, and both of them are far from the heart, the vital part."[1698] *These are judgments here threatened to the serpent, visible and invisible.*

(5) ***Finally, the benefits implicitly and explicitly promised for the woman and her seed, are several and excellent.*** Not to dispute now: (i) whether under the serpent's curse for ruining mankind, be not implied a contrary blessing intended for mankind?[1699] (ii) Whether under the serpent's deep debasement for debasing man and causing him to fall, there be not implied contrariwise some hope of lapsed man's advancement again to a more honorable condition? Which things yet seem very probably to be insinuated. Yet these mercies and benefits seem clearly intended. Namely: (a) God's free love, rich grace and commiseration to the woman and mankind lapsed, in setting her at enmity against Satan, by familiarity with whom she was undone. In which enmity against Satan, seem to be implied, *enmity against sin*, whereunto Satan tempts: amity and reconciliation with God, from whom Satan tempts, namely: repentance from dead works and reconciliation to God. (b) Such a seed of the woman as should not only be distinct, but quite opposite unto the serpent's seed, namely: *principally* and *peculiarly*, Christ: *secondarily*, all that are Christ's. This is contained in the enmity of the two seeds. (c) A continued conflict of the woman's seed against the serpent and his seed, and at last an absolute victory over Satan and his seed when they have done their worst. *It* (the woman's seed) *shall bruise thine head: and thou* (serpent) *shalt bruise his heel*.[1700] But of these things more fully in the following aphorisms. Thus of the sense of the words.

[1698] Serpens ictus corporis, quantumvis graves, sustinere potest sine periculo. Sed si caput vel minima virgula series, statim extinguitur. Luth. in Gen. cap. 55. p. 193. b. To. 3.
[1699] Genesis 3:14
[1700] Genesis 3:15

Section 3

The positions or aphorisms, resulting from these words thus briefly unfolded, touching God's first discovery of his Covenants of Promise, from Adam until Noah, are several, namely:

1. Immediately upon Adam's fall, God revealed a gracious promise touching man's recovery.

2. This promise of man's recovery was revealed very imperfectly and obscurely.

3. This first promise of lapsed man's recovery was revealed in Christ, the seed of the woman.

4. This first promise in Christ revealed lapsed man's recovery in the enmity threatened between the woman and the serpent, between her seed and his seed; and in the events or fruits of that enmity.

5. This first promise revealed in Christ the seed of the woman, though it had not the name and formality of a covenant; yet had it the nature, substance and reality of a covenant. These five aphorisms being distinctly opened and cleared, the first discovery of God's Covenant of Faith, in the first remarkable period of time, from Adam until Noah (which was above 1050 years, as chronologers observe out of the history of Genesis) will be sufficiently unfolded.

Aphorism 1

Hence, immediately upon Adam's fall, God revealed a gracious promise touching man's recovery.

Here note: (1) that after the fall God revealed a promise touching man's recovery. (2) That this promise was revealed immediately upon Adam's fall. (3) That this promise was most gracious. (4) Corollaries ensuing hereupon.

(1) That *after the fall God revealed a promise touching man's recovery*, is evident:

[1] *By the heavy and dreadful doom which God pronounced upon the serpent for ruining man by his subtle seducements.* This doom was fourfold, as has been shown. A doom not only in justice and wrath against the serpent: but also in mercy, favor, and compassion to man seduced by the serpent, as the particulars thereof evince. Now in God's explicit denouncing of the serpent's destruction for seducing man, seems to be comprised of an implicit promise of man's salvation, though seduced by Satan.

[2] *By the enmity which God has put between the woman and the serpent, and between their respective seeds.* For, where there is enmity against the serpent Satan who tempts unto evil; there must be a nature and principle contrary both to Satan, and to sin, whereunto Satan tempts. What can this principle be, but repentance, etc? And where there is enmity expressed against Satan: there is reconciliation, amity, and union implied with the Lord God. This imports man's recovery.

[3] *By the utter victory promised to the woman's seed over the serpent, in bruising the serpent's head.* The serpent overthrew the woman: but the woman's seed shall overthrow the serpent, and all the *works of the devil*, sin and death.[1701] Satan is not subdued, till sin and death be subdued. Now sin and death being bruised in the head, and subdued: man is delivered from his

---

[1701] 1 John 3:8, Hebrews 2:14-15, 1 Corinthians 15:54-58

deadly enemies and recovered. For (as Luther said well), "sin and death are the head of the serpent."[1702]

(2) That *the promise of man's recovery was revealed immediately upon Adam's fall*, seems clear by the series and order of the history. For Adam, in all probability, fell on the selfsame day in which he was created, being the same day made and marred, formed and deformed, as has been formerly shown:[1703] and was on the same day wherein he sinned, cast out of paradise, stripped of all his paradise privileges, and sentenced to several miseries, yet after his fall, and before his sentence or ejection out of paradise, whilst God was pronouncing sentence upon the serpent (who first offending, was first doomed).[1704] Even then the Lord promises *the enmity of the woman and her seed against the serpent and his seed, and the bruising of the serpent's head by the woman's seed*.[1705] *Una eademque dies vulnus opem {que} tulit*; one and the same day brought on both the woman and the cure, the malady and the remedy. In the serpent's *malediction* is comprised the sinner's *benediction*.

Whilst God denounces the serpent's damnation, he proclaims the sinner's salvation. This promise is not directed to the woman, deceived by the serpent: nor yet to Adam, deceived by the woman; but it is expressly directed to the serpent; for, as yet God continues his speech to the serpent, and this is part of his doom, *and I will put enmity between thee and the woman, and between thy seed and her seed*, etc.[1706] How is it directed to the serpent? Not as a promise (for God intended no promise nor saving mercy to him), but only as a threatening. Everything therein is destructive to the serpent: not only the curse and his debased posture, but also the enmity, and the bruising of the serpent's head. What could vex and punish the serpent worse than to be ruined by the seed of the woman whom he had ruined? So then it is a promissory threatening and a minatory [threatening] promise. As minatory it

---

[1702] "Diabolis caput sunt & mors peccatum." Luther in Genesis fol.55, b. Tom.1
[1703] See in Book 2, Chapter 1, Aphorism 6, Particular 3
[1704] Genesis 3 throughout & duly considered
[1705] Genesis 3:14-15, etc. See Book 2, Chapter 2, Aphorism 1.11
[1706] Genesis 3:14-15, etc.

was against the serpent; as promissory it was for sinners seduced by the serpent. It is as Samson's lion with honey in his bowels. The lion of the threatening is for the serpent's ruin; the honey of the promise is for the sinner's refreshment.

(3) That *this promise was most gracious*, may appear in several ways, namely:

[1] By the extreme misery into which man was plunged by his fall; before, and when this promise was made. For, at that time man was wholly under the deadly penalty of the broken Covenant of Works admitting of no mercy – the Covenant of Faith in Christ the seed of the woman being as then wholly unknown to him as a remedy. This was the utmost misery that ever mankind was in, or can be in on this side of hell from the beginning until the end of the world. Consequently God's promise of the recovery out of this extremest misery must needs be supereminently gracious.

[2] *By the complete sufficiency of the remedy promised for man's recovery out of this most extreme misery*, namely, the seed of the woman, that is peculiarly and primarily Jesus Christ God-man, to be born of a woman who is *able to save to the utmost*.[1707] Nor man, nor angel, nor any mere creature in the world could have appeased infinite justice offended, and so have recovered man offending, had not Jesus Christ this *seed of the woman* undertaken and effected it. The promise then must needs be most gracious, that contrary to all merit, tenders to man most wretched, the only all-sufficient and efficacious remedy.

[3] *By the speediness of the promise*. Had God promised recovery to Adam nine hundred years after his fall, it had been a glorious act of grace:[1708] but that he promised this recovery so immediately after his fall the selfsame day, this proclaims divine grace double glorious. Oh the riches of the glory of God's grace to wretched man, that would not suffer him to lie despairing in his misery for one day; that would not permit Satan the old serpent to insult over him and his misery for one day; that would not suppress the yearning of his

---

[1707] Hebrews 7:25
[1708] Genesis 5:5

bowels of mercy to miserable undone man for one day; that would not defer the publication of the soul-reviving gospel of Christ, the sinner's salvation, the serpent's damnation, for one day!

(4) *Corollaries hence.* Did God immediately upon Adam's fall reveal a gracious promise touching man's recovery? Then,

[1] **See here the antiquity of the gospel.** The word {*gospel*} is from the ancient Saxon {*Godspell*}, that is, {*good-speech*}, as some think:[1709] it is *glad tidings from God touching lapsed sinners' recovery and restitution*. Such glad tidings is peculiarly styled *the good word of God*:[1710] and is published not only since Christ under the New Testament, but long before Christ under the Old Testament. And they that reject or despise the Old Testament as not gospel, do neither understand what the Old Testament, nor the gospel mean. The gospel, the glad tidings of sinners' recovery, was published presently upon man's fall: probably on the selfsame day whereon man was corrupted, yea and created. And after that, still more and more cleared, by Scriptures in all succeeding ages. The gospel then is almost as ancient as the creation of the world. Hence it's styled, for the great antiquity of it, *the everlasting gospel*.[1711] And to this effect, it is said that the *un-lying God has promised eternal life before the world began*.[1712] Greek: *Before times of ages*: or, *before ancient times*. Here (as Calvin well notes)[1713] we are not to carry the promise to before all times, but to most ancient times, even from the foundation of the world. Thus the gospel is most ancient. And good things, the more ancient, the more excellent, as most like to God himself, *who is from eternity*.[1714]

[2] **Man's recovery was at first but promised.** It was not actually effected and performed until the fullness of time,[1715] which was many

---

[1709] Henry Ainsworth on Psalm 40:10
[1710] Hebrews 6:5
[1711] ευαγγελιον αιωνιον, Revelation 14:6
[1712] Titus 1:2
[1713] John Calvin on Titus 1:2
[1714] Psalm 90:1
[1715] Galatians 4:4-6

thousands of years after the fall; until then, man's recovery did hang only in the promises like water in the clouds or like fruit in the blossoms. And yet this recovery only promised, was for those times effectual and sufficient for the elect's salvation living in those days: God's promise being sure and infallible to all believers. But now in these later times man's recovery – promised of old – is actually performed and accomplished. And *performed recovery* far surpasses *promised recovery*.

[3] **God's incomparable love to mankind is singularly to be admired and adored, in that immediately upon man's fall he would graciously promise man's rise and recovery.** For, if we duly consider the author promising, the blessing promised, the object to whom the promise was made, the season when the promise broke forth, and the parties to whom the promise was denied, it will appear that God's free love to mankind is most wonderful indeed.

{1} *The author promising man's recovery is God.* That God, who by a word made the whole world, and, the world becoming corrupt, could by a word have unmade the world again, and have created another world.[1716] That God, who depends upon no creature, has no need of man, not of any work of his hands to add unto him. If man should be saved, what does God gain? If man should perish, what does God lose? Yet such his love to man, that he who has no need of man, promises recovery unto man.

{2} *The blessing promised, is lapsed man's recovery.* In his enmity against the serpent, amity and reconcilement with God is promised: and in his bruising the serpent's head, victory over Satan. O happy restoration! Man un-recovered, would have been as wretched as the devil's; man recovered, will become as blessed as the angels.

{3} *The object of this promised recovery* is lapsed man, corrupted man, apostate man, worthless, loveless, liveless, hopeless, helpless man, dead in sin, enmity against God, without God in the world, wholly unfit for heaven, a vassal of Satan, a child of wrath, and an heir of hell. And will the holy Lord

---

[1716] Genesis 1 with Psalm 33:9

cast his eye upon such a wretch, such a detestable lump of wickedness, more full of sin than any toad of poison, so as to restore him?

{4} *The season of this promise of recovery, was immediately upon Adam's fall*. Man, presently upon his creation, made haste to damn himself; God, presently upon man's fall, made haste to save him. As a tender father speedily snatches up his fallen child from the ground, from fire or water, and hugs it in his arms compassionately, so the heavenly father snatched our first parents speedily from their lapsed, hopeless state, far worse than of fire or water, by the hand of this promise, and embraced them in the bosom of his love most tenderly. This was love indeed. *Speedy kindness is double kindness*.[1717]

{5} Finally, *the parties to whom this promise was denied, were lapsed angels*. They were above man by creation: man becomes far above them by restoration. The angels fall, and find no mercy, no promise, etc., but woeful curses, sharp threatenings and severe judgements; man falls, and yet he finds rich mercy, and saving promises of restoration.[1718] Is the inferior creature thus respected, when the superior is neglected? Is man healed, when angels are left incurable? Is lapsed man saved, and fitted for heaven; when lapsed angels are damned and fixed in hell? Here's an admirable love, a discriminating love to mankind, forever to be adored.

[4] **God takes more pleasure in sinners' recovery, then in sinners' ruin**. This is evident,

{1} In that, so immediately upon their ruin he most sweetly promises their recovery. As most unwilling, that mankind should remain at all in their lapsed state.

{2} In that since then, God so often testifies that he has no delight in sinners' destruction. To this effect God interrogates, *Have I any pleasure at all that the wicked should die? Saith the Lord God: and not that he should return from his ways and live?*[1719] Yea, God positively asserts, *I have no pleasure in the death of him that dieth, saith the Lord God: wherefore turn your selves, and live*

[1717] Bis dat qui cito dat; nil dat qui munera tardat.
[1718] Genesis 3:14-15, compared with Jude 6
[1719] Ezekiel 18:23

ye.[1720] And if this be not tenderly enough expressed, he swears; *As I live, saith the Lord God, I have no pleasure in the death of the wicked, but that the wicked turn from his way and live: turn ye, turn ye from your evil ways; for why will ye die, O house of Israel?*[1721] How emphatically!

Doubt: If God has more pleasure in sinners' recovery, than in sinners' ruin, then why did God permit the fall, and upon man's fall, punish him with death?

Answer: God permitted the fall, that he might glorify himself the more in fallen man's recovery. For, as Augustine well: "God is so good, that he would not suffer evil to be, were he not able," and did he not intend to "bring greater good out of that evil."[1722] Hereby: (i) the weakness of the most perfect creature, left to itself, is discovered. (ii) The mysteriousness of the lapsed creature's recovery is occasionally revealed. (iii) The condemnation of the old serpent the devil and Satan is aggravated.[1723] (iv) The just rejection and condemnation of reprobate persons is prosecuted. And, (v) in all the glory of God's power, freedom, justice, mercy, etc., is most illustriously advanced.

Though God permitted man's fall, yet in that permission, he neither did man any wrong at all, for he was not bound to uphold man, but left him in a perfect, yet mutable state; nor was he any cause of man's sin directly or indirectly, for he neither necessitated him to evil by creation or constitution of his nature, man being made upright, free, and able to all good;[1724] nor did God tempt him to evil by his providential dispensation, but only left him to himself to stand or fall.[1725]

{3} Man being fallen, God justly punishes the impenitent with death. Not that he has any pleasure in the sinner's death as it is the destruction of his creature, but only as it is a due act or expression of his truth and justice for his own glory against sin and sinners.

[1720] Ezekiel 18:32
[1721] Ezekiel 33:11
[1722] Augustine, ad. Enchiridion, ad Laurent Chapter 100 Tom. 3
[1723] Genesis 3:14-15
[1724] Ecclesiastes 7:29
[1725] James 1:13

[5] ***How advantageously has God improved Adams' fall, in promising his recovery immediately upon his fall?*** What greater mischief or disadvantage ever came into the world, then by *Adam's apostasy*? For, thereby Adam and all his posterity to the end of the world were utterly undone, and involved under death: hereby Satan had most notably wreaked his malice upon mankind, and brought them under his diabolical tyranny, and thereby the glory of the creator was deeply obscured and eclipsed, his noblest creature on earth being ruined, and set against him in most extreme enmity. Yet all these disadvantages the Lord has turned to great advantage by this blessed promise, namely:

{1} *To the increase of man's felicity.* Man was happy before his fall by a natural, mutable and finite righteousness in his own person: but he becomes more happy since his fall by a supernatural, immutable and infinite righteousness in the person of the promised seed. Before, upon continuance of his obedience, he should have had a continued life in paradise on earth, since upon his faith in Christ, he shall have eternal life in paradise which is the third heavens. Thus Adam's greatest loss is improved to his greatest gain.

{2} *To the aggravation of Satan's misery.* Satan was miserable before man's fall, for not keeping his first estate, being *reserved in chains under darkness unto the judgment of the great day*;[1726] but became much more miserable by effecting man's ruin, being thereupon doomed to a fourfold judgment.[1727] Then he envied man's natural happiness so as to overthrow it; now he shall twice so much envy man's supernatural happiness, which he can never overthrow, but must eternally be overthrown by it. Thus the Lord has out-shot Satan in his own bow; he has cut off this Goliath's head with his own sword.

{3} *To the illustration of his own glory.* Before man's fall, God was much glorified by man's creation: since his fall, much more glorified by his restoration. Before, by man's integrity of nature: since, by man's integrity of grace. Before, God was glorified in his wisdom, freedom, power and goodness:

[1726] Jude 6
[1727] Genesis 3:14-15

since, he is glorified not only in these his perfections, but also in his free grace, mercy, bowels of commiserations and long-suffering.

[6] ***Has God thus laid a foundation of sinners' recovery in his promise? Then let us, as children of this our heavenly Father, resemble him, in endeavoring to recover lapsed sinners.*** Are we ourselves converted and recovered from a state of sin, to a state of righteousness? Then let us endeavor by conviction, admonition, exhortation, example, and by all means possible to win and gain poor lost souls unto God: especially such as are more near and dear unto us. Let the converted minister labor to convert the people committed to him, the converted husband to gain his carnal wife, and the converted parents and masters to win their carnal children and servants. For,

{1} This is a duty required and to be endeavored, not only of ministers publicly and especially: but also of particular Christians privately and in their place.[1728] *Brethren* (says Paul to the Galatians), *if a man be overtaken in a fault, ye which are spiritual, restore such an one with the spirit of meekness.*[1729]

{2} This the godly have desired and endeavored. One convert soul, would have (if it were possible) all the world also converted. David, begging restoration from his fall, upon his restoring promises: *Then will I teach transgressors thy ways, and sinners shall be converted unto thee.*[1730] Paul, once converted, was a happy instrument of the conversion of many.[1731] And he says of himself: *Though I be free from all men, yet have I made myself servant to all, that I might gain the more: and unto the Jews, I became as a Jew, that I might gain the Jews: to them that are under the law, as under the law, that I might gain them that are under the law: to them that are without law as without law, (being not without law to God, but under the law to Christ) that I might gain them that are without law. To the weak, became I as weak, that I might gain the weak. I am made all things to all men, that I might by all means save some.*[1732]

[1728] Acts 26:18
[1729] Galatians 6:1. See also Jude 22-23, Leviticus 19:17, Matthew 18:15-17, Luke 17:3-4
[1730] Psalm 51:12-13
[1731] Acts 9 & 26:16-18
[1732] 1 Corinthians 9:19-23

{3} For the gaining of sinners, the Lord has given particular directions: how some are to be won with sweetness, love and meekness; others with fear and terror. *Of some have compassion, making a difference; and others save with fear, pulling them out of the fire.*[1733]

{4} The act of winning souls is a high and excellent point of skill, most-desirable. *He that winneth souls, is wise:*[1734] spiritually, savingly wise indeed – for himself and others, for this and the world to come.

{5} How much good does this bring to the parties converted! *Their eyes are opened, they are turned from darkness to light, and from the power of Satan unto God, that they may receive forgiveness of sins, and inheritance among them which are sanctified by faith which is in Christ.*[1735] And James says: *Brethren, if any of you do err from the truth, and one convert him: let him know, that he which converteth the sinner from the error of his way, shall save a soul from death,* (and one soul is better worth then all the treasure of this world),[1736] *and shall hide a multitude of sins.*[1737]

{6} Finally, how advantageous will the conversion of sinners prove to the instruments of their conversion! Hereby they shall sweetly resemble the compassionating God, who presently upon Adam's fall held forth his golden scepter to him, his sweet promise of recovery. And it's no small happiness to be like unto the most happy God. Hereby also they shall treasure up for themselves a great reward for a better world. For, *They that be wise shall shine as the brightness of the firmament: and they that turn many unto righteousness, as the stars, for ever and ever.*[1738]

Thus *immediately upon Adam's fall, God revealed a gracious promise touching man's recovery.* This is the first aphorism.

[1733] Jude 22-23, Galatians 6:1
[1734] Proverbs 11:30
[1735] Acts 26:28
[1736] Matthew 16:29
[1737] James 5:19-20
[1738] Daniel 12:3

Aphorism 2

Hence, this promise of man's recovery was revealed very imperfectly and obscurely.

For the clearing of this, consider three things, namely:

(1) *That this promise of man's recovery was revealed very imperfectly and obscurely*, is plain in several ways.

[1] In that this promise is not here fully and wholly expressed, but in part only implied. namely. In the *enmity of the woman and her seed against the serpent and his seed*, explicitly threatened: the reconciliation and amity of the woman and her seed with God, is contrariwise implicitly promised.[1739] And that which is not plainly expressed but only implied is imperfectly and obscurely revealed.

[2] In that this promise so far as it is expressed is laid down very generally and remotely: *the woman's seed shall bruise thine head*, said the Lord to the serpent.[1740] This is all that's expressed. Now though this for the materiality of it be a promise that the woman's seed should ruin the serpent who had deceived the woman, yet for the formality or manner of it, being uttered and directed only to the serpent, it is only a threatening of his destruction by the woman's seed. And what is here promised, is propounded very remotely and generally. For it is not declared particularly and distinctly, {1} what this woman's seed shall be for person and office, {2} when this seed of the woman should bruise the serpent's head, nor {3} how this seed should bruise the serpent's head. But only in the general, the seed of the woman shall bruise the serpent's head. Now all generals are very imperfect and obscure.

[3] In that this discovery of the promise of man's recovery comes far short of all following discoveries thereof, if they be compared together. As in the opening of them hereafter will more fully appear.

[1739] Genesis 3:14-15
[1740] Genesis 3:15

(2) *Why was this promise of man's recovery thus obscurely and imperfectly revealed?*

Answer: [1] Because, this promise was the first promise, the first daybreak of salvation, and the very first gospel that ever was preached unto sinners. Therefore it was the most obscure and most imperfect of all the promises. When God at first created the world, he proceeded from the most obscure and imperfect state of the creature, to the more clear and perfect, till at last he came to the most perfect. At first he created the confused mass or lump, and the earth was without form and void, darkness being upon the face of the deep; then he created things without life; as light, the firmament, dry land, and seas.[1741] After these he created things that had life but no sense, as grass, herbs and trees. After these, things that had life and sense but no reason, as fowls, fishes, beasts and creeping things. Last of all he created them that had life, sense, and reason, as man and woman that were most perfect of all. In like sort when God re-created the lapsed world of mankind, and revealed this new work of his by covenant and promise, he laid open this mystery in his promises and covenant, not all at once but by degrees. This first degree being darkest; the last clearest of all. As the first model of a building; the first lineaments of a picture; the first draught of covenants and articles of agreements, etc., are still most rude, imperfect and obscure.

[2] Because this promise was the remotest and at greatest distance of all other from the performance and accomplishment thereof in the actual exhibition of the woman's seed. Between this promise, and Christ's death whereby he specially bruised the serpent's head, there were almost four thousand years.[1742] Adam and the fathers of the old world through this longest promissory perspective looked at Christ a great way off, and therefore they beheld him more dimly and obscurely. Every object, the further away it is, the more darkly and imperfectly it is beheld; the nearer, the clearer.

[1741] Genesis 1 throughout
[1742] Some place Christ's death in Anno Mundi 3960 (Broughton); some in Anno Mundi 3952, *The Sacred Chronology* by Roger Drake p.73

[3] Because, when this promise was revealed, God's church was (to say the best) but in its primordial foundation, in its extreme infancy, yea but an *embryo*; this very promise being the first foundation-stone whereon it was built in Christ. Consequently, the capacity and apprehension of the church, most weak, imperfect and obscure. God therefore suits them with the most imperfect and obscure discovery of the promised recovery: gives them the first elements – the ABC of the gospel – as they were able to receive it.[1743] God reveals not what himself is able to reveal, but (such is his indulgence, and condescension) what his people are able to receive from time to time.

[4] Because, from this first promise, till the actual performance of man's recovery in the recovering seed of the woman, God intended still a clearer and clearer manifestation of this mystery from age to age, till at last the full noontide or perfect day of the New Testament should be discovered most brightly and gloriously. By this gradual discovery, the church's faith and hope are more and more nourished and encouraged against fainting: the worth and desirableness of the promised seed is more and more displayed day by day: and the glory of divine wisdom, grace, mercy and goodness is still afresh magnified with greater and greater degrees of exaltation. Therefore, this first discovery is most dark and imperfect: that so there might be a more excellent and observable progress, from the darkest to the brightest, from the lowest to the highest revelation of man's recovery in Christ. Pareus also gives several causes of the obscurity of this first promise. See them in the footnote.[1744]

[1743] Quicquid recipitur, recipitur ad modum recipientis.

[1744] "There seem to be three causes why this promise was laid down thus obscurely and figuratively:
1. Because of the devil, to whom God would have this promise remain obscure, that he might be exercised with perpetual fear, and might envy and suspect all women bringing forth children from that time till the exhibition of Christ, lest they should bring forth the promised seed which was to bruise his head .For if the mystery of the incarnation remained a long time hid from the angels themselves, how much more from Satan? Ephesians 3:9.
2. For the first parents and their faithful posterity, whose faith and invocation God would exercise by this obscurity, and stir up in them a more ardent desire of the promised seed, and diligence in searching out the time and manner of the redemption to come. As Peter testifies of the prophets, that they diligently searched and inquired of the grace and salvation that was to come upon us. 1 Peter 1:10.

(3) *Corollaries resulting hence*, are these, namely:

[1] Hence, *the wisdom and goodness of God in his gospel-dispensations is very observable*. He reveals not the mystery of Christ, and of sinners' recovery by him, all at once, nor in full clearness and perfection at first; but most obscurely. Otherwise, {1} the glory of a full discovery would have dashed and dazzled his people's weak apprehensions in those days of the church's most extreme infancy.[1745] {2} The faith and hope of his church would not have so increased and grown by degrees from dimness to clearness. {3} Nor the desirableness of Christ have been more and more desirable from age to age, according to the sweet and comely order of God's discovery. In these regards the wisdom and goodness of God is the more notable in this way of discovery.

[2] Hence, *the gospel at first had very weak and small beginnings*. This obscure and imperfect revelation of man's recovery was the first out-breaking of it. Though afterwards it has increased to wonderful perfection. Hence, Christ compares it to *a little leaven, which at last leavens the whole lump, and to a small grain of mustard seed, which groweth at length to such a tree that the fouls lodge in the branches of it*.[1746] And Christ is compared to a little *stone cut out of the mountain without hands, that became a great mountain, and filled the whole earth*.[1747] As the greatest river at first arises from a small spring, or as the waters of the sanctuary that at last became impassable, were at first but up to the ankles.[1748] Who then would despise the day of small things? Who would

---

3. For the seed itself, Christ, for whole manifestation and glory, a clearer light was reserved; that between the grace of the Old and New Testament there might be kept an eminent difference, as between morning and midday. Meanwhile God was not wanting to the weakness of the fathers; but in several ways relieved their faith by immediate conference with them, revelations, dreams, oracles, visions and prophecies. And this same promise of the woman's seed at first given more obscurely and more generally, by little and little he made clearer, when he restrained it to a certain nation, to a certain tribe, to a certain family, to a certain person, to a certain place, and at last to a certain time."
David Pareus in his commentary on Genesis 3:15

[1745] Nimis vehemens sensibile destruit sensum.
[1746] Matthew 13:31-33
[1747] Daniel 2:34-35, 44-45
[1748] Ezekiel 47:3-5

not greatly prize the least beginnings or discoveries of the gospel? The whole gospel (which now has filled all the world) was at first wrapped up in the narrow womb of this mother-promise.

[3] Hence, *the church and people of God after the fall, in the beginning of the world were very darkly and obscurely instructed in the mystery of Christ.* They did but grope after him, as in the dawning of the day: they did but dimly discover him afar off; and yet sufficiently for their salvation in those times, if they believed; and for their condemnation, if they believed not. How much better has God provided for us under the New Testament, upon whom the ends of the world are come, having most clearly, fully and with open face displayed Jesus Christ and the glad tidings of sinners' recovery by him, as in the noontide of clearest evangelical glory! Oh how faithful, obedient, and thankful should we be beyond them? But if we neglect so great a salvation, such clear gospel manifestations, how shall we escape?![1749] Where shall we appear?!

[1749] Hebrews 2:1-3

Aphorism 3

Hence, this first promise of lapsed man's recovery was revealed in Christ, the woman's seed.

For clearing of this, let us see: (1) that this first promise was revealed in Christ, the woman's seed. (2) What meant the revealing of this promise, in Christ, the woman's seed. (3) Why this first promise was revealed in Christ, the seed of the woman. (4) What corollaries result hence.

(1) <u>**That this first promise of lapsed man's recovery was revealed in Christ, the seed of the woman**</u>, is evident for:

[1] This text declares expressly, that *the seed of the woman shall bruise the serpent's head*.[1750] Now this is the principal promise of this Scripture: comprising in it lapsed man's recovery; and this promise is revealed in Christ *the seed of the woman*. For God does not barely promise that *the serpent's head shall be bruised*, but also that *the serpent's head shall be bruised by the seed of the woman*. At one and the same time that the bruising of the serpent's head is promised, the seed of the woman, Christ, is promised to bruise his head. Consequently, this first promise of man's recovery is revealed in Christ the seed of the woman.

[2] This seed of the woman that should bruise the serpent's head is no other than Christ, namely: *primarily*, Christ personal, God-man; *secondarily*, Christ mystical, his church, his mystical body, they that are Christ's. Not only the person of the mediator is styled {*Christ*} in Scripture;[1751] but also the mystical body of Christ (in regard of her spiritual oneness and sameness with him) is denominated {*Christ*}.[1752] *As the body is one, and has many members, and all the members of that one body, being many, are one body: so also is*

[1750] Genesis 3:15
[1751] John 1:41 & 3:28
[1752] 1 Corinthians 12:12-14

Christ, that is, *Christ mystical.* Now as *the seed of the serpent* is here taken collectively, for all the wicked: so *the seed of the woman* is to be taken collectively, not only for the *eminent seed,* Christ's person, who is the seed recovering: but also for the *secondary seed,* Christ's mystical body, which is the *seed recovered.* Both bruise the serpent's head: Christ personal *primitively* by his own power; Christ mystical *derivatively* by the power of Jesus Christ the head, as afterwards shall appear. Consequently this promise of sinners' recovery by bruising the serpent's head, is revealed in Christ, primarily, peculiarly, and especially in Christ personal, the God-man.

(2) **What meant the revealing of this first promise in Christ, the seed of the woman?**

Answer: The revealing of this first promise in Christ, the seed of the woman, seems to have intended these four things, namely: [1] that this promise was grounded on Christ, and led to him, as the bruiser of the serpent's head, the recoverer of lapsed sinners. [2] That Christ, in order to this bruising the serpent's head, and recovering of lapsed sinners, should in future time be incarnate and take flesh [from] a woman.[1753] [3] That Christ, the bruiser of the serpent's head, should not only be the incarnate seed of the woman, but beyond that, the omnipotent God. [4] That those sinners who in and by Christ should bruise the serpent's head, should become a joint-seed with Christ, contradistinct from the seed of the serpent.

[1] ***That this first promise was grounded on Christ, and led to him, as the bruiser of the serpent's head, the recoverer of lapsed sinners.*** The words of the text speak this plainly, saying, *I will put enmity between thee and the woman, and between thy seed, and her seed: it shall bruise thine head.*[1754] All the promises of God have their foundation and confirmation in Christ the mediator: being *in him yea, and in him amen.*[1755] And so this primitive promise, this ancient gray-headed promise, was founded and settled on him.

[1753] The original has "of a woman"
[1754] Genesis 3:15
[1755] 2 Corinthians 1:20

Before man's fall, the promise of the Covenant of Works was grounded and settled on man himself: since the fall, the promise of the Covenant of Faith is founded only upon Christ. It's a new kind of promise, and has a new foundation. As God's Covenant made to Abraham was *confirmed in Christ*,[1756] or (as the Greek implies) *confirmed towards Christ*; that is, established upon him, and leading unto him; so this first promise was confirmed in Christ also. This promise is like that *star in the east*, that directed the wise men unto Christ.[1757] This promise is as the shell; Christ as the kernel in it. This promise, the precious cabinet; but Christ the most precious jewel in this cabinet.

[2] *That Christ, in order to this bruising of the serpent's head, and recovering of lapsed sinners, should in future time be incarnate, and take flesh of a woman.* He therefore that's here promised to bruise the serpent's head, and consequently to rescue sinners from the serpent, is styled {*the seed of the woman*}. Not the seed of the woman, for present; but for future. If Christ the seed of the woman should bruise the serpent's head, then Christ was presupposed and implied first to become the seed of the woman by being made flesh, and then being incarnate to bruise the serpent's head.

Doubt: Then, the serpent's head was not bruised, Satan not destroyed, nor lapsed sinners recovered, till the fullness of time, which was above three thousand nine hundred years after the world's creation, and man's corruption; for until about that time (as Scripture[1758] and several chronologers[1759] evidence) Christ became not the seed of the woman, was not made flesh. What became then of all mankind before Christ? Did they perish? Or could they be saved by the seed of the woman, before the seed of the woman was?

{*Answer* 1}: Christ the eternal Son of God became the seed of the woman in several ways, namely: by decree, by promise, and by performance. By God's decree, eternally determining it before the foundation of the world. Hence the

---

[1756] Galatians 3:17
[1757] Matthew 2:9
[1758] Galatians 4:4-5, Daniel 9:24-26, Luke 1 & 2 throughout
[1759] H. Broughton's *Consent of Scripture*, General view of Holy Scripture, p.338, etc., London 1640, *Sacred Chronology*, p.73, 1648

scattered Jews are said to be *redeemed by the precious blood of Christ, as of a lamb without blemish, and without spot, who verily was foreordained before the foundation of the world, but manifest in these last times.*[1760] By God's promise in the beginning of time declaring it. *The seed of the woman shall bruise the serpent's head.*[1761] And by God's performance of his purpose and promise, actually exhibiting Christ in our flesh in fullness of time.[1762] Now God's decree of Christ's incarnation before all time, and his promise hereof in the beginning of time, were as sure as his actual performance in fullness of time. Therefore in all these respects he became the woman's seed.

{*Answer* 2}: Christ the seed of the woman, did proportionally bruise the serpent's head, *intentionally, virtually,* and *actually. Intentionally,* according to God's decree, Christ being intended and ordained to that end. Virtually, according to God's promise, the virtue of Christ's victory over Satan extending itself to all the elect from the very foundation of the world. *Jesus Christ being the same yesterday, and today, and forever.*[1763] Hence, he is called, the *lamb slain from the foundation of the world*:[1764] for this reason among others, because the virtue of his blood shed in fullness of time extended itself even to the elect from the world's first foundation, as the sun at midday extends his light and influence backwards towards the east, and forwards towards the west, as well as to the very place where he is. And in this sense, that of our savior's to the Jews may be interpreted: *before Abraham was, I am.*[1765] As if Christ had said: *I am, not only in mine eternal divinity, but also in the virtue and efficacy of my mediatorship, long before Abraham.* As Calvin well expounds the place.[1766] And by this virtue of Christ's office was Satan

---

[1760] 1 Peter 1:18-20
[1761] Genesis 3:14-15, Luke 1:69-71
[1762] Galatians 4:4
[1763] Hebrews 13:8
[1764] Revelation 13:8
[1765] John 8:58
[1766] "Some think that this applies simply to the eternal Divinity of Christ, and compare it with that passage in the writings of Moses, *I am what I am,* (Exodus 3:14). But I extend it much farther, because the power and grace of Christ, so far as he is the Redeemer of the world, was common to all ages." John Calvin on John 8:58

destroyed from the beginning of the world. Actually Christ *bruised the serpent's head* by his actual incarnation and officiating in our flesh; as after will more fully appear.[1767]

{*Answer* 3}: All mankind therefore before Christ's actual incarnation did not perish. All the elect were saved by the same Jesus Christ from the foundation of the world. By faith they realized Christ promised unto them as present and performed. Abraham *rejoiced to see* his *day* by faith, and *he saw it, and was glad.*[1768]

[3] *That Christ, the bruiser of the serpent's head, should not be only the incarnate seed of the woman; but beyond that, the omnipotent God.* Otherwise, as mere man, he could not have fully bruised the serpent's head, and have perfected the recovery of sinners. Because lapsed man was now wholly enthralled under the dominion of Satan.

[4] *That those sinners, who in and by Christ should bruise the serpent's head, should become a joint seed with Christ, contradistinct from the seed of the serpent.* Therefore he does not say {*seeds*} in the plural, but {*seed*} in the singular number: and *it*, not *they, shall bruise the serpent's head.* Referring this victory over, and destruction of the serpent, to the woman's seed; that is, *principally*, to Christ who bruises him by his own power; *less principally*, to them that are Christ's, who bruise him by Christ's power. None can actually share with Christ in bruising the serpent's head, till they conform to Christ, ceasing to be the *serpent's brood*, and becoming the *woman's seed*.

(3) <u>Why was this first promise of sinners' recovery thus revealed in Christ, as the woman's seed?</u>

Answer: For these causes especially.

[1] Because *lapsed man, without reference and respect to Christ, this seed of the woman, is wholly incapable of any promise of mercy from God.* And this, whether we consider man's sin; God's truth: or God's justice. {1} Man's sin in

---

[1767] 1 John 3:8, John 16:11, Colossians 2:15, Hebrews 2:14-15
[1768] John 8:57

falling from God, was an offense against an infinite majesty, an infinite glory: and therefore in itself deserved a kind of infinite punishment, even *eternal death*.[1769] This is the most proper adequate wages of sin. Now where sin has deserved infinite punishment: the sinner in himself considered, must needs be incapable of all promise of mercy. {2} God's truth threatened man with certain death in case of disobedience, against the Covenant of Works:[1770] man falling from his obedience, the threatened judgment must needs be inflicted according to the inviolable truth of God, who cannot lie nor alter,[1771] had not God provided surety to undertake for him. {3} God's justice is so infinite and exact, that it must needs *render to every one according to his works, without respect of persons*;[1772] unless full satisfaction be made to offended justice, which is infinite. Finite lapsed man, considered without any respect to Christ, can never make satisfaction to infinite justice; therefore no promise of mercy can have place towards lapsed man without reference to Christ. That therefore lapsed man might be rendered capable of God's promise and mercy, the promise of his recovery is revealed in Christ the woman's seed.

[2] Because, *there is no other way in the whole world for lapsed sinners' recovery but by Jesus Christ*, the seed of the woman. *Neither is there salvation in any other: for there is none other name under heaven given among men, whereby we must be saved*.[1773] Besides him, without him, all the creatures on earth, all the saints and angels in heaven, are not able to save one soul, or to expiate one sin. Therefore the promise of sinners' recovery, that it might be sufficiently revealed, was revealed in Jesus Christ the woman's seed.

[3] Because, God (from eternity foreseeing man's fall) *had eternally decreed lapsed sinners' recovery by Jesus Christ the seed of the woman*. Thus Peter says: *Ye were not redeemed with corruptible things, as silver and gold, from your vain conversation,—but with the precious blood of Christ, as of a lamb without blemish and without spot. Who verily was fore-ordained before*

[1769] Romans 6:23
[1770] Genesis 2:17-18
[1771] Titus 1:2, James 1:17
[1772] Romans 2:6, 12
[1773] Acts 9:12

the foundation of the world, but was manifest in these last times for you.[1774] Hereupon Peter calls them, *Elect according to the foreknowledge of God the Father, through sanctification of the Spirit unto obedience, and sprinkling of the blood of Jesus Christ.*[1775] By which passages it's clear that God eternally fore-ordained the redemption of lapsed sinners by Christ's spotless blood: which blood he had, not as the eternal Son of God, but as the seed of the woman. Therefore proportionably, this first promise of sinners' recovery was revealed in Christ as the seed of the woman in order to accomplish this decree.

[4] Because God *peculiarly intended, in the recovery of lapsed mankind, to glorify his son Jesus Christ the seed of the woman, most eminently.* And this especially: {1} in his *person*;[1776] {2} in his *office*;[1777] {3} in the *states* wherein he executed his office;[1778] and, {4} in the effects of his office. In all which, Christ God-man incomparably surpasses all men, all saints, all angels, and all creatures in the whole world.[1779] Hereupon God revealed this first promise of sinners' recovery in Christ the seed of the woman, as the first inlet and inchoation of Christ's intended glory.

(4) **Corollaries hence resulting**. Seeing, *this first promise of lapsed man's recovery was revealed in Christ the woman's seed*; then,

[1] *Lapsed man's recovery from his state of sin and death, is not from within, but from without himself: even from Christ the seed of the woman.* Man could *ruin* himself; but being ruined, could not *repair* himself. Man could *fall*; but being fallen could not *raise himself* again. Man that was wholly upright, could become a sinner: but being a sinner, could not possibly make himself *righteous*. Man that was perfect yielded himself to be *bruised by the serpent*, but being so bruised, had no power to *bruise the serpent's head*, nor to rescue himself from his tyranny. No less, no other, than Christ, the

---

[1774] 1 Peter 1:18-20
[1775] 1 Peter 1:1-2
[1776] John 1:14, 1 Timothy 3:16, Isaiah 9:6
[1777] John 5:22-23
[1778] John 13:31-32 & 17:1-2, Acts 3:13-15
[1779] John 17:10 & 16:14, 2 Thessalonians 1:12

supereminent seed of the woman, could possibly effect lapsed man's recovery. Christ therefore is here promised for that end. But God would never have promised Christ for lapsed man's recovery, could lapsed man have possibly wrought his own recovery. Now lapsed man could never have recovered himself from sin and death: {1} Because lapsed man has neither skill, nor power, nor will to recover himself. Not skill, for his *mind* and *heart* are blinded by sin and Satan the God of this world,[1780] so that he neither knows, nor can know the things of God, but counts them foolishness.[1781] Yea he is mere *darkness*, and cannot comprehend God's light not power,[1782] for lapsed man is *without strength*, without all acceptable saving strength to spirituals.[1783] He is *not of himself sufficient to think anything as of himself.*[1784] He is *dead in trespasses and sins.*[1785] *In the gall of bitterness and bond of iniquity.*[1786] *Taken captive by the devil at his will.*[1787] Nor finally has lapsed man any will or true desire to recover himself. *Every imagination of the thoughts of his heart being only evil*, and that *continually.*[1788] *Having his conversation in the lusts of his flesh, and fulfilling the desires* (Greek: the *wills*) of the flesh and of the mind. {2} Because *lapsed man could never fulfill the broken Covenant of Works, so as to be sufficient for his own recovery*. For he could neither fulfill it in an *active*, nor in a *passive* way. Not in an *active way*, being wholly unable to yield unto it perfect and perpetual personal obedience,[1789] partly because he has already broken it and partly because he has no principle of ability left in him at all whereby he might for the future keep it. Nor in a *passive way*, for lapsed man could not, by any manner of sufferings for quantity or quality, for kind or degree, in soul or body, ever satisfy God's infinite justice offended: infinite

---

[1780] 2 Corinthians 4:4, Ephesians 4:18
[1781] 1 Corinthians 2:14
[1782] Ephesians 5:8, John 1:5
[1783] Romans 5:6
[1784] 2 Corinthians 3:5
[1785] Ephesians 2:1
[1786] Acts 8:23
[1787] 2 Timothy 2:26
[1788] Genesis 6:5
[1789] Genesis 2:17, Galatians 3:10

justice offended, requiring infinite satisfaction for such offense. Now no mere finite person can give infinite satisfaction, nay a finite sinner can give no satisfaction at all. Now without complete fulfilling of the Covenant of Works passively and actively, there is no possibility of recovering lapsed sinners. For either this broken Covenant must be *repaired* or the penalty of it must be *endured*. {3} Because *lapsed man is wholly opposite to his own recovery, and wilfully set upon his own ruin*. The *wisdom of the flesh is enmity against God: for it is not subject to the law of God, neither indeed can be.*[1790] The Lord Christ, the recoverer of sinners, *came unto his own, but his own received him not.*[1791] And he says of the Jews, *Ye will not come unto me that ye might have life.*[1792] And to Jerusalem, *How often would I have gathered thy children together, even as a hen gathers her chickens under her wings: and ye would not!*[1793] Yea the Jews said of Christ: *We will not have this man to reign over us.*[1794] And God by the prophet lamentingly expostulates with them for their wilful disposition to their own destruction: *Why will ye die O house of Israel?*[1795] {4} Because, *lapsed man cannot of himself accept recovery already wrought by Christ, and tendered in Christ: much less can he work out his own recovery*. Christ is accepted by faith: and faith is not of ourselves, it is the gift of God.[1796] And Christ says: *No man can come unto me, except the father which has sent me draw him.*[1797] {5} Finally, *because lapsed man could never have devised nor imagined his recovery by Christ according to the Covenant of Faith, which is a mere supernatural mystery made known only by divine revelation*: much less could he have effected or brought about his own recovery. How do these considerations dash asunder those fond opinions of *universal grace*, of carnal man's ability and *free will* in *spirituals*! How may these things abase carnal man to the dust, annihilate all his excellencies in reference to his

---

[1790] Romans 8:7-8
[1791] John 1:11
[1792] John 5:40
[1793] Matthew 23:37
[1794] Luke 19:14
[1795] Ezekiel 18:31-32
[1796] John 1:12 with Ephesians 2:8
[1797] John 6:44

happiness, drive him to despair in himself, and enforce him to seek beyond and above himself for salvation!

[2] *The same Jesus Christ, God-man, who saves sinners now in the end of the world, was the sole savior of sinners in and from the beginning of the world.* The promise of *bruising the serpent's head*, and consequently of rescuing poor sinners from the serpent's thraldom, was established in the *seed of the woman*: and Jesus Christ is primarily and eminently this seed of the woman. That of the apostle's is emphatical: *Jesus Christ the same yesterday, and today, and forever.*[1798] Christ the same in office and substantial benefits or effects of his office, *yesterday*, in all the time of the Old Testament from the beginning of the world until his incarnation; *today*, in all these times of the New Testament from Christ until the end of the world; and *forever*, in the world to come. Though the same Christ was under the Old Testament represented as *promised* and under the New Testament as *performed*. Under the Old Testament *darkly* and *typically*; under the New *clearly* and *fully*. Yet in both *sufficiently* for salvation.

[3] *The promise of sinners' recovery since the fall, has a firmer foundation than the promise of sinners' life and felicity before the fall.* Before the fall, the promise of life and happiness was grounded upon man's mutable obedience,[1799] but since the fall the promise of sinners' recovery is founded upon Christ and his immutable merit.[1800] That, upon man's finite righteousness; this, upon Christ's infinite righteousness. How sweet is the gospel, beyond the law! How precious is the Covenant of Faith, beyond the Covenant of Works! How glorious is the grace of God as a redeemer, beyond the bounty of God as a creator!

[4] **Finally,** *lapsed sinners should peculiarly eye Christ, in this and all God's promises for their recovery*. For in them, all Christ is the promised recoverer, the kernel, the marrow, and the soul of the promises.

[1798] Hebrews 13:8
[1799] Genesis 2:17
[1800] Genesis 3:14-15

Aphorism 4

Hence, *this first promise in Christ, revealed lapsed man's recovery, in the enmity threatened between the woman and the serpent, between her seed and his seed, and in the events of that enmity.*

This aphorism comprises in it the substance of this text, and the chief mystery of sinners' recovery, as revealed in this first promise. Therefore for the more satisfactory clearing of it, consider: (1) that in God's explicit threatenings against the serpent, are contained implicit promises for sinners' recovery. (2) What degree of sinners' recovery is promised, under the enmity between the serpent and woman, between his seed and her seed, threatened? (3) What are the events or fruits of this enmity? And how far the recovery of lapsed sinners is therein further revealed. (4) What corollaries or necessary consequences may flow from all?

(1) That, **in God's explicit threatenings against the serpent, are contained his implicit promises for sinners' recovery**, may be evinced, [1] *from the mutual relation and reference, between promises and threats.* They are in the nature of relatives; the one being expressed, the other are proportionally implied. Relatives mutually place and displace one another. God *expressly threatened* death in case of disobedience; and therein *implicitly promised* life in case of obedience.[1801] So here, he expressly threatened judgements to the serpent deceiving man: and implicitly promised mercies to man deceived by the serpent. [2] *From the procuring cause of these threatenings.* The procuring cause that moved God to thunder out these threatenings against the serpent, was his seducing and overthrowing of mankind. *The woman said, the serpent beguiled me and I did eat. And the LORD God said unto the serpent, because thou hast done this, thou art cursed*

[1801] Genesis 2:16-17

above all cattle, etc.[1802] The serpent then being expressly threatened for ruining man; God seems implicitly to promise the restoring of man. As man's ruin provoked God's indignation against the serpent *ruining*, so man's ruin as it were moved God's commiseration towards sinners *ruined*. But if these two arguments be less cogent, the third that here follows is more clear and convincing. [3] *From the particulars of God's threatenings against the serpent*, this is most clear. These passages in the text are formally threatenings as directed to the serpent, but materially they are promises as intended for mankind. May we not at least obscurely read in the serpent's *curse*, man's *blessing*? In the serpent's *debasement*, man's *advancement*? In the enmity of the woman and her seed against the serpent, their consequent enmity against sin and contrary amity with God? And in the bruising of the serpent's head by the woman's seed, the full deliverance of the woman and her seed from the serpent and all his mischief; and if so, then the explicit threatenings of the serpent's ruin for deceiving man, have in them implicit promises of lapsed man's recovery from the serpent's deceivings.

(2) **What degree of sinners' recovery is implicitly promised, under the enmity between the serpent and woman, between his seed and her seed, explicitly threatened?**

Answer: Not to insist upon mercies implied in the two first threatenings:[1803] in this enmity of the woman and her seed against the serpent and his seed expressly threatened, these steps or degrees of lapsed man's recovery seem to be implicitly promised. namely: [1] an enmity of the woman and her seed against sin, the work of the old serpent.[1804] [2] A contrary reconciliation and amity of the woman and her seed, to and with God. View a little the enmity threatened, and then the degrees of recovery implied.

[1] *The enmity expressly threatened* is twofold, namely: {1} *corporeal*, between the corporeal serpent and the woman with her seed, serpents having a

---

[1802] Genesis 3:13-15
[1803] Genesis 3:14
[1804] 1 John 3:8, John 8:44

natural antipathy against mankind, and mankind against serpents, so as to endeavor mutually one another's corporal ruin. {2} *Spiritual*, of the woman and her seed, namely: Christ and his members against the old serpent the devil, and his seed, namely: all the wicked of the world. This spiritual enmity consists especially in their contrariety of (i) *natures*, (ii) *affections*, and (iii) *actions*. (i) *They have contrary natures*. They are from above;[1805] these are from beneath.[1806] *They are not of this world*, but by Christ *chosen out of the world*: these are of this world.[1807] *They* are supernaturally holy and righteous:[1808] *these* naturally unholy and unrighteous.[1809] Thus their natures are contrary: and hence flows all other contrariety. (ii) *They have contrary affections*.[1810] *They* love God, godliness, the godly, and the light manifesting these from their contraries:[1811] *these* hate God, Godliness, the godly, and the light discovering their deeds and ways of wickedness.[1812] (iii) *They have contrary actions. They* walk in sobriety, righteousness and holiness, oppugning the contrary intemperance, unrighteousness and impiety in Satan and his seed.[1813] *These* do walk in all impiety against God, unrighteousness, cruelty and persecution against Christ and the godly, and intemperance in themselves.[1814] This their spiritual enmity against each other reciprocally. Now God is not the author of this sinful enmity of Satan and his seed, against the woman and her seed; that proceeds originally from themselves. But God is the author of the judicial enmity of the woman and her seed, Christ and his members against the serpent and his seed. Notwithstanding, God is the most wise orderer, over-ruler and disposer of them both.

[1805] John 3:3, 7
[1806] Psalm 17:14
[1807] John 15:19
[1808] Ephesians 4:24, Colossians 3:12
[1809] 1 Timothy 1:9-10
[1810] 1 Timothy 1:9-10
[1811] Psalm 18:1 & 116:1, 1 John 5:1-3, Psalm 119:20, 97; John 3:21
[1812] Romans 1:30, Luke 19:14, Romans 8:7, John 15:18-19, 1 John 3:12-16, John 3:20
[1813] Titus 2:12-13, Luke 1:6, Psalm 26:5 & 119:136
[1814] Ephesians 2:1-3, 1 Peter 4:4, 1 John 3:12, Galatians 4:29

[2] *The degrees of sinners' recovery implicitly promised under this threatened enmity,* are chiefly two, namely: {1} *an enmity of the woman and her seed against sin, the work of the old serpent the devil.*[1815] For if they are set in enmity against Satan and his seed the wicked, not as creatures, but as wicked, then consequently, they must much more have enmity against sin and wickedness, called the deeds and lusts of the devil.[1816] They cannot have enmity against sin, but by having principles of grace and holiness infused, contrary unto sin. This implies the new-creation and renovation of their natures, the principling of them with faith and repentance especially, whereby sin is more peculiarly opposed. And these are sweet degrees of sinners' recovery. {2} *A contrary reconciliation and amity of the woman and her seed with God.* For, how can there be an enmity against Satan, and against his seed, and against sin, all of which are most contrary to God: but there must be contrariwise, a reconciliation and amity with God, implied? They cannot be at enmity against Satan, his seed and sin, but only by contrary natures and principles bestowed upon them from God. And God never bestows truly gracious principles, opposite to sin, Satan, and his seed: but only upon such as he reconciles to himself and actually accepts in Jesus Christ by effectual calling and conversion. Put all these together: *enmity against Satan and his seed, enmity against sin,* by *principles contrary both to sin and Satan*; and *amity with God*: how excellent degrees are these of lapsed man's *recovery*!

[3] *What are the events or fruits of this enmity? And how far the recovery of lapsed sinners is therein further revealed? Answer*: The events or fruits of this enmity here mentioned are only two, namely: {1} the bruising of the serpent's head by the seed of the woman. {2} The bruising of the heel of the woman's seed, by the serpent. *It shall bruise thine head, and thou shalt bruise his heel.*[1817] But yet in these two, the recovery of sinners is very notably discovered and promised.

[1815] Psalm 119:124, 1 John 3:8
[1816] 1 John 3:8, John 8:44
[1817] Genesis 3:15

{1} *The bruising of the serpent's head by the seed of the woman*, denotes the destruction of Satan the old serpent, together with all his mischief, power and policy by temptations,[1818] sin,[1819] death,[1820] and all the harbingers of death, afflictions whereby he opposes the elect of God. These are the serpent's head, wherein all his mischief and danger lies, and these shall be wholly ruined by the seed of the woman, namely: *primarily*, by Christ, the eminent seed. *Secondarily*, by all that are Christ's, through Christ's power and victory. (i) Christ bruises the serpent's head in his own person for his elect. (ii) Christ bruises the serpent's head in the persons of his elect: and by them, through his power.

(i) *Christ bruises the serpent's head, (namely, temptations, sin, death and afflictions) in his own person, for his elect*: and that in several ways. (a) *By his incarnation and taking human flesh*. Hereby he became our near kinsman, our brother, that so the right of our redemption might be his, and he become actually capable of destroying Satan, as the seed of the woman.[1821] *In fullness of time, he was made of a woman, made under the law, to redeem them that were under the law.*[1822] *For this end was the son of God manifested, that he might destroy the works of the devil.*[1823] And it is observed by some, that when Christ was born, all the devil's false and lying oracles, cried up in the world, did cease. (b) *By his life and conversation on earth*. Herein Christ overcame the devil's capital temptations, by his innocency, by Scripture, by his divine power and wisdom: that in his conquests, his members might be more than conquerors.[1824] He also overcame all the malice, reproaches, calumnies, penalties and perfections of Satan's instruments, by his spotless purity, holiness, patience, and other divine accomplishments. (c) By his death, and the virtue, efficacy, and merit thereof. Hereby Christ bruised the serpent's head

---

[1818] Genesis 3:2-6, Matthew 4:1-12, 2 Corinthians 11:3 & 2:11, Revelation 2:24
[1819] 1 John 3:8, Ephesians 2:2, 6:11-12
[1820] Hebrews 2:14
[1821] Leviticus 25:25, etc., Ruth 4:4, 6, Hebrews 2:14-17, Galatians 4:4-5
[1822] Galatians 4:4-5
[1823] 1 John 3:8
[1824] Matthew 4:1-12

meritoriously and *mysteriously*. For, (1) he destroyed sin by becoming *sin for us*.[1825] By being made a *sacrifice for sin, he condemned sin in the flesh: that the righteousness of the law might be fulfilled in us*. (2) He crucified the cross by being crucified on the cross, he destroyed death by dying, and he buried the very grave by being buried in the grave.[1826] Why? Because he was crucified, died, and was buried, as an all-sufficient surety for sinners, for his elect. Therefore he – fully discharging our debt – wholly canceled our bonds and crossed the debt book which was against us. *Christ has redeemed us from the curse of the law, by becoming a curse for us*.[1827] (3) He also by death *destroyed him that had the power of death, that is the devil.—and having spoiled principalities and powers, he made a show of them openly, triumphing over them in it*.[1828] So then, Christ by dying destroyed the devil, spoiled him, and triumphed openly over him: for as much as by death he has reformed us from Satan's power, and redeemed us to himself. Hereupon said Origen, "Two are understood to be fixed to the cross: visibly Christ, of his own will, for a time; invisibly the devil against his will, for evermore."[1829] Therefore the eye of faith (says Davenant)[1830] beholds Christ on the top of the cross, as it were sitting in his triumphant chariot; but the devil at the lower part thereof, fast chained to the cross, and trampled under Christ's feet. (d) *By his resurrection the third day from the dead*. By death, Christ conquered and crushed the serpent's head: by his resurrection he evidently declared and demonstrated the truth of this his conquest. *Having loosed the pains of death, because it was not possible that he should be holden of it*.[1831] Herein Christ showed himself a true Samson indeed: for as he arose at midnight and carried away both gates, posts and bars of the city wherein he was imprisoned;[1832] so Christ about midnight, early in

---

[1825] 2 Corinthians 5:21, Isaiah 53:6, Romans 8:3-4
[1826] Hebrews 2:14-17
[1827] Galatians 3:13
[1828] Hebrews 2:14-15 with Colossians 2:15
[1829] Duo in cruce affixi intelliguntur; Christ us visibiliter, sponte sua, ad tempus; Diabolus invisibiliter, in|vitus, in Perpetuum. Origen
[1830] Davenant, in his exposition on Colossians 2:15
[1831] Acts 2:24
[1832] Judges 16:2-3

the morning arose carrying away as it were the gates and bars of the grave wherewith he was imprisoned.[1833] (e) *By his ascension into heaven*. For, when Christ ascended upon high, *he led captivity captive*,[1834] that is, Satan and every enemy that captivated his people, he then led captive. He chained them all to his triumphant chariot as his subdued slaves, and victoriously gloried over them. And after his ascension, he sent forth his Spirit *to convince the world of righteousness, because he went to the Father; and of judgment, because the prince of this world is judged*.[1835] (f) *By his glorious session at God's right hand in highest heavenly majesty*. For, hereby God has exalted him, *Far above all principality, and power, and might, and dominion, and every name that is named, not only in this world, but also in that which is to come*.[1836] And has put all things under his feet, and gave him to be the head over all things to the church. So that hereby Christ the head of the church is become head over all things to the church: even over the devil, and all his church's enemies. They are all put under his feet and brought under his subjection. (g) Finally, *by his coming to judge the world at the last day*, Christ shall completely and perfectly bruise the head of the old serpent the devil for evermore. For, the devil and his angels which are *reserved in chains of darkness, till the judgment of the great day*,[1837] shall then be cast *into the lake of fire and brimstone*, prepared for them by God, where they with all the wicked *whose names are not written in the book of life, shall be tormented day and night for ever and ever*.[1838]

Thus by these seven degrees, Christ the eminent seed of the woman in his own person bruises the serpent's head, until at last he has obtained over him a total and final victory for us. Christ bruises the serpent's head in the persons of his elect, and by them, through his own power and victoriousness communicated to them. And this he does in them by several degrees. Namely:

[1833] Matthew 28:1-2
[1834] Psalm 68:19, Ephesians 4:8
[1835] John 16:8-11
[1836] Ephesians 1:20-22, Philippians 2:9-11
[1837] Jude 6
[1838] Revelation 20:10, 15; Matthew 25:41

(i) By *calling and converting them effectually from darkness to light, and from the power of Satan unto God, through the preaching of the gospel.*[1839] Even the elect of Christ, whilst in their carnal state, are wholly under the reign and dominion of Satan, *taken captive by him at his will.*[1840] Yea, Satan keeps them in his power, as a strong man armed keeps his palace and goods in peace: until Christ – a stronger-than-Satan – comes, disarms him, and despoils him. So that of our savior's in Luke seems intended: *When a strong man armed keeps his palace, his goods are in peace. But when a stronger then he shall come upon him, and overcome him, he taketh from him all his armour wherein he trusted, and divideth his spoils.*[1841] Satan's first practice against mankind was to turn them away from God by unbelief, etc.[1842] The returning of lapsed man again to God by faith and repentance in conversion, is his first blow that he gives to the bruising of the serpent's head. Then *they are delivered by God from the power of darkness into the kingdom of the Son of his love.*[1843]

(ii) *By sanctifying them throughout in soul and spirit and body.*[1844] *Christ is made of God, sanctification to them.*[1845] He gives them his Spirit,[1846] furnishing them with the holy habits of all saving graces. By which gracious principles infused, they are *mortified* to sin, but *vivified* to holiness and righteousness, so that they walk not any longer as formerly, according to the course of this world, *according to the prince of the power of the air, the spirit that now worketh in the children of disobedience*:[1847] but they begin to *walk as Christ walked*, who *destroyed the works of the devil.*[1848] By this sanctification, the saints bruise the old serpent's head; whilst Satan's black image is obliterated out of the soul, and the beauteous image of God implanted instead

---

[1839] Acts 26:17-18, Ephesians 4:7-8, etc.
[1840] Ephesians 2:1-3 with 2 Timothy 2:25-26
[1841] Luke 11:21-22
[1842] Genesis 3 throughout
[1843] Colossians 1:12-13
[1844] 1 Thessalonians 5:23
[1845] 1 Corinthians 1:30
[1846] Romans 8:9, Galatians 5:22-23
[1847] Ephesians 2:1-3
[1848] 1 John 2:6 & 3:8

thereof. Whilst the soul, which was a den of devils and cage of all filthiness, becomes a spiritual temple for the Holy Ghost.

(iii) *By adopting them into God's family and household.* Lapsed man naturally has the devil for his father;[1849] and therefore is of the devil's family, yea is the devil's palace:[1850] but he supernaturally becomes a *fellow-citizen with the saints, and of the household of God*, by the Spirit of adoption.[1851] This is an eminent degree of sinners' recovery, and consequently of bruising the serpent's head.

(iv) *By justifying them freely*, sprinkling his blood upon their consciences by faith so that all their sins are remitted, and their persons accounted as righteous as if sin had not been committed by them.[1852] He is made unto them *righteousness: yea, the Lord their righteousness*.[1853] He – having for them more righteousness than they have unrighteousness and more pardons than they have debts – fully acquits them in the court of heaven, from death and damnation: *there being no condemnation to them that are in Christ.*[1854] Hereby then *they are delivered from death, and from him that* (as an executioner) *had the power of death, the devil*:[1855] and may triumph with the apostle: *Who shall lay any thing to the charge of God's elect? It is God that justifieth; who is he that condemneth? It is Christ that died.*[1856] Their justification is virtually Satan's condemnation.

(v) *By assisting them powerfully in their sharpest conflicts with Satan, so that they victoriously prevail.* Satan fights against Christ's members two ways. By temptations, and by tribulations. (a) By temptations, and herein he has his

---

[1849] John 8:4
[1850] Luke 11:21-22
[1851] Ephesians 2:19, Romans 8:15
[1852] Romans 3:22-27, 1 Peter 1:2, Hebrews 12:14, 2 Corinthians 5:21
[1853] 1 Corinthians 1:30, Jeremiah 23:6
[1854] Romans 8:1
[1855] Hebrews 2:14-15
[1856] Romans 8:33-34

devices,[1857] *depths,*[1858] extreme *subtleties,*[1859] and *indefatigableness*:[1860] endeavoring one while to draw them from the faith and truth of the gospel to error; another while from a good conscience unto unconscionable and sinful courses. Against the former of these the apostle notably intimates the Lord's potent assistance, saying: *I beseech you brethren, mark them which cause divisions and offenses, contrary to the doctrine which ye have learned, and avoid them. And the God of peace shall bruise Satan under your feet shortly.*[1861] That is, God shall bruise under your feet Satan, who is the principal author of schisms, errors and offenses, against the truth. Against the latter of these, the Lord among other parts of the spiritual armor, does especially afford us *the sword of the Spirit, the word of God,*[1862] whereby Christ so utterly spoiled Satan in his most capital temptations; and *faith, his peculiar gift, which is a shield whereby we quench all the fiery darts of the wicked.*[1863] For faith carries the tempted to the promises, and to Christ, and there cools and quenches the burning poison of Satan's temptations. (b) By *tribulations,* Satan also fights against Christ's members. But they are still sufficiently assisted therein, being either preserved from them, supported under them, delivered out of them, or advantaged by them. Christ says to the angel of the church in Smyrna: *Fear none of those things which thou shalt suffer: behold the devil shall cast some of you into prison, that ye may be tried and ye shall have tribulation ten days: be thou faithful unto death, and I will give thee a crown of life.*[1864] Christ overcame Satan in every way, but especially by his blood and death: Christ's members shall also proportionably overcome the serpent and bruise his head every way, but peculiarly by their sufferings and tribulations. When they seem most conquered by Satan, they shall be the greatest conquerors of Satan.

[1857] 2 Corinthians 2:11
[1858] Revelation 2:24
[1859] 2 Corinthians 11:3
[1860] 1 Peter 5:8
[1861] Romans 16:17-20
[1862] Ephesians 6:16-17
[1863] Ephesians 6:16 & 2:8
[1864] Revelation 2:10

(vi) Finally, Christ in his members shall bruise the serpent's head, *by advancing them triumphantly above the old serpent, the devil, and all his angels, at the day of judgment.* Then they shall totally and finally trample him under foot forever, so as never to be bothered by[1865] him more. And this especially three ways, namely: (a) *by their victorious resurrection from the dead.* Then all that sleep in Jesus, shall awake out of the dust, and put on incorruption, power, spiritualness and glory: quite shaking off all bonds of death, and fetters of the grave.[1866] *Then shall be brought to pass the saying that is written, death is swallowed up in victory. O death, where is thy sting? O grave, where is thy victory?*[1867] Consequently, as then they shall have full victory over death and grave, so they shall have victory over him that had power of death and grave, the devil. This bloody executioner shall no more kill them by death; this cruel jailor shall no more imprison them in the grave. (b) By their glorious judging of the world; yea even the devil and his angels shall be doomed by them. *Do ye not know, that the saints shall judge the world?—know ye not that we shall judge angels?*[1868] How shall this be! Christ shall judge as *supreme*: saints as *subordinate*, or as *assessors*. Christ by his mediatory authority: saints by *acclamation* to, and *approbation* of Christ's sentence. What? Shall the devil and his angels, the old serpent and his seed, be at last judged and doomed by the saints, and hear from them, go ye cursed? How shall they then bruise the serpent's head in pieces? (3) By their celestial cohabitation with Christ for evermore. After Christ has said, *come ye blessed*, etc.[1869] They shall ascend with Christ triumphantly into heaven, and so *be ever with the Lord*. They in heaven; Satan in hell. They in joys unspeakable; Satan in woes and torments intolerable. They far above all of Satan's malice and darts of temptation; Satan far below all hopes of help or consolation. Thus, the *seed of the woman*, Christ shall *bruise the serpent's head*. Christ personal, by his own power: Christ mystical by Christ's power.

[1865] Original reads: "molested with"
[1866] 1 Thessalonians 4:13-18, 1 Corinthians 15:42-43, etc.
[1867] 1 Corinthians 15:54-57
[1868] 1 Corinthians 6:2-3
[1869] Matthew 25:34, 46; 1 Thessalonians 4:17

{2} *The bruising of the heel of the woman's seed by the serpent, comes next to be considered: and thou shalt bruise his heel.*[1870] That is, thou corporeal serpent, shalt (from thine enmity against the woman and her natural seed) bruise and offend, not their principal part, head or heart; but their less principal part, the *heel*. And thou incorporeal serpent, Satan, shalt (from thine enmity against the woman and her spiritual seed, Christ and his elect) bruise and offend, not the principal, but less principal and lowest part of Christ and his elect, the heel. If the heel only be crushed, there's less danger – it's far from the heart, it may be healed again, and the party will live – but if the head or heart be crushed and bruised, that will be capital and mortal. So great is the disparity between these parties here at enmity, as Mercerus well notes.[1871] They shall both conflict and fight against one another, yet with this difference: the serpent can only reach and bruise the heel of the woman's seed, but the woman's seed shall crush the very head of the serpent. The disadvantage therefore shall wholly lie on the serpent's side. Thus generally. More particularly this metaphor of the serpent's bruising the heel of the woman's seed, looks: (i) primarily at Christ the eminent seed. (ii) Secondarily, at them that are Christ's: both shall be bruised by him.

(i) *Primarily, this has reference to Christ, the most eminent seed of the woman.* The serpent should bruise his heel. In the serpent's bruising of the heel of Christ, who should bruise the serpent's head, we may note three things especially. Namely: (a) God's permission of this bruising, (b) God's limitation of it, and (c) God's ordination of it.

(a) *God's permission of this bruising of Christ's heel, by the old serpent, the devil and Satan.* Could not the devil touch one of the Gadarene's swine, without Christ's permission? How then should he touch or

---

[1870] Genesis 3:15

[1871] "Vide magnum discrimen inter Christi & Satanae pugnam, quod in vocibus Capitis & Calcanci ostenditur. Caput Satanae Christus petit & conterit, in quo totum robur, quo contrito totum corpus Conteritur & perit; totum ejus regnum & potentiam evertit, ac ejus ministros, peccatum, mortem, ac insernum, etc. At Satanas non nisi Calcaneum ejus petit, id est, leviora & infirmiora, etsi valide eum oppugnet, & delere conetur totis viribus Christi regnum, non tamen petit nisi Calcaneum, &c." John Mercer. in Genesis 3:15.

bruise Christ's heel, without God's permission? Those words: *and thou shalt bruise his heel*,[1872] as they are directed to the serpent are not *preceptive* but only *permissive*. And as they have reference to the seed of the woman, they are prophetical and *promissory* rather than *minatory*: the serpent's bruising Christ's heel being Christ's way to the bruising of the serpent's head.

Question: But how did the serpent (God permitting it) bruise the heel of Christ, in his own person? ***Answer***: Satan the old serpent, bruised Christ's heel many ways: these ways especially. (1) *By his audacious and impudent temptations*,[1873] frequently troubling Christ, though not tainting or corrupting Christ at all. They afflicted Christ. They infected him not. The blasphemousness and wickedness of them could not choose but grieve Christ's spirit: but they neither did nor could defile Christ's spirit. (2) *By multiplied tribulations and afflictions* raised up against Christ, all his life long, through Satan's instigation. As soon as he was born, Herod Ascalonita sought to kill him, and lest he should miss him, murdered all the infants in Bethlehem two years old and under, so that Christ's mother was forced to fly with him into Egypt, till Herod's death.[1874] As soon as he appeared in his public ministry in order to the accomplishment of his mediatorship, this own people the Jews received him not,[1875] but rejected him,[1876] hated him,[1877] despised him,[1878] opposed him,[1879] reviled, reproached and blasphemed him,[1880] stiling him a sinner,[1881] a sabbath breaker,[1882] a blasphemer,[1883] a Samaritan that had a devil,[1884] mad,[1885] a gluttonous man, and a wine-bibber, and a friend of

---

[1872] Genesis 3:15
[1873] Matthew 4:1-12, Mark 1:12-13, Luke 4:1-14
[1874] Matthew 2:13-19
[1875] John 1:11
[1876] Matthew 21:42, Mark 8:31, Luke 14:25
[1877] Luke 10:14, John 15:18, 25
[1878] Mark 9:12
[1879] Hebrews 12:2-3
[1880] Luke 22:63-65
[1881] John 9:24
[1882] John 9:14-16
[1883] Mark 2:7, Luke 5:21
[1884] John 8:48
[1885] John 10:20, Mark 3

publicans and sinners,[1886] a caster out of devils through Beelzebub the prince of devils, etc.[1887] Yea they plotted against him how they might entangle him, apprehend him, and destroy him,[1888] *they sent officers to take him*, who were so taken with him, they were not able to lay hands on him,[1889] and at last *they gave Judas thirty pieces of money* to betray him unto them, that they might put him to death.[1890] To all these villainies, the devil instigated them, hence Christ says of them, *Ye do that which ye have seen with your father*. And—*Ye are of your father the devil, and the lusts of your father ye will do. He was a murderer from the beginning*, etc.[1891] Were not all these tribulations raised up by Satan against Christ, as so many bruisings of his heel? (3) Finally, by a *grievous, painful, shameful, causeless and cursed death of Christ upon the cross*, extremely embittered and aggravated to him, by passages antecedent, concomitant, and consequent thereunto.[1892] This was the greatest blow or bruise upon Christ's heel by Satan. Satan put it into Judas' heart to betray him to this end and to that purpose strongly entered into Judas.[1893] And Christ says to the Jews acting this horrible tragedy: *This is your hour, and the power of darkness*.[1894] Thus Satan bruised Christ's heel by God's permission.

(b) **God's limitation of Satan's bruising of Christ the woman's seed.** He should bruise his heel – his meanest and lowest part – but only his heel. He must not bruise nor touch his head, his heart, his breast; or other his superior and more principal parts, wherein his life, sense, wisdom, power, etc., were radically seated. He should only annoy his meaner inferior outward part, his heel. More particularly, the serpent could not touch the Godhead of Christ, the personal union between his Godhead and manhood, the essence and immortality of his human soul, the incorruptibility of his human body, the

---

[1886] Mark 11:19, Luke 7:34
[1887] Mark 3:22, Matthew 12:24
[1888] Psalm 2:1-2, Acts 4:25-28, Mark 12:12-13, John 11:53
[1889] John 7:32, 45-46
[1890] Matthew 26:15
[1891] John 8:38, 41, 44
[1892] Luke 23 throughout, Galatians 3:13
[1893] John 13:2, 27
[1894] Luke 22:53

spotless purity and innocency of his person, nor the sufficiency and efficacy of his mediatory office. (1) *The serpent could not bruise or touch Christ's Godhead.* For the Godhead is impassible; can not suffer or die at all, being a mere act altogether eternal[1895] and unchangeable,[1896] infinitely above the reach or activity of all created beings or infernal devils whatsoever. (2) *The serpent could not bruise the personal union between the Godhead and manhood of Christ.* For, from the first moment of Christ's conception according to his humanity, it was indivisibly and personally united to the second person in the Trinity, and never after separated – no not in death itself. By death, Christ's body was separated from his soul, but his divinity neither from his body nor soul. For: [1] then, during Christ's death, he should have had an actual subsistence in his humanity, namely: his soul in paradise,[1897] his body in the sepulcher,[1898] distinct from his deity: which cannot be, seeing Christ united not to his deity any human person distinctly of itself subsisting, but only the true and perfect human nature never subsisting but in personal union with Christ's Godhead. As the mistletoe is united to the apple tree into one tree, that mistletoe never subsisting distinctly of itself but only in the apple-tree. [2] Then also Christ should have ceased to be *Immanuel, God-man, God with us*;[1899] and consequently for so long, he should have ceased to be our mediator, and have been totally conquered for a time by sin, death and Satan. [3] And then, this would have been the serpent's bruising not only of his heel, but also of his head. (3) *The serpent could not bruise the essence, and immortality of Christ's human soul.* His soul was *surrounded with sorrow* for our sins to the death:[1900] but was not bruised *to death*, as his body was.[1901] When his dead body was in grave: his living soul was *in paradise*.[1902] That was mortal, and died: this immortal and could not die. (4) *The serpent could not bruise and destroy the*

[1895] Psalm 90:2
[1896] James 1:17
[1897] Luke 23:43
[1898] Luke 23:52-53
[1899] Matthew 1:23, John 1:14, 1 Timothy 3:15
[1900] περίλυπος, Matthew 26:38
[1901] Matthew 10:28
[1902] Luke 23:43

incorruptibility of Christ's human body. God *left not his soul in hell* (that is, his person or life, in the state of the dead), *nor suffered his holy one to see corruption.*[1903] His body was brought into the grave, but not at all corrupted or putrefied in the grave. (5) *The serpent could not bruise or destroy the spotless purity and innocence of his person.* The serpent could *tempt* him but could not *taint* him,[1904] could afflict him with many sufferings, could not infect him with any sin, could bring him to yield up his *spirit,* but not at all to yield up the least degree of his *spiritualness*; could deter him from good, or draw him to evil, by all his serpentine subtleties, but he still remained both in *conception, birth, conversation and death, holy, harmless, undefiled, and separate from sinners.*[1905] His *innocence* always triumphed over the serpent's *iniquity.* (6) Finally, *the serpent could not bruise, or at all prejudice the sufficiency or efficiency of Christ's mediatory office.* Notwithstanding all the bruises which he had from the serpent in his *heel* through *temptations, tribulations,* and *death,* yet he did once in his *state of humiliation,*[1906] and does still in his *state of exaltation,*[1907] faithfully discharge and fulfill his mediatory office in all the parts and functions of it, prophetic, [1908] priestly,[1909] and kingly,[1910] to the full pleasing and satisfying of God,[1911] redeeming and recovery of his elect,[1912] ruin and destruction of all his and their enemies.[1913] Yea Satan's bruising his heel by temptations, tribulations and death, through God's over-ruling hand helped forward the execution of his office as in the next branch will appear. Thus Satan bruised but Christ's heel, and that through God's restraint and limitation of him.

[1903] Psalm 16:10-11, Acts 13:34-38
[1904] Matthew 4:1-12, John 14:30
[1905] Hebrews 7:26
[1906] Philippians 2:6-8
[1907] Philippians 2:9-11, Ephesians 1:20-22
[1908] John 3:2, 17:6-7, Luke 24:45, John 14:26, Acts 2:2-4, etc.
[1909] Hebrews 9:25-28 & 7:24-27 & 9:24
[1910] Psalm 2:6, Hebrews 7:1-3 with Psalm 110:1, 4; 1 Corinthians 15:24-26
[1911] Matthew 3:17, Ephesians 5:2
[1912] Hebrews 9:12 & 10:14
[1913] Romans 8:3, Hebrews 2:4, 15; Colossians 2:14-15

(c) ***God's ordination and overruling disposal of Satan's bruising Christ's heel***, comes in the last place to be considered, and it is very mysterious. For, by Satan's bruising Christ's *heel*, Christ bruises Satan's *head*. Jesus Christ was tempted by Satan, that he might conquer his temptations, and fortify us against them.[1914] Christ was exercised with manifold afflictions and sufferings from Satan: that he might overcome all sufferings,[1915] *be touched with the feeling of our infirmities, in that he was in all points tempted like as we are, yet without sin*,[1916] and *that he might be a merciful and faithful high-priest in things pertaining to God, to make reconciliation for the sins of the people: for in that himself has suffered being tempted, he is able to succour them that are tempted*.[1917] Yea, Christ was (through Satan's subtlety) put to death, and buried in the grave: that so he might be the death of death, the plague of the grave, *that through death he might destroy him that had the power of death, that is the devil: and deliver them who through fear of death, were all their life time subject to bondage*.[1918] Thus mysteriously and wonderfully has the Lord overruled, ordained, and disposed all the bruisings of *Christ's heel* to be the bruises of the *serpent's head*. The serpent *hurts* Christ but thereby *kills* himself; he is slain with his own weapon as Goliath was beheaded with his own sword. Christ tramples upon temptations by being tempted, triumphs over sufferings by sufferings, afflicts afflictions by being afflicted, crucifies the cross by being crucified, curses the very curse by becoming a curse, deadens death by dying, buries the grave by being buried in the grave, and in all these destructively bruises the serpent's head, while the serpent only afflictingly bruises his heel. O the depth of the wisdom and dispensations of God!

Thus of the serpent's bruising the heel of the woman's seed, as it has reference to Christ, the eminent seed, primarily.

[2] ***Secondarily, this has reference to them that are Christ's***. As Christ's heel was bruised, so their heel shall be bruised by the serpent also

---

[1914] Matthew 4:1-12
[1915] John 16:33
[1916] Hebrews 4:15
[1917] Hebrews 2:17-18
[1918] Hebrews 2:14-15, Colossians 2:14-15

proportionally. The members must be conformed to the head, and drink of the same cup with Christ. They are the *woman's seed* also, as opposite to the *serpent's seed*. Christ the primary, they the secondary seed. As Christ had the *primary*, so they shall have the *secondary bruise in the heel* by the serpent. This their bruise is, {1} permitted, {2} limited, and {3} overruled by God.

{1} **Permitted.** God permits Satan the old serpent to bruise the heel of Christ's members, by temptations, afflictions, and death. (i) By temptations. *Satan desires to have them, to sift them as wheat: desiring to find them, or make them, not wheat, but chaff*.[1919] David was tempted by Satan to number the people.[1920] Paul himself, who *was caught up into the third heaven, into paradise*,[1921] had *a thorn in the flesh, the messenger of Satan to buffet* him.[1922] And Satan has his depths,[1923] his devices[1924], his serpentine subtleties,[1925] sometimes transforming himself into an angel of light that he may deceive,[1926] sometimes as a roaring lion,[1927] walking about, seeking whom he may devour, always watching[1928] and compassing the earth to and fro,[1929] to do mischief. (ii) By afflictions. Satan the old serpent raises many a storm against Christians, against the godly.[1930] Satan (through God's permission) brought a terrible tempest, yea a whirlwind of afflictions upon Job. And Christ says to the church in Smyrna, *the devil shall cast some of you into prison, that ye may be tried, and ye shall have tribulation ten days*.[1931] *The dragon, the devil, persecuted the woman which brought forth the man-child*, namely, the primitive church, which brought forth Christ mystical: *and the woman flying into the*

[1919] Luke 22:31
[1920] 1 Chronicles 21:1
[1921] 2 Corinthians 12:2-4
[1922] 2 Corinthians 12:7
[1923] Revelation 2:24
[1924] 2 Corinthians 2:11
[1925] 2 Corinthians 11:3
[1926] 2 Corinthians 11:14
[1927] 1 Peter 5:8
[1928] 1 Peter 5:8
[1929] Job 1:7 & 2:2
[1930] Job chapters 1 & 2
[1931] Revelation 2:10

wilderness, the serpent cast out of his mouth water as a flood, after the woman; and went to make war with the remnant of her seed, which keep the commandments of God, and have the testimony of Jesus Christ.[1932] (iii) By death, Satan has been a *murderer from the beginning*, for he brought death upon all mankind.[1933] Yea a murderer of saints from the beginning; for *Cain was of that wicked one, and slew his brother, because his own deeds were wicked, and his brother's righteous.*[1934] What massacres and butcheries were ever executed upon the saints, but the devil (who had the power of death) was the prime agent therein?[1935] The beast, *that bare the woman*, the scarlet-whore *of Babylon, drunken with the blood of the saints, and with the blood of the martyrs of Jesus, ascended out of the bottomless pit, and received his power, and seat, and authority from the dragon*, the devil. [1936]

{2} **Limited**. Satan shall bruise them that are Christ's; not wherein he pleases, but wherein God permits, only in their *heel*. Their heel he shall bruise: beyond their heel he shall not bruise. God that bound the sea, saying: *Thus far shalt thou go, and no further, and here shall thy proud waves be stayed*,[1937] has bound Satan also, intimating: *thus far shalt thou bruise, and no further, and here shall thy proud rage be stopped*. He may bruise them so as *to tempt them, to afflict them*, and perhaps *to kill their bodies*, but when he has done his worst, he shall never be able to bruise them, so as: (i) to tempt, afflict, or kill them at his pleasure; (ii) to kill their immortal souls at all; (iii) to detain their dead bodies perpetually in the grave; (iv) to destroy God's image in them; (v) to separate them from the love of God which is in Christ Jesus our Lord, or, (vi) to deprive them of their eternal inheritance in heaven.

(i) *Satan cannot tempt, afflict, or kill them at his pleasure.* For, that they are tempted, afflicted or slain, is only by divine permission. And God (that

---

[1932] Revelation 12:13-17
[1933] John 8:44, Genesis 3:1-7, Romans 5:12
[1934] 1 John 3:12
[1935] Hebrews 2:14-15
[1936] Revelation 13:1-2, 4 & 17:4-8
[1937] Job 38:11

numbers the very hairs of their head,[1938] *tells their wanderings*,[1939] *and puts all their tears in his bottle*) limits all circumstances, whether of time, place, person, manner, etc. *The devil shall cast some of you* (not all) *into prison* (not into grave, or hell) *that ye may be tried* (not destroyed), *and ye shall have tribulation ten days* (not ten months, ten years, or forever).[1940] In Job's case, Satan might touch all that he had, but not himself,[1941] and afterwards, Job himself was permitted to be under Satan's hand, but not his life.

(ii) *Satan shall not kill their immortal souls*, though he may afflict and kill their mortal bodies. It's God's sole prerogative to be able *to kill both body and soul, and cast them into hell*.[1942] And when they are dissolved by death, the body returns to the earth as it was, and the spirit to God that gave it.[1943]

(iii) Satan shall not detain their bodies perpetually in the grave. For, (a) God *will redeem their soul from the power of the grave, for he shall receive them*.[1944] (b) God is their God: therefore *they all live to him and shall rise again*.[1945] (c) Christ their head is risen, as a *last Adam*, as *the first-fruits from the dead*: therefore they that are Christ's shall rise by virtue of his resurrection.[1946] (d) If we believe that Jesus died, and rose again, even so they also who sleep in Jesus, will God bring with him.[1947] They do but *sleep in Jesus*; therefore they shall *awake in Jesus*. And when they that are Christ's shall rise again at Christ's coming, then *death and grave shall be swallowed up in victory*, the risen saints triumphing, *O death where is thy sting, O grave where is thy victory?—thanks be to God who giveth us the victory through our Lord Jesus Christ.*[1948]

[1938] Matthew 10:30
[1939] Psalm 56:8
[1940] Revelation 2:10
[1941] Job 1:12 & 2:6
[1942] Matthew 10:28
[1943] Ecclesiastes 12:7
[1944] Psalm 49:15
[1945] Luke 20:37-38
[1946] 1 Corinthians 15:20, 22
[1947] 1 Thessalonians 4:14, etc.
[1948] 1 Corinthians 15:54-57

(iv) Satan shall never so bruise them, as to destroy God's image in them. The natural image of God in man, concreated[1949] with man, he quickly destroyed;[1950] but the supernatural image of God, newly created in the elect, he shall never destroy.[1951] (a) This is a seed *remaining in them*, so that *they cannot sin*, namely, as the unregenerate sin.[1952] (b) This is everlasting life, namely: the beginning, principle and foundation of everlasting life, and therefore it can never perish.[1953] Everlasting life has no end. (c) Whom God *calls, he justifies, and whom he justifies, he glorifies*.[1954] Satan may through temptations obscure, darken and enfeeble God's image in them, may shake, wound and weaken their graces, but shall never finally or totally overthrow them.

(v) Satan *shall never so bruise them, as to separate them from the love and favor of God in Christ, or pluck them out of his hand* by temptations, tribulations or death.[1955] He may separate them from their dear friends, but never from their dearest Christ. He may separate their heads from their bodies, and their bodies from their souls, but shall never separate either soul or body from the Lord. *Who shall separate us from the love of Christ? Shall tribulation, or distress, or persecution, or famine, or nakedness, or peril, or sword? Nay in all these things we are more than conquerors through him that loved us. For I am persuaded that neither death, nor life, nor angels, nor principalities, nor powers, nor things present, nor things to come, nor height, nor depth, nor any other creature shall be able to separate us from the love of God, which is in Christ Jesus our Lord*.[1956]

(vi) Finally, *Satan shall never so bruise their heel, as to deprive them of their eternal inheritance in heaven*. He may perhaps dim their evidences for their inheritance so that they might suspect and question their title, but he shall neither destroy their title nor deprive them of their inheritance. For, (a)

[1949] That is, created at the same time, along with
[1950] Genesis 1:26-27, Ecclesiastes 7:29 & 3:1-7
[1951] Ephesians 4:24, Colossians 3:11
[1952] 1 John 3:9
[1953] John 17:3 & 10:28-29
[1954] Romans 8:30
[1955] John 10:28-29
[1956] Romans 8:35-39

this inheritance, or kingdom was *prepared for them from the foundation of the world*, yea before the foundation of the world.[1957] (b) *God that cannot lie, hath promised them eternal life before times of ages.*[1958] (c) Christ is ascended up into heaven *to prepare a place for them, and will come again to receive them to himself.*[1959] (d) The *inheritance incorruptible and undefiled, and that fades not away, is reserved in heaven for them.*[1960] And *they are begotten again unto a lively hope of this inheritance, being kept* (Greek: *kept as in garrison*) *by the power of God through faith unto salvation.*[1961] Thus Satan (though permitted to bruise the heel of Christians, yet) is limited in his bruising. He shall bruise but their heel.

{3} **Overruled**. Satan as he is permitted to bruise and limited in bruising, so in this his bruising them he is overruled by God, ordering and most wisely disposing all the temptations, tribulations and corporal death, where with their heel is bruised, to their great advantage; but to Satan's disadvantage, even the bruising of his head.

(i) Their temptations by Satan, God overpowers and orders for their good and Satan's ruin. For, (a) hereby they are so buffeted that they are preserved from spiritual pride *lest they should be exalted above measure* with the abundance of spiritual dignities and privileges conferred upon them.[1962] (b) Hereby, they are driven to fly to God for succor by prayer, and to wrastle more fervently with the Lord for deliverance. For this (says Paul) *I besought the Lord thrice, that it might depart from me,*[1963] that is, I besought him often: a definite number being put for an indefinite. Violent temptations awaken to vehement supplications, whilst they discover Satan's power and subtlety, together with our own weakness and simplicity to withstand him. (c) Hereby they come to have such experience of the all-sufficiency of divine grace against

---

[1957] Matthew 25:34
[1958] Titus 1:2
[1959] John 14:2-4
[1960] 1 Peter 1:4
[1961] 1 Peter 1:3-5
[1962] 2 Corinthians 12:7
[1963] 2 Corinthians 12:8

all Satan's temptations, and of God's perfecting his strength in their weakness; that they glory in their infirmities, afflictions, and temptations, that upon this occasion the power of Christ may rest upon them the more conspicuously.[1964] (d) Hereby they have many opportunities both of exercising their complete armor – their graces – in this conflict against Satan:[1965] (armor is wont to rust in times of peace) and of exalting their comfortable experiences and thankful triumphs upon their conquest of Satan. *The shield of faith quenches all the fiery darts of the wicked.*[1966] And if they *resist the devil*,[1967] they have this promise that he shall fly from them, and that God *will shortly tread him under their feet*.[1968]

(ii) Their tribulations and afflictions raised up against them by Satan, the Lord overpowers, and orders for their benefit, but Satan's prejudice. For by their afflictions: (a) their sins are scoured off, and destroyed.[1969] As rust is rubbed off by a sharp file, or as dross is purged out by a vehement fire. (b) Their wanderings from God are reclaimed, and they reduced from stray-courses. *Before I was afflicted, I went astray; but now have I kept thy word.*[1970] (c) Their spiritual state and graces are proven and tried; that they may be discovered to be gold and not dross, by coming out of the furnace and fining pot, refined and purified.[1971] The fire makes the mettles more shining and precious, and afflictions makes the saints' graces more orient and glorious. Job's faith, patience, and uprightness were rendered much more illustrious by his great distresses, as the sun shows largest face in lowest state.[1972] (d) Their graces and duties are improved and increased. The pomander smells the better for rubbing the camomile scents the more fragrantly for treading upon, the *musical instrument* makes sweet melody when struck with a skilful hand, and

---

[1964] 2 Corinthians 12:9-10
[1965] Ephesians 6:13, etc.
[1966] Ephesians 6:16
[1967] James 4:7
[1968] Romans 16:20
[1969] Isaiah 27:9
[1970] Psalm 119:67, 71
[1971] Revelation 2:10, 1 Peter 1:6-7 & 4:12
[1972] Job 3:15 & 19:25, 10:27; James 5:11, Job 1:1, 8 & 2:3, 9

some trees by beating become doubly fruitful: so afflictions better our graces and obedience. *He for our profit, that we might be partakers of his holiness.*[1973]—*We glory in tribulation; knowing that tribulation works patience, and patience experience, and experience hope, and hope maketh not ashamed.*[1974] When did David breathe out more ardent love, zeal and affections to God, or perform more accurate spiritual obedience to God, or pour out more servant heaven-piercing prayers to him; then when under his greatest afflictions? *As Israel, the more they were afflicted, the more they grew:*[1975] the palm tree, the more it's pressed downward, the more it contends upwards or as the birds in the spring, tune their notes most sweetly, when it rains most sadly. (e) Their filial relation to God is strengthened and confirmed, whilst God does correct and *chastise* them as *children*, not neglect and despise them as bastards.[1976] (f) Their condemnation with the wicked is prevented. *When we are judged, we are chastened of the Lord, that we might not be condemned with the world.*[1977] The cattle destined to slaughter are put into the fattest meadows whilst they that are reserved for use must bite on the bare commons. *The men of this world have their portion in this life,*[1978] and *receive their good things here,*[1979] because they shall be tormented hereafter, but the people of God here receive their evil things, because hereafter they shall be comforted. (g) Finally, their eternal glory and happiness in heaven shall be promoted and increased by their present tribulations. *Our light affliction, which is but for a moment* (Greek: the momentary lightness of our affliction) *works for us a far more exceeding and eternal weight of glory* (Greek: works for us an eternal weight of glory from hyperbole to hyperbole).[1980] The Greek here transcends the emphasis of our English tongue. The greater the cross now, Christianly

---

[1973] Hebrews 1:10
[1974] Romans 5:3-5
[1975] Exodus 1:12
[1976] Hebrews 12:5-8
[1977] 1 Corinthians 11:32
[1978] Psalm 17:14
[1979] Luke 16:32
[1980] 2 Corinthians 4:17

managed, the greater shall their crown be forever when Christianity comes to be rewarded.[1981]

(iii) *Their corporal death*, finally, the Lord overrules and orders for the healing of their bruise, but for the bruising of the serpent's head. Forasmuch as: (a) by death, they are fully freed and delivered from all their sins, *the works of the devil*, from which they could not fully be released while life lasted.[1982] Death delivers the saints but devours their sins, as the Red Sea delivered Israel but drowned and swallowed up the Egyptians. (b) By death they are set far above the gunshot of all Satan's temptations. As they are freed from sin: so they are freed from all temptations unto sin. (c) By death they are set free from all their labors, sorrows and miseries in this vain vexing world. *Blessed are the dead that die in the Lord,—that they may rest from their labours.*[1983] Their heads shall no more ache; their eyes be dim; their ears deaf; their heart sad; their spirits faint; nor their limbs feeble, etc. *They shall hunger no more, neither thirst any more, neither shall the sun light on them, nor any heat* (they shall be freed from both privative and positive miseries), *for the lamb, which is in the midst of the throne, shall feed them, and shall lead them unto living fountains of waters, and God shall wipe away all tears from their eyes.*[1984] (d) By death they shall make a happy change, namely: of visibles for invisibles, of shadows for substances, of terrestrials for celestials, and of temporals for eternals. They shall exchange sorrows for joys, troubles and conflicts for triumphs, faith for fruition, baseness for glory, society with sinners for the fellowship of glorious saints and angels, and earth for heaven itself. (e) Finally, by death they shall presently come to see God,[1985] to be with Christ,[1986] and to enjoy God in Christ immediately face to face, which is far best of all. They shall see him, admire him, love him, delight in him, and be ravished with him for evermore, as being the reward of rewards, the fullness of joy, the jubilee of

---

[1981] Luke 6:21-23, Matthew 5:10-11
[1982] Romans 6:7, 1 John 3:8
[1983] Revelation 14:13
[1984] Revelation 7:16-17 & 21:4
[1985] Matthew 5:8, 1 John 3:2
[1986] Philippians 1:23

gladness, the heaven of heaven, and the very glory of glory. Thus, the serpent's bruising of the heel of God's people, is wonderfully poured-over and disposed by God for their best, but for the bruising of the serpent's head.

Hitherto of the enmity between the serpent and the woman, his seed and her seed, and of the fruits of that enmity, namely: the bruising of the serpent's head by the seed of the woman Christ and his members, and the bruising of the heel of the woman's seed by the serpent, explicitly threatened: and therein of lapsed sinners' recovery implicitly promised.

(4) *__Corollaries hence resulting are several__*. Did this first promise in Christ reveal lapsed man's recovery in the enmity threatened between the woman and the serpent, between her seed and his seed, and in the events or fruits of that enmity? Then,

[1] *__God's threatenings are not to be slighted, or neglected by lapsed sinners, no nor by God's own redeemed people themselves: but to be duly weighed and considered__*. For, besides that God's threatenings may have a manifold and good use upon them, {1} cautioning them against sin,[1987] {2} quickening them, to duty,[1988] {3} discovering God's justice and truth,[1989] and {4} preserving thèm from threatened judgements;[1990] {5} there may be sweet and precious promises wrapped up in the bowels of the threatenings. As here in the threatening of Satan's destruction expressed, the very first promise of lapsed man's restitution is implied (these words are pronounced against the serpent, only in a minatory [threatening] way: but are intended for the benefit of mankind, in a promissory way).[1991] Therefore let us, when threatenings are before us, intentively view them on every side. We may find sweetest roses and lilies amongst these thorns, honeycombs in the bellies of these lions, and precious stones in the heads of these serpents. Let's therefore dive into them narrowly, and not fly from them as once Moses from his rod becoming a

---

[1987] Genesis 2:17, Exodus 20:4-7
[1988] Jonah 3:4-5
[1989] Genesis 2:17 with 3:19, Romans 5:12
[1990] Jonah 3:4-5, 10
[1991] Genesis 3:14-15

serpent,[1992] but rather let us take these serpents by the tail and handle them so that they may become a useful and comfortable rod in our hands.

[2] ***Behold here the riches of God's love, bowels of mercy, and commiserating grace to lapsed man; in that before he came to sentence man for his fall, he revealed the mystery of man's recovery from his fall.*** According to their order of sinning; first the serpent, then the woman, and last of all the man offended:[1993] so God proportioned his order of sentencing and judging them for sin, first dooming the serpent,[1994] then the woman,[1995] and lastly the man.[1996] Now before God comes to pronounce sentence upon woman or man, whilst he was now judging the serpent, he reveals man's blessing in the serpent's curse,[1997] man's advancement in the serpent's debasement, man's amity with God in the serpent's mutual enmity with man, man's bruising the serpent's head in the serpent's bruising of his heel, and man's restitution and salvation in the serpent's condemnation and destruction. Oh, what haste did God make to be gracious! How did his bowels yearn and roll within him most compassionately, over lapsed man, till he had published this gospel, these glad tidings of his recovery! Man hasted to his ruin by sin; God hasted to his recovery by the woman's seed. Man hasted to break the old Covenant of Works; God hastened to establish a new Covenant of Faith that should never be broken. Who can behold this *height and depth and length and breadth of divine love* to loveless man, to loathsome sinners, and not admire it, and adore it![1998]

[3] ***How notably is the depth of lapsed man's misery hereby intimated!*** In the *remedy*, we may read the *malady*: in the *recovery*, the *ruin*. What is the remedy here propounded for man's recovery? *The enmity of the woman and her seed, against the serpent and his: and the woman's seed's*

[1992] Exodus 4:3-4
[1993] Genesis 3:1-7
[1994] Genesis 3:14-15
[1995] Genesis 3:16
[1996] Genesis 3:17-19
[1997] Genesis 3:14-15, well considered, as has been explained.
[1998] Ephesians 3:18

bruising the serpent's head, as the serpent bruises its heel.[1999] What and how great is the misery of lapsed man herein implied? Namely: {1} his amity with the serpent, the devil, and with the deeds of the devil. Naturally carnal man is the *serpent's seed*, and *of his father the devil, and the lusts of his father he will do.*[2000] This miserable and damnable amity which is the very worst in the world, God cures by planting a supernatural enmity in man against Satan and sin. {2} His enmity against God and all his ways. *The carnal mind is enmity against God, and is not subject to the law of God, nor indeed can be. So then, they that are in the flesh, cannot please God.*[2001] This enmity against God, the Lord removes by destroying the cause of this enmity with God, namely, amity with Satan and sin. And this amity with Satan and sin is destroyed by the seed of the woman, *bruised in his heel* by the serpent, but *bruising the head of the serpent*. {3} His extreme thraldom and bondage under Satan, sin, and the wages of sin, death, the serpent's head: from which he could not be delivered but by *bruising the very head of the serpent* (which is especially sin and death) by Christ the seed of the woman. {4} His actual estrangement from Christ and from all saving interest in him, until he should cease to be *the serpent's seed* and become *the woman's seed* in and with Christ. Oh how complex is this misery of carnal man compounded of these four deadly poisons, amity with sin and Satan, enmity against God, bondage under Satan and sin, and estrangement from Christ the only remedy against them all! Sit down in the dust, O carnal man, break thine heart with sighs and sobs at this thine undone condition. Rest not contented in thy carnal state, lest thou be undone forevermore.

[4] ***This first promise, though very dark and obscure, yet comprehended in it much gospel in a few words.*** It is a compendious abstract or epitome of the gospel. The first sweet glimpse of evangelical glory. Come and see: herein are disclosed these glad tidings, namely: {1} that lapsed man should not still continue lapsed, but in time be most graciously recovered. {2} From what evils and miseries lapsed man should be recovered. namely.

[1999] Genesis 3:15
[2000] John 8:44
[2001] Romans 8:7-8, Colossians 1:21

From amity with Satan and sin, from enmity against God and his ways, and from the serpent's head: that is, his tyranny, power, mischief and subtlety, especially by sin, death and hell. {3} How and by whom lapsed man should be recovered from these evils. Not immediately by himself or his own power, which was quite lost: but mediately by an intervening mediator, the seed of the woman. For God's truth and justice must be fulfilled and satisfied, which lapsed man could never have effected. {4} What this mediator, this recoverer of lapsed man, must be for a person, namely: the *seed of the woman*: therefore he must be a *true and perfect man*. And yet he must be stronger than the serpent, then Satan, able to *bruise his very head*: therefore he must be the mighty God.[2002] God-man, Immanuel: in one person.[2003] {5} In what way this mediator, Christ God-man should effect lapsed man's recovery. Namely, by discharging his *mediatory office*. Two eminent branches of which office are here notably insinuated: (i) his priestly function in suffering for sinners: the serpent bruising his heel. (ii) His kingly office, in subduing his and their spiritual enemies, Satan, sin, death and hell; he *bruising the serpent's head*, thereby crushing and overthrowing all his policy, power and kingdom. {6} Who they are that shall partake of this recovery. Not all lapsed mankind universally without exception: but only *the woman and her seed*, as contradistinct to the serpent and his seed, namely: all the elect of God in Christ, through faith unto salvation.[2004] All that in this sense become the *joint seed of the woman with him*, shall *jointly* with him *bruise the serpent's head*. But as for the serpent and his seed, Christ would not so much as pray for them, much less would be bruised for them.[2005] {7} Finally, how they that shall be recovered by this Christ, the eminent seed of the woman, shall become actual partakers of him, and of recovery by him: namely, by mere grace, on God's part; and by faith, on theirs. This recovery of them by Christ, is offered them by God of mere grace, without respect to any worth in them, or merit by

---

[2002] Isaiah 9:6
[2003] Isaiah 7:14, Matthew 1:23, John 1:14, 1 Timothy 3:16
[2004] John 10:15, Ephesians 5:25-27
[2005] John 17:9

them, which is none at all; yea, quite contrary to what they deserved, being wholly in their lapsed state, and having deserved only death by their fall. And being a recovery without them of mere grace, how can it become theirs but by the appropriating and applying act of faith?

These evangelical mysteries seem to be sweetly couched and comprised in this primitive promise. O it is a pregnant, teeming promise, the *mother-promise* of the gospel – yea, the *great grandmother promise* of all the promises of God in the whole Scripture. Well spoke that learned Mercerus of it: "O excellent promise, and more then necessary to our first parents, without which they could never have endured to have lived, but their conscience accusing them, they would a thousand times have been guilty of their own death, when they should see themselves as authors to derive so many and great evils to all their posterity."[2006] And as this golden promise preserved our first parents from despair under their dreadful fall, so the faithful fathers in the first age of the world lived upon this promise especially, if not only, and drew waters of consolation out of this well of salvation, for the first 1536 years of the world.

[5] Then *lapsed sinners are actually in a state of recovery, when this enmity against the serpent and his seed, together with the fruits of this enmity (namely. bruising the serpent's head, and having only their heel bruised by the serpent), are effectually implanted in them, wrought by them, or belonging to them.* For God, explicitly threatening these three things to the serpent, therein implicitly promised and revealed the recovery of sinners, as has been explained: consequently when these three things are actually fulfilled and verified in any lapsed sinners, they are actually partakers of their promised recovery. But how may we know: {1} that we have true enmity against the serpent? {2} That we have bruised and do bruise the

---

[2006] "O Promissio|nem egregiam, & primis parentibus nimis qūam necessariam, sine qua vivere nunquam sustinuissent, sed conscientia accusante millies sibi mortem constivissent, cum se tot ac santorum malorum in omnem posteritatem suam derivandorum authores viderent, John Mercer in Praelect. ad Gen. 3. 15.

serpent's head? And: {3} that the serpent does but bruise our heel, when he does his worst against us?

Answer: These three things will be very comfortable indeed to be known. And they may be discovered severally by these evidences ensuing, namely: {1} **that we have true enmity against the serpent implanted in us**, may be convincingly and comfortably cleared to us: (i) by the causes of this enmity, (ii) by the effects thereof; and, (iii) by amity with them that are contrary to Satan.

(i) *By the causes, grounds or foundations of this enmity*. If they be in us: this enmity against Satan the old serpent is in us. The *cause* being put and present, the *effect* is put and present also. Now the grounds whence our enmity against the serpent principally arises, are especially these three. Transmutation of our state, dissimilitude to the serpent thereupon, and enmity against sin, flowing from both: (a) *Transmutation of our state*. When we, who are naturally the seed of the serpent, and *of our father the devil*,[2007] become supernaturally the seed of the woman, as opposite and contradistinct to the seed of the serpent, and children of our heavenly Father the Lord God,[2008] then the foundation is laid of our enmity against Satan. For, whilst we are wholly Satan's, we love Satan and his lusts: but when our state and condition is quite changed, and we become God's people, we cannot choose but have enmity against Satan, who is so contrary both unto God and all godliness. (b) *Dissimilitude to the serpent, upon our transmutation of state*. Our state and condition being changed, from carnal to spiritual,[2009] from natural to supernatural,[2010] from sinful to sanctified,[2011] from dead in sin to alive in grace,[2012] from diabolical to divine,[2013] etc., we thereupon become extremely unlike to the serpent, who were before like unto him. He, *the father of the lies*; we, *the children of truth*.[2014] He, *the prince of darkness*; we, *light in*

[2007] John 8:44
[2008] 2 Corinthians 6:7-18
[2009] John 3:3, 5-6
[2010] 1 Corinthians 2:14-15
[2011] 1 Corinthians 6:9-11, Titus 3:3-5
[2012] Ephesians 2:1-10
[2013] John 8:44, 1 John 3:12 with 2 Peter 1:4
[2014] John 8:44, 1 John 3:19

the Lord and children of the light.[2015] He, an *unclean spirit*; we, *clean through the word*, and *sanctified by the Spirit.*[2016] He, *the god of this world*; we, *not of this world, as Christ is not of this world, but chosen by him out of the world*, etc.[2017] Here is great dissimilitude. Now as similitude and likeness is the foundation of *love* and *amity*, like will love his like: so *dissimilitude* and unlikeness is the ground of *hatred* and *enmity*. Are we spiritually become unlike to the serpent? Then we have enmity against the serpent. (c) *Enmity against sin* flows from both the former. If we are changed from our carnal to a gracious state, and thereby are become quite unlike Satan the old serpent: consequently hence inevitably results in us an enmity against sin. *The flesh lusteth against the Spirit, and the Spirit against the flesh: and these are contrary one to the other.*[2018] If then we have a true contrariety and enmity in us against sin, that is: (1) against sin as it is sin especially and principally. (2) Against all sin, consequently, without partiality. (3) Against our own sins most of all. We have in us also a true enmity against the serpent, and consequently have actual part in this precious promise, and in recovery from our sinful state here promised.

(ii) *By the effects or fruits of this enmity*. If they are in us: enmity against the serpent is in us. Where the proper effect is, there the cause is producing that effect. These fruits are three, namely: *hatred of the serpent, resisting his dominion*, and *conflicting against him*. (a) *Hatred of the serpent is an effect of enmity against the serpent*. Hating is an act or fruit of enmity. Hence Christ says in the parable, *those that hated him, were his enemies.*[2019] And David, *Do not I hate them that hate thee? I hate them with a perfect hatred, I count them mine enemies.*[2020] Proportionally to hate the serpent the devil, as a serpent, as a devil, for his wicked works, etc., arises from enmity, and argues enmity against him. (b) *Resisting his dominion*. We cannot endure being under his dominion

---

[2015] Ephesians 6:12 & 5:8
[2016] Matthew 12:43, John 15:3, 1 Corinthians 6:11
[2017] 2 Corinthians 4:4, John 15:19
[2018] Galatians 5:17
[2019] Luke 19:14, 27
[2020] Psalm 139:21-22

and reign, whom we hate, if we can help ourselves. Christ's *citizens, that hated him, said we will not have this man to reign over us.*[2021] In resisting his dominion, they express their hatred against him. Thus if we truly resist Satan's reign over us, not enduring that he should *take us captive at his will,*[2022] nor that he should act and sway in us, as *he worketh in the children of disobedience*:[2023] then we have enmity against Satan. (c) *Conflicting against him, and his temptations.* Enmity breeds opposition: contrariety of natures causes mutual and destructive conflicts. Fire and water fight one with another, because they are contrary to each other: so Christ's members being contrary to Satan, through the divine nature in them, do as spiritual *well-armed soldiers* and enemies fight and war against him,[2024] as also Christ their chief-captain did fight against him.[2025] And herein they discover their enmity against Satan.

(iii) *By our amity with God, his ways and people, which are contrary to Satan, we discover our enmity against Satan.* They that truly love God and his ways, cannot choose but hate the devil and his works.[2026] They that truly love God's people as his seed cannot choose but to hate the wicked as the serpent's seed.[2027] To love both at once, or to hate both at once, is impossible. And by the rule of contraries, the loving of one implies the hating of that which is contrary thereunto.

{2} *That we have, and do bruise the serpent's head*, we may comfortably conclude on these and like grounds, namely:

(i) *When through the power of the gospel and spirit of Christ we are rescued from the power of Satan, in our effectual conversion.*[2028] Then Satan's power is broken, *his armor wherein he trusted is taken from him,*[2029] and we are no

---

[2021] Luke 19:14
[2022] 2 Timothy 2:25
[2023] Ephesians 2:2 & 6:12
[2024] Ephesians 6:11, etc.
[2025] Matthew 4:1-12, Hebrews 2:10
[2026] Psalm 97:10
[2027] 1 John 5:1, Psalm 16:3 & 26:4-5 & 139:21-22
[2028] Acts 26:17
[2029] Luke 11:21-22

longer *taken captive by him at his will.*[2030] This is our first degree of bruising the serpent's head, through Christ plucking us out of his hand.

(ii) *When we are completely armed with the panoply or whole armor of God.* Then we bruise the serpent's head fundamentally. For then God furnishes us with principles and foundations of strength, namely, the habits of victorious graces, whereby we are *enabled, not only to wrestle against flesh and blood, but also against principalities, against powers, against the rulers of the darkness of this world, against spiritual wickedness in high places, yea to withstand in the evil day*: yea, *to quench all the fiery darts of the wicked, and having done all to stand.*[2031] This is our second degree of bruising the serpent's head, when we are sufficiently principled by grace against him.

(iii) *When we actually resist the devil, so that he flies from us.*[2032] Then we actually bruise his head, crushing him in his politic and potent temptations. A *flying* enemy is a *foiled* enemy. Now we resist Satan: (a) by rejecting and slighting his temptations, not revolving them or meditating upon them in our thoughts. It's hard to touch pitch and not to be defiled: to ponder upon Satan's temptations, and not to be polluted with his temptations. As Satan *darts* them at us: so must we fling them away out of our thoughts presently, as a poisoned gloss.[2033] To roll them around in our mind, is to open a door to Satan to enter into our hearts. (b) By repelling them (if violent, impetuous, and reiterated) by *the whole armor of God,*[2034] according to the peculiar property of every piece. As temptations to error, heresy or hypocrisy: by *the girdle of truth*. To looseness or unrighteousness in heart or life: by *the breastplate of righteousness*. To discouragements, apostasy, etc., by reason of the rough ways of tribulation, etc.: by *the shoes of the preparation of the gospel of peace*. All fiery darting temptations: by the shield of faith. All temptations to doubt or despair of God's love, or our own salvation: by the helmet of hope. All temptations, in a word, to any sin, or from any duty: by *the sword of the*

[2030] 2 Timothy 2:25
[2031] Ephesians 6:12-19
[2032] James 4:7
[2033] Ephesians 6:16
[2034] Ephesians 6:12, etc.

Spirit, the word; and by *prayer*. We fight on foot with Satan, by the *shoes of the gospel*, etc.; we fight on horseback with him, by *prayer*; we fight as garrisoned in a castle, by *faith* and *hope*. (c) By occasional improvement of Satan's temptations, to act the contrary graces and duties so much more vigorously. As, when he tempts to *diffidence*, we strive more earnestly to *believe*. When he tempts to *pride*, we strive to be so much more *humble*, etc., thus we undermine Satan in his own works, and countermine his mines. (d) *When sin is pardoned and subdued; then we bruise the serpent's head indeed*. Our sins are his *works*.[2035] His *armor wherein he trusts*.[2036] His *strongholds*, by all of which he naturally has power over us.[2037] When our sins therefore are pardoned to us and subdued in us: his works are destroyed, his armor taken from him, and his strongholds cast down, and slighted. (e) Finally, *when the curse and terror of death are removed from us, then Satan's head is bruised by us*. For, Satan as an executioner, *hath the power of death*, in reference to the serpent's seed, *keeping them still in bondage through fear of death*,[2038] yea of the utmost *curse of death*.[2039] But both curse and terror of death are removed from them that are Christ's; *virtually*, by the merit of Christ's death and resurrection;[2040] actually, by the Spirit of grace and sanctification, changing their cursed state into a blessed state, and suppressing their fears by the predominance of faith, love, and Christian magnanimity.[2041]

{3} *That Satan the old serpent does but bruise our heel, when he does his worst against us*; may be comfortably clear to us: (i) *whilst our head is safeguarded by the hope of salvation*. The *hope of salvation* is compared to a *helmet*.[2042] A helmet guards the head, the principal part of the body, wherein the senses outward and inward, the animal spirits and rational soul itself are especially seated. A wound or blow there is very dangerous. So the hope of

---

[2035] 1 John 3:8, John 8:44
[2036] Luke 11:22
[2037] 2 Corinthians 10:4
[2038] Hebrews 2:14-15
[2039] Galatians 3:10
[2040] Galatians 3:13
[2041] 1 Corinthians 6:11, Ephesians 2:3-6, Titus 3:3-6, 1 John 4:17-18
[2042] Ephesians 6:17, 1 Thessalonians 5:8

salvation, guards as it were a Christian's head and spiritual senses. Whilst he keeps up his hope of salvation, the main is safe: he shall not despair. (ii) *Whilst the heart is defended by the breast-plate of righteousness, faith, and love.*[2043] The heart is another principal part: the seat of the vital spirits; the first that lives, the last that dies in a man: the breastplate defends the heart. Thus a good conscience, integrity, faith in God, and love to him, defend the heart of Christians in comfort and peace with God, against all Satan's suggestions, accusations, and temptations. Job's faith and uprightness held up his heart from fainting under all his trials and sorrows.[2044] (iii) *Whilst all our Christian vitals are preserved safe by the girdle of truth, shield of faith, and sword of the Spirit.*[2045] If Satan bruise not, touch not the vitals: he only bruises our heel. The *girdle of truth* preserves from error and hypocrisy; the *shield of faith*, preserves from diffidence, unbelief, and all Satan's fiery darts; and the sword of the Spirit, not only defends the whole of a Christian but also *offends* Satan, and every enemy to a Christian. All's well if we be thus preserved. (iv) *When the serpent's temptations rather afflict us than infect us; rather distress us than defile us; rather correct us than corrupt us; then Satan bruises but our heel.* Satan's temptations *troubled* Christ, but did not *taint* him at all.[2046] The more we are troubled by them, the less we are tainted with them, and the more we are conformed to Christ, whose heel alone was bruised by them. (v) *Finally, when both the temptations and tribulations, which Satan raises up against us, become our advantages, rather than our disadvantages* (as has formerly been explained), *then he only bruises our heel.*[2047] He shakes our tops; but our roots fix the faster. He casts us into a furnace, but the dross being consumed, our gold becomes the purer. He treads us under foot, but our heavenly spices and graces smell the sweeter. By these things we may discover whether we are actually brought into a state of recovery by Jesus Christ.

[2043] Ephesians 6:14, 1 Thessalonians 5:8
[2044] Job 13:15-16 & 19:25-27 & 27:1-11 & 31 throughout
[2045] Ephesians 6:14, 16-17
[2046] Matthew 4:1-12
[2047] 2 Corinthians 12:7-10, Revelation 2:20

[6] *These threatenings were not so terrible to the serpent and his seed, but they were as comfortable to the woman and her seed.* To the serpent and his seed they express nothing but destruction: to the woman and her seed (implying promises in them) they intend nothing but recovery from destruction. What a ground of manifold comfort is this Scripture to poor lapsed sinners? As: {1} that the serpent for seducing and overthrowing mankind, should be cursed, debased, opposed by the enmity of the woman and her seed against him, and bruised in his head by the woman's seed.[2048] Thus the deceiver is deceived: the destroyer is destroyed. {2} That in the enmity of the woman and her seed, against the serpent and his seed, should so notably be implied their enmity also against sin, *the work of the devil*;[2049] but their amity and reconcilement with God, the enemy of the devil. {3} That the seed of the woman (Christ *primarily* by his own power, they that are Christ's *secondarily* by Christ's power), should bruise the very head of the serpent: that is, utterly and irrecoverably destroy Satan, sin, death and hell, even all the powers of darkness. {4} That the old serpent the devil and Satan, when he should do his worst against Christ and them that are his, by temptations, tribulations, or corporal death, should but bruise their lowest and meanest part, their *heel*. {5} That Satan's bruising of their heel *afflictingly*, should be the very way for the woman's seed to bruise Satan's head *destructively*. Oh here is a very fountain of comfort overflowing! Various comfort, mysterious comfort, saving comfort.

[7] *This first promise, revealing such grace and mercy to lapsed sinners, did and does oblige poor sinners to all possible gratitude.* Here the day of salvation did first dawn up on the world, and the dayspring from on high did first visit us.[2050] Here the sluice of commiserating grace was first opened, and the streams of mercy began first to flow out to sinners. Here the everlasting gospel was first preached,[2051] the all-sufficient mediator and

---

[2048] Genesis 3:14-15
[2049] 1 John 3:8, John 8:44
[2050] 2 Corinthians 6:2, 2 Peter 1:19, Luke 1:77-78
[2051] Revelation 14:6

redeemer was first tendered; and lapsed sinners' recovery in him was first revealed, here life is promised to sinners, before death was pronounced upon them for sin, and the heavenly paradise is set open for them, before the earthly paradise was shut against them. Here, here, therefore is no ordinary matter of thankfulness offered unto sinners. If *the morning-stars sang together, and all the sons of God shouted for joy*,[2052] at the world's creation, how much more should lapsed sinners – and with them heaven and earth – sing and shout together for joy, at their own restoration? As for us, if we have any part in this primitive promise, let us abound in thankfulness to the God of this promise: and thus, by *punctual recognition* and notice-taking of this mercy in all its proportions, dimensions, and amplifications. By *singular estimation* of this mercy according to its excellency. By *suitable retribution*, or *rendering* to the Lord again according to this benefit.[2053] {1} Believing this promise without staggering, that it shall completely be performed. {2} Loving the Lord with all endeared affections who has thus *loved us first* from the foundation of the world.[2054] {3} *Maintaining* an irreconcilable enmity against the serpent and his seed, until we bruise his head, and be *more than conquerors through Christ that loves us.*[2055]

Thus, this first promise in Christ revealed lapsed man's recovery, in the enmity threatened between the woman and the serpent, between her seed and his seed, and in the fruits or effects of that enmity.

[2052] Job 38:6-7
[2053] Psalm 116:12, 2 Chronicles 32:24-26
[2054] 1 John 4:19
[2055] Romans 8:37

Aphorism 5

Hence, this first promise revealed in Christ the seed of the woman, though it had not the name and complete formality of a covenant; yet had it the nature, substance and reality of a covenant, and that the Covenant of Faith.

This aphorism is very evident by what has been said already of this famous and primitive promise,[2056] and may be yet further cleared, and that briefly, by a distinct consideration of: (1) the author, (2) parties, (3) matter, and, (4) form of this promise, which are for substance the same with those of the Covenant of Faith, though very dimly and obscurely revealed in this first promise.

(1) The *author*, or efficient cause of the Covenant of Faith, is only God, and that of his mere mercy and commiserating grace, as has been shown:[2057] and the same God, of mere commiserating grace and mercy was the efficient cause, or author of this promise. For, *The LORD God said unto the serpent, because thou hast done this, thou art cursed—and I will put enmity between thee and the woman*, etc.[2058] So then, the Lord God immediately revealed this promise. And nothing but mere mercy and riches of commiserating grace to lapsed sinners could be imagined to move him here unto. They being wholly deprived of all acceptableness, amiableness, and moral goodness: and involved in the bondage of sin and death.

(2) The *parties* to the Covenant of Faith (as has been proven)[2059] are, God blessed forever, on the one hand, and Jesus Christ the last Adam, with all his elect seed on the other hand: and these selfsame are the parties to this promise.

[2056] Genesis 3:14-15
[2057] Book 2, Chapter 2, Aphorism 2, Section 1
[2058] Genesis 3:14-15
[2059] Book 2, Chapter 2, Aphorism 2, Section 2

For: [1] God is the party promising, to put enmity, etc.[2060] [2] Christ and his elect seed (who with Christ the eminent seed, are collectively comprised under this phrase, *the seed of the woman*,[2061] as contradistinct from, and opposite to the seed of the serpent) are the party restipulating, to accept these promised mercies by faith, and to walk worthy of them; as after will more appear. This promise was not settled upon Adam, as the first covenant and promise was. It was not so much as directed to Adam, but to the serpent; and to the serpent, not under the form of a promise, but of a threatening.[2062] But it was settled upon the woman's seed, that is, on Christ and on them that are Christ's according to the election. The seed of the woman shall bruise thine head, and thou shalt bruise his heel.

That question which is moved by some, may here receive a brief solution, namely: whether all and singular the children and posterity of Adam, which should after the fall be brought into the world, were with Adam comprehended in this first promise, in this first dispensation of the Covenant of Faith: as they were all comprised in and with him in the first Covenant of Works standing and falling with him.[2063]

Resolution: This query may be resolved,

{1} *Concedendo*, by way of concession. It is granted that not only Adam but also all and singular persons that should ever descend from him by natural propagation were comprised with him in the Covenant of Works. So that he standing, they stood; he lapsing, they fell. As has formerly been sufficiently cleared.[2064]

{2} *Denegando*, by way of negation. It is utterly denied, that all and every one of Adam's posterity were comprehended with him in this first promise or dispensation of the Covenant of Faith since the fall, as they were comprehended with him in the Covenant of Works before the fall. For:

[2060] Genesis 3:14-15
[2061] Genesis 3:15
[2062] Genesis 2:17
[2063] Genesis 2:26-17, Romans 5:12 to the end, 1 Corinthians 15:21-22
[2064] Book, 2 Chapter 1, Aphorism 3

(i) The Covenant of Works, God made with Adam immediately as with a public person, founding it upon Adam's natural integrity and ability to keep it: and therefore if Adam had persisted in his integrity and kept the covenant, all his posterity had persevered and kept covenant with him, partaking the blessings of the covenant: but God did not make this first promise, to the first Adam immediately, as to a public person, nor directed it to him at all in the promulgation of it.[2065] For before God came to sentence the man or woman, while he was now dooming the serpent and directing his speech only to him, he publishes this excellent promise of man's recovery by Christ, the seed of the woman, to the terror and confusion of the serpent. This promise then was founded not upon the first Adam at all, but immediately only upon Jesus Christ, the seed of the woman, as a last Adam – and in him it is mediately extended to all his spiritual posterity.

(ii) This first promise makes a plain distinction between two contrary seeds,[2066] namely, the *seed of the serpent*, and the *seed of the woman*; and of a hereditary enmity between them. And it speaks destruction to the serpent's seed: victory and restoration to the woman's seed. Therefore, though these two contrary seeds might be under the outward administration of this promise, as Cain and Abel were,[2067] yet could they not both be under the inward efficacy, grace and consolation thereof. The woman's seed, Christ and they that are Christ's, are all comprised within this promise in this sort, but the serpent's seed, who *are of their father the devil, and will do his lusts*,[2068] devilish reprobates, are not the woman's seed, nor thus comprised in the promise with them.

(iii) Many thousands and millions in the world, if they never come to enjoy so much as the outward administration of this promise, or of any other evangelical dispensation – pagans, Turks, etc. – how shall they be comprised

---

[2065] Genesis 3:14-16, etc.
[2066] Genesis 3:15
[2067] Genesis 4:3-4, etc.
[2068] John 8:44

under this promise in respect of the inward efficacy, grace, or consolation thereof?

(iv) These two covenants – of works and faith – are most different. That was in a sort natural to man; this merely supernatural. That founded immediately upon Adam himself without a mediator; this founded not upon man but upon Jesus Christ the mediator. That conditioning for perfect and perpetual obedience in Adam's own person; this conditioning for true faith in Christ's person and obedience. Therefore, though all Adam's posterity were comprised with him under that covenant, it does not follow that they must be comprehended under this: but rather the contrary.

(3) The *matter* of the Covenant of Faith is either promised or restipulated. Promised on God's part, namely: the recovery of lapsed man out of the state of sin and death to a state of righteousness and life by Jesus Christ. *Restipulated* on the part of Christ and his seed, namely: Christ's accepting and undertaking of a mediatory office to effect this recovery, and his seed's accepting Christ and these promised mercies by faith, with resolution to walk worthy of them according to the gospel.

In like sort the matter of this eminent primordial promise is either promised on God's part, or restipulated on the part of the woman's seed.

[1] ***The matter promised explicitly on God's part*** is,

{1} That a spiritual *enmity should be put between the woman and her seed, the serpent and his seed*.[2069] And consequently, that the woman and her seed should have enmity against sin and amity with God, which could not be without conformity to God and contrariety to sin by supernatural grace, nor without renouncing and departing from sin by true repentance.

{2} That *the seed of the woman should bruise the very head of the serpent*,[2070] that is, utterly destroy the old serpent the devil, and Satan with all his policy, dominion, and deeds, whether sin or death. Consequently, that lapsed sinners in and by Christ should be recovered from the state of sin and

---

[2069] Genesis 3:15
[2070] Genesis 3:15

death, and become conquerors of the serpent himself that had plunged them into that estate: and that Jesus Christ for the obtaining of this victory for them, should with them become true and perfect man, the seed of the woman; and not only perfect man, but should above them be the mighty God, above the serpent, and so able to bruise the serpent's head.

{3} That, in order to Christ's bruising the serpent's head, *the serpent should bruise his heel*.[2071] Christ should be *consecrated through sufferings and death, that he might destroy him that had the power of death the devil*.[2072] Consequently, herein God promised that Christ should be a priest in suffering *bruises in his heel*, and a king in inflicting *bruises on the serpent's head*. Now in these matters and mercies promised, sinners' recovery from the state of sin and death to the state of righteousness and life by Jesus Christ is promised.

[2] ***The matter restipulated implicitly on the part of the woman's seed***, is either *on the part of Christ*, or *of his elect seed and members*.

{1} On the part of Christ: (i) that he would submit to that low state of incarnation and become the woman's seed.[2073] His incarnation was deep humiliation. (ii) That he would, as the woman's seed, abase himself to be bruised in his heel, by the serpent, namely, even to sufferings, and death;[2074] that hereby he might bruise the serpent's head, and recover his elect out of his dominion. (iii) That all his elect should become a joint *seed of the woman* with himself, opposite to the *seed of the serpent*, that with him and by virtue of his bruises, they might *bruise the serpent's head* also.

{2} On the part of Christ's seed and members: (i) that they would accept Christ, and these promised mercies in him, by faith. This faith they implicitly restipulated, for (a) without faith neither Christ, nor any benefit promised by him, can be received.[2075] (b) Without faith they could not bruise the serpent's

---

[2071] Genesis 3:15
[2072] Hebrews 7:28 & 2:10, 14-15
[2073] Hebrews 10:5-9
[2074] Hebrews 10:9-10
[2075] John 1:11-12, Ephesians 3:17

head, quench his fiery darts,[2076] conquer sin,[2077] and overcome the world.[2078] (c) The fathers of the old world enacted faith, and by their faith were accepted of God, which could not have been without this mutual agreement between God and them touching faith. *By faith the elders obtained a good report.*[2079] By faith Adam after the promise named his wife Eve, living, in hope of life to him, and his, promised.[2080] *By faith Abel offered unto God, a more excellent sacrifice than Cain, by which he obtained witness that he was righteous, God testifying of his gifts.*[2081] *By faith Enoch was translated that he should not see death, and was not found, because God had translated him: for before his translation he had this testimony, that he pleased God. But without faith it is impossible to please him.*[2082] These testimonies may evince that these ancient saints knew how necessarily faith was required of them by this first promise. Yea: (d) they offered sacrifices, and that by God's appointment, otherwise God would not have accepted them:[2083] and these sacrifices being types of Christ, testified their faith in Christ.

(ii) That they would walk worthy of Christ and these promised mercies to all well-pleasing, according to evangelical rule. For: (a) faith being required in them, love and-good-works were also required: *faith working by love,*[2084] and being naturally *fruitful in good works,*[2085] as the way to heaven: though not the cause of heaven. (b) Their course and good works are highly commended, as godly: Enoch and Noah walked with God, *Noah was a just man and perfect in his generations;*[2086] as *accepted of God,*[2087] and well-pleasing before him, which

---

[2076] Ephesians 6:16
[2077] Acts 15:9
[2078] 1 John 5:4-5
[2079] Hebrews 11:2
[2080] Genesis 3:20
[2081] Hebrews 11:4
[2082] Hebrews 11:5-6
[2083] Genesis 4:4, 7
[2084] Galatians 5:6
[2085] James 2
[2086] Genesis 5:22 & 6:9
[2087] Genesis 4:4, 7 & Hebrews 11:6

could not be, had not God required them of them, and consequently, they implicitly restipulated them.

(4) Finally, *the Covenant of Faith has its **form**,* namely: *inward*, the mutual compact or agreement of the federates: *outward*, the various manners of administrations. So here this primitive promise had its *inward* and *outward* form also.

[1] *The inward form of it,* was the mutual agreement between the federates or parties to the covenant touching matters promised, and restipulated, which agreement was *partly* expressed and *partly* implied, as has been noted.

[2] *The outward form of it,* was that visible form, way, or manner of God's administering this promise, and of the affairs of his church and people under this promise, in the first notable period of time from Adam until Noah, in all which form or manner of administration there are evident characters and intimations of the *Covenant of Faith in Jesus Christ.* And this may be briefly thus represented. Man having broken the Covenant of Works, and God having promised lapsed sinners recovery by Christ the seed of the woman, after this promise thus dealt with him and his posterity, namely:

{1} *He pronounced a heavy sentence upon both the woman and the man, for their first sin, whereby they broke the Covenant of Works.*[2088] That so he might more experimentally convince them of the sinfulness of that sin, more deeply bruise and humble them for it, and contrariwise more eminently display the glory and sweetness of the first promise revealing their recovery both from sin and misery.

{2} *He not only drove them out of the garden of Eden, but also guarded the tree of life therein from them, with cherubims and a flaming sword, which turned every way to keep the way of the tree of life.*[2089] Why? Not that God envied them eternal life, for he had now but

---

[2088] Genesis 3:16-20
[2089] Genesis 3:23-24

newly promised it to them in Christ.[2090] Nor that the tree of life could have made them live forever if they had tasted it, for the Covenant of Works being broken, the sacraments or tokens thereof were evacuated and of no force.

But, that hereby God might teach them, not to delude and deceive themselves with vain hopes of life from the Covenant of Works or the external use of the tokens thereof, whilst they had already broken that covenant irreparably: but wholly now to apply themselves for life and happiness to the promise, or Covenant of Faith, in Christ, the woman's seed.[2091]

{3} *He clothed Adam and Eve, his wife, with coats of the skins of dead beasts.* This he did: (i) partly to cover their nakedness and shame, the fruit of their sin. (ii) Partly to make them yet more sensible of the shame and beastliness of their sin and apostasy so that both their nakedness and their clothing might tend to remind them of, and humble them for their sin – as Calvin well notes.[2092] (iii) Partly to instruct them touching the necessity of being clothed spiritually with Christ to be crucified, and his righteousness; for covering their deformity from the pure eye of God. (iv) Partly to remember them daily of their mortality contracted by sin.[2093] That under those dead skins, they had dying bodies.

{4} *He instituted and ordained sacrifices, under this first dispensation of his promise and covenant in this first period of time from Adam until Noah.*

That sacrifices were then of God's institution and appointment, we have just cause to think, for: (i) God *clothed Adam and his wife with coats of*

[2090] Genesis 3:15

[2091] Genesis 3:15

[2092] "The reason why the Lord clothed them with garments of skin appears to me to be this: because garments formed of this material would have a more degrading appearance than those made of linen or of woolen. God therefore designed that our first parents should, in such a dress, behold their own vileness – just as they had before seen it in their nudity – and should thus be reminded of their sin." John Calvin. "They were clothed with coats of skins for a perpetual memorial of their disobedience." John Chrysostom

[2093] Pelliceae vestes significant mortalitatem. Corpus enim Adami ab initio fuit tenuius & mollius, nec omnino mortale, sed mediae conditionis inter mortale & immortale. Nazianzen. Orat. 2. de Pasch.

skins.[2094] Of what skins? Justin Martyr is of the opinion that God did not kill beasts, and clothe them with their skins, but rather immediately created skins by his word of command, and so clothed them.[2095] Yet this opinion seems scarcely probable; because it's strange to think that God should create beasts' skins without the beasts, nor do we find any color for any such act in the whole Scripture. Calvin thinks that "God imposed this task upon Adam and Eve, that they should make themselves coats of skins."[2096] Some conceive that these skins were skins of beasts created before Adam's fall; and that after his fall God slew some of those beasts, clothing them with their skins, by his commanding word, and that he taught them to offer the dead bodies of those beasts in sacrifice.[2097] For, God doubtless would not have the bodies of those beasts lost and useless. And seeing the *eating of flesh* was not permitted till after the flood,[2098] what other use can we imagine their bodies to be put unto, besides that of sacrificing? This also is the more probable, because in the story of Genesis, presently after man's expulsion from Eden, there is mention of Adam's two first sons, and of their *sacrificing* (and this without any intervening command expressed),[2099] wicked Cain bringing his offering to God, as well as righteous Abel. (ii) Abel is said *by faith to offer unto God a more excellent sacrifice than Cain.*[2100] He could not have offered any sacrifice by faith, unless the Lord had appointed that sacrifice: God's appointment and institution of his worship, being the ground of our faith, in worshiping. (iii) God accepted in those days the sacrifices of righteous persons. *He had respect to Abel, and to his offering: but to Cain and his offering he had not respect.*[2101]

[2094] Genesis 3:21
[2095] Justin Martyr, Question & Response 49 to the orthodox
[2096] John Calvin's commentary on Genesis 3:21
[2097] "Adam and Eve were clothed with skins, as it should appear, with skins of beasts, to shew their beastliness, which God for them had slain to offer for sacrifice, to teach them the use thereof. For no doubt God would not destroy beasts to have them spoiled, seeing that Adam was not to eat any." *The General view of the holy Scriptures.* p. 19. London 1640.
[2098] Genesis 9:2-4
[2099] Genesis 4:1-6
[2100] Hebrews 11:4
[2101] Genesis 4:4-5

And when *Noah offered burnt-offerings, the LORD smelled a sweet savour*,[2102] Hebrew: *a savor of rest*. Now had their sacrifices been of human invention, and not of divine institution; they would have been *will-worship*, and God would never have accepted them, but rather would have abhorred them. But to what end and use did God appoint sacrifices under this first dispensation of the promise?

Answer: For several excellent ends, namely: (a) for the more clear convincing of lapsed sinners of their sin and misery. *Of their sin*: because, *in their sacrifices there was a remembrance of sin*,[2103] which needed such sacrifices, frequently renewed. Every sacrifice for sin, being an implicit arraignment and condemnation of the sinner. Of their misery by sin, the death of those sacrifices implying that the due wages of their sins were death, unless divine justice had full satisfaction.[2104] (b) For the familiar instructing of lapsed sinners touching the remedy against sin and death. The death therefore of those sacrifices typified the death of Christ the true sacrifice,[2105] the true *lamb of God taking away the sins of the world*.[2106] These sacrifices were types, instructing them in the mystery of Christ the antitype. (c) For ratifying the first promise in Christ's blood, as it were sacramentally; they being in the nature of visible signs, pledges and tokens annexed to the promise. The bruising of the heel of the woman's seed denoted Christ's blood, establishing the promise *meritoriously*: the sacrifices, typifying Christ's blood, established the promise *sacramentally*. In these sacrifices Christ and his death being typified, Christ may be said to be the *lamb slain from the foundation of the world*.[2107] (d) For a visible means and way of divine worship, whereby they testify their faith, devotion, homage, and obedience unto God, as his own people.

[2102] Genesis 8:20-21
[2103] Hebrews 10:3
[2104] Romans 6:23
[2105] Hebrews 9:9-15
[2106] John 1:29, 36
[2107] Revelation 13:8

{5} *He confirmed and further strengthened this first grand promise*, by: (i) promises, (ii) mercies, (iii) threats, and, (iv) judgements. (i) By *promises* encouraging faith, obedience, etc., according to the grand promise.[2108] (ii) By *mercies* heaped as rewards upon believers and well-doers, walking uprightly. Thus God testified his acceptance of the person and sacrifice of righteous Abel.[2109] *Enoch walking with God; God took him, that is, translated him that he should not see death.*[2110] Noah being *just and upright in his generations, and walking with God*, was preserved in the ark by water, when the whole world was drowned.[2111] (iii) By *threatenings* denounced against all unbelievers and evildoers contrary to this first promise. Thus wicked Cain is threatened with imminent judgment for sin – *If thou dost not well, sin lies at the door*:[2112] with the earth's barrenness, with a vagabond life, etc. The wicked world also, and for their sins, every creature breathing therein is threatened after 120 years to be destroyed, except those that were preserved with Noah in the ark.[2113] (iv) By *righteous judgments* upon the unbelievers and ungodly of that first age. Thus God cursed Cain from the earth, and set a dreadful *mark upon him*;[2114] probably thought to be a continual, miserable and horrid quaking of his body for murdering his brother Abel.

{6} *He for a long time contended and strove with the wicked world to bring them to faith, repentance and reformation of their evil ways*: that so in Christ the seed of the woman they might have bruised the serpent's head. *And the LORD said, My Spirit shall not always strive with man; for that he also is flesh: yet his days shall be a hundred and twenty years.*[2115] God's Spirit strove with them three ways especially: (i) by the great patience and long-suffering of God, leading them to repentance;[2116] yea, after God had

---

[2108] Genesis 4:7
[2109] Genesis 4:4
[2110] Genesis 5:24 with Hebrews 11
[2111] Genesis 6:9, 17-18
[2112] Genesis 4:7, 12
[2113] Genesis 6:3, 7, 13, 17 & 7:4
[2114] Genesis 4:11, 15
[2115] Genesis 6:3
[2116] Romans 2:4

determined in the time of Noah to destroy the world, yet this long suffering waited for their return 120 years.[2117] (ii) By *preaching* to them (which are now *spirits in prison*) by the patriarchs of the old world,[2118] especially by Enoch the seventh from Adam (whose prophecy Jude recites),[2119] and by Noah the eighth person (the eighth saved in the ark but the tenth from Adam) *a preacher of righteousness*, so called because he preached both by his doctrine and by his practice in building the ark that God's *righteous judgment* would come upon the world, and also the *righteousness of Christ by faith* whereby they might escape God's judgments. (iii) By his secret illuminations, convictions, motions and stirrings in the hearts of many, causing them to make a saving use of God's patience, and the patriarchs preaching unto them.

{7} **Finally, when the world generally neglected and despised God's precious promise of lapsed sinners' recovery in Christ the seed of the woman, and were swallowed up with violence and all manner of wickedness incorrigibly: then the Lord brought in the flood upon the world of the ungodly,**[2120] **in the midst of their impiety and security, and destroyed them all.**[2121]

Thus this first administration of the Covenant began at the world's first corruption by sin, and ended at the world's first general destruction by the flood. Thus this first promise, though it had not the name and complete formality of a covenant; yet if the author, parties, matter and form thereof be duly considered, it had the nature and reality of a covenant.

Hitherto of God's Covenants of Promise, as discovered and administered in the first notable period of time, from Adam to Noah. namely, till about the 480th year of Noah's age (for about that time God renewed the Covenant with Noah), which was about the 1536th year from the world's creation and the first promise's publication.

[2117] 1 Peter 3:20
[2118] 1 Peter 3:18-20
[2119] Jude 14-15
[2120] 2 Peter 2:5
[2121] Genesis 6 with Matthew 24:37-38, Luke 17:26-27

Chapter 2

Of the discovery and administration of the Covenants of Promise, in the second period of time: from Noah until Abraham.

The second remarkable period of time wherein the Lord God pleased to renew the Covenant of Faith, in reference to Christ promised, was from Noah until Abraham, namely: from the 480th year of Noah's life, or thereabouts,[2122] being the 1536th year from the world's creation till about the 71st year of Abram's life, when the promise of Christ was first made to Abram[2123] (as the author of *Sacred Chronology* clears it)[2124] which was in the 2079th year of the world. This period was very short, being but about 542 years, yet it was enlarged somewhat by the repetition of this covenant when Abram was 99 years old, and so it was extended to 571 years.[2125]

As this period of the covenant's administration was very short, so I shall proportionally contract myself in opening it with all convenient brevity. And for clearness sake I shall insist upon these three aphorisms especially, namely:

1. *That the Lord God, having determined to destroy the old world for its extreme wickedness, established his Covenant with righteous Noah, to save him, his family, and a seed of the creatures in the ark, from the common destruction.*

2. *That God, having destroyed the wicked old world by a flood of waters, not only resolved with himself, but also established his Covenant with Noah, with his seed, and with the creatures, never to destroy the earth any more by a flood. Annexing the rainbow as a token of the covenant.*

[2122] Compare Genesis 6:3 with 7:6
[2123] Genesis 12:1-3 with Acts 7:2-4
[2124] Roger Drake, Sacred Chronology, Difficulty 2, p.36
[2125] Genesis 17:1

3. *That these covenants of God with Noah, were a renewed discovery of the Covenant of Faith, touching sinners' salvation by Jesus Christ.* Some writers who purposely handle the subject of God's Covenants of Promise yet omit this period of the Covenant's discovery. Why, I know not – unless upon opinion that this Covenant of God with Noah was not the Covenant of Faith. This therefore I shall in this third aphorism endeavor to evince, after I have first briefly opened the two former aphorisms to make way thereunto.

Aphorism 1

The Lord God, having determined to destroy the old world for its extreme wickedness, established his Covenant with righteous Noah, to save him, his family, and a seed of living creatures in the ark, from the common destruction.

This aphorism may be briefly (1) confirmed, (2) explained, and (3) applied in certain corollaries or inferences thence resulting.

(1) For **_confirmation_**, it is clear that thus the Lord covenanted with Noah, from the historical narrative that Moses made hereof: *And God said unto Noah, the end of all flesh is come before me: for the earth is filled with violence through them; and behold I will destroy them with the earth. Make thee an ark of gopher wood, etc. And behold, I, even I do bring a flood of waters upon the earth, to destroy all flesh wherein is the breath of life, etc. But with thee will I establish my covenant: and thou shalt come into the ark; thou, and thy sons, and thy wife, and thy sons' wives with thee: and of every living thing of all flesh, two of every sort shalt thou bring into the ark, to keep them alive with thee: they shall be male and female.*[2126] These words clearly and fully prove the truth of the whole aphorism. And this is the very first place wherein the word בְּרִית *berith* or {*covenant*} is used in the whole Bible. Let us the more heedfully mind the meaning of it.

(2) For **_explanation_** of this federal transaction of God with Noah, consider: [1] what this word covenant means, [2] how God established his covenant with Noah, [3] who were the parties to this covenant, [4] what were the matters covenanted between them, and [5] what the occasion and end of this covenant is.

[2126] Genesis 6 throughout, especially verses 13-14, 17-19

[1] **What this word בְּרִית** *berith*, or, *covenant*, means, has been formerly at large explained in opening the *general nature of the covenant*.[2127] Here therefore no more needs to be super-added.

[2] *How God established his covenant with Noah: seeing he says, With thee will I establish my covenant?*[2128] Here he only promised to establish his covenant with Noah: but when, or how did he perform this promise?

Answer: {1} The Hebrew phrase וַהֲקִמֹתִי אֶת-בְּרִיתִי, *hakimothi et-berithi*, that is, *I will establish* (or, *make firm*; or, *make firmly to stand*) *my covenant*, is very emphatical. The word וַהֲקִמֹתִי, *I will establish*, is derived from קוּם, *koom*, which signifies either *to rise up*, or, *firmly to stand*. According to the former signification, it may be rendered, *I will lift up my covenant*: or, *I will make my covenant rise up*; that is, *I will make a covenant with thee*. An allusion to the customary manner of covenanting, wherein a *statue*, or a *stone*, or *heap of stones*, etc., was wont to be lifted up by the parties covenanting, to testify their agreement,[2129] as Oleaster has observed.[2130] According to the latter signification, it may be translated: *I will firmly-establish my covenant*, or, *I will firmly ensure my covenant*, or *make it stand sure*.[2131] For when a covenant is kept, it is said to stand; when it is broken, it is said to *fall*. This latter signification is herein thought more apposite and fit: denoting the firmness, sureness and faithfulness of God's covenant. {2} Though God promised to Noah, *I will establish my covenant with thee*, yet this promise of God was his establishment of his covenant. Here (says that learned Rivet)[2132] the Hebrews enquire, how God says he would establish his covenant, which he had not yet made. But both are in one and the same moment, for when it is entered into, it

---

[2127] See Book 1, Chapter 2, Aphorism 1
[2128] Genesis 6:8
[2129] Genesis 28:18, etc., & 31:44-45 to the end of the chapter.
[2130] Oleaster, Commentary on Genesis 6:18
[2131] "I will establish, that is, make sure and stable, and faithfully keep my Covenant. For so the word importeth, and other Scriptures open it. As, establish thou (2 Samuel 7:25) is expounded, Let it be faithful, (or, sure) 1 Chronicles 17:23. And to establish the words of a Covenant (2. Kings 23:3) is to do (or perform) them (2 Chronicles 34:31). and to continue in doing them, Galatians 3:10. with Deuteronomy 27:26." Henry Ainsworth Annot. on Genesis 6:18.
[2132] Andre Rivet in Genesis 9 Exercit. 53

is established. So then, God's publishing his Covenant to Noah, was his establishing his Covenant with him.

[3] *Who were the parties to this covenant?* The text, and the aphorism express them, namely: God and Noah.

God was the *author* of this Covenant, and the *party* promising and covenanting with Noah, to save him, when the whole world should be drowned.[2133] And God revealed this covenant *expressly*, and formally, styling it a covenant: not only *implicitly*. Nor did he express and declare this Covenant to Noah, *mediately* by the ministry of man, angel or creature: but *immediately* by his own lively voice; and this of mere *grace*.[2134] So that this Covenant was divine, in regard to the foundation of it; *eminent, excellent*, and *sure*, in respect of the publication of it.

Noah was the party restipulating certain duties to God, as God promised certain benefits to him. Noah's restipulation was partly *explicit*, partly *implicit*, as after will appear.[2135] Consider a little, who this Noah was, whom God thus honored with his covenant.

{1} For his *pedigree* or natural *descent*, he was the son of Lamech, etc.,[2136] the tenth from Adam, in a direct line: and by Noah's three sons, Shem, Ham, and Japheth, was the whole earth overspread and planted.[2137]

{2} For his *name*: Noah signifies *rest proceeding from comfort*, or *comforter*, or *restorer*. His father Lamech gave him this name, saying: *This same shall comfort us concerning our work and toil of our hands, because of the ground which the LORD hath cursed*.[2138] A prophetic denomination of him, who was to be a type of Christ the true Noah, in building the ark, and offering sacrifices,[2139] whereupon *the LORD smelled a savour of rest*, and promised no more to curse the earth for man's sake.[2140] In this name given to his son,

---

[2133] Genesis 6:13, etc., 18
[2134] Genesis 6:18
[2135] Genesis 6:18
[2136] 1 Chronicles 1:1-4, Genesis 5 throughout
[2137] Genesis 9:19
[2138] Genesis 5:29
[2139] Henry Ainsworth also speaks to this effect, Annotation on Genesis 5:29
[2140] Genesis 8:21

Lamech's faith is observable, not only touching the comfortable restoring of the drowned world by Noah, but also touching the restoring of ruined mankind by Jesus Christ, the *seed of the woman*.

{3} For his *religion*, God himself gives him high and ample commendation, both in Old and New Testament. For: (i) he was a *just and righteous person before God in his generations*.[2141] A righteous man in the midst of the unrighteous world, yea *an heir of righteousness which is by faith*.[2142] The Scripture names three persons eminent for righteousness, and Noah was one of those three, yea the first of those three,[2143] not only righteous in himself, but also *a preacher of righteousness* to the world.[2144] (ii) He was a *perfect and upright man*,[2145] without hypocrisy, guile, or deceit in his religion. He had the power as well as the form of godliness in him. (iii) He *walked with God*.[2146] His habitual course of life and conversation was with his God, when the world walked in wickedness. God was his God reconciled in Jesus Christ. For *can two walk together unless they be agreed?*[2147] The *guide* of his *actions*, the *center* of his *motions*, the *loadstone* of his *affections*, the *companion* of his *life*, and the chief end of all his *aims* and *undertakings*. Blessed Noah thus walking with God, thus having sweet communion with God in a wicked world, had a *heaven on earth*, yea as it were a *heaven in hell*. (iv) He excelled in faith, believing things revealed of God, though unseen.[2148] (v) He had a holy awe and fear of God and his judgments.[2149] (vi) He was notably obedient to all God's commands, though against greatest difficulties and discouragements, especially in that stupendous act of making the ark.[2150]

[2141] Genesis 6:9 & 7:1
[2142] Hebrews 11:7
[2143] Ezekiel 14:14, 20
[2144] 2 Peter 2:5
[2145] Genesis 6:9
[2146] Genesis 6:9
[2147] Amos 3:3
[2148] Hebrews 11:7
[2149] Hebrews 11:7
[2150] Genesis 6:22, Hebrews 11:7

{4} For his *privileges*: God invested him with many, and those most remarkable. For: (i) he was singularly preserved by divine grace from the general corruption that in his times had overrun the whole world.[2151] (ii) He alone with his family was saved in the ark which he made at God's appointment: when the whole world besides was universally drowned with a deluge of waters.[2152] (iii) He alone is accepted in *covenant* with God touching his and his family's salvation from the flood, 120 years before the flood came.[2153] (iv) He was of the period of the old world, and the beginner of the new world; the *omega* of that, the *alpha* of this, having lived before the flood 600 years, and living 350 years after the flood,[2154] so that he was compared to Janus with two faces. And in respect of this new world, replenished by him and his family, he was as another Adam: all mankind being reduced to him, and flowing from him. (v) He – in making the ark and therein saving his family with himself from the dreadful flood which destroyed the world of the ungodly – was a special type of Christ, as afterwards shall appear. (vi) Finally, of him *according to the flesh Jesus Christ came, who is over all, God blessed for ever. Amen.*[2155] This was that Noah with whom God established his Covenant.

[4] ***What were the matters, or things covenanted between God and Noah?*** Answer: the subject matter of this covenant is twofold: {1} promised, on God's part, and {2} restipulated, on Noah's part.

{1} On God's part, the matter promised was the preservation and salvation of Noah and his family with a seed of living creatures in the ark, from the destructive flood of waters, wherewith the whole world should be drowned.[2156] This God promised, and this he punctually performed to Noah, and to them that were with him in the ark, according to his covenant.

{2} On Noah's part the matters restipulated by him, and which God required of him, were: (i) *Faith*, to believe God, warning him of things not

---

[2151] Genesis 7:1
[2152] Genesis 7:23
[2153] Genesis 6:3, 17-18, etc.
[2154] Genesis 7:6 & 9:28
[2155] Luke 3:36, Romans 9:5
[2156] Genesis 6:17-18 & 7:23

seen as yet,[2157] namely that God would destroy the whole world with a flood, at the end of 120 years. That God notwithstanding would save him, his family and a seed of the creatures in an ark, for replenishing the world anew. The apostle ascribes this to his faith. And without both the *assenting* and *applying* act of faith, Noah could never have entertained or depended upon this divine revelation, nor have done what God prescribed. (ii) *Obedience* to God's will and warning, namely: (a) In *preparing an ark for the saving of his house*.[2158] A strange, a difficult, a chargeable, a wearisome and tedious work for 120 years together. (b) In providing and laying up food in the ark for himself, and for all in the ark with him, for the space of a whole year: for as long as they were in the ark.[2159] (c) In entering into the ark: he, his house, and the creatures, as God had commanded him.[2160] (d) In persisting in his *righteousness, integrity*, and *walking with God*:[2161] for which God so commended him, and rewarded him.[2162] God's *commending* and rewarding him for these excellencies was an implicit *commanding* and indenting with him to continue therein, nor can it be reasonably thought anything besides that Noah thus understood the Lord and implicitly resolved and contracted with him to persevere in these acceptable virtues and practices.

[5] **What was the occasion and end of the Lord's making this covenant with Noah?** The occasion of God's establishing this Covenant with Noah, was double, namely:

{1} *The extreme wickedness of the old world, for which God determined to destroy it with a flood.*[2163] Hereupon God took occasion to reveal his Covenant to Noah. The wickedness of the old world was extreme. For: (i) piety and true religion were overgrown with wickedness and great ungodliness.[2164] The preaching of Enoch and Noah, the patience and long-suffering of God, and the

---

[2157] Hebrews 11:7
[2158] Hebrews 11:7
[2159] Genesis 6:21
[2160] Genesis 7:7-11 & 8:13-14
[2161] Genesis 6:6-9
[2162] Genesis 6:9 & 7:1
[2163] Genesis 6 throughout
[2164] Genesis 6:5

striving of God's Spirit with them, little or nothing availing to bring them to repentance and reformation.[2165] (ii) Equity and righteousness to man was swallowed up with tyranny, violence, and oppression.[2166] Giants became great tyrants, and the earth was filled with violence. (iii) Sobriety and temperance were overthrown, *partly* by their intemperate *eating and drinking* to excess, not for necessity.[2167] Partly by their intemperate and disordered marriages, for satisfaction of their lusts, rather than for procreation of a holy seed. *The sons of God saw the daughters of men, that they were fair; and they took them wives of all which they chose.*[2168] The godly families *in the church*, matched promiscuously with the wicked posterity of Cain *out of the church*; for *Cain departed from the presence of the LORD.*[2169] This brought a wicked confusion into godly families. (iv) All this sinfulness of the old world was exceedingly heightened by these heinous aggravations, namely:

(a) The extensiveness and universality thereof. Not only Cain's family had degenerated, but *the whole earth was corrupt, all flesh had corrupted his way upon the earth.*[2170] (b) The intensiveness of this general corruption, wholly and continually depraving all their inward principles. *God saw that the wickedness of man was great in the earth, and that every imagination* (Hebrew: *figment*) *of the thoughts of his heart was only evil continually* (Hebrew: *every day*)[2171] – what? Not only works and words, but the very thoughts of man's heart: yea the figment or imagination of his thoughts: yea, every imagination; was evil, only evil: continually evil. How emphatically! Again, *the earth was filled with violence.*[2172] (c) Their deep security in all their wickedness; *till the very day that Noah entered into the ark, and they knew not until the flood came and took them all away.*[2173] (d) Their final impenitence: God's *patience and*

[2165] Jude 14-15, 2 Peter 2:5, Genesis 6:3
[2166] Genesis 6:4, 11
[2167] Luke 17:26-27
[2168] Genesis 6:2, Luke 17:27
[2169] Genesis 4:16
[2170] Genesis 6:11-13
[2171] Genesis 6:5
[2172] Genesis 6:13
[2173] Matthew 24:38-39

long-suffering, the *preaching of Noah*, and the *striving of God's Spirit* with them, nothing at all prevailing with them to reclaim them; but they were then drowned, and now remain *spirits in prison*.[2174]

{2} *The singular godliness of Noah in the midst of all the world's wickedness*:[2175] this was the other occasion of God's covenanting with him to save him, when the world should be destroyed.

The *end* or *intent* of God, in making this Covenant with Noah, seems especially to be fourfold, namely: (i) thereby to signify his peculiar love, grace, and mercy to righteous Noah,[2176] and that familiarly in a covenant way, when his justice, severity and wrath should be so dreadfully revealed from heaven against the unrighteous world. (ii) Thereby to encourage Noah the more effectively to undertake and accomplish that chargeable, difficult, dangerous, and tedious task of framing the ark: seeing in that ark God assured him, and his, of preservation, as Calvin well observes.[2177] (iii) Thereby to instruct Noah and his family in the mystery of the *Covenant of Faith*, touching the salvation of God's elect family by the *true Noah, Jesus Christ*, and by the *streams* of his blood, as we shall see afterward. (iv) Thereby to let all in after ages see that God *knoweth how to deliver the righteous, but to reserve the unjust to exemplary punishment*.[2178]

(3) **Corollaries**, or **inferences** hence resulting. Hence,

[1] *The sin of the old world was exceeding great, and reached up to heaven: seeing that it was plagued with so great a judgment.* The earth was filled with violence, and it was filled with vengeance. The sin was universal, and the judgment universal. All flesh had corrupted his way on earth: and all flesh is swept away from off the earth. Oh, heavy punishment! Oh, heinous sinfulness!

[2] *The fruit of sin is bitter, woeful and deadly: though the acting of sin seem never so sweet and delightful.* The eating of the forbidden fruit was

---

[2174] 1 Peter 3:18-20
[2175] Genesis 6:9 to the end of the chapter, & 7:1
[2176] Genesis 6:8
[2177] John Calvin's commentary on Genesis 6:18
[2178] 2 Peter 2:3-11

pleasing to Adam and Eve,[2179] but the *curse* that followed upon them, all mankind, and the whole creation, was gall and wormwood.[2180] The old world's impiety, unrighteousness, intemperance, mixed marriages, security, etc., were delightfully acted, but when the flood took them all away for these things, the dead carcasses of man and beast being spread like dung upon the face of all the habited earth, they were dismally plagued. Beware of the first and smallest beginnings of sin: *it will be bitterness in the end*.

[3] *The wrath of God, after means of grace and long waiting of his patience without fruit, is most severe against the ungodly.* To the old world, Enoch prophesied, Noah preached righteousness, and God's long suffering waited 120 years in his time for the world's reformation, but all were utterly disappointed and ineffectual, therefore God swallowed them up at once with a flood, husbands and wives, parents and children, masters and servants, young and old, male and female, bond and free, man and fowl and beast, they were all drowned together, not one of them was left, but those with Noah in the ark. Had not Noah preached, and God waited so long for them, their judgements had been more tolerable; but when they despised all means of grace, and tyred out all God's patience, then *the wrath of God came upon them to the uttermost.* Oh *it is a fearful thing to fall into the hands of the living God*,[2181] in this case! The greater God's patience, and means of grace on earth, if fruitless, the greater will be the damnation and torments of the wicked in hell. The longer God is in drawing his bow of patience, the deeper will be the wounds of the arrows of his vengeance. Though he has leaden heels, yet he has iron hands. When he is long before he strike, he strikes home when the blow comes. *It shall be more tolerable for Tyre and Sidon, than for thee Chorazin, and Bethsaida: for Sodom and Gomorrah than for Capernaum (that was lifted up to heaven in the means of grace) at the day of judgment.*[2182] Why? Because they had more means of grace than these. What city was honored like Jerusalem

---

[2179] Genesis 3:6
[2180] Genesis 3:16-20, Galatians 3:10, Romans 8:20-22
[2181] Hebrews 10:31
[2182] Matthew 11:20-25

with means of salvation? And what city was ever laid so low in judgements for despising those means? If England should abuse all God's patience and be incurable under all God's means and medicines; where shall England appear?

[4] *Oh how precious treasures are piety and integrity that preserve from public judgments and common calamities.* Upright Noah is alive and safe in the ark, when the wicked are rolling, gasping and dying in the merciless waves. The giants of those times with all their power, greatness, violence, tyranny and wealth, could not save themselves from drowning: but *Noah's righteousness delivered him from death.*[2183] Who would not be in love with piety and integrity? Piety and integrity will bring us into God's ark: these will preserve us when the transgression of the ungodly shall destroy them.

[5] *The Lord knows how to preserve the righteous when the wicked are destroyed.* He had an ark for Noah, when the old world is choked in the flood.[2184] He had Zoar for Lot when Sodom and Gomorrah are consumed with fire and brimstone.[2185] He had a safe refuge for Jeremiah even in prison, when Jerusalem is taken.[2186] Let us therefore sincerely walk with him, and depend upon him in greatest extremities, for *none can deliver in this sort.*[2187]

[6] *The Lord preserves his people by means ordinarily*: Noah, by an ark. Lot by flight from Sodom, etc. Yet sometimes those means are strange means: Noah was saved from drowning, by the same *waters* that drowned the world.[2188] Israel was preserved from the Egyptians, by the same waves that overwhelmed the Egyptians.[2189] Jonah was delivered from the belly of the sea, by being swallowed up by the belly of the whale.[2190] Therefore we use means but we trust God. To depend upon God without use of means is to tempt God and endanger ourselves; to depend upon means and not upon God is to despise God and idolize means.

[2183] Proverbs 11:4
[2184] Genesis 6:18, etc.
[2185] Genesis 19:20-22
[2186] Jeremiah 38:28 & 39:11-14
[2187] Daniel 3:29
[2188] 1 Peter 3:20
[2189] Exodus 14 & 15
[2190] Jonah 1:15, 17

[7] God's Covenant is his people's evidence or security for their salvation. By the fall of Adam we have forfeited all, both temporals and spirituals. Without a new contract or agreement with God, we are outlaws and can claim nothing. God, by covenant, interests us in Christ, and through Christ, in *all things*.[2191] Noah himself had no security for his salvation from the flood until God secured him by covenant; nor have Noah's posterity any protection from a second deluge but by God's other covenant with him and them.[2192] Nay, without God's Covenant, what evidence or security could lapsed sinners have for their spiritual recovery or eternal salvation? God's Covenant then is the *great charter* of our salvation. By this we have and hold all. How should we then study and value God's Covenant and labor to be federate parties with God therein?

[2191] 1 Corinthians 3:21-23
[2192] Genesis 8:20-22 & 9:8-18

Aphorism 2

The Lord God having destroyed the wicked old world by a flood of waters, not only resolved within himself, but also covenanted with Noah, with his seed, and with the creatures, never to destroy the earth anymore by a flood: annexing the rainbow for a token of the Covenant.

This was God's second covenant with Noah: his additional covenant super-added to the former. For clearing of it, this aphorism (as the former) shall be: (1) confirmed, (2) opened, and, (3) applied.

(1) Confirmed this aphorism may be, in the principal branches of it, by evident Scripture testimonies. As,

[1] that God resolved and determined with himself, after the world's destruction by the flood, never to destroy it again by a flood of waters. *And Noah went forth of the ark,—and Noah builded an altar unto the LORD, and took of every clean beast, and of every clean fowl, and offered burnt-offerings on the altar. And the LORD smelled a sweet savour, and the LORD said in his heart* (there's his determination with himself), *I will not again curse the ground any more for man's sake,* (though the imagination of man's heart be evil from his youth); *neither will I again smite any more every thing living, as I have done. Henceforth all the days of the earth, seed-time and harvest, and cold and heat, and summer and winter, and day and night shall not cease.*[2193]

[2] That God covenanted this with Noah, with his seed, and with all living creatures. *And God spake to Noah, and to his sons with him, saying: And I, behold I, establish my covenant with you, and with your seed after you, and with every living creature that is with you, of the fowl, of the cattle, and of every beast of the earth with you, from all that go out of the ark, to every beast of the earth. And I will establish my covenant with you; neither shall all flesh be*

[2193] Genesis 7:21-23 with 8:20-22

cut off any more by the waters of a flood, neither shall there any more be a flood to destroy the earth.[2194]

[3] That God also annexed the rainbow as a sign or token to this covenant, *And God said, This is the token of the covenant, which I make between me and you, and every living creature that is with you, for perpetual generations; I do set my bow in the cloud, and it shall be for a token of the covenant between me and the earth. And it shall come to pass, when I bring a cloud over the earth, that the bow shall be seen in the cloud: and I will remember my covenant, which is between me and you, and every living creature of all flesh, and the waters shall no more become a flood to destroy all flesh. And the bow shall be in the cloud; and I will look upon it, that I may remember the everlasting covenant between God and every living creature of all flesh that is upon the earth. And God said unto Noah, this is the token of the covenant, which I have established between me and all flesh that is upon the earth.*[2195] By this heap of words and variety of expressions touching the tokens of God's Covenant with Noah, we may perceive both what need Noah and his sons had to be comforted against a future flood, the deluge now newly past leaving such prints of astonishment and amazement upon their spirits; and also how solicitous the Lord was by those reiterated phrases to raise up their faith and confidence for future, above their present fears and despondencies. And in the last clause, he summarily and emphatically recapitulates the whole, *this is the token of the covenant which I have established,* etc. Yea (as Mercerus notes) some among the Jews think that by these words, God demonstrated a rainbow in the cloud to Noah for the strengthening of his faith.[2196]

(2) **Explained**, and opened this aphorism may be also, by inquiring into, and unfolding of these particulars, namely: [1] the causes and occasion of this Covenant, [2] the parties covenanting, [3] the matters covenanted, and [4] the token of this Covenant, the bow in the cloud.

[2194] Genesis 9:8-11, Isaiah 54:9
[2195] Genesis 9:12-17
[2196] Joan Mercer in praelec ad Genesis 9:7

[1] **The causes and occasion of this Covenant may be thus declared.** {1} The efficient cause, or author of it, was God. God spake to Noah, saying: *And I, behold I establish my covenant with you.*[2197] {2} The inward impulsive or moving cause, can be imagined to have been none other, but his own mere grace and commiserating mercies to Noah, and the small remnant with him surviving the flood. {3} The outward impulsive or moving cause was twofold: (i) *Less principal and typical*, namely: Noah's altar and burnt offerings offered thereon to God, in which God smelled a sweet savor, and whereupon he took occasion to resolve and covenant never more to destroy the world with a flood.[2198] (ii) *More principal and anti-typical, or typified*: namely: Jesus Christ and his offering himself up a sacrifice for sin to God upon the altar of his Godhead, where in he was *an odor of a sweet smell to God*.[2199] And this was the outward moving cause of God's covenanting both his elect's recovery and, the world's restitution and preservation in reference thereunto; as shall after more appear. {4} The final cause, or end intended in this Covenant, was: (i) partly to assure Noah and his posterity of his great mercy intended to the world, notwithstanding man's sin, in that it should never more be destroyed by a flood of waters.[2200] (ii) Partly to instruct him and his seed, that as sin brought destruction upon the creature: so Christ satisfying God's justice for sin, should bring restitution and preservation to the creature. (iii) Partly to glorify the riches of God's grace, mercy and loving-kindness in both.

[2] **The parties covenanting are:** {1} God, on the one hand. God as appeased and smelling a savour of rest, upon Noah's sacrifices in this notion God establishes this Covenant. {2} Noah and his sons, and their seed, and all living creatures, on the other hand.[2201] Here (as Calvin notes)[2202] there are three degrees of federates with God mentioned, or (as Pareus)[2203] four, namely:

[2197] Genesis 9:8-9
[2198] Genesis 8:20-22
[2199] Ephesians 5:2 with Heb.
[2200] Genesis 8:20-22 & 9:8-11
[2201] Genesis 9:8-10, 12, 15-17
[2202] Calvin on Genesis 9:9
[2203] Pareus on Genesis 9:9, etc.

(i) Noah himself. The parent and common father of the new world: the second Adam. With whom the Lord had established his covenant towards the period of the old world. God honored this righteous, sincere, and heavenly man with the first place. (ii) Noah's sons, Shem, Ham, Japheth, who were saved with Noah in the ark. The females are implied and included in the males. (iii) Their seed after them, namely: all the posterity of Noah, and of his sons, till the end of the world, for perpetual generations.[2204] In this branch, we are comprehended – and all mankind. God covenants not only with his people, but with their seed, and with their seed's seed, that keep covenant with him, even to all generations.[2205] This Covenant therefore in some sort concerns all the world. Oh the infinite bounty of the Lord in his federal administrations! (iv) All living creatures, fowls, beasts, and creeping things. Them also being created for man, God takes into covenant with man. Noah was confederate with God herein, and the other three sorts were as sub-federates under him. But here some doubts may arise, and are to be removed.

[**Doubt 1**]: *Seeing as God established his covenant not only with Noah, but with his sons, and their seed also, God seems to admit into covenant with himself the wicked as well as the righteous: for Ham was ungodly, and cursed by his own father; and more of the posterity of these three sons of Noah were wicked than godly.*[2206] *Consequently, God covenants not only with Christ and his seed, but also with the seed of the serpent.*[2207] *And godliness alone has not the promise of this and the life to come.*

Resolution: This is a material doubt. Thus conceive:

{1} God never covenants with the *seed of the serpent*, formally *as such*; nor makes promises to the ungodly in that notion as they are ungodly. For then God should approve them in their evil and equalize them to his elect: both of which it is impossible for God to do.

[2204] Genesis 9:12
[2205] Isaiah 59:20-21
[2206] Genesis 9:22, 24-27
[2207] 1 Timothy 4:8

{2} Since the fall, the Covenant of Faith and all the promises of it are (as has been shown)[2208] settled upon Christ, and in him upon them that are his, and that are godly, in one respect or another: or at least upon others, with reference to the godly, and for the benefit of Christ's members. Thus promises were made to wicked Cyrus, with reference to his church: God intending him to be a noble instrument of her good, etc.[2209] Now people may be said to be godly, or to be Christ's in several ways, namely: *actually, virtually, professedly*. (i) *Actually*, when they are truly implanted into Christ already by their effectual calling, and are really sanctified.[2210] Of these there is no doubt, but God's Covenant and promise are actually and formally theirs. As called and sanctified, they are within the Covenant.[2211] Such a one was Noah, here first named in this covenant with God. And probably such were Shem and Japheth, his sons. (ii) *Virtually* and *potentially*, when they are in a capacity or possibility of becoming Christ's. Thus all that are elected, though many of them be as yet unborn,[2212] are Christ's virtually according to election; and God establishing his Covenant with those that are his, and with their seed, must needs intend all such before they are in being. Thus God takes in here not only Noah and his sons, but their seed also, (iii) *professedly*, men may be said to be Christ's, and godly, when they make a true profession of Christ, and of godliness: and this either in themselves, as adult grown up to years of discretion,[2213] or in their Christian parents, as infants which by reason of being so born are counted federally holy, and in covenant with their parents.[2214] And thus, God entered into covenant not only with Noah, Shem, and Japheth, but also with Ham, he at that time professing godliness with his pious father and family, and not discovering his lewdness until after this Covenant was made.[2215] Yea, he entered into covenant with their seed as well as with

---

[2208] 2 Corinthians 1:20, 1 Timothy 4:8, Section before in Book 2, Chapter 2, Aphorism 2
[2209] Isaiah 44:28 & 45:1-5
[2210] Romans 8:28-30
[2211] Acts 2:39
[2212] Romans 11:5
[2213] Acts 8:13
[2214] 2 Corinthians 7:14
[2215] Genesis 9:8-18 with verse 22, etc.

themselves, their seed professing godliness *implicitly* and *fundamentally* in their parents. If then the Lord admit both root and branches, parents and their seed into his covenant jointly, how unwarrantable and dangerous are the acts of Anabaptists who forbid infants of such parents to partake of the initiating sign and token of the Covenant?

{3} In God's Covenants, we must further distinguish between the *outward administration* and common benefits thereof which come short of salvation: and the *inward efficacy* and special benefits thereof which reach unto salvation. In the former sense, all the seed of Noah and of his sons were comprehended in this covenant, and thereby secured against any other universal deluge of water, but in the latter sense only the elect of their seed are comprised in this covenant, as tending to secure them from eternal perdition in Christ.

[**Doubt 2**]: *But how and in what sense can God be said to establish his covenant with the brute creatures, fowls, beasts and creeping things, that can neither understand God's promises, nor restipulate any performances?*

Resolution: {1} Some say that this covenant here made with Noah, etc., was absolute, and required no conditions on the creature's part: and such an absolute covenant may be made even with brute creatures, though they neither understand it nor restipulate. But every covenant consists in mutual agreement. *Explicit* or *implicit*. Promises may be absolute without restipulation, but not covenants. And in this covenant, we shall find some things restipulated.

{2} Others resolve better, who say: God covenanted here with these brute creatures, not properly and directly for themselves, but improperly, indirectly and relatively, with reference and relation to mankind, that they should not any more be generally destroyed with a flood. For as at first these creatures were all made for man's use and service,[2216] and were afterwards drowned in the flood, not for their own sakes, but for man's sin;[2217] so now while man

---

[2216] Genesis 1:26-28
[2217] Genesis 6 throughout

should continue in this world, God covenants that these creatures should continue also for his service and benefit.

[3] The matters covenanted in this covenant are, either on God's part, or on the part of Noah, his sons and their seed. God on his part covenanted that he would nevermore destroy the earth and the living creatures therein with an universal deluge, as he had done, but that the natural courses and revolutions of times and seasons, should successively continue till the world's end.[2218] Herein therefore God has given notable security and assurance that the whole earth shall no more be drowned with a *general flood*. Yet this hinders not, but that:

{1} Particular persons and places may be destroyed with floods of waters, and outbreaking of the unruly sea, as has come to pass both in England and in foreign countries. Particulars and individuals may be destroyed by waters, but not the whole universe.

{2} The whole world, (though it shall not be destroyed by a flood and streams of waters, yet) may be destroyed with streams of fire. *For the heavens shall pass away with a great noise, and the elements shall melt with fervent heat, the earth also and the works that are therein shall be burnt up.*[2219] Noah, *his sons, and their seed* on their part, at least *implicitly* restipulate with God: (i) To believe this promise of God, that the earth and the living creatures therein shall no more be destroyed generally with the waters of a flood. (ii) To believe in Christ the true sacrifice appeasing God's wrath against the world, and restoring stability to the perishing creature, and so becoming the foundation of this and of all God's Covenants and promises. (iii) To make use of the rainbow appearing, as a sign or token of this covenant, for strengthening their faith therein.

[4] The token of the Covenant is God's bow in the cloud,[2220] as has formerly been expressed from the text. For better understanding of this token,

---

[2218] Genesis 8:21-22 with 9:8-18
[2219] 2 Peter 3:10
[2220] Genesis 9:12-18

consider: {1} what bow this is, {2} when this bow was set in the cloud, and {3} what manner of sign or token it was, and is, in respect of this covenant.

{1} What bow this is, which is added as a token of this covenant, may be concluded from that phrase, *I will set my bow in the cloud*.[2221] That is, the *rainbow*, which is the most beautiful of all the meteors, and most admirable both in its generation and figure. Hence the poets call it *filiam thaumantis*, that is, *the daughter of that God which is most wonderful*.[2222] It is called a *bow*, because it resembles a bended bow in the figure of it; a bow in the cloud, because there only it appears: the rain-bow, because it naturally signifies rain; iris, in Latin from the word {Ἶρις}, *to foretell*, because it still foretells some natural, or supernatural thing. The rainbow is an image or representation of a bow or semicircle of many colors arising in a moist waterish cloud from the various reflections and refractions of the sunbeams thereupon. The chief colors of the rainbow are three: namely: a *reddish* color uppermost, a *greenish* color middlemost, a *waterish* color lowest, and sometimes there appears a *yellowish* color, from the commixture of the red and green. Further discourse about the natural mysteries in the rainbow, I leave to the natural philosopher, as not so pertinent to my present purpose.

{2} When this rainbow was set in the cloud, is variously disputed. Some think it was first set in the cloud at that very time when God made this covenant with Noah. Mercerus says, Rashi was of this opinion,[2223] and that at the same time as God spoke these words to Noah, he brought a dewy cloud into the air with a rainbow in it, showing it to Noah, saying, *this is the token of the covenant*, etc. Others rather conclude that whether at that time God showed the bow to Noah or not, the rainbow did appear in the clouds long before that time,[2224] there being the selfsame natural causes to produce this natural effect of the rainbow before as well as since the flood, and no impediment hindering such production. The rainbow might be before the

---

[2221] Genesis 9:13
[2222] Videatur B Kekerma 1. Syllem. Physic. lib. 6. sub finem.
[2223] John Mercer on Genesis 9:17
[2224] David Pareus on Genesis 9:12, Andre Rivet in Genesis 9, Exercitation 60, sub finem - John Calvin, commentary on Genesis 9:13

flood, from the beginning, as a natural effect of natural causes – but until after the flood when God made this covenant, it never was a *sign* or *token of a supernatural covenant*.

{3} What manner of sign or token of the Covenant the rainbow was, we may thus conceive. *Signs or tokens are things that signify and betoken some other thing to the mind, besides what they represent unto the sense. Signs are either natural, or voluntary and instituted.*

(i) *Natural* signs are they which of themselves, and in their own nature signify something present or future. (a) Present, as smoke is a sign of fire, paleness of some disease, etc. Such signs are merely significative. (b) Future, as the *red evening* fore-signifies a fair day,[2225] the red morning a foul day; the rainbow signifies rain shortly to come, etc.[2226]

(ii) *Voluntary* or *instituted* signs are such as signify, not of their own nature, but only according to the will or pleasure of the author or institutor thereof. Thus the passover signified Christ,[2227] bread his body,[2228] wine his blood, and here the *rainbow* signifies *security*, that the world shall no more be generally drowned with a flood. So then the rainbow which physically and *naturally* denotes rain, *theologically*, supernaturally and by institution signifies fair weather and security from rain and a flood. It's not a *natural*, but an *instituted sign*.[2229] When we look upon it, we are not so much to take notice

---

[2225] Matthew 16:3
[2226] Matthew 16:4
[2227] 1 Corinthians 5:7
[2228] 1 Corinthians 11:23-25
[2229] "The rainbow was no natural, but an instituted sign, and therefore it may seal the assurance of the promise, though there were no correspondence between it and the thing signified: and yet it was the fitter to be a sign of security from the future flood.
1. Because of the place, which is in the clouds of heaven, whence the rain came that drowned the world before.
2. Because the bow is bended upwards towards God, not towards the creature below, as when it is taken in hand to shoot at a mark: Nor is there in the bow any arrow, which is said to be made ready upon the string, when hurt is intended, Psalm 11:2.
3. Because the rainbow commonly appears with rain, and so where men might begin to fear this judgment, there they may take comfort against it, in that it is a sign of his covenant for safety.

of its *natural*, as of its *supernatural* and *instituted signification*, and of God's great favor in resolving never to drown the world again, remembered thereby. Thus God sometimes makes use of contrary means, for our good. The rainbow then confirms and seals the certainty of God's Covenant, and our assurance thereof – not by *natural signification*, but by *supernatural institution*. Those conjectures of some are more witty than solid and weighty, who thus interpret the natural colors of the rainbow namely: the *waterish color*, which is lowest, to signify the flood past, the *greenish color*, which is in the midst, to signify the mercy present, and security against another general flood; and the fiery color, which is highest, to signify the future destruction of the world by fire, as Peter intimates.[2230]

(3) **Applied** this aphorism may be in these brief ensuing corollaries. Hence,

[1] Noah was *singularly honored and favored of God*, in that God established his covenant twice with him; namely: *before* the flood, to assure him that himself and family should not perish with the wicked world;[2231] *after* the flood, to assure him that he would never bring such another flood upon the world.[2232]

[2] *The greatness of God's commiserating grace and mercy to mankind is to be observed and admired in this dispensation*. Especially in that: {1} God's judgment upon the old world is closed up with mercy to the new, though as sinful as the old. {2} This mercy is tendered in a covenant, and that a covenant upon divine record. {3} This covenanted mercy is assured by a sacrament: the rainbow. {4} This mercy, so far as temporal, is extended to all – to the wicked, as well as to the godly – yea to creatures irrational, neither understanding the nature nor obligation of the Covenant, as well as to rational creatures.

---

4. Because the rainbow appears not but when there is a clearness and a brightness In some part of the sky: but at the general flood it was all black with rain."
See the late annotations on Genesis 9:13
[2230] 2 Peter 3:20
[2231] Genesis 6:18, etc.
[2232] Genesis 9:8-18

[3] *There shall never be another general flood to drown the world,*[2233] nor shall the natural revolution and course of seed-time and harvest, cold and heat, summer and winter, day and night cease by any general judgment, while this earth continues.[2234]

[4] *When we see God's bow in the cloud, we should heedfully remember God's severity in drowning the world for sin, and God's goodness assuring the new world that it shall never be drowned with a general flood any more.*

[2233] Genesis 9:11
[2234] Genesis 8:21-22

Aphorism 3

These two Covenants of God, established with Noah, before and after the flood, for saving Noah and his family in the ark by water from perishing with the wicked world, and for preserving the world from future destruction by a general flood, were a renewed discovery and administration of the Covenant of Faith, touching sinners' salvation by Jesus Christ.

The two former aphorisms I have briefly opened, for the better clearing of this. In them, God's Covenant with Noah has been explained in reference to the temporal benefits therein expressed in this, God's Covenant with Noah, is to be unfolded in reference to spiritual benefits and mysteries under those temporals implied. In the two former aphorisms, we have seen the outside of these covenants; in this, we shall behold the inside also. For more full satisfaction herein, consider:

(1) That these Covenants of God with Noah were a renewed discovery and administration of the Covenant of Faith touching sinners' recovery and salvation by Jesus Christ. (2) What was the spirituality, or spiritual meaning of this covenant. (3) What additional things are annexed to this federal administration, more than to the first from Adam until Noah. And consequently, what differences and agreements there were between these two dispensations. (4) Corollaries or inferences from the whole.

(1) That *these two Covenants of God with Noah, before and after the general flood were a renewed administration of the Covenant of Faith, touching sinners' recovery and salvation by Jesus Christ*, may be evinced by these ensuing arguments, namely:

[1] All God's Covenants and promises since man's fall were founded, established and principally accomplished in Jesus Christ the sinner's savior. *For all the promises of God in him* (that is, in Jesus Christ) *are yea, and in him*

Amen, unto the glory of God: as has been formerly explained.²²³⁵ The same Christ for substance being tendered in them all: in several ages, variously. Why then shall Jesus Christ – and the mystery of sinners' salvation by him – be excluded from these covenants and promises to Noah? It's granted that Christ was revealed in these covenants with Noah, very dimly, obscurely, and but implicitly; and it cannot be denied, but that in all the several administrations of the Covenants of Promise before Christ's coming in the flesh, Christ was represented very obscurely, especially in the first administrations, when divine grace in him began but to dawn and break forth to the world. Yet in the first promise, which is darkest of all, we have found Christ and sinners' recovery by him intended and implied:²²³⁶ {1} in the seed of the woman, {2} in the enmity between the seed of the woman and the serpent, {3} in the bruising of the serpent's head by the woman's seed, and, {4} in the serpent's bruising of his heel. Why then should it seem a thing incredible or impossible to find out Christ, and sinners' salvation by him: {1} in Noah's and his family's salvation in the ark by water from destruction, {2} in his sacrifices offered, {3} in God's promises of his and the world's preservation from all such floods for future, and, {4} in the rainbow confirming the same? Surely there were some glimmerings of Christ, in Noah, the ark, the waters, salvation thereby, the altar, sacrifices, rainbow, etc., as after may more distinctly appear.

[2] Noah by his faith, being moved with fear at God's warning and making his ark, became heir of the righteousness which is by faith. *By faith Noah being warned of God of things not seen as yet, moved with fear, prepared an ark, to the saving of his house, by the which he condemned the world, and became heir of the righteousness which is by faith.*²²³⁷ In which words note: {1} the foundation of Noah's faith, namely: God's warning him of things unseen as yet. God's will and warning by his word is the ground of our faith. {2} The commendation of Noah's faith by the excellent effects, fruits or advantages thereof, notably flowing from one another, namely: (i) a reverential awe and

---

²²³⁵ 2 Corinthians 1:19-20 with 1 Timothy 4:8, Galatians 3:17, Hebrews 13:8
²²³⁶ Genesis 3:14-15
²²³⁷ Hebrews 11:7

respect to God and to his warning revealed, being moved with fear. (ii) Hereupon an obediential *preparation of an ark*, (a) primarily, *for the saving of his own house*. (b) Secondarily, *for the condemning of the world*. In his building of which ark he condemned the world two ways: partly, by his faith and obedience in building it: hereby he condemned the unbelieving and disobedient world. Partly, by his preaching to the old world whilst he did build it – every knock upon the ark for 120 years together being as a penitential sermon to the world of the ungodly. Hereby he condemned the obstinate and impenitent world. (c) Consequently from both, a true title to, and *heirship of the righteousness which is by faith*, even as an heir has right and title to his inheritance. This *righteousness by faith* is that perfect righteousness of Jesus Christ, which God of his mere grace imputes to them that by faith accept and receive the same, having renounced all self-righteousness, and all other ways of sinners' justification whatsoever.[2238] It's called {*God's righteousness*}[2239] because it is a righteousness whereof God is author, which alone God will accept, and which consists in the perfect obedience of him who is God as well as man. It's styled {*the righteousness by faith*}, or *of faith*, because it is instrumentally apprehended and applied only by faith.[2240] It is opposed to the *righteousness of the law*, called *our own righteousness*,[2241] which consists in our own perfect and perpetual personal fulfilling of the law:[2242] this being not our own, but Christ's righteousness, perfectly fulfilling the law, and undergoing the curse thereof for us,[2243] and making his righteousness ours by faith.[2244] Of this *righteousness of Christ*, Noah became heir, whilst by faith he reverenced God's warning touching the flood, and prepared an ark according to God's Covenant with him, for his family's salvation. Hence therefore it is evident that Noah, in all this *federal transaction* between God and him, had a special eye to Christ

---

[2238] Romans 3:21-22
[2239] Romans 3:21-22, Matthew 6:33, Romans 10:3
[2240] Romans 3:22 & 10:6
[2241] Romans 10:3-6, Philippians 3:9
[2242] Romans 10:5, Galatians 3:10
[2243] Romans 5:17-19, Galatians 4:4-5, 3:12-14
[2244] Romans 3:24-25

by faith, and that beyond the *temporal salvation* of his house in the ark by waters from the general deluge, he beheld and apprehended the *spiritual salvation* of Christ's house the church, and peculiarly of himself from the wrath of God by Jesus Christ and his blood; otherwise how could this *act of his faith* have made him *heir of Christ's righteousness*? None can inherit Christ's righteousness, but by faith in Christ. Consequently this Covenant of God with Noah, touching his *salvation in the ark by water*, principally intended the great salvation by Christ: and so was an administration of the Covenant of Faith.

[3] Noah was a singular type of Christ; the ark, a figure of the church; and the temporal saving of his house with himself in the ark by water, a special type of the salvation of Christ's elect in the church by Jesus Christ. Consequently, God's Covenant with Noah touching the saving of him and his family in the ark by water from the common destruction upon the wicked world, intended herein to signify the elect's salvation by Christ through faith, and so this covenant was the *Covenant of Faith* renewed with Noah touching sinners' recovery and salvation by Christ. The *consequence* is clear. The *antecedent*, consisting of three distinct branches, may be thus evidenced also in order.

{1} ***Noah was a singular type of Christ.*** The Scriptures not obscurely intimate this,[2245] and learned writers both ancient and modern affirm it.[2246] Parallel them a little, and then see how notably Noah adumbrated and resembled Jesus Christ.

(i) Of Noah it was foretold, that he should *comfort his family concerning their work and toil, and the curse of the ground.*[2247] Whereupon he was named Noah, that is, *resting, comforting,* or *restoring,* as before was noted. Of Christ

---

[2245] Matthew 24:37-39, Luke 17:26-27, 1 Peter 3:20-22

[2246] "Christ was represented also in Noah and in that ark of the whole world." Augustine, exposition in John, Tractate 9, p.80, A. Basil, 1569, Tom. 9, H. Broughton in *The general view of holy Scripture*, p.42, London 1640. Dr. Thomas Taylor in his *Christ Revealed*, chapter 3.

[2247] Genesis 5:29

also it was foretold that *he should save his people from their sins,*[2248] whereupon he was called Jesus, a savior, that *he should preach good tidings unto the meek; should bind up the broken-hearted; should proclaim liberty to the captives, and the opening of the prison to them that are bound; should proclaim the acceptable year of the LORD; should comfort all that mourn; should give unto the mourners in Sion beauty for ashes, the oil of joy for mourning, the garment of praise for the spirit of heaviness.*[2249] And how sweetly does Christ allure distressed souls to himself! *Come unto me all ye that labor and are heavy-laden, and I will give you rest; take my yoke upon you,—and ye shall find rest unto your souls.*[2250]

(ii) When *all flesh had corrupted his ways,*[2251] and the whole world was overflowed with extreme wickedness, yet *Noah was a just, and upright man, walking with God, and found grace in the eyes of the LORD.*[2252] So Jesus Christ, in the most corrupt times wherein he lived, was perfectly just,[2253] *did nothing amiss,*[2254] had *no guile in his mouth,*[2255] was *holy, harmless, undefiled, and separate from sinners,*[2256] *increased in favor with God and man,*[2257] and was *the Son of his Father's love.*[2258]

(iii) Noah was a priest, a prophet, and a king. (a) A *priest*, for *he builded an altar unto the LORD; and took of every clean beast, and of every clean fowl, and offered burnt-offerings upon the altar.*[2259] (b) A *prophet*, for he was *a preacher of righteousness* to the old world.[2260] And, (c) a *king*, for the flood having drowned the whole world except himself, and his family, Noah was the

---

[2248] Matthew 1:21
[2249] Isaiah 61:1-3, Luke 4:18-21
[2250] Matthew 11:28-29
[2251] Genesis 6:12
[2252] Genesis 6:8-9
[2253] Matthew 27:19, Psalm 45:6-7
[2254] Luke 23:41
[2255] Isaiah 53:9
[2256] Hebrews 7:26
[2257] Luke 2:40, 51
[2258] Colossians 1:13
[2259] Genesis 8:20
[2260] 2 Peter 2:5

sole monarch of the whole earth: and by his three sons, Shem, Ham, and Japheth was the whole earth over-spread; and all creatures subdued under them.[2261] So Christ was: (a) a *priest*, yea our *great high priest*,[2262] both making satisfaction to God's justice for our sins by offering up his manhood once upon the altar of his Godhead,[2263] and by making continual intercession in heaven for us.[2264] (b) A *prophet*, revealing unto sinners God's will touching their salvation,[2265] and *opening their understandings* to discern the same.[2266] (c) A *king*, conquering and subduing us to himself,[2267] applying his benefits to us purchased and revealed; governing,[2268] and guarding us,[2269] and crushing all his and our enemies under his foot.[2270]

(iv) Noah built a material ark, for the saving of his natural posterity therein from the general deluge of water, according to God's Covenant.[2271] So Jesus Christ builds a spiritual ark, his church, for the saving of all his elect, his supernatural posterity therein, from the deluge of God's wrath.[2272]

(v) Noah sacrificing *burnt-offerings to God, God smelled a savour of rest*, and took occasion hereby to promise and covenant with Noah never to destroy the world with a flood of waters, making his bow in the cloud a sign or token of the Covenant.[2273] So Jesus Christ *by the eternal Spirit offering up himself without spot to God*,[2274] *and giving himself for us an offering and a sacrifice to God for a sweet smelling savour*,[2275] the Lord hereupon has established *a new and everlasting covenant* with them that are Christ's, never to destroy them

---

[2261] Genesis 9:1-3, 19
[2262] Hebrews 4:14
[2263] Hebrews 9:14, 28 & 10:10-19
[2264] Hebrews 7:24-25 & 9:24, 1 John 2:1
[2265] John 1:18 & 15:15 & 20:31; 1 Peter 1:10-12
[2266] Luke 24:45
[2267] Psalm 110:2-3, Acts 15:14-17
[2268] Isaiah 33:22
[2269] Isaiah 32:1-2
[2270] 1 Corinthians 15:25, Psalm 110:1
[2271] Genesis 6:14 to the end
[2272] Hebrews 3:3, 6, Matthew 16:18
[2273] Genesis 8:20-22 & 9:8-18
[2274] Hebrews 9:14
[2275] Ephesians 5:2

for their sins by the deluge of his wrath, but to be *merciful to their iniquities, and remember their sins no more*; yea to *be their God, and that they shall be his people*,[2276] adding baptism[2277] and the Lord's supper[2278] as tokens and seals of this covenant.

(vi) The dreadful storm of the flood being over, *Noah sent forth out of the ark a dove, which returned to them into the ark with an olive branch* (an emblem of peace and comfort) *in her mouth*, signifying that the waters were abated.[2279] So Jesus Christ – the terrible storm and tempest of his passion and death for our sin being over – sends forth his Holy Spirit[2280] (sometimes appearing in the form of a dove)[2281] the author of comfort, peace and joy in the hearts of his people,[2282] *witnessing with their spirits that they are God's children*,[2283] that their sins are pardoned, their peace with God is concluded, and the flood of his wrath is forever turned away.

(vii) Finally, Noah was a restorer of the world ruined by the flood of waters: his sons over-spread the whole earth, and the creatures which he preserved and provided for in the ark replenished the world.[2284] So, and much more eminently, Jesus Christ is the restorer of the whole world, dissipated, scattered, broken, cursed and ruined for man's sin by the flood of God's wrath: redeeming, preserving and propagating his church throughout the whole world, restoring and ordering all creatures for the good of his church. *In the dispensation of the fulness of times, God has gathered together in one all things in Christ, both which are in heaven, and which are in earth, even in him; And has put all things under his feet: and gave him to be head over all things to the church.*[2285] And of Christ it is said, *He is before all things, and by him all things*

[2276] Hebrews 8:8 to the end & 13:20
[2277] Matthew 28:19, Acts 2:38-39
[2278] Matthew 26:26-28, 1 Corinthians 11:20, 23-25
[2279] Genesis 8:8-11
[2280] John 16:7, Acts 2 throughout
[2281] Matthew 3:16-17
[2282] John 16:7 & 14:16-17, Romans 14:17
[2283] Romans 8:16
[2284] Genesis 9:19
[2285] Ephesians 1:10, 20-23

consist. And he is the head of the body, the church: who is the beginning, the first-born from the dead, that in all things he might have the preeminence. For it pleased the Father that in him should all fullness dwell. And (having made peace through the blood of his cross) by him to reconcile all things unto himself by him, I say, whether they be things in earth, or things in heaven.[2286] Thus Noah, in reference to this federal transaction of God with him, notably resembled Jesus Christ. And therefore how can we but conclude that God's Covenants with Noah were intended for an administration of the *Covenant of Faith* touching sinners' recovery by Jesus Christ?

{2} ***The ark of Noah was a notable type of the church of Christ.*** The apostle Peter intimates so much, in the judgment of Jerome,[2287] Augustine,[2288] Jerome again,[2289] Cyprian,[2290] and other later writers[2291] hold that Noah's ark was a type of Christ's church, yet in the accommodation of the resemblance, they run out into some niceties and curiosities which will hardly abide a strict examination. Pitch we upon those things which seem more solid herein.

Now the ark of Noah did notably adumbrate and resemble the church of Christ, (especially the church visible) in these particular respects, namely:

(i) The ark was built by Noah as the master-builder, ordering all things therein according to God's Covenant and command, having inferior workmen under him.[2292] The church – the house of the living God – was built by Jesus

---

[2286] Colossians 1:17-20, Herewith well compare and consider Romans 8:19-24, 2 Peter 3:13, Acts 3:21, which ascribe to Christ the creating of a new heavens and a new earth, and the restitution of all things.

[2287] 1 Peter 3:20-21. Arca Noe Ecclesiae typus fuit, dicente Petro Apostolo: In Arca Noe, pauci, id est, octo animae, etc. Jerome advers. Luciferianos. p. 145. A. Basil. 1553 [Hom.] 2. "Noah's ark was a type of the Church, as the apostle Peter says – 1 Peter 3:20: In Noah's Ark, few, that is, eight souls, etc."
<https://www.newadvent.org/fathers/3005.htm> [Accessed 6/14/2023]

[2288] Augustine, City of God, 15.26.5 & in Dialog Question 65, p.691, q.51, etc. Tom. 4. Basil. 1569. *Praecipuè verò in lib. 12. contra Faust. Manichaeum cap. 14. ad 21. Tom. 6.*

[2289] Jerome. advers. Luciferian. p. 145. A. etc. Tom. 2. Basil. 1553.

[2290] Cyprian ad Novatianum Haereticum. num. 3, 4, 5, 6. p 476. An. Dom. 1593.

[2291] D. Taylor of Types. Chap. III.—H. Broughton in the General view of the holy Scriptures. pp. 50-51. London 1640. And that learned Rivet in Gen. 6. Practices. 53

[2292] Genesis 6:22

Christ, hence it is called his own house.[2293] And particular churches are styled *the churches of Christ*.[2294] And Jesus Christ has his inferior master-builders under him, namely: *apostles, prophets, evangelists, pastors and teachers, for the perfecting of the saints, for the work of the ministry, for the edifying of the body of Christ:*[2295] some of these Christ constituted as *master-builders* to lay the foundation, as the extraordinary officers, *apostles*, etc.[2296] Others as under-builders to build upon their foundation laid, *Jesus Christ himself being the chief cornerstone*.[2297]

(ii) The material ark was a long time in building by Noah, namely: from God's first establishing his Covenant with Noah, until the end of the old world, which was 120 years.[2298] The spiritual ark the church is a longer time in building by Christ, even from God's *first promise* established on *the seed of the woman*,[2299] until the end of the world that now is, and Christ's second coming; for till then the gospel ordinances, and officers are to continue for the gathering and building of his church.[2300] And the received opinion of the Jews is, as it was created in six days, so it will continue for 6000 years.

(iii) The ark was builded of gopher wood, a wood well-scenting and lasting; the planks thereof closed fast together, *and pitched within and without with pitch*, that neither rain from above, nor floods from below might enter, or sink the same.[2301] The church also is builded of lasting and well-scenting gopher-wood, namely: *trees of righteousness*,[2302] *saints by calling*,[2303] really or apparently such; a knit and joined together in love,[2304] with this (as Augustine

---

[2293] Hebrews 3:3, 6
[2294] Romans 16;16
[2295] Ephesians 4:12
[2296] 1 Corinthians 3:10
[2297] Ephesians 2:20
[2298] Genesis 6:3, 17-18, and chapter 7 throughout; 1 Peter 3:19-20
[2299] Genesis 3:15
[2300] Matthew 28:19-20, 1 Corinthians 11:26
[2301] Genesis 6:14
[2302] Isaiah 61:3
[2303] Romans 1:7, 1 Corinthians 1:2
[2304] Colossians 2:2, Song of Solomon 8:7-8

has it)[2305] *they are pitched within and without, maintaining the unity of the Spirit in the bond of peace,*[2306] whereby they are kept from sinking under temptations or tribulations. *Jerusalem is as a city that is compact together.*[2307] *In Christ all the building fitly framed (or compacted) together, grows unto a holy temple in the Lord.*[2308]

(iv) The material ark had a window to let in light to them that were therein.[2309] The spiritual ark the church has her window, her spiritual light – even Jesus Christ the light of the world – who by his word and Spirit illuminates all his house. *Jesus said, I am the light of the world: he that followeth me, shall not walk in darkness, but shall have the light of life.*[2310]

(v) The ark had but *one door* to go in and out at.[2311] The church also has but one door for the elect sheep of Christ to enter in at for salvation. This door is Christ alone. *I am the door of the sheep* (says Christ). *By me if any man enter in, he shall be saved; and shall go in and out and find pasture.*[2312] *No man comes unto the Father but by Christ.*[2313] *Neither is there salvation in any other: for there is no other name under heaven given among men whereby we can be saved.*[2314] Yea there is a door unto this door Christ: for (as Augustine notes), "The side and heart of Christ pierced and opened by the spear, the wound in Christ's side, is the way into Christ, for hence the sacraments did flow whereby believers are initiated."[2315]

[2305] "Bitumen enim significat Charitatem," etc. Aug. Dialog. Quest. LXV. quest 66. Tom. 4. Machine translation: "For bitumen signifies charity", etc.
[2306] Ephesians 4:3
[2307] Psalm 122:3
[2308] Ephesians 2:21
[2309] Genesis 6:16
[2310] John 8:12
[2311] Genesis 6:16
[2312] John 10:7, 9
[2313] John 14:6
[2314] Acts 4:12
[2315] Augustine, City of God, 15.26.5

(vi) The ark was made with *lower, second* and *third stories*, for the variety of creatures.[2316] So in the church there are several storeys and degrees:[2317] all not in a level of equality. Some are governors, rulers, officers; some are governed, ruled, and without special office.[2318] Again, among officers, some were extraordinary, and to continue but for a time, as apostles, prophets, evangelists, *Are all apostles, are all prophets?* etc.[2319] Some ordinary, and to continue until the end, as pastors, and teachers, elders, deacons. As the natural body has several members: and several offices for all these members.[2320] And amongst the community of the faithful, *some are babes in Christ: some are grown men, having their senses exercised to discern between good and evil*;[2321] some are *weak in the faith*: some are *strong*, and comparatively *perfect* in regard to others.[2322] And as the God of order has thus ranked his people in the church, in their several places, functions and stories as it were, so they should know and keep their places respectively. Yea in heaven itself, wherein the church shall be triumphant, *there are many mansions*;[2323] and as here degrees of grace; so there degrees of glory; *some shall shine as the brightness of the firmament, some as the stars for ever and ever.*[2324] For the *Lord will render to every one according to his works, both for kind and degree.*[2325]

(vii) The ark had in it all variety of creatures, both *clean* and *unclean*: wolf and lamb, sheep and goats, etc.[2326] Yea in it was a cursed Ham, as well as a holy Noah and a blessed Shem.[2327] So the visible church, the spiritual ark has in it people of all nations, tongues and languages, of all sexes, ages, conditions, and

---

[2316] Genesis 6:16
[2317] Habuit Arca nidos suos; Ecclesia pluremas mansiones. Jerome. advers. Luciferians p. 145 Tom. 2. Basil 1553. Machine translation: "The ark had its nests; the church has many rooms."
[2318] Hebrews 13:17, 24, 1 Thessalonians 5:12-13, 1 Timothy 5:17-18
[2319] 1 Corinthians 12:28, Romans 12:4-8
[2320] Romans 12:4-5, 1 Corinthians 12:12, etc.
[2321] 1 Corinthians 3:1-2, Hebrews 5:12-14
[2322] Philippians 3:15, 1 Corinthians 2:6
[2323] John 14:2
[2324] Daniel 12:3
[2325] Romans 2:6
[2326] Genesis 6:19-20 & 7:8-9, 14
[2327] Genesis 9:18-19, 25-26

degrees: Jews and Gentiles; noble and ignoble; rich and poor; wise and foolish; bond and free; male and female; young and old.[2328] In this *field*, also are *tares* as well as *wheat*;[2329] in this *net*, *bad*, as well as *good* fish;[2330] in this *house*, *foolish*, as well as *wise virgins*;[2331] in this ark, hypocrites and reprobates, as well as the sincere and elect. Hereupon said Jerome: "As in the ark were kinds of all creatures, so in the church are men of all nations and manners. As there the leopard and the kids, the wolf and the lambs, so here the righteous and sinners, that is, golden and silver vessels remain with wooden and earthen vessels."[2332] In the visible church, God's house, are as well *vessels to dishonor*, as *vessels to honor*; as well *vessels of wrath*, as *vessels of mercy*.[2333]

(viii) Finally, the ark with them that were therein, was exposed to storms and tempests, winds and waves, rain and floods, such as the world never saw since nor before, by which it was extremely endangered to be split in a thousand pieces upon rocks or mountains, or to be overturned and overwhelmed in the deep, all the world being nothing but one entire sea. Thus the church on earth with all the people of God therein are liable to the most rugged tempests of afflictions and persecutions of all sorts and degrees. *Time is come that judgment must begin at the house of God*.[2334] *In this world* (says Christ to his disciples) *ye shall have tribulation*.[2335] *Many are the afflictions of the righteous*, says David.[2336] *Yea and all that will live godly in Christ Jesus, shall suffer persecution*,[2337] and, *Through much tribulation we must enter into the kingdom of God*.[2338] Hereupon said Jerome, "The ark was endangered in

---

[2328] Acts 2:5-14, 41; Colossians 3:11, Galatians 5:6, 1 Corinthians 1:26 to the end of the chapter
[2329] Matthew 13:24-31, 38-44
[2330] Matthew 13:47-53
[2331] Matthew 25:1-13
[2332] Jerome, Dialogue against the Luciferians, p.145, Tom 2, Basil, 1553.
[2333] Romans 9:21-23
[2334] 1 Peter 4:17-18
[2335] John 16:33
[2336] Psalm 34:19
[2337] 2 Timothy 3:12
[2338] Acts 14:22

the flood: the church is endangered in the world."[2339] And before him, Cyprian said, "The ark did bear a figure of the church; and the tossing of the ark to and fro with winds and billows, a figure of persecution."[2340] The ark could have no rest, until it came to Mount Ararat; nor shall the church and people of God have any perfect rest, until they come to the celestial Ararat, those mountains of spices. Thus the ark (to mention no more particulars) did notably resemble the *visible church* of Christ. And therefore in God's Covenant with Noah touching this ark, *explicitly*, why may we not understand God's Covenant of Faith in Christ touching his church *implicitly*?

{3} Finally, *the saving of Noah, his family and the living creatures in the ark by waters, from perishing by the flood, was a remarkable type or figure of the salvation of the household of God in the ark of his church by Jesus Christ from perishing by the deluge of divine wrath*. The words of Peter are most clear for this: *The long-suffering of God waited in the days of Noah, while the ark was preparing, wherein few, that is, eight souls were saved by water. The like figure whereunto, even baptism doth also now save us* (note the putting away of the filth of the flesh, but the answer of a good conscience towards God) *by the resurrection of Jesus Christ.*[2341] Thus parallel and accommodate the *type* to the *antitype*; the *figure* to the thing *prefigured*.

(i) They only that were in the ark with Noah, were saved from the flood of waters, when all the world besides, without the ark, were drowned.[2342] Likewise, they only that are within the church with Jesus Christ are saved from the wrath of God, when all the world without the church are swallowed up by divine vengeance for their sins. The known maxim is, "Outside the church there is no salvation."[2343] Ordinarily it is so; I dispute not what God may do extraordinarily. But the apostle informs us that such as are *aliens to the commonwealth of Israel, are without Christ, strangers from the covenants of*

[2339] Jerome, Dialogue against the Luciferians, p.145, Tom 2, Basil, 1553
[2340] Cyprian, to the heretic Novatian, p.476, 1593.
[2341] 1 Peter 3:20-21
[2342] Genesis 7:21-23
[2343] "Extra ecclesiam non est salus"

promise, having no hope, and without God in the world.[2344] And therefore as such, they are in a sad incapacity of salvation. Hereupon said Augustine, "Whosoever he be, and whatever manner of person he is, a Christian he is not, that is not in the church."[2345] And again elsewhere he says: "Firmly hold, and nothing doubt, that not only all pagans, but also all Jews, heretics, and schismatics, who finish this present life outside the catholic church, shall go into everlasting fire prepared for the devil and his angels."[2346]

(ii) They that were saved in the ark *were saved by water.*[2347] They were saved by water, from water; by the flood, from the flood. For the waters lifted up the ark and them therein above the peril of drowning. So the church is saved: (a) *Sacramentally* by water, namely: by the way of baptism, which in regard to its signification and end, is salvifical:[2348] *He that believes and is baptized, shall be saved.*[2349] (b) *Spiritually* by the blood of Christ justifying,[2350] and by the Spirit of Christ sanctifying[2351] – both signified by water. Christ's blood washes away the guilt, Christ's spirit washes off the filth of sin. Thus we are saved by the flood of Christ's blood and water, from the flood of God's wrath.[2352] Yea as Augustine notes, "They in the ark were saved by wood and water: so we in a sort in Christ are saved by wood and water,"[2353] namely: by his death, *who himself bare our sins in his own body on the tree,*[2354] and out of whose side, pierced with the spear, gushed both blood and water for the cleansing away of our sins. What does it signify that Noah was delivered by water and wood? Water signifies baptism, wood the cross, as Noah was delivered by water and wood: so also the church is delivered by baptism and the signal of his passion.

[2344] Ephesians 2:12
[2345] Augustine, de Tempor. Sermon 181, p.993, Tom. 10, Basil, 1569.
[2346] Augustine, de Fide ad Pet. Diaconum, p.234 DC Tom. 3, Basil 1569.
[2347] 1 Peter 3:20, Genesis 7:17
[2348] 1 Peter 3:21
[2349] Mark 16:16
[2350] 1 John 1:7, Ephesians 5:25-27
[2351] 1 Corinthians 6:11
[2352] 1 Peter 3:24, 1 John 5:6
[2353] Augustine, Dialog, Quae. 65, Q.51, Tom. 4
[2354] 1 Peter 2:24

(iii) They that were saved in the ark by water and wood, were saved *by being lifted up above the earth*. So they that are saved by Christ's blood, are saved by being lifted up above the earth by his *resurrection* and *ascension* also.—*The like figure whereunto, even baptism doth also now save us, by the resurrection of Jesus Christ: who is gone into heaven, and is on the right hand of God.*[2355] When Christ meritoriously and effectually wrought our salvation, he by his resurrection came out of the earth, and by his ascension went far above the earth, even into heaven: when Christ actually applies his salvation to us, Christ *risen* makes us *rise with him*: Christ ascended, makes us ascend after him;[2356] Christ *sitting in heaven, makes us set our affections above, not on things on the earth, and our conversations are in heaven also.*[2357]

(iv) They that were saved in the ark were saved therein with Noah, who forsook his own habitation to dwell with them in the ark and with them to be tossed up and down with winds and waves that they might be saved with him. So they that are saved in the ark of the church, are saved by Christ's gracious and powerful presence, therefore Christ himself left his heavenly throne for a while, and entered solemnly into the church by *baptism*;[2358] and therein dwelt with us, exposing himself to all storms and tempests, waves and billows, rocks and dangers of affliction and persecution, etc., to save us from them. *He carried our griefs and bare our sorrows* so that our griefs and sorrows might be turned into joy.[2359] He was content to undergo *our storms* with us so that we might enjoy *his calms* with him. He was tossed with us on *our sea* so that we might anchor with him in his haven. He was *afflicted* with us in all our *afflictions* so that we might be *affected* with him in all his *consolations*.[2360] He was involved in *our curse* so that he might impart to us his *blessedness*.[2361] He was *wounded* and *bruised* for our iniquities so that we might *be healed* by his

---

[2355] 1 Peter 3:20-22
[2356] Colossians 3:1-2, Ephesians 2:5-6
[2357] Philippians 3:20
[2358] Matthew 3:16-17
[2359] Isaiah 53:3-5
[2360] Isaiah 63:9
[2361] Galatians 3:13-14

stripes.[2362] He was condemned for *our crimes* so that we might be cleared by *his condemnations*. He was imprisoned in *our chains and fetters* so that we might be set at liberty by *his imprisonment*. He was crowned with *our thorns* so that we might be crowned with *his triumphs*. He *died with us* so that we might *live with him*. He was *buried with us* so that we might *rise with him*. He became sin with us so *that we might be the righteousness of God in him*.[2363] Thus Christ endangers himself with us, for our safety. While Christ is in the ship, in the ark, all is safe, though (as once the apostles) in greatest storms and hazards. The ship of the church had long ere this day been split, sunk, wrecked and broken in pieces, had not Christ been in the ship to rebuke the waves and tempests.

(v) They that were saved in the ark from the flood, were saved by God's special providence, guiding and ordering the ark. For it was heavy-laden, yet had neither anchor nor cable, mast, helm, sails nor tackling, neither pilot, mariner nor skilful steersman; yet at last it landed safely on *mountains of Ararat*, which signifies, *take-away-fear*.[2364] So they that are saved in the church by Christ from divine wrath, are saved by God's singular providence, most eminently acting in providing Christ for them, in *tendering* and *applying* Christ to them, and in *preserving* them in Christ unto the end.[2365]

(vi) They that were saved in the ark, were saved according to God's Covenant.[2366] So they that are saved by Christ, are saved according to God's Covenant and promises in him, both under Old and New Testament. God's truth and faithfulness herein, is their shield and buckler, and their tower of salvation.

(vii) They that were saved in the ark were but few, namely: *eight souls*, when the whole world besides was drowned.[2367] So they that are saved by

---

[2362] Isaiah 63:5-6
[2363] 2 Corinthians 5:21
[2364] Genesis 8:4
[2365] 1 Peter 1:5
[2366] Genesis 8:4
[2367] 1 Peter 3:20

Christ (though in themselves a *multitude*, which none can number, yet)[2368] in comparison of those that perish, are exceedingly few.[2369] Christ's flock is but *a little flock*.[2370] *Many are called, few are chosen*, etc.[2371]

(viii) Finally, they that were saved from the flood of waters, were assured from God after their deliverance was completed, that there should be nevermore any such *flood to drown the earth*.[2372] So they that are saved by Christ, after the accomplishment and completing of their salvation, are assured *there shall be no more sea:*[2373] no more sea of affliction. But that *God shall wipe away all tears from their eyes: and there shall be no more death, neither sorrow, nor crying, neither shall there be any more pain*.[2374] Thus the saving of Noah and his family in the ark by water from the flood, was an observable type of our salvation by Christ from divine wrath. Therefore God's Covenant with Noah – thus to save him and his in the ark by water – was for substance the Covenant of Faith for saving sinners by Jesus Christ. And under that *temporal* and *typical*, this *spiritual* and *eternal* salvation was intended. Seeing then, Noah was a type of Christ herein – the ark a type of the church; and the saving of his house, etc., with Noah in the ark by waters from perishing in the flood, a type of the saving of God's people in the church by Christ from perishing by God's wrath – it is clear that God's Covenant with Noah was a renewed administration of the Covenant of Faith. Thus of this third argument.

{4} God's Covenant with Noah and his family, *not to curse the ground any more for man's sake*,[2375] by destroying the earth with a general flood of waters, notwithstanding the imagination of man's heart remained evil from his youth, notably indicates God's Covenant of Faith in Christ, by whom alone the curse due for sin is removed, though sin in his people be

---

[2368] Revelation 7:4, 9
[2369] Matthew 7:13-14, Luke 13:24
[2370] Luke 12:32
[2371] Matthew 22:14 & 20:16
[2372] Genesis 8:20-22 and 9:9-18
[2373] Revelation 21:1
[2374] Revelation 21:4
[2375] Genesis 8:20-22 & 9:8-18

not wholly extinguished and obliterated. *Christ has redeemed us from the curse of the law, being made a curse for us; for it is written, cursed is every one that hangs on a tree.*[2376] To this effect says one very appositely, "Touching this place of Genesis, taking away of the curse (notwithstanding man's corrupt heart remaining) is a notable testimony of God's rich mercy in Christ, by whom we are freed from the curse (Galatians 3:13, Revelation 22:3, Zechariah 14:11). For the covenant now made concerning the waters with Noah, was a figure of that spiritual and eternal covenant of peace with us in Christ, as is shown in Isaiah 54:8-10."[2377] So he.

And I add, that God's covenanting to curse the ground no more with a general flood forever, though man's heart remained corrupt, the more clearly signifies to us God's Covenant of Faith in Christ, touching sinners' recovery and salvation, because God took occasion to make this covenant, upon *Noah's sacrificing of burnt-offerings upon an altar to him, whereupon God smelled a sweet savour of rest, and said in his heart, I will not again curse the ground any more,* etc.[2378] God made this Covenant, being pacified with Noah's burnt-offerings. How could Noah's burnt-offerings pacify God, or afford any sweet savor to God? Not in, and of themselves: for the bodies of beasts burnt, of themselves send forth an offensive savor. Not from any merit of Noah: for though he was righteous, yet his righteousness was of faith, not of works;[2379] and he was subject to sinful frailties.[2380] How then? Only as types of Christ's death for our sins, that sacrifice of sacrifices which was the substance, end and scope of all the sacrifices under the Old Testament. This was *the sacrifice to God for a sweet smelling savor.*[2381] This was the true cause of appeasing God's wrath, of removing the curse, and of God's gracious covenanting with Noah no more to drown the world with a flood. Consequently this Covenant in the

---

[2376] Galatians 3:13
[2377] Henry Ainsworth in his Annotations on Genesis 8:21
[2378] Genesis 8:20-22
[2379] Hebrews 11:7
[2380] Genesis 9:21, etc.
[2381] Ephesians 5:2

secret and spiritual intendments of it was a renewed discovery of the Covenant of Faith touching sinners' recovery in Christ Jesus.

{5} **As the rainbow is made a *token of this Covenant of God with Noah*,**[2382] **a sign and pledge of divine favor, mercy and peace: so Jesus Christ our Lord is represented in Scripture,** sometimes as *sitting upon a throne, there being a rainbow round about the throne, in sight like to an emerald*;[2383] sometimes as *a mighty angel descending from heaven, clothed with a cloud, and a rainbow upon his head*, etc.[2384] In both which places (as that learned Rivet well notes),[2385] "There is mention of a rainbow (which God has made a token of mercy and peace) that we may acknowledge Christ's throne to be compassed about with mercy, and that he shows this mercy in his countenance, when he manifests himself unto his people. But especially, we have that rainbow in his face, whereby we are certain, not only that the waters shall no more universally overflow the earth; but also and chiefly that we are not to fear the flood of God's wrath, since Christ has pacified the Father, whom whilst God beholds, he remembers his mercy and promises, which in him are yea and amen. Therefore Christ appears crowned with a rainbow, as the messenger of grace and peace. For he is the prince of peace, and our peace, Isaiah 9:6, Ephesians 2:14." So he.

The rainbow then, which as a token of mercy was annexed to Noah's Covenant, is thence used to signify divine mercy to sinners in Christ Jesus, whereby we are given to understand, that the rainbow was not only given as a confirmatory token against a universal flood of waters: but also as a consolatory token in Christ against the flood of God's wrath. And so the rainbow leads us even to Christ himself, and to the Covenant of Faith in him. Hence says another, "As the Covenant made with Noah concerning the waters, is applied to the spiritual Covenant made with us in Christ, Isaiah 54:9-10. So the rainbow (the sign of that Covenant) is also applied for the sign of grace

---

[2382] Genesis 9:12-18
[2383] Revelation 4:3
[2384] Revelation 10:1
[2385] "Sed negligendum non est quod Ioan scribit. In circuitu throni fuisse Iridem, etc." Andre Rivet in Genes. 9. Exercise 9, sub fin.

from God to his church, Revelation 4:3, 10:1, Ezekiel 1:28."[2386] And Augustine says, "What is signified by this rainbow but the reconciliation of the world, which is known to be done by the dispensation of the incarnate word?", etc.

{6} **Finally, several judicious writers account this Covenant of God with Noah before and after the flood, the Covenant of Grace and faith in Christ, and think, that under this temporal salvation from the flood expressed, the spiritual and eternal salvation of God's elect from the deluge of God's wrath is implied.** This therefore is no new or singular opinion, though those that purposely treat of God's Covenant, do omit this gradual discovery and distinct administration of the Covenant of Faith to Noah.

Learned and judicious Rivet says of this covenant: "*Et quamvis foedus illud tantum spectare videatur praesentem vitam*, etc." "And though that covenant seem only to respect this present life; yet we must ascend higher, to the thing signified. For it is the Covenant of Grace, which looks at some other thing than the use of temporal life for a few years."[2387]

That learned and laborious Pareus says thus: "*Quaestio hîc est, an idem hoc foedus sit, an aliud ab eo, quod cum deo nunc habemus? Respondeo, est idem & diversum,*" etc., namely: "A question here arises, whether this covenant be the same with that which we have now with God, or another different from it? I answer, it is the same, and distinct. It is the same in respect of eternal grace by Christ, and in respect of the obligation of moral obedience. For, this substance of the covenant, that is, of the mutual stipulation of God and the elect, is the same, and perpetual in both testaments: promulgated in paradise; the seed of the woman, etc., repeated to Noah here and in chapter 9, tied to the family of Abraham in chapters 15, 18, and 17:2, and repeated to Moses and the Israelites, Exodus 24. At last, it is most fully declared and confirmed by the ministry and blood of Christ. Therefore, Christ is mediator of the everlasting covenant, Hebrews 13:20. The same both now and of old is the way of

---

[2386] Henry Ainsworth in his Annotation on Genesis 9:13
[2387] Andre Rivet in Genesis 6, Exercitation 53, p.271, Lugd. 1633

salvation by Christ, Hebrews 13:18, Acts 15:11. But this covenant differs in circumstances and manner of administration. God propounded this gratuitous covenant in one sort to the fathers, and in another to us.

(i) To the fathers he added certain external promises: as, of preservation in the flood, to Noah; of giving the land of Canaan to Abraham; not so to us.

(ii) To them he gave other signs and burdens: before the flood, sacrifices; after the flood, the rainbow to Noah; circumcision to Abraham; the passover to Moses and the Israelites; yea, sacrifices, ceremonies, festivals, and innumerable other laws, wherein as in a cloud or dark garment the promise of grace was involved. For all the legal shadows did show Christ: but more obscurely, as when the sun is seen through the clouds. To us he has given other signs, clearer and fewer, the shadows disappearing at Christ's coming. By reason of this diversity, the covenant, which is but one in substance, is said to be twofold: Old and New. And the Old is abolished because the promise of grace has put off its legal robe wherewith it was covered of old as with a cloud. But the New is everlasting, both in substance and administration, because another change of rites and sacraments is not to be expected before the last day: for as much as we are commanded to break the Lord's bread, and show forth the Lord's death, until he come."[2388]

How fully and clearly has he expressed himself in this matter!

That learned and accurate textual, Mr. Ainsworth, thus expresses himself: {*and thou shalt enter*}, etc. "This explains the covenant made on God's part, that he would save Noah and his household from death by the ark; and on Noah's part, that he should through faith and obedience make and enter into the ark, so committing himself to God's preservation, Hebrews 11:7. And under this, the Covenant or testament of eternal salvation by Christ, was also implied: the apostle testifying, that the antitype, or like figure hereunto, even baptism, does now also save us (1 Peter 3:21), which baptism is a seal of our salvation, Mark 16:16."[2389]

[2388] David Pareus commentary on Genesis 6:18 & 9:6
[2389] Henry Ainsworth in his Annotation on Genesis 6:18

That pious, judicious and industrious Perkins (who did more good service to the church of God with his left hand, then many do with both; like a spiritual Ehud stabbing the Romish Eglon with his left-handed pen)[2390] says, "Thus we have seen in some sort how the ark saved Noah and his household, and what this his household was. Now besides this end and use of the ark, we are further to know that whereas this saving of them was but a corporal deliverance from a temporal death, this ark has also a spiritual use which we may not omit: for as many of Noah's family as were true believers, it was a means to save them another way, even to save their souls. For it taught them many things.

(i) It was an assurance of God's love unto their souls. For if he were so careful to save their bodies from the flood, they thereby assured themselves he would be as good unto their souls, which they knew to be far more precious and excellent.

(ii) It showed them how to be saved. For as they saw no safety – nothing but present death, out of the ark – so it taught them, that out of God's church, and out of God's favor, no salvation could be expected; and so it taught them to labor to be in God's favor, and members of his true church.

(iii) They saw they were saved from the flood by faith and obedience. For, first Noah believed God's word that the flood should come; then he obeyed God's commandment, and made the ark as he was commanded. And thus he and his by believing and obeying were saved through the ark: and without these the ark could not have saved them. This taught them more particularly how to be saved, namely, by believing God, and obeying God, and else no salvation. For when they saw their bodies could not be saved without them; it assured them much less could their souls be saved without faith and obedience.

(iv) Lastly, this deliverance by the ark was a pawn unto them from God, assuring them of salvation if they believed in the Messiah. For seeing God so fully performed his promise unto them for their bodily deliverance upon their

---

[2390] Dextera quamtum vis fuerat tibi manca, docendi Pollebas mira dexteritate tamen

believing: they thereby might assure themselves, he would perform his promise of salvation unto them upon their faith and true obedience."[2391]

So he. In his judgment therefore, the temporal salvation of their bodies in the ark by water, did instruct them touching the spiritual and eternal salvation of their souls in the church by Christ. Whence it is clear, that God's Covenant with Noah in the temporal salvation expressed, intended the spiritual and eternal salvation implied.

Thus, in Noah, we have found Christ. In the ark, the family or church of Christ. In the *saving of Noah's family in the ark by waters from perishing in the flood*, the saving of the church and elect of God by Jesus Christ, and his death, from perishing in the deluge of God's wrath. In Noah's *altar and burnt-offerings affording a savour of rest to God*, the true altar and sacrifice Jesus Christ, who offered up himself for our sins, *an odor of a sweet smell to God*.[2392] In the rainbow, the token of mercy and peace, the mercy, favor, love, and peace of God towards us in the face of Christ. And consequently, in that Covenant of God with Noah for corporal preservation, we have found the Covenant of Faith dispensed to him in Christ touching sinners' spiritual recovery and eternal salvation. And so the first thing is cleared, *that God's Covenants with Noah before and after the flood, were a renewed discovery and administration of the Covenant of Faith touching sinners' salvation by Jesus Christ*. The next thing to be inquired into, is, *the spirituality of these Covenants of God with Noah*, as they are a renewed administration of the Covenant of Faith touching sinners' eternal salvation by Jesus Christ. For it is already cleared by sundry arguments, that under temporals explicitly covenanted, spirituals were implicitly intended and comprised.

(2) What the spirituality, or spiritual meaning of these covenants of God with Noah, as a renewed administration of the Covenant of Faith, is, has partly been discovered by the arguments formerly produced to prove the thing; and may further appear, by considering briefly, [1] the

---

[2391] Mr. William Perkins in his commentary on Hebrews 11:7
[2392] Ephesians 5:2

author, [2] parties, [3] matter, and [4] form of these covenants, as a Covenant of Faith in Christ, touching sinners' salvation.

[1] The **author** of these covenants with Noah, etc., as a Covenant of Faith, was God.[2393] God was author of them, immediately by lively voice revealing them to Noah, as a gracious preserver, deliverer and merciful savior of a remnant of mankind from deserved destruction.[2394] In this notion God was author hereof, the impulsive cause moving him hereunto, was *inward*, and *outward*. {1} *Inward*: his own mere grace and commiserating favor to Noah and his family.[2395] {2} *Outward*: the satisfactory and sweet-smelling sacrifice of Jesus Christ, typified in Noah's sacrifices which were a savour of rest to God, and an occasion of God's Covenant with him.[2396]

[2] The **parties** to these covenants, as a Covenant of Faith, were chiefly two, namely: {1} on the one hand, as the *party covenanting*: God, as a gracious, compassionate, and merciful savior of a remnant of lost mankind in Christ. {2} On the other hand, as the *party restipulating*, in Noah and his family, Christ (as a true Noah, a true comforter, and author of rest and peace, to cursed and tyred sinners), and his family, his spiritual household in him. *Typically*, Noah and his family; *anti-typically* or spiritually, Christ and his family, the church, his spiritual seed, are here federates with God.

[3] **Matters** covenanted in these two covenants, as a distinct administration of the Covenant of Faith, are: {1} on God's part, and {2} on Christ's part (as the true Noah) and his seed's.

{1} **God on his part graciously covenanted and promised:**

(i) That the spiritual household of Christ the true Noah (though very few in comparison of the world) should be spiritually and eternally saved from the deluge of God's wrath, when the whole world besides should utterly perish therein. For under the *temporal and corporal salvation of Noah's family from*

[2393] Genesis 6:13, 18, etc. & 9:8-18
[2394] Genesis 8:20-22 & 9:8-18
[2395] Genesis 6:8, etc.
[2396] Ephesians 5:2 with Genesis 8:20-22 & 9:8-18

the flood of waters, we are to understand the *spiritual and eternal salvation of Christ and his family from the flood of God's wrath.*[2397]

(ii) That they who should be spiritually and eternally saved from the deluge of God's wrath and vengeance, should be saved only in the ark of God's church with and by Jesus Christ the true Noah. No living creature on earth was saved without the ark, all died in the flood, except they that were with Noah in the ark: so all without the church eternally perish; they only that are with Christ in his church are eternally saved[2398]— *And the Lord added to the church daily such as should be saved.*[2399] But first they were *added to the church*, then *saved*. Yea therefore *added to the church, that they might be saved.*

To this purpose said Cyprian notably of the church of Christ: "By her fructifying we are brought forth; by her milk we are nourished; by her spirit we are animated. The spouse of Christ cannot be defiled with adultery, she is incorrupt and chaste: she knows one house, most chastely preserves the sanctity of one chamber. She keeps us to God, she assigns the sons which she has begotten to a kingdom. Whosoever segregated from the church, is joined to an adulteress, he is separated from the promises of the church. Nor shall he come to Christ's rewards, who relinquishes Christ's church. He is an alien, he is profane, he is an enemy. He cannot have God as a father that has not the church as a mother. If any could escape who was without the ark of Noah: then may he escape that is without the church. So here, without the ark, none escaped drowning: without the church none escape damning."[2400]

And as all that shall be saved, shall be saved only in the church: so they are to be saved only with and by Christ therein. Peter says, *eight persons were saved in the ark*, but *by water*:[2401] so we must be saved in the church, but by Christ, figured by water. Christ is the only *way to the Father*,[2402] the only *saving door*

[2397] 1 Peter 3:20-21
[2398] Ephesians 2:12
[2399] Acts 2:47
[2400] Cyprian, on the Unity of the Church, Section 5, p.297, 1593 edition
[2401] 1 Peter 3:20-21
[2402] John 14:6

of the sheep,[2403] the only *mediator between God and man*,[2404] the *only name given whereby we can be saved*.[2405] So then in this Covenant, under the type of Noah, Christ as a comforting savior of his house from God's wrath, is most sweetly promised of God.

(iii) That they who should be saved by this true Noah Jesus Christ in the ark of his church, should be saved by virtue of his death and resurrection. This Peter intimates in his accommodation of the type to the antitype. *While the ark was preparing, wherein few, that is, eight souls were saved. The like figure whereunto, even baptism doth also now save us, by the resurrection of Jesus Christ, who is gone into heaven, and is on the right hand of God.*[2406] When Christ purchased and wrought out our salvation, he effected it chiefly two ways: (a) By his death and humiliation. *Dying for our sins, and bearing the curse of our sins in his own body on the tree*,[2407] for the full satisfying and pacifying of divine justice: so that now there needs no more *sacrifice for sin*.[2408] (b) By his resurrection from the dead, and exaltation. Hereby he justified himself to be the Son of God, a righteous person, and a triumphant conqueror of sin, death, grave, and all the powers of darkness:[2409] and this for our justification, that we might be over these enemies joint conquerors with him.

Proportionably when Christ applies unto us salvation purchased, he does it two ways: (a) By *mortifying* and burying our old man with him, that sin should no longer live and reign in us.[2410] (b) By *vivifying* and raising up the new man with him: that *as Christ rose from the dead, so we should walk in newness of life*.[2411] Both these are signified by baptism. (1) *Our death with Christ*, by our going into the water, or being in or under the water in baptism. Hence these phrases, *we are baptized into his death: we are buried with him by*

[2403] John 10:7, 9
[2404] 1 Timothy 2:5
[2405] Acts 4:12
[2406] 1 Peter 3:20-21
[2407] Romans 4:25, 1 Corinthians 15:3, 1 Peter 2:24, Galatians 3:13
[2408] Ephesians 5:2 & Hebrews 10:5-19
[2409] Romans 1:4, 1 Timothy 3:16
[2410] Galatians 5:24, Colossians 3:3, 5, 8; Ephesians 4:22
[2411] Ephesians 2:4-6, Colossians 3:1, etc., Romans 6:4

baptism into death; we are planted together in the likeness of his death.[2412] (2) *Our life and resurrection with Christ*, by our coming out of, or from under the water of baptism. Hence we are said to be *buried with him by baptism into death, that like as Christ was raised up from the dead; so we also should walk in newness of life.*[2413] And it is styled, *our planting in the likeness of his resurrection.*[2414] Thus (as Peter intimates)[2415] we are saved *meritoriously* by Christ's death and resurrection; *actually*, by the effectual application of both these to us; sacramentally by baptism signifying and sealing both these to us.

Now of both these the saving of Noah's family in the ark by water, was a type, for: (a) Noah's entering into the ark and his house with him, was a kind of typical death and burial; as Mr. Perkins has well observed, "They went into the ark as dead men into a grave. They were buried in the ark, and the ark in the waters: they were deprived of human society, fresh air, gladsome light, and of the comfort of earthly creatures. Yet this was God's way to save them from death and grave, as it were by death and grave. If Noah's family will be saved alive with him, they must go into the grave with him. So if Christ's family will be eternally saved by him, they must go into the grave with him, being spiritually mortified, crucified and buried with him."[2416] (b) Noah's coming out of the ark alive and his family with him, when all the world was drowned and dead, was a kind of typical reviving and resurrection from the dead. They came out of the ark as out of the grave; and that into a new world. If Noah's family will be saved with him, they must also come out of the ark with him. Had they not come out at last, they would have perished there. So if Christ's family will be saved with him eternally, they must be quickened and rise again with him. As they must die with him to sin, so they must live with him to righteousness. Thus in this covenant with Noah, God typically represented sinners' salvation by Christ's death and resurrection in their entering into and

---

[2412] Romans 6:3-5
[2413] Romans 6:4
[2414] Romans 6:5
[2415] 1 Peter 3:20-21
[2416] Mr. William Perkins in his commentary on Hebrews 11:7

coming out of the ark. And this is one high point, and a principal mystery of the gospel.

(iv) That Christ's family and elect saved by him once from the flood of God's wrath should never eternally perish by the deluge of his wrath, as Noah and his family, saved from the flood of waters, receive a covenant from God that neither they nor the living creatures on earth should ever anymore be destroyed by a flood of waters.[2417]

(v) Finally, that they who are spiritually and eternally saved by Christ, shal have all necessary temporal blessings superadded to them in Christ. *Seek first the kingdom of God, and his righteousness, and all these things shall be added unto you.*[2418] Thus in the type, Noah's family was not only saved in the ark with Noah; but also for their sakes, a seed of the living creatures were saved in the ark with them for their after use and service; the free use of the creatures is granted to them, the earth and creatures being put under their power in subjection; and the continued course and revolution of times and seasons, without danger of being destroyed anymore, by an universal flood of waters, is assured to them.[2419] So in Christ, *all are ours, the world, and life, and death, and things present, and things to come, all are ours; and we are Christ's; and Christ is God's.*[2420] These things God covenanted and promised on his part.

{2} Christ (the true Noah) and his family; on their part restipulated respectively different things, namely: (i) that Jesus Christ would prepare and build a spiritual ark, his church, wherein his elect family should be saved from wrath to come: whereby the world of the ungodly should be destroyed.[2421] (ii) That the elect of Christ should come into this ark, should enter into this church with Jesus Christ, and therein abide with him, for their salvation. Christ entered into his church by baptism, that with himself he might save all his elect in his church.[2422] That his elect may actually partake salvation by

---

[2417] Genesis 9:9-18
[2418] Matthew 6:33, 1 Timothy 4:8, Hebrews 1:3 with Romans 8:17
[2419] Genesis chapters 6-9
[2420] 1 Corinthians 3:21-23
[2421] Matthew 16:18
[2422] Matthew 3:16-17

Christ, they must enter Christ's ark, and remain therein with Christ. These things Christ and his family restipulated, under the type of Noah and his family, on their part.

[4] The *form* of these covenants of God with Noah, as a renewed administration of the Covenant of Faith in Christ, was twofold, namely: {1} *Inward*, the reciprocal and mutual obligation of the federate parties to each other. {2} *Outward*, the way and manner of this covenant's administration. This Covenant of Faith from Noah until Abraham was revealed, dispensed and administered in this sort.

(i) It was explicitly styled *a covenant*,[2423] *a covenant for perpetual generations*,[2424] Hebrew: *For generations of eternity*; *an everlasting covenant*,[2425] Hebrew: *a covenant of eternity*. This was the first express mention and denomination of a *covenant* between God and man. And this *covenant everlasting*, in that hereby God assured Noah, that the world should never again be destroyed by a general flood. Proportionably hereunto God in his *covenant of peace* has assured his people, that *he would not be wroth with them, but have mercy on them with everlasting kindness.*[2426]

(ii) It was made by God's immediate voice to Noah: clearly therefore a divine covenant.[2427]

(iii) It was limited to *Noah and his family as the type*;[2428] to Christ and his church visible as the antitype. All others were aliens from the covenants of promise.

(iv) It was revealed and represented under the visible temporal preservation of Noah and his family in a material ark from the flood of waters; and their *certioration*, or assuring of them and their seed, that the earth should no more be destroyed with a general flood of waters. Under which the elect of

---

[2423] Genesis 6:18 & 9:9-13, 15, 17
[2424] Genesis 9:12
[2425] Genesis 9:16
[2426] Isaiah 54:7-10
[2427] Genesis 6:13 to the end, & 9:9-18
[2428] Genesis 6:18 & 9:8-9

Christ are assured of their spiritual and eternal salvation in the church by Jesus Christ, through his death and resurrection, etc., from the deluge of God's wrath and vengeance for sin and iniquity.[2429]

(v) It was confirmed strongly in two ways. (a) By God's sacred and inviolable oath. *For this is as the waters of Noah unto me: for, as I have sworn that the waters of Noah should no more go over the earth; so have I sworn that I would not be wrath with thee, nor rebuke thee*, etc.[2430] (b) By God's eminent and visible sacrament, *the rainbow in the cloud*: the solemn ratifying sign and seal of this covenant.[2431] So that this covenant as dispensed to Noah was most firm, sure and inviolable.

(vi) Finally, this covenant-administration had many temporal blessings annexed thereunto. As: (a) the continued revolution of *seed time and harvest, cold and heat*, etc., *while the earth remaineth*.[2432] (b) The fruitfulness of mankind on earth.[2433] (c) Dominion over the creatures.[2434] (d) Enlarged liberty to have not only herbs, but the flesh of the creatures for food, etc.[2435] So true is that saying of our savior, *Seek first the kingdom of God and his righteousness, and all these things shall be added unto you*.[2436] And that of Paul's: *Godliness has the promise of the life that now is, and of that which is to come*.[2437]

Thus of the spiritual meaning of these covenants of God with Noah.

(3) **What additionals were annexed to this second federal administration from Noah until Abraham, more than were to the first dispensation of the promise from Adam until Noah**; may now appear by what has already been declared. And consequently what *agreement* and *difference* there was between these two dispensations.

[2429] 1 Peter 3:20-22
[2430] Isaiah 54:9-10 with Genesis 8:21; See Henry Ainsworth's annotations thereupon
[2431] Genesis 9:12-18
[2432] Genesis 8:22
[2433] Genesis 9:1, 7
[2434] Genesis 9:2
[2435] Genesis 9:3-4
[2436] Matthew 6:33
[2437] 1 Timothy 4:8

[1] *Additionals* to this federal dispensation, beyond the former, were these: {1} The express name of *A COVENANT*:[2438] this being the first time that the transaction between God and his people, is called *a covenant* in the whole scripture. {2} The express mention of the parties with whom God made this covenant, namely: Of the parties restipulating with God: *Noah, his sons, and their seed*.[2439] {3} A new and more clear representation of sinners' recovery and salvation by Christ, under the type of *Noah's saving his family in the ark by water, from perishing with the world of the ungodly*.[2440] {4} A notable establishment and confirmation of this covenant: (i) By God's sacred oath.[2441] (ii) By God's sacramental token: the rainbow.[2442] That by these two, Noah and his sons – and we in them – might have strong consolation, in hope and assurance of divine performance. {5} An express declaration of this covenant's perpetuity, until the end of the world.[2443] {6} Certain accessory promises of several temporal blessings.[2444]

[2] *Agreement* and *difference* between this federal dispensation, and the first promissory administration, stands thus:

{1} They agree in substance, both of them having: (i) the same author, God.[2445] (ii) The same parties covenanting, namely: God on the one hand; Christ and his elect seed taken from among lapsed mankind, on the other hand. (iii) The same foundation, namely: God's mere grace in Christ. (iv) The same matter promised and covenanted, namely: recovery of sinners from state of sin and death to righteousness and life by Jesus Christ. (v) The same end, the assuring and securing of sinners of their salvation and recovery, if by faith they will accept Christ according to God's covenant. *Herein they agree for substance.*

[2438] Genesis 6:18
[2439] Genesis 6:18 & 9:8-9
[2440] 1 Peter 3:20-22, Hebrews 11:7
[2441] Isaiah 54:9-10 with Genesis 8:21. See Henry Ainsworth's annotation there.
[2442] Genesis 9:12-18
[2443] Genesis 9:9, 12, 16
[2444] Genesis 8:22 & 9:1-4, 7
[2445] Genesis 3:15 with Genesis 6:18 & 9:8-9

{2} *They differ in circumstance, and in some accidental considerations.* For:

(i) That was laid down but as *a promise*; this, as a formal and complete *covenant*.[2446]

(ii) Of that, God was author as a destroyer of lapsed man's enemy the serpent; of this, God was author, as lapsed man's preserver, deliverer and savior from death and destruction.[2447]

(iii) That mentioned no parties restipulating with God, being neither directed expressly to Adam, nor to his wife, but to the serpent, though the promised benefit thereof was intended to them; not to the serpent, but this expressly mentions parties restipulating with God, namely: Noah, his sons, and their seed, and under them we are also principally to understand, Jesus Christ, the true Noah, and his seed.[2448]

(iv) That led to Christ more generally, as *the seed of the woman*,[2449] intimating that Christ should come of some woman that should be in the world, but neither expressing nor excluding any nation, family, or person: but this led to Christ more particularly, as to descend of Noah's family, by which *the whole earth was overspread*,[2450] excluding all other families and women from this privilege of bringing forth Christ into the world, that were not in a direct line from Adam till Noah.

(v) That represented Christ as *the seed of the woman at enmity with the serpent's seed, bruised in his heel by the serpent*,[2451] but bruising the head of the serpent, that old serpent the devil and Satan, who had bruised and undone mankind: this represented Christ as the *antitype of Noah*, a true *comforter* and *savior* of his elect family, in his ark of the church, by his own death and humiliation, resurrection and exaltation. So that Christ is here more clearly revealed as the sinner's recoverer, than in the first promise.

[2446] Genesis 3:15 with Genesis 6:18
[2447] Genesis 3:15 with Genesis 6:17-18, etc
[2448] Genesis 3:14-15, etc., with 6:18 & 9:8-10, etc
[2449] Genesis 3:15
[2450] Genesis 9:19
[2451] Genesis 3:14-16 with 1 Peter 3:20-22

(vi) That was established without any oath of God, or *sacramental token*;[2452] only *sacrifices* were added thereunto,[2453] which had as it were a sacramental confirming nature, but this was established, both by God's sacred inviolable *oath, wherein it was impossible for God to lie*;[2454] and also by his eminent sacramental token: *the rainbow in the cloud*.[2455] Hereby God sweetly provided for the *stronger consolation* of his people.

(vii) That was not styled everlasting, or perpetual, but this was named *an everlasting covenant, for perpetual generations*.[2456] Though for substance they were both equally everlasting in respect of Christ, and man's spiritual recovery by him.

(viii) Finally, this superadded more temporal blessings and promises, then that, and more clearly. That *implicitly* signified and promised the woman's conception and bringing forth of children, in the curse pronounced upon her, and the man's eating of bread all his days by his labor, in the curse propounded upon him (which words some do very well interpret to be both, a command, a threatening, and a promise to man);[2457] but this *explicitly* declared diverse notable promises and temporal blessings,[2458] as has been formerly declared.

In these things these two first federal dispensations do principally agree and differ.

(4) **Corollaries from the whole, are briefly these:**

[1] ***God's Covenants with Noah before and after the flood, revealed not only a corporal and temporal, but also a spiritual and an eternal salvation***. That corporal and temporal salvation in the ark from the flood of waters, with security to the world for ever after from such a general flood, typically resembling and representing the spiritual and eternal salvation of

---

[2452] Genesis 3:14-15
[2453] Genesis 3:21 with 4:3-5
[2454] Isaiah 54:9-10, Hebrews 6:18
[2455] Genesis 9:12-18
[2456] Genesis 3:15 with Genesis 9:12, 16
[2457] Genesis 3:16-19
[2458] Genesis 9:1-4, 7

lapsed sinners in the church by Christ from the flood of God's wrath and vengeance.

Doubt: But seeing God's later Covenant with Noah extended to the whole world, to save all mankind from any such general flood for future: does not this typically favor the doctrine and opinion of universal redemption by Christ?

Resolution: No. For: {1} it has already been cleared that in the former dispensation of the first promise, there was no footing for the opinion of universal redemption, nor proportionably was there in this, which for substance is one and the same with that.[2459] {2} If this Covenant should in this regard favor *universal redemption*, because the corporal benefit thereof is extended to all mankind in the whole world, then by the same argument, *spiritual redemption* should by this Covenant belong to brute beasts and other living creatures, for even they reap the benefit of this Covenant, and God is said to make it with them as well as with mankind. But this were most absurd to imagine. {3} These Covenants with Noah revealed a double salvation: an *outward* corporal and temporal salvation, and an *inward* spiritual and eternal salvation principally intended and typified thereby. This latter belongs only to the elect family of the true Noah, Jesus Christ, and to the new world planted and replenished by him spiritually. The former salvation which is but outward and corporal from all such future floods is (in and for the benefit of Christ's elect and saved family) extended even to all the wicked in the world, and to brute creatures themselves.

[2] *They who treat of God's Covenants with man in Christ purposely, and yet totally omit this excellent federal dispensation to Noah, seem too much to neglect the gradual order and method of God's federal administrations, and to bury in too much silence this eminent transaction of God with Noah, which was the very first in the world*

[2459] See Book 3, Chapter 2, Aphorism 2, Doubt 1. Also see the Question in Aphorism 5 of Chapter 2 of this book.

expressly styled a covenant.[2460] And that it was *a Covenant of Faith* in Christ, has been already proved.

Here I ingenuously confess, I dare not make so large a leap over this *federal transaction* as some have done: but have diligently examined and enquired into the mystery of it: {1} lest I should darken or eclipse the glory of God's grace, goodness, mercy, and wisdom herein, by an unthankful silence. {2} Lest I should disturb the order and deface the beauty of God's dispensations of grace which he has purposely revealed in certain gradual discoveries. {3} Lest I should prejudice and prevent myself or others of that spiritual benefit and edification which (I hope) through God's blessing may be reaped by the opening of this *covenant* in order.

[3] ***This federal dispensation is much fuller and clearer than the first***: as has been evidenced in many particulars. Such is God's grace, wisdom and goodness to his church and people, that as her capacity of receiving grows, so his dispensations and discoveries of mercy grow towards her.

[4] Finally, ***God's Covenant with Noah, etc., being a Covenant of Faith in Christ, it may be both a useful and comfortable subject even for our meditation and contemplation***. The substance of it, being the same with this under the New Testament. And both the temporal blessings *expressed*, and the spirituals *implied*, reaching to every one of us and our families, as well as to Noah and his family. How many lectures may we read to ourselves, of Christ, in Noah, of the church, in the ark, of *the salvation of Christ's family in his spiritual ark by his death and streams of his blood*, in the saving of Noah's family in the ark from perishing by water, of *the acceptableness of Christ's death and sacrifice of himself to God*, in the gratefulness of Noah's sacrifice to him, and in a word, of *that divine mercy, grace and favor towards sinners, that encompasses his throne, and shines in his face abundantly*, in the rainbow, that token of divine grace and commiseration? Sometimes let us converse with *Noah*, who *walked with God*.[2461] Let's mark his faith and patience in *building his ark*; Christ's more in

---

[2460] Genesis 6:18
[2461] Genesis 6:9

building his church. Let's consider his *entering into,* and *coming out of the ark,* to save his family, but much more Christ's *entering into* and *coming out of the grave,* to save his people. Yea as they of old were buried with Noah in the ark, and as it were drowned in the ark in the waters, that they might not be buried and drowned with the wicked world: so let us die, and be buried with Christ spiritually, that we may not die and be buried eternally. Let's make sure we are of Christ's elect family, and get we into his spiritual ark indeed, so that in this way we may be saved from the flood of God's indignation, which will swallow up all the wicked of the world for evermore.

Hitherto of God's Covenants of Promise, as dispensed in the second eminent period of time, from Noah till Abram, namely: from the 480th year of Noah, Anno Mundi 1536 until the 70th or 71st year of Abram, Anno Mundi 2079, the time of God's first promise to Abram, which was precisely 430 years before Israel's going out of Egypt, and the giving of the law.